JESUS

the Messianic Herald of Salvation

EDWARD P. MEADORS

HENDRICKSON PUBLISHERS

Hendrickson Publishers, Inc.
P. O. Box 3473
Peabody, Massachusetts 01961-3473

ISBN 1–56563–268–0

Hendrickson Publishers' edition published by arrangement with J. C. B. Mohr
(Paul Siebeck), Tübingen.

JESUS THE MESSIANIC HERALD OF SALVATION, by Edward P. Meadors © 1995
J. C. B. Mohr (Paul Siebeck), P.O. Box 2040, D-72010 Tübingen, Germany.

First printing —March 1997

Printed in the United States of America

Library of Congress Cataloging-in-Publication Data

Meadors, Edward P., 1964–
      Jesus, the messianic herald of salvation   /   Edward P. Meadors.
      Originally published: Tübingen: J.C.B. Mohr (Paul Siebeck), c1995.
      Includes bibliographical references and indexes.
      ISBN 1–56563–268–0 (paper)
      1. Bible. N.T. Mark—Criticism, interpretation, etc.   2. Q hypothesis
(Synoptics criticism)   I. Title.
    BS2585.2.M42   1997
    226'.066—dc21   97–2498
                                                                          CIP

Preface

This book is a response to the growing scholarly assumption that the hypothetical Gospel source "Q" was a document composed in multiple stages which reflect the varying theological biases of a developing community. According to this commonly held premise, the transmitters of Q had their own idiosyncratic view of Jesus and his message, which differed to such a significant extent from Mark, that Q is now considered by many to be a composition stemming from a 'second sphere of early Christianity.' In a fresh examination of the evidence, I shall challenge this "critical orthodoxy" and attempt to demonstrate that Q stands in close harmony with Mark and is based on the teaching of the historical Jesus.

In the pages that follow, I hope to clarify that many characteristic themes of Q (wisdom, prophecy, the Son of Man) are present equally and in similar ways in Mark. The primary theme of both Q and Mark, the Kingdom of God, will be examined in detail to determine if, and to what extent, the content of Q is dissimilar to Mark, and thus to what extent Q is deserving, if at all, of the variant heritage dubbed 'second sphere.' Further, I shall argue that the juxtaposition of the categories of wisdom, prophecy, apocalyptic and eschatology in Q has a historical precedent in the Book of Daniel, which contains the same agglomeration of ideas and which almost certainly influenced Jesus. This will open up the way to claiming that these themes in Q have their origin in a combination of ideas taught by Jesus, and that therefore the hypothesis of successive layers of Q redaction is redundant.

I shall contend that Q and Mark, rather than contradict one another, collaborate in revealing important insights into the early church's understanding of the mission of Jesus. Although the 'Messianic Secret' has long been thought to be distinctive of Mark, Q, by not containing the Christ title, conceals the messianic identity of Jesus in a way that is thoroughly consistent with Mark. Both hypothetical sources tie the proclamation of the Gospel—the good news that eschatological salvation has come through Jesus to those desiring the benefits of his ministry—closely to Jesus himself. They present Jesus' teaching and acts in a way that implies his identity as the eschatological herald of salvation (Isa. 61:1f.), the anointed wise Messiah, who came to defeat Satan and gather God's people for salvation in the Kingdom of God.

Thus in the end I hope to verify from what Q and Mark say, rather than from what they do not say, that, so far from being *Gemeindetheologie*, the product of an esoteric community, Q belongs to the mainstream of a tradition rooted in early apostolic memories of what Jesus said and did during his earthly ministry.

It is both a pleasure and an honor for me to acknowledge the outstanding people who have contributed to my development as a student of the New Testament. To Drs. C. Hassell Bullock and J. Julius Scott of Wheaton College and Wheaton College Graduate School, I express thanks for the model of Christian excellence they each displayed as lecturers during my years of college and M.A. study. As this book is a revision of my Ph. D. thesis written at the University of Aberdeen (1993), I am greatly indebted to the encouragement and scholarly criticism of my doctoral supervisor Prof. I. Howard Marshall. I also owe a debt of gratitude to Dr. Max Turner, now of London Bible College, who read and skilfully criticized several papers related to this publication. The editorial corrections and suggestions for revision rendered by Dr. Ruth Edwards of Aberdeen and Dr. Ronald Piper of St. Andrews, my internal and external examiners respectively, have made this book far better than the thesis that preceded it.

It is a great privilege for me to have J.C.B. Mohr (Paul Siebeck) as my publisher. My thanks extend to Profs. Martin Hengel and Otfried Hofius for accepting my work in the WUNT 2. Reihe. Prof. Hengel's initial interest and subsequent suggestions have been a continuing source of encouragement in the laborious task of revision. I also wish to thank Ilse König of J.C.B. Mohr (Paul Siebeck) for her patient, cheerful help in the physical production of this book, and to John Yates, Woody Hengel, and Dr. Kathe Gabbe, colleagues who proofread significant portions of the manuscript. Likewise, I am in debt to my students at Beeson Divinity School, who helped compile my indexes, and to my secretary, Mrs. Sandra McDonald, who assisted me in corresponding with Tübingen via the Samford University fax machine.

Most importantly, I am thankful for my family. The kindness, love, and support of my father-in-law and mother-in-law, Mr. and Mrs. Roger McDonald, have been a constant source of encouragement and joy. The love and blessing of my parents, Dr. and Mrs. Marvin P. Meadors Jr., have undergirded my life and work with happiness, balance, and strength. My little assistants in this enterprise, Edward Jr. and Davis Weston, have kept my priorities straight and provided a helpful excuse for the disorder of my office. Finally, this book is dedicated to my precious, loving wife, Kathy, who celebrates with me the joy of salvation in Christ.

Edward Paul Meadors   Christmas 1994

Table of Contents

Abbreviations

ANTJ	Arbeiten zum Neuen Testament und Judentum.
AsSeign	*Assemblées du Seigneur.*
Bauer	W. Bauer, *A Greek-English Lexicon of the New Testament and Other Early Christian Literature*, ET, Ed. W.F. Arndt and F.W. Gingrich; 2nd ed. rev. F.W. Gingrich and F. W. Danker, University of Chicago Press, 1979.
BBB	Bonner biblische Beiträge.
BDB	E. Brown, S.R. Driver, and C.A. Briggs, *Hebrew and English Lexicon of the Old Testament*; Oxford: Clarendon, 1907.
BET	Beiträge zur evangelischen Theologie.
BETL	Bibliotheca ephemeridum theologicarum lovaniensium.*
BFTh	Beiträge zur Förderung christlicher Theologie.
BGBE	Beiträge zur Geschichte der biblischen Exegese.
BHT	Beiträge zur historischen Theologie.
BJRL	*Bulletin of the John Rylands Library.*
BR	*Biblical Research.*
BTB	*Biblical Theology Bulletin.*
BZ	*Biblische Zeitschrift.*
BZAW	Beihefte zur *ZAW.*
BZNW	Beihefte zur *ZNW.*
CBQ	*Catholic Biblical Quarterly.*
CBQMS	*CBQ* Monograph Series.
CGTC	The Cambridge Greek Testament Commentary.
EKKNT	Evangelisch-katholischer Kommentar zum Neuen Testament.
ETL	*Ephemerides theologicae lovanienses.*
ExpT	*Expository Times.*
ÉThR	*Études théologiques et religieuses.*
Even-Shoshan	Abraham Even-Shoshan, *A New Concordance of the Old Testament*, Jerusalem: "Keryat Sefer," 1984.
FB	Forschung zur Bibel.
FRLANT	Forschungen zur Religion und Literatur des Alten und Neuen Testaments.
FS	Festschrift.
FTS	Frankfurter theologische Studien.
GNS	Good News Studies.
HibJ	*Hibbert Journal.*
HTKNT	Herders theologischer Kommentar zum Neuen Testament.
HTR	*Harvard Theological Review.*
HUCA	*Hebrew Union College Annual.*
IBS	*Irish Biblical Studies.*
ICC	International Critical Commentary.

---

* All Biblical Quotations are taken from the New American Standard Bible.

JAAR	*Journal of the American Academy of Religion.*
JBL	*Journal of Biblical Literature.*
JBR	*Journal of Bible and Religion.*
JQR	*Jewish Quarterly Review.*
JSJ	*Journal for the Study of Judaism.*
JSNT	*Journal for the Study of the New Testament.*
JSNTSS	*JSNT* Supplement Series.
JSOT	*Journal for the Study of the Old Testament.*
JSOTSS	*JSOT* Supplement Series.
JTC	*Journal for Theology and Church.*
JTS	*Journal of Theological Studies.*
KBANT	Kommentare und Beiträge zum Alten und Neuen Testament.
LD	Lectio divina.
MNTC	Moffatt New Testament Commentary.
NCBC	New Century Bible Commentary.
NIGTC	The New International Greek Testament Commentary.
NovT	*Novum Testamentum.*
NovTSup	*Novum Testamentum* Supplements.
NTD	Das Neue Testament Deutsch.
NTOA	Novum Testamentum et orbis Antiquus.
NTS	*New Testament Studies.*
RB	*Revue biblique.*
RGG	*Die Religion in Geschichte und Gegenwart.*
RHPR	*Revue d'histoire et de philosophie religieuses.*
SANT	Studien zum Alten und Neuen Testament.
SBLDS	Society of Biblical Literature Dissertation Series.
SBLMS	Society of Biblical Literature Monograph Series
SBLSPS	Society of Biblical Literature Seminar Papers Series.
SBM	Stuttgarter biblische Monographien.
SBS	Stuttgarter Bibelstudien.
SBT	Studies in Biblical Theology.
SE	*Studia Evangelica.*
SJT	*Scottish Journal of Theology.*
SNTSMS	Society for New Testament Studies Monograph Studies.
SNTU	Studien zum Neuen Testament und seiner Umwelt.
ST	*Studia theologica*
StNT	Studien zum Neuen Testament.
SUNT	Studien zur Umwelt des Neuen Testaments.
TB	Theologische Bücherei.
TDNT	G. Kittel and G. Friedrich, Eds., *Theological Dictionary of the New Testament,* 10 vols., ET (Grand Rapids: Eerdmans, 1964-76).
TDOT	G. Johannes Botterweck and Helmer Ringgren, Eds., *Theological Dictionary of the Old Testament,* 7 vols., ET (Grand Rapids: Eerdmans, 1974-).
TExH	Theologische Existenz heute.
THKNT	Theologischer Handkommentar zum Neuen Testament.
TQ	*Theologische Quartalschrift*
TSK	*Theologische Studien und Kritiken.*
TTZ	*Trierer theologische Zeitschrift.*
TU	*Texte und Untersuchungen.*
TynB	*Tyndale Bulletin.*
TZ	*Theologische Zeitschrift.*
UBS	United Bible Societies.
VT	*Vetus Testamentum.*
VTS	*VT* Supplements.

WBC	Word Biblical Commentary.
WMANT	Wissenschaftliche Monographien zum Alten und Neuen Testament.
WUNT	Wissenschaftliche Untersuchungen zum Neuen Testament.
ZAW	*Zeitschrift für die alttestamentliche Wissenschaft.*
ZNW	*Zeitschrift für die neutestamentliche Wissenschaft.*
ZTK	*Zeitschrift für Theologie und Kirche.*

Chapter 1

The Study of Mark and Q

I. The Source Analysis of Mark and Q

The problem of the relationship between Mark and the hypothetical sayings source Q[1] dates as far back as the origin of the two source theory in the mid-nineteenth century formulations which Karl Lachmann,[2] C.H. Weiße,[3] and Heinrich Holtzmann[4] developed in Germany. When Lachmann, Holtzmann, and other early source analysts[5] reasoned that the puzzling literary relationship between

---

[1] The siglum "Q" was apparently first used by Johannes Weiss (1863-1914). See Frans Neirynck, "The Symbol Q (= Quelle)", *ETL* 54 (1978) 119-125. J.G. Eichhorn (*Einleitung in das Neue Testament,* Leipzig [1804] 344-367) is credited as being the first to theorize that Matthew and Luke independently drew from a common literary source (*Vorlage*) which was a Greek translation of a Hebrew or Chaldean-Syriac sayings source. Soon thereafter Friedrich Schleiermacher (*Über die Zeugnisse des Papias von unsern ersten beiden Evangelien, TSK* 8 [1835] 570-590) proposed that Eusebius' quotation of Papias' "Ματθαῖος μὲν οὖν 'Εβραΐδι διαλέκτῳ τὰ λόγια συνετάξατο" (III, 39:16) was not a reference to Matthew's Gospel, but rather to a collection of Jesus' sayings which went back to the apostle Matthew. For exhaustive bibliographies on Q, see: Frans Neirynck and F. Van Segbroeck, "Q Bibliography," *Logia,* Ed. Joël Delobel; Leuven: Leuven UP (1982) 561-586; David M. Scholer, "Q Bibliography: 1981-1989", *SBL Seminar Papers* 28, Ed. David J. Lull; Atlanta: Scholars Press (1989) 23-38. Scholer's bibliography is revised annually in SBL.

[2] Lachmann (1793-1851) proposed a source whose order Mk. best preserved (*Urmarkus*) and a second source (*Quelle*) which accounted for the parallels between Mt. and Lk. (*De ordine narrationum in evangeliis synopticis, TSK* 8 [1835] 570-590).

[3] *Die evangelische Geschichte kritisch und philosophisch bearbeitet.* Leipzig (1838) Bd. 1, 3-138. Weiße later supported a literary relationship between the two sources in *Die Evangelienfrage in ihrem gegenwärtigen Stadium,* Leipzig (1856) 146.

[4] The importance of Holtzmann's work rests in its conviction that Mk. and Q developed totally independently from one another: "Hauptsache ist und bleibt also, unsere zweite Quelle, als von Matthäus und Lucas benutzt, vollkommen selbständig neben A hinzustellen und jedes Abhängigkeitsverhältnis zwischen diesen Quellen selbst abzuweisen." In *Die synoptischen Evangelien, ihr Ursprung und geschichtlicher Charakter,* Leipzig (1863) 140. Holtzmann used A as the symbol for UrMarkus. Quotation taken from Rudolf Laufen, *Die Doppelüberlieferungen der Logienquelle und des Markusevangeliums,* BBB 54; Bonn: Hanstein (1980) 62.

[5] Other early advocates of the two-source theory include: Ch. G. Wilke (*Der Urevangelist oder exegetisch kritische Untersuchung über das Verwandtschaftsverhältnis der drei ersten Evangelien,* Dresden-Leipzig: 1838), and H. Ewalds (*Die drei ersten Evangelien,* Göttingen: 1850). Wilke

Matthew, Mark, and Luke was solved best by the theory that Matthew and Luke used two primary sources the obvious question arose: What is the relationship between the two? How can the similarities and differences in language and content between the two earliest witnesses to the Jesus tradition be explained?

In time five major solutions to this problem were advanced: (1) Mark used Q as a direct literary *Vorlage*; (2) Q drew directly from Mark; (3) Mark quoted Q from memory; (4) Q was a growing document—some early parts were known to Mark while later materials entered the sayings collection after Mark's completion; (5) literary independence—Mark and Q drew from common oral or written traditions independently from one another. Each position has been modified with various corollaries and each has supporters among modern and contemporary adherents to the two-source theory.[6]

Attempts to prove literary dependence either way falter primarily on the difficulty of isolating exactly where Mark or Q take up their counterpart's characteristic vocabulary or style. Where does Mark contain remnants of Q redaction—a phenomenon itself difficult to isolate?[7] And where Q appears to contain elements of Markan style how certain is it that apparent Markan elements in Q do not result from Matthew's or Luke's conflation of Q with Mark? As a result of these difficulties, the predominant opinion at present favors literary independence.[8]

---

furthered the theory of Markan priority; Ewalds argued that oral traditions could be traced back to the oral expressions of Jesus.

[6] For exhaustive bibliography supporting each position see R. Laufen, *Die Doppelüberlieferungen*, 69-76, 394-400; P. Vassiliadis, "Prolegomena to a Discussion on the Relationship between Mark and the Q-Document", *Deltion Biblikôn Meletôn* 3 (1975) 31-46; M. Devisch, "La relation entre l'évangile de Marc et le document Q", in *L'Évangile Selon Marc*, BETL 34, Ed. M. Sabbe; Leuven: Leuven U.P. (1976) 59-91.

[7] D. Catchpole ("The Mission Charge in Q", *Semeia* 55 (1992) 150, 51) has recently defended W. Schenk ("Der Einfluss der Logienquelle auf das Markusevangelium", *ZNW* 70 [1979] 141-65) in arguing that Mark may have used Q. According to Catchpole Lk. 10:13-15par. has been taken up by Mark. However, Catchpole's evidence is not persuasive. He claims Mark takes up δύναμις from Q (Lk. 10:13-15) in 6:2, 5; 5:30; 6:14, yet δύναμις is hardly unique to Q (Mk. 10x; Q 1x). The other correspondences he sees between Mk. and Q 10:13-15 are conceptual (e.g., repentance and the kingdom go together in Mk. 1:14, 15 and in Lk. 10:11,13-15) rather than redactional and thus do not demand literary dependence. Such similarities, in our opinion, are no greater than would be expected of two independent documents drawing on the same tradition.

[8] So M. Devisch, "La relation entre l' évangile de Marc et le document Q", 83, 91; J. Dupont, "La transmission des paroles de Jésus sur la lampe et la mesure dans Marc 4, 21-25 et dans la tradition Q", *Logia*, 201-236 (236); P. Vassiliadis, "Prolegomena to a Discussion on the Relationship between Mark and the Q Document", 45; W.G. Kümmel, *Introduction to the New Testament*, London: S.C.M. (1975) 70; R. Pesch, *Das Markusevangelium* I, Freiburg: Herder (1976) 30. See further the long list of adherents to this position in R. Laufen, *Die Doppelüberlieferungen*, 73-76.

II. The Theological Comparison of Mark and Q

Among early source critics consensus existed in the belief that Mark and Q both provided authentic witnesses to the life and teaching of the historical Jesus. H.J. Holtzmann's conviction of the historical value of Mark and Q is representative of the era:

> But the most striking evidence of all for the credibility of both sources lies in the artless congruence of the material content of Jesus' discourses. Finally, attention must be drawn to how perfectly homogeneous are the two sources with respect to the material that in general they offer for a more searching attempt to define the moral character of Jesus. . . . We may perhaps characterize it as the most precious result of our investigations that by them we are enabled to draw a rather definite picture of the historical character of the person of Jesus and of the activity that filled his span of life.[9]

The desire to identify the authentic teaching of Jesus gradually led to christological and theological harmonizations of Mark and Q. Similar status was attributed to the two sources, so that independently of each other Bernhard Weiß[10] and B.W. Bacon[11] defined Q as a primitive Gospel form. F.C. Burkitt[12] and later Emmanuel Hirsch[13] even went so far as to attribute portions of Luke's passion and

---

[9] *Die synoptischen Evangelien. Ihr Ursprung und ihr geschichtlicher Charakter.* Quotation from W.G. Kümmel, *The New Testament, The History of the Investigation of its Problems*, Tr. S.M. Gilmour and H.C. Kee; London: SCM (1973) 153. Similarly, A. Jülicher (*Einleitung in das Neue Testament*, Leipzig: J.C.B. Mohr [1894] 222), "Das 2 in der synoptischen Literatur benutzte Quellen werk dient dem Zweck, wertvolle Aussprüche des Heilands in authentischer Form den Nachkommen zu überliefern"; F.C. Burkitt (*The Gospel History and Its Transmission*, Edinburgh: T&T Clark [1906] 147), "Where Q and Mark appear to report the same saying, we have the nearest approach that we can hope to get to the common tradition of the earliest Christian society about our Lord's words"; B.H. Streeter (*The Four Gospels* , London: Macmillan [1924] 191), ". . . Q was a document of very early date and represents a peculiarly authentic tradition"; A. Harnack (*The Sayings of Jesus*, Tr. J.R. Wilkinson; London: Williams and Norgate [1908] 249), "Our knowledge of the teaching and the history of our Lord, in their main features at least, thus depends upon two authorities independent of one another, yet composed at nearly the same time. Where they agree their testimony is strong, and they agree often and on important points. On the rock of their united testimony the assault of destructive critical views, however necessary these are to easily self-satisfied research, will ever be shattered to pieces"; C.H. Dodd (*The Parables of Jesus*, London: Nisbet [1935] 34), "We are therefore left with Mark and Q . . . criticism has yet provided us with any better *organon* for approximating to the original tradition of the words and works of Jesus than is supplied by a careful study and comparison of these two."

[10] *A Manual of Introduction to the New Testament*, Tr. A.J.K. Davidson. 2 vols, New York: Funk & Wagnalls, 1887-89.

[11] "The Nature and Design of Q, the Second Synoptic Source", *HibJ* 22 (1923-24) 674-88.

[12] *The Gospel History and Its Transmission*, 134-145; *idem, The Earliest Sources of the Life of Jesus,* Boston: Houghton Mifflin (1910) 109-110.

[13] "Fragestellung und Verfahren meiner Frühgeschichte des Evangeliums", *ZNW* 41 (1942) 106-24.

resurrection narratives to Q. Hence Q was interpreted against the theological background of Mark.[14]

The first attempts to compare the theological contents of Mark and Q came from Julius Wellhausen[15] and Adolf von Harnack.[16] With opposing results both scholars focused on the source question. Wellhausen argued that Q was dependent upon Mark and hence later. Harnack countered that Q was independent and earlier, the lack of a Passion narrative being directly related to the source's audience: "the compilation in Q was intended solely for the Christian community and was addressed to those who did not require the assurance that their Teacher was also the Son of God."[17] However, the two essentially agreed that both Mark and Q presented the teachings of Jesus in an atmosphere presupposing the Passion and resurrection of Jesus. Both therefore failed to recognize christological antithesis between Mark and Q as each identified Q as a collection of Jesus' sayings which were originally gathered together for catechetical purposes.[18]

In England the relation of Mark and Q was understood in much the same way. B.H. Streeter in his enormously influential book *The Four Gospels* reasoned that both Mark and Q were written at a time when the oral tradition of Jesus' life, death, and resurrection was preached and well known. Mark met the demand of the Church of Rome that a history of the "Founder's life" be recorded following the deaths of Peter and Paul,[19] while Q was written to "supplement, not to supersede, a living oral tradition."[20] Like Wellhausen and Harnack, Streeter did not perceive a christological problem emanating from Q's omission of Passion emphasis:

> The Passion and its redemptive significance could readily be taught in oral tradition. But ethical teaching implies detailed instruction which sooner or later necessitates a written document. Such a document is found in the Didache, which obviously presupposes a general knowledge of the central facts of the Christian story. Similarly Q was probably written to supplement an oral tradition.[21]

---

[14] For a comprehensive history of the study of Q from from a form critical perspective, see John S. Kloppenborg, *The Formation of Q*, Philadelphia: Fortress Press (1989) 1-39.

[15] "Markus verglichen mit Q," *Einleitung in die drei ersten Evangelien*, Berlin: Druck und Verlag von Georg Reimer (1905) 73-89.

[16] "A comparison of Q with the Gospel of St. Mark," *The Sayings of Jesus*, 193-246.

[17] *Ibid.*, 235.

[18] Wellhausen, *Einleitung in die drei ersten Evangelien*, 84-85: "Die Sprüche werden da nicht bloß an eine Geschichte angeknüpft, sondern getragen von einem größeren lehrhaften Zusammenhang"; Harnack (*The Sayings of Jesus*, 203): ". . . Q was a compilation of the sayings of our Lord, made with the aim of giving authoritative teaching (and that principally ethical)."

[19] *The Four Gospels*, 497.

[20] *Ibid.*, 229.

[21] *Ibid.*, 292.

The classification of Mark as a Gospel containing the story of Jesus' life and Passion, and the classification of Q as a catechetical sayings-source thus ruled the day both in Germany and in England where T.W. Manson[22] and Vincent Taylor[23] soon followed Streeter's lead. The compatibility of Mark and Q was therefore hardly questioned—Q being a supplement to the Passion kerygma which Mark represented.

III. The Rise of Form Criticism

The emergence of form criticism, however, brought a new perspective to the comparison as New Testament scholars addressed for the first time the question of how Mark's literary form compared with the literary form of Q. The answer to this question was initially thought self-evident: Mark, displaying all the features characteristic of a Gospel (teachings within the narrative framework of Jesus' ministry, death, and resurrection) was deemed a full-scale Gospel, while Q, being considerably shorter (roughly 230 verses) and composed primarily of sayings, was recognized as a simple collection of Jesus' sayings.

The distinction between narrative and sayings material led to previously unconsidered conclusions regarding the relationship of the traditions behind Mark and Q. Martin Dibelius, for example, believed Mark and Q represented two different traditions of transmission within the development of the Gospels: "the words of Jesus were handed down under other conditions than were the narratives of His acts."[24] Q represented a tradition in which the sayings of Jesus were gathered for a hortatory end, while Mark represented an attempt to "explain the Passion of Jesus beforehand by means of practical remarks and also by carrying through his theory of a Messianic secret."[25] A distinct christological perspective formed the structure of Mark. In contrast Q lacked christological orientation

---

[22] "...there is no Passion-story because none is required, Q being a book of instruction for people who are already Christians and know the story of the Cross by heart", *The Sayings of Jesus,* London: SCM Press (1949) 16.

[23] "The simplest and most natural view is that Q began as a sayings-source pure and simple. ... Q was an innovation prompted by the needs of catechetical instruction. ... Writing at Rome between 65 and 70 A.D., Mark had unique advantages. ... The Petrine stories and a knowledge of the progress of events derived from Peter, supplied him with an outline into which he inserted single stories and small collections of primitive material in such a way as to show how Jesus, the Messiah, came to His Passion and His Cross." *The Formation of the Gospel Tradition,* 2nd ed.; London: Macmillan (1949) 182, 186, 187.

[24] *From Tradition to Gospel*, Tr. B.L. Woolf, Cambridge: James Clarke & Co. (1971) 238.

[25] *Ibid.*, 246, 260.

because it was collected for hortatory purposes.[26] Dibelius therefore still maintained a catechetical orientation behind Q and understood Q to be christologically compatible with Mark.

Similarly, in *The History of the Synoptic Tradition*, R. Bultmann described Q as a collection of dominical sayings to which the Church added later Jewish proverbs, laws, prophecies, and sayings from traditional wisdom. Though Bultmann was more sceptical of the authenticity of Jesus' sayings, he too understood Q to be a collection of speech material in contrast to Mark, which combined Palestinian traditions with "new motives in the Hellenistic Church which produced the shaping of the traditional material into a Gospel."[27] With the contrast in forms correlated a contrast in christology: "In Q he (Jesus) is above everything else the eschatological preacher of repentance and salvation, the teacher of wisdom and the law. In Mark he is a $\theta\epsilon\hat{\iota}o\varsigma$ $\check{\alpha}\nu\theta\rho\omega\pi o\varsigma$, indeed more: he is the very Son of God walking on the earth."[28] Yet, the most important "new motive" according to Bultmann, was the death and resurrection kerygma:

> The tradition had to be presented as an unity from the point of view that in it he who spoke and was spoken of was he who had lived on earth as the Son of God, had suffered, died, risen and been exalted to heavenly glory. And inevitably the centre of gravity had to be the end of the story, the Passion and Resurrection. Mark was the creator of this sort of Gospel . . .[29]

With those before him, Bultmann identified Mark and Q as two different stages within the formation of the Christian Gospel. Q met the needs of paranesis and catechism while Mark satisfied the need for a narrative uniting the Palestinian sayings tradition with the story of Jesus' death and resurrection.

IV. Theological Disparity between Mark and Q

The identification of Q as a mere collection of Jesus' teachings did not satisfy later form critics who championed Q's omission of a passion narrative as evidence that alternative theological factors motivated the formation of Q. Indeed, the lack of a passion narrative soon emerged as material evidence cited to support the hypothesis that Q represented a distinct theological tradition. Q therefore began to be viewed as a document which was collected, composed, and edited around

---

[26] On the lack of christology in Q, Dibelius writes, "It is perfectly certain that the sayings were not brought together at first for the sake of their Christological interest." *Ibid.*, 246.

[27] *The History of the Synoptic Tradition*, 2nd ed., Tr. John Marsh, Oxford: Basil Blackwell (1968) 369; see also 101f.

[28] *Ibid.*, 241.

[29] *Ibid.*, 371.

specific theological purposes which were distinctly different from Mark which focused on the Passion kerygma. The established classification of Mark as kerygma and Q as didache was challenged.[30] Günther Bornkamm's early appraisal of the composition of Q is indicative of the changing perspective on Mark's relationship to Q:

> Indessen läßt sich ein großer Teil seiner Überlieferung und das Motiv der Sammlung in keiner Weise als blosse Paränese verstehen, die das Passionskerygma der Gemeinde ergänzen sollte. Dieses ist in Q überhaupt noch nicht vorausgesetzt. Q ist vielmehr von einer anderen theologischen Konzeption geprägt.[31]

Bornkamm raised the question: If Q presents theological conceptions other than the passion kerygma, what theological conceptions does it emphasize? If Jesus' death and resurrection are insignificant, what emphasis *does* Q place upon Jesus—does Q have a christology, and if so how can it be defined?

The first major attempt to affirm that Q did, indeed, have a christology was carried out by Bornkamm's student H.E. Tödt. In his work on the present, future, and suffering Son of Man sayings, Tödt came to the conclusion that the christology of Q was a Son of Man christology: "There is a second, independent source, then, located in the Q stratum of the productive development of the Son of Man sayings. Christology as it springs up here is a Son of Man Christology."[32] Not finding evidence of Jesus' suffering or humility in Q, Tödt identified the reteaching of Jesus' teaching as the motivating factor behind the collection. Q therefore retransmitted the primary burden of Jesus' proclamation—the eschatological expectation of the Son of Man.

From a different perspective J.M. Robinson and Helmut Koester produced a second attempt to uncover the original thought behind Q in their dual work *Trajectories through Early Christianity*. Pursuing Bultmann's suggestion that many of the sayings in Q represent Logia or wisdom sayings,[33] they considered Wisdom to be the controlling factor in the genre to which Q belongs. Robinson, after an extensive survey of ancient literature, concluded that the Q genre belonged to a trajectory of "sayings of the sages" ($\lambda\acute{o}\gamma o\iota\ \sigma o\phi\tilde{\omega}\nu$) which he traced from Jewish wisdom literature through later gnostic writings.[34] In the same volume,

---

[30] Here we simply mean by 'kerygma' the early Christian preaching which identified Jesus' death and resurrection as the means of redemption and salvation. By 'didache' we simply mean the instructional or teaching material of the early Church.

[31] "Evangelien, synoptische", RGG Bd. 2; Tübingen: J.C.B. Mohr (1958) 759.

[32] *The Son of Man in the Synoptic Tradition*, Tr. D.M. Barton, London: SCM (1963) 235.

[33] *History of the Synoptic Tradition*, 69-107.

[34] "Logoi Sophon: On the Gattung of Q", in *Trajectories through Early Christianity*, Ed. H. Koester and J.M. Robinson, Philadelphia: Fortress Press (1971) 71-113.

Koester wrote of an early stratum of Q in which Jesus' radicalized eschatology of the kingdom and his revelation of divine wisdom were dominant motifs. Koester surmised that the Gospel of Thomas—which like Q lacks passion emphasis— derived from this early version of Q.[35] In a separate article he further claimed that the pre-Christian Jewish wisdom myth springing from the Wisdom of Solomon, Philo, and 2 Enoch was applied to Jesus in Q (in addition to Matthew, Philippians 2, John's prologue, and Hebrews). According to Koester, the sayings tradition gradually expanded to include more and more sayings in which Jesus functioned as Wisdom's envoy.[36] Q then represented a totally different, yet more authentic christology than the christology found in Mark:

> . . . the most original Gattung of the Jesus tradition—the *logoi sophon*—which, in the canonical gospels, became acceptable to the orthodox church only by radical critical alteration, not only of the form but also of the theological intention of this primitive Gattung. Such critical evaluation of the Gattung, *logoi*, was achieved by Matthew and Luke through imposing the Marcan narrative-kerygma frame upon the sayings tradition represented by Q.[37]

In contrast to previous comparisons of Mark and Q, Robinson and Koester proposed that Q's identification of Jesus as a messenger of Wisdom was incongruous with Mark's Passion oriented christology and thus required "radical critical alteration" before being combined with Mark.

Robinson's and Koester's work stands as a watershed in Q studies. Since its publication, the majority of major works on Q have approached the Sayings Source as a document containing not only a different literary tradition, but also a primitive christology unlike the christology of Mark. In the first redactional study of Q, Dieter Lührmann asserted that Q exalted Jesus not for his kerygmatic significance, but for his eschatological position. Where Mark placed importance on Jesus' death and resurrection, Q emphasized the coming judgement: "Jesus is not the pronouncement, but rather the content of pronouncement is the coming judgement in which Jesus will save his community as the Son of Man."[38]

---

[35] "One Jesus and Four Primitive Gospels", in *Trajectories through Early Christianity*, 186.

[36] "The Structure and Criteria of Early Christian Beliefs", *Trajectories through Early Christianity*, 221. Koester maintains essentially the same perspectives in *Ancient Christian Gospels*, London: SCM (1990) 128-171: "Thus Q can not be seen as a teaching supplement for a community whose theology is represented by the Pauline kerygma. Q's theology and soteriology are fundamentally different" (160).

[37] Helmut Koester, "Gnomai Diaphoroi: The Origin and Nature of Diversification in the History of Early Christianity", *Trajectories through Early Christianity*, 135.

[38] *Die Redaktion der Logienquelle*, WMANT 33; Neukirchen-Vluyn: Neukirchener Verlag (1969) 96, 97.

Similarly, Paul Hoffmann in his study of the theology of Q de-emphasized the ignificance of the Passion kerygma in Q in favor of the christological ronouncement of Jesus as the exalted Son of Man:

> Die Logienquelle enthielt, soweit die Überlieferung erkennen läßt, keine Ostergeschichten; es fehlt in ihr auch ein Beleg für das Auferstehungs-Kerygma, wie es z. B. 1 Kor 15,3ff überliefert wird. Die Funktion, die in der urchristlichen Tradition der Auferstehungs-aussage zukommt (Erweis der Hoheitsstellung Jesu und Legitimation der Sendung der Jünger), übernimmt also in Q die Mt 11,25-27 bezeugte Erfahrung, daß Jesus, der Sohn, den Auserwählten seine Menschensohnwürde offenbarte.[39]

Like Lührmann, Hoffmann found the centre of Q in the christological significance of Jesus' future arrival as the Son of Man.[40] Where Mark emphasized Jesus' death and resurrection in the past, Q emphasized Jesus' return as the Son of Man in the future.

From a similar perspective, Siegfried Schulz, author of the first full commentary on Q, attempted to distinguish different christological traditions behind Mark and Q. Agreeing with Tödt that Q's christological perception was not that of the Passion kerygma,[41] he claimed polemical interaction existed between the traditions behind Mark and the more recent Q material:

> Aber im Unterschied zur vormarkinischen Gemeindetradition findet der kerygmatische Rückgriff auf den irdischen Jesus innerhalb der jüngeren Q-Stoffe in Zeichen der göttlichen Sophia statt bei gleichzeitiger polemischer Ablehnung der vormarkinischen Wundermann- und Gottmensch-Christologie![42]

Schulz explained the conflict as two different early Christian communities' struggle for existence. A Hellenistic Gentile community motivated the writing of Mark's Gospel in contrast to a Hellenistic Jewish community which composed Q. Thus Schulz explained Mark and Q on the basis of an apparent plurality of kerygmatic design within early Christianity.[43] As a result, the goal of Schulz's commentary was to define the kerygma of the Q community.

---

[39] *Studien zur Theologie der Logienquelle*, Münster: Verlag Aschendorff (1972) 140.

[40] "Die Identifikation Jesu mit dem kommenden Menschensohn ist theologiegeschichtlich gesehen von größter Bedeutung: indem Jesus als der "Angelpunkt" der Geschichte erkannt wurde, gewann jener unscheinbare, anscheinend gescheiterte Beginn in Palästina weltgeschichtliche Bedeutung." *Ibid.*, 142.

[41] "Richtig ist schließlich auch, daß diese christologische Konzeption nicht dem Passionskerygma untergeordnet werden darf, das durch die vormarkinischen und vor allem vorpaulinischen Traditionsstoffe repräsentiert wird, wie es immer wieder geschehen ist." *Q, Die Spruchquelle der Evangelisten*, Zürich: Theologischer Verlag (1972) 31.

[42] *Ibid.*, 483.

[43] "Vom hellenistisch-heidenchristlichen Markus-Evangelium aus beurteilt, ist die heute noch erkennbare, judenchristliche Q-Quelle jedenfalls kein vollständiges, sondern nur ein

In a detailed attempt to contrast Q and pre-Markan tradition, U. Luz in 1975[44] identified eschatology as the major point of distinction between the two. In agreement with Hoffmann, Luz accepted the existence of a Q Group whose explicit christology focused on Jesus as the coming Son of Man/world ruler. The christology of the pre-Markan material centred on the authority evident in the miracles and work of the *earthly* Jesus. Whereas Jesus' miracles in Q are infrequent and draw attention to realized eschatology as signs of the inbreaking of the kingdom of God, Jesus' miracles in Mark never come in combination with the kingdom of God but instead serve a kerygmatic function by constituting the post-Easter community's faith in the saving power of Jesus himself.[45] Where Mark incorporates Q variants, Mark's versions invariably contain less eschatological interest.[46] Further, while Q lacks a biographical framework comparable to Mark's, Mark lacks almost entirely the kind of eschatological paranesis which appears determinative for the future judgement advocated by Q. Theological differences, then, between Mark and Q are commensurate with their formal differences. While narratives, wonder stories, apophthegms, and legends dominate the Markan tradition, Q contains apocalyptically oriented sayings and prophetic words. Luz, in this article, therefore addressed two different early Christian perspectives of Jesus: the Q group focused upon the future return of Jesus as the Son of Man, and the Markan community focused upon the earthly authority of Jesus.[47]

With similar presuppositions, Richard Edward's *Theology of Q* identified Q's theology as a complex combination of wisdom, prophetic, and eschatological

---

<<Halbevangelium>>! Aber solche traditionsgeschichtlichen Urteile verabsolutieren Standpunkte, berücksichtigen aber gerade nicht die Pluralität kerygmatischer Konzeptionen des Urchristentums." *Ibid.*, 40.

[44] "Das Jesusbild der vormarkinischen Tradition." In *Jesus Christus in Historie und Theologie*, FS H. Conzelmann, Ed. G. Strecker, Tübingen: J.C.B. Mohr (1975) 347-374.

[45] *Ibid.*, 355: "Grundlegend für die hier sehr reich fließende markinische Überlieferung ist, daß hier von den Wundern Jesu in besonderer Weise gesprochen wird: sie sind konstitutive für den Glauben der nachösterlichen Gemeinde und ein integraler Teil der Wirksamkeit des irdischen Jesus, nicht primär des Anbruchs des Reiches Gottes."

[46] *Ibid.*, 353: "In der Perikope vom Beelzebul (Mk 3, 22. 24-29 [30]) fehlen die beiden eschatologisch aus gerichteten Logien Lk 11.19, 20. Das Fehlen von V. 20 ist besonders wichtig: eine eschatologische Deutung der Wunder vom Anbruch des Gottesreiches her findet sich in der markinischen Überlieferung nicht."

[47] Edward Schillebeeckx (*Jesus*, New York: Seabury [1979] 423) offers a very similar perception to that of Luz: "The difference between the two communities lies in the fact that the Marcan congregation, which would appear not to acclaim any immediate salvific activity of the risen Christ prior to the Parousia, puts its faith in the ministry of the earthly Jesus in toto, and not just in his eschatological message of judgment and of mercy near at hand, as in the earliest phase of the Q tradition, which is therefore interested only in Jesus' preaching (logia) and hardly at all in his miracles."

themes. He maintained that the Q community knew of Jesus' death, but did not interpret the cross kerygmatically:

> It is the thesis of this study that Q preserves such a non-*kerygmatic* approach. Salvation is promised to those who respond to Jesus as the Son of Man and who are prepared for his imminent return. The death of Jesus is understood as a feature of the last days before the coming of the Kingdom when the forces of evil attempt to destroy those who speak in YHWH's name. The fate of the prophets has always been persecution, misunderstanding, and often death; as Jesus died at the hands of those who claim to be God's people, so those who follow in his steps can expect persecution. His death is highly significant, but it is not the basis of salvation.[48]

Edwards agreed that there was a plurality of kerygmatic understanding within the early Church. Q contains a message of salvation, but salvation bound to Jesus' imminent return as the Son of Man. Jesus' death is important as a model for the prophets who follow him, but the cross does not represent an act performed for the forgiveness of sins or as a means of salvation. Where Mark places emphasis on Jesus' death and resurrection, Q emphasizes Jesus' role as a prophet of the end times.

This growing consensus again set the tone in Dieter Zeller's short commentary on Q. In this work he agrees with previous writers on Q that the omission of Passion history suggests christological emphasis of another kind. Within Q, Jesus' death does not bring the forgiveness of sins because the Q community was able to appeal directly to God for forgiveness (Lk. 11:4).[49] Instead the Q community understood Jesus' death as the typical fate of a prophet of the Wisdom of God. Likewise the Q community placed limited importance on Easter. The resurrection was significant only in that it confirmed that Jesus would return as the Son of Man in the final judgement.[50] Zeller concludes that Q proclaims a kerygma which is not Jesus' death, but Jesus' message of the coming kingdom of God. Through the sending out of charismatic messengers the salvation of the coming kingdom is offered to the sick and poor. Where Mark contains a death and resurrection kerygma, Zeller believes a kingdom of God kerygma exists in Q.[51]

---

[48] *A Theology of Q*, Philadelphia: Fortress Press (1976) 149. The italics are Edwards'.

[49] "In Q wird der Tod Jesu nur einmal als Entschwinden angedeutet (Lk 13:35); er is nicht als Sühnesterben verstanden, die Vergebung Gottes braucht nicht erst durch ihn erwirkt zu werden, sondern die Q-Gemeinde bittet den Vater im Himmel direkt darum (Lk 11:4), freilich von Jesu Wort ermuntert, daß Gott barmherzig ist (vgl. Lk 6,36)." *Kommentar zur Logienquelle*, Stuttgart: Verlag Katholisches Bibelwerk (1984) 97.

[50] "Ostern hat für sie nur indirekt Bedeutung, weil sie -- trotz der Ablehnung Jesu durch Israel -- seine Sache weiterführen und ihn als den Menschensohn zum Gericht erwarten." *Ibid.*, 97.

[51] "Aber im Traditionskern enthält Q nicht nur Paränese, sondern durchaus auch Kerygma, eben die Botschaft Jesu vom nahen Reich Gottes (Lk 10,9). . . . Schließlich bleibt für uns –bei

In the most comprehensive study of Q to date in English, John Kloppenborg takes up the task left by Robinson and Koester to define the literary genre of Q in its historical setting. He compares Q with a vast range of ancient sayings collections to conclude that visible literary shifts took place in the evolution of Q as it developed from a mere collection of instructions to a proto-biography. Important to our present discussion, however, is his conviction that Schulz and others are correct in their assumption that Q represents an unique christological tradition:

> Q apparently conceived of the death of Jesus in accordance with the deuteronomistic pattern: it was the expected fate for a messenger of Sophia. Hence, at precisely the point at which one would expect influence of either the passion kerygma of the Crucified and Risen Messiah, or the narratives of the passion with their apologetic use of the OT, and the motif of the suffering Just One, Q moves in an entirely different direction. This is best explained by supposing, as Schulz does, that Q represents a theologically autonomous sphere of Christian theology.[52]

Kloppenborg agrees that the "autonomous sphere of Christian theology" that Q represents placed primary significance on the call to repentance in light of the coming judgement. Jesus' Passion experience is not the focus of Q, but rather Jesus' call to repentance and his proclamation of the kingdom of God.[53] With Schulz he believes "the reason why Q has a different view of the passion than that of the kerygma (or even the Marcan passion story) is that it derives from a different orbit of tradition."[54]

The endeavour to confirm variance between Mark and Q has been attempted through recourse to the study of genre. W. Kelber, for instance, following the seminal works of J. M. Robinson and H. Koester, claims that Q represents a genre of tradition dominated by an "oral ontology of language". With this technical phrase Kelber argues that the formula of speech characteristic of Q originally authorized its representatives to speak with "prophetic authority" so that their sayings bore the authority not of the past historical Jesus but of the exalted Lord Jesus in the present. Mark, in contrast, with the textual form of Gospel, "created the counterform to oral speech" and in so doing created a "gospel christology . . .

---

allen Schwierigkeiten einer >Übersetzung< –wichtig, daß die Logienquelle in radikaler Absage an die Welt die Verkündigung der nahen Gottesherrschaft ins Zentrum stellt." *Ibid.*, 98, 99.

[52] *The Formation of Q*, Philadelphia: Fortress Press (1987) 27.

[53] "The idiom of Q is controlled not by a philosophic notion of freedom, but by a historical and soteriological schema of God's constant invitation of Israel to repent, and by the expectation of the imminent manifestation of the kingdom – an event which calls forth a radical response in its adherents, and which produces conflict and polarization in the world. . . . Q, by contrast, does not appear to hold out much hope for the repentance and salvation of 'this generation.' All that awaits it is judgment." *Ibid.*, 324.

[54] *Ibid.*, 26.

an alternative to oral christology." Where Q stressed the present authority of Jesus as the inspiration of the community prophets, Mark's christology, in reaction to Q emphasized the Jesus of the past and his historical death.[55] M. E. Boring similarly argues that the paucity of sayings in Mark reflects its author's distrust of prophetic sayings: "To counteract this tendency, Mark took a step at once paradoxical and radical: he presented the message of the living Lord in a narrative form in which the post-Easter Jesus, in the narrative story line, says nothing."[56]

From a variety of perspectives, therefore, the absence of a Passion interest in Q has emerged as the decisive factor leading many scholars to reconsider the theological relationship between Mark and Q. Indeed, a growing number of scholars accept the lack of Passion emphasis within Q as verification for the conclusion that Mark and Q bear witness to two distinctly different christological traditions within early Christianity.[57] Among these scholars it is said that Mark's christology represents the orthodox beliefs of early Christians who attributed redemptive and soteriological significance to Jesus' death and resurrection. The christology of Q, in contrast, bears witness to the achievement of a separate group within first-century Palestine who placed little or no emphasis on Jesus' death and resurrection. Among scholars devoted to the study of Q, the following words of Burton Mack represent the growing consensus:

> The remarkable thing about the people of Q is that they were not Christians. They did not think of Jesus as a messiah or the Christ. They did not take his teachings as an indictment of Judaism. They did not regard his death as a divine, tragic, or saving event. And they did not imagine that he had been raised from the dead to rule over a transformed world. Instead, they thought of him as a teacher whose teachings made it possible to live with verve in troubled times.[58]

---

[55] *The Oral and the Written Gospel*, Philadelphia: Fortress (1983) 206-211.

[56] *The Continuing Voice of Jesus*, Louisville: Westminster/John Knox Press (1991) 243-245.

[57] The dominant alternative to this theory is the view that the passion narrative co-existed with Q in different settings within the same church. Adherents to this view include: Ulrich Wilckens, "Tradition de Jésus et Kérygma du Christ: la double historie de la tradition au sein du christianisme primitif", *RHPR* 47 (1967) 1-20; Ernst Käsemann, "On the Subject of Primitive Christian Apocalyptic", in *New Testament Questions of Today*, London: SCM Press (1969) 82-107, esp. 121f.; Horst R. Balz, *Methodologische Probleme der neutestamentliche Christologie*, WMANT 25, Neukirchen-Vluyn: Neukirchener Verlag (1967) 170-71; O. H. Steck, *Israel und das gewaltsame Geschick der Propheten*, WMANT 23, Neukirchen-Vluyn: Neukirchener Verlag (1967). For criticism of this view see Kloppenborg, *ibid.*, 24-26.

[58] *The Lost Gospel*, Rockport: Element (1993) 4.

V. The Problem

Our survey demonstrates the discord that exists between 19th and early 20th-century two-source critics who perceived Mark and Q to be primary sources which together attested to the genuine teaching of the historical Jesus, and numerous contemporary scholars who dissociate Mark and Q into two different spheres of early Christianity which contrast sharply on basic concepts including eschatology, christology, soteriology and discipleship. The problem at hand, therefore, is the relation of Mark and Q: Are their differences real or exaggerated, significant or minor? Is the evidence valid which scholars interpret to imply a sharp distinction in form and content between these two bodies of synoptic material? Are the two really comparable in every respect? Should we demand of Q all that Mark contains? Is the growing consensus correct—that Q's lack of a Passion narrative implies its origin within a Q community which developed a christology in which Jesus' death and resurrection was either unknown or insignificant? Does Q contain unique eschatological expectation? Does comparison of Mark and Q provide evidence of a "plurality of kerygmatic design" within early Christianity? Do Mark and Q represent two opposing christological traditions?[59] Does the author of Mark present a Gospel which is christologically incompatible with the Sayings Source Q, or is Mark simply a fuller more developed christological statement whose emphasis is not counter to the perspective of Q, but simply goes beyond Q?

VI. The Purpose and Scope of this Study

The purpose of this book is to make a fresh comparison of the Q materials with the Gospel of Mark in order to determine whether the two are compatible christologically. In contrast to those scholars who speak of a self-contained christology within Q or of an evolving christology within Q, we shall show that Q is best understood as Matthew's and Luke's independent utilization of highly valued Greek recordings of Jesus' teachings. The fact that Matthew and Luke both absorb the Q material into their gospels suggests that the two Evangelists respected both the historicity of the Q tradition and the channel(s) of transmission through which Q passed. Obviously christology was the motivating force behind the

---

[59] William Farmer goes so far as to complain that the study of the theology of Q in itself affects the Christian faith: "the present and growing theological interest in "Q" makes it clear that theories about the Gospels can affect faith. Is the cross and resurrection of the Church's preaching grounded in the apostolic witness central to our faith or not? This question of "Q" is no mere academic question. It vitally affec*~ \ow we construe the Apostolic witness of the New Testament, . . ." In "The Church's St. ..c in the Question of 'Q' ", *Perkins Journal* 39 (1986) 17.

writing of Matthew and Luke. It must be questioned, therefore, whether the writers of these two passion-oriented Gospels[60] would both have incorporated sayings of Jesus that originated or were created by a Q community which attributed very little significance to Jesus' death and resurrection. Moreover, it must be asked whether the authors of Matthew and Luke would *both* have combined two sources which were christologically incompatible. More likely, the authors of Matthew and Luke sensed a need to supplement Mark's passion narrative with additional evidence characterizing the content of Jesus' earthly teaching. Therefore, using Matthew and Luke as clues, the differences between Mark and Q may be explained by the likelihood that the authors of Matthew and Luke had before them sayings materials which were either unavailable to Mark or which Mark chose not to use for reasons which were not christological in nature. Simply stated, our purpose is to demonstrate that Jesus' words and acts recorded in Q are compatible christologically with the testimony of Mark's Gospel.

We will attempt to substantiate this argument first by assessing the themes previously thought particularly characteristic of Q (wisdom, prophecy, the Son of Man) and addressing the question of the compatibility of these concepts with Mark. Second, we will compare and contrast Jesus' teaching on the kingdom of God in Q and Mark. Occurring ten times in the Q material and fourteen times in Mark, the kingdom of God is a primary interest of both bodies of synoptic material.[61] G. Bornkamm, the teacher of both Tödt and Lührmann, wrote of the Q collection: "Ihr Hauptmotive ist Jesu Predigt vom Kommen der Herrschaft Gottes und dem Eingang in das Reich (Lk. 11, 20; Mt. 13, 31; 8, 11f; 11,2)."[62] And in regard to Mark, R. Pesch is representative when he writes: "Gottes Herrschaft ist nach dem Bericht des Markus der zentrale Begriff von Predigt und Lehre Jesu."[63] If Q is the production of an ancient 'variant' community whose christology, soteriology, and eschatology were formulated without interest in the passion of Jesus, a comparison with passion-oriented Mark should expose the uniqueness of Q. If, however, it can be shown that Jesus is saying and doing the same or similar kinds of things in Mark and Q and with similar emphases, it must be questioned whether narrow assessments of Q are valid, and whether the hypothesis of an

---

[60] Passion-oriented at least to the extent that both contain lengthy passion accounts.

[61] Q: Lk. 6:20b//Mt. 5:3; Lk. 12:31//Mt. 6:33; Lk. 11:2//Mt. 6:9f.; Lk. 7:28//Mt. 11:11; Lk. 10:9//Mt. 10:7; Lk. 11:20//Mt. 12:28; Lk. 13:18, 19//Mt. 13:31-32; Lk. 13:28, 29//Mt. 8:11, 12; Lk. 16:16//Mt. 11:12, 13; Mark: 1:14, 15; 4:11, 26, 30; 9:1, 47; 10:14, 15, 23, 24, 25; 12:34; 14:25.

[62] "Evangelien, synoptische", in RGG Bd. 2, 759. So also Burton Mack (*The Lost Gospel*, 123), "There is only one term in all of Q^1 that refers to the movement and its purposes. That is the term kingdom of God, . . ."

[63] *Das Markusevangelium* I, HTKNT, Freiburg: Herder (1977) 107.

esoteric Q community is necessary. The purpose of this study is to expose the weaknesses of previous appraisals of Q and to clarify the compatibility of Mark's Gospel with the teaching of Jesus as it is evidenced in the Q material. If Q scholars are asking the right question, and if Q does, indeed, have an unique christology, Q's witness to Jesus' teaching of the kingdom of God should emerge as distinct from Mark's development of the same theme.[64] If, however, Mark corroborates the basic message of Jesus' teaching in Q, the lack of a Passion narrative must be questioned as a valid criterion for attributing an unique christology to Q.

---

[64] So Burton Mack (*The Lost Gospel*, 48), "A theme that is common both to Q and to the gospels takes on different meanings in each literary context. When read in Q these themes are better understood if their gospel connotation is avoided."

Chapter 2

The Q Community Hypothesis

I. Introduction

In both Markan and Q studies, scholars have approached matters of christology, soteriology, and theology with the presupposition that distinct historical communities either actively or latently participated in shaping the documents with which they were associated. A corollary to Form Criticism, *Gemeindetheologie* postulates that the earliest synoptic traditions, including Jesus' sayings, were shaped according to the practical needs and social situations of the people who valued, recorded, and passed them on. Accordingly, careful analysis of Gospel material yields evidence qualifying the theological perspectives of the specific communities which transmitted synoptic tradition. From Mark's Gospel we can distil the theological perspectives of Mark's church. From Q we can decipher the christological bias or *Tendenz* of the community or group which recorded and edited the teachings of Jesus which we now find in parallel form in Matthew and Luke.

Gemeindetheologie, however, occasions historical problems particularly in its application to the study of Q. While virtually all Q scholars agree that Q contains at least some authentic teaching of Jesus, little explanation has been offered as to where Holtzmann, Jülicher, Harnack and others went wrong when they attributed most if not all the Q material to the historical Jesus. Isolation of Q community bias is difficult because Q does not contain explicit statements of purpose such as Lk. 1:1 or explicit statements of belief such as Mk. 1:1. Where does distinctive Q influence enter in? How is the conjecture that the Q community composed sayings of Jesus more convincing than the conclusion which served as its precedent—that Q contains largely what Matthew and Luke say it contains—Jesus' teaching? In passing from dominical teaching to community creation what landmarks indicate the distinction and in what way are those landmarks inappropriate to Jesus' thought? Is the distinction compelling or is it dubious?

Explicit Biblical evidence documenting the life of those who passed on Jesus' teaching does not exist. Hence G. Theissen, a pioneer into sociological study of the first followers of Jesus, admits the limits of his own method: "Scepticism on grounds of methodology is understandable and legitimate. We know very little. Much must remain conjectural. Nevertheless, scientific work is legitimate as long as better and worse hypotheses can be weighed against one another."[1] Our purpose in this chapter is to define what scholars are saying about the carriers of the Q tradition and to weigh the value of the Q community hypothesis.

II. The Q Community in Recent Discussion

A. Siegfried Schulz

Siegfried Schulz speaks of two successive Q communities: an early Palestinian Jewish community and a later Hellenistic Jewish community. He boldly asserts that the form of Palestinian Jewish Christianity which stands behind the oldest Q material is an eschatological movement which stands in fervent expectation of an imminent end, and which cannot be likened to any other salvation community (*Heilsgemeinde*) in Israel. The Q community is unique in that it offers no predications as "the True Israel" or the "New Israel" nor does it adopt the titles "the chosen" or "the saints" which were characteristic of the early Aramaic speaking community of Jerusalem. "The oldest Q community regards itself as the community of the endtimes."[2] The community lived in an atmosphere in which all pronouncements were carried by the unwavering hope of the imminent arrival of the kingdom of God, when the Son of Man would appear before the throne of God and redemption would be given to the faithful and harsh judgement to unbelievers.

Central to Schulz's understanding of the earliest Q community is his notion of an "Apocalyptic Enthusiasm" among the Q group. He accepts fully Ernst Käsemann's conjecture[3] that Mt. 12:32; 10:32 par. reflect prophetic pronouncements within the community while Mt. 10:15, 11:22, 24; 12:42f. par. reveal the community's focus on the eschatological future. In turn, Mt. 7:2; 23:12, 10:26f., 39 par. indicate an apocalyptic awareness within the community, and Mt. 11:20-24; 7:22; 8:11f. par. represent prophetic pronouncements of curse.[4] Thus Schulz identifies within Q (which he classifies amongst the oldest writings of

---

[1] ET. *The First Followers of Jesus, A Sociological Analysis of the Earliest Christianity*, London: SCM (1978) 3.

[2] *Q–Die Spruchquelle*, 168-69.

[3] Schulz adopts the concept from Ernst Käsemann who originally spoke of an "Apocalyptic Enthusiasm" in *Die Anfange christlicher Theologie*, Versuche II; Göttingen (1960) 82-104. However, Schulz's overall understanding of the tradition of Q differs sharply from Käsemann's contention that the Q tradition co-existed with the Passion tradition within the same early Churches.

[4] *Q–Die Spruchquelle*, 33-34.

Christian tradition) a prophetic-apocalyptic enthusiasm which awakened an imminent expectation of the parousia through Easter. This old community order reflected apocalyptic enthusiasm in its strict adherence to the law (Mt. 5:12; 10:19f.; 13:16f. par.). The entire community thought of itself as standing in the sequence of OT prophets. Charismatic leadership in the form of prophecy and the prophetic was the only kind of leadership or organization possible for such a group. Community membership was characterized by the possession of the spirit as the pledge of the forthcoming parousia and the envisioned power of their mission. Enthusiasm and apocalypticism were united as an inner necessity.[5]

From these observations, Schulz eliminates Jerusalem as the possible location of the original Q group because its leadership originally came from the twelve. Instead he opts for a location within Transjordanian Syria-Palestine. From Mt. 5:18, he further reasons that the community must have adhered stringently to the law of Moses, and as a result kept the observation of circumcision and adhered to the Jerusalem temple cult—they did not consider themselves a new religion separate from Judaism.

Thus, for Schulz, the unifying force behind the oldest Q community was the eschatological expectation of an imminent end event. The community assumed a prophetic role in announcing the coming end and the judgement associated with it. They identified their own charismatic tendencies (the filling of the spirit) as evidence that the end was near. Schulz dates the work of this community as contemporary with the oldest pronouncement models in Mark.[6] He believes the kerygma of this group is pre-Pauline, and even goes so far as to say that "the false brothers" in Ga. 2:4 may have belonged to this oldest Q community. In Acts 6-8, Ga. 1:15-2:14, and Ro. 15:30f., he finds as characteristics of "these" Hebrews: an apocalyptic expectation of the end, an expressed loyalty to the Mosaic Law, and participation in the Jerusalem temple.[7]

Whereas the Palestinian Q community exclusively drew on prophetic tradition, the later Hellenistic Jewish community produced a variety of new literary forms of expression: historic narrative, apophthegms, apocalyptic words (even an apocalypse), parables, and "I words" which reflect back on the significance of the earthly Jesus. Schulz believes the final polished Q tradition is not to be found in Palestinian origins, but in the more recent Hellenistic-Jewish community which is best sought in the Transjordan-Decapolis.[8]

The primary activity which set this community apart from the Palestinian

---

5 *Ibid.*, 33, 34.

6 *Ibid.*, 481, 482.

7 *Ibid.*, 166, 67.

8 *Ibid.*, 481.

tradition was its "kerygmatic recourse" to the words and deeds of the earthly Jesus. The more recent community developed a new theological perspective that expected the apocalyptic arrival of Jesus as the Son of Man. From the enthusiastic prophetic sayings in which Jesus was originally announced as the present-raised Son of Man, now come the words of the earthly Jesus as the endtime prophet for the approaching Son of Man parousia. Kerygmatic recourse to the words and deeds of Jesus develop from three causes: 1) the delay of the parousia; 2), kerygmatic reaction to the Markan material; and 3), the diminishment of prophetic enthusiasm evidenced by the secondary use of the prophetic introductory formula λέγω ὑμῖν.[9] This process continued during the phase of tradition when the Q materials were collected, and above all in the redaction of Q. At the end of this phase, Jesus speaks throughout Q as the earthly Nazarene, the Son of God and the Son of Man. The Hellenistic-Jewish Q community has come to grips with the delay of the parousia.

In summary, Siegfried Schulz identifies two historical communities behind Q: a very early Syrian-Palestinian community and a later Transjordanian Hellenistic Jewish community. The later community developed from the first but supplemented its tradition with recourse to the words and deeds of the earthly Jesus in an attempt to understand the delayed parousia. Both communities understood themselves in relation to the OT prophetic tradition, and both actively awaited the eschatological end event. The earlier community, however, displayed a charismatic vitality which did not survive into the life of the latter.

C. Dieter Lührmann

Dieter Lührmann in *Die Redaktion der Logienquelle* attempts to unveil and explain the layers of redaction within the sayings source. The supposition that antagonism to Israel is worked into Q redactionally[10] leads Lührmann to the conclusion that the community of Q must have been a group belonging to Gentile Christianity and one which faced opposition and persecution from the Jews. Hence the judgement motif which pervades Q. Lührmann defends his case by noting the frequency of the threat-word form (*Drohworte Gattung*) in Q.[11] Drawing from Bultmann's conclusions,[12] he argues that the use of "*Drohworte*" by the Q community conforms to OT tradition of prophetic judgement against Israel. Recognizable

---

[9] *Ibid.*, 482.

[10] *Die Redaktion der Logienquelle*, 31.

[11] *Ibid.*, 37, 57.

[12] *Die Geschichte der Synoptischen Tradition*, FRLANT 29; Gottingen (1921) 118.

features of the Q community are their opposition to Israel and their pronouncement of judgement against Israel.[13]

Lührmann believes the Q community was an eschatologically oriented group. However, he believes that it was aware of a delayed parousia from the beginning.[14] In his chapter on the eschatology of Q, he refers to three sayings groups which were inserted secondarily by the community to explain the delay of the parousia: 1) the call for watchfulness Lk. 12:39f., 42-46//Mt. 24:43f., 45-51; 2) the parable of the pounds Lk. 19:12-27//Mt. 25:14-30; and 3), the section on the day of the Son of Man Lk. 17:24, 26-30, 34f., 37//Mt. 24:27f., 37-41.

Thus Lührmann describes the Q community as a Gentile entity existing in opposition to the established Judaism of its day. The primary activities of the community with regard to Q included redaction in which the editors altered existing traditions and inserted additional parables and sayings reflecting their tension with the Jews and their awareness of the delayed return of the Son of Man. The use of *Drohworte* suggest that the community was engaged in prophetic activity emphasizing judgement. For these reasons he assigns the Q redaction to a Hellenistic community existing sometime in the 50's or 60's A.D.[15]

D. Paul Hoffmann

Written in response to Lührmann's work, Paul Hoffmann's *Studien zur Theologie der Logienquelle* emphasizes apocalyptic experience as the motivating force behind the Q material. Just as Paul's mission was validated by an apocalyptic experience (Gal. 1:12), so the Q community legitimated their mission through the apocalyptic words of Jesus.[16]

> Both the compilation of sayings about the work of the messengers and the logion Mt. 11:27/Lk 10:22 go back to the community; thus, they already presuppose the *post-Easter* situation. Through the Apocalyptic-Sayings, the work of the messengers is legitimated *after Jesus' death*. The Apocalyptic language reveals the origin of their present pronouncement and their existence as a group.[17]

---

[13] *Die Redaktion der Logienquelle*, 93.

[14] D. Catchpole follows Lührmann in perceiving the delay of the parousia in Q. See "Q, Prayer, and the Kingdom: A Rejoinder", *JTS* 40 (1989) 379; *idem*, "The Mission Charge in Q", *Semeia* 55 (1992) 157.

[15] *Ibid.*, 88. Here Lührmann notes the inconsistency of Biblical scholarship in locating the geographical location of the Q community: Wellhausen placed Q within Jerusalem while Harnack preferred a location in Galilee. Lührmann concludes that an exact determination of the location of Q's community is impossible.

[16] *Studien zur Theologie der Logienquelle*, 140-142.

[17] *Ibid.*, 139, 140. The translation is ours, the italics are Hoffmann's.

The "apocalypse of the Son", Lk. 10:21, 22//Mt. 11:25-27, determines the origin of the group's confession, and provides motivation for collecting the sayings of Jesus. The Q community was an apocalyptic group. They interpret Jesus' teachings, death, resurrection, and exaltation entirely from an apocalyptic perspective.[18] The Q confession, therefore, is the apocalyptically oriented identification of Jesus with the eschatological Son of Man who will bring judgement at the endtime. The coming Son of Man in Lk. 17:30 presupposes apocalyptic tradition.[19] Likewise, the mention of the coming Son of Man in Lk. 12:40 and the comparison of his appearance with lightning in Lk. 17:24 presuppose that the Son of Man will come into this world from the mystery of the beyond—a presupposition grounded in apocalyptic tradition.

Hoffmann differs from Lührmann in arguing that the group expected an imminent rather than a delayed parousia. He claims that the commissioning of the twelve in Lk. 10:2-16//Mt.9:37f.; 10:7-16, 40; 11:20-27 suggests an imminent expectation in which the end is described as the endtime harvest of God. He further argues that Lk.12:39, 42 par. and Lk. 19:12 par. can be understood in the framework of an imminent eschatology in which the inbreaking takes place within one's own lifetime or generation. It is thus possible to combine the delay statements with an imminent expectation, and correct to order the expectation of these statements horizontally. Time is understood in relation to the imminent coming of the Son of Man.[20]

With Lührmann and Schulz, Hoffmann agrees that the Q community understood itself in succession with OT prophets. In addition, he believes that the prophetic traditions within Q were intertwined with elements drawn from a background of Wisdom tradition. For example, in Jesus' encounter with the disciples of John the Baptist found in Lk.7//Mt.11, the sayings in Mt.11:18, 19 par. mark the Wisdom tradition while vs. 5 presupposes a prophetic tradition. The image of the endtime prophet (Isa 61:1) combines with the presentation of sending through Wisdom.[21]

Hoffmann surmises the Q tradition presupposes a charismatic prophetic missions movement. The community members believed they were sent by Jesus

---

[18] If I interpret Hoffmann correctly, he believes the resurrection and exaltation of Jesus were apocalyptic in that these events were originally experienced as visions by the Q community. Thus, it follows in terms of general content that Q's emphasis on the teaching of the Son of Man, the end-time judgment, and the coming Kingdom of God represent topics characteristic of apocalyptic literature.

[19] Hoffmann assimilates the apocalyptic tradition behind the coming Son of Man sayings in Q with that of the Ethiopic Enoch. Jesus is raised to Son of Man status in the same way as Enoch –his words become the words of the future judge. See I Enoch 71:14-17. Ibid., 141.

[20] *Ibid.,* 36-38, 49.

[21] *Ibid.,* 231-233.

to announce the message of the nearness of the Kingdom in expectation of His coming as the endtime Son of Man. Imminent expectation and miraculous healings were characteristic of the group's work. Like John and Jesus their task was the work of endtime prophets. Their work was primarily oriented toward Israel. The greeting of peace (Lk. 10:5//Mt. 10:11, 12) associated the Q group with the endtime prophets. Hoffmann locates the group historically during the conflict between the insurrectionists and the pacifists in the years before the Jewish-Roman War, actively passing on the words of the Son of Man Jesus .[22]

D. Athanasius Polag

Athanasius Polag identifies the work and self-understanding of the Q community in two successive stages of redaction: an earlier major collection (*Die Hauptsammlung*) and a later redaction (*Spät Redaktion*).[23] He proposes that the editors of the major collection originally received through tradition a small collection of pericopes, *Die Kernstücke* (Lk. 6:27-38; 7:18-26; 10:4-11; 11:14-23 par.), to which they added the bulk of the Q material (Lk. 3:7-4:13; 6:20-7:1a; 7:18-35; 10:1-16; 11:1b-13; 11:14-26; 11:29-36; 11:37-52; 12:1-12; 12:22-53; 12:54-16:18; 17:1-10; 17:23-35 par.). The Q corpus was finally completed, according to Polag, with a later phase of editing whose contribution can be seen in Lk.7:1b-10//Mt. 8:5-10, 13; Lk.7:27//Mt. 11:10; Lk. 7:28//Mt. 11:11; Lk. 10:21, 22//Mt. 11:25-27; Lk. 10:23, 24//Mt. 13:16, 17; Lk. 12:10//Mt. 12:31, 32; Lk. 12:49-53//Mt. 10:34-36; Lk. 12:47, 48//Mt. 5:19.

Evidence for redactional activity in the formation of the major collection (*Die Hauptsammlung*) exists in the nature of its arrangement into sayings groups (*Spruchgruppen*), while clues to the late redaction are found in the organization, introductions, and conclusions to individual groups.[24] In the evolution of Q the task of the editors was: (1) the review of the materials at hand, (2) the clarification of language peculiarities, (3) the analysis, arranging, and grouping of the sayings, and (4), the comparison of the choice of materials with the original Jesus tradition.[25]

Because Polag understands the Q tradition as the culmination of a two-stage editorial process rather than as a uniform tradition which remained unchanged throughout its transmission (an *Überlieferungsgeschichte* as opposed to a

---

[22] *Ibid.,* 331-334.

[23] *Die Christologie der Logienquelle,* WMANT 45; Neukirchener Verlag: Neukirchen-Vluyn, 1977.

[24] Polag (7-8) lists 11 saying groups (*Spruchgruppen*).

[25] *Ibid.,* 6.

Traditionsgeschichte), he carefully avoids speaking of Q's community as a single unified historical group. Rather he directs attention to the identity of the carriers of the Q tradition—*die Träger* or *die Tradenten*. The carriers of the "major collection" of Q were probably the leading men of the community. Four possible groups, however, could have passed on the material of the "late redaction": the leaders of the community, the missionaries sent out by the community, the early Christian prophets and the teachers of the community. In rejecting the first three groups Polag cites the uncertainty of the role the community leaders played in the transmission of tradition outside of Jerusalem, and the omission of Jesus' sayings in early Christian missionary preaching. Polag rejects prophets as the carriers of "the sayings of the Lord tradition" because he associates early Christian prophecy with the filling of the spirit. The title "prophet" implied special spiritual attributes (*Geistbegabung*)[26]—an influence not significant in Q. He concludes that the community teachers were the bearers and carriers of the Q tradition. The activities of the Q teachers were probably similar to those of contemporary Jewish teachers: they directed worship, administered ethical exhortation, and interpreted Jesus in light of scripture.[27]

Polag attempts to identify the *Sitz im Leben* of the Q community by identifying the possible areas of early Christian life in which the sayings of the Lord may have been used. In turn he considers the breaking of bread, prayer in the service of God, and gatherings for special occasions such as baptism. Citing the inappropriate use of Jesus' sayings in each of these contexts, he goes on to attempt to isolate the community *Sitz im Leben* in the functions of missionary pronouncement, dialogue with enemies of the community, personal exhortation, and the instruction of new community leaders. However, because Q's lack of a faith formula rules out a missions setting, Polag concludes that the most probable *Sitz im Leben* for the community exists in the preservation and transmission of the words of the Lord for the purpose of instructing believers in post-baptism catechism. In turn, a new *Sitz im Leben* came into being in the late redaction stage as new christological perspectives arose either on account of a different circle of carriers (*Tradenten*) whose presuppositions for the interpretation of Jesus' sayings was different, or because a new application of the collection was taken over (e.g., in the service of worship).[28]

Polag therefore does not envision a static isolated Q community. Instead, he proposes a series of contributors who were responsible for the passing on of the Q

---

[26] *Ibid.*, 26.
[27] *Ibid.*, 23-30.
[28] *Ibid.*, 17-21

material. The most important were the teachers who organized the sayings into groups during the *Hauptsammlung* stage, and the editors who arranged, introduced, and concluded the sayings groups during the period of late redaction.

E. Walter Schmithals

In his introduction to the first three gospels, Walter Schmithals[29] reconstructs yet another framework for the development of the Q tradition. Schmithals agrees with Polag that behind the sayings source existed a unique community and a distinct line of carriers. Q was not originally a sayings collection but a composition which developed by degrees. Schmithals divides the Q material into two layers of tradition—Q[1] and Q.

Q[1], the original layer, exists in the Q/Mk doublets.[30] Schmithals stresses that Q[1] was not christological in purpose. Instead he perceives the circle carrying Q[1] as a group active in responding to a small apocalypse which came into being in A.D. 40 when Caligula placed his statue in the Jerusalem temple.[31] The author(s) of Q[1] was convinced that this desecrating event would bring in the end of the age. This apocalypse ignited the missionary thrust and the interim ethic characteristic of Q. Schmithals describes the Q[1] community with detail: their language was Aramaic and their geographic location was probably within Galilee (Lk 10:13). Their mission was not directed to Gentiles, as references to the Gentile mission do not exist within Q[1]. Jesus' disciples bear no influence on this first layer, as the twelve are not mentioned. The change of the ages (*Äonenwende*) is first encountered with the activity of John the Baptist (Lk. 16:16//Mt. 11:12f.; Lk. 7:28 par.). Jesus is identified as the successor to John and nothing more. He continues

---

[29] *Einleitung in die drei ersten Evangelien*, Berlin: Walter de Gruyter (1985) 384-404.

[30] *Ibid.*, 399-402.

[31] Gerd Theissen (*The Gospels in Context*, Edinburgh: T&T Clark [1992] 203-234) similarly envisions the collecting of the sayings of Jesus in Q as a response to the Caligula crisis. He persuasively demonstrates how the temptation narrative could have been applied to the social context of Palestine in 40's A.D. Less persuasive, we believe, is his case that the temptation narrative represents the *terminus a quo* for Q. He argues that in Mt. 4:9//Lk. 4:7; Mt. 4:10//Lk. 4:8 προσκυνέω should be taken as prostration. Jesus' refusal to fall prostrate before Satan represents the Q Christian's refusal to honor Gaius Caligula, who regularly demanded subjects to prostrate themselves in his presence as to a god. However, it is not clear that προσκυνέω can be confined to this context in Q where the Lk. version lacks the word πεσών from Mt. 4:9. Similarly, it is a bold conjecture that προσκυνήσεις was inserted secondarily by the Q scribes into Dt. 6:13; 10:20 (LXX diff. MT) to admonish against prostration before Caligula, when the same word is found in Dt. 6:13 in the OT versions of Codex Alexandrinus, Justin, Clement of Alexandria, Origen, Cyril and Chrysostom. It is easier to believe that Q is here following the same OT text type as these witnesses as opposed to Theissen's (216, 17) conviction that all of the above assimilated Dt. 6:13 in their Old Testaments to the quotations in Q (Mt. 4:10//Lk. 4:8).

John's activities of announcing the coming of the kingdom of God and proclaiming the coming of the Son of Man.

Interestingly, Schmithals cites the Jewish wars (A.D. 66-70) as a second apocalyptic event within Q^1, in addition to Caligula's desecration in AD 40. This event renewed an acute imminent expectation of the end among the carriers of Q^1 (Lk 11:49-51 par.). The previous small apocalypse was now reinterpreted in light of the new apocalyptic situation. Thus apocalyptic elements dominate Q^1. The earliest carriers of the Q^1 tradition do not confess Jesus as the Christ nor do they pronounce him as the Coming Son of Man—Judge.

In contrast, the task of the Q redaction was purely christological.[32] The universal scope of the Gospel and the Gentile mission emerge as the redactional motives. Where John was previously seen as a prophet on par with Jesus, he is now given the role of Jesus' forerunner (Lk. 3:1-22). The redactor adopts a Hellenistic image to paint Jesus as the Son of God (Lk. 4:1-13par) in what Schmithals calls an artistic narrative (*kunstvollen Erzählung*)—the redactor apparently uses the same tool in Lk. 10:22par. In Lk. 7:18-23 John renews his role as predecessor and Jesus affirms that he is the coming one by reference to his deeds. The redactor goes further in Lk. 9:57-62. Here Jesus unmistakably identifies himself with the Son of Man of Q^1. In Lk. 13:31 the redactor identifies Jesus with personified Godly Wisdom, and finally with the parable of the pounds the redactor concludes Q^1 with the presentation of the coming judge as the present leader of the community. Thus Schmithals concludes that all christological material in Q is the work of creative redaction.

Central to Schmithal's thesis is his understanding of Q^1's and Q's relationship to Mark.[33] Q^1 was composed prior to Mark around A.D. 75[34] and subsequently used by Mark. Q was written later as a supplement to Mark's Gospel. Schmithals proposes that Mark took over the Q^1 material in an attempt to win over the Q^1 group to the christological Kerygma of the early Church. When Mark's purpose was achieved, christological and universal elements were added to Q^1 in the Q redaction. Thus Q^1 ultimately was absorbed into the early Christian (christological) community. Schmithals even goes so far as to say that the author of Mark and the author/redactor of Q come from the same school. Following Q's completion, Mark and Q were carried in different directions. It is not surprising, therefore, that different versions were eventually used by Matthew and Luke.

---

[32] *Ibid.,* 396-399.

[33] *Ibid.,* 398, 399, 402-404.

[34] *Ibid.,* 403.

F. Rudolf Laufen

Rudolf Laufen represents a consensus among Q scholars in arguing that Jesus' commissioning address in Lk. 10:1-16 par. reflects the practical problems facing the church situation in which the Sayings Source developed. The section addresses the material needs of the community missionaries. It suggests the members of the Q community have embarked on a mission to the Gentiles in which their primary purpose is to repeat Jesus' proclamation of an imminent parousia— the nearness of the kingdom of God.[35] In contrast to Hoffmann, Laufen asserts that the impetus for the Q mission is not apocalyptic but eschatological and christological: "Die Gottesherrschaft und damit das Eschaton ist in Jesus, dem Auferstanden und als Menschensohn zum Gericht zurückerwarteten, bereits angebrochen und in der Person der Glaubensboten (Sendungsmotiv) nahe."[36] The preaching of the kingdom of God is the centre of the Q pronouncement, but not with apocalyptic colouring. The christological accent which had already come forth from the mouth of the historical Jesus (Lk. 11:20//Mt. 12:28) was decisive for the orientation of Q, so that in contrast to Schmithals, Laufen observes continuity between Jesus' own christological understanding and the christological perspectives of the Q community.[37] Apart from the commissioning address, Laufen does not offer a specific *Sitz im Leben* for the entire Q collection.

G. Risto Uro

In his monograph *Sheep Among the Wolves*, R. Uro focuses his research on the mission instructions of Q, concluding that they passed through three successive stages. The earliest collection defended the rights and lifestyle "of the wandering, ascetic preachers who were the charismatic authorities of the Christian movement in the Palestine of the first decades after Jesus' crucifixion."[38] The purpose of these charismatic preachers was to gather the eschatological people of God and "to proclaim the immediate coming of God's reign, as was also done by the historical Jesus."[39] The second phase of instruction came into being as a result of the negative Jewish response to the mission of stage 1. At this second phase, prophetic cries of divine judgement entered the Q material to reprimand "the recalcitrance of the Jewish people." Finally in stage three, in the final redaction of

---

[35] *Die Doppelüberlieferungen der Logienquelle und des Markusevangeliums*, 289.

[36] *Ibid.*, 290.

[37] *Ibid.*, 294.

[38] Helsinki: Suomalainen Tiedeakatemia (1987) 241.

[39] *Sheep Among the Wolves*, 241.

Q, the materials of the previous two stages are applied practically to the "ecclesiastical" and "didactic" purposes of the Q community. From stage 1 to stage 3, Q reveals a long tradition history which concludes in "a mature ecclesiastical situation" some time around 70 C.E.[40]

H. Migaku Sato

M. Sato, in *Q und Prophetie,* locates Q's beginnings in the pre-Easter group of Jesus' disciples. Easter compelled the Q disciples to renew the pronouncement of their master's message and to identify the risen Jesus with the Son of Man / World ruler. The Q circle was distinguished by two divisions: wandering preachers and settled members of the community.[41] The community's preoccupation with the endtime sets it apart from the early Jerusalem community. The Q community was prophetically orientated. The purpose of the *Q-Jünger* was to prophesy, and like the followers of OT prophets, to pass on the word of their master: "Daneben übten die Q-Jünger "Jüngerprophetie" aus, wobei genauso wie in Alten Testament die "Meisterspruche" eine entscheidende Rolle spielte."[42] Hence the Q ethos follows that of the OT prophets and their circle of followers: homelessness, separation from family, sacrifice of material possessions. Finally, the disciples were characterized by their identification with Jesus—the master prophet and Son of Man. The *Q-Jünger* attempted to follow Jesus' lifestyle even to the point of sharing his violent fate.[43]

I. John Kloppenborg

John Kloppenborg identifies three compositional layers within Q.[44] The genre of sapiential instruction typifies the first stage. Characteristic components include clusters of admonitions "which take the form of sapiential *Mahnsprüche* (i.e., imperatives with aphoristic motive clauses), prefaced by programmatic aphorisms and sometimes concluded by warnings to heed the words of the sage."[45] The

---

[40] *Ibid.,* 241, 243, 271.

[41] Here Sato is dependent on the sociological works of G. Theissen: *Sociologie der Jesusbewegung. Ein Beitrag zur Entstehungsgeschichte des Urchristentums,* München: 1977; *Studien zur Soziologie des Urchristentums,* Tübingen: J.C.B. Mohr (Paul Siebeck), 1983.

[42] *Q und Prophetie,* WUNT 2. Reihe 29; Tübingen: J.C.B. Mohr (Paul Siebeck), 1988, 408.

[43] *Ibid.,* 407-408.

[44] *The Formation of Q,* 1989. Kloppenborg provides a valuable summary of his findings in his recent article: "Literary Convention, Self-Evidence and the Social History of the Q People", *Semeia* 55 (1992) 80-81. Our summary statements below are based on this article.

[45] *Semeia* 55 (1992) 80.

second compositional layer is characterized primarily by prophetic and polemical statements against "this generation." Many of these statements are structured as *chreiai*—sharp pointed sayings voiced by specific persons in specific situations. All the apocalyptic Son of Man sayings and all the Q material which deals with the relationship of Jesus and John occurs at this secondary stage. The final stage of Q redaction, according to Kloppenborg, appears with the Temptation story and the few sayings which reflect concern for Torah (Lk. 11:42c; Lk. 16:17). Thus behind Q exists a literary evolution from "instruction" to "proto-biography." At different stages in the evolution process, Q resembled instructions, gnomologium, and *chreiai* collections while its historicizing elements were inserted in the final redaction.

Kloppenborg's compositional theory has implications for the study of the tradition history of Q. Defining Q as a "Sayings Gospel", he denies that Jesus' death was perceived as salvific by the Q community, and claims that Jesus' resurrection was not a motivating impetus for the Q *Tradents*.[46] Q represents a second kerygma independent of other *kerygmata*. Behind each of the three layers of composition, there exists a separate social background. The social location of the first stage exists within the "scribal sector" of the cities and villages of Galilee, Perea, Iturea and the region of the Decapolis. The second, polemical stratum of Q, distinguishes itself as "Israel." Their counterparts were the Pharisees with whom they struggled for "social dominance." They socialized in the market places of the larger cities. The final stage of Q reflects a new heightened emphasis of Torah and the Temple. By this time the Q people have learned to engage with the Pharisees using their own law and logic.

J. Myung-Soo Kim

Myung-Soo Kim in his published Ph.D. thesis *Die Trägergruppe von Q-Sozialgeschichtliche Forschung zur Q-Überlieferung in den synoptischen Evangelien*, attempts, as his title suggests, to identify the social background of the carriers of the Q tradition. Kim's study is unique in its comparison of Q-theology with Minjung Theology (a Korean version of South American Liberation Theology), but his description of the social origin of the Q group is quite familiar. The Q community considers itself the eschatological community of the endtime: "Diese eschatologische Bewußtsein der Q-Gemeinde wäre dann die entscheidende Triebkraft der Jesusbewegung."[47] The community did not identify Jesus as the Messiah, but furthered the teaching of the earthly Jesus, following his wandering

---

[46] "'Easter Faith' and the Sayings Gospel Q", *Semeia* 49 (1990) 71f., 90.

[47] *Die Trägergruppe von Q*, Ammersbek bei Hamburg: Verlag an der Lottbek (1990) 309.

lifestyle in its missionary activity. Hence the kingdom of God was the centre of its message and healing the sick was its primary activity. The rejection of the community leaders was a consequence of following the roles of Jesus and John the Baptist as prophets of endtime judgement. Their purpose was primarily social—to gather and free the people of God (social outcasts).

Kim sees the Q community as composed of three groups: 1) wandering prophets—the community leaders; 2) stationary sympathizers to the movement; and 3), the socially underprivileged—the addressees of the Q mission. He singles out the third group as most important: "Diese sozial diskriminierte Gruppe war ja keine periphere Gruppe in der Jesusbewegung der Q-Gemeinde, sondern die zentrale Gruppe."[48] Kim locates the Q community, an anonymous circle of Jesus' followers, in northern Palestine and Southern Syria. Their work concluded around 70 C.E.

K. Burton Mack

In his book *The Lost Gospel* (1993) subtitled *The Book of Q & Christian Origins*, Burton Mack traces five stages in the history of the Q community. He correlates each successive stage within the community to the shifting identity and teaching of Jesus. He thus presupposes "the attributed teachings (of Jesus) were the expression of the group's ethos and behavior."[49]

Q[1], the first stage, is composed of aphorisms which Mack likens to Cynic teaching. The early community reacted to rival philosophies by means of Cynic-like arguments and injunctions. Their perspective was rooted not so much in Judaism as in the background of Greek philosophy, politics, and governance. They perceived Jesus to be a Cynic-like sage.[50]

The Q community entered a second stage with the organization of blocks of material. Select imperatives represent community rules created *ad hoc* and secondarily attributed to Jesus. Jesus, no longer the speaker of aphorisms, has become an advocate of proverbial wisdom. The community has developed into a series of small groups.[51]

The shift between Q[1] and Q[2], the third stage, is characterized by growing social distress and conflict "within close circles of acquaintance."[52] Because of

---

[48] *Ibid.*, 364.

[49] 202.

[50] 115. For the specific Q passages which Mack attributes to each stage see pp. 81-102 and their explanation on p. 72.

[51] 203.

[52] 204.

developing conflict, judgement terminology entered into the speech of Jesus at this stage.

The authors of Q^2, the fourth stage, present Jesus as a prophet pronouncing judgement and apocalyptic threat in response to those who had risen up to frustrate the Q mission.[53] Because of family splits and a reduction in numbers within the group, Q^2 shows an increased interest in defining the attributes of faithful followers. In place of the aphorisms and imperatives used in previous stages, Q^2 is characterized by dialogue, controversy stories, epic tradition, parables and apocalyptic pronouncements. Jesus' authority continues to escalate and specific charges against Pharisees and lawyers enter in. Also at this level the figures of Wisdom, son of man, and John break into the Q tradition.[54]

Q^3, the fifth stage and the last embellishment to the document, takes place after the Jewish-Roman war. The Q community and its portrait of Jesus assimilate to forms of Judaism it once opposed. Jesus, once the Cynic-like sage, has become the Son of God of Lk. 10:21, 22 and the temptation narratives.

The great achievement, therefore, of the Q community, according to Mack, was its creation of a complex Jesus myth whose varied components reflect the ebb and flow of the community's social experience. This "Jesus myth" had separate origins and was totally unrelated to the "Christ myth" represented in the Gospels and the writings of Paul.

Conclusion

The above descriptions of the Q community attempt to define how Q may have developed in an atmosphere in which the passion and resurrection kerygma was not the christological focus. In our estimation, however, each effort fails to produce a convincing scenario mainly due to the sheer lack of historical data supporting the existence of an isolated Q community or series of communities. It is very difficult to analyze sayings as indicators of the social climate of Q, since it is very uncertain that isolated sayings do not come from preceding tradition. As Gerd Theissen warns, "We need to keep in mind that the texts give us no direct picture of the social environment of the Sayings Source; all we have is an interpretation of it based on a number of traditions."[55] Thus specific conclusions are based on speculation and fantasy.

On the other hand, little attempt is made to discredit the Q materials to the historical Jesus. The discrepancy existing between these scholars over the

---

[53] 134.

[54] 149.

[55] *The Gospels in Context*, 221.

geographical and historical placement of the supposed Q group raises doubts as to what can be accurately said in an argument which begins from silence. Moreover, we wonder if the speculative ease with which Schulz, Lührmann, Hoffmann, and Schmithals resort to theologically packed literary forms, redactional layers, and traditional backgrounds is consistent with the sharp scepticism with which they approach the historicity of Jesus' teaching. We are not persuaded that Hoffmann's hypothesis of apocalyptic enthusiasm provides a better solution to the origin of Q than the simple claim that Q was collected for teaching purposes and was motivated by the actual events of Jesus' ministry. Would not Jesus' miracles and his radical preaching about the nearness of the kingdom of God have motivated an enthusiasm of their own—enough to stimulate the memories of those who witnessed them?

A methodological weakness of the community enterprise as described in the accounts of Schulz, Schmithals and Mack is not only the lack of historical evidence documenting the Q community(s), but also the scarcity of qualitative information documenting the *Sitz im Leben* of its supposed counterpart—the Jerusalem community. Can there be any doubt that the transmitters of Jesus' sayings had additional religious beliefs beyond those contained in the 230 or so verses contemporary scholars are now attributing to Q? And is there any reason to doubt that mainstream Christians including those in Jerusalem would have valued the earthly teaching of their risen Lord? Are the questions posed to Q appropriate? For instance why is it surprising that Q, as a collection of Jesus' sayings, does not refer to the Twelve,[56] when in Mark Jesus himself only refers to the twelve once (14:20)?

Another difficulty with the Q community hypothesis is the unconscious manner in which Jesus' teaching suddenly becomes community pronouncement. How strong is the evidence that the Q community was involved in polemical activity against the nation of Israel? Lührmann's (and subsequently Kloppenborg's) claim that Jesus' opposition to "this generation" ($\dot{\eta}$ $\gamma\epsilon\nu\epsilon\dot{\alpha}$ $\alpha\ddot{\upsilon}\tau\eta$) represents a redactional infusion by the Q community suffers by comparison to Mark where Jesus adopts the same phrase repeatedly (8:12, 38; 9:19; 13:30) in polemical contexts.[57] Multiple attestation suggests authenticity rather than community origin. The specific opponents addressed in Q include: Chorazin, Bethsaida, and Capernaum (Lk. 10:13-15 par.), Galilean cities through which

---

[56] An implicit reference to the Twelve may occur in Lk. 22:28-30//Mt. 19:28. See G.R. Beasley-Murray, *Jesus and the Kingdom of God*, Grand Rapids: Eerdmans (1986) 273-277.

[57] *Die Redaktion der Logienquelle*, 8. Hoffmann, Schulz, and Laufen follow Lührmann in perceiving judgment as a major motive of the Q community: *Studien zur Theologie der Logienquelle*, 303; *Q die Spruchquelle*, 323-378; *Die Doppelüberlieferungen der Logienquelle und des Markusevangeliums*, 286, 287.

Jesus undoubtedly travelled; Satan (Lk. 4:1-13; 11:17-26 par.) with whom Jesus clashes not only in Q but also in Mark and in the Gospel of John; the Pharisees and experts of Jewish law (Lk. 11:46, 52 par.) whom Jesus confronts throughout the Gospels; and finally, the hardened people of Jerusalem (Lk. 13:34, 35 par.) who traditionally rejected God's messengers in the Old Testament and continued to do so outside of Q in the New Testament (Acts 20:22f.; 1 Th. 2:14, 15). Hence a unique Q community bias cannot be constructed on the basis of polemical material.

Similarly, the evidence for a *distinct* Q mission is not compelling. Multiple attestation (Mk. 6:7-13; Lk. 9:1-6; 10:1-12; Mt. 9:37f.; 10:5-16), according to F. Hahn, leaves "no doubt" that Jesus himself commissioned disciples during his lifetime.[58] What aspects of Lk. 10:1-16 par. suggest a unique Q mission? R. Laufen notes the lack of explicit reference to the Q mission,[59] but nonetheless supposes redactional handiwork in the introduction (10:2) and in the conclusion (10:16) of the Q commissioning address. However, "the Lord of the Harvest" spoken of in Lk. 10:2 par. refers not to the risen Lord Jesus as Laufen suspects, but to God (Isa. 18:4; 27:12; Jer. 51:53; Hos. 6:11; Joel 3:13; Mt. 3:12; 13:30, 39). The authenticity of 10:2 is a strong possibility.[60] The language of Lk. 10:16 par. is unique to Q only in nuance. Jesus voices the Shaliah principle—that disciples are as one with their sender—not only in Q but also in Mk. 9:37//Lk. 9:48 and John 5:23; 12:44,45; 13:20.[61] With such a plurality of Gospel witnesses, evidence does not support Lk. 10:16 par. as the unique *Tendenz* of the Q community. What Laufen says of the Q Redactor, in our opinion, could with more force be said of Jesus himself: "Der Q-redaktor ist überzeugt, daß die Menschen in den Boten der βασιλεία, die in Jesus gekommen ist, Gott selbst begegnen, will er der Urheber aller Sendung ist."[62]

What about more specific aspects of the Q mission? The divide among the above Q scholars on the question of whether Q is oriented around imminent expectation of the parousia or the parousia's delay largely reflects the lack of sure evidence to qualify either conclusion. It is telling that while all the above scholars agree that foremost the Q community was an eschatologically oriented group,

---

[58] *Mission in the New Testament*, London: SCM (1965) 32; Similarly M. Hengel, *The Charismatic Leader and His Followers*, Edinburgh: T&T Clark (1981) 74.

[59] *Die Doppelüberlieferungen der Logienquelle und des Markusevangeliums*, 285: "Während in den Logien, die als zum Grundbestand der Rede gehörig bestimmt wurden, von Sendung explizit gar nicht gesprochen wird und vermutet werden mußte, daß eine redaktionelle Einleitung die Situation der Jüngersendung angab, nimmt das Motiv in der Q-Fassung breiten Raum ein."

[60] See Davies and Allison, *The Gospel According to Saint Matthew*, Vol. II; Edinburgh: T&T Clark (1991) 149.

[61] See I.H. Marshall, *The Gospel of Luke*, Grand Rapids: Eerdmans (1978) 426.

[62] *Die Doppelüberlieferungen der Logienquelle und des Markusevangeliums*, 286.

according to R. Bultmann the most distinctive feature of Jesus' own teaching is its eschatological fervour.[63] And even if we skeptically reduce the body of authentic Q Son of Man sayings to those where Jesus speaks of a future Son of Man not explicitly identified with himself (Lk. 12:8//Mt. 10:32),[64] we are still left, on the basis of this limited information, with Jesus himself promoting eschatological expectation. Could not what these scholars ascribe to Q community eschatology be more accurately said of Jesus' own future expectations?

Furthermore while Schulz, Laufen, and Schmithals confidently speak of a Q mission to the Gentiles, U. Luz reaches exactly the opposite conclusion: "die Q-Stoffe zwar Jesus punctuelle Offenheit gegenüber Heiden überliefern, aber nirgendwo die Existenz einer Heidenmission voraussetzen."[65] How can one group of scholars qualify a mission which another astute scholar cannot even discover?

In addition, scholarly consensus does not support Schmithal's and Schulz's respective proposals of a complex development of Q tradition in which christological material entered in at only a late stage. The important Q saying Lk 11:20//Mt 12:28 whose authenticity is "one of the assured results of modern criticism"[66] depicts Jesus anointed with the spirit, bearing authority over demons, and in some way mediating the power of the kingdom of God. Jesus is not speaking as an ordinary figure. From the beginning, the Q material was important for its content in relation to the person of Jesus, his authority, and his relation to God and the eschatological rule of God.

In our opinion Burton Mack's vision of a Hellenistically oriented community is seriously mistaken. The conceptual background of all the Q material is Jewish, a fact verified by the abundant quotations and allusions to the Old Testament in Q and by Q's prominent themes (kingdom of God, Son of Man, wisdom, prophecy) which in their Q contexts are all indebted to Jewish backgrounds and which are entirely foreign to Cynic philosophy.

---

[63] Hence Bultmann (*History of the Synoptic Tradition*, 162) writes of Lk. 11:20//Mt. 12:28: ". . . it is full of that feeling of eschatological power which must have characterized the activity of Jesus."

[64] As is done by: R. Bultmann, *The History of the Synoptic Tradition*, 152; G. Bornkamm, *Jesus of Nazareth*, New York: Harper & Row (1961) 161; H.E. Tödt, *The Son of Man in the Synoptic Tradition*, 55-60; A. J. B. Higgins, *Jesus and the Son of Man*, Philadelphia: Fortress (1964) 24, 57-60.

[65] *Das Evangelium nach Matthäus* (Mt 1-7), EKK 1/1 Köln: Benzinger; Neukirchen-Vluyn: Neukirchener Verlag (1985) 59. So also Uwe Wegner, *Der Hauptmann von Kafarnaum*, WUNT 2. Reihe 14; Tübingen: J.C.B. Mohr (Paul Siebeck), 1985, 334.

[66] Davies and Allison, *The Gospel According to St. Matthew* II, 339. See also R. Bultmann, *The History of the Synoptic Tradition*, 162; E. Käsemann, *Essays on New Testament Themes*, SBT 41, London: SCM (1964) 39.

On the whole, it is far from certain that there ever was an isolated *distinct* Q community[67] which represented a "second sphere of Christianity." Detailed refutation of supporting evidence is impossible because Q community life is not grounded in secular history or Biblical literature. The above reconstructions are purely imaginative. It is impossible to precipitate Q community *Tendenz* from the sayings of Jesus. While the sayings of Jesus had to have been recorded and passed on by someone, the anonymity of that person, group, or community is important. They did not desire to pass on memory of themselves, and we may err in speculating that they desired to reorient qualitatively the authoritative teaching of their master.

However, if the above scholars do not agree fully on the historical details of the Q community, they do find a small parcel of common ground on its theological perspectives. Each agrees that the community was eschatologically focused on the end event when Jesus would bring in the kingdom of God and judge the world as the apocalyptic Son of Man. They further agree that the Q community identified its mission in sequence with the prophetic tradition of suffering and rejection, and eventually came to understand Jesus as a rejected prophet of Wisdom. The task at hand is to question if these conclusions accurately represent the content of Q, and then to discover exactly how unique these theological perspectives are to Q in comparison with Mark. If it can be shown that the Q material complements Mark in the themes which the two have in common, the process of projecting the content of Q onto a kerygmatically diverse community will be rendered unnecessary.

---

[67] Here we share the skepticism of Ben Witherington III (*The Christology of Jesus*, Philadelphia: Fortress [1990] 223), "Thus, the argument that there ever was a Q community is based on silence because it is methodologically unsound to base conclusions on this matter purely on sayings from the Synoptics. One cannot first assume there was a Q community and then select certain synoptic sayings to bolster such an assumption."

Chapter 3

Wisdom Christology in Q

I. Introduction

Rudolf Bultmann in *The History of the Synoptic Tradition* observed that many of Jesus' sayings reflect wisdom forms and traditions. Though Bultmann did not trace the pedigree of any one saying or a group of sayings to a single wisdom tradition, he did raise the possibility that synoptic sayings could have been borrowed from Jewish wisdom traditions by the early church and subsequently placed on the lips of the historical Jesus.[1] More recently Robinson's and Koester's theory that Q belongs to a wisdom genre, a trajectory of "sayings of the sages" (λόγοι σοφῶν),[2] has influenced many NT scholars that "wisdom" is a major theme inherent to Q's christology and its form.[3] Hence J. Kloppenborg's influential monograph on Q bears the subtitle *Trajectories in Ancient Wisdom Collections*.[4]

---

[1] *The History of the Synoptic Tradition*, 108: "Naturally these examples can never in any instance indicate the source of a particular logion. It is perhaps possible in some cases to trace the history of an individual saying. But the most important thing is that these examples of parallel subject-matter show the Synoptic sayings can be understood in relationship with Jewish 'Wisdom' and that we must therefore consider the possibility that they may in part derive therefrom."

[2] For the contribution of Robinson and Koester to the study of Q, see above Ch. 1 pp. 7-8.

[3] R.S. Sugirtharajah ("Wisdom, Q, and a Proposal for a Christology", *ExpT* 102 [1990] 42-45) argues that "the portrait that emerges of Jesus in Q is that of a popular and impressive sage" (45). Sugirtharajah stresses the universal nature of Jesus' wisdom teaching, comparing it to Buddhist thought, as Jesus' purpose in Q is to "illustrate God's concern for human beings and to promote solidarity within the community thereby making social injustice unacceptable" (45). The Q material, however, more than once places ultimate stress upon the listener's relationship with Jesus in particular (Lk. 6:22, 23par.; 10:16 par.; 10:22 par.; 11:23 par.; 12:8, 9; 14:25-27 par.) and in doing so contradicts universalist theology.

[4] *The Formation of Q*, Philadelphia: Fortress Press, 1989. Kloppenborg's thesis is that behind Q exists a literary evolution from "instruction" to "proto-biography." At different stages in the evolution process, Q resembled instructions, gnomologium, and *chreiai* collections while its historicizing elements were inserted in the final redaction. Kloppenborg supposes the Wisdom myth or some sort of unifying concept of wisdom was present throughout this process although he does not explain how the many different aspects of Q are subsumed under the rubric of

In a separate article entitled "Wisdom Christology in Q," Kloppenborg concludes: "The Christological reflection in Q—which takes its theological materials from the trajectory of reflective mythology associated with late Jewish Wisdom—was not so much a matter of reflection on the historical Jesus as on the present situation of the community . . ."[5] In projecting the wisdom contours in Q onto the self-understanding of the Q community, Kloppenborg plays down the significance of the historical Jesus and argues that the members of the Q community considered themselves to be the "true σοφοί" because they held rights to the "revelation of God which leads to salvation."[6]

From another angle, Ronald A. Piper's *Wisdom in the Q - Tradition* focuses on the phenomena of aphorisms ("short, pithy sayings") in the double tradition. He identifies and comments on five collections of aphoristic sayings in the double tradition,[7] two other collections with a similar structure,[8] a group of isolated

---

wisdom. Kloppenborg's presuppositions are the weakness of his work. First, his work will only convince the strictest of form critics because his presupposition that "meaning in texts is 'genre-bound'" (p. 2) is the foundation for his study of Q against the background of Egyptian and Near Eastern sayings collections, pre-Byzantine gnomic collections, and later Greek *chreiai* collections. These ancient writings in fact have very little in common with the content of the Q sayings, whose conceptual background is firmly entrenched in Jewish thought. Kloppenborg fails to trace the pedigree of a single Q saying to such backgrounds. In addition, Kloppenborg builds his argument upon the tentative foundation that "Q was composed originally in Greek" (64). While few deny that the Mt/Lk agreements suggest that the two evangelists shared a Greek copy of Q, the original language of the sayings within Q is much more difficult to ascertain. M. Black ("The Aramaic Dimension in Q with notes on Luke 17:22 and Matthew 24:26 (Luke 17:23)", *JSNT* 40 [1990] 33-41) has recently taken Kloppenborg to task for ruling out the possibility of translation Greek in Q, while the findings of R. Martin (*Syntax Criticism of the Synoptic Gospels*, Lewiston/ Queenston: Edwin Mellen Press, 1987) contradict Kloppenborg: "the Q documents used by Luke and Matthew were Greek texts which prior to Luke's and Matthew's use of them, had been translated from a Semitic language" (98). Finally, the greatest weakness of Kloppenborg's book is its failure to deal with the content of Q. This weakness again springs from his radical form-critical methodology: "This illustrates the importance of the framing devices and formulae for determining the overall genre. Content is not enough because it is too often ambiguous" (38). We do not agree. Much material in Q is neither ambiguous nor comparable to ancient Greek sayings collections. Kloppenborg emphasizes form/genre comparisons to the detriment of careful exegesis.

[5] "Wisdom Christology in Q", *Laval Théologique et Philosophique* 34 (1978) 147; cf. Celia Deutsch (*Hidden Wisdom and the Easy Yoke: Wisdom, Torah and Discipleship in Matthew 11:25-30*, JSNTSS 18, Sheffield: JSOT Press, 1987): "Thus, there is already in Q a Wisdom Christology in which Jesus is identified with personified Wisdom. . . . Thus, we might say that the Q community assumes the Wisdom myth, in a limited fashion, to describe certain of Jesus' functions" (103, 104).

[6] *Ibid.*

[7] Mt. 7:7-11//Lk. 11:9-13; Mt. 6:25-33//Lk. 12:22-31; Mt. 7:1-5; 15:14; 10:24-5//Lk. 6:37-42; Mt. 7:16-20; 12:33-35//Lk. 6:43-5; Mt. 10:26-33//Lk. 12:2-9

[8] Mt. 5:44-8//Lk. 6:27-36; Lk. 16:9-13

aphoristic sayings outside the aphoristic collections,[9] and aphorisms used in eschatological announcements.[10] In these collections Piper detects a "clear design of argument" which follows four distinct steps: (1) a general opening maxim; (2) a supporting argument; (3) "further new illustrations and arguments in a rhetorical question formulation, typically being double rhetorical questions"; and (4), a concluding saying which draws together the collection's argument and "provides the interpretative key for the collection as a whole."[11]

This pattern of argument, according to Piper, is unique to the double-tradition material, and supports, together with the 'divine Sophia' logia in Q, the likelihood that behind Q was "a unique sapiential activity deriving from one stream of the synoptic tradition and thus probably from one circle in the early church."[12] Although the subject of Piper's book is not christology, he concludes "there is a tendency in the double-tradition material to emphasize Jesus' genuineness as a messenger of God rather than to insist always on his uniqueness."[13]

S. Schulz likewise places importance on wisdom in Q. Blended with the themes of prophecy and judgement, Schulz argues that, within Q, wisdom in the form of pre-existent heavenly Sophia has taken over the salvation function in the history of Israel in the apocalyptic endtimes by sending her last two envoys—John the Baptist and Jesus. The exclusive place of Jesus as the last envoy of heavenly Sophia distinguishes him from the dead prophets and envoys of Israel. Unlike his predecessors, Jesus was raised to God as the secret Son of Man who would appear together with Sophia in the next age to assume the role of the apocalyptic Son of Man. Jesus' death, however, is not the salvation event, but the fate destined him as a prophet. The wisdom faith of the early Q prophets (in apocalyptic enthusiasm) released the message that the Nazarene did not remain in death but was raised to God and now has sent the Spirit of the endtimes.[14]

On this point P. Hoffmann concurs with Schulz: Jesus' death conforms to the scenario of the typical end of those sent by Sophia; his fate falls in line with all messengers of Wisdom—the prophets before him and the disciples after him.[15]

---

[9] Mt. 10:25a//Lk. 6:40; Mt. 9:37-8//Lk. 10:2; Mt. 10:10b//Lk. 10:7b

[10] Mt. 24:28//Lk. 17:37b; Mt. 3:10b//Lk. 3:9b; Mt. 25:29//Lk. 19:26

[11] *Wisdom in the Q - Tradition*, Cambridge: C.U.P. (1989) 193.

[12] *Ibid.*, 194, 196.

[13] *Ibid.*, 194. Piper is not successful in our opinion in arguing away the comparable sayings' collections in Mark (2:19-22; 4:21-5; 9:42-50). The one Markan collection he takes up at length renders his conclusion that "in isolated cases Mark had access to a tradition shared with the double-tradition material, but not necessarily directly from the Q-source" (200). This statement seems to contradict his argument for the distinctiveness of aphoristic sayings' collections in Q.

[14] *Q–Die Spruchquelle*, 168, 169, 482, 483.

[15] *Studien zur Theologie der Logienquelle*, 187-190.

In modern research, however, the most avid proponent of wisdom christology in Q and indeed within the entire NT has been Felix Christ. Christ agrees that the Synoptic Gospels present Jesus as the messenger and prophet of Wisdom, but in contrast to others Christ stresses that Matthew, Luke (implicitly), and Q present Jesus as Wisdom herself: "Jesus erscheint also gleichzeitig als Träger der Weisheit und als Weisheit selbst."[16] Surveying five prominent wisdom passages within Q (Lk. 7:29; 10:21; 10:22; 11:49-51; 13:34f. and par.), he concludes that Jesus speaks as personified Wisdom in each of these passages. Uniquely, Christ attributes a "high" christology to Q in that he perceives Jesus' pre-existence in Lk. 10:22, and even goes so far as to equate Jesus with God:

> Nicht weniger möglich ist, das Jesus sich als die Weisheit wuste. Könnte es nicht sein, das er mit den Titeln Menschensohn und Sohn auf das größe Geheimnis hinweisen wollte, das hier mehre ist als David, mehr als Salamo, mehr als Moses, Joseph, Jakob, Abraham, Henoch, Adam, mehr als der Messias, mehr als Engel, nämlich—wer dürfte es aussprechen?—Gott selbst in seiner Weisheit?[17]

Thus, Christ is convinced that Q christology is wisdom christology.[18]

In explaining the relationship between wisdom and the Son of Man, Christ contends that the two figures appear alternately for the same purpose.[19] He applies to Q the theory of Oscar Cullmann that Jesus originally combined the traditions of the exalted Son of Man (Dn. 7, 1 Enoch 46) and the OT suffering servant of God (Isa. 53). The combination of roles fit Q where Jesus plays both exalted Son of Man and rejected spokesman of Wisdom—a combination of roles played outside of Q exclusively by Jesus the suffering Son of Man.[20]

The consensus, however, among most Q scholars is that Schulz is correct in suggesting that Jesus represents an envoy of Sophia within Q and not Sophia herself. In Q Jesus is nowhere explicitly identified as Wisdom. Jesus, rather, is

---

[16] *Jesus Sophia*, Zürich: Zwingli-Verlag (1970) 73.

[17] *Ibid.*, 93.

[18] Cf. W.A. Beardslee, "The Wisdom Tradition and the Synoptic Gospels", JAAR 35 (1967) 236: "On the side of Christology, it is a striking fact that Q, already at a very early date, interpreted Jesus by means of the analogy of transcendent Wisdom, or possibly even identified Christ as the Wisdom of God."

[19] *Jesus Sophia*, 69.

[20] Cf. Oscar Cullmann, ET *The Christology of the New Testament*, Philadelphia: Westminster (1963) 161 f. Christ's orientation of Wisdom in Q at times seems to predetermine his identification of redactional layers. As a result, his reconstructions are unconvincing. Most of the statements he makes about Wisdom could more validly be said of God. For criticism of Christ see: Lührmann, *Die Redaction der Logienquelle*, 99; M. Jack Suggs, *Wisdom, Christology, and Law in Matthew's Gospel*, Cambridge: Harvard U.P. (1970) 96; Graham M. Stanton, "On the Christology of Q", in *Christ and Spirit in the New Testament*, Ed. B. Lindnars and S.S. Smalley, FS C.F.D. Moule; Cambridge: C.U.P. (1973) 25-40.

the final representative of the prophets. His fate marks him as one of the many
rejected messengers of Sophia. With this understanding Jack Suggs writes, "If by
'Wisdom Christology' one means only that Jesus is here interpreted as Sophia's
envoy who brings her truth to men, then the term may be applied."[21] Similarly
James Dunn asserts, "The presentation for Jesus is clear, consistent and obviously
deliberate, so that we can speak quite properly of a Q christology in which Jesus is
understood as the messenger of Wisdom."[22] In the pages that follow we will
address this question: *How clear, consistent, and deliberate is Jesus' role as
messenger of wisdom in Q?*

II. The Q Sayings believed to present Jesus as an Envoy of Wisdom

In this chapter we will examine the form of 'wisdom christology' advocated by
Suggs and Dunn in order to discover the merits and weaknesses of this approach
to Q. Our second and more important objective is to present an alternative way of
understanding the presence of wisdom—namely, as an attribute of Jesus which is
entirely consonant with his messiahship. To the extent that we are successful in
the latter, we will be able to narrow the gap between the Jesus of Q and the Jesus
of Mark. However, before accepting or rejecting the above explanations for the
presence of wisdom themes in Q, we turn to the four passages within Q which are
said to reveal Q's wisdom thought most clearly.

A.   Luke 7:30-35//Matthew 11:16-19

The verbal parallels between these two passages commonly designate them as two
recensions of the same Q *Vorlage* in which Jesus responds to "this generation"

---

[21] M. Jack Suggs, *Wisdom, Christology, and Law in Matthew's Gospel*, 28. Suggs is
followed by, among others, R.G. Hamerton-Kelly, *Pre-existence, Wisdom and the Son of Man: a
study of the idea of pre-existence in the New Testament,* Cambridge: C.U.P. (1973) 35: "He is
not, however, identified as pre-existent Wisdom herself; he is rather, her final envoy." Arland D.
Jacobson, "The Literary Unity of Q", *JBL* 101/3 (1982) 388: "The integration of the figure of
Wisdom into the deuteronomistic sketch of history served to draw John and Jesus into Israel's
Heilsgeschichte as the last in a series of Wisdom's envoys." This article provides a summary of
Jacobson's Ph.D. thesis "Wisdom Christology in Q", Claremont Graduate School, 1978.

[22] James D.G. Dunn, *Christology in the Making*, 205. Similarly Charles E. Carlston
writes: "Q reflects a tendency, known elsewhere in early Christian literature but particularly clear
in Gnosticism, to concentrate not on the death of Jesus but on his teaching and to understand the
resurrection not as the overcoming of sin and death but as the vindication of God's envoy and the
validation of his ministry." In "On 'Q' and the Cross", *Scripture, Tradition, and Interpretation*, Ed.
W. Gasque and William S. LaSor, Grand Rapids: Eerdmans (1978) 30.

which has rejected first John and now Jesus himself. In our discussion the concluding saying is the most important as it reveals the section's wisdom orientation. The distinction between Luke's "Wisdom is justified by all of her children" and Matthew's "Wisdom is justified by her works" leads most scholars to conclude that Luke's τέκνα, being the more difficult, is original as opposed to Matthew's ἔργα which refers back to Jesus' works in Mt. 11:2 (τὰ ἔργα τοῦ χριστοῦ). ἔργα, then, bears evidence of Matthew's secondary redaction of Q.[23] This reasoning leads Suggs to the conclusion that Jesus and John are the children of Wisdom in Q, in contrast to Matthew where Jesus is personified Wisdom.[24]

There are, however, a number of difficulties with Sugg's position. First, πάντων in Luke 7:35 forces a translation which reads "all of her children" rather than "her children" or "her (two) children."[25] This problem is circumvented, however, if one reasons with Dunn that "all" was inserted by Luke (as it is one of Lk's favourite words) possibly referring back to "all the people" in Lk. 7:29.[26] In this case Matthew, Luke, and Q have three different readings: (Mt) Jesus is Wisdom; (Lk) Wisdom's children are all who have responded positively to the teaching of Jesus and John; and (Q), Jesus and John are the envoys of Wisdom. However, the identification of Jesus and John as "the children of wisdom" is not explicit in Q.

A second possibility is that πάντων is original to Q and refers back not to Lk. 7:29, but to πάντων in Lk. 7:18. In this case 7:35 concludes the entire section (7:18-35) with the claim that Wisdom's children are πάντων τούτων (7:18)—the things that Jesus was doing, i.e., Matthew's works. The validity of this position is supported by the unity of the Q section in both Lk. 7:18-35 and Mt. 11:2-19c where the acts of Jesus bear witness to his identity—both positively and negatively (Lk. 7:22,32 par). Moreover, this explains ἔργα in Mt. 11:19 as Matthew's development of a thought already present in his Q source.

Yet a third possibility is offered by H. Gese and M. Hengel who argue that Luke passes on the original gist of Q in which case Lk. 7:35 refers back to Lk. 7:29, so that the children of Wisdom are the common people and tax collectors who are wise in recognizing the present unfolding of God's plan of salvation and so accept and obey the teaching of Jesus and John.[27] These "children of wisdom"

---

[23] J. Kloppenborg, "Wisdom Christology in Q", 130 n 7; J. Suggs, *Wisdom, Christology, and Law in Matthew's Gospel,* 57-58; W.D. Davies and Dale Allison, *The Gospel According to St. Matthew* II; Edinburgh: T&T Clark (1991) 264.

[24] *Wisdom, Christology, and Law in Matthew's Gospel,* 35f.

[25] I.H. Marshall, *The Gospel of Luke,* 304.

[26] *Christology in the Making,* 197, 198.

[27] H. Gese, "Wisdom, Son of Man, and the Origins of Christology: The Consistent Development of Biblical Theology, in *Horizons in Biblical Theology,* Vol 3 (1981) 57 n 3; M.

respond in repentance to the preaching of John and react with joy at the endtime blessings which radiate from Jesus' ministry (Lk. 7:34 par.).

With these different explanations before us, a secure conclusion as to the identity of the children of wisdom is difficult to reach. The second and third options stand or fall on the hypothesis that Lk. 7:18 and Lk. 7:29 represent the original versions of Q—a hypothesis many scholars would reject. In favour of the first option is the fact that Jesus and John and their respective ministries provide the major subject material of the entire Q section (Lk. 7:18-35//Mt. 11:2-19) which the wisdom saying concludes. Yet in this block of material Jesus and John do not serve in the same capacity.

A difficulty with the theory that Lk. 7:35//Mt. 11:19 identifies Jesus and John as envoys of Sophia—and hence of equal significance in the minds of the first transmitters of Q—is the preceding verse (Lk. 7:34//Mt. 11:19a) where Jesus qualitatively distinguishes his ministry from that of John by assuming the epithet Son of Man. If it is maintained that the earliest Q community appraised Jesus as a mere envoy of Sophia—having the same ontological status as John—then the same should be said for the Son of Man. Yet, there is no evidence to compel us to the conclusion that Lk. 7:35 is more original than Lk. 7:34 as the two sayings occur in the same sequence in Matthew and Luke. Is Q identifying Jesus the Son of Man as a rejected envoy of Wisdom? If so, the image on the one hand complements the Markan portrait of Jesus as the suffering Son of Man, while on the other hand it appears unique to the apocalyptic Son of Man tradition where the one like a son of man in Dan. 7 and the Son of Man in I Enoch 46 are not characterized by rejection and suffering, but by exaltation and power.[28]

In any case, if they are fellow messengers of Sophia, Jesus' eschatological significance greatly surpasses that of John. Indeed, the distinction between John and Jesus is repeatedly raised throughout this passage: (1) John's messengers come asking if Jesus is the "coming one", whom John and his disciples have been eagerly expecting; (2) Jesus indirectly says "yes", that he is the expected one by identifying the works he is doing, and adds the authoritative remark: "Blessed is he

---

Hengel, "Jesus als messianischer Lehrer der Weisheit und die Anfänge der Christologie", in *Sagesse et Religion*, Colloque de Strasbourg (Oct. 1976/ Vendôme 1979): "Die Kinder der Weisheit, die «wahrhaft Weisen» , sind die «'ammê ha-aräs» , die Zöllner und Sünder, die der Botschaft des Täufers und Jesu Folge leisten, die «Rechtfertigung» geschieht dadurch, daß sie dem darin offenbar werdenden Heilsratschluß Gottes «Recht geben», ihn anerkennen"(155). So also H. Schürmann, *Das Lukas Evangelium*, Freiburg: Herder (1969) 428.

[28] Suggs attempts to explain this difficulty by citing the emphasis of Wisdom in the Similitudes of I Enoch and by associating Wisdom with Spirit in Lk. 12:10//Mt. 12:32. However, while the word σοφία does not occur in Lk. 12:10 par., the wisdom motifs in I Enoch in no way detract from the exalted status of the Son of Man figure: *Wisdom, Christology, and Law in Matthew's Gospel*, 48-55.

who does not stumble upon me";[29] (3) Jesus identifies John as the preparer (7:27), and the greatest of those born of women (7:28); yet the least in the kingdom of God are greater than he (7:28); and (5), the parable of the playing children (7:32) contrasts the stern message of John with the joyous ministry of Jesus—John is condemned as an ascetic, Jesus is called a glutton (7:34). Clearly, then, John and Jesus emerge with different roles within this Q passage. If the Q community did proclaim Jesus and John as the final emissaries of Sophia, they understood them as distinctly different from the prophets before them, and distinctly different from each other. Most importantly, Jesus' acts reveal an association with the eschatological "Day of the Lord"—an association distinct from wisdom tradition.

This leads to a crucial weakness in a strict wisdom interpretation of this Q passage or of Q in general, as the content of Q is not confined to a wisdom background. The attempt to categorize the sayings that do contain partial wisdom terminology to a single confined stratum of tradition is purely speculative and unnecessary to a first-century Jewish background where wisdom, prophecy, and eschatology were not mutually exclusive. In Lk. 7:18-23[30] Jesus responds indirectly to John's question,"Are you the coming one?" by citing his works of healing and preaching to the poor. His response alludes to OT ideas found in Isa. 29:18f.; 35:5f.; 42:6, 7 and 61:1. Drawing attention to the prophecies of old, Jesus asserts that his work is evidence that the eschatological day of the Lord is dawning. His acts are not those of Wisdom's envoy, but of God himself, God's agent (Isa. 35:4f.), or God's Servant (Isa. 42:7). He proclaims "good news to the afflicted" (Isa. 61:1), but, in distinction to the OT prophet, Jesus performs the acts which bring remedy to those in need.[31] Therefore, in view of its OT background, the eschatological eminence of Jesus' ministry goes beyond paradigms existing in ancient wisdom writings.

Finally, the question consistently arises as to the proper understanding of wisdom. Is the contemplation of σοφία the unique source of Q revelation, or is

---

[29] It is important to note that Jesus does not say "Blessed is he who does not stumble upon (my words)", but rather "Blessed is he who does not stumble upon me" (ἐν ἐμοί). Ironically Jesus, the bringer of good news, pronounces a warning to John, the prophet of eschatological judgement. Thus, this Q passage emphasizes the response to Jesus as the criterion for blessing or woe – not the response to Jesus' words or the Wisdom which Jesus mediates.

[30] The authenticity of Mt. 11:5-6//Lk. 7:22-23 is for the most part unquestioned by NT scholarship. Beasley-Murray notes the opinions of Bultmann and Polag: "Bultmann writes of these sayings,'The immediacy of eschatological consciousness is given such emphatic expression . . . that it is impossible for any Jewish tradition to provide an origin' (HST, p.126). A. Polag observes, 'The entire wording appears to be uninfluenced by later Christological terminology' " (*Die Christologie der Logienquelle*, Neukirchen-Vluyn, 1977, 38). In G.R. Beasley-Murray, *Jesus and the Kingdom of God*, 357; cf. 80-83.

[31] I.H. Marshall, *The Gospel of Luke*, 292.

wisdom here merely to be understood as a personalized quality or attribute of God?[32]

B.   Luke 10:21, 22//Matthew 11:25-27

The exclusive relationship between the Father and the Son in Mt. 11:27//Lk. 10:22 has conceptual parallels with wisdom traditions where only God knows Wisdom and only Wisdom knows God.[33] Just as Wisdom reveals divine secrets, so Jesus mediates hidden revelation (Wis. 9:1-18; 10:10).[34] However, with the exception of Felix Christ, few scholars claim that this passage equates Jesus with Wisdom.[35] Instead it is argued that this is another Q passage which presents Jesus "as Wisdom's eschatological envoy . . . as the righteous man *par excellence* who knows God as Father and has the task of bringing God's final wisdom to men."[36] Or phrased differently, Jesus is seen as "Sophia's finest and final representative, as the mediator of eschatological and divine revelation."[37]

Both Suggs and Dunn cite as the closest parallel to this saying Wis. 2:13-16 where "godless men" contemplate the disgusting nature of the "just man":

> He professes to have knowledge of God, and calls himself a child of the Lord. He became to us a reproof of our thoughts; the very sight of him is a burden to us, because his manner of life is unlike that of others, and his ways are strange. We are considered by him as something base, and he avoids our ways as unclean; he calls the last end of the righteous happy, and boasts that God is his father.

The similarities between this wisdom passage and Mt. 11:25-27//Lk. 10:21f. are obvious: the just man is equipped with a knowledge of God and refers to God as his father. Moreover, the comparison is appealing because of the description of the just man who has an odd life-style, and who pronounces eschatological blessings on the just—characteristics commonly attributed to Jesus within Q. From these conceptual parallels, Suggs concludes that the Wisdom of Solomon provides the background for the revealed knowledge and the intimate relationship in Mt. 11:25-27.[38]

---

[32] So F. Bovon, *Das Evangelium nach Lukas*, EKK III/1; Zürich/Neukirchen-Vluyn: Benziger Verlag/Neukirchener Verlag (1989) 382.

[33] James D.G. Dunn, *Christology in the Making*, 198. Dunn gives the following references: Job 28:1-27; Sir. 1:6, 8; Bar. 3:15-32; Prov. 8:12; Wis. 7:25f.; 8:3f.,8f.; 9:4, 9, 11.

[34] Davies and Allison, *Matthew* II, 272.

[35] For the case against the equating of Jesus and Wisdom in this passage see: James D.G. Dunn, *Christology in the Making*, 199.

[36] James D.G. Dunn, *ibid.*, 200.

[37] M. Jack Suggs, *Wisdom, Christology, and Law in Matthew's Gospel*, 97.

[38] Suggs, *ibid.*, 92.

But this application of the evidence is misleading for several reasons. First, the "just man" of the Wisdom of Solomon is not a single individual, but a generic typical figure who represents the nation of Israel. Therefore it is uncertain that the "just man" can convincingly be equated with Jesus. Second, it is not at all obvious that the "just man" is an envoy or disciple of Sophia in the wisdom text itself. It is not the relationship of the "just man" and Wisdom which is in view, but the relationship between the "just man" and God—the "just man" professes a special relationship with God not with Wisdom. Third, the quoted text clearly portrays Wisdom, not as a sender, but as an emissary: "Send her forth from the holy heavens and dispatch her from your majestic throne, so that she may labor at my side and I may learn your pleasure" (9:10). Fourth, because the wisdom text cited is dependent upon the LXX version of Isaiah,[39] the ideas inherent to Lk. 10:21, 22 par. may only reflect an Isaianic background which is coloured by wisdom terminology.

Job 28:12-28, Wis. 9:13, 17, and Bar. 3:29-31 provide a wisdom background from which Jesus could adopt terminology for describing the mutually exclusive knowledge between the Son/Jesus and the Father/God in Lk. 10:21, 22//Mt. 11:25-27. The passage has numerous points of contact with the ministry of Jesus. Rather than viewing the "wise" and "understanding" as the opponents of the Q community,[40] it is far more plausible in our estimation to identify this group as the religious leaders of Jesus' day—the Pharisees and Lawyers who conflict with Jesus throughout the Synoptic Gospels and explicitly in Q (Lk. 11:39, 42, 43, 46, 52 par.). The "babes" need not be the members of the Q community, but rather they may be identified as Jesus' original followers—the poor, the sick, the lame— all those who were blessed by the power of the kingdom of God as it was manifested in the life of Jesus (Q: Lk. 6:20b//Mt. 5:3; Lk. 7:22, 23//Mt. 11:4-6). The "things" given to the "babes" need not be identified as some form of esoteric knowledge which forms the embryo of later gnosticism. Instead the gift given the recipients of Jesus' ministry is the knowledge that eschatological power is indeed present in Jesus, just as he has claimed. The arrival of the kingdom of God is real to these who have experienced it for themselves. The babes have received this knowledge because they have willingly accepted the blessings of Jesus' ministry, in contrast to Pharisees and Lawyers (the supposedly wise), who, having eyes to see and ears to hear, refused Jesus all the same (cf. Mk. 4:11, 12), and even

---

[39] Winston (*The Wisdom of Solomon: A New Translation with Introduction and Commentary*, 119, 120) writes that Wisdom 2:12 is "Virtually a quotation from the LXX version of Isa 3:10," while in v. 13 "the suffering and vindication of the child of God is a homily based chiefly on the fourth Servant Song in Isa 53:12 . . . ,"

[40] *Contra* Celia Deutsch, *Hidden Wisdom and the Easy Yoke*, 104, *et al.*

attempted to prevent others from experiencing the saving benefits of Jesus'
ministry (Lk. 11:52//Mt. 23:13), which they reject. The truly wise, therefore,
according to Jesus' message, are not those who have fitted themselves into some
sort of esoteric wisdom trajectory, but simply those who have recognized the truth
of Jesus' proclamation and have acted as a result of their need for Jesus' help by
following Jesus and believing the message which he preached. These are the
blessed, the babes, and the poor.

C. Luke 11:49-51//Matthew 23:34-36

The predominant scholarly conclusion is that Luke's version of this passage is the
more original, as it is unlikely that Luke would have substituted a wisdom saying
for an "I saying" of Jesus.[41] Many scholars argue that Matthew's replacement of
"the Wisdom of God" with the first person "I" proves the author of Matthew
consistently equated Jesus with personified Wisdom and thus championed a "high"
wisdom christology. The background of Luke's phrase ἡ σοφία τοῦ θεοῦ is
unclear and thus the center of debate.[42]

Of all the wisdom sayings it is said that this one most clearly represents Sophia
sending her prophets and apostles (Lk.) or prophets, wise men, and scribes (Mt.).
The passage portrays the envoys of Wisdom in their archetypical role—that of
rejection and suffering. These features lead Suggs to conclude that within Q Jesus
is best understood against the background of rejection and persecution of
Wisdom's envoys. This saying, then, is not an authentic saying of the historical
Jesus, but the quotation of a "lost wisdom-apocalypse" which the Q community
attributed to Jesus—a figure considered to be a prophet of Wisdom: "The recently

---

[41] On the redaction of this passage, see David E. Garland, *The Intention of Matthew 23*,
Leiden: E.J. Brill (1979) 171f.

[42] I.H. Marshall lists five prominent positions: (1) the phrase is a Lucan insertion: Adolf
Schlatter, *Das Evangelium des Lukas*, 2nd ed., Stuttgart (1960) 521; W.G. Kümmel, *Promise and
Fulfillment*, London: SCM (1957) 80; (2) the "Wisdom of God" is the name of a lost Jewish
apocryphal book: Rudolf Bultmann, *Die Geschichte der synoptischen Tradition*, 4th ed.;
Göttingen (1958) 119; Walter Grundmann, *Das Evangelium nach Lukas*, THNT 3; Berlin: (1966)
249; (3) the phrase could be a self-designation of Jesus: Tatian; N. Geldenhuys, *Commentary on
the Gospel of Luke*, London (1950) 346 – Geldenhuys also supports the next view (342); (4) the
phrase may mean 'God in his wisdom' – a personal trait of God: J.M. Creed, *St. Luke*, London
(1930) 167; T.W. Manson, *The Sayings of Jesus*, 102; F.W. Danker, *Jesus and the New Age*,
St. Louis (1972) 146; (5) the reference is to divine or personified Wisdom: O.H. Steck, *Israel und
das gewaltsame Geschick der Propheten*, 224; U. Wilckens, "σοφια", *TDNT* VII, 515; Felix
Christ, *Jesus Sophia*, 125f.; M. Suggs, *Wisdom, Christology, and Law in Matthew's Gospel*,
19f.; S. Schulz, *Q–Die Spruchquelle*, 340. Prof. Marshall considers the last view to be the most
convincing. See I.H. Marshall, *Luke*, 502-506.

martyred prophet of Wisdom, whose death is a sign of impending judgement, must be the one on whose lips her oracle is placed—Jesus himself."[43]

This reasoning, however, is unsatisfactory for three reasons: it misrepresents the wisdom sources upon which it is based, it does not do justice to the text at hand, and the supposed "lost wisdom-apocalypse" is entirely speculative.[44] According to Suggs, Q is oriented within a history which is "the story of the rejection and persecution of Wisdom's envoys." In his discussion of Lk. 11:49-51//Mt. 23:34-36 he leads the reader to assume this "rejection" motif has a pre-history in Isa. 5:8-10,18-24; Prov. 1; 8:12; I En. 91:12-17; 93; Wis. 2:10-15, 17-18; 10-11; 7:27. Yet in reading these sources it quickly becomes apparent that not one envoy of Sophia exists in any of them.[45] Wis. 7:27, which Suggs hails as the summary of the wisdom motif, describes the work of Sophia in "holy souls," but this reference says nothing about Wisdom's envoys: "Though but one she can do everything, and abiding in herself she renews all things; generation by generation she enters into holy souls and renders (κατασκευάζει) them friends of God and Prophets" (7:27). κατασκευάζω, according to Bauer, in this case carries the meaning 'to make ready' in the spiritual or mental sense.[46] Wisdom in 7:27 is therefore an attribute characteristic of friends of God and prophets. Yet there is no evidence that Sophia is sending out envoys—sending verbs such as ἀποστέλλω or πέμπω are not present. *Thus, the motif of Wisdom sending her envoys is unclear in the wisdom text itself.*

In addition Suggs fails to disprove the authenticity of Lk. 11:49//Mt. 23:34. εἶπεν rules out the possibility that Jesus was identifying himself with Wisdom in the Lucan version (Jesus would have used the present form λέγει to do so), but it is unclear how the tense disproves the sayings' authenticity.[47] M. Hengel has rightly cautioned that the historical span of time reflected upon in these verses goes beyond deuteronomistic tradition, so that the pericope's pedigree cannot be

---

[43] M. Jack Suggs, *ibid.*, 26.

[44] The hypothesis of a lost document was original to Bultmann (to my knowledge) : "In Q this saying was a quotation from some lost writing, which Matthew has put straight into the mouth of Jesus", *History of the Synoptic Tradition*, 114.

[45] In response to Suggs, Marshall D. Johnson's penetrating article shows that the concept of Wisdom's envoys lacks evidence within any of the references which Bultmann originally cited: Wis. 7:27; Sir. 24:32-34; Bar. 3:38; Shepherd of Hermas I. 2. 2; II. 4. 1; III. 1. 6; Gregory of Nyssa; illustrations in early medieval manuscripts; and the Mandaean and Manichaean literature. We echo Johnson's response: "In light of the fact that for both Bultmann and Suggs the motif of Wisdom's envoys is essential for the understanding of the Christology of Q and Mt., it is striking that neither deals with this motif critically or at length." Marshall D. Johnson, "Reflections on a Wisdom Approach to Matthew's Christology", *CBQ* 36 (1974) 47.

[46] Bauer, 418.

[47] M. Jack Suggs, *Wisdom, Christology, and Law in Matthew's Gospel*, 18.

confined to a "deuteronomistic" background. In no way is it certain that the "prophets" and "apostles" are those sent by the early church. The phrase, more likely, is a hendiadys referring to the single body of messengers sent by God to the people of Israel.[48] ἀποστόλους (messengers) need not be understood in the technical sense of early church apostles.

On the other hand authenticity can be supported from two perspectives. Either the saying "gave a bird's eye view" of Israel's history ascribed to personified Wisdom without any particular text in view,[49] or the phrase ἡ σοφία τοῦ θεοῦ may be considered a personification of an attribute of God in which case the meaning would be "God, in His wisdom, said."[50] In either case the Q saying could very well go back to Jesus himself in a situation in which Jesus compared the Scribes and Pharisees to those in Israel's history who rejected the obedient followers of God who are spoken of in the OT. The inclusion of Abel marks the "rejected" as an unspecified group—we have no reason to perceive Abel as a rejected *prophet* of Sophia (even in view of Wis. 10:3).

The interpretation of ἡ σοφία τοῦ θεοῦ as a circumlocution is certainly preferable to the hypothesis of a lost wisdom-apocalypse. The genitive of description is the genitive case's most extensive syntactical use in the NT,[51] and makes the most sense in this case where Israel's history is being viewed as a whole (from Abel to Zechariah). If personified Wisdom were in view, one must wonder why the Q text did not simply attribute the sending directly to Sophia rather than to the "Wisdom of God." In any case, the saying emphasizes the role of the Pharisees and their "spiritual" ancestors who rejected the obedient followers of God in the past. It need not have any definitive bearing on the person of Jesus at all.

The wisdom theme inherent in Lk. 11:49-51//Mt. 23:34-36 appears much the same as that in Lk. 10:21, 22//Mt. 11:25-27. Jesus rebukes his antagonists who reject the offer of salvation which God offers through the ministry of Jesus himself. The Jewish antagonists who by merit assume the role of "the wise" ironically act in foolishness by rejecting the greatest representative ever sent by God. And to disregard the sovereignty which God mediates through his chosen spokesmen is to incur God's wrath. Hence the degree of the punishment

---

[48] "Jesus als messianischer Lehrer der Weisheit und die Anfänge der Christologie", 157.

[49] James D.G. Dunn, *Christology in the Making*, 201.

[50] T.W. Manson, *The Sayings of Jesus*, 102.

[51] F. Blass and A. Debrunner, *A Greek Grammar of the New Testament and Other Early Christian Literature*, Tr. Robert W. Funk, Chicago: University of Chicago Press (1961), 95f.; H.E. Dana and J.R. Mantey, *A Manual Grammar of the Greek New Testament*, New York: Macmillan (1957) 75f.

correlates with the degree of foolishness. Because Jesus' adversaries have rejected God's greatest emissary, they incur the guilt due those who from Abel to Zechariah spilt the blood of the righteous: "Truly I say to you, all these things shall come upon this generation" (Lk. 11:51b//Mt. 23:36; cf. Mk. 12:1-9). "This generation" represents the group of Jesus' contemporaries who renounced Jesus' message and his ministry. Therefore the message of wisdom inherent in this passage again relates to the question of how one responds to the message and ministry of Jesus: the wise respond in obedience, the foolish respond with hostility.

D.   Luke 13:34-35//Matthew 23:37-39

The fourth passage commonly cited as evidence that Q expresses a wisdom christology in which Jesus exists in the role of an envoy of Wisdom does not mention wisdom explicitly nor does it allude to a specific wisdom text. It is argued, nonetheless, that the saying reflects the history of Wisdom sending prophets (Prov. 9:3; Wis. 6:16; Sir. 24:7-12; I En. 42:1f.), while "hen" imagery meshes with the maternal imagery of the wisdom text of Sirach 15:1. The speaker, therefore, is Wisdom, while Jesus is understood to be one of the rejected prophets of Sophia. This scheme is particularly appealing in the Lucan context where the passage is immediately preceded by Jesus' statement that it is necessary for him to go to Jerusalem to be rejected as a prophet (13:33).[52]

Yet the text does not allow such a reading. Once again it must be confirmed that the history of Wisdom sending prophets is undocumented and highly speculative. The mother hen, rather than an image of Sophia, is best understood against its OT background as a metaphor for God himself (Deut. 32:11; Ruth 2:12; Ps. 17:8; 36:7; 57:1; 61:4; 63:7; 91:4; Isa. 31:5). Strict dependence on Sirach is unlikely as its emphasis is on learning wisdom—a concept not present in this Q text. And while it is true that Sophia is like a mother or young wife to the God-fearer in Sirach 15:1, 2, it still must be emphasized that in this text Sophia does not send envoys or prophets. In addition, the wisdom scheme fails to provide a context for the concluding verses whose background is clearly from Jer. 12:7; 22:5; Ps. 118:26—passages not commonly associated with wisdom.[53] And finally, the rejection described here is fitting to the rejection Jesus met throughout

---

[52] James D.G. Dunn, *Christology*, 203; M. Jack Suggs, *Wisdom*, 63-70. Bultmann writes, "the whole verse has to be understood in the light of the myth of divine Wisdom, in which, after Wisdom dwells on the earth and calls men to follow her in vain, leaves the world, and man now searches for her in vain." *The History of the Synoptic Tradition*, 115.

[53] R.T. France, *Matthew–Evangelist & Teacher,* Exeter: Paternoster Press (1989) 305.

his ministry—the saying need not be attributed to Sophia who is in fact not mentioned.[54]

Like Lk. 7:35; 10:21-22; and 11:49-51, the call to Jerusalem addresses the plight of Jesus' contemporaries who reject the salvation which is available in Jesus' ministry. Jesus has come to perform the messianic act (Ps. Sal. 17:26) of gathering the people to take part in the eschatological blessings associated with the coming of God as described in the OT (Lk. 6:1; 7:22f; 13:28, 29par.). Yet the people of Jerusalem refuse this offer and so incur judgement upon themselves. Jerusalem, like the "wise" in Lk. 10:21, ironically acts with indifference at the presence of its savior.

Conclusion

Despite the many who champion a wisdom christology in Q, the evidence does not warrant this appraisal. In an important article, Marshall Johnson has clearly shown that the motif of Sophia sending messengers is virtually non-existent in OT and intertestamental wisdom literature. Therefore, if the Q community proclaimed such a christology, it was the first to do so. However, such is not the case because the references to $\sigma o \phi \iota a$ in Q are seldom and very difficult to interpret. They do not represent early statements of community christology.[55] The placement of Q within the "trajectory" of a wisdom myth beginning with the Wisdom of Solomon and ending with the Gospel of Thomas exaggerates the similarities between the sayings of Jesus and wisdom sources, and underestimates the uniqueness of Jesus within Q. There exists therefore no evidence that Q or the Q community ever interpreted Jesus along the lines of a "wisdom myth" or proclaimed a wisdom christology which contrasted in some fashion with the general portrait of Jesus as proclaimed in the Synoptic Gospels. There is in fact a growing consensus that the "wisdom myth" itself is a concept which lacks textual support in the ancient wisdom writings.[56]

---

[54] So David E. Garland, *The Intention of Matthew 23*, (195-96): "In both gospels it is Jesus who is identified as the speaker and there is no reason why Jesus – who saw his mission field as the lost sheep of the house of Israel – could not have utilized a traditional picture and applied it to himself."

[55] Cf. A. Polag, *Die Christologie der Logienquelle*, 137: "Der Begriff ἡ σοφία begegnet in Q sehr selten. Seine Verwendung ist gegenüber dem Spruchmaterial sekundär, aber nicht betont."; W.A. Beardslee, "The Wisdom Tradition and the Synoptic Gospels", *JAAR* 35 (1967) 237: "Almost no mythology of σοφία is expressed in Q."

[56] So Bernhard Lang: "A critical analysis of the relevant textual evidence yields the result that in antiquity *there never has been such a Wisdom Myth.* The idea is a mere invention and construction of modern scholarship." In *Wisdom and the Book of Proverbs: An Israelite Goddess Redefined*, 141, 142. Italics Lang's.

III. The Wisdom features of Jesus' teaching against the Background of OT and Early Jewish Writings

While we are not convinced that in Q Jesus is Wisdom personified, or an envoy of Wisdom, or that in Q wisdom thought provides the overarching conceptual framework for understanding Jesus, it is indeed true that many of the Q sayings contain wisdom terminology and elements of wisdom thought.[57] Q does bear evidence that Jesus incorporated wisdom traits into his pedagogical style. Lk. 12:24//Mt. 6:26, for example, clearly alludes to earlier wisdom proverbs found in Ps. 104:27 and Job 38:41. Wisdom in Q, as an attribute of Jesus' teaching, corroborates the testimony of Mark where Jesus' wisdom occasions amazement and rejection—features which anticipate Jesus' passion experience. Furthermore, wisdom as an attribute of Jesus' teaching should not motivate a variant appraisal of Q, because wisdom in OT and early Jewish literature is an attribute given by God to his chosen messengers, including important Israelite kings and the expected Messiah. Thus the wisdom dimension in Q could have been valued by the early church for its content which implicitly confirmed Jesus' identity as the anointed Messiah sent by God to share and to inaugurate the mystery of his kingdom. In this case, Jesus' wise teaching in no way contradicts his identity as Messiah.

In the OT, חכם (LXX: σοφία / σοφός) occurs 26 times as a verb and 135 times as an adjective or as a noun. The noun חָכְמָה occurs 147 times while the plural form חָכְמוֹת appears 4 times. 73 times the root occurs in the historical books, 41 in the prophets, 13 in the Psalms, and 180 in wisdom literature itself.[58] Because the English translation "wise" or "wisdom" is not always an exact indication of the Hebrew meaning in these references, OT scholars have failed to agree on a precise definition of the term.[59]

---

[57] See R. Bultmann, "'Dominical Sayings' 1. *Logia* (Jesus as the Teacher of Wisdom)", in *The History of the Synoptic Tradition*, 69-108.

[58] Georg Fohrer, "σοφία", *TDNT*, 476-496.

[59] Gerhard von Rad (*Old Testament Theology*, Vol 1, 418) defined wisdom: "practical knowledge of the laws of life and of the world, based on experience." R.N. Whybray (*The Intellectual Tradition in the Old Testament*, Berlin: Walter de Gruyter [1974] 72f.) calls wisdom "an intellectual tradition" in Israel "a set of ideas, or an attitude to life." James L. Crenshaw ("Prolegomena" in *Studies in Ancient Israelite Wisdom*, New York: KTAV [1976] 3) describes wisdom as "the quest for self-understanding in terms of relationships with things, people, and the Creator." R.E. Murphy ("Wisdom Theses", in *Wisdom and Knowledge*, Papin FS, Ed. J. Armenti, Philadelphia: Villanova Press [1976] 187-200) claims: "Biblical wisdom issues from the effort to put order in human life." Alexander A. Di Lella (*The Wisdom of Ben Sira*, New York: Doubleday [1987] 32, 33) broadens the definition to two basic forms: (1) "recipe wisdom" which "deals with every day attitudes, beliefs, customs, manners, and forms of behavior one should have toward God, one's fellows, and the world at large if one is to live fully and well as a faithful Israelite", and (2) "existential wisdom" – "the goal of supplying the believer with a

For the tradition-critic further problems arise because wisdom thought runs through a large percentage of the OT and is particularly noticeable in the prophetic literature. If we consider how Jesus, how a hypothetical "Q community", or even how Matthew or Luke would have reflected on the OT, it is extremely unlikely that they would have understood Jesus' Q sayings against a single confined OT tradition, because the concepts of wisdom and prophecy (including characteristic forms, themes, and vocabulary) which modern scholars have dubbed "traditions" are virtually blended together in the OT.[60] In Q these themes are not unique except in their relation to Jesus. Jesus is the speaker, the actor, and the source of unity within Q. Q is not primarily a collection of wise sayings, or a collection of prophetic sayings, but rather a collection of Jesus' teachings which contain these themes (or means of communication) because they serve the objectives of Jesus' ministry. While textual evidence does not support the OT as the background for a confined esoteric wisdom myth or line of trajectory, there are good grounds, we believe, for claiming OT and intertestamental Jewish wisdom as a strategic source from which Jesus could articulate his teaching on the kingdom of God.

Wisdom provides a strategic background for Jesus' teaching on the kingdom of God because in the OT and in early Jewish writings wisdom is directly related to the revelation of the kingdom of God. This is clearly seen in Wis. 10:9, 10a:

> Wisdom rescued from troubles those who served her. When a righteous man fled from his brother's wrath, she guided him on straight paths; she showed him the kingdom of God, and gave him knowledge of angels;

---

theodicy, or a plausible legitimation of God's ways in view of the existence of moral and physical evil." Finally, G. Fohrer ("σοφία", *TDNT* VII, 482) cites four pervasive uses of wisdom in the OT: (1) knowledge built on human experience; (2) the courtly ideal of the cultured and trained "whole man"; (3) the post-exilic concept of wisdom as a form of divine revelation; and (4) secular wisdom subordinated to faith in Yahweh – "the fear of the Lord." For a good treatment of the definition of Wisdom, see: Dianne Bergant, *What are they saying about Wisdom Literature?* New York/Ramsey: Paulist Press (1984) 3-19.

[60] For an exhaustive list of references of wisdom form, style, theme, motif, vocabulary, and references to "the wise" in prophetic literature, and prophetic influence in wisdom see: Donn F. Morgan, "Wisdom and the Prophets," *Studia Biblica* I (1978) 209-244. For the interaction of wisdom and prophecy in the OT see: J. Lindblom, "Wisdom in the Old Testament Prophets", *VTS* (1955) 192-204; J. Fichtner, "Isaiah among the Wise," in *Studies in Ancient Israelite Wisdom*, Ed. J.L. Crenshaw; New York: KTAV (1976) 421-438; J. Crenshaw, *Studies in Ancient Israelite Wisdom*, 9-13; R.N. Whybray, *The Intellectual Tradition in the Old Testament*; Berlin: Walter de Gruyter (1974); W. C. McKane, *Prophets and Wise Men*, London: SCM (1965); R.B.Y. Scott, "Priesthood, Prophesy, Wisdom, and the Knowledge of God," *JBL* 80 (1961) 3: "...there is evidence for a certain mingling of the functions of prophet, priest, and sage, and of a common element in their teachings"; E.W. Heaton, *The Hebrew Kingdoms*, Oxford: Oxford UP (1968) 175f.

Wisdom in the OT is an attribute characterizing God's royal authority. As Marc Zvi Brettler states: "God's *hokmah* was often understood as an entailment of the metaphor 'God is king'.[61] True wisdom is an attribute exclusive to Israel's God—the wisdom of all other nations is folly. To illustrate this truth we will address three OT texts which demonstrate the superiority of God's sovereignty over human wisdom. Because wisdom is an element directly related to God's sovereignty and kingship in the OT, we can understand why Jesus adopted wisdom language into his teaching which focused on this very theme—the kingdom of God.

A.   Joseph, the Spokesman of Godly Wisdom

The first episode takes place in the Genesis account of Joseph's rise to success in Egypt, when "all the magicians of Egypt, and all its wise men" (41:48) failed to interpret Pharaoh's dreams. The foil to the magicians and wise men of Pharaoh's court, of course, is Joseph: "the Lord was with Joseph, so he became a successful man" (39:2), and thus Joseph was able to reveal accurately the meaning of Pharaoh's dreams. It is important to note that nowhere in Gn. 39-47 is it mentioned that Joseph achieved superior status as a result of personal attributes or ability—his prosperity hinged on his relationship with God (Gn. 40:8; 41:16; 41:32). This fact is born out in his promotion where even Pharaoh comprehends the act of God:

> Then Pharaoh said to his servants, "Can we find a man like this, in whom is a divine spirit?" So Pharaoh said to Joseph, "Since God has informed you of all this, there is no one so discerning and wise as you are. You shall be over my house, and according to your command all my people shall do homage; only in the throne I will be greater than you." And Pharaoh said to Joseph, "See, I have set you over all the land of Egypt" (Gn. 41:38-41).

Pharaoh reasons that Joseph is discerning and wise because God has spoken to him. Wisdom, therefore, appears as a mode of revelation. Joseph subsequently is described as both containing "a divine spirit" and as being "discerning and wise"—the two phrases appear almost synonymous.[62] Finally, because of his obedience to God, Joseph is made a ruler over Egypt. Throughout the story Joseph's success walks hand in hand with his humility before the sovereignty of God.

---

[61] *God is King: Understanding an Israelite Metaphor,* Sheffield: JSOT Press (1989) 54. For wisdom as an aspect of God's royalty, see esp. pp. 53-55.

[62] On the close relation of the wisdom of God and the Spirit of God in the OT and Jewish literature, see M. Hengel, "Jesus als Messianischer Lehrer der Weisheit und die Anfänge der Christologie", 166f.

Joseph's obedience to God results both in his acquisition of power and in the deliverance of his people: "And God sent me before you to preserve for you a remnant in the earth, and to keep you alive by a great deliverance" (Gn. 45:7).

B. Israel's Exodus: A Paradigm for the Wise Response to God's Sovereignty

Israel's exodus from Egypt provides the second episode in which God proves superior to human wisdom in dominating the affairs of human government. As in Joseph's story, the Egyptian monarch of the Exodus is surrounded by wise men, sorcerers, and magicians (Ex. 7:11) who regularly advise Pharaoh on difficult issues. The story poses on the one side of the battle Pharaoh and his wise men[63] and on the other side Moses and Yahweh—when Yahweh acts, Pharaoh boasts that his magicians can work equivalent wonders. In the ten ensuing plagues, however, the tricks and deceptions of Pharaoh's advisers prove no match to the sovereign power of God. After only the third plague, when not being able to cover the earth with gnats, the magicians surrender and plead with their stubborn ruler: "This is the finger of God" (8:19). But Pharaoh resists this warning, and not until the seventh plague does he appear to understand his plight: "I have sinned this time; the Lord is the righteous one, and I and my people are the wicked ones" (Ex. 9:27). Pharaoh's appeal secures temporary relief from God's wrath, but the battle still wages because Pharaoh will not submit to the authority of God. That is Pharaoh's lack of wisdom: "But as for you and your servants, I know that you do not yet fear the Lord God" (Ex. 9:30). The Exodus is wisdom encapsulated: God is sovereign over nature, life, death, and the kingdoms of the earth. The foremost hero of the story is not Moses, but God: God acts in power, delivers his people (Ex. 14:30), and receives exaltation (8:10). And most importantly for our purposes, while witnessing God's power, the Israelites learn wisdom: "And when Israel saw the great power which the Lord had used against the Egyptians, the people feared the Lord, and they believed in the Lord and in His servant Moses" (14:31). Through this understanding we perceive at a very early stage the concept of the kingdom of God:

> The place, O Lord, which Thou hast made for Thy dwelling, The sanctuary, O Lord, which Thy hands have established. "The Lord shall reign forever and ever." For the horses of Pharaoh with his chariots and his horsemen went into the sea, and the Lord brought back the waters of the sea on them; but the sons of Israel walked on dry land through the midst of the sea. (Ex.15:17-19).

---

[63] Sorcerers and magicians were considered wise men in ancient Egypt. See S.H. Blank, "Wisdom", 853, 854.

Through the history of the exodus, the Israelites learn wisdom through experience: God alone is sovereign and His reign will never end.[64] The wise are those who recognize the presence of God's sovereign rule and respond accordingly with obedience to the Lord and to His chosen servant Moses. The wise act intelligently in the present on the basis of what they have learned about God in the past.

C. Wisdom in the Book of Daniel

The third and most telling OT account which correlates wisdom with the realization of God's reign occurs in the book of Daniel.[65] In addition to being a prophet, Daniel along with Hananiah, Mishael, and Azariah is described as being "Good-looking, showing intelligence in every branch of wisdom, endowed with understanding, and discerning knowledge" (1:4; cf. 1:17, 20; 2:12-14, 48; 5:11-15).[66] Daniel, however, exceeds his peers in comprehending "all kinds of visions and dreams" (1:17), so that Nebuchadnezzar promotes him to chief prefect over all the wise men of Babylon (2:48). Wisdom is a vehicle of revelation from God to Daniel, who functions as a wise man in the court of the king.

---

[64] See J.R. Boston, "The Wisdom Influence upon the Song of Moses", *JBL* 87 (1968) 201: "The enemy who vaunts himself over Yahweh is described in vs. 28 as one for whom counsel has perished and in whom there is no understanding." For the linguistic parallels between Moses' song and wisdom literature see Boston pp. 201-202.

[65] In addition to Daniel's status as a "wise man", and the obvious wisdom phraseology, Daniel contains numerous wisdom traits: in ch. 4 the tree image (4:4f.) is a wisdom feature (Jud. 9:8-15; 2 Kgs. 14:9; 1 Kgs. 5:13); and the theme of humbling the proud monarch alludes to aphorisms in the wisdom tradition (Pro. 16:5-7,12). See P.W. Coxon, "The Great Tree of Daniel 4", in *A Word in Season*, FS W. McKane, Ed. J.D. Martin and P.R. Davies, JSOTSS 42 (1986) 91-111. J.G. Gammie notes the parallels between Daniel's wisdom and that of the servant of Isaiah, "On the Intention and sources of Daniel i-vi," *VT* 31 (1981), 284. Belshazzar's decadent feast has been described as an illustration of wisdom literature's warnings against "power, sex, and drink", John E. Goldingay, *Daniel*, WBC 30, Dallas: Word (1989) 113. The court conflict in Ch. 6 contains several wisdom motifs including features of wisdom teaching, and "the traditional wisdom-triangle: the powerful, but witless dupe–the righteous wise–the conniving schemer" (Pr. 6:12-19; 14:30, 32, 35; 24:16; 29:12). Goldingay, *Daniel*, 122. Root forms of the wisdom word שָׂכַל (be prudent: give attention to, consider, ponder (BDB, 968), occur more in Daniel than any other O.T. book except Proverbs (and Psalms, if the word מַשְׂכִּיל "contemplative poem" is included), Goldingay, *Daniel,* 249. See also R.S. Wallace, *The Lord is King: The Message of Daniel,* Downers Grove: IVP, 1979.

[66] In reference to 1:20 Kalugila writes, "The term *hokmah* is here parallel to insight (*binah*). The *hokmah* referred to is probably technical knowledge, which was regarded as supernatural, divine, i.e. given by Yahweh and superior to the wisdom of the king's magicians. The *hartummim* and *assapim*, "the magicians and the enchanters", were special classes of wise men who played a major role at the king's court, but were defeated by the Jewish youth. Thus the Israelite religion is represented as superior to that of the Babylonians", *The Wise King*, 76, 77.

The parallels to Joseph's story are numerous.[67]   Daniel's ascension to authority, like Joseph's, occurs as a result of his correct interpretation of the ruling monarch's dream—a task which the Babylonian wise men could not perform (2:2,12f.). And as with Joseph, human genius does not characterize Daniel; his wisdom comes directly from God (2:28, 30).

In Daniel, perhaps as in no other OT book, the transience of earthly kingdoms contrasts with the eternal reign of God. But the important observation we propose is that Daniel attributes the revelation of historical and supernatural events to God's gift of wisdom:

> Let the name of God be blessed forever and ever, for wisdom and power belong to him. And it is he who changes the times and the epochs; He removes kings and establishes kings; He gives wisdom to wise men, and knowledge to men of understanding. It is He who reveals the profound and hidden things; He knows what is in the darkness, And the light dwells with Him. To Thee, O God of my fathers, I give thanks and praise, For Thou hast given me wisdom and power; Even now thou hast made known to men what we requested of thee, for thou hast made known to us the king's matter. (2:20-23; cf., Lk. 10:21//Mt. 11:25)

Twice in this passage Daniel attributes "wisdom and power" to God: first in relation to God's sovereignty over history and the kings of the earth; and second, in affiliation with God's gift to Daniel himself. Because God has given Daniel "wisdom and power", he is able to reveal the unknown to Nebuchadnezzar. The wisdom which Daniel communicates to the king addresses directly the sovereignty of God over heaven (v. 19), Israel (v. 23), and "times and epochs" (v. 23)—"the successive epochs ruled by one king or another, one empire or another."[68]

In Ch. 2, God's sovereignty emerges even more strongly when both the rise and fall of historical nations (vv. 36-43) and the establishment of the divine kingdom are revealed to Daniel in his interpretation of the King's dream:

> And in the days of those kings the God of heaven will set up a kingdom which will never be destroyed, and that kingdom will not be left for another people; it will crush and put an end to all these kingdoms, but it will itself endure forever. (2:44)

Daniel's ability to interpret Nebuchadnezzar's dream and consequently to prophesy the rise and fall of historical earthly kingdoms and the kingdom of God, depends solely on God's gift of "wisdom and power" (2:23). God's wisdom, then, directly reveals God's own sovereignty over history. John E. Goldingay comments: "The wisdom being referred to here is not the quality of being wise but

---

[67] See L.A. Rosenthal, "Die Josephsgeschichte mit den Büchern Ester und Daniel verglichen", *ZAW* 15 (1895) 278-84.

[68] John E. Goldingay, *Daniel*, 55, 56.

the possessing of knowledge (about history) that stems from being the deciding factor (in history) and issues in being alone able to grant knowledge (about history)."[69] The wisdom which God reveals through Daniel is that God is sovereign over history.

Therefore, with Joseph, Moses, and Daniel as foils, we can see how appropriate it was, against the theology of the OT, that Jesus assumed the role of a wisdom teacher or wise prophet when he embarked on his Galilean ministry to proclaim the good news of the kingdom of God. He spoke with authority about the mystery of the kingdom of God as only a wise man could—a wise man whose wisdom comes not from the traditions of the courtly sages, but a wise man whose wisdom is received directly from the true source of wisdom—from the God of Israel, the creator, king, and sovereign Lord of the universe.

IV. Wisdom and Kingship

The OT writers also associate wisdom with the successful reign of Israel's kings.[70] As von Rad put it, "the king was the foremost champion and promoter of all searching after wisdom."[71] And more recently, L. Kalugila has written:

> A king could not perform his duties without divine wisdom—consequently royal wisdom was esteemed in the kingship ideology of the ancient Near East. By wisdom a king could obey the will of his god(s) with humility and thereby rule successfully. Royal wisdom helped him to be a righteous king, without wisdom a king would plunge his country into chaos. A king therefore was expected to seek wisdom through prayer.[72]

In fact, it is from within the king's court that Hebrew wisdom literature is said to originate.[73]

---

[69] *Ibid.,* 56.

[70] S.H. Blank, "Wisdom", *The Interpreter's Dictionary of the Bible,* New York: Abingdon (1962) 855.

[71] *The Theology of the Old Testament,* Edinburgh: Oliver & Boyd (1962-65) 34.

[72] *The Wise King: Studies in Royal Wisdom as Divine Revelation in the Old Testament and Its Environment,* Lund: Gleerup (1980) 132.

[73] See R.B.Y. Scott, "Solomon and the Beginnings of Wisdom in Israel", in *Wisdom in Israel and in the Ancient Near East,* VT Sup 3, Eds. M. Noth and D.W. Thomas; Leiden: E.J. Brill (1960) 84-101; Glendon E. Bryce, "Wisdom and Kingship in the Religion of Israel", in *A Legacy of Wisdom: the Egyptian contribution to the Wisdom of Israel,* Lewisburg: Bucknell U.P. (1979) 189-210.

A. David the Wise King

David, though not traditionally associated with Israel's wise, exhibits leadership features which determine the success of his reign. As Saul's advisers describe him, David's qualifications are impressive: "Behold, I have seen a son of Jesse the Bethlehemite who is a skillful musician, a mighty man of valour, a warrior, one prudent in speech, and a handsome man; and the Lord is with him" (1 Sm. 16:18). The most outstanding attribute of David is that Yahweh is with him (1 Sm. 17:37; 18:12, 14, 28; 20:13; 2 Sm. 5:10); each episode of his life implies that his success as a leader hinges on his direct obedience to God. Because of this relationship to Yahweh, David aptly responds to the plea of the wise woman (2 Sm. 14:2: אִשָּׁה חֲכָמָה) from Tekoa who calls out:

> Please let the word of my lord the king be comforting, for as the angel of God, so is my lord the king to discern good and evil. And may the Lord your God be with you. (2 Sm. 14:17).

The correlation exists between David's unique relationship with God and his ability to judge between good and evil, so that David's insight leads the woman to appraise him: "But my lord is wise, like the wisdom of the angel of God, to know all that is in the earth" (2 Sm. 14:20). Because the Lord is with David, the woman from Tekoa describes him as a man of incomparable wisdom.

B.   Solomon

Yet, it is not David but Solomon who emerges as the archetypal OT wise man.[74] For in response to God's offer of "anything" (1 Kgs. 3:5), Solomon prays for the exact attribute which the Tekoa woman ascribed to David: "an understanding heart to judge thy people to discern between good and evil" (1 Kgs. 3:9). Hence Solomon receives a wise and discerning heart (1 Kgs. 3:12). The narrative unveils the relationship of wisdom and successful kingly rule. Solomon already reigns as king before his prayer, yet he perceives his inability to reign successfully—he needs wisdom. As Simon J. DeVries writes, "God has made Solomon ruler; now

---

[74] So K.I. Parker, "Solomon as Philosopher King? The Nexus of Law and Wisdom in 1 Kings 1-11", *JSOT* 53 (1992) 76: "The ideal king is one who (a) renders justice throughout the realm (see 1 Sm. 12.3-4; 2 Sm. 8.15; 23.3-4; Ps. 72.1-4; Isa. 16.5; Jer. 21.5; 22.3-4,15-17), (b) lives according to the law of Jahweh (see Deut. 17.14-20; Pss. 18.21; 132.12), and (c) is wise, that is, one who 'fears Jahweh' (see Prov. 1.7; 8.14-16; 9.10; Ps. 11.10; Job 28.28; Isa. 11.2-3a; 9.6)."

let him provide Solomon with what he needs to rule."[75] The account in 2 Chronicles makes the relationship of wisdom and power more clear:

> And God said to Solomon, Because you had this in mind, and did not ask for riches, wealth, or honor, or the life of those who hate you, nor have you even asked for long life, *but you have asked for yourself wisdom and knowledge, that you may rule My people,* over whom I have made you king, wisdom and knowledge have been granted to you. (1:11, 12a)

Wisdom, then, during the reigns of both David and Solomon, produces successful monarchial rule.[76]

Solomon's wisdom likewise develops from his relationship to God. The process takes place in 1 Kgs. 3:1f. where Solomon makes his pilgrimage to Gibeon to worship and sacrifice. Here he receives his blessing at a point of absolute devotion to Yahweh: "Now Solomon loved the Lord" (3:3). His kingdom grows in proportion to the capacity of his wisdom which comes directly from God:

> So King Solomon became greater than all the kings of the earth in riches and in wisdom. And all the earth was seeking the presence of Solomon, to hear his wisdom which God had put in his heart. (1 Kgs. 10:23, 24; cf. 2 Chr. 9:22, 23)

Solomon's fame emanates from the glory of his kingdom and from his status as a wise man, but again we emphasize that, as with other OT figures, Solomon's wisdom comes directly from God.

The post-exilic writer of Chronicles offers the clearest association of wisdom with kingly reign, but in Chronicles Solomon sits not on an earthly throne (1 Kgs. 10:9), but on the throne of God. Here, in assessment of Solomon's rule, the Queen of Sheba announces:

> How blessed are your men, how blessed are these your servants who stand before you continually and hear your wisdom. Blessed be the Lord your God who delighted in you, setting you on His throne as king for the Lord your God; because your God loved Israel establishing them forever, therefore He made you king over them, to do justice and righteousness. (2 Chr. 9:7, 8)

Here the proximity of wisdom to rule on God's eternal throne and the resulting establishment of justice and righteousness lead us again to suggest a close correlation between wisdom and kingship; and here, even more than in Daniel,

---

[75] *1 Kings*, Waco: Word (1985) 52.

[76] R.B.Y. Scott writes that this form of wisdom – the ability of the successful ruler – represents the most authentic and certainly "pre-deuteronomistic" concept of Solomonic wisdom, "Solomon and the Beginnings of Wisdom in Israel", 84-101.

wisdom is associated with rule on God's throne.[77] The close relationship between the Davidic dynasty and the kingdom of God is evident throughout Chronicles (1 Chr. 17:14; 28:5; 29:23; 2 Chr. 13:8), so that M. Selman claims: "it is clear that the Chronicler believed that the kingdom of God was made known through the Davidic dynasty."[78] We have in Chronicles a direct relationship between wisdom and the kingdom of God. God's gift of wisdom to Solomon results in his successful reign over Israel and, in Chronicles, over God's kingdom. This wisdom is not a human attribute but a gift from God dependent on obedience to God.

C. Hezekiah

In addition to David and Solomon, OT history attributes wisdom to King Hezekiah of Judah. Biblical parallels between Hezekiah on the one hand and David and Solomon on the other are numerous. Hezekiah, for instance, is the first king since Solomon to have literary associations and the first to rule over an undivided kingdom.[79] Hezekiah, likewise, possessed immense wealth (2 Chr. 32:22-23, 27-29; 1 Kgs. 5:1, 4, 14; 10:21-25; Isa. 39). Furthermore, the language used by the author of 2 Kgs. 18:5-7 to describe Hezekiah strongly resembles that applied earlier to David:

> He trusted in the Lord, the God of Israel; so that after him there was none like him among all the kings of Judah, nor among those who were before him. For he clung to the Lord; he did not depart from following Him, but kept His commandments, which the Lord had commanded Moses. And the Lord was with him; wherever he went he prospered. And he rebelled against the king of Assyria and did not serve him.

Hezekiah trusted the Lord and the Lord was with him—thus his reign as king was successful. During his reign specific levitical reforms took place (2 Chr. 29:5-19), temple worship was restored (2 Chr. 29:20-36), and the Passover was reinstituted (2 Chr. 30:13f.), so that the Chronicler claims "there was nothing like this since the days of Solomon the Son of David, king of Israel" (2 Chr. 30:26). The most dramatic episode of Hezekiah's reign occurs in the successful deterrence of Sennacherib of Assyria, where Hezekiah appeals to the sovereign rule of God: "O Lord, the God of Israel, who art enthroned above the cherubim, Thou art the God,

---

[77] In Chronicles, God's kingdom is represented by his throne: 1 Chr. 17:14; 2 Chr. 28:5; 29:23. See M. Selman, "The Kingdom of God in the Old Testament", *TynB* 40.2 (1989) 164-165.

[78] "The Kingdom of God in the Old Testament", 167.

[79] R.B.Y. Scott, "Solomon and the Beginning of Wisdom in Israel", in *Studies in Ancient Israelite Wisdom*, Ed. J.L.Crenshaw, New York: KTAV (1976) 84-101.

Thou alone, of all the kingdoms of the earth. Thou hast made heaven and earth" (2 Kgs. 19:15). Hezekiah's prayer encapsulates the wisdom axiom that Yahweh rules "all the kingdoms of the earth."

Noting the similarities between Solomon and Hezekiah, R.B.Y. Scott reasons that "he set out to foster a national revival, taking Solomon as his model. In particular he became a patron of wisdom literature, more effective though less famous than his predecessor."[80] In fact, however, the OT only associates with Hezekiah the wisdom passage recorded in Isa. 38:9-20 and the transcription of Proverbs 25-29. Proverbs 25-29, though, displays how later generations attributed the recording of wisdom literature to Hezekiah's court.[81]

V. Wisdom and the Kingdom of God

Moving from specific monarchs to wisdom literature at large, the association of wisdom with kingly rule is maintained. This is especially true of Proverbs where kings are a primary subject.[82] Hence C.H. Toy noted that "Throughout Proverbs the source of royal success is wisdom; . . ."[83] Thus personified wisdom cries out:

Counsel is mine and sound wisdom; I am understanding, power is mine. By me kings reign, and rulers decree justice. By me princes rule, and nobles, all who judge rightly. (Pr. 8:14-16)

In this passage and in Proverbs as a whole, Wisdom's bond to Yahweh is always in view (8:13, 27).[84] Wisdom in OT and Jewish literature is inseparable from the personality of Israel's God.

When we reach other writings of the Diaspora, the relation of wisdom and power appears clearly in Philo where the wise man is king:

So we read, "he ran thither and taketh him thence" (1 Sm. X. 22f.), because, while lingering amid such vessels of the soul as body and sense perception, he was not competent to listen to the principles and rules of kingship—and we pronounce wisdom to be kingship, for we announce the wise man to be a king. (Migr Abr 197)

---

[80] *Ibid.*, 275.

[81] Another OT king to whom wisdom literature is attributed is the mysterious King Lemuel of Proverbs 31.

[82] 8:15; 14:28, 35; 16:10, 12-15; 19:12; 20:2, 8, 26, 28; 21:1; 22:11; 22:29; 24:21; 29:4, 14; 30:27, 28, 31; 31:3, 4.

[83] *Proverbs*, Edinburgh: T&T Clark (1899) 168.

[84] Thus in 21:1 it is not strange that the king is subservient to Yahweh rather than to wisdom.

... the Sage alone is a ruler and king, and virtue a rule and a kingship whose authority
is final. (De Somniis 2:244b)

Hence J.J. Collins writes, "For Philo, kingdom ($Bασιλεία$) is the rule of the wise
man, and it is established by God (Abr. 261). 'Kingdom' ($Bασιλεία$) can even be
defined as wisdom . . ."[85] Wisdom, therefore, was not confined to a streamlined
trajectory within ancient Jewish perception,[86] but represented a divine mystique
specifically associated with royalty.

Most importantly, the OT portrait of wisdom as "experiential knowledge" is
bonded indelibly with the realization of God's sovereign rule over man and nature
both present and future. Wisdom addresses God as creator, judge, and king.
Further, the OT consistently exposes the inferiority of human wisdom to the
almighty wisdom and power of Yahweh. This is not only true in the stories of
Joseph, Moses, and Daniel, but also in the literary prophets where the wisdom of
Egypt (Isa. 19:11f.), Babylon (Isa. 47:10), Edom (Jer. 49:7), Tyre (Eze. 28:3;
Zch. 9:2), and Jerusalem (Isa. 29:14; Jer. 8:9) fall in confrontation with the
sovereign power of God. True wisdom for the Israelite and later the Jew
characterizes a life lived in complete obedience to the call and direction of Yahweh
(Dt. 32:28f.). Such a theological orientation to daily life characterizes the literary
prophets (Isa. 33:6; 43:11-13; 45:20; Mic. 6:9; Jer. 9:23, 24; 10:9-10), the Psalms
(111:10), and the wisdom books proper where wisdom is "the fear of the Lord"
(Pr. 1:7; 9:10; 15:33; 31:10; Job 28:28). In the OT, wisdom directly relates to the
international political scene as Yahweh appears as the giver of wisdom (Pr. 2:6;
Job 38:36; 1 Kgs. 3:12f.) and it is by wisdom that kings reign (Pr. 8:15). Above
all else, however, one fact predominates—Yahweh rules. Thus the authors of the
wisdom books of Sirach and the Psalms of Solomon write:

I give you thanks, Lord and King:
I praise you, my Savior God!
I proclaim your name, my life's refuge. (Sir. 51:1)

O Lord, thou art our king for ever and ever,
For in thee, O God, shall our soul glory. (Ps. Sal. 17:1)

The Lord is our King for ever and ever. (Ps. Sal. 17:46)

---

[85] "Kingdom of God in the Apocrypha and Pseudepigrapha", in *The Kingdom of God in 20th-
Century Interpretation*, Ed. Wendell Willis, Peabody: Hendrickson (1987) 88. For "Basileia" in
Philo, see also K.L. Schmidt, "$Bασιλεία$ ($του$ $θεοῦ$) in Hellenistic Judaism", *TDNT* I, 574-76.
For Wisdom in Philo, see Celia Deutsch, *Hidden Wisdom and the Easy Yoke*, JSNTSS 18;
Sheffield: JSOT Press (1987) 81-90.

[86] *Pace* J.M. Robinson, "Logoi Sophon: On the Gattung of Q", *Trajectories through Early
Christianity*, 71-113.

The sovereignty of God, then, is firmly entrenched in wisdom literature. The wise are those who respond in obedience to God's sovereignty by relying completely upon God as they recognize Him to be the source of life and the king over all history.

VI. Wisdom and Messiahship

When the OT and early Jewish writers associate wisdom with the courts of kings and with kings themselves, it comes as no surprise that Isaiah, Jeremiah, and the writer of the Psalms of Solomon affiliate wisdom with the the messianic Davidic king:

> And the Spirit of the Lord will rest on Him, the spirit of wisdom and understanding, the spirit of counsel and strength, the spirit of knowledge and the fear of the Lord. (Isa. 11:2)

> Behold, the days are coming," declares the Lord, "When I shall raise up for David a righteous Branch; and He will reign as king and act wisely and do justice and righteousness in the land. (Jer. 23:5)

> He shall judge the nations and the peoples with the wisdom of his righteousness. (Ps. Sal. 17:31)

> Blessed are they that shall be in those days: for they shall see the goodness of the Lord which he shall bring to pass for the generation that cometh, under the rod of the chastening of the Lord's anointed in the fear of his God: in the spirit of wisdom and of righteousness and of might. (Ps. Sal. 18:7, 8)

These prophetic passages which come to us from multiple sources clarify that wisdom is a chief characteristic of the expected messianic king. Wisdom combines with other messianic traits including power (Isa. 11:2; Ps. Sal. 18:7, 8), righteousness (Jer. 23:5), the endowment with the "Spirit of the Lord" (Isa. 11:2), and the authority to judge (Ps. Sal. 17:31). However, even the wise Messiah submits to the sovereignty of God as the Messiah is, according to Ps. Sal. 18:8, *"anointed in the fear of his God; in the spirit of wisdom and of righteousness and of might."*

The correlation between wisdom and strength surfaces again as a coalition of attributes characteristic both of the "Elect One" as envisioned in the Similitudes of I Enoch and of the Messiah championed in the Isaiah Targum:

> Because the Elect One standeth before the Lord of spirits, and his glory is for ever and ever, and his might to generations of generations. And in him dwells the spirit of wisdom, and the spirit which gives insight. (49:2b, 3a)

And the elect One shall in those days sit on his throne, and all the secrets of wisdom shall come forth from the meditation of his mouth, for the Lord of spirits hath appointed him and hath glorified him. (51:3)

Yet before the Lord it was a pleasure to refine and to cleanse the remnant of his people, in order to purify their soul from sins; they shall see the kingdom of their Messiah, they shall increase sons and daughters, they shall prolong days; those who perform the law of the Lord shall prosper in his pleasure; from the slavery of the Gentiles he shall deliver their soul, they shall see the retribution of their adversaries. They shall be satisfied with the plunder of their kings; by his wisdom shall he make innocents to be accounted innocent, to subject many to the law; and he shall beseech concerning their sins. (Targ. Isa. 53:10, 11)[87]

It is important to note that the wise Messiah described in these writings is a figure of authority empowered to administer judgement—*the wise Messiah is judge.* Hence, there is common to the OT prophets, the OT historical books, the Psalms of Solomon, the Isaiah Targum, Philo and the Similitudes of I Enoch, a direct correlation between the endowment with wisdom and the roles of kingship and messiahship. When such is the case, it seems extremely likely that Jesus would have evoked a singular response and would have raised the question as to his own identity when he spoke as a wise man in regard to the kingdom of God. Hence M. Hengel may well be correct when he writes that the implications of Jesus' wisdom fit the contours of the Messianic secret as it unfolds in the Synoptic Gospels.[88]

In conclusion there appears to be a common denominator in all of these ancient Jewish writings: wisdom and power belong together as attributes given by God to his appointed authorities on earth.[89] The specific content of wisdom is not so much characterized by personal intellect but by obedience to and acknowledgment of the sovereignty of God. Wisdom is an attribute of God's anointed kings and messengers on earth. The wise are those who recognize God's kingship and as a result respond to God with reverence and homage.

VII. Wisdom and God's Reign through Jesus in Q

The OT and extra-biblical wisdom passages we have highlighted suggest a close relationship between God's gift of wisdom and his revelation of power. This background suggests that Jesus' association with wisdom in Q may signify not only Jesus' teaching prowess but also his supreme authority as God's agent of

---

[87] Bruce Chilton, *The Isaiah Targum*, Edinburgh: T&T Clark (1987) 104, 105.

[88] Hengel argues that the original Messianic secret, the question of the unique authority of Jesus, is evident in the Q saying Lk. 11:31f.//Mt. 12:41f. See "Jesus als messianischer Lehrer der Weisheit und die Anfänge der Christologie", 151.

[89] Thus Kalugila writes, "It is an essential principle that wisdom is consistently regarded as a divine prerogative", *The Wise King*, 134.

power. If Kalugila's statement is true that: "royal wisdom in Israel helps us to understand what manner of a Messiah the Israelites expected,"[90] what are we to make of Jesus' association with wisdom—is it a hint of his Messiahship?

As we have noted previously, wisdom motifs stand in the background of the important Q saying Lk. 10:21, 22//Mt. 11:25-27 (Job 28:25-28; Pr. 8:22-30; Sir. 1:1-10; Bar. 3:27-38; Wis. 8:3) where Jesus takes up the role of son of God as the unique mediator of God's knowledge to men.[91] Against the background of OT prophecy, Jesus' unique relationship to God explains his unparalleled awareness of the kingdom of God in Q. But Jesus' remarkable power and authority may also be in view. Numerous scholars have recognized the parallels between this saying and Dn. 7:13ff. in asserting that Jesus thanks the Father for not only transferring knowledge but also power and authority.[92] The critical point of debate surrounds the meaning of ταῦτα (Lk. 10:21//Mt. 11:25): whether power or knowledge is in view. Against the wisdom background we have cited, however, wisdom, knowledge, and power exist together as benefits of God bestowed upon his chosen agent—frequently the king. Hence Bo Reicke's proposal that ταῦτα refers to both knowledge and authority is plausible.[93] Indeed, the ability to reveal God is the source of authority for the prophets and the means of successful rule for kings in OT and early Jewish literature. In regard to these figures, then, knowledge is power. The same may also be true for Jesus in Lk. 10:22//Mt. 11:25 where ταῦτα probably originally referred "to the gospel of the kingdom, attested by the preaching and mighty works of Jesus." [94] A similar situation exists behind Jesus' saying in Mk. 4:11 where Jesus assumes the power to mediate "the mystery of the kingdom of God." Jesus' ability to reveal mysteries implies his anointing with wisdom (like that of Daniel) and implies his unique relationship to God.

The association of Jesus' wisdom with power also figures in Lk. 11:31//Mt. 12:42:

> The Queen of the South shall rise up with the men of this generation at the judgement and condemn them, because she came from the ends of the earth to hear the wisdom of Solomon; and behold, something greater than Solomon is here.

---

[90] *Ibid.*, 134.

[91] I.H. Marshall, *Luke,* 437, 438.

[92] See the list of scholars supporting this position in I.H. Marshall, *Luke,* 436.

[93] *TDNT* V, 895.

[94] I.H. Marshall, *Luke,* 434; cf. W. Grundmann, *Das Evangelium nach Lukas,* 215; J. Kloppenborg agrees: "The original referent of ταῦτα in 10:21 is probably the same: the events which signal the presence of the kingdom." *The Formation of Q,* 197; Similarly, S. Schulz, *Q–Die Spruchquelle,* 217; P. Hoffmann, *Studien zur Theologie der Logienquelle,* 110; W.D. Davies, "Knowledge in the Dead Sea Scrolls and Matthew 11:25-30", *HTR* 46 (1953) 137.

The OT background for this saying, both in 1 Kgs. 10 and in 2 Chr. 9, presents Solomon's intellectual wisdom in tension with his monarchial wealth and power:

> When the queen of Sheba perceived all the wisdom of Solomon, the house that he had built, the food of his table, the seating of his servants, the attendance of his waiters and their attire, his cupbearers, and his stairway by which he went up to the house of the Lord, there was no more spirit in her. (1 Kgs. 10:4, 5)

> So King Solomon became greater than all the kings of the earth in riches and in wisdom. (1 Kgs. 10:23; 2 Chr. 9:22)

> And he was the ruler over all the kings from the Euphrates River even to the land of the Philistines, and as far as the border of Egypt. (2 Chr. 9:26)

The queen of Sheba is awestruck both by Solomon's wisdom and by his kingdom. When therefore Jesus exclaims "Something greater than Solomon is here," he boasts an authority which surpasses that of Israel's wealthiest, wisest, and—by territorial merit—most powerful king. *Here is one greater than the Son of David!* This emphasis accords with the irony of Jesus' observation that even ancient Gentiles were more capable than Jesus' generation in comprehending God's sovereignty as mediated through human channels. According to Beasley-Murray, the Ninevites and the Queen of Sheba will judge, "since they gave heed to the word of God that was delivered to them by Jonah and Solomon, whereas Jesus' generation would not listen to God's ultimate messenger and was blind to the divine sovereignty at work in him."[95]

What does it mean that something greater than Solomon or Jonah is here? If we accept Solomon as the archetypal wise king and Jonah as representative of the prophets, surely the emphasis of Jesus' comparison must rest upon his status as revealer of God's decree—the message revealed in Jesus is greater than the wisdom Solomon exuded or the call to repentance which Jonah preached. These sayings do not tell us specifically what Jesus' message is, but they do qualify the importance of Jesus' pronouncement, as it surpasses in importance all previous expressions of Godly wisdom. The authority of Jesus' words correspond with his superior rank. His status as supreme revealer of God's kingdom beckons a public affirmative response by his generation. Jesus subsequently is amazed that his generation cannot comprehend the power which he claims both in his prophetic speech and in his words of wisdom. Hence the failure to heed Jesus' words will result in judgement.

Lk. 11:49-51//Mt. 23:34-36 attests to the combination of wisdom decree and assumption of power in Jesus' teaching. Jesus announces a wisdom saying and

---

[95] *Jesus and the Kingdom of God*, 172.

then he pronounces judgement, a warning or threat in which he assumes the authority and knowledge to foretell the fate of his generation: $\nu\alpha\grave{\iota}$ $\lambda\acute{\epsilon}\gamma\omega$ $\acute{\upsilon}\mu\hat{\iota}\nu$, $\acute{\epsilon}\kappa\zeta\eta\tau\eta\theta\acute{\eta}\sigma\epsilon\tau\alpha\iota$ $\acute{\alpha}\pi\grave{o}$ $\tau\hat{\eta}\varsigma$ $\gamma\epsilon\nu\epsilon\hat{\alpha}\varsigma$ $\tau\alpha\acute{\upsilon}\tau\eta\varsigma$ (Lk. 11:51//Mt. 23:36). Power, knowledge, and judgement decree combine in Jesus' words: he announces wisdom and administers a sentence of judgement. Israel's history unfolds a paradigm of wisdom and folly, *Heilsgeschichte* and *Unheilsgeschichte*. Jesus beckons his audience to choose the former by following himself the authoritative, true, messenger and mediator of the wisdom and power of God. The combination of attributes—wisdom, power, and authority to judge—are exactly those expected of the Davidic Messiah. Jesus' teaching in Q, therefore, conforms to, at least in part, various expectations of the coming Davidic Messiah.[96]

The same combination of wisdom and power occurs in Lk. 13:34//Mt. 23:37-39 where a lament containing numerous wisdom images (cf. Sir. 24:7-12; 1 En. 42; Wis. 7:27f.) is followed by a prophecy of judgement and an affirmation of Jesus' exalted status as "the one who comes in the name of the Lord." Here again a wisdom saying and a prophetic statement of future judgement combine to draw attention to Jesus' power as revealer of God. Again Jesus announces a negative future sentence against those who have rejected his message (in this case his offer of protection). Whatever the source for the Jerusalem saying, it is important to note that in Q Jesus is the speaker: the contemplation of Jerusalem's history of apostasy, the sentence of future negative judgement, and the "$\lambda\acute{\epsilon}\gamma\omega$ $\acute{\upsilon}\mu\hat{\iota}\nu$" saying draw attention to Jesus' unique status and power. Jesus displays knowledge over history, power as judge, and distinguished identity as the special messenger of God (Ps. 118:26).

In conclusion, the nuances of wisdom found in these Q passages signify the power and authority of Jesus and his message. Jesus' wisdom implies his closeness to the God of Israel because God is the dispenser of wisdom in the OT to major figures including Israelite kings and Daniel the prophet/wise man who

---

[96] R. Riesner (*Jesus als Lehrer*, WUNT 2. Reihe 7; Tübingen: J.C.B. Mohr [Paul Siebeck] 1981) argues that Jesus' wisdom teaching implies his messiahship: "Das Wirken als Lehrer und sein außergewöhnlicher Hoheitsanspruch standen für Jesus nicht unverbunden nebeneinander, da er als "messianischer Lehrer der Weisheit auftrat"(499). Similarly G. Ziener (*Die Theologische Begriffssprache im Buche der Weisheit*, BBB 11; Bonn: Hanstein, 1956): "Wenn Christus . . . sagt, daß hier mehr ist als Salomo, dann wird er sich als den messianischen Weisheitslehrer verstehen, der auch Weish. 6,1ff. unter dem Namen Salomos spricht" (120; Quote from Riesner, *Ibid.*, 331). Also making this observation is K. Berger, "Die königlichen Messiastraditionen des Neuen Testaments", *NTS* 20 (1974) 3-9, 28-37, 44: "Weisheit und Herrschaft über Dämonen sind daher kein Gegensatz zur Figur des endzeitlichen Davididen, sondern diesem aufgrund der Salomo-Typologie zugeordnet" (8). Berger elsewhere argues that the Father/Son relationship between Jesus and God is grounded in Jewish Wisdom tradition: "Zum traditionsgeschichtlichen Hintergrund christologischer Hoheitstitel", *NTS* 17 (1971) 391-425 (422-24).

prophesied the future kingdom of God. Yet in Q Jesus surpasses even these figures. His direct relationship to God—as a son to a father/as the one "who comes in the name of the Lord"—makes him superior to historical wise men and prophets. Jesus' wisdom and power associate his authority with divine attributes of God (cf. Job 13:13: "With Him are wisdom and might; To Him belong counsel and understanding"). Hence, Paul Hoffmann writes:

> Im Q-Logion tritt Jesus an die Stelle, die in der apokalyptischen Tradition Jahwe oder die Weisheit einnehmen; gerade in dieser Funktion wird er der "Sohn" genannt. Er ist es auch, nicht Gott oder die Weisheit, der die Jünger sendet und zu wirkmächtiger Ankündigung der Nähe der Herrschaft Gottes bevollmächtigt.[97]

Hoffmann, O.H. Steck[98], and more recently J. Kloppenborg have observed that in Lk. 10:3,16//Mt. 10:16, 40 Jesus appears as the sender of missionaries—a task which "places Jesus in the position of God or Sophia, as sender of the eschatological envoys."[99] Hoffmann explains Jesus' assumption of God's role on the basis of a speculative apocalyptic post-Easter revelation of Jesus' Sonship to the Q group,[100] while Kloppenborg explains the association as "intelligible in the context of the instructional genre."[101] Hoffmann, we believe, accurately identifies Lk. 10:22//Mt. 11:27 as the key to understanding Jesus' exalted status, his knowledge, and authority in Q. But while Hoffmann asserts a post-Easter *Sitz im Leben*, Jesus' words of judgement and his salvific acts (Lk. 7:18-23//Mt. 11:4-6; Lk. 11:20//Mt. 12:28) must arise from an authority invested in Jesus himself. Lk. 10:22//Mt. 11:27 explains the source of this authority. It is true that in Q Jesus is never called the messiah (ὁ χριστός), but sonship, wisdom, divine authority, and the administration of judgement are all messianic characteristics which Jesus assumes in Q, as he does in Mark where such characteristics imply his messiahship.

It is not necessary, then, to postulate an organizing wisdom myth behind Q or a particular wisdom genre trajectory. Wisdom serves as an appropriate speech form for Jesus to communicate his unique relationship with God. Wisdom enables Jesus to identify God as the source of his power. Kloppenborg rightly draws attention to the fact that Jesus' Q sayings contain wisdom which "reorients towards the new reality of the kingdom (6:20b) and God (6:35, 36; 11:9-13; 12:4-7, 22-31,

---

[97] *Studien zur Theologie der Logienquelle*, 139.
[98] *Israel und das gewaltsame Geschick der Propheten*, 286.
[99] J. Kloppenborg, *The Formation of Q*, 319.
[100] *Studien zur Theologie der Logienquelle*, 140.
[101] *The Formation of Q*, 319.

33-34)."[102]   What Kloppenborg does not emphasize, however, is Jesus' role in mediating this new reality.   Jesus is the person through whom God mediates knowledge, power, and the awareness of the kingdom of God.   Wisdom[103]and prophecy draw attention to the fact that God's revelation of the kingdom is in Jesus.[104]

VIII. Wisdom and Power in Mark 6:2

We confirm our argument by turning to Mark. Mk. 6:2 provides the only occurrence of the word σοφία in the second Gospel. The majority of scholars attribute the vocabulary of 6:2a to Markan redaction, and accept 6:2b-6a as traditional.[105] Mk. 6:2b is an important foil to our preceding discussion of the dual characteristics of wisdom and power in Jesus' Q teachings because the same traits are attributed to Jesus here:

> καὶ πολλοὶ ἀκούοντες ἐξεπλήσσοντο λέγοντες, Πόθεν τούτῳ ταῦτα, καὶ τίς ἡ σοφία ἡ δοθεῖσα τούτῳ καὶ αἱ δυνάμεις τοιαῦται διὰ τῶν χειρῶν αὐτοῦ γινόμεναι;

The first phrase addresses the amazement of the crowd (ἐξεπλήσσοντο) after they have heard the teaching of Jesus. For our purposes, the fact that the crowd appears "amazed" or "overwhelmed" indicates that, for Mark, Jesus' teaching by itself incited a qualitative response to Jesus from his listeners. The following three questions explain the crowd's amazement: they are overwhelmed by Jesus' wisdom and power. The first question, "From where did he get these things" (Πόθεν), asks the origin of Jesus' wisdom and miraculous work. If not inherited from family (6.3), is Jesus' power divine or satanic (cf. Mk. 3:22; Lk. 11:19, 20//Mt. 12:27, 28)? For Mark, of course, the source of Jesus' strength is never in question: He is "Christ, the Son of God" (1:1) who was anointed with the spirit at his baptism (1:10). Jesus' power and wisdom come from God. The second question connotes as much: Jesus' wisdom is not learned in the academic sense, but it is given to him (καὶ τίς ἡ σοφία ἡ δοθεῖσα τούτῳ). And against the

---

[102] Cf. James Wood, *Wisdom Literature*, London: Duckworth (1967) 123, 124.

[103] *Ibid.*, 320.

[104] Thus we agree with M. Hengel who writes: "Die Beziehung seiner Botschaft zur Weisheit sowohl von der Form als auch vom Inhalt her steht keinesfalls im Gegensatz zur eschatologischen Ausrichtung seiner Predigt auf die Gottesherrschaft – zumal diese ja nicht mehr nur eine rein zukünftige, sondern zugleich bereits anbrechende Größe ist." In "Jesus als messianischer Lehrer der Weisheit und die Anfänge der Christologie", 166.

[105] R. A. Guelich, *Mark* I, Dallas: Word (1989) 306; R. Pesch, *Markus* I, 316.

background of the OT and Jewish sources we have cited, the thought that Jesus is endowed with God's wisdom immediately raises the question of his messiahship. Such reasoning leads R. Pesch to conclude: "Daß die wahre Weisheit des 'Gesalbten' von Gott gegeben ist, ist klar. Die Leute von Nazaret weisen also mit ihrer Frage einen sich aus Jesu Lehre aufdrängenden Messiasanspruch zurück. Wenn Jesus die Weisheit aus sich selbst hat, ist er ein Pseudochristus."[106]

The same implications are raised by Jesus' miracles,[107] so that with the third question the crowd asks about the source of Jesus' power. Yet, at this point of his Gospel, Mark does not provide an explicit answer to the crowd's questions. Rather he allows the implications of Jesus' ministry to remain implicit. For our purposes, it is significant to observe that in Q Jesus raises the very same question (the source and meaning of his miracles) in his answer to John the Baptist whose disciples come asking "Are you the expected one?" (Lk. 7:22//Mt. 11:3). In this passage as in Mk. 6:2, Jesus allows his miracles to speak for themselves. He does not explicate the meaning of the miracles, but he does make certain that his acts of power, at least in part, contain the answer to his identity. Similarly, it is important to observe that in Q the basis for blessing or woe is not the comprehension of wisdom, but rather the manner in which one responds to Jesus: "Blessed is he who keeps from stumbling over me" (Lk. 7:23//Mt. 11:6).

Thus we have in Mk. 6:2b a parallel to the wisdom passages we have cited in Q. Jesus' attributes of wisdom and power coexist in provoking a singular response from Jesus' audience. In contrast, however, to Bethsaida, Chorazin, Capernaum and "this generation" in Q, Jesus' audience in this Markan episode does comprehend something unique in Jesus—they are "amazed" or "overwhelmed." Yet like the Q audience, the people of Nazareth in Mk. 6 fail to see in Jesus what they should—they are not moved to repent: "And he wondered at their unbelief" (6:6a). In Mark, therefore, Jesus' wisdom is a sign of the unique power invested both in Jesus himself and in his message.[108] Mk. 6:1-6 presents Jesus as wise man (6:2a), prophet (6:4), and miracle worker (6:2, 5)—a combination of roles which subtly address the question: "Where did this man get these things?" With this combination of attributes, the Jesus of Mark compares

---

[106] *Markus* I, 317, 318.

[107] So R. Pesch, *Markus* 1, 318: "Wie mit der Frage nach der Weisheit, so weisen die Synagogenbesucher mit der Frage nach den Machttaten Jesu (vgl. zu 6,14-16), die mit der ersten sachlich zusammengehört, den sich aus Jesu Machttaten aufdrängenden messianischen Anspruch zurück. Wenn Jesus Wunder nicht in Gottes Macht wirkt (und dies demonstriert, vgl. zu 8,11f), ist er ein Pseudomessias, kann er für besessen erklärt werden (3, 22.30)."

[108] The close proximity of wisdom and power in both Q and Markan traditional material argues for the genuineness of the dual concept. The fact that the Markan passage and each of the Q sayings are set in Jesus' homeland further leads to this conclusion.

with the kind of Messiah expected in numerous OT and early Jewish texts and matches the Jesus of Q.

Conclusion

Evidence does not suggest that Q contains either a full-blown wisdom christology in which Jesus equals Wisdom incarnate or a more implicit wisdom christology in which Jesus appears as an "envoy" or "emissary" of Sophia. Against the background of the OT and early Jewish writings, Jesus' endowment with wisdom, his wise teaching, and the authority he assumes in announcing judgement against the Pharisees and "this generation" combine as attributes which fit important Jewish descriptions of the expected Messiah. In Q Jesus is a wise teacher who acts authoritatively in pronouncing judgement.

Chapter 4

Jesus the Prophet in Q

I. The Role of Early Christian Prophets in the Q Tradition

Our discussion of the hypothetical Q community addresses the conviction of some scholars that the Q community understood itself in relation to the OT prophets and as a result actively participated in prophetic activity. Siegfried Schulz builds the foundation of his study of Q upon Ernst Käsemann's thesis that ". . . prophecy (and the prophet-directed community) was the vehicle of enthusiasm in Jewish Christianity after Easter, as it was to be in later Gentile Christianity."[1] In locating the early Q community in Palestine, Schulz assumes prophetic activity among its members. Similarly, Paul Hoffmann believes the Q tradition presupposes a charismatic prophetic missions movement in which the Q community members understood themselves in the prophetic tradition—like John and Jesus their task was the work of end-time prophets (Isa. 61:1).[2] Of crucial importance, therefore, to the study of the Q material is the phenomenon of creative Christian prophecy— are there sayings within Q which originally sprang from Christian prophets and were only subsequently placed in the mouth of Jesus? For if Q is the product of early Christian prophets, it may be argued that the Q material must be defined in prophetic terms in contrast to Mark's christology which develops in narrative form and climaxes in Jesus' passion.[3] Hence our present task is to address the

---

[1] Ernst Käsemann, "The Beginnings of Christian Theology", in *New Testament Questions of Today*, Tr. W.J. Montague, London: SCM (1969) 92; Siegfried Schulz, *Q–Die Spruchquelle*, 33, 34.

[2] *Studien zur Theologie der Logienquelle*, 332f. Dieter Lührmann ("Jesus und Seine Propheten", in *Prophetic Vocation in the New Testament and Today*, Ed. J. Panagopoulos, SNT XLV; Leiden: E. J. Brill (1977) 213, 15, 17) argues that the commissioning address in Q (Lk. 10:1-16//Mt. 9:37-38; 10:5-14, 21-23, 40) represents the clearest prophetic tradition in which Jesus and his disciples work in continuity to OT prophets. However, Jesus' authority in Lk. 10//Mt. 10 supersedes the rights of OT prophets as Jesus, and not Jahweh, is the sender here. OT prophets did not commission missionaries.

[3] E.g., M. Eugene Boring, *The Continuing Voice of Jesus*, Louisville: Westminster/John Knox (1991) 242-246: "The most probable reason for Mark's hesitating use of the Q material is

supposed evidence supporting the existence of prophetically created sayings and to discuss the validity of that evidence to see whether it does lead legitimately to the conclusion that Q originated from a prophetic impetus other than the historical 'earthly' Jesus. And finally, we ask: Does Jesus' role as a prophet in Q in any way contradict the Markan material—particularly Mark's passion account?

A. Richard Edwards

Defining prophecy as "a means whereby new, revelatory information or data is presented in a declarative manner", Richard Edwards cites four pieces of evidence which support the existence of prophecy within Q:

> (1) Prophets are mentioned 6 times in Q: Lk. 6:22-23 (Mt. 5:11-12), Lk. 7:26 (Mt. 11:9, 11), Lk. 10:23-24 (Mt. 13:16, 17), Lk. 11:47-51 (Mt. 23:29-32, 34-36), Lk. 13:34, 35 (Mt. 23:37-39), Lk. 16:16 (Mt. 11:12, 13).
> (2) "The lego humin introductory formula has often been considered as an indication of prophetic activity and is quite prominent in Q."
> (3) "A traditional characteristic of prophetic speech is its style of announcement rather than argument. The prophet, it is argued, speaks as a messenger of YHWH who announces his (YHWH's) will and the results of present action. Sayings with this proclamatory force are found in Q primarily in a variety of judgment and warning sayings." (e.g., Lk. 10:12 (Mt. 10:15), Lk. 10:13-15 (Mt. 11:20-24), Lk. 12:8-9 (Mt. 10:32-33), Lk. 3:17 (Mt. 3:12).
> (4) Q displays an interest in John the Baptist and his preaching of judgment, and makes use of quotations from the Old Testament prophetic books.[4]

Edwards admits that the evidence is of "varying strength and usefulness." Nevertheless he contends that the evidence is sufficient to suggest one aspect of the Q community's self-understanding. On the origin of the sayings, he further admits, "it is far from certain that any or all of these sayings originated with the community. That is an issue which current methods cannot solve."[5] In another publication, however, Edwards asserts more strongly the possibility of creative prophecy in Q:

> If there are prophets in the Q community who are inspired to speak in Jesus' name, the words of such a prophet could be considered to be the words of Jesus, not the mere words of a human disciple. As time passes, the sayings of the "historical" Jesus could be combined with the sayings of the risen Lord which were spoken through a prophet. As a result, both sayings would be repeated by the community as sayings of Jesus

---

to be found in his suspicion of the genre that it represents: the post-Easter revelations of the risen Lord" (244).

[4] Richard A. Edwards, "Christian Prophecy and the Q Tradition", in *SBL 1976 Seminar Papers*, Ed. George MacRae; Missoula: Scholars Press (1976) 123, 124.

[5] "Christian Prophecy and the Q Tradition", 124.

which should be remembered and heeded. Our twentieth-century distinction between the "historical" Jesus and a "prophetic disciple" could easily be a meaningless (even perverse) "splitting of hairs" to the Q community.[6]

In essence Edwards is saying hypothetically that the Q community ascribed the same authority to Christian prophets as they ascribed to the historical Jesus. In the collection process the sayings of the historical Jesus and the oracles of early Christian prophets gradually became indistinguishable.

However, such a supposition is not supported by Edwards' data. The evidence Edwards cites is characteristic of the synoptic gospels in general and thus does not prove a heightened prophetic awareness within the Q community whose very existence we have come to consider suspect. Six references to prophets is not disproportionately high within the synoptic gospels (Mt. 39x; Lk. 31x; Mk. 7x). The prophetic origin of the $\lambda\acute{\epsilon}\gamma\omega$ $\acute{v}\mu\hat{\iota}\nu$ phrase is highly questionable (see discussion below). Could not Jesus have spoken with "proclamatory force" as a messenger of YHWH? And while Q shares with the Gospels as a whole an interest in John the Baptist, we fail to see how interest in John suggests heightened prophetic awareness among the first transmitters of Q. Quotations from OT prophetic books likewise prove very little, as the prophets are alluded to and quoted throughout the entire NT.

B. Siegfried Schulz

From another angle Siegfried Schulz identifies "prophetic enthusiasm" as the force generating the oldest Q material. The prophets of Schulz's Palestinian Q community were apparently different from those of OT tradition in that they did not speak through YHWH, but through the exalted spirit of Jesus.[7] As a mouthpiece of the present living spirit of Jesus, Schulz contends that prophets were the leaders and authorities of the oldest Q community. Thus, the oldest Q sayings do not go back to the "earthly" historical Jesus, but to the prophets through whom spoke the exalted Lord himself.[8] The prophets passed on the sayings of the exalted Lord in expectation of the imminent end event when salvation would be realized with the appearance of the Son of Man.

Schulz's scheme, however, is largely built upon the form critical assertions of Ernst Käsemann. If Käsemann's postulations hold up to criticism, Schulz's foundation remains solid. The most important theory postulated by Käsemann,

---

[6] *A Theology of Q*, Philadelphia: Fortress Press (1976) 49.

[7] *Q–Die Spruchquelle*, 64.

[8] *Ibid.*, 60.

and subsequently adopted by Schulz, is the formula *Sätze heiligen Rechtes* (sentences of holy law).[9] "Sentences of holy law" are structured in the form of a chiasmus with the same verb in both the protasis and apodosis. The protasis is introduced by the casuistic legal form "if anyone" or "whoever," and the apodosis follows the style of apodictic divine law.[10] The apodosis typically has the future passive form of the verb and characterizes God's eschatological activity (primarily judgement). The major theme communicated by the form, according to Käsemann is *jus talionis* (retributive justice): "It is evident that the *jus talionis* is being promulgated here: destruction to the destroyer. And at the same time God is being defined with unsurpassable brevity and clarity as the God who rewards every man according to his works."[11] In "sentences of holy law" Käsemann claims the eschatological activity of God is anticipated in the immediate future by the speaker: "The *jus talionis* is, as the future tense of the apodosis shows, located on the eschatological level; and this is possible because, according to the view which lies behind the saying, the Last Day is immediately imminent."[12] Examples of "sentences of holy law" include: Mt. 10:32, Mk. 8:38, Ro. 2:12, 1 Co. 3:17, 14:37, 38, Ga. 9:6 and Rev. 22:18, which apparently represents the original *Sitz im Leben* for the prophetic proclamation.

Most important to our present discussion, as it is the foundation of Schulz's book, is Käsemann's conviction that early Christian prophets were responsible for producing "sentences of holy law." Prophets were the only ones capable of administering such judgement:

> It is therefore prophecy's function of leadership in the community which finds expression in the sentences of holy law. Such leadership, on the other hand, would scarcely have been able to develop in Jerusalem since the strong community there necessitated very early on a tighter organization under the apostles and a presbyterate. Prophecy can only have possessed a leadership function within the small communities of Palestine, where the oppressed faithful needed to gather round a charismatic man.[13]

Käsemann's theory is attractive to some scholars because it provides formal support for the belief that Christian prophecy played a central role in the formation of early Christian tradition. However, Käsemann's dichotomy between Jerusalem

---

[9] Ernst Käsemann, "Sentences of Holy Law in the New Testament", in *New Testament Questions of Today*, 66-81.

[10] David E. Aune, *Prophecy in Early Christianity and the Ancient Mediterranean World*, Grand Rapids: Eerdmans (1983) 166, 167. As the footnotes contest, a large part of the following discussion is dependent on Aune's research.

[11] "Sentences of Holy Law in the New Testament", 67.

[12] *Ibid.*, 67.

[13] *Ibid.*, 68, 79.

and Galilee can no longer be considered valid as a result of the diversity known to exist in both locations during the first century A.D.[14]

Käsemann's other conclusions have been heavily criticized. David Aune notes four problems inherent to the "sentences of holy law" formula: (1) the connection between early Christian prophecy and "sentences of holy law" is assumed rather than proven; (2) the formulation of the sentences is not legal, but that of conventional wisdom; (3) there are wide variations which characterize similar sayings throughout early Jewish and early Christian literature; and (4), it cannot be proven that Jesus could not and did not use a speech form similar to that proposed by Käsemann in the "sentences of holy law."[15] Two major weaknesses therefore mark Käsemann's proposal. The first weakness is the simplicity of the form. Käsemann unconvincingly attaches a simple almost generic form to a very specific hypothetical group—early Palestinian Christian prophets. The second relates to the ambiguous manner in which Käsemann surrounds "sentences of holy law" with broad theological ramifications—his conclusions are based on broad generalizations which lack firm support. Such a lack of evidence has led David Hill to conclude: "It would seem that the attribution of the so-called 'sentences of holy law' to Christian prophets is really presupposed by Käsemann: at best it is only a hypothesis, but one which has been elevated to the level of assumed fact by reason of its frequent reiteration."[16]

Schulz reiterates Käsemann's findings without contributing further evidence to the theory. He offers five sources of proof for the prophetic-apocalyptic scheme which he believes originated with the earliest Q community:

1) the λέγω ὑμῖν formula
2) the beatitudes (blessings/*Makarismen*) existing in "Palestinian Q"
3) the "woe" sayings (*Weherufen*) in the oldest Q
4) the existence of eschatological *jus talionis* within Q
5) the existence of τίς ἐξ ὑμῶν phrases within the oldest part of Q.[17]

Cumulatively, this evidence leads Schulz to conclude that prophets were responsible for the original body of Q material: "Hinter allen diesen prophetisch-apokalyptischen Verkündigungsformen steht eindeutig die Gewißheit dieser

---

[14] I.H. Marshall, "Palestinian and Hellenistic Christianity: Some Critical Comments", *NTS* 19 (1972-73) 271-87; M. Hengel, ET *Judaism and Hellenism*, 2 Vols.; London: SCM, 1974; *idem*, *The 'Hellenization' of Judaea in the First Century after Christ*, Philadelphia: Trinity Press International, 1990.

[15] *Ibid.*, 166-168, 237-240.

[16] David Hill, "On the Evidence for the Creative Role of Christian Prophets", *NTS* 20 (1974) 273.

[17] *Q–Die Spruchquelle*, 57-66.

Propheten, den Geist der Endzeit zu besitzen, der in ihrer Mitte als Kraft der Prophetie gegenwärtig und wirksam ist."[18] Before accepting or rejecting Schulz's ideas, the above forms must be explained and weighed carefully.

The λέγω ὑμῖν formula occurs fourteen times in Q. The origin of the phrase is heavily debated within Q studies[19] and, indeed, in each of its occurrences within the Gospels. Scholars classify individual references as either the work of Matthaean, Lukan, or Q redaction,[20] or as the precipitate of an earlier tradition. Added complexity surrounds the phenomenon of the expanded form ἀμὴν λέγω ὑμῖν which occurs in eight of the Matthean references (5:26; 8:10; 10:15; 11:11; 13:17; 18:13; 23:36; 24:47) but nowhere in the Lukan version of Q. F. Neirynck suggests that ἀμήν was added by Matthew in 8:10b; 11:11a; 10:15; 23:36 diff. Lk. 7:9, 28; 10:12 and 11:15 and omitted by Luke probably in 12:44 (ἀληθῶς diff. Mt. 24:47), 15:7 (diff. Mt. 18:13) and possibly in 10:24 (diff. Mt. 13:17) and 12:59 (diff. Mt. 5:26).[21] The Lukan omissions can be explained as the work of the final Lukan redaction,[22] or as the editorial work of pre-Lukan tradition.[23] It is certain, however, that ἀμήν cannot be pinned down exclusively to the evangelist Matthew as the word appears repeatedly in Mark (13x) and John (25x). Since no exact Hebrew equivalent has been found for the Greek New Testament formula, and since the exact phrase with the prefatory amen exists only on the mouth of Jesus in the NT and differs in usage from its OT predecessors as an introductory formula rather than a responsive call, it may be attributed to the authentic speech of Jesus.[24] As such the phrase implies Jesus' authority and his claim to be God's prophetic spokesperson.

Schulz believes the λέγω ὑμῖν formula originated within the prophetic-enthusiasm of the earliest Q community. Assuming a history of religions

---

[18] *Ibid.*, 64.

[19] Extensive bibliographical data and a survey of the dominant positions on the λέγω ὑμῖν formula within Q can be found in Frans Neirynck, "Recent Developments in the Study of Q", *Logia*, 29-75, esp. 56-69. Neirynck concludes, "it appears that in most instances where the λέγω ὑμῖν formula is peculiar to Matthew or to Luke it can be assigned to Matthaean or Lukan redaction. Q redaction is probable in 6,27 (?); 10,12; 11,51; 12,22. Other instances in Q are more likely traditional" (p. 69).

[20] λέγω ὑμῖν occurs in 9 references peculiar to Luke, and 8 times in references peculiar to Matthew. W. Schenk believes 10 of the 14 Q occurrences go back to Q redaction: *Synopse zur Redenquelle der Evangelien: Q Synopse und Rekonstruktion in deutscher Übersetzung mit kurzen Erläuterungen*, Düsseldorf: Patmos (1981) 92.

[21] "Recent Developments in the Study of Q", 69.

[22] I.H. Marshall, *Luke*, 536.

[23] Joachim Jeremias, *Die Sprache des Lukasevangeliums. Redaktion und Tradition im Nicht-Markusstoff des dritten Evangeliums*, Göttingen: Vandenhoeck & Ruprecht (1980) 126.

[24] Cf. R.E. Brown, *The Gospel According to John* I; New York: Doubleday (1966) 84; J. Fitzmyer, *Luke* I, 536; Davies and Allison, *Matthew* I, 489, 90.

perspective, he identifies the literary background of the λέγω ὑμῖν sayings in apocalyptic sources: the Ethiopic Enoch (91:18; 94:1, 3, 10; 99:13; 102:9), and the Testament of the Twelve Patriarchs (Test. Rub. 1:7; 4:5; 6:5; Test. Levi 16:4; Test. Benj. 9:1). ἀμήν did not enter into the Q material until the later Hellenistic-Jewish phase (due to the fact that ἀμήν is not found in the Pauline corpus). Thus, the full ἀμὴν λέγω ὑμῖν formula is a combination of ἀμήν from Jewish tradition and λέγω ὑμῖν from prophetic-enthusiastic tradition.

In brief Schulz argues: (1) Käsemann's "Sätze heiligen Rechtes" theory is valid and confirms that the oldest Palestinian Christian community originated in apocalyptic-enthusiasm and participated in prophetic activity; (2) the λέγω ὑμῖν phrase derives from apocalyptic sources rather than an OT or Pharisaic background and thus must have originated in an early apocalyptically enthused community; (3) the λέγω ὑμῖν phrase is not validated through recourse on the OT scriptures or on the sayings of the historical Jesus, but rather the formula emanated from early Christian prophets; and (4), the mere presence of λέγω ὑμῖν helps restore the community behind Q: "Das λέγω ὑμῖν als prophetisch-apokalyptische Grundformel ist also der Schlüssel zur Interpretation dieses ältesten juden-christlichen Enthusiasmus der Q-Gemeinde."[25]

Schulz accurately observes that λέγω ὑμῖν is distinct from OT usage as Jesus does not assert God's authority ("thus says Yahweh"), but his own ("I say to you"). Schulz's other premises, however, are questionable. Is it clear that λέγω ὑμῖν entered Q through apocalyptic sources? And, if the phrase did enter through apocalyptic channels, can we extrapolate from this supposition that the Q community was apocalyptically enthusiastic and active in prophetic activity? Most importantly, can we conclude that λέγω ὑμῖν sayings derived from Christian prophets rather than from Jesus himself?

On all counts, the evidence suggests that Schulz's conclusions are unwarranted. In addition to the above references, Aune offers examples of the "I say to you" saying which come not only from apocalyptic literature, but also from the LXX, Greek magic papyri, and the Pauline corpus.[26] The likelihood, therefore, that λέγω ὑμῖν sayings can be pinned down to a narrow apocalyptic background is naught. Furthermore, a clear connection has yet to be established between the λέγω ὑμῖν phrase and early Christian prophecy. Much depends upon sheer speculation.

---

[25] *Q–Die Spruchquelle*, 61. For the λέγω ὑμῖν phrase see pp. 57-61.

[26] *Ibid.*, 164, 392: Prov. 24:38; 31:2 (LXX), the Greek Magic Papyri IV. 2088; XII. 131; XII. 1074; XXXVI. 286; LVIII. 8, and Paul in Ro. 11:13; 1 Co. 6:5; 15:51; Ga. 5:2; 1 Th. 4:15; Aune notes also Jubilees 36:11; Teachings of Silvanus (VII, 4) 93:24; 94:5; Treatise on Resurrection (I, 3) 48:20; 50:13.

On the other hand, if one adheres strictly to the criterion of dissimilarity, the redaction-critical study of Victor Hasler[27] and the semantic/form critical analysis of Klaus Berger[28] together have greatly reduced the validity of Jeremias' argument that λέγω ὑμῖν represents the *"ipsissima vox Jesu."* The existence of the phrase within the LXX proves that it is not unique to Jesus.

However, authenticity is not dependent on the criterion of dissimilarity—a criterion rapidly falling into disrepute. The uniqueness of the phrase is not in its form or its semantic quality, but in the manner in which Jesus uses it. In none of the references which Berger cites does the OT prophet speak with his own authority (including Ezekiel), he always speaks the words of the Lord. In contrast Jesus speaks by his own authority. Authenticity is suggested by the fact that the synoptic gospels constantly attest to the unparalleled authority displayed by Jesus—the λέγω ὑμῖν phrase is consonant with such authority. Jesus is distinctly different from the prophets before him: "something greater than Jonah is here!" (Lk. 11:32//Mt. 12:41).

Schulz's second piece of evidence, the blessings or beatitudes (*die Makarismen*), suggest prophetic activity owing to their two-part form and their eschatological orientation. Schulz claims Lk. 6:20f.//Mt. 5:3f. represent the three occurrences of the blessing form in the Palestinian Q material. Wisdom tradition apparently provides the background for the beatitudes, but Schulz notes similarities to apocalyptic sources (I Enoch 58:2; 99:10; 103:5; and the Apk. Bar. 10:6; 48:23; 54:10). Making no attempt to explain the relation of apocalyptic and wisdom, he concludes: "Die Heilrufe von Lk 6,20b f. par dagegen sind Einzelsprüche judenchristlicher Propheten, durch den eschatologischen Geist inspiriert!"[29]

In assigning the beatitudes to Christian prophets, Schulz again assumes much with little textual support. It is well known that Jesus' sayings often conform to a two-part structure with the first part focusing on the present and the second part on the future—the eschatological element being combined with the Jewish apocalyptic conception of two ages. When Schulz identifies Lk. 6:20b f. as Christian prophetic speech, he makes the assumption that Jesus could not have spoken: (1)

---

[27] Victor Hasler, *Amen*, Zürich: Hotthelf-Verlag (1969). Hasler believes the phrase appeared within Jewish-Hellenistic communities and was thus secondary.

[28] Klaus Berger, *Die Amen-Worte Jesu*, Berlin: Walter de Gruyter, 1970. Despite his claims, Berger in no way destroys the theory that the λέγω ὑμῖν phrase reflects the self-consciousness of Jesus: "Die Theorien von der christologischen Relevanz oder der Bedeutung der Amen-Einleitung für das Selbstbewusstsein Jesu sind so zwar hinfällig geworden, . . ."(28). The phrase has christological relevance to the extent that it reflects the unique authority assumed by Jesus. The infrequent references to the phrase in pre-NT literature do not disprove the formula's authenticity.

[29] *Q–Die Spruchquelle*, 61.

in a two-part structure, (2) eschatologically, (3) prophetically, and (4), with apocalyptic orientation. Each assumption is poorly based.[30]   Further, it may also be worth noting that the first beatitude which Schulz attributes to the prophets does not have the verb of the second part in the future tense, but in the present: Μακάριοι οἱ πτωχοί, ὅτι ὑμετέρα ἐστὶν ἡ βασιλεία τοῦ θεοῦ (Lk. 6:20b//Mt. 5:3). This saying, at least, is orientated towards the present though it no doubt has future implications.   Schulz very well may have drawn his conclusions on the prophetic orientation of the beatitudes from Bultmann who listed all of the beatitudes under the heading "Prophetic and Apocalyptic Sayings."[31] Even Bultmann's comments, however, were made with very little explanation.

The "Woes" (*Weherufen*) constitute Schulz's third piece of evidence supporting the prophetic activity of the original Q community. According to Schulz the woe sayings occur seven times in the oldest Q material[32] and were originally prophetic words of judgement addressed to Pharisees condemned in the approaching apocalyptic judgement because they failed to follow the law of God. Like the blessing form, woes spring from a Wisdom background and resemble apocalyptic speech found in I Enoch 94:6, 7, 8; 95:5f.; 96:4-8. Schulz does not explain the prophetic origin of the sayings, but allows his earlier reasoning to determine the prophetic identification: the two-part structure, the presence of *jus talionis* and the eschatological judgement motif. Perhaps he also draws from Bultmann who classified the woe sayings in the category of "Prophetic and Apocalyptic Sayings."[33] Once again, however, one must question if Jesus could not have spoken in this manner.

Fourthly, Schulz adopts Käsemann's theory of "eschatological *jus talionis*" as proof of early Christian prophecy within Q.[34] He offers Lk. 12:8 as an example of a "sentence of holy law" within the oldest Q material. The above discussion of "sentences of holy law" should suffice as a response to *jus talionis* as evidence for the prophetic creation of Jesus' sayings. However, it is fair to question again

---

[30] The frequency of the sayings of Jesus which follow the two-part structure and contain eschatological content points toward authenticity rather than inauthenticity (cf., David E. Aune, *ibid.*, 166). Furthermore, it seems highly unlikely that Jesus would not have incorporated apocalyptic ideas into his speech as apocalyptic flourished in his day and is the most likely source (Dan 7) from which Jesus applied the Son of Man title to himself. It would be very difficult to prove that Jesus did not speak prophetically in regard to future events due to the frequency of synoptic references in which Jesus does prophecy, and to the witness of Jesus' contemporaries who identify him as a prophet.

[31] Rudolf Bultmann, *The History of the Synoptic Tradition*, 2nd ed., 109.

[32] Lk. 11:39b-41, 42, 43, 44, 46, 47, 48, 52 par.

[33] *The History of the Synoptic Tradition*, 111f.

[34] *Q–Die Spruchquelle*, 62.

whether Jesus could not have spoken of an eschatological judgement in which man's reward or punishment would be determined by man's response not to God's law as Schulz asserts, but to God's work being accomplished in Jesus himself.

Schulz's fifth and final piece of evidence is the "who among you" ($\tau i \varsigma \ \dot{\epsilon}\xi \ \dot{\upsilon}\mu\tilde{\omega}\nu$) phrase which he cites in two Palestinian Q entries (Mt. 7:9 par.; Lk. 12:25 par.). He fully accepts the conclusion of H. Greeven[35] that $\tau i \varsigma \ \dot{\epsilon}\xi \ \dot{\upsilon}\mu\tilde{\omega}\nu$ was a traditional speech form which originally existed as a prophetic introductory formula. The saying does not exist in Pharisaic rabbinic literature or in late apocalyptic Jewish literature but only a few times in the OT prophets (Isa. 43:13; 50:10; Hag. 2:3).

Schulz provides no explanation of how the phrase reveals prophetic origin, nor does he justify or add support to Greeven's hypothesis. The references in Isaiah and Haggai fail to prove that later "who among you" phrases emanated from prophets only. Further, Klaus Berger has shown that the phrase was in use within the Hellenistic world[36]—a fact which lessens the likelihood that it entered the synoptic gospels through the Palestinian Q community. In fact the phrase is not unique to Q, but occurs four times in material peculiar to Luke (11:5; 14:28; 15:4; 17:7). Most importantly the saying quite possibly reflects the original language of Jesus as David Aune opines: "Although the introductory expression itself, therefore, may be either Palestinian or Greco-Roman, when used in combination with the 'lesser to greater' argument it is a unique and distinctive pattern of speech used by Jesus."[37] The phrase has no contemporary Greek parallel either in extra-biblical sources or in the speech of known early Christian prophets.

In conclusion, Schulz's argument is not convincing. It is, indeed, doubtful that the supposed Palestinian Q sayings originally sprang from the mouths of early Christian prophets. Schulz assumes that the form critical conclusions of Käsemann, Hasler, and Greeven can be accepted without question and subsequently applied to the hypothetical Palestinian Q community. Casual appeal to apocalyptic sources as support for the "apocalyptic enthusiasm" of the early Q group lacks credence as we know from the complexity of ascertaining a confident date for the Similitudes of Enoch—the apocalyptic source Schulz bases much of his theory upon. Finally, a solid argument can be made that each of the forms Schulz refers to can go back to the historical Jesus, which makes the prophetic

---

[35] H. Greeven, " 'Wer unter euch . . . ?' " in *Wort und Dienst* 3, (1952) 86-101.

[36] Klaus Berger, "Zur Frage des traditionsgeschichtlicher Wertes apokryphen Gleichnisse", *NovT* 17 (1975) 58-76.

[37] *Ibid.*, 166.

theory unnecessary. As speculative hypotheses multiply, the phenomenon of early Christian prophecy grows less and less convincing.

C. Eugene Boring

In an attempt to define the interplay between the sayings of the risen Jesus and the traditional sayings attributed to the historical Jesus, Eugene Boring identifies two criteria which characterize those of prophetic origin: (1) they exist independently of a narrative context, and (2) are secondary—church products rather than the words of the historical Jesus.[38] Sayings which meet these two criteria are subsequently classified as prophetic if they adhere to the characteristics of early Christian prophecy which Boring traces from the primary sources of OT prophecy, contemporary Judaism, Hellenistic prophecy, Revelation, Paul, the Deutero-Pauline letters, Luke/Acts, Matthew, the Didache, the Gospel and letters of John, and Hermas.

The result of Boring's work is a very large body of prophetic sayings. In his exhaustive section on Q, he produces the following statistics:

> Q contains 79 sayings-units, containing 3652 words, which could have circulated independently of a narrative context. Of these 79 sayings-units, 42 sayings-units, containing 1803 words, are from Christian prophets or have been significantly reshaped by them. 22 sayings (28%) containing 802 words (22%) originated from Christian prophets; 20 sayings (25%) containing 1001 words (27%) bear the marks of prophetic, representing 49% of the words in the Q sayings-units.[39]

Such statistics lead Boring to conclude that Jesus' words and a few of his deeds provided the original nucleus of the Q material. However, it was not the historical Jesus, but the exalted Jesus who spoke through the prophets of the Q community and inspired their prophetic lifestyle: "What Jesus of Nazareth had said became dissolved in what the post-Easter Jesus said through his prophets."[40] By the time of the Q redaction the distinction between the words of the earthly Jesus and the exalted Jesus was no longer apparent.

As impressive as Boring's statistics are, the assumed framework behind them lacks credibility. Like Schulz, Boring perceives prophetic handiwork behind formal peculiarities: the $\lambda\acute{\epsilon}\gamma\omega$ $\acute{\upsilon}\mu\hat{\iota}\nu$ phrase, "sentences of holy law", chiasmus, antithetic parallelism, and the "eschatological correlative."[41] We judge the

---

[38] M. Eugene Boring, *Sayings of the Risen Jesus,* Cambridge: C.U.P., 1982.

[39] *Ibid.,* 195, 196. For references to the Q sayings see p. 180.

[40] *Ibid.,* 182.

[41] The eschatological correlative ($\kappa\alpha\theta\grave{\omega}\varsigma/\ddot{\omega}\sigma\pi\epsilon\rho$ $\dot{\epsilon}\gamma\acute{\epsilon}\nu\epsilon\tau o$ ($\mathring{\eta}\nu$) ... $o\ddot{\upsilon}\tau\omega\varsigma$ $\check{\epsilon}\sigma\tau\alpha\iota$) was originally proposed by Richard Edwards ("The Eschatological Correlative as *Gattung* in the New

prophetic origin of these phrases to be dubious. Moreover, Boring's methodology is *a priori* favourable to the prophetic origin of Jesus' sayings. His second criterion, "Secondary Origin," is altogether unsatisfactory as few sayings can be classified as such according to broad scholarly consensus—certainly not the percentage assumed in the statistics above. He repeatedly assumes secondary origin without sufficient textual or critical support. Furthermore, sayings that do not fit into the narrative context can be legitimately ascribed to an earlier source of authentic sayings rather than a spurious source of Christian prophecy. A setting for the sayings of Jesus within the early Church can be found for all the sayings of Jesus, yet scholars have failed to demonstrate how this disproves authenticity. He unjustifiably pins the prophetic tag to sayings which express interest in the Holy Spirit, legal matters, and eschatology—themes prominent in prophetic literature, but obviously not monopolized by early Christian prophets.

The guiding presupposition of Boring's second volume, *The Continuing Voice of Jesus,* is as follows:

> Sayings of Christian prophets may comprise not only new, post-Easter revelations; they may also take up and re-present words from the tradition, including pre-Easter words of Jesus of Nazareth. They are here called "prophetic" because they are presented in the community not as what Jesus once said but as what the post-Easter exalted Lord now *says.*[42]

But is this true? He presents no evidence (nor does anyone else) that the post-Easter community valued Jesus' sayings apart from their origin within Jesus' earthly ministry where all of the synoptic evidence agrees in placing it. Jesus' earthly teaching remained determinative in the post-Easter situation because the Jesus who spoke of himself in a veiled manner as Son of Man on earth was now vindicated as exalted Son of Man in heaven. When Boring writes: "But there is a great difference in whether words of Jesus are understood as the remembered words of a past historical figure who is now dead, or understood as spoken in the present by one who still lives,"[43] he makes the false assumption that those who

---

Testament", *ZNW* 60 [1969] 9-20), who claimed the form only existed in Q. However, subsequent scholarship has successfully disproven his theory. Critics of the eschatological correlative include: Anton Vögtle, "Der Spruch vom Jonaszeichen", in *Das Evangelium und die Evangelien*, KBANT, (Düsseldorf: 1971), 116, 117; John S. Kloppenborg, *The Formation of Q,* 129; David E. Aune, *Prophecy in Early Christianity,* 168, 169; D. Schmidt, "The LXX Gattung 'Prophetic Correlative' ", *JBL* 96 (1977) 517-522. In addition to Schmidt's findings in the LXX, Aune has found many correlatives paralleling Edwards' model in the Hebrew OT so that he is able to say, "There is no reason to regard the prophetic correlative either as a form unique to the LXX or as a distinctively prophetic form" (168).

[42] *The Continuing Voice of Jesus,* 16.
[43] *Ibid.,* 19.

recorded and transmitted Jesus' earthly sayings could only have done so if the sayings were in a process of continually being voiced by Jesus through prophets in the present. Clearly this supposition is unnecessary. The earliest Christians did not consider Jesus to be dead, rather the resurrection itself certified that what Jesus once said was true and had now been vindicated. The resurrection, therefore, was a logical stimulus motivating the collection of Jesus' pre-Easter teaching.

Further, it is strange to us that the exalted Lord did not speak explicitly *as the exalted Lord* as he does in the book of Revelation. While Boring assumes that the risen Christ became the determinative factor in the formation of the Jesus tradition, the reversal of identity does not suggest that this was actually the case—if exalted sayings were placed on the mouth of the earthly Jesus, it would seem that the earthly Jesus and not the exalted Jesus was in fact the authoritative source of instruction for the community.

In addition, Boring's argument is not plausible when he asserts that Paul's letters ". . . are our *earliest* Christian documents, containing our earliest references to Christian prophecy. . . . They contain prophetic *formulae and oracles* from Paul himself and other early Christian prophets."[44] Yet when this is apparently the case, why does not Paul voice Son of Man sayings or speak of the kingdom of God in terms more familiar to synoptic vocabulary where prophetic sayings are apparently rampant? Is not the same risen Lord inspiring both? And why is it that "Luke's interest in prophecy does not extend to the careful preservation and handing on of prophetic oracles themselves."[45] If Boring is correct, is it not strange that in Acts there is not a single instance in which Christian prophets voice sayings comparable to those which Boring isolates in Q—a very prominent component in Luke's Gospel?

D. Migaku Sato

Migaku Sato defines Q as a kind of "Prophetic book" or "book of a prophet" whose creation was determined by the prophetic activity of the circle succeeding Jesus. The Q disciples were, like the OT disciples of the prophets, carriers of the words of their master and also prophets in their own right. The Elijah-Elisha relationship emerges as the closest parallel to the Q phenomenon, and is the model on which the Q group consciously established its continuation of Jesus' prophetic

---

44 *Ibid.*, 59.
45 *Ibid.*, 74.

office. To these Q carriers belongs a wandering lifestyle characterized by homelessness, lack of family, poverty, and defenselessness.[46]

The foundation of Sato's study is his hypothesis that the OT passes along the *Prophetenbuch* as the major literary type (*Makrogattung*) which eventually became the literary genus of the Q source. As opposed to other *Makrogattungen* prevalent in NT times (gospels, testaments, apocalypses, wisdom sayings collections, etc), the "book of a prophet" claims the godly origin of its collected words which were originally voiced by divinely appointed prophets. The "prophet's book" contains selections of prophetic *Mikrogattungen*, transcriptions of words from oral tradition, and specific compositional characteristics: thematic blocks, a framework (*Rahmungstechnik*), catch-word association, conclusion with a hymn, chronological arrangement, and conclusion with a salvation promise or condemnation statement.[47] Sato finds all these elements within Q.

He identifies four major characteristics representing the ground structure of prophecy within Israel:

1) The special intervention of God (*Gottergriffenheit*). A vertical manifestation of the deity of God to the prophet.
2) Actual Addressees—A horizontal relationship from the endowed prophet to his audience.
3) Eschatology—the background of the prophetic phenomena is an atmosphere in which the present and future are bound.
4) Connection with the prophetic tradition which 3 criteria make evident: a) use of specific prophetic *Mikrogattungen* (smaller forms), b) the use of prophetic images (fire, swords, etc.), c) reference to earlier prophets.[48]

Sato, likewise, finds each of these elements within Q. However, unlike Käsemann, he does not believe there was one exclusive unifying *Mikrogattung* espoused by early Christian prophets. Thus the Q prophets took over a number of prophetic *Mikrogattungen* including the call narrative (*Berufungserzählung*), the vision narrative (*Visionserzählung*), the condemnation word (*Unheilswort*), the salvation word (*Heilswort*), the salvation oracle (*Heilsorakel*), the admonition or warning word (*Mahnwort*), and the woe (*Weheruf*). The *Mahnwort* is an example of a *Mikrogattung* taken from another tradition (Wisdom) and revived prophetically.

These observations lead Sato to claim that Q originally resembled an OT "prophet's book"—its closest parallel existing in 1 Kgs. 19:19-21 with the Elijah-Elisha relationship. He reasons that Jesus assumed the prophetic role exemplified

---

[46] Migaku Sato, *Q und Prophetie*, 375, 406-411.

[47] *Ibid.*, 76-95.

[48] *Ibid.*, 96-106.

by the OT prophets, the hypothetical prophets behind 1 Enoch 94-104, and finally John the Baptist (Sato claims Jesus was an original disciple of John).[49] Q developed prior to Easter. Jesus assumed the *Meisterprophet* role, and the disciples recorded his sayings. Subsequently, Easter moved the disciples to re-pronounce the pronouncements of their master and contribute prophecies of their own. Simultaneously, Jesus became identified with the Son of Man-world ruler. The Q circle existed in two divisions: a stationary group which carried out editorial work (Sato sees three redactions behind Q), and a wandering group which transmitted the Jesus tradition.[50]

The parallels Sato cites are legitimate. However, his hypothesis that the Q *Tradenten* modeled themselves after Elisha fails to recognize the fact that Elisha achieved known prophetic status in his own right apart from Elijah, and was subsequently identified explicitly as a prophet by the OT writers. The Q community on the other hand prophesied anonymously (if they prophesied at all), and were never identified as prophets in the NT. A plausible parallel, therefore, between Elisha and the hypothetical "Q prophets" is still lacking. Second, the *Makrogattung* and *Mikrogattungen* are ambiguous features which cannot be specified as characteristics of one particular group within first-century Palestine. Third, that a prophetic speaker lies behind I Enoch 94-104 is purely imaginative. Fourth, Sato does not prove the prophetic origin of a single Q saying, but openly admits, "Eine klare Entscheidung für oder gegen die Echtheit war sehr oft kaum möglich."[51] Having read Aune and Hill, he still attributes numerous sayings of Jesus to early Christian prophets without first identifying why such sayings could not have originated from Jesus—a prophetic figure by scholarly consensus. Finally, and most importantly, Sato fails, in our opinion, to weigh in his conclusions the uniqueness of the historical Jesus and the uniqueness of Jesus' relationship with his disciples.[52] Sato agrees that a prophetic parallel cannot be found for the Jesus of the Q material:

---

[49] *Ibid.,* 372. See also p. 374.

[50] *Ibid.,* 106-108. For Sato's theory of the redaction of Q see p. 380. Sato identifies the prophetic sayings most likely not going back to Jesus to be: Lk. 12:10; Lk. 11:49-51 par.; Lk. 13:34 par.; Lk. 7:33f.; Lk. 10:13f.; Lk. 12:11f. par.; Lk. 17:23 (24) par.; Mt. 10:23; Lk. 6:22f. par. (p.301). He makes this classification as a result of the *Mikrogattungen* existing in these verses.

[51] *Ibid.,* 302.

[52] Thus, Martin Hengel writes: "Despite all the things they have in common, however, attention must be drawn to *one* essential difference between the call to follow Jesus and the story of Elijah and Elisha, and this difference basically applies to all Old Testament call-narratives. There, the *person who calls* is ultimately God himself: whether he is commissioning a prophet to his vocation (1 Kings 19.15-18;1 Sam 16.1f.; 1 Kings 11.31f.) or whether he himself is calling through the medium of a vision. Jesus' call to follow him cannot on the other hand be traced

Der wichtigste Punkt jedoch, der Q über die Makrogattung "Prophetenbuch" hinausrücken wird, besteht vor allem in der Gestalt des Sprechers Jesus selbst: Jesus in Q nimmt als für Heil am Eschaton entscheidende Person die göttliche Stellung ein. Daraus stammt auch die einmalige christologische Gliederung der Stellung des Propheten ist in den altestamentlichen Prophetenbüchern nicht geschehen.[53]

But is the Q material unique because of the special development of the Q *Makrogattung* as it occurred in a now unknown prophetic community or is the content of Q unique to prophetic tradition simply because Jesus himself, while exhibiting prophetic attributes, went beyond the normal confines of prophetic behaviour? To maintain his thesis Sato is ultimately forced to assume that the unique characteristics emerging from Jesus' sayings (unique to OT tradition and to NT history) point not to the exceptional nature of the historical Jesus, but to the unique activity of the Q prophets, and to the special character of the "prophet's book" Q:

Die Jünger waren also sowohl Tradenten als auch Propheten - ein Phänomen, das zwar in der Alttestamentlichen Prophetie zu beobachten ist, aber in den anderen charismatischen Strömungen des Urchristentums nicht vorkommt. Der Unterschied zu den alttestamentlichen Prophetenjüngern ist der, daß in Q der Meisterprophet Jesus de facto an die Stelle Jahwes trat. Darum ist die Q-Prophetie ein einzigartiges Phänomen in der Geschichte der israelitischen Prophetie; dies verursachte auch den Sondercharakter des "Prophetenbuches" Q.[54]

This in our opinion is the weakness of Sato's thesis and the weakness of the theory of Christian prophecy as the original source of Jesus tradition within the synoptic Gospels. It is not reasonable to explain what we know—that Jesus was a prophet and spoke prophetically oriented sayings—by what we do not know—that early Christian prophets channelled sayings of the exalted Lord Jesus which at a later date were secondarily attributed to the earthly Jesus.

Conclusion

F. Neugebauer,[55] David Hill, J.D.G. Dunn, and D. Aune have cast considerable doubt on the supposed evidence verifying the existence within the Gospels of sayings of the exalted Jesus spoken through Christian prophets. *No explicit or*

---

back to any other source; according to the Synoptic account the call is empowered by Jesus' own *messianic authority*." The italics are prof. Hengel's. *The Charismatic Leader and His Followers*, Tr. James C.G. Greig, Ed. John Riches; Edinburgh: T&T Clark (1981) 16-17.

[53] *Ibid.*, 95.

[54] *Ibid.*, 408.

[55] "Geistsprüche und Jesuslogien", *ZNW* 80 (1962) 218-28.

implicit factual evidence points to the prophetic origin of any synoptic sayings of Jesus. On the other hand, the NT evidence we do have does not support the post-Easter prophetic origin of Jesus' synoptic sayings. Conclusions based upon the findings of form criticism are untenable.[56]   Where Luke quotes a prophetic utterance, he names the prophet explicitly (Acts 11:27; 13:1f.; 21:9f.). The book of Revelation attributes sayings of the risen Jesus directly to the risen Jesus through the servant John. No attempt is made in Revelation to place such material back onto the lips of the earthly Jesus.[57]   And as Dunn notes, for Paul "there is a qualitative distinction between Jesus-tradition and the inspiration of the present, and the one is not a complete substitute for the other (1 Cor 7:10, 25, 40)."[58] Some very simple facts should not be forgotten. The burden of proof must remain with those who perceive Christian prophetic creation within Q, because early Christian prophets are never alluded to therein and the exalted Lord Jesus is never referred to as a stimulus for prophetic speech—a strange fact considering the prominent role attributed to him by these scholars.[59]

---

[56] Perhaps later form critics should have heeded Dibelius' warning: "But the greatest doubts arise when we consider the literary category of Q, . . . we must be careful not to speak with too great self-confidence of Q as a definitely ascertained entity", *From Tradition to Gospel*, 234.

[57] Elisabeth Schüssler Fiorenza assumes "The Logia source Q and the pre-Matthean tradition also indicate the leadership of prophets in the primitive Palestinian or Syrian church," but Fiorenza like so many others assumes such activity without offering tangible support. On the question of Revelation, she concludes (in support of D. Hill!) ". . . that John has an exceptional position among the other prophets", *The Book of Revelation: Justice and Judgment*, Philadelphia: Fortress Press (1985) 146.

[58] "Prophetic 'I'-Sayings and the Jesus Tradition: The Importance of testing Prophetic Utterances Within Early Christianity", *NTS* 24 (1978) 179. In *Jesus and the Spirit*, London: SCM (1975) 173, Dunn is more open to the possibility of Christian prophecy and the Jesus tradition: "Prophetic oracles in the first person which may have become counted among sayings of Jesus include Matt. 10.5 (possibly); 18.20 (almost certainly) and Luke 11.49-51 (probably)." However, even Matt. 18:20 (the almost certainly saying) is suspect as Davies and Allison (*Matthew* II, 790) caution when they observe that if Paul could write 1 Cor.5:3-5 it is not beyond reason that Jesus, while on earth, could have said something like Matt.18:20.

[59] The articles of Gerald Hawthorne ("Christian Prophets in the Gospel Tradition", in *Tradition and Interpretation in the New Testament*, FS E.E. Ellis; Grand Rapids: Eerdmans [1987] 119-133) and Robert J. Miller ("The Rejection of the Prophets in Q", *JBL* 107/2 [1988] 225-40) do not alter our conclusion. Hawthorne openly admits the lack of foundation upon which his argument builds: ". . . there is no 'concrete evidence' for such a role played by Christian prophets in the formation of the gospel tradition, and no critical methodology has as yet been developed by which such a role can be detected and demonstrated. . . . I have no illusions of being able to prove that a single utterance of the risen Lord spoken by a prophet actually became part of the dominical sayings . . ." (123). Miller's argument is more bold but less convincing, as it depends entirely on the shaky presupposition of a prophetically inspired Q community: "So Q's accusation needs an additional premise to make sense. Since this premise is not in the text, we can best suppose that it was supplied by the lived context, that is, the actual experience of the Q community" (230). One hypothesis is not proven by another. Miller's premise is not as convincing as its *textual* precursor – that Jesus himself was a prophetic figure who was rejected by his generation.

Moreover, if one takes into consideration the entire body of Q material, it appears unlikely that the Q community had a prophetic christology in the narrow sense. The complex combination of Son of Man sayings, the preaching of the kingdom of God, and the numerous wisdom motifs require more advanced christological understanding on the part of those who transmitted the Q sayings— here Jesus appears to be more than a master prophet.

On the other hand, it is entirely possible that the prophetic elements within Q reflect Jesus' own prophetic self-understanding. The anointing of the Holy Spirit at Jesus' baptism, Jesus' prophetic visions (Lk. 10:18, 21; Mt. 11:25-27), Jesus' symbolic acts (entry into Jerusalem, cleansing the temple, cursing the fig tree, Lord's Supper, etc.), Jesus' prophetic foresight (Mk. 10:39, 14:8 par., 14:30), Jesus' insights into the innermost thoughts of people (Mk. 2:5,8; Lk. 6:8; 9:47), and Jesus' prediction of a violent death all reflect prophetic characteristics of Jesus manifested outside of the Q material. No doubt these traits led many of Jesus' contemporaries to proclaim him to be a prophet (Mk. 6:15; 8:28; Mt. 21:11 etc.). Therefore, if the Q sayings are authentic one would expect them to have a prophetic flavour.[60]

Jesus' association with prophets coupled with the omission of Passion allusions within Q does not necessarily indicate that Q represents a group whose form of prophecy set it apart from mainstream early Christianity. Many of the prophetic characteristics thought peculiar to Q are evident throughout the NT. Especially noteworthy is the following passage from Paul's first letter to the Thessalonians:

> You, my friends, have followed the example of the Christians in the churches of God in Judaea: who have been treated by your own countrymen as they were treated by the Jews, who killed the Lord Jesus and the prophets and drove us out, and are so heedless of God's will and such enemies of their fellow-men that they hinder us from telling the Gentiles how they may be saved. (2:14-16a)

In this epistle, whose early date and authenticity most scholars accept, Paul speaks of Jesus' death, the death of the prophets, and the rejection of himself and his followers in a similar vein. Conflict with the Jews is clearly apparent in Paul's comment on the churches in Judea. In this passage, however, Paul obviously is not equating Jesus, the prophets, and the Thessalonians. The christological emphasis in other parts of the letter prohibits such conjecture. If Paul mentions the tradition of the prophets together with Jesus' death, and the rejection of Paul

---

[60] The above examples and references are dependent on David Hill, *New Testament Prophecy*, London: Marshall, Morgan & Scott (1979) 49-69. See also J.D.G. Dunn, *Jesus and the Spirit*, 83; J. Jeremias, *New Testament Theology*, 77f.; E. Boring, *The Continuing Voice of Jesus*, 56f.

himself, it would seem that Q scholars have perhaps misinterpreted Q when they assume an esoteric prophetic community as the determinitive factor behind the emergence of the Q material. If so, the same should be said of Paul's community.

In conclusion we believe that Q bears witness to the prophetic qualities of Jesus' mission including Jesus' endowment with the spirit, his miracles, his pronouncements, and his prophecies. But that the Q sayings reflect a prophetically active community of early Christian prophets is unfounded. Like its synoptic environment, Q presents Jesus in a very unique role in relation to prophetic tradition. Jesus' endowment with the spirit coincides with the events emanating from Jesus' ministry which signify the presence of God's saving rule among men (Lk. 11:20//Mt. 12:28; Lk. 7:22f.//Mt. 11:2f.). Q bears witness to the fact that Jesus' prophetic acts are more than eschatological signs—they bear witness to eschatological events at hand! Moreover, by proclaiming "I say to you" rather than "the Lord says", Jesus speaks with unique authority unlike the prophets before him. As a prophet, he was most unusual.

II. The Old Testament Prophets and Jesus' Preaching
of the Kingdom of God in Q

The book of Isaiah contains, in tension with one another, a presentation of wisdom thought, frequent warnings of impending judgement, an emphasis on ethical behaviour, the pouring out of the spirit, and the address of God as "Father". Isaiah shares with the Q material specific references to Sheol, Sodom and Gomorrah, Jerusalem and the literary forms of the"blessing" and "woe." As we have seen, these similarities led M. Sato to conclude that Q, like Isaiah, is a prophetic work, the product of early Christian prophets.

A major problem, however, with the hypothetical early Christian prophetic origin of Q springs from Jesus' emphasis on the kingdom of God and his self-identification as the Son of Man, because these two themes are not found in the early Christian prophecies in Acts and the Pauline corpus. A more plausible explanation for the prophetic character of Q, we believe, exists in the probability that Jesus himself was familiar with OT prophetic books and hence adopted prophetic language to his teaching style and polemical language.

In many ways prophetic speech provided the perfect medium through which Jesus could present his gospel of the kingdom of God. For God's sovereignty functions at the heart of OT prophecy: the prophets' call, the filling of the spirit, the warning of judgement, the call to repentance, the call to ethical behaviour, eschatological predictions, the appeal to act in view of God's coming salvation— all the outward manifestations of prophecy bear in common a direct relation to

God's unrivalled sovereignty. Hence Walter Eichrodt wrote of the classical prophets: ". . . all their utterances are dominated by the incomparable greatness of their God."[61]

The same emphasis on God's sovereign authority is clearly present in Jesus' teaching which focuses on the rule of God. Though Jesus is not identified directly in Q as a prophet as elsewhere in the Gospels,[62] Q does contain passages which associate Jesus' calling, his acts, and his teaching authority with his possession of the Holy Spirit (Lk. 4:1//Mt. 4:1; Lk. 12:10//Mt. 12:32)—an endowment which affiliates Jesus with the prophets.[63] And as a prophet Jesus would have assumed divine authority. In Q, therefore, when Jesus speaks with the recognizable forms of prophecy he does a radical thing—he speaks with an authority by which his words reveal the direct decrees of Yahweh the sovereign God of all the earth—the same authority which bolstered Isaiah, Jeremiah, and all the true OT prophets. Yet Jesus' sayings assume authority previously unmatched.

None of Jesus' prophetic predecessors could match Jesus' knowledge of God's sovereignty and the knowledge of how God was acting—especially in relation to the prophetic figure himself. Jesus' direct speech about the kingdom of God is unique to prophetic speech and raises the question of Jesus' identity. Who could say such things and from where could he get such authority? The general observation must be made that Jesus' adaptation of prophetic speech immediately necessitates a response from his audience, not only to the legitimacy or illegitimacy of Jesus' prophetic status, but also to the legitimacy of Jesus' message. With this observation in mind, we adopt Georg Fohrer's definition of the "the oracle" and "the threat" as the two characteristic forms of OT prophecy:

> An oracle is usually marked by the introduction kô 'āmār yhwh (sebā'ôt), a cultic liturgical formula. An oracle always declares the immediate future to be favourable or unfavorable on the basis of the present situation, thereby granting the person concerned the chance so to act in the present moment so as to secure the good or avoid the evil through his conduct.[64]

Using Fohrer's definition as our model, we see that Jesus' proclamations in Q maintain the basic strategy of the oracle, but from a radically new perspective. The

---

[61] Walter Eichrodt, ET *Theology of the Old Testament,* Vol I; Philadelphia: The Westminster Press (1961) 350.

[62] Mk. 6:15 par.; 8:28 par.; Mt. 21:11, 46; Lk. 7:16; Jn. 4:19; 6:14; 7:40, 52; 9:17; by Pharisaic circles: Lk. 7:39; 24:19; Mk. 8:11par.; arrested as a false prophet: Mk. 14:65; Lk. 22:63.

[63] Thus Jeremias: "To possess the spirit of God was to be a prophet", *New Testament Theology* I, 78.

[64] Georg Fohrer, *Introduction to the Old Testament,* Tr. David Green; New York: Abingdon (1968) 353.

OT oracles cry out for unconditional alignment to God's sovereignty either directly through seeking Yahweh's protection in political confrontations or indirectly through obedience to Yahweh's ethical standard; but Jesus' oracles, while maintaining ethical standards, cry out for a positive response to Jesus himself: Lk. 12:8//Mt. 10:32; Lk. 10:13-15//Mt. 11:21-24; Lk. 11:31, 32//Mt. 12:41-42; Lk. 13:34//Mt. 23:37; Lk. 10:23//Mt. 13:16; Lk. 6:22//Mt. 5:10; Lk. 7:23//Mt. 11:5, 6. The words are not 'of the Lord' but of Jesus. Jesus' oracle in Q, God's message revealed through the prophet, declares the future to be a blessing or woe on the basis of the listener's present response to Jesus himself. The prophet, therefore, is a vital part of the message which he preaches—a phenomenon alien to OT precursors.

But the content of Jesus' prophetic message is also the kingdom of God. The kingdom of God in addition to Jesus himself appears in Q as the basis for future approval (Lk. 12:31//Mt. 6:33). The kingdom of God is inextricably bound to Jesus' appearance (Lk. 16:16//Mt. 11:12), his mighty acts (Lk. 11:20//Mt.12:28), and the authority which he transmits to his disciples (Lk. 10:9, 11//Mt. 10:7). As a prophet, Jesus claims ability to identify future members of the kingdom (Lk. 13:29//Mt. 8:11; Lk. 6:20//Mt. 5:3); he perceives the present activity of the kingdom (Lk. 10:9, 11//Mt. 10:7; Lk. 11:20//Mt. 12:28); and he claims ability to define the kingdom (Lk. 13:18-20//Mt. 13:31-33). In view of the fact that OT prophets never use the phrase "the kingdom of God", Jesus' speech is all the more startling. Jesus' prophetic speech raises the question as to Jesus' identity: *Here is more than Jonah!* And if Jesus is recognized as more than a prophet, while recognizing the diversity of first-century expectation concerning the coming anointed one, we do not go too far in suggesting that Jesus' anointing with the spirit, his wisdom, his miraculous healings, and his unsurpassed authority combine to imply his messiahship within Q. Though in Q Jesus does not receive the title Χριστός, as he does not in Mark, each attribute suggests messiahship. To this extent Q is compatible with the so-called "Messianic Secret."

In Jesus' oracles, as with the OT prophets, God's sovereignty is always in view. Nowhere, for instance, is God's sovereignty at center stage more than in the Lord's Prayer: Πάτερ, ἁγιασθήτω τὸ ὄνομά σου,

ἐλθέτω ἡ βασιλεία σου (Lk. 11:2//Mt. 6:9b, 10a).[65]
Here and in all the "kingdom of God" sayings, the "kingdom" can only be understood in relation to God's sovereign rule. As a prophet in Q, Jesus addresses the dynamic kingship of God. It is no wonder, therefore, that Jesus,

---

[65] The origin of the Lord's Prayer is of course very controversial, though major works on Q consistently address the passage as a Q saying. See: J. Kloppenborg, *Q Parallels,* Sonoma: Polebridge (1988) 84.

like the OT prophets, emphasizes ethics and humility as requirements of the kingdom—these attributes are the prophetic response to God's righteousness and sovereignty.[66] God is in view, not human achievement.

We agree, then, that Jesus appears in Q as a prophetic figure, but the content of Jesus' prophecy sets Jesus apart. In addition to expressing prophetic knowledge of the kingdom of God, Jesus also conveys qualitative knowledge of the Son of Man. There can be no doubt, in our opinion, that Jesus applies this phrase *to himself* twice in Q (Lk. 7:34//Mt. 11:19; Lk. 9:58//Mt. 8:20). Further, Jesus and the Son of Man both seem to be the basis for future blessing in different contexts: in Lk.12:8//Mt. 10:32 the future Son of Man's acts of judgement are based on man's present response to Jesus, while in Lk. 6:22//Mt. 5:11 future blessing depends on present obedience to the Son of Man. Hence Jesus and the Son of Man inextricably bind in Jesus' prophetic speech within Q. Just as Jesus expresses future knowledge of the kingdom of God, he also claims prophetic knowledge of future activity of the Son of Man: Lk. 11:30//Mt. 12:40; Lk. 12:8//Mt. 10:32; Lk. 12:10//Mt. 12:32; Lk. 12:40//Mt. 24:44; Lk. 17:24//Mt. 24:47; Lk. 17:26//Mt. 24:37; Lk. 17:30//Mt. 24:39. There is a relationship, then, within Q between the kingdom of God and the Son of Man: the knowledge of both is revealed through the prophetic words of Jesus; both are qualified as future blessings; and, both inseparably bind to the person of Jesus.

Jesus' negative words draw further attention to his prophetic identity. In Q Jesus directs specific woes[67] against: (1) the Galilean cities which failed to repent and believe at the sight of his miracles (Lk. 10:13//Mt. 11:22); (2) against lawyers who legislated picky rules (Lk. 11:46//Mt. 23:4) and prevented others from acquiring a saving knowledge of God (Lk. 17:1//Mt. 18:7); and (3), against the Pharisees, who followed religious laws meticulously while neglecting the basic OT mandates for justice (Lk. 11:42//Mt. 23:23), who failed to act humbly before God by seeking places of honour in the synagogue and market place (Lk. 11:43//Mt.23:6, 7), and who transmitted defilement (Lk. 11:44//Mt. 23:27, 28) rather than a message of salvation leading to God. The general force of the woes materializes in Lk. 17:1//Mt. 18:7 where Jesus verbally attacks those who set

---

[66] E.g., Lev. 19:14, 18; 25:18; 26:15, 43; Dt. 10:18, 19a; 32:3b, 4; Isa. 3:14; 10:2; 42:21; 45:8, 13; Jer. 5:28; 7:3-7; 22:3; Eze. 22:29; Zch. 7:9, 10; Mal. 3:5

[67] οὐαί is the LXX translation of the Hebrew OT the word for "woe" (אוֹי), "an impassioned expression of grief", (BDB,17) which occurs 24 times (Even-Shoshan, 23) all in the prophets except Num. 21:29; 24:23; 1 Sm. 4:7, 8; Pr. 23:29. An alternate word (הוֹי) – an expression of dissatisfaction and pain often preceding a judgement threat (BDB, 223) – occurs 51 times (Even-Shoshan, 284) all in the prophets except for 1 Kgs. 13:30. הוֹי is used 25 times against Israel, and 11 times against foreign nations. See Claus Westerman, *Basic Forms of Prophetic Speech*, Tr. Hugh White; London: Lutterworth (1967) 190.

stumbling blocks—an image which can only stand for obstacles preventing a saving knowledge of God. Most importantly, however, it must be noted that Jesus directs woes against those who reject Jesus himself (Lk. 10:13f.//Mt. 11:21f.). No other prophet was the basis for blessing and woe.

The woes indirectly serve as indicators of the immense authority which Jesus assumed as a prophet. In challenging the Pharisees and lawyers, he claims authority to judge and sentence the religious leaders of his day. While the Son of Man will condemn in the future, *Jesus judges now*. The fact that Jesus' threats resemble in form the threats of OT prophets only accentuates the bite of his judgement and the validity of his charge—not only is Jesus claiming that he himself speaks God's verdict, but he alleges that his verdict is supported by the authority of scripture—the source which the Pharisees and lawyers boast mastery of.

Finally, Q testifies to the unique authority of Jesus' prophetic knowledge in Lk. 10:22//Mt. 11:27:

> All things have been handed over to me by my Father, and no one knows who the son is except the father, and who the father is except the son, and anyone to whom the son wills to reveal him.

Against the background of OT prophetic literature, this saying communicates clearly what many other Q sayings attest indirectly—Jesus' unparalleled prophetic knowledge and power come directly from God with whom Jesus shares a unique relationship. In Q this unique relationship between God the Father and Jesus the Son results in Jesus' unique authority and explains both Jesus' remarkable perception of the activity of the kingdom of God, and Jesus' prophetic knowledge of how the Son of Man will judge. In Q at large and in the Matthean and Lukan settings "All things" refers both to Jesus' knowledge of the activity of God's kingdom and his power to perform miracles.[68] Both Jesus' knowledge and his power signal his unique relationship to God. In Jesus is the power and knowledge of the sovereign God.

In Q, then, the basis for blessing and woe is God's revelation of power manifested in Jesus—a power which beforehand had never appeared in human form:

> Blessed are the eyes which see the things you see, for I say to you, that many prophets and kings wished to see the things which you see, and did not see them, and to hear the things which you hear, and did not hear them. (Lk. 10:23, 24//Mt. 13:16, 17; cf. Lk. 11:31, 32//Mt. 12:41, 42)

---

[68] See Bo Reike, "$\pi\hat{\alpha}\varsigma$, $\ddot{\alpha}\pi\alpha\varsigma$", *TDNT* V, 895.

The Queen of the South shall rise up with the men of this generation at the judgment and condemn them, because she came from the ends of the earth to hear the wisdom of Solomon; and behold, something greater than Solomon is here. The men of Nineveh shall stand up with this generation and condemn it, because they repented at the preaching of Jonah; and behold, something greater than Jonah is here. (Lk. 11:31, 32//Mt. 12:41, 42)

The most natural interpretation of these sayings is that prophets and kings desired to see the things that were going on in Jesus' ministry. Solomon and Jonah are being identified as inferior to a specific figure—namely Jesus who is performing controversial acts and subsequently facing rejection by a portion of his listeners. In view of Fohrer's contrast between the positive and negative OT prophetic sayings,[69] we can see that Jesus surpasses OT precedents: he not only announces "a favourable turn of fortune" in Lk.10:23, 24//Mt. 13:16, 17 and "disaster" in Lk. 11:31, 32//Mt. 12:41, 42, but he claims that fortune or ruin depends directly upon one's response to Jesus himself and his message.

Conclusion

Addressing Jesus' Q sayings against the background of OT prophecy, we can formulate the following conclusions: First, Jesus does speak and act as a prophet in Q; second, Jesus' Q sayings maintain prophetic awareness of the sovereignty of God; third, Jesus' prophetic authority in Q is startling and unique—his knowledge and power come directly from God as from a father to a son; fourth, Jesus' prophetic awareness holds in tension his perception of the reign of the kingdom and his role as the Son of Man; and fifth, proper response to Jesus himself and his message is the basis for prophetic blessing and woe in Q.

Jesus' prophetic character in Q does not contradict his messiahship any more than does Jesus' prophetic role in Mark, Matthew, Luke, or John (4:19, 44; 6:14; 7:40; 9:17).[70] In Mark and Q the attributes which imply that Jesus is a prophet—healing miracles, the anointing with the spirit, prophetic foresight, divine authority—corroborate, like the attribute of wisdom, Jesus' identity as Messiah according to various streams of ancient Jewish expectation (Isa. 11:1f.; Jer. 23:5; Ps. Sal. 18:7, 8; I En. 49:2b, 3a). Jesus' prophetic demeanour in Q accords fully

---

[69] "The positive prophetical saying is a declaration of salvation or a promise, which, in a present state of distress, announces a favourable turn of fortune, . . . The negative prophetic saying is a threat, with or without motivation, announcing imminent disaster on account of human sin,"*Introduction to the Old Testament,* 353, 354.

[70] So F. Schnider, "Die Prophetenchristologie und der Anspruch Jesu", Ch. 8 in *Jesus der Prophet*; Göttingen: Vandenhoeck & Ruprecht (1973) 259: "Jesu Anspruch ist absoluter Art. Jesus ist nicht einer der Propheten, sondern "der Prophet" als der absolute Heilbringer, der alle eschatologischen Erwartungen erfüllt und in radikaler Nähe zum Vater steht."

with the role Jesus plays in Mark, where Jesus identifies himself as a prophet (6:4), where second parties address Jesus as a prophet (6:15; 8:23), where Jesus adopts the λέγω ὑμῖν phrase,[71] pronounces woes (13:17; 14:21) and is in fact mocked as a false prophet before the Sanhedrin (Mk. 14:65; cf. Lk 22:63-65) immediately before Jesus is sentenced to death—a sentence which accords to the sort of death required of false prophets in the OT (Dt. 18:20).[72] Jesus' prophetic character in Q, therefore, corroborates Mark's passion account.

---

[71] σοὶ λέγω: 2.11; 5:41; ἀμὴν λέγω ὑμῖν: 3:28; 9:1, 41; 10:15, 29; 11:23; 12:43; 13:30; 14:9, 18, 25, 30; λέγω ὑμῖν: 9:13; 11:24.

[72] See J. Jeremias, *Theology of the New Testament*, 77, 78; R. Pesch, *Markus* 2, 441; I.H. Marshall, *Luke*, 845; F. Schnider, *Jesus der Prophet*, 158.

Chapter 5

Daniel and the Conceptual Background of Q

I. Introduction

The OT provides the conceptual background for the Q sayings of Jesus. Jesus alludes to OT figures, he adopts OT language and form into his pedagogical style, and he quotes and alludes to specific OT texts. Because his audience was familiar with the OT, Jesus used wisdom and prophetic styles heuristically as means of communicating his relation to God and his relation to the message he preached—the kingdom of God. A comparison of themes indicates that Daniel in particular provides the most likely conceptual background for the major components of Jesus' Q sayings.

Conceptual Parallels among Daniel, I Enoch and Q

	Q (Lk.)	Daniel	I Enoch
The Son of Man	6:22; 7:34; 9:58; 11:30; 12:8; 12:10; 12:40; 17:24; 17:26; 17:30; 22:28	"One like a Son of Man" (7:13)	46:2,3,4; 48:2f.; 62:5,7,9,14; 63:11; 69:26, 27, 29; 71:14, 17
The kingdom of God	6:20b; 7:28; 10:9; 11:12; 11:20; 12:31; 13:18f.; 13:20, 21; 13:28; 13:29; 16:16[1]	2:44; 3:33; 4:29; 7:13, 14, 18, 27	
Wisdom	7:35; 11:31; 11:49 diff. Mt. 23:34	חָכְמָה : 1:4, 17, 20; 2:20, 21, 23, 30; 5:11, 14	32:3; 37:1-4; 42:1-3; 48:1; 49:1; 51:3; 61:7, 11; 63:2; 82:2, 3; 84:3; 91:10; 93:8, 10; 94:5; 98:3; 101:8; 104:12; 105:1
Allusion to OT Prophetic Books	passim	9:24 and passim	108:6 and passim

---

[1] H. Schürmann ("Das Zeugnis der Redenquelle für die Basileia-Verkündigung Jesu", *Logia*, 121-200) addresses fifteen KG sayings in Q. Those not listed above include: (1) 9:61 diff. Mt.; (2) 12:32 diff. Mt. (3) Mt. 5:19; (4) Mt. 23:13 diff. Lk. 11:52.

Judgement	$\kappa\rho\acute{\iota}\nu\omega$: Lk. 6:37; 22:30 $\kappa\rho\acute{\iota}\sigma\iota\varsigma$: 10:14; 11:31; 11:32	7:22, 26	10:6, 12; 16:1; 22:11; 55:4; 84:4; 91:7, 9; 97:3; 100:4, 10; 104:5
Evil Powers	$B\epsilon\epsilon\lambda\zeta\epsilon\beta o\acute{\upsilon}\lambda$: 11:15; 11:19 $\delta\iota\acute{a}\beta o\lambda o\varsigma$: 4:2; 4:13	Ch.7 "The Four Beasts"	"Satan" 40:7; 53:3; 65:6; 67:4; 69:4
Forecast of the End	11:30; 12:8, 9; 12:10; 12:40; 17:24; 17:26; 17:28	2:28, 29; 6:26; 7:9-12, 26-27; 8:19, 23; 9:24-27; 10:14; 11:4; 12:8; Ch. 12.	10:2, 6,15; 16:1; 18:14; 19:1; 22:4, 11, 13; 54:6; 65:6; 84:4; 93:4; 94:9; 98:10; 100:4; 102:10; 103:8; 104:5

Our chart indicates that the major conceptual images which scholars cite as characteristic of Q exist within Daniel and the Similitudes of I Enoch—a co-existence of imagery not shared by any other pre-Christian literature. This is an important observation in response to tradition critics who isolate and interpret Q according to a single speculative OT or Hellenistic tradition. For in Daniel the concepts of the kingdom of God and "one like a son of man" exist in an atmosphere of wisdom and prophecy where apocalyptic features abound in anticipation of endtime judgement. When this combination of features merges in Daniel—wisdom, prophecy, judgement, eschatology—a text dated well before the life of Jesus, there is no solid reason to deny that Jesus could have combined them in his perception of his own ministry.

II. The Relation of Daniel and I Enoch in Determining the Conceptual Background of the Q Sayings of Jesus

A. The Son of Man

1. Daniel 7

What can be said with certainty about the "one like a Son of Man" (כְּבַר אֱנָשׁ) in Daniel 7:13, 14 is that he is a divine though humanlike figure who comes before the Ancient of Days to receive kingly authority. First in verse 14, the Ancient of Days bestows upon the humanlike figure dominion/sovereignty (שָׁלְטָן). 7:14b qualifies the dominion/authority of the manlike figure as an authority which will last forever (שָׁלְטָנֵהּ שָׁלְטָן עָלַם) and which will not pass away (דִּי־לָא יֶעְדֵּה). The Aramaic word שָׁלְטָן occurs 14 times in Daniel[2]—each time in direct reference to

---

[2] *Even-Shoshan*, 1106.

kingly authority.[3] In two instances שָׁלְטָן refers to the earthly dominion of the Babylonian monarchs: 6:27(26) refers to the sovereignty of Darius' kingdom while 4:19(22) expresses the rule of Nebuchadnezzar "which reaches the end of the earth." שָׁלְטָן also describes the authority or dominion of the beasts in Dn. 7, the authority given to the Leopard-like figure in 7:6, the dominion which is taken away from the beasts in 7:12, and the authority of the small horn which is crushed in 7:26. Further, in 7:27a, שָׁלְטָן describes the dominion of all the kingdoms under the heaven which will be given to the saints of the Highest One. The usage of שָׁלְטָן, however, which most closely resembles the dominion bestowed upon the "one like a son of man" in 7:14 occurs in those references which describe the rule of God. In 3:33b (4:3b) Nebuchadnezzar proclaims that the dominion of the "highest God" will last from generation to generation (וְשָׁלְטָנֵהּ עִם־דָּר וְדָר). Similarly, in 4:31, Nebuchadnezzar again praises the "Highest One," announcing that his rule lasts forever (שָׁלְטָנֵהּ שָׁלְטָן עָלַם), while later, after Daniel survives the lions' den, King Darius declares that Daniel's God's "rule will persist to the end" (עַד־סוֹפָא וְשָׁלְטָנֵהּ).[4] Hence Daniel qualifies both God's rule and the manlike figure's rule as eternal in nature.[5] The vocabulary used to describe the authority bestowed upon the "one like a son of man" (שָׁלְטָנֵהּ שָׁלְטָן עָלַם) in 7:14b is remarkably close to that associated with God in 3:33b and 6:27b, while the phrase is in fact exactly the same as that describing God's eternal rule in 4:31 (שָׁלְטָנֵהּ שָׁלְטָן עָלַם). Therefore, the authority of "the one like a son of man" surpasses that of earthly kings or the beast-like figures of Dn. 7.

The second gift awarded to the "one like a son of man" is honor יְקָר. The masculine noun occurs seven times in Daniel—each in reference to royalty.[6] From the king Daniel receives royal honor in return for interpreting the king's dream (2:6), while elsewhere in Daniel the term is applied only to the royal honor of Nebuchadnezzar (2:37; 4:27, 33). Like dominion, God gives (5:18) and takes away (5:20) honor from the king. In 7:14, then, honor represents a royal gift bestowed upon the "one like a son of man" by God.

---

[3] *BDB*, 1115.

[4] Goldingay's translation, *Daniel*, 120.

[5] עָלַם "forever" occurs twice in Ezra (4:15,19) and 18 times in Daniel where the word is used exclusively to describe rulership: in reference to earthly kings in the generic phrase "long live the king" (2:4; 3:9; 5:10; 6:7, 22); in reference to God's eternal rule (2:20, 44 (2x); 3:33; 4:31 (2x); 7:27b(?)); in reference to the Son of Man's rule (7:14); and in reference to the rule given to the "saints" (7:18, 22, 27a); *BDB*, 1106; *Even-Shoshan*, 881. The phrase "עִם־דָּר וְדָר " ("generation after generation") occurs only twice in Daniel (3:33; 4:31) both times in reference to God's eternal rule.

[6] *BDB*, 1096; *Even-Shoshan*, 489.

The third gift given to the "manlike figure" in Dn. 7:14 is a kingdom or kingship (מַלְכוּ). The feminine Aramaic noun מַלְכוּ occurs 54 times in the book of Daniel.[7] The term is used to describe the earthly kingdoms of Nebuchadnezzar (4:15, 26, 27; 5:7, 11, 16, 20, 29), Darius (6:1, 2, 2, 4, 5, 8, 27a), Cyrus (6:29b), the kingdom of iron established on earth in Dn. 2:40, 41, 42, and the evil kingdom of the fourth beast in Dn. 7:23, 24.

In reference to God, מַלְכוּ occurs in Dn. 2:44 (x3) for the permanent kingdom which God will set up to crush all earthly kingdoms. The same term appears in two instances (3:33; 4:31) on the lips of Nebuchadnezzar in his exalted tributes to God's eternal kingdom (reign). In comparing 3:33 with 4:31, the Aramaic words מַלְכוּ (kingship) and שָׁלְטָן (dominion/sovereignty) occur juxtaposed in each verse, but interestingly they swap modifiers from the first instance to the next:

Daniel 3:33 (4:3)	Daniel 4:31 (4:34b)
מַלְכוּתֵהּ מַלְכוּת עָלַם וְשָׁלְטָנֵהּ עִם־דָּר וְדָר	שָׁלְטָנֵהּ שָׁלְטָן עָלַם וּמַלְכוּתֵהּ עִם־דָּר וְדָר
His kingdom is an everlasting kingdom and his dominion is from generation to generation.	For his dominion is an everlasting dominion and his kingdom endures from generation to generation.

In both verses, emphasis rests upon the eternal omnipotent sovereign rule of God. God's kingdom and his rule (dominion) have no end. In a slightly different syntactical framework, the combination of Aramaic terms occur again in 6:27— again in reference to God's power: (וּמַלְכוּתֵהּ דִּי־לָא תִתְחַבַּל וְשָׁלְטָנֵהּ עַד־סוֹפָא). Elsewhere in Daniel מַלְכוּ refers to the sovereignty which God exercises over all human kingship (5:21: אֱלָהָא עִלָּיָא בְּמַלְכוּת אֲנָשָׁא). God gives sovereignty/rulership (מַלְכוּ) to human kings (2:37; 4:14, 23), and he takes sovereignty away (4:28; 5:21, 26, 28).

With this Danielic portrait of God's omnipotent kingship in view, the authority attributed to the "one like a son of man" in 7:14b appears remarkable. The same combination of terms used previously to describe God's authority apply in 7:14b to the manlike figure: שָׁלְטָנֵהּ שָׁלְטָן עָלַם דִּי־לָא יֶעְדֵּה וּמַלְכוּתֵהּ דִּי־לָא תִתְחַבַּל. His rule (שָׁלְטָנֵהּ) will be forever and his kingdom (וּמַלְכוּתֵהּ) will never be destroyed. Therefore, the authority which the "one like a son of man" yields is, in fact, the authority of God. His rule is God's rule; his kingdom is God's kingdom; his authority is God's authority.[8]

---

[7] *Even-Shoshan*, 672; *BDB*, 1100.

[8] The relation of the manlike figure to the "saints of the Highest One" (Dn. 7:18, 22, 27) is complex. The combination of terms cited as unique to God and the "one like a son of man" are

The unique authority which Jesus exhibits in Q is therefore accounted for if Daniel is a significant part of the conceptual background for Jesus' teaching. For just as the 'one like a son of man' inherits the authority of God, so Jesus in Q yields on earth the authority to judge his generation, the authority to commission disciples as missionaries, and the prerogative to announce with authority the nearness of the kingdom of God—an event directly related to his own earthly ministry (Lk. 7:22, 23//Mt. 11:4-6; Lk. 11:20//Mt. 12:28). In Q Jesus wields exalted authority which recalls the dominion and sovereignty bestowed on the manlike figure in Daniel 7.

2. The Son of Man and the Kingdom of God in the Similitudes of 1 Enoch

While the exact date of the Similitudes remains an open question, several facts exist which advise caution when discussing the relation of the Similitudes to the NT in general and to the Q sayings in particular. First, while it is true that general similarities of thought and language do exist between the Similitudes and the

---

here applied to the saints. In 7:18 the "saints" receive a kingdom which they will rule forever (מַלְכוּתָא עַד־עָלְמָא). In 7:22, following God's judgement, the saints take possession of the kingdom (וּמַלְכוּתָא הֶחֱסִנוּ קַדִּישִׁין); and, in 7:27a, the sovereignty (מָלְכוּתָה), the dominion (שָׁלְטָנָא), and the greatness (רְבוּתָא) of all the kingdoms under the heavens are given to the saints. The center of controversy, however, regarding the relationship of the "saints" and the "one like a son of man" focuses on 7:27b: whether the third person singular pronominal suffixes of מַלְכוּ[תֵה] and לֵהּ refer to (a) the saints in 7:27a, (b) God in 7:27a, or (c) the manlike figure in 7:14. In favor of (a) is the fact that לְעַם קַדִּישֵׁי עֶלְיוֹנִין is a construct form and as such can be modified by a singular form; in favor of (b) are the facts that עֶלְיוֹנִין immediately precedes מַלְכוּתֵה and מָלְכוּתָה modifies עֲלָי (the Highest) in Dn. 4:31 where the surrounding language is very close to that in 7:27b. In favor of (c) is the fact that מַלְכוּתֵה together with שָׁלְטָנֵהּ modifies the "one like a son of man" in 7:14b. The majority of OT commentators have opted for (a), thus translating the phrase "its (the people's) kingship will be one that stands forever; every authority will honor and show obedience to it": (so Hartman and Di Lella, *Daniel*, New York: Doubleday (1978) 207; R.H. Charles, *Daniel*, Oxford: Clarendon (1929) 195; J.E. Goldingay, *Daniel*, 143). Arthur J. Ferch (*The Son of Man in Daniel 7*, Berrien Springs: Andrews UP [1983] 175-180), however, opts for (b) or (c). He finds it difficult to comprehend the saints as the object of worship and obedience in 27b, and emphasizes that in 27a the saints receive the sovereignty of all kingdoms under the heavens. C. Caragounis (*The Son of Man*, 72) argues strongly for (c) claiming: "Vs 14 is parallel only to vs. 27b, whereas the first part of vs. 27 corresponds with vv. 18 and 22. Vs. 14 sets forth the 'dominion', 'glory' and 'kingly rule', the 'dominion' and the 'greatness' *of the kings under the whole heaven* (!) as given to the saints." Though Caragounis' identification of the Son of Man as the 'Most High' in vv. 18, 22, 25, and 27 is questionable (p.75), the extremely close parallels between 4:31, 7:14, and 7:27 favor either options (b) or (c), in which case the translation would be "His kingdom will be an everlasting kingdom, and all the dominions will serve and obey Him" (NASB).

Synoptic Gospels,[9] the fact remains that specific quotations of I Enoch do not exist and allusions to the parables are limited to two possible instances in Matthew (19:28, 25:31). Even in Charles' exhaustive list of parallels, the Similitudes show no influence on Q sayings.[10] Thus there is not a direct literary relationship between the Q sayings of Jesus and the Parables of I Enoch. Second, the similarities of thought and language that do exist appear to be better explained as independent developments of Daniel rather than the reflection of Jesus or the Q community on the Similitudes.[11] Finally, the expression "kingdom of God" which is so prevalent in the Q sayings does not exist at all in the Similitudes, while God is called king in only one passage (I En. 63:2-4).[12] In this respect the Q

---

[9] See R.H. Charles' list of examples: *The Book of Enoch*, Oxford: Clarendon (1912) xcv-ciii., and the thorough comparative study of I Enoch and the Gospel of Matthew by J. Theisohn, *Der auserwählte Richter. Untersuchungen zum traditionsgeschichtlichen Ort der Bilderreden des äthiopischen Henoch.* SUNT 12, Göttingen: Vandenhoech & Ruprecht, 1975.

[10] *The Book of Enoch*, cii-ciii.

[11] Caragounis perceives allusions to Daniel and the Parables in the following Q passages (though he does not refer to them as Q sayings): (A) Lk. 17:24//Mt. 24:27 to Dn. 7:13 (p. 170); (B) Lk. 9:58//Mt. 8:20 to Dn. 2:38; 4:9, 18 (p.176); (C) Lk. 13:19//Mt. 13:31 to Dn. 2:38; 4:12, 18; (p.177); (D) Lk. 12:8, 9//Mt. 10:32-33 to Dn. 7:10, 13 (p. 202). He sees in (E) Lk. 17:26//Mt. 24:37 the association of Noah with the Son of Man's coming an allusion to I En. 60-69 (p. 170) and (F) Lk. 22:30b//Mt 19:28 a "direct quotations from the *Parables*" – I En. 45:3; 51:3; 55:4; 61:8; 62:2 (p. 171). The suggested allusions to the Parables, however, are not secure evidence for supposing Q knowledge of the Similitudes because, unlike Lk. 17:26, 27//Mt. 24:37, 38, the Similitudes present an exalted apocalyptic Noah figure, while ἐπί θρόνου δόξης αὐτοῦ ("the direct quotation from the *Parables*" in Mt. 19:28) does not exist in the Lukan version. Hence even if ἐπί θρόνου δόξης αὐτοῦ is a direct quotation from I Enoch (which is by no means certain), the quotation only proves that the writer of Matthew knew the Similitudes. In addition to Caragounis's data, Lk. 20:18//Mt. 21:44 may be a direct Q allusion to "the stone which crushes" in Dn. 2:35,45. Though Mt. 21:44 has traditionally been considered an interpolative assimilation to Lk. 20:18, which has resulted in its omission from all recent reconstructions of Q, there exist serious reasons for questioning the classification of Mt. 21:44 as an interpolation. First, the external evidence does not convince: ℵ *B C L W Z* (Θ) 0138 ƒ1.13 𝔐, the Vulgate, the Curetonian Syriac, the Peshitta, the Harklean Syriac and the Coptic witnesses all support the inclusion of Mt. 21:44, while the verse is omitted by D, some of the Old Latins, the Sinaitic Syriac and Eusebius. In citing 21:44 as an interpolation, most commentators have followed Westcott and Hort's theory that the combination of D with the Old Latin and Syriac texts represents the original form of the NT text (K. and B. Aland, *The Text of the New Testament*, Grand Rapids: Eerdmans,1987, 232); however, recent discoveries of papyri have disproved this theory so that Aland calls it "a relic of the past" (232). In addition to the external evidence, the inclusion of 21:44 is supported by the fact that the wording of Mt. 21:44 and Lk. 20:18 are not the same – thus it is not a clear example of assimilation. Further, Metzger (*A Textual Commentary on the Greek New Testament*, UBS, 1975, 58) points out, that if 21:44 were an interpolation, "a more appropriate place for its insertion would have been after vs. 42." If 21:44 is genuinely Matthean, Lk. 20:18//Mt. 21:44 must be considered an independent logion which the authors of Mt. and Lk. have placed in proximity to a Marcan saying (12:10). It would then be a composite Q allusion to Dn. 2:34-35, 44-45 and Isa. 8:14-15.

[12] We agree that the theme of "kingship" goes beyond word studies. However, as J.J. Collins ("The Kingdom of God in the Apocrypha and Pseudepigrapha", 89) notes, where the

sayings show closer affinity with Daniel where the kingdom of God is a central theme (3:33; 4:29; 7:13-14, 18, 27).[13]

Comparison of the Q sayings of Jesus with the Similitudes of I Enoch does not suggest literary dependence of one upon the other despite the fact that a pre-Christian date for the Similitudes is possible. Most likely the teachings of Jesus and the Similitudes of I Enoch reflect two parallel movements of thought leading back to the book of Daniel. James H. Charlesworth may well be correct:

> . . . under the influence of the Enoch traditions (1 En. 62-63, 69), perhaps indirectly through oral traditions, Jesus used the term Son of Man to stress his own charismatic authority that amazed his contemporaries (see Mk. 1:22, 7:37, 11:18, Mt. 7:28; Lk. 4:32, 19:48; Jn. 7:46). Perhaps the apocalyptic and judgmental form of his message caused him to talk about the coming powers of judgment attributed to the Son of Man—which probably did not denote another future figure—and here again he may have been influenced by the apocalyptic Enoch traditions (1 En. 62, 69).[14]

In the Similitudes of 1 Enoch, the Son of Man figure is a supernatural person who sits on God's throne (5:13) which is, in effect, his throne (62:3, 5; 69:27, 29). He possesses universal dominion (62:6) and is judge over all (41:9; 69:27).[15] The Enochic Son of Man exerts authority over kings, the mighty, the strong, the powerful, and sinners (46:4-7; 69:27). The Son of Man both reveals "the treasures of that which is hidden" (46:2) and is revealed by "the wisdom of the Lord" to the righteous (48:7) and the elect (62:7; 69:26). He is pre-existent (48:3), he resides with the Head of Days (46:2; 48:2; 62:7), shares his righteousness (71:14), and receives worship from "all who dwell on earth" (48:5), specifically from "the mighty kings and the exalted and those who rule the earth" (62:9), who supplicate for mercy from Him. The Enochic Son of Man is a messianic figure (48:10). Though he is also a negative figure who judges men, angels (41:9), demons (55:4), and all who deceive (69:27f.), the Similitudes emphasize his presence with the elect as an important aspect of future salvation: "And the righteous and elect shall be saved on that day" (62:13) . . . And with that Son of Man shall they eat and lie down and rise up for ever and ever" (62:14; cf. 71:17).

---

theme exists within the Similitudes "the kingship of God is viewed primarily in its negative aspect, in the destruction of the kings of the earth." In contrast, the "Kingdom of God" in both Daniel and the Q sayings has both positive and negative aspects with the positive benefits of the kingdom being the emphasis.

[13] Cf. 2:21, 39f., 44; 4:3, 17, 25, 32, 34f.; 5:18-21, 30; 6:26; 7:12, 18, 22, 26f.; 8:21-25; 10:13, 20; 11:36; 12:7.

[14] *Jesus Within Judaism*, London: SPCK (1988) 42.

[15] Son of Man occurs sixteen times in the Similitudes: 46:1, 2, 3, 4; 48:2; 62:5, 7, 14; 63:11; 69:26, 27, 29 (2x); 70:1; 71:14, 17.

One of the few aspects of 1 Enoch that recent scholarship has agreed upon[16] is that the Similitudes develop their basic concept of the Son of Man from Daniel 7.[17] Comparison of 1 Enoch 46 to Dn. 7 makes this conclusion unavoidable. C. Caragounis, for instance, cites twenty-five points of agreement between the two passages in concluding, "1 En. 46 has in general taken his schema over from Dan. 7."[18]   G.K. Beale, also noting in 1 En. 46-47 parallels in thematic structure and frequent literary allusions to Dn. 7, calls 1 En. 46-47 a "Daniel 7 midrash."[19] Beale concludes, "the observation that 1 Enoch 46-47 is a Daniel 7 midrash helps to explain why the 'son of man' theme is taken up repeatedly in the remainder of the Similitudes."[20]

Hence the Similitudes of 1 Enoch illustrate how "the one like a son of man" in Dn. 7:13 developed into a messianic figure in later Judaism—into "the Son of Man."[21]   Negative results from comparing the Similitudes to the Q sayings of

---

[16] Two notable dissenters from this view are F.H. Borsch who sees no dependence of 1 En. 46-47 on Dn. 7 (*The Son of Man in Myth and History*, London: SCM, 1967, p.149), and M. Casey (*Son of Man*) who notes the similarities between the passages but claims there is "no 'Son of Man' concept" in either Daniel (p. 35) or 1 Enoch (112).   Casey is able to reach this conclusion by interpreting all the Similitudes in light of 71:14, where Enoch attains Son of Man status. J. J. Collins (*NTS* 38, 1992, 454), however, has recently shown that 1 En. 70:1 "makes a clear distinction between Enoch and the Son of Man, which cannot be avoided."   Moreover, Casey's reasoning is inconsistent. First he writes: "Enoch was pre-existent, like other righteous people (1 Enoch 70:4; cf. 39:4f.). He was born, and lived his life on earth. During this life he saw visions, including visions of himself as the eschatological judge. He did not die, but was exalted to heaven, where he was greeted by God. There he is now, shortly to reappear at the end as the eschatological judge" (106). To this figure, Casey reasons that the author of the Similitudes applied Dn. 7:13, "which explains why he chose to use the term 'son of man' rather than any other word for man in his descriptions of his heavenly hero. He used it, not as a title, but as an ordinary expression for 'man'" (107). But further on he writes, "He appears to have taken the כ in כבר אנש as an indication of the difference between an ordinary man, and a man who has been exalted to heaven as Enoch is in 1 Enoch 70-71(111)." Hence Casey is forced to admit that for Enoch "Son of Man" is indeed more than an ordinary expression for 'man'.

[17] R.H. Charles, "The Son of Man: its Meaning in Jewish Apocalyptic and the New Testament", *1 Enoch*, 306; M. Black, *1 Enoch*, Leiden: E.J. Brill (1985) 188; C. Caragounis, *The Son of Man*, 101-111; Seyoon Kim, *"The 'Son of Man' as the Son of God"*, 15; B. Lindars, "Enoch and Christology", *ExpT* 92 (1981) 295-299; E. Sjöberg, *Der Menschensohn im Äthiopischen Henochbuch*, Lund: Gleerup, 1985, 46.

[18] *The Son of Man*, 101.

[19] *The Use of Daniel in Jewish Apocalyptic Literature and in the Revelation of St. John*, New York: Lanham (1984) 105; M. Black also refers to 1 En. 46-47 as midrash on Dn. 7: "The Eschatology of the Similitudes of Enoch", *JTS* 3 (1952) 3; Similarly, N. Perrin, "The Son of Man in Ancient Judaism and Primitive Christianity, A Suggestion", *BR* 11 (1966) 18.

[20] *The Use of Daniel in Jewish Apocalyptic Literature and in the Revelation of St. John*, 106.

[21] 1 Enoch 70:1 represents the only instance in the Similitudes in which Son of Man might be used other than as a title. M. Black, citing an Ethiopic corruption of the text, translates the phrase "the name of a son of man was raised up," and reasons that if this were the original reading

Jesus render it unlikely that the "Son of Man" figure in Q derives from 1 Enoch, yet the Similitudes offer positive evidence in that they prove that in at least one ancient Jewish document the titular use of "Son of Man" did derive from Dan. 7. Q's combined interest in the kingdom of God, the Son of Man, wisdom, prophecy, and endtime judgement suggest that Q is equally dependent upon Daniel or traditions traceable to Daniel.

B. Wisdom

1. Wisdom in Daniel: The 'Court Tales'

As we illustrated in Chapter 3, wisdom is an important feature in the book of Daniel. Wisdom vocabulary is common. The noun wisdom (חָכְמָה) occurs ten times;[22] the verb be prudent, ponder, have insight (שָׂכַל) occurs ten times,[23] and the Aramaic noun insight (שָׂכְלְתָנוּ) occurs five times.[24] Daniel attends the Babylonian and Persian monarchs as a wise man who reveals to pagan kings the reality of God's sovereignty. If wisdom is "practical knowledge of the laws of life and of the world, based on experience,"[25] we may define Danielic wisdom in particular as *the public acknowledgement of God's sovereignty*. This wisdom is revealed through God's gift of wisdom, but is also learned from previous human experience.

The first six chapters of Daniel present five successive episodes (court tales) which develop the theme of wisdom as the positive acknowledgement of God's omnipotent rule. Wisdom in Daniel is derived from God and superior to that of

---

rather than "that Son of Man," the text would have described Enoch's ascension to heaven in terms similar to that of Elijah. If "that Son of Man" were original, Black reasons a Christian scribe subsequently may have altered the "oblique" reference to Enoch to the "theologically loaded" term "son of man." If this were the case we would have in 70:1 an example of the pronominal use of ברנשא/ברנש which Geza Vermes espouses in his circumlocution theory. Yet this reasoning is speculative at every point: the relation of Ch. 70 to the rest of the Similitudes is a mystery; the textual difficulties of 1 Enoch are formidable, and Christian interpolations in the Similitudes are unproven and in many ways illogical. M. Black, *I Enoch*, 250 n. 1; G. Vermes, "The use of ברנש/ברנשא in Jewish Aramaic."

[22] Daniel 1:4, 17, 20; 2:20, 21, 23, 30; 4:11 (x2), 14. Our word counts are taken from *Even-Shoshan*, pp. 368, 69, 1142-43.

[23] Daniel 1:4, 17; 7:8; 9:13, 22, 25; 11:33, 35; 12:3, 10. This 'wisdom' word occurs more in Daniel than any other book in the OT except for Proverbs. See Goldingay, *Daniel*, 249.

[24] Daniel 5:11, 12, 14.

[25] Gerhard von Rad, *Old Testament Theology*, Vol 1, 418.

pagan sages.[26] We see this first in ch. 2 where, after Daniel rehearses Nebuchadnezzar's dream and interprets its meaning, the king responds in awe: "Surely your God is a God of gods and a Lord of kings and a revealer of mysteries, since you have been able to reveal this mystery" (2:47). Then in ch. 3, when God saves Shadrach, Meshach and Abednego, the pagans comment: "How great are his signs, and how mighty are his wonders! His kingdom is an everlasting kingdom, and his dominion is from generation to generation" (4:3). In. ch. 4 at Daniel's successful interpretation of Nebuchadnezzar's dream, the Babylonian monarch responds in worship to the eschatological sovereign power of God: "I blessed the Most High and praised and honoured him who lives forever; for his dominion is an everlasting dominion, and his kingdom endures from generation to generation" (4:34b). 4:37 recaps the wisdom which the king has learned experientially, "Now I Nebuchadnezzar praise, exalt, and honor the King of heaven, for all his works are true and his ways just, and he is able to humble those who walk in pride."[27] Wisdom relates directly to God's rule. The next episode occurs to Daniel himself during the reign of Nebuchadnezzar's son Belshazzar, who faces the penalty for his foolish disregard for God's rule. Unable to translate the foreign writing on his palace wall, he commissions Daniel, whom he recognizes to have a spirit of the gods, illumination, insight, and extraordinary wisdom (5:14). Because of Belshazzar's pomp before God, the inscription translates into punitive judgement: "God has numbered your kingdom and put an end to it. . . . you have been weighed on the scales and found deficient. . . . your kingdom has been divided and given over . . ." (5:25-28). The writing on the wall was the content of wisdom—God rules heaven and earth and woe to those who reject him. The final episode which develops the theme of wisdom as the positive acknowledgement of God's omnipotent rule occurs in Ch. 6 where Daniel faces the dilemma of whether or not to obey the king's decree which forbade worship of any god but the king (6:7-9). Daniel refuses, of course, and worships his God as before, so that he is cast into the lion's den. After the four previous episodes, however, there can be no doubt that God will save Daniel. Even King Darius expresses this confidence: "Your God whom you constantly serve will himself deliver you" (6:16). And so the story goes: God saves Daniel and the conspirators

---

[26] Hence, D.S. Russell, *The Old Testament Pseudepigrapha,* London: SCM (1987) 54: "The story of Daniel is told to show, beyond a peradventure, that this Babylonian wisdom cannot begin to compare with that wisdom given by God to his own people Israel."

[27] Thus E.W. Heaton writes, "The wisdom vouchsafed to Daniel and the confession of Nebuchadnezzar proclaim God's rule no less than the investiture of the 'one like unto a son of man', and these, combined with the shattering of the Image, must have quickened the faith of Israel in the dark days of Antiochus Epiphanes no less effectively than the destruction of the beasts", *Daniel,* London: SCM (1956) 124.

are eaten by the lions. Finally King Darius' decree at the story's conclusion provides the interpretive capstone—the wisdom message:

> I make a decree that in all the dominion of my kingdom men are to fear and tremble before the god of Daniel; for he is the living God and enduring forever, and his kingdom is one which will not be destroyed, and his dominion will be forever. He delivers and rescues and performs signs and wonders in heaven and on earth, who has also delivered Daniel from the power of the lions.(6:26, 27)

In these five episodes, therefore, man learns through experience that God is sovereign over heaven and earth.

In the book of Daniel, then, *true wisdom is the understanding that God rules.* This is the wisdom that God mediates to Daniel, and this is the wisdom which the kings learn in episode after episode. Thus Ch. 12 provides a fitting conclusion to a book characterized throughout by political turmoil. It is those who have insight (הַמַּשְׂכִּלִ֑ים) who lead many to righteousness. John J. Collins writes:

> The resistance of the maskilim is not based only on future expectation but also on the present experience of wisdom. This wisdom enables them to withstand persecution and to transcend suffering and death. It gives them immediate, if only partial, access to a higher world which must wait for its full political manifestation until the time of the end. This does not mean that they opt out of the political situation. Rather, their wisdom enables them to withstand the kingdom of the beasts in the name of heaven which will ultimately destroy all human kingdoms.[28]

In Q Jesus advocates a similar form of wisdom. Like Daniel's kingdom language, Jesus' kingdom sayings in Q exist in a wisdom framework—Jesus' teaching, dominated by the kingdom of God, is wisdom: "But seek for his kingdom, and these things shall be added to you" (Lk. 12:31//Mt. 6:33). The story of the wise and foolish builders communicates a similar message (Lk. 6:47-49//Mt. 7:24-27). Whether or not Matthew's "wise man" ($\dot{\alpha}\nu\dot{\eta}\rho$ $\phi\rho\acute{o}\nu\iota\mu\sigma\varsigma$) is original, this passage presents Jesus making the claim that his audience's response to his teaching will determine either its resistance to hardship (if the response is positive) or its collapse (if the response is negative). Whereas in Daniel man's acknowledgment of God's sovereignty is all important, in Q importance rests upon man's response to Jesus' teaching—which, of course, centers upon the kingdom of God. Both demand a positive response to God's rule, though Q emphasizes a positive response not only to God's rule, but to God's rule and revelation through Jesus

---

[28] *The Apocalyptic Vision of the Book of Daniel*, Missoula: Scholars Press (1977) 210. Collins compares and contrasts Daniel with the Testament of Moses and the Wisdom of Solomon (210f). See also E.W. Heaton, *Daniel*, who places Daniel in the tradition of Ben Sira (160). On the wise in 12:1-4, P.R. Davies writes: "their witness rests not on their power to resist but the power of their God to assert his sovereignty", *Daniel*, Sheffield: JSOT Press (1985) 110.

(Lk. 10:16//Mt. 10:40). Jesus is the difference. Such a transfer of authority—from God to Jesus—is accounted for if Jesus in Q assumes the role of the Danielic Son of Man.

2.   Wisdom in the Similitudes of 1 Enoch

"The Second Vision which he saw, a vision of wisdom, which Enoch saw" (37:1a).

"Until now there has not been imparted (to anyone) from the Lord of spirits such wisdom as I have received, according to my powers of understanding (and) the good pleasure of the Lord of spirits" (37:4).

This opening coupled with frequent references to wisdom[29] leads P.G.R. De Villier to conclude that wisdom is the over-riding interest of the Similitudes,[30] while James Muilenburg has claimed wisdom together with eschatology to be the Parables two dominant emphases.[31] The term "wisdom" occurs throughout the Similitudes with different meanings in different contexts. Ch. 42 presents wisdom fully hypostatized[32] in a form reminiscent of Pr. 1-9. U. Wilckens regards this passage as the clearest example of the supposed "wisdom myth" in Jewish literature.[33] Black, however, notes that "'wisdom' is not usually connected with apocalyptic visions and the expression seems to be unique."[34] Outside of Ch. 42 "fountains of wisdom" (48:1) adorn the scene in which the Son of Man is named before the Chief of Days, while "the wisdom of the Lord of Spirits reveals the Son of Man to the holy and righteous" (48:7). Further, the "spirit of wisdom" indwells the "Elect One" (49:3), so that "all the secrets of wisdom shall come forth from the meditation of his mouth" (51:3). No indicators exist within the Similitudes, however, that the "Son of Man" or the "Elect One" is wisdom personified.[35] Both figures transmit wisdom because God has blessed them: the "wisdom of the Lord" reveals the "Son of Man," while the "Elect One" expresses wisdom because "the

---

[29] 37:1-4; 42:1-3; 48:1, 7; 49:1, 3; 51:3; 61:7, 11; 63:2; 69:8

[30] "Revealing the Secrets. Wisdom and the World in the Similitudes of Enoch", *Studies in I Enoch and the New Testament.* Neotestamentica 17; Annual Publication of the NT Society of South Africa: Stellenbosch (1983) 50-68.

[31] "The Son of Man in Daniel and the Ethiopic Apocalypse of Enoch", *JBL* 79 (1960) 199.

[32] Ulrich Wilkens defines hypostasis "a rather obscure term designed to denote something midway between simple metaphor and direct personification", "σοφία", *TDNT* VII, 507.

[33] *Ibid.*, 508.

[34] *I Enoch*, 194.

[35] *Contra* Wilkens who likens wisdom to the "SM" especially in relation to pre-existence: "σοφία", 504.

Lord of Spirits hath appointed him and hath glorified him" (51:3). 63:2 clarifies that wisdom is an attribute characterizing God's sovereignty:

> Blessed is the Lord of spirits and the Lord of kings,
> And the Lord of the mighty and the Lord of the exalted,
> And the Lord of glory and the Lord of wisdom. (cf. 63:3)

In a fashion similar to the five episodes in Daniel, 1 Enoch 63 unveils wisdom as the reality of God's universal sovereignty which earthly kings learn through experience:

> "We have now learned that we should glorify
> And bless the Lord of kings and him who rules over all kings.
> And they shall say:
> Would that we had a respite to glorify, praise and give thanks before thy glory!
> And now we long for a brief respite and find it not:
> We pursue it but obtain it not:
> And light has vanished from before us,
> And darkness shall be our dwelling-place for ever and ever.
> For before him we have not given thanks,
> Nor glorified the Name of the Lord of spirits, nor glorified our Lord in all his works,
> but our trust has been in the sceptre of our kingdom, and in our own glory.

Because the "mighty kings" (63:1) trust in their earthly glory (63:7) they face suffering and tribulation in the end (63:8)—a time when even they will bow before God's universal sovereignty. As in Daniel, the wise in the Similitudes are those who praise the "Lord of Spirits" (First of Voices) "with wisdom" (61:7); they are the "holy ones," the "host of the Lord," "the Cherubim, Seraphim, and Ophannim," "the angels of power," "the angels of dominion," the "Elect One," and "the other powers on the earth and over the water."   "On that day" these beings will raise one voice "in the spirit of wisdom" and bless the name of the Lord of Spirits "forever and ever" (61:10-11).   Wisdom in 1 Enoch as in Daniel leads the wise to acknowledge God's sovereignty.

C. Prophecy

1. Prophecy in Daniel

One only has to look at the index of Biblical sources at the back of any good commentary on Daniel to see that Daniel draws heavily from the literary prophets, especially Isaiah, Jeremiah, Ezekiel, and to a lesser extent Amos and Zechariah.[36]

---

[36] Dn. 2 shares with Isa. 40-66 the major theme of the contrast between the helplessness of the Babylonians' spiritual resources and the power and wisdom of the God of Israel to effect and to

Daniel, furthermore, shares important prophetic themes including the sentencing of monarchs with sin and judgement, symbolic visions (Isa. 24-27; Eze. 38-39; Joel 3; Zch. 9-14), concern with the purity of temple (Dn. 8:11, 13, 14; 9:17, 24, 26), and the present interpretation of history as a decisive factor in determining the events which will bring God's judgement (especially on pagan kings).[37] It is not surprising, then, that subsequent history came to recognize Daniel as written prophecy.[38] Hence Goldingay writes: "For Josephus, as for the Greek Bible, Qumran, Jesus, and the NT writers, Daniel is a prophet and has similar authority to the prophets within the Hebrew canon . . ."[39] Most importantly, however, Daniel adopts and furthers a prophetic theology in which God rules universally and indiscriminately over heaven and earth.

2. Prophecy in the Similitudes of I Enoch

Like Daniel, the Parables of I Enoch are firmly rooted in OT prophecy. According to R.H. Charles' index there are twenty-five OT prophetic passages directly connected to or closely paralleled with the Similitudes' text.[40] Of these, twenty-one allude to Isaiah. Not only do the Similitudes borrow figures of speech from Isaiah, but they describe the "Elect One" (39:6) as exhibiting the "righteousness"

---

interpret history (Isa. 41:1-7, 21-29; 44:25-26; 47:9-15); the image of silver, gold, bronze and iron which turn to clay; the image of God as Lord of hidden things (Isa. 45:3, 7); and, the image of nations and kings doing homage to the exiles and their God (Dn. 2:46, 47; Isa. 45:3, 14; 49:23; 60:6-7, 14). Like Daniel, Isaiah promises the Lord's Kingship (44:6; 52:7). Dn. 2:10-12 parallels the contempt for Babylonian sages in Isa. 40-55. Daniel 7 also has notable parallels with the literary prophets: it is written prophecy (Dn. 7:1, 2; cf. 8:26; 12:4; Isa. 8:1, 16; 30:8; Jer. 30:2; 36:2; 51:60; Eze. 43:11; Hab. 2:2) that shares with the prophets the vision of the historicized sea monster (Dn. 7:2, 3; Isa. 27:1; 51:9-10; Eze. 29:3. Elsewhere Dn. 9:2 refers directly to Jeremiah the prophet and his prophecy of "seventy years," while the vision of God enthroned in 9:1 parallels the same image in Eze.1:26-28 (see Goldingay, *Daniel,* 37, 149, 160). For the many allusions to the prophets in chs. 10-12, including those to the servant passages of Isa., see Goldingay, *ibid.,* 284-285. See also André Lacoque, ET *Daniel,* London: John Knox (1979) 6, 183, 204, 232; S.B. Frost, *Old Testament Apocalyptic,* London: Epworth, 1952; P. von der Osten-Sacken, *Die Apokalyptik in ihrem Verhältnis zu Prophetie und Weisheit,* TExH 157; Munich: Kaiser, 1969; P.D. Hanson, *The Dawn of Apocalyptic,* Philadelphia: Fortress, 1979.

[37] Goldingay, *Daniel,* 323.

[38] On the canonical status of Daniel as a prophetic book, see Klaus Koch, "Is Daniel Also Among the Prophets?", *Interpreting the Prophets,* Philadelphia: Fortress (1987) 237-248.

[39] *Daniel,* xxx.

[40] Isaiah: 5:14 (I En. 56:8); 5:24 (48:9); 13:8 (62:4); 14:11 (46:6); 14:14 (68:4); 21:3 (62:4); 21:10 (56:6); 26:17 (62:4); 27:1 (60:7); 33:7 (40:8a); 34:6 (62:12); 40:26 (43:1); 42:1 (39:6); 42:6 (48:4b); 43:5, 6 (57:1); 45:1 (60:3c); 49:12 (57:1); 61:2 (48:4c); 65:17 (45:4); 66:22 (45:4); Jeremiah: 10:13 (28:3); Amos: 5:24 (39:5d); Zechariah: 2:1, 2 (61:1, 2); Malachi: 4:1 (48:9).

and "faithfulness" of the "Righteous Branch" of Isa. 11:5. Further, they describe the sovereignty of the "Lord of Spirits" (43:1; 45:4) with language borrowed from Isa. 40:26; 65:17; 66:22, which exalt the creative power of Yahweh. And the Parables of Enoch also equip the Son of Man with characteristics of Isaiah's Servant.[41] The description of the Enochic Son of Man as "the light of the Gentiles" is a clear allusion to the Servant Songs in Isa. 42:6; 49:6, while the description of him as "the hope of those who are troubled in their heart" recalls Isa. 61:1, 2 where the prophet (servant?) is anointed "to bind up the broken hearted." Hence the author of the Similitudes has clothed his major figures with attributes well known to the reader of Isaiah. As in Daniel, wisdom and prophecy coexist.

D. Eschatology

1. Eschatology in Daniel

Daniel's eschatology has one characteristic which is not debatable—in the end God will rule. Within Daniel four expressions exist which translate into the English phrase "the end." The first phrase "the end of the days" (קְצָת הַיָּמִים) occurs in 1:18 where it designates the closure of a period of time set by the king. Hence R.H. Charles writes: "This phrase is never used eschatologically in our author and never refers to the advent of the Kingdom." Charles' negative assessment also holds true for the second phrase "end of years" (קֵץ שָׁנִים), which occurs in 11:6 to specify an indefinite length of time.

The third phrase, "the latter days" (אַחֲרִית יוֹמַיָּא), however, does refer to the "last days" or "the end time" specifically in relation to the coming of God's kingdom. The phrase occurs fourteen times in the OT, four times as a technical term. Hos. 3:5 uses the phrase in reference to the endtime when God will save the righteous, while Eze. 38:16 uses it to define the endtime when God will judge the wicked (Eze. 38:16). Daniel uses אַחֲרִית יוֹמַיָּא twice as a technical term (2:28; 10:14). The "final days" in 2:28 refers directly to the content of Nebuchadnezzar's dream including vv. 44, 45 which prophesy the establishment of God's eternal kingdom:

> And in the days of those kings the God of heaven will set up a kingdom which will never be destroyed, and that kingdom will not be left for another people; it will crush and put an end to all these kingdoms, but it will itself endure forever. (2:44)[42]

---

[41] Thus M. Black writes, "The Son of Man is the Servant of the Lord", *I Enoch*, 210.

[42] 2:45b clearly refers back to 2:28: "the great God has made known to the king what will take place in the future; so the dream is true, and its interpretation is trustworthy."

The content of this passage qualifies "the latter days" as a time when God will act authoritatively: (a) he will set up a kingdom for a specified people; (b) his kingdom will devastate, destroy, and terminate the ruling pagan monarchies symbolized in vv. 31-43; and (c), his kingdom will endure forever. The second use of יֹמַיָא אַחֲרִית also occurs at the beginning of a dream interpretation, but this time Daniel is the dreamer and the one "who resembled a human being" (10:16) is the interpreter: "Now I have come to give you an understanding of what will happen to your people in the latter days, for the vision pertains to the days yet future" (10:14). 10:14 anticipates Chs. 11 and 12 which prophecy the establishment and extinction of kingdoms from the rule of Cyrus to Antiochus IV. At least part of the interpretation, however, describes not only the future but specifically the "endtime." 12:1-4 cannot be applied to earthly history but only to the final judgement when some will awake to everlasting life and others to "disgrace and everlasting contempt" (12:2). Hence both uses of אַחֲרִית יֹמַיָא refer to the end: 2:26 to the establishment of God's kingdom at the end of history, and 10:14 to the final judgement.[43]

The fourth phrase denoting the end (עֵת־קֵץ) occurs five times in Daniel (8:17; 11:35, 40; 12:4, 9). R.H. Charles claimed, "This phrase is always used eschatologically in our author and refers definitely to the advent of the kingdom."[44] Though עֵת־קֵץ does not specifically modify God's kingdom in any of these passages, Charles' statement remains accurate as a result of the content of Chs 1-7, where God's kingdom is consistently anticipated in the future as a rule which will endure forever. Chs. 8-12, where all the occurrences of עֵת־קֵץ exist, then, presuppose God's final rule though they emphasize the confrontation of ancient historical kingdoms (11:40) and the negative period of persecution at the hands of pagan kings. It is noteworthy though that Antiochus' assumption of God's power (8:24; 11:29-12:3 esp. v. 36) represents the major event preceding the book's climax in 12:4f. Thus the pervading theme of God's sovereignty remains in view through the repugnant description of the king who challenges his authority. Close examination of the phrase in each context noted actually yields very little qualitative information describing the end event itself, because the descriptive language only addresses events leading up to the end. The imagery of Chs. 11 and 12 is mysterious and the language allusive, so that J. Goldingay

---

[43] Thus Horst Seebass' article "אַחֲרִית", *TDOT* I, 207-212: "This expression is clearly used as a technical term in Dnl. 2:28 (Aramaic) and 10:14. In both passages the translation 'future times' is possible, but it is not what the author intended. . . . The point of the vision does not lie in the course of future events, but in the destruction of the colossus and in the coming of an indestructible kingdom (v. 44). Thus the outcome of the future is what is intended, and not the future in general" (211, 212).

[44] *Daniel*, 394.

cautions that "exegesis must preserve this allusiveness."[45] Yet it is also true that Daniel does anticipate a specific albeit mysterious "end of time" (12:4, 9), which has one characteristic that the text of Daniel as a whole demands—when this time comes God's kingdom will prevail (2:44, 45; 3:33 [4:3]; 4:31, 32 [4:34, 35]; 6:27).

2. Eschatology in the Similitudes of I Enoch

The first Parable:
When the congregation of the righteous shall appear,
And sinners shall be judged for their sins
And driven from the face of the earth. (38:1)

The first parable in the Similitudes lays the foundation for the eschatological tenor of Chs. 37-71 as a whole. As M. Black wrote nearly forty years ago, "The main eschatological theme is that of an impending world judgement 'as in the days of Noah', but on a grander scale."[46] The 'grander scale' which Black refers to is the future cosmic judgement which the Lord of Spirits and the Elect One (Son of Man) will sentence. The Similitudes lack historical points of contact such as those which characterize Daniel. In I Enoch judgement is universal and complete: sinners shall be destroyed "from the face of the earth" (45:6); military hardware will be destroyed "from the surface of the earth" (52:9); and angels of punishment will bring "judgement and destruction on all who abide and dwell on the earth" (66:1; cf. 54:9). The recipients of this chastisement are the kings and the mighty ones of the earth (38:5), who will be bound with the "fetters of Satan" (53:4), that "they be destroyed" (53:5), being cast into a deep valley of burning fire (54:1, 2). In Ch. 68 the sphere of judgement moves beyond earthly kings to the supernatural realm where Michael responds to the archangel Raphael: "The power of the Spirit seizes me and makes me tremble because of the severity of the sentence regarding the secrets, the punishment of the angels. Who can endure the severity of the sentence . . ." (v. 2). Thus the Similitudes describe a future judgement which will be universal and cosmic.[47]

What is the reason for judgement? The accused face guilt for denying the Lord of Spirits (45:1; 67:10), for denying the "testimony of the holy ones" (45:1), and

---

[45] *Daniel*, 291.

[46] "The Eschatology of the Similitudes of Enoch", *JTS* 3 (1952) 2. Black's article does not define a specific "eschatology" for the Similitudes. His emphasis, rather, focuses on the relation of Ch. 71 to the rest of the Parables and the identification of the Enochic Son of Man.

[47] In Ch. 46 the "powerful" are also cosmic figures who deny the Lord of Spirits; they are described as "those who rule the stars of heaven" (vs. 7).

for denying the "Anointed One" (48:10). Doom results from unrighteousness and the failure to repent (50:45; 54:10). The angels of punishment will attack the kings who rule the earth because they have oppressed the elect (62:11). But most importantly the future day of judgement assesses individuals' loyalty. Thus the kings will confess their tragic flaw: "For before him we have not given thanks, nor glorified the name of the Lord of spirits, nor glorified our Lord in all his works, but our trust has been in the sceptre of our kingdom, and in our own glory" (63:7). Hence the cause of damnation is spiritual sin: "Their spirits (the kings) are full of lust, so that their bodies are punished, for they have denied the Lord of spirits; and they see their punishment daily, and yet they believe not in his Name" (67:8). As a result, the kings face eternal torture, "they will pay in their spirits for ever and ever" (67:9).

The Similitudes' perspective of the end, however, is not entirely negative. Though emphasis focuses on punitive judgement, the salvific fate of the holy ones consistently serves as a foil to the punishment of the wicked. While the kings embody unrighteousness, the Similitudes' author applies the epithet "the righteous" to the elect. While the kings will face eternal damnation, "the righteous and elect" will abide beneath the wings of the Lord of spirits (39:7) experiencing peace (58:4), rest (39:4, 5)[48] and eternal life (58:3). On the day of judgement the righteous and elect will be saved (62:13), and thereafter they will dwell with the Son of Man forever (62:13; 71:16, 17: SM=Enoch). And if judgement impends universally, so too does the offering of salvation: the Gentiles will witness the victory of "the righteous" that they may repent and be saved (50:2, 3).[49] And finally, in contrast to the king's guilt in denying the Lord of spirits, "the righteous" continually praise his name (39:12, 13; 41:7, 8).

Like Daniel, the Similitudes' portrait of the endtime judgement bears numerous conceptual similarities to the literary prophets' concept of the "Day of the Lord" (especially 60:6, 24, 25). However, Daniel and the Similitudes (to a greater extent) move beyond the prophets to project the end as a universal and cosmic event in which judgement will be final. The major characteristic which colours the end-event in both is the reality of God's (the Lord of spirit's) rule:

> And they shall bless and glorify the Lord of spirits and the Lord of kings,
> And the Lord of the mighty and the Lord of the exalted,
> And the Lord of glory and the Lord of wisdom.
> Every secret thing will be brought to light;

---

[48] The description of the "elect and holy" in this context is of angels; elsewhere the expression describes human saints (62:8; 38:4). The distinction leads some to suspect textual corruption in Ch. 39: R.H. Charles, *I Enoch*, 74; See M. Black, *I Enoch*, 196.

[49] Elsewhere the Son of Man is described as the "light of the Gentiles" (48:4).

Thy power is from generation to generation,
And thy glory for ever and ever. (63:2, 3a)

Daniel and the Similitudes presuppose God's rule. Judgement results from denying his sovereignty.

E. Apocalyptic Imagery in Daniel and the Similitudes of I Enoch

The address to encourage the faithful, animal symbolism, the supremacy of God, eschatology, judgement, heaven, hell, angels, demons, special revelation to ancient heroes and the broad interpretation of history combine differently in Daniel and the Similitudes of I Enoch to lead commentators to register both these documents as primary representatives of ancient apocalyptic literature. One truism apocalyptic literature reveals or at least presupposes in its revelation is the sovereignty of God in past, present, and future history.[50] Hence the apocalyptic writers chose as their heroes ancient biblical figures who had experienced first hand God's sovereign power in the past (Enoch, Moses, Noah, Ezra). Through these figures, the apocalyptic writers address a contemporary audience warning some while consoling others that man's present response to God (homage or denial) will dictate his damnation or salvation in God's final judgement. The present, then, is understood in light of a future which is dominated by God's absolute sovereignty. What holds true for apocalyptic literature in general is especially true for Daniel and the Similitudes of I Enoch, perhaps because all apocalyptic literature looks back to Daniel as its literary model. In any case, one thing remains clear and incontrovertible: apocalyptic imagery, despite its mysterious symbols, announces, reveals and anticipates God's complete sovereignty.[51]

---

[50] On the past, present, and future aspects of apocalyptic, see C. Rowland, *The Open Heaven*, London: SPCK, 1982.

[51] Thus the following definitions of apocalyptic: "Apocalypse – the anticipatory raising of the curtain to display the final scene – is a way of conveying, pictorially and in symbol, the conviction of the ultimate victory of God", C.F.D. Moule, *The Birth of the New Testament*, London: Black (1962) 103; "An apocalypse is a book containing real or alleged revelations of heavenly secrets or of the events which will attend the end of the world and the inauguration of the Kingdom of God", G.E. Ladd, "Apocalyptic", *Evangelical Dictionary of Theology*, Grand Rapids: Baker (1984) 65. Thus D.S. Russell (*The Method and Message of Jewish Apocalyptic*, 285) writes, "The apocalyptists are interested, not so much in the process of history, as in the goal of history which, to them, is the kingdom. Or rather, they are interested in the course of history in the measure in which it leads to its completion and fulfillment in the kingdom. The Gentile kingdoms, like the Greek supremacy of the Seleucids and Ptolemies which seemed so overwhelming and terrible, are shown as phases in a world process whose end is the kingdom of God. There is an inevitability about the course of history because there is absolute certainty

Parallels between Q and the apocalyptic aspects of Daniel and I Enoch are limited.[52] Despite the fact that Lk. 17:22-24, 26-35, 37//Mt. 10:39; 24:17-18, 26-28, 37-39, 40-41 has often been called "the Q apocalypse,"[53] and despite N. Perrin's identification of Q as "the first literary evidence in the NT for the existence of Christian apocalyptic . . .,"[54] the Q sayings bear several important distinctions from what is commonly called "apocalypse":

> 'Apocalypse' is a genre of revelatory literature with a narrative framework, in which a revelation is mediated by an otherworldly being to a human recipient, disclosing a transcendent reality which is both temporal, insofar as it envisages eschatological salvation, and spatial insofar as it involves another, supernatural world.[55]

The differences are obvious: though Q is revelatory in nature it does not have a "narrative framework" nor is revelation mediated to Jesus in Q through an angelic or heroic intermediary. In Q revelation comes directly from God to Jesus (Lk. 10:21, 22//Mt.11:25-27). With references to Jonah, Noah and Lot, Jesus alludes directly to the OT but he does not elevate these figures to the status of heavenly mediators (as, for instance, the Similitudes elevate Noah: 60:8; 65:1f.; 67:1).[56] Nor is it evident that an "apocalyptically enthusiastic" Q community produced prophetic sayings and subsequently placed them on the lips of Jesus. ὁ ᾿Ιησοῦς occurs only five times in the parallel sayings: three times in the temptation

---

about the establishment of the kingdom of God. This conviction is based on their faith in God who 'ruleth in the kingdom of men and giveth it to whomsoever he will'" (Dn. 4:17).

[52] Responding to A. Polag who minimizes apocalyptic influence on Q, P. Hoffmann writes: "Die Reduktion apokalyptischer Elemente, die sich in den ältesten synoptischen Sprüchen vom kommenden Menschensohn feststellen läßt, geschieht gerade *im Rahmen der apokalyptisch geprägten Erwartung* eines kommenden Richters und Heilsmittlers. Auf sie verweisen die Motive des Kommens (Lk 12,40), des Tages des Menschensohnes (Lk 17,24), die mit seinem Kommen verbundene Gerichtserwartung (Lk 11,30), sein universales Erscheinen wie der Blitz (Lk 17,24)." *Studien zur Theologie der Logienquelle,* 95. Italics are Hoffmann's.

[53] Among others: Beasley-Murray, *Jesus and the Kingdom of God,* 313; S. Schulz, *Q–Die Spruchquelle,* 277.

[54] *The New Testament. An Introduction. Proclamation and parenesis, myth and history,* 74.

[55] J.J. Collins, "Introduction: Towards the Morphology of a Genre", *Semeia* 14 (1979) 1-20.

[56] A. Polag cites the following differences between Q and apocalyptic: (a) Jesus' statements about the present activity of the Kingdom cannot be harmonized with the apocalyptic emphasis of the absolute separation of the aeons; (b) the strict dualism of heaven and hell, above and below which characterizes apocalyptic literature does not compare with Q where the decisive eschatological event is now between man and Jesus; (c) Q refuses to provide objective esoteric information about the end event; (d) present salvation is possible for men now in Q which is an impossibility within the apocalyptic framework of the separation of the aeons: *Die Christologie der Logienquelle,* 125, 126.

narrative, once in the story of the centurion's servant, and only once at the beginning of a saying.[57]

Yet without exaggerating the parallels, the conceptual similarities between Q and Daniel are probably not accidental. As opposed to originating in an early Christian atmosphere of apocalyptic enthusiasm, the apocalyptic features of Q may best be explained as Jesus' apocalyptic awareness which stems from his own interpretation of Daniel.

James H. Charlesworth has written that "the impact of Jewish apocalypticism and apocalyptic thought upon Jesus is undeniable and pervasive."[58] In Q Jesus is to some extent an apocalyptic figure.[59] As he does in Mk. 4:11,12, Jesus reveals in Q through his teaching and his acts the mystery of the kingdom of God. Jesus reveals things of God hidden from the ordinary observer—most notably his own sonship (Lk. 10:21, 22//Mt. 11:25-27). As the man-like figure in Dn. 7:13 receives power and dominion from the Ancient of Days, so in Lk. 10:22//Mt. 11:27: "All things have been handed over to me by my father, and no one knows who the son is except the father, and who the father is except the son, and anyone to whom the son wills to reveal (ἀποκαλύψαι) him." In favour of the authenticity of this controversial verse is its compatibility with what we find throughout Q where Jesus reveals the father as Abba (Lk. 11:2//Mt. 6:9), and where Jesus speaks authoritatively about the Son of Man and what the Son of Man will do when he is revealed at the end of time. Throughout Q Jesus is both the revealer of Godly mystery and the one upon whom depends the blessings of the kingdom of God. In Lk. 22:28-30//Mt. 19:27, 28[60] in a manner similar to Lk. 10:21, 22 par., Jesus gives to his persevering disciples what the *Father* has given to him—a

---

[57] Lk. 4:1//Mt. 4:1; Lk. 4:8//Mt. 4:10; Lk. 4:12//Mt. 4:7; Lk. 7:9//Mt. 8:10; Lk. 9:58//Mt. 8:20. "καὶ εἶπεν αὐτῷ ὁ 'Ιησοῦς" which is consistent in the Lucan versions (4:8, 12; 7:9; 9:58) appears to be the more original usage as Luke "generally avoids this phrase while Matthew likes it" (3:15). So Davies and Allison (*Matthew* I, 368) who cite J. Jeremias, *Die Sprache des Lukasevangeliums*, 39-41, 117. Other possible occurrences of ὁ 'Ιησοῦς in Q include Lk. 4:4; 7:3, 4, 6; 9:62 which, however, have no Matthean counterparts, and Mt. 8:13, 22; 11:4, 7; 11:25; 18:22; 22:1 which have no Lucan counterparts. Hence there exists no clear evidence that the Q sayings were in large measure created and subsequently placed upon the lips of Jesus because the name Jesus is not frequent in Q. The sayings' genuineness, rather, seems to be assumed in the transmission process.

[58] *Jesus within Judaism*, 42.

[59] Arland D. Jacobson identities apocalyptic characteristics in Q Lk. 3:7-9, 16-17; 10:13-15, 21; 12:8-9, 39-40, 42-46, 51-53, 54-56; 13:26-27, 28-29, 34-35; 17:24, 26-30, 34-35. See his article "Apocalyptic and the Synoptic Sayings Source Q", *The Four Gospels*, FS F. Neirynck; Leuven: Leuven U.P. (1992) 403-419.

[60] For the inclusion of Lk. 22:28-30 in Q, see J. Kloppenborg, *Q Parallels*, 202. For the authenticity of the passage and the relation of the Matthean and Lukan versions, see G.R. Beasley-Murray, *Jesus and the Kingdom of God*, 273-277.

kingdom: "and just as my Father has granted me a kingdom ($\kappa\alpha\theta\dot{\omega}\varsigma$ $\delta\iota\dot{\epsilon}\theta\epsilon\tau\dot{o}$ $\mu o\iota$ $\dot{o}$ $\pi\alpha\tau\dot{\eta}\rho$ $\mu o\upsilon$ $\beta\alpha\sigma\iota\lambda\epsilon\dot{\iota}\alpha\nu$), I also grant you ($\kappa\dot{\alpha}\gamma\dot{\omega}$ $\delta\iota\alpha\tau\dot{\iota}\theta\epsilon\mu\alpha\iota$ $\dot{\upsilon}\mu\hat{\iota}\nu$) that you may eat and drink at my table in my kingdom, and you will sit on thrones judging the twelve tribes of Israel." The two passages have clear parallels: the Father/Son relationship between Jesus and God, the intermediary role of Jesus, the identification of the disciples of Jesus as the recipients of the kingdom of God and its associated blessings. In view of these parallels, a Danielic interpretation of Lk. 10:21, 22 par., becomes more legitimate because the conceptual background of Daniel 7:9 is probably behind the throne image in Lk. 22:30b. In giving the disciples the authority to rule over the twelve tribes of Israel, Jesus as the Son in Lk. 22:30 gives what the Father has given to him—namely the authority, dominion, and kingdom which the Ancient of Days gives to the 'one like a son of man' in Daniel 7:13, 14. Jesus, whose sonship is implied in Lk. 22:28-30 assumes the authority and function of the manlike figure in Dn. 7:13, 14. Therefore, in Lk. 10:21, 22//Mt. 11:25-27 we may not have a divergent line of Q tradition or a separate layer of Q redaction but rather the explanation of the authority which Jesus bears throughout Q. The saying corroborates what Jesus says and does elsewhere.[61] Jesus' authority is that of God's son—a figure mysteriously related to the Son of Man in Daniel 7. That the two figures were related in Jesus' mind is more likely, in our opinion, than the conjecture that one or the other or both were the christological achievements of Q redaction.

1. The Suffering Saints

A final conceptual parallel we suggest between Daniel and Q is the image of the "suffering saints" which plays a prominent role in Dn. 7:18, 21, 22, 25, 27. The major characteristics of the "saints" are as follows: (1) the "saints" are inseparably bound to God—they are God's people (vv. 18, 22, 25, 27);[62] (2) the "saints" will receive a kingdom in the future (v. 18); (3) they will possess that kingdom forever (vv. 18, 27); (4) they will face persecution (by the little horn) and will, in fact, be overpowered for a time (vv. 21, 25); (5) they will be saved by the Ancient of Days and will emerge on the positive side of God's judgement (v. 22); and (6), at the

---

[61] For the authenticity of this verse and an extensive list of scholars who support or deny its authenticity, see J. Fitzmyer, "Abba and Jesus' Relation to God", *A Cause de L' Évangile*, FS J. Dupont; Cerf: Publications de Saint-André (1985) 35-38. Fitzmyer basically supports the previous claims of J. Jeremias who argued for the authenticity of Lk. 10:22.

[62] "Saints of the Highest One"(קַדִּישֵׁי עֶלְיוֹנִין) is a bound structure in which the second element (עֶלְיוֹנִין) delimits the first (קַדִּישֵׁי). The second element is in the genitive relationship. Hence the "saints" belong to or are possessed by God. This is their primary attribute; *BDB*, 1110.

judgement the saints will receive the sovereignty, the dominion, and the greatness of all the kingdoms under heaven.

With the image of the Danielic saints before us, we turn to Q where we take up specifically the first three beatitudes. The majority of commentators have rightly understood the first beatitude against the background of Isa. 61: "The Spirit of the Lord is upon me, because the Lord has anointed me to preach good news to the poor" ($\pi\tau\omega\chi o\hat{\imath}\varsigma$). Lk. 6:21//Mt. 5:4 ($\kappa\lambda\alpha\acute{\iota}o\nu\tau\epsilon\varsigma$//$\pi\epsilon\nu\theta o\hat{\upsilon}\nu\tau\epsilon\varsigma$) alludes to $\pi\epsilon\nu\theta o\hat{\upsilon}\nu\tau\alpha\varsigma$ in Isa. 61:2.

The beatitude may represent a composite allusion to the blessings of Isa. 61 as characteristic of the kingdom in Daniel 7. In that case, as G. Friedlander states: "In the Gospels, the "saints" become the disciples of Jesus."[63] Conceptual parallels between the Q beatitudes and Dn. 7 include the following: In each the saved experience persecution (Lk. 6:22//Mt. 5:11); the Danielic saints and the NT "blessed" each receive explicitly the reward of a kingdom; and, each receives eschatological hope as present comfort (cf. Dn. 12). Each of these Danielic parallels merge in composite fashion with the images emerging from the background of Isa. 61.[64] Further, if the Lucan version of Lk. 6:22//Mt. 5:11 is original (Lk.'s $\tau o\hat{\upsilon}$ $\upsilon\acute{\iota}o\hat{\upsilon}$ $\tau o\hat{\upsilon}$ $\dot{\alpha}\nu\theta\rho\acute{\omega}\pi o\upsilon$ rather than Mt.'s $\dot{\epsilon}\mu o\hat{\upsilon}$),[65] the language of the beatitudes assume a note of crisis in which Jesus' followers experience direct persecution as a result of their association with the Son of Man—a figure derived from Dn. 7. Thus if we add up the conceptual images in the "Q Beatitudes" we discover that the conceptual parallels to Daniel 7 are notable despite the fact that purely linguistic allusions to Isa. 61:1f. coexist. Is the coexistence of imagery surprising? Not when we take into account the fact that the conceptual background of Daniel dominates the Q sayings of Jesus throughout while Isa. 61:1f. serves as the only explicit OT reference which Jesus adopts in the Q sayings

---

[63] *The Jewish Sources of the Sermon on the Mount*, New York: KTAV (1969) 18.

[64] It is true, however, that ancient Jewish texts did draw from Isa. 61 in describing eschatological events (Acts 10:38; 11QMelch 2.4, 6, 9, 13, 17, 20; Tg. Ps.-J. to Nem 25.12 and Midr. Ekhaf on Lam. 3.50. See M.P. Miller, "The Function of Isa 61:1-2 in 11 Q Melchizedek", *JBL* 88 (1969) 467-469; J.A. Sanders, "From Isaiah 61 to Luke 4", *Christianity, Judaism, and other Greco-Roman Cults,* FS Morton Smith; Leiden: E.J. Brill (1975) 75-106.

[65] So J. Jeremias, "Die älteste Schicht der Menschensohn-Logien", *ZNW* 58 (1967) 159-172. J. Fitzmyer, *Luke* I, 635 argues that Matthew's "because of me" is the original owing to the fact that Matthew has added Son of Man elsewhere (16:13) thus rendering it hard to understand why he would have omitted it here. Fitzmyer reasons, "the use of the title scarcely refers to the coming Son of Man; it is rather used of Jesus in his active earthly ministry, what he has been doing." However, Mt. is also capable of omitting Son of Man (16:21) while Fitzmyer's statement presupposes a purely eschatological use of the phrase on the mouth of Jesus. Within Q Lk. 7:24//Mt. 11:19 and Lk. 9:58//Mt. 8:20 are two references where Jesus applies Son of Man to his earthly existence. Hence the Lucan form may be original (so: H. Schürmann, *Lukasevangelium*, 334 n. 62; S. Schulz, *Q–Die Spruchquelle*, 453 n. 77; I.H. Marshall, *Luke*, 253.

to identify himself and to interpret his mission (Lk. 7:22//Mt. 11:5). A powerful case can be made that both OT passages served as prominent sources for the authentic thought of Jesus.[66] In this case, Q merely transmits the combination of emphases from Daniel 7 and Isaiah 61 which were in fact central to the eschatological perspective of Jesus himself.

Conclusion

The overwhelming diversity of Q allusions and quotations to the OT (see Appendix A), and its thoroughly Jewish conceptual imagery, require that Q's background be classified as Jewish. The Son of Man, the kingdom of God, the theological form of wisdom in Q, and Q's prophetic features are all Jewish in nature. Strict form critical studies (such as the formidable work of John Kloppenborg) do not do justice to this fact. The "proposition that meaning in texts is 'genre bound' "[67] clearly does not hold up when the content of the Q sayings is compared to the content of the ancient Egyptian and Near Eastern sayings collections, pre-Byzantine, Byzantine and Medieval gnomic and chriae collections which have been cited as formal relatives of Q.[68] The major emphases of Q, namely, the Son of Man and the kingdom of God, do not figure in these documents.

Because the major conceptual images of Q find parallels in Daniel and because there is not a direct link between Q and the Similitudes of I Enoch, we conclude that Daniel is the most likely source for the conceptual background of Q. Where else do the broad conceptual images of wisdom, prophecy, apocalyptic, and

---

[66] On Dn. 7, see Caragounis, *Son of Man*; and S. Kim, *The 'Son of Man'" as the Son of God*. Regarding Isa. 61:1f. see also Lk. 4:18. M. Hengel writes "Wenn wir nach einem alttestamentlichen «Messianischen» Text suchen, der den Anspruch Jesu verständlich macht, so dürfen wir uns weder an den für die Entwicklung der späteren Christologie so bedeutsamen Texten wie Ps 2 oder 110, auch nicht an Jes 11 und selbst nicht an den eigentlichen Gottesknechtliedern Deuterojesajas orientieren, sondern an einem Wort wie Jes 61,1-3, das freilich die Gottesknechttradition voraussetzt und weiterführt. ... Dieses vollmächtige Trostwort eines unbekannten Propheten der nachexilischen Zeit charakterisiert jedoch im Grunde das ganze Wirken Jesu, seine Verkündigung der befreienden Liebe des Vaters gegenüber den Verlorenen und Ausgestoßenen in Israel, wie auch seine Heilungen und Exorzismen." In "Jesus Als Messianischer Lehrer der Weisheit und Die Anfänge der Christologie", 181, 182. On the compatibility of Daniel and the Isaiah "Servant Songs" see: W. Manson, *Jesus the Messiah*, London: Hodder and Stoughton (1948) 99, 171; F.F. Bruce, "Qumrân and Early Christianity", *NTS* 2 (1955, 56), 176.

[67] *The Formation of Q*, 2.

[68] See *The Formation of Q*, "Appendix I "Ancient Sayings Collections", 329-341 and index pp. 374-377. Recently Kloppenborg ("Literary Convention, Self-Evidence and the Social History of the Q People", *Semeia* 55, 1992, 77-102) has located the "formative stratum" of Q (stage 1 of the 3 he proposes) "in the villages and large towns of Galilee" (100). In this article he refrains, however, from bringing this finding into the linguistic or tradition critical debates.

eschatology coexist with specific interests in the kingdom of God and the Son of Man? There is not, however, abundant one to one literary contact between Daniel and Jesus' Q sayings at large—the parallels are primarily conceptual. Clearly the Q 'Son of Man' has traits unrelated to the figure of "one like a son of man" in Daniel. Further, a good case can be made that the Q figure is less developed than the Enochic Son of Man, which explicitly bears characteristics of a pre-existent messiah.

Q shares with OT prophecy and Jewish apocalyptic literature an atmosphere of crisis. For the latter two, crisis emerges from a world situation hostile to God's righteousness and sovereignty—primarily the pagan consequences of the Assyrian conquests, the Babylonian exile, and the Seleucid dynasty. In Q, however, we do not find internal evidence of a political event which could have motivated the creation of Jesus' sayings.[69] For instead of a crisis producing Jesus' sayings, the reverse appears to be the case—Jesus' proclamation of the kingdom produced crisis.[70] It is here that the themes of prophecy, wisdom, and eschatology combine: Jesus pronounces the nearness of the kingdom, he prophesies the judgement of the Son of Man, he admonishes his listeners that the wise are those who seek the kingdom (Lk. 12:31//Mt. 6:33), and he boldly claims that his work represents the action of God (Lk. 10:16//Mt. 10:40; Lk. 10:22//Mt. 11:25-27). For Q, the nearness of the kingdom of God in Jesus' proclamation is the crisis: "Allow the dead to bury their own dead; but as for you, go and proclaim everywhere the kingdom of God" (Lk. 9:60, 62//Mt. 8:21, 22). Thus there can be no doubt that S. Schulz correctly perceives "enthusiasm" at the heart of Q.[71] But we part company with Schulz on the question of origin: is "apocalyptic enthusiasm" explained by a historical event not mentioned in Q (so Schulz, Theissen) or did Jesus' radical proclamation of the nearness of the kingdom of

---

[69] *Contra* Paul Hoffmann, who conjectures political conflict between the "Q community" and Jewish nationalists as the event which produced the recording of Q, "Die Anfänge der Theologie in der Logienquelle", *Gestalt und Anspruch des Neuen Testaments,* Würzburg: Echter Verlag (1969) 147-51. We do not deny categorically the *possibility* that an external event occasioned the composition of Q, but we find the 'enthusiasm' resulting from Jesus' teachings and acts to be the more probable stimulus for the active memory of the figure(s) responsible for transmitting Q at the point of its inception.

[70] On this issue, we cite W.D. Davies: "Q sets the ethical teaching of Jesus in its utterly radical or critical context as part of the drawing near to the Kingdom, that is, that teaching is not primarily a catechetical necessity or an addendum to the gospel but itself part of the Gospel. This helps us to appreciate, in the third place, that the ethical teaching of Jesus in Q was preserved not merely as catechetically useful, and not only as radical demand, but as *revelatory*: it illumines the nature and meaning of the coming of the Kingdom as demand, which is the concomitant of the coming of the Kingdom as grace. . . . In Q, crisis and commandment are one." *The Setting of the Sermon on the Mount,* Cambridge: C.U.P. (1964) 386. Italics Davies'.

[71] *Q–Die Spruchquelle,* 33.

God produce an enthusiasm of its own, which stimulated the disciple's memory of Jesus' teaching? We opt for the latter explanation.

It is equally unlikely that major themes of Q existed as separate strata and were mutually exclusive at the time of Jesus. The apocryphal psalm 11QPs^a XXVII illustrates how unnecessary such categorizations are:

> David son of Jesse was wise and brilliant like the light of the sun; (he was) a scribe, intelligent and perfect in all his ways before God and men. YHWH gave him an intelligent and brilliant spirit, and he wrote 3,600 psalms and 364 songs to sing before the altar for the daily perpetual sacrifice, for all the days of the year; and 52 songs for the Sabbath offerings; and 30 songs for the New Moons, for Feast days and for the Day of Atonement. In all, the songs which he uttered were 446, and 4 songs to make music on behalf of those stricken (by evil spirits). In all, they were 4,050. All these he uttered through prophecy which was given him from before the Most High.[72]

This "midrashic account" of king David's literary achievements characterizes David as an intelligent writer of psalms who exhibits wisdom, a spirit given him by YHWH, the ability to cast out evil spirits through music, and the inspired ability to prophecy. Do David's different attributes represent diverse layers of redaction created by the Qumran scribes? Rather each attribute complements the other in forming the kingly ideal. To the same extent in Q, Jesus' wisdom, his anointing by the Holy Spirit, his prophetic awareness, his power to expel demons,[73] and his intelligence as a teacher combine to affirm his uniqueness and imply his messianic authority. The parallels to the figures of David and Solomon are unmistakeable.

In view of the images which converge in Daniel, it would have been possible for Jesus to have drawn together the images of the Son of Man, the kingdom of God, judgement, prophecy, wisdom and various apocalyptic figures of speech and applied them to his mission. These themes are all appropriate to his kingdom of God emphasis and are not unique to Q. The identifications of Jesus as prophet, wise man, Son of Man, and proclaimer of the kingdom of God appear understandable in light of the OT background where God's sovereignty motivates the prophets to pronounce judgement and the Day of the Lord, where God in his sovereignty bestows and removes wisdom and power from earthly potentates, where God's absolute sovereignty leads the writer of Daniel to pronounce the kingdom of God to be the sovereign power of the universe, and where God, as the Ancient of Days, gives dominion, glory and a kingdom to the one like a Son of Man. The fact that these themes existed together prior to Jesus supports the

---

[72] Taken from G. Vermes, *The Dead Sea Scrolls in English*, London: Penguin (1987) 213, 14.

[73] Note also the combination of wisdom and miracle in 4Q185.

argument that Jesus could have combined them in the manner that we find them in Q. Because wisdom, prophecy, eschatology, and apocalyptic are present in Daniel—a document which precedes Jesus chronologically—these concepts may have been amalgamated already within Jesus' perspective of his own ministry. Hence modern theories which attribute an individual layer of redaction to a single theme may be considered superfluous.

Chapter 6

The Son of Man and the Q Material

I. Introduction

In this chapter we will address the contemporary Son of Man debate and give reasons for the view that Mark and Q refer to the Son of Man in ways not altogether dissimilar. We will critically analyze and respond to the major attempts to explain the Son of Man sayings on the basis of redactional expansion of Q. Does Q contain a Son of Man christology which reflects the bias of its editor(s)? And finally, we will examine the major themes in Q against the background of Daniel 7. A number of scholars contend that Jesus could have used the Aramaic equivalent of Son of Man both as a veiled reference to himself and more explicitly in allusion to the figure of Dn. 7:13, 14.[1] In this chapter we will examine this hypothesis and attempt to provide additional support for it from an investigation of Q. The Q material seems to support this conclusion as Q contains both idiomatic and Danielic sayings. Problems of Q redaction, creative exegesis, and layers of Q redaction may simply be explained by Jesus' interpretation of his mission on the basis of Daniel. As we have seen, the parameters of Q compare very well with the conceptual background of Daniel—the Son of Man is only one such feature. The fact that the major themes in Q fit the conceptual background of Daniel suggests that Daniel may be the implicit conceptual background for the generic Son of Man sayings which do not explicitly quote or allude to Dn. 7:13, 14.

II. The Linguistic Problem

Jesus' self-designation "the Son of Man" is common to both Mark (14x)[2] and Q (10x).[3] The phrase occurs as a self-reference, *in some sense*, exclusively on the

---

[1] Recently J. J. Collins ("The Son of Man in First Century Judaism", *NTS* 38, 1992, 448-466) has argued persuasively that 4 Ezra 13 and the Similitudes of 1 Enoch allude to the 'one like a son of man' in Daniel 7, an individual heavenly being and not a collective symbol. In both works the Son of Man is a messianic figure (465).

[2] Mk. 2:10, 28; 8:31, 38, 9:9, 12, 31; 10:33, 45; 13:26; 14:21 (x2), 41, 62

lips of Jesus within the NT except for Jn. 12:34, where the crowd questions Jesus about the meaning of his own words ("how can *you say*, 'The Son of Man must be lifted up'? Who is this Son of Man?"), and the third person reference in Acts 7:56,[4] where the dying Stephen sees the Son of Man in heaven standing at the right hand of God. There is little agreement, however, among NT scholars as to whether the phrase ὁ υἱὸς τοῦ ἀνθρώπου (or its Aramaic equivalent) originated with Jesus or with the early Church. Moreover, consensus does not exist even among those who take seriously the absence of the phrase in the NT apart from Jesus' sayings and as a result attribute an Aramaic precursor for ὁ υἱὸς τοῦ ἀνθρώπου to Jesus himself on the basis of the criterion of dissimilarity. The shortage of an adequate supply of extant Aramaic material to draw from in ascertaining the Semitic pedigree of the Greek phrase has led to a plurality of hypotheses for its origin. Furthermore, the symbolic nature of the "one like a son of man" (כְּבַר אֱנָשׁ) in Daniel 7 prevents scholarly consensus as to the identity and the significance of the figure to which allusion is definitely made in a select body of synoptic sayings.[5] Because the "one like a son of man" in Dn. 7:13 is not explicitly a 'titular' messianic figure, and because sufficient evidence does not exist to prove the pre-Christian origin of the Similitudes of Enoch (where the Son of Man designation "that man" is applied to a messianic figure clearly on the basis of Dn. 7 in I En. 46:1, 3),[6] many scholars fail to believe that Jesus could have

---

[3] Lk. 6:22//Mt. 5:11; Lk. 7:34//Mt. 11:19; Lk. 9:58//Mt. 8:20; Lk. 11:30//Mt. 12:40; Lk. 12:8//Mt. 10:32; Lk. 12:10//Mt. 12:32; Lk. 12:40//Mt. 24:44; Lk. 17:24//Mt. 24:27; Lk. 17:26//Mt. 24:37; Lk. 17:30//Mt. 24:39. Two other Son of Man sayings which theoretically could have originally belonged to Q are Mt. 10:23 which lacks a Lukan parallel altogether and Mt. 19:28 whose supposed variant Lk. 22:28-30 does not contain ὁ υἱὸς τοῦ ἀνθρώπου. H. Schürmann (*Traditionsgeschichtliche Untersuchungen zu den synoptischen Evangelien*, Düsseldorf: Patmos-Verlag [1967] 140, 150-56) argues for the inclusion in Q of Mt. 10:23 after Mt. 10:19//Lk. 12:11-12 on the basis of similarity in form and content. Mt. 10:23 originally concluded the sayings chain now found in Lk. 12:(1) 2-10 par. Davies and Allison (*Matthew* 2, 188) tentatively attribute 10:23 to Q but place it in the Q missionary discourse (Mt. ch. 9,10; Lk. 10) on the basis of content. Both conjectures stand or fall on Luke's hypothetical omission of the saying. The differences between Mt. 19:28 and Lk. 22:28-30 are extensive and complex, though a host of scholars trace the two versions to one Q original (see J. Kloppenborg, *Q-Parallels*, 202). An equal number of scholars do not trace the sayings to Q. For the inclusion of Mt. 19:28//Lk. 22:28-30 in Q, the saying(s) authenticity, and its content, see G.R. Beasley-Murray, *Jesus and the Kingdom of God*, 273-277.

[4] In Rev. 1:13 and 14:14 the phrase ὅμοιον υἱὸν ἀνθρώπου "one like a Son of Man" occurs in reference to Jesus as the risen Danielic Son of Man. However, in these references the phrase is not used as a self-reference, and both verses lack the article.

[5] For a survey of recent scholarly suggestions on the identity of the figure in Dn. 7:13, 14, see John E. Goldingay, *Daniel*, Dallas: Word (1989) 169-172.

[6] See Morna Hooker, *The Son of Man in Mark*, London: SCM (1967) 46-47.

adopted an Aramaic form of ὁ υἱὸς τοῦ ἀνθρώπου with the intention of identifying his messianic identity with the figure of Dn. 7 although it is agreed that the Greek/Aramaic tradition may so identify him.[7]

As a result a dichotomy has developed in the classification of synoptic Son of Man sayings. On the one hand there exist sayings which clearly compare Jesus with the figure of Dn. 7:13, 14. In these references the Son of Man must be taken as a technical designation for a messianic figure who functions in a manner which recalls Dn. 7:13, 14. The Son of Man is that Son of Man (Dn. 7) who yields supernatural power and authority to judge on the eschatological day of the Lord. On the other hand there exist sayings which do not clearly allude to Daniel either linguistically or conceptually. In such sayings, it is suggested, the phrase ὁ υἱὸς τοῦ ἀνθρώπου represents the Greek translation of an Aramaic idiom of self-reference. The original form of the Aramaic idiom and the connotations which the idiom originally yielded are both matters of debate. Three contemporary theories stand out.[8] First, according to G. Vermes, ὁ υἱὸς τοῦ ἀνθρώπου may translate בר נשא/בר נש which was originally used by Jesus as a surrogate or circumlocution for the first person pronoun "I". According to Vermes's study of ancient Aramaic documents this Aramaic idiom was particularly appropriate in dangerous situations or situations requiring humility.[9] The idiom was capable of being used by Jesus to say things true of himself but not necessarily true of everyone else. Second, B. Lindars, in contrast to Vermes, suggests that the idiomatic use of the generic idiom בר אנשא deflects, in an ironic fashion, the thought from Jesus to his eschatological mission. Jesus originally voiced בר אנשא in reference to himself but not exclusively to himself, "it also means anyone else in his position, therefore the prospective disciple who stands before him."[10] Third, M. Casey, adopting many of the same examples used by Vermes, postulates an idiomatic usage very close to that advocated by Lindars. The Aramaic phrase בר אנש(א), according to Casey, was an idiom any Aramaic speaker could take up and use "in either the definite or

---

[7] For a critical summary of the major solutions to the Son of Man problem see C. Caragounis, *The Son of Man Vision and Interpretation*, Tübingen: J.C.B. Mohr (Paul Siebeck) 1986, 9-33; I.H. Marshall, "The Synoptic Son of Man Sayings in Recent Discussion", *Jesus the Savior*; 73-99; Idem, "The Son of Man in Contemporary Debate", idem, 100-120; J. Dunn, *Christology in the Making*; 86f.; R.A. Hare, *The Son of Man Tradition*, Minneapolis: Fortress, 1990; Davies and Allison, "Excursus VI", *Matthew II*, 43-53.

[8] For the distinction between the views of Vermes, Lindars, and Casey, see I.H. Marshall, "Son of Man", in *Dictionary of Jesus and the Gospels*, Ed. J.B. Green, Scott Mcknight, and I.H. Marshall; Downers Grove/Leicester: Intervarsity (1992) 775-781; idem, "The Son of Man and the Incarnation", *Ex Auditu* 7 (1991) 29-43.

[9] "Appendix E, The Use of בר נשא/בר נש in Jewish Aramaic", in Matthew Black, *An Aramaic Approach to the Gospels and Acts*, Oxford: Clarendon (1967) 310-330.

[10] *Jesus Son of Man*, London: SPCK (1983) 181, 183.

indefinite state, in a general statement in order to say something about himself, or sometimes himself and a group of associates. He would normally do so in order to avoid sounding exceptionally exalted or feeling exceptionally humiliated."[11] In authentic sayings, therefore, Jesus used the self-reference (בר אנש(א in statements "believed by him to be true of other people as well as of himself."[12] Casey, Vermes, and Lindars agree the phrase was never used by Jesus messianically or in reference to Daniel 7.

The search for an Aramaic solution to the Son of Man debate is well founded and helpful particularly with regard to the difficult versions of the saying found in Mk. 3:28, 29//Mt. 12:31; Lk. 12:10//Mt. 12:32, 33, where Mark's "the sons of men" and Q's "the son of man" probably represent two divergent attempts to translate into Greek the ambiguous Aramaic generic singular בר נשה which in this instance likely did not allude originally to the figure of Daniel 7.[13]

However, the Aramaic idiom(s) theories proposed by Vermes, Casey, and Lindars are not fully satisfactory. The generic idiom is an arbitrary criterion upon which to classify authenticity. The authors assume an ambitious knowledge of what could have and what could not have been said in Aramaic despite the great shortage of extant Aramaic material from the time in question. Further, we have doubts that the handful of supposed genuine sayings should be read in the manner proposed by these authors.[14] When Jesus refers to the Son of Man as a glutton and drunkard, a friend of tax collectors and sinners (Lk. 7:34//Mt. 11:19), is he really identifying himself through generic idiom with a class of persons with whom he identifies? If so what are we to make of the parallel tradition in Mk. 2:15-17? The simplest explanation is that Jesus is here referring to himself in particular.

A position mediating between the first view (that Son of Man sayings can be explained wholesale on the basis of Daniel 7) and the second (that the only "authentic" sayings are those which can be understood idiomatically) is the

---

[11] "General, Generic and Indefinite: The Use of the Term 'Son of Man' in Aramaic Sources and in the Teaching of Jesus", *JSNT* 29 (1987) 52. An updated summary of Casey's point of view may be found in his book *From Jewish Prophet to Gentile God*, Cambridge: James Clarke & Co (1991) 46-54 [48].

[12] *Son of Man The Interpretation and Influence of Daniel 7*, London: SPCK (1979) 228.

[13] So R. Pesch, *Markus* I, 217; I.H. Marshall, *Luke*, 516-19; J.D.G. Dunn, *Jesus and the Spirit*, 49-52. The saying does not originate from early Christian prophecy. See D. Aune, *Prophecy in Early Christianity and the Ancient Mediterranean World*, 240-42; J.D.G. Dunn, "Matthew 12:28//Luke 11:20 –A Word of Jesus?" in *Eschatology and the New Testament,* FS G.R. Beasley-Murray; Peabody: Hendrickson (1988) 37 n. 21: "It is not in the nature of charismatic movements to accept criticisms of the charismatic founder and to include them among his revered sayings!" *Contra* M.E. Boring, *The Continuing Voice of Jesus*, 219-21.

[14] On this problem see especially I.H. Marshall, *Ex Auditu* 7 (1991) 29-43.

position advocated by James Dunn who asserts that Jesus may have adopted the Aramaic expression and used it with different emphases in different situations. Because the conceptual background found in Dn. 7 is not wooden, but incorporates kingdom terminology, specifies a direct relationship between the "one like a son of man" and the Ancient of Days, specifies a symbolic relationship between the "one like a son of man" and the suffering saints (7:18, 27), and points toward future vindication, Jesus may have alluded to the Danielic 'one like a son of man' as "an expressive symbol for his whole ministry, his present role and anticipated suffering as well as his future vindication."[15] Along similar lines I.H. Marshall advances the opinion that:

> 'Son of Man' is used throughout the sayings of Jesus as a way of referring to himself in a manner intended to recall its use in the OT. It would thus be a self-designation based on the quasi-titular use of the phrase rather than upon its putative use as a simple circumlocution for 'I'. At the same time, the phrase was ambiguous and would not necessarily be recognized as titular by Jesus' hearers.[16]

This perspective depends not upon one uncertain interpretation of a small group of sayings but accounts for every kind of synoptic Son of Man saying (present, suffering, future, idiomatic, Danielic) without attributing artificial categories of sayings to the very early Church and without categorically denying that the historical Jesus could have interpreted his ministry against the background of the OT. In favour of Jesus' own recourse on Daniel, whether or not he was familiar with the Son of Man traditions associated with the Similitudes, is Jesus' unusual use of *abba* and *amen* which demonstrate "that he was deliberately innovative in the linguistic sphere. He was not, that is, bound by conventional usage."[17] While Casey identifies primarily 'earthly' sayings as authentic because they accord with his understanding of the Aramaic idiom, and future sayings as secondary because they often allude to Dn. 7 and accord with early Christian preoccupation with the end,[18] it is problematic to Casey that there are on the one hand present Son of Man sayings which allude to Dn. 7,[19] and future Son of Man sayings which do not

---

[15] *Christology in the Making*, 86.

[16] "The Son of Man in Contemporary Debate", *Jesus the Saviour*, 118 n. 69.

[17] Davies and Allison, "The Son of Man", Excursus VI in *Matthew* II, 47. That *abba* was in some sense unique to Jesus, has recently been defended by J. Fitzmyer, "Abba and Jesus' relation to God", in *A Cause de L'Évangile*, FS J. Dupont; Cerf: Publications de Saint-André (1985) 16-38.

[18] *Son of Man*, 237, 38.

[19] Lk. 12:8//Mt. 10:32; Lk. 9:58//Mt. 8:20. See: Davies and Allison, *Matthew* II, 214-15; C. Caragounis, *The Son of Man*, 175-179; *Pace* M. Casey, *Son of Man*, 229.

allude to Daniel.[20] The distinction, therefore, between present and future is not clear. That the early Church created Son of Man sayings is a hypothesis dependent on the unlikely scenario that at an early stage the Church reflected christologically on Dn. 7, but very quickly abandoned the process never to take it up again.[21] The position advocated by Dunn and Marshall, in contrast, represents a step forward as it gains external support from dominical sayings which do not take up the Son of Man phrase but which nonetheless contain authoritative commands.[22] Seeing no reason to doubt categorically the frequent $\lambda\acute{\epsilon}\gamma\omega$ $\acute{\upsilon}\mu\hat{\imath}\nu$ sayings in which Jesus does openly assert his own authority, we remain open to the possibility that Jesus could have associated his authority (both present and future) with the authority which the Ancient of Days gives the man-like figure in Dn. 7. Such a likelihood becomes greater both in view of Jesus' relationship to God (Lk. 10:22) and the authority which Jesus assumes in speaking knowledgeably about the kingdom of God—a specific entity given the man-like figure in Daniel. Furthermore, the view of Dunn and Marshall does not depend on a dramatic shift in meaning in the translation from Aramaic to Greek. Certainly a shift in meaning took place as occurs in any translation, but Casey, in our opinion, is unreasonable when he categorically denies on the one hand the possibility that Jesus could have identified himself with the figure of Dn. 7, while on the other hand openly agreeing to the likelihood that Aramaic-speaking Christians were the first to make the connection between Jesus and the 'man-like figure':

> If the term בר אנש was already known from sayings of Jesus, it would for this reason reinforce the suggestion, which could be made on the grounds of the content of Dan 7.13, that כבר אנש was in fact Jesus, and such was ancient exegetical method that the mere occurrence of the term in the text of Dan. 7.13 could be the origin of the suggestion that the man-like figure was Jesus even among Aramaic-speaking Christians.[23]

---

[20] Lk. 17:24//Mt. 24:27; Lk. 17:26//Mt. 24:37; Lk. 17:30//Mt. 24:39. This is a particular shortcoming of Casey's book: "Further analysis of inauthentic sayings which do not appear to make use of Dan. 7 lies altogether beyond the scope of this book"(238).

[21] As Lindars himself admits: "In early Christian thought there is very little sign of the use of Dan. 7, and the absence of it from both Paul and Hebrews is remarkable", *Jesus Son of Man*, 15.

[22] On this point see especially the "I" sayings discussed by I.H. Marshall, "The Son of Man and the Incarnation", 34, 35: "The important point which emerges is that Jesus can and does speak with authority about his own role as the leader of the disciples. This suggests that the rather minimalist Christology found by Lindars does not square with the rest of the evidence. It also suggests that the case that Jesus did not assert his authority openly or speak about himself openly and directly is not sound."

[23] *Son of Man*, 235.

Yet, when the earliest Aramaic Christians were able to make the connection between Jesus' Aramaic idiom and the language of Dn. 7, why is it not possible that Jesus could have identified himself with the figure of Dn. 7:13,14, when Jesus no doubt equally knew the scriptures?

III. The Son of Man in Mark and Q

Where does this lead us in our study of Q and its relation to Mark? Both Mark and Q contain present 'authentic' Son of Man sayings which conform to the different forms of idiomatic Aramaic usage as outlined by Casey, Lindars, and Vermes (Mk. 2:10, 28; Lk. 7:34//Mt. 11:19; Lk. 9:58//Mt. 8:20; Lk. 12:10 diff. Mt. 12:32).[24] Of these the two Markan references address the Son of Man's authority on earth to forgive sin (2:10) and to rule the Sabbath (2:28). The Q sayings, in contrast, deal primarily with the humility of the Son of Man who is deemed a drunkard (Lk. 7:34//Mt. 11:19), and whose lifestyle is characterized by homelessness (Lk. 9:58//Mt. 8:20). The distinction, however, between authority (Mk.) and humility (Q) does not warrant special appraisal in view of the authority which Jesus assumes throughout Q and the humility which characterizes Jesus as the suffering Son of Man in Mark. The validity of interpreting such sayings in the generic sense derives from the difficult tradition behind Mk. 3:28; Lk. 12:10 diff. Mt. 12:32 (Q), where the Markan phrase τοῖς υἱοῖς τῶν ἀνθρώπων proves a generic translation is a *possible* rendering of the underlying Aramaic whatever the Aramaic phrase may have been. For our purposes, however, it suffices to say that contradiction between the present 'idiomatic' Son of Man sayings in Mark and Q does not seem apparent.

Similarly, both Mark and Q contain future-oriented Son of Man sayings which allude to Dn. 7:13, 14 (Mk. 8:38; 13:26; 14:62; Lk. 12:8//Mt. 10:32[25]; Lk. 12:40//Mt. 24:44,[26] Lk. 17:24//Mt. 24:27[27]). The direct quotations of Dn. 7:13, 14 in Mk. 13:26 and 14:62 have no counterparts in Q. Yet the allusions to Daniel

---

[24] M. Casey, *Son of Man*, 236; G. Vermes, *Jesus the Jew*, London: Collins, 1973; Lindars omits Mk. 2:28 (*Jesus Son of Man*, 29-60).

[25] On the dependence of Lk. 12:8//Mt. 10:32 on Dn. 7:13, 14, see C. Caragounis, *Son of Man*, 202, 3; Davies and Allison, *Matthew* II, 214, 215.

[26] See M. Casey, *Son of Man*, 190. *Pace* I. Havener, (*Q: The Sayings of Jesus*, Wilmington: Michael Glazier, 1987, p. 75): "Since Q never quotes Daniel 7:13 nor even clearly alludes to the passage, it is difficult to speak of a Christian midrash, that is, an explanatory interpretation in rabbinic fashion, of Daniel 7:13 in the Q parousia son of man sayings. Indeed, the Christological significance of son of man is greatly diminished, . . ."

[27] For this saying's dependence on Dn. 7, see G. Vermes, *Jesus the Jew*, 178-79. *Pace* M. Casey, *Son of Man*, 189.

7 in Q suffice to prove that Q compares favorably with Mark in identifying ὁ υἱὸς τοῦ ἀνθρώπου with that Son of Man in Dn. 7:13. *Both Mark and Q contain Son of Man sayings traceable to Dn. 7.* Q contrasts with Mark, however, in containing future Son of Man sayings which do not directly allude to Daniel 7 (Lk. 17:26//Mt. 24:37; Lk. 17:30//Mt. 24:39). What to make of this, if anything, is uncertain in a Mk/Q comparison. However, these sayings are important in that they transcend the idiom/Daniel dichotomy and so raise the question whether the early Church could have created such sayings where the particular figure referred to is not explained or defined in kerygmatic fashion on the basis of the OT. On the other hand, if future sayings whose vocabulary does not depend on Daniel are authentic—as Bultmann, Colpe and others have suggested[28]—and yet only understandable on the basis of Daniel or an independent tradition traceable to Daniel, the way is open to the possibility that Daniel may be in view in other 'authentic' Son of Man sayings which do not directly quote or allude to Dn. 7— i.e., sayings identified as idiomatic by the scholars above. In this case Lk. 7:34//Mt. 11:19 and Lk. 9:58//Mt. 8:20 fully reflect the irony of Jesus' situation— the rejected one is in fact the same as 'that one' who will judge at the parousia.

In summary, our findings lead us to conclude that there is no appreciable difference between Mark and Q at least among the present and future Son of Man sayings. Both contain allusions to Daniel 7 and both contain apparent examples of the idiomatic usage of בר אנש(א).

IV. Recent Study of the Son of Man in Q

Recent studies attempt to explain how and why the Son of Man sayings entered Q on the basis of preconceived notions about the *Sitz im Leben* of the Q community and the redactional activity of the Q editor(s). The purpose of this section is to analyze these theories and to reach a conclusion as to their validity. What is the significance of the Son of Man in Q? Is there evidence that Q contains a Son of Man christology which is incompatible with the passion oriented christology of Mark's Gospel?

A. H.E. Tödt

There is a distinction between the Son of Man sayings in Mark and Q which has occasioned special attention. H.E.Tödt, who was later to be followed by many,

---

[28] C. Colpe,"υἱὸς τοῦ ἀνθρώπου", *TDNT* VIII, 430-61; R. Bultmann, ET *Theology of the New Testament,* London: SCM (1952) 28-32.

originally observed that of the three groups of Son of Man sayings in the Synoptic Gospels (present Son of Man sayings, future Son of Man sayings and suffering Son of Man sayings) only the first two groups can be found in Q:

> In Q there are sayings on the coming Son of Man and on the Son of Man in his present activity side by side, neither confused nor combined with each other. In the first group of sayings Jesus speaks of the Son of Man as of another in the future. In the second group Jesus speaks of the Son of Man when speaking of his own present activity on earth. In the former group the sovereignty of the Son of Man is unrestrictedly transcendent; in the latter, the sovereignty of the Son of Man is not that of a transcendent being.[29]

Consequently, Tödt identified the future Son of Man sayings as the authentic utterances of Jesus: Mt. 24:27 par.; 24:37, 9 par.; Lk. 11:30; Mt. 24:44 par.; Lk. 12:8, 9, while ascribing the present sayings to the community: "they retained the differentiating form of the authentic sayings of Jesus when forming a Son of Man saying of their own."[30] The purpose of the present sayings was essentially to designate Jesus' authority. Accordingly, Tödt did not believe that Jesus applied the name/title Son of Man to himself, but instead he envisioned another transcendent being who would come bringing judgement in the future. The post-Easter community utilized the authentic Son of Man sayings to explain the delayed parousia by attributing the future sayings to the historic Jesus and then created new "present" Son of Man sayings of their own. In so doing the community redefined Jesus' christological expectation and in essence created their own Jesus/Son of Man christology.

Therefore, Tödt came to the conclusion that Q, independent of Mark, represents a specific form of Son of Man christology:[31] "There is a second, independent source, then, located in the Q stratum of the productive development of the Son of Man sayings. Christology as it springs up here is a Son of Man Christology."[32] Furthermore, because no evidence of Jesus' suffering or humility exists in Q, the center of the Q material rests in the re-teaching of Jesus' teaching. Because Jesus' teaching was perceived to be the eschatological expectation of the Son of Man, Tödt believed the Q community existed in expectation of an imminent return of the Son of Man. The great christological awareness of the group existed in their identification of Jesus as the Son of Man.

---

29 *The Son of Man in the Synoptic Tradition*, 124.

30 *Ibid.*, 65.

31 Similarly J. Gnilka, "Das Christusbild der Spruchquelle", Kapitel VII: in *Jesus Christus nach frühen Zeugnissen des Glaubens*, München: Kösel-Verlag (1970) 113: "Die Christologie der Spruchquelle ist primär Menschensohn-christologie."

32 *The Son of Man in the Synoptic Tradition*, 235.

However, Tödt's attempt to explain Q's christology with the present and future Son of Man scheme fails to convince for a number of reasons. In addition to suffering sayings, Mark contains present sayings which identify Jesus' earthly authority (2:10, 28; 14:21, 62), and future sayings which focus on Jesus' eschatological role as Son of Man (8:38; 13:26). Because Mark contains different sayings whose content matches that of the Q Son of Man sayings, there is little evidence that the supposed Q community put forth a Son of Man christology which was uniquely its own. Tödt's argument hinges on Q's silence (passion) rather than on what Q says positively about Jesus.

His scheme fails to take into account the diverse portraits of Jesus which exist in Q where Jesus is in fact *rejected* by his generation, and where he appears as the teacher of wisdom (Lk. 6:12, 20a; Mt. 5:1, 2), as the Son of God (from the mouth of Satan: Lk. 4:1-13; Mt. 4:1-11), as the expected one whose present acts bear witness to who he is (Lk. 7:19; Mt. 11:2, 3), as the performer of miracles (Lk. 7:22f.; Mt. 11:4f.), as the teacher and administrator of the kingdom of God (Lk. 11:20; Mt. 12:28), as the sender of missionaries (Lk. 10:2b; Mt. 9:37, 38), as the unapologetic judge of the religious practices of his day (Lk. 11:39-52; Mt. 23:25f.), and as the one who refers to God as "Father" (Lk. 10:21, 22; Mt. 11:25f.) Clearly, then, Q goes beyond the present and future Son of Man designations in its portrayal of Jesus. Most importantly, Tödt has provided us with no credible evidence that Q originally contained a christology which was diverse and incompatible with the passion oriented christology of Mark.

A bold community hypothesis is not needed to explain the apparent lack of suffering Son of Man sayings in Q. While a comparison of the Son of Man sayings in Mark and Q reveals that Tödt's analysis was basically correct—there are no Son of Man sayings in Q which predict Jesus' death and resurrection, and there is certainly not a Q saying whose content compares with that of Mk. 10:45, his theory has convinced very few scholars who have studied the Son of Man issue in detail.[33] His christological proposal is methodologically unsound because of the possibility that Matthew or Luke could have taken from Q a suffering Son of Man

---

[33] O.J.F. Seitz, "The Rejection of the Son of Man; Mark Compared with Q", *Studia Evangelica* (1982) 451-465; I.H. Marshall, "The Synoptic Son of Man Sayings in Recent Debate", *NTS* 12 (1965, 66) 327-51; Christopher Tuckett, "The Present Son of Man", *JSNT* 14 (1982) 58-82. We, however, cannot accept Tuckett's claim that the SM sayings in Mk. 2:10, 28 fit the description of suffering sayings as opposed to authority sayings. Mk. 2:10 is explicitly a present authority saying "ἵνα δὲ εἰδῆτε ὅτι ἐξουσίαν ἔχει ὁ υἱὸς τους ἀνθρώπου ἀφιέναι ἁμαρτίας ἐπὶ τῆς γῆς", and 2:28 explicitly describes the SM as Lord (κύριος) or master of the Sabbath. Suffering terminology is entirely lacking in both sayings.

saying that the other omitted (e.g., Lk. 9:22; 17:25).[34] Our knowledge of the original contents of Q is imprecise, and it is naive to think that modern reconstructions of Q mark the limits of the knowledge and theology of the Q redactors.[35] Most importantly, however, Tödt's study fails to weigh the extent to which various Q sayings present Jesus as a rejected figure. Lk. 7:34//Mt. 11:19, for instance, presents Jesus the Son of Man as a despised and debased figure: "The Son of Man has come eating and drinking; and you say, "Behold, a gluttonous man, and a drunkard, a friend of tax-gatherers and sinners!"[36] In this saying, it is Jesus himself, not his message, which is repelled. The woes to the cities of Chorazin and Bethsaida in Lk. 10:13-15//Mt. 11:21-23 likewise evince a portrait of Jesus as a rejected figure: "Woe to you, Chorazin! Woe to you, Bethsaida! For if the miracles had been performed in Tyre and Sidon which occurred in you, they would have repented long ago, sitting in sackcloth and ashes." The "woes" present Jesus' frustration that the people of his homeland have failed to comprehend the significance of his miracles and as a result have rejected his mission. And finally, the lament over Jerusalem and the call for disciples to bear their own cross (Lk. 14:27//Mt. 10:38) further reflect the reality that Jesus in his earthly life was a rejected figure who endured suffering.[37] He was somehow unacceptable to his homeland. Such Q evidence corroborates the rejection Jesus experiences in the Galilean section of Mark (2:6, 7, 18, 23, 24; 3:1, 2, 22, 30; 6:4; 7:1-5; 8:11f.).[38]

Closely linked with this evidence is the fact that though there are no Son of Man sayings in Q which address the vicarious benefits of Jesus' death, Lk. 9:58//Mt. 8:20 does describe in ironic terms the humble nature of Jesus' earthly ministry: "The foxes have holes, and the birds of the air have nests, but the Son of

---

[34] Hans F. Bayer (*Jesus' Predictions of Vindication and Resurrection*, WUNT 2. Reihe 20; J.C.B. Mohr [Paul Siebeck] 1986, 212) has made a plausible case for the Q origin of Lk. 9:22//Mt. 16:21f. Lk. 17:25 is included in Q by A.M. Hunter, *The Work and Words of Jesus*, London: S.C.M. (1973) 179.

[35] Hence Marinus de Jonge (*Christology in Context*, 83), "It is extremely unlikely, however, that the communities in which the sayings of the Q collection were handed down knew no other traditions about Jesus' life, death, and resurrection/exaltation. Q's implicit Christology cannot have represented the whole understanding of Jesus by any Christian congregation."

[36] The authenticity of this verse has recently been defended: Douglas R.A. Hare, *The Son of Man Tradition*, Minneapolis: Fortress Press (1990) 259-264. So also E. Schweizer, "Der Menschensohn", *ZNW* 50 (1959) 200.

[37] On the basis of Lk. 14:27//Mt. 10:38, M. Hengel has argued that Q refers to the suffering of Jesus and that the Q transmitters were aware of the passion predictions ("Kerygma oder Geschichte", *TQ* 151 [1971] 334).

[38] So O.J.F. Seitz, "The Rejection of the Son of Man; Mark Compared with Q", 465.

Man has nowhere to lay his head."[39] This saying like Lk. 7:34//Mt. 11:19 does not conform to the generic rendering "a son of man," "any man," or "a man" as the correct translation of ὁ υἱὸς τοῦ ἀνθρώπου. As all men are not homeless and considered to be gluttonous drunkards, the epithet "the son of man" most naturally refers here to Jesus in particular.[40] While we agree with G.R. Beasley-Murray that Bonnard and Colpe "go beyond what the text warrants" when they cite this verse as a direct allusion to the suffering Jesus experienced on his way to the cross, we must not overlook the plain fact that this saying in its Q form does present Jesus as both the Son of Man and as a homeless afflicted figure.[41] Hence the imagery of Lk. 9:58//Mt. 8:20 has led M. Black to write: "Q is not, however, without sayings where Jesus refers to himself as Son of Man in his humanity and humiliation (Matthew 8:20; 11:19 and parallels); and such sayings belong more properly to "the suffering" Son of Man group of sayings than to the Parousia tradition."[42] The trichotomy between present, future, and suffering Son of Man sayings is, therefore, not nearly as defined as the demarcations which Tödt and Bultmann set.[43]

Furthermore, we wonder whether preoccupation with the silence of Q has not obscured the important similarities between the present and future Son of Man sayings in Mark and Q. Surely it is significant that both Mark and Q contain future Son of Man sayings whose vocabulary M. Casey and M. Black trace back to Dn. 7:13 (Q Lk. 12:40//Mt. 24:44; Lk. 17:24//24:27; Mk. 8:38; 13:26; 14:62).[44] Likewise it must not be overlooked that Mark's present Son of Man sayings which focus upon Jesus' authority to forgive sins (2:10) and to heal on the Sabbath

---

[39] For the authenticity of Lk. 9:58//Mt. 8:20 see: Douglas Hare, *The Son of Man Tradition*, 271-73; R. Bauckham, "The Son of Man: 'A Man in My Position' or 'Someone'?", *JSNT* 23 (1985) 25; W.G. Kümmel, *Die Theologie des Neuen Testaments nach seinen Hauptzeugen Jesus, Paulus, Johannes*, GNT 3; Göttingen: Vandenhoeck & Ruprecht (1969) 71-72.

[40] *Pace* M. Casey, "The Jackals and the Son of Man", *JSNT* 23 (1985) 10.

[41] G.R. Beasley-Murray, *Jesus and the Kingdom of God*, 235, 236; P. Bonnard, *L 'Évangile selon Saint Matthieu*, Neuchatel: Delachaux & Niestle (1963) 118; C. Colpe, "υἱὸς τοῦ ἀνθρώπου", *TDNT* VIII, 433.

[42] "The Son of Man Passion Sayings in the Gospel Tradition", *ZNW* 60 (1969) 2.

[43] Bultmann claimed the earthly suffering SM sayings arose within the Hellenistic community where the original meaning of the apocalyptic title SM was no longer understood – only so could the title be applied to Jesus on earth: *History of the Synoptic Tradition*, 155; *Theology of the New Testament* I, 30. Cf. C.K. Barrett, *Jesus and the Gospel Tradition*, Philadelphia: Fortress Press (1968) 32, 79f.

[44] M. Casey, *The Son of Man*, 190; *idem, Jewish Prophet and Gentile God*, 150f. Casey, of course, does not believe the sayings were originally voiced in Aramaic by Jesus. M. Black, "The Aramaic Dimension in Q with notes on Luke 17:22 and Matthew 24:26 (Luke 17:23)", *JSNT* 40 (1990) 33-41. See also G. Vermes, "Appendix E", *An Aramaic Approach to the Gospels and Acts*, 321-329.

(2:28) complement the overall authority which Jesus assumes throughout Q where Jesus' authority surpasses that of the Roman centurion (Lk. 7:6f.//Mt. 8:6f.), where Jesus delivers punitive woes to the Pharisees and teachers of the law, and where Jesus claims that God's power is visible in his miracles and exorcisms (Lk. 7:22f.//Mt. 11:4f.; Lk. 11:20//Mt. 12:28). Apart from where Q is silent, the witness to Jesus as the Son of Man in Mark and Q is remarkably consistent.

These considerations lead us to the conclusion that though Q does not contain a saying which predicts the suffering and death of the Son of Man, the content of one Q saying (Lk. 9:58//Mt. 8:20) and the implied context of five others (Lk. 7:34//Mt. 11:19; Lk. 10:13-15//Mt. 11:21-23; Lk. 10:16//Mt. 10:40; Lk. 13:34, 35//Mt. 23:37-39; Lk. 14:27//Mt. 10:38) do present Jesus as a rejected human figure in Q. We agree that Q differs from Mark in what Q does not contain—that is a Son of Man saying loaded with redemptive implications such as Mk. 10:45. But the positive point we are trying to make is that this distinction is not extraordinary. The material Q does contain concerning the earthly ministry of Jesus complements rather than contradicts the gospel of Mark. The early church could have interpreted these sayings in light of their "kerygmatic" or "orthodox" belief that Jesus died on the cross for the forgiveness of sins. Indeed, it is hard to understand why the early church would have retained the homelessness and rejection sayings outside of this context, and it is illogical that a Q community created such sayings, if it focused the entirety of its attention on the parousia of Jesus the Son of Man.[45]

B.   Siegfried Schulz

Subsequent works have not found Tödt's narrow classification of Q's "Son of Man christology" to be convincing.[46]   However, many do agree that the Son of Man phrase must have been an editorial addition made by the carriers of the Q

---

[45] We therefore concur with Arland J. Hultgren's assessment of Lk. 11:49-51//Mt. 23:34-36; Lk. 13:34//Mt. 23:37, and Lk. 14:27//Mt. 10:38, when he writes: "Given these allusions to the crucifixion, it goes without saying that the Q community would have had to reflect on the question of why Jesus had been put to death and what that might mean", *Christ and His Benefits*, 21.

[46] A.J.B. Higgins, *The Son of Man in the Teaching of Jesus*. Cambridge: CUP (1980) 125: "The Son of Man christology originated neither in pesher interpretation of Ps. 110.1 and Dan. 7.13, nor in the theology of Q, but in Jesus' own preaching"; D.R.A. Hare, *The Son of Man Tradition*, 218: "the existence of the earthly sayings in the hypothetical document must be counted as valid evidence *against* the alleged Son of Man Christology. The proposal that an apocalyptic title was so quickly demoted to a simple self-designation devoid of apocalyptic coloration must be deemed very improbable"; O.J.F. Seitz, "The Rejection of the Son of Man; Mark Compared with Q", *Studia Evangelica* (1982) 451-465; I.H. Marshall, "The Synoptic Son of Man Sayings in Recent Debate", *NTS* 12 (1965, 66) 327-51.

tradition who anticipated Jesus' coming as the future Son of Man. Like Tödt, Siegfried Schulz identifies two different phases in the christological application of Son of Man within Q. Schulz, however, goes beyond Tödt to locate the development of Son of Man within two different Q communities. He argues that at the beginning of the Christian movement we do not find proclamation of the historical Jesus ("nowhere does one find in the oldest Q material kerygmatic recourse on the Nazarene"),[47] but prophetic-apocalyptic enthusiasm. Yet if the early Q community was preoccupied with charismatic apocalyptic enthusiasm focused upon the future end-event—why Jesus? Schulz responds to this question by reasserting his theory of "apocalyptic enthusiasm": The oldest Palestinian Christians believed the endtime had begun and that the promised Spirit was being poured out by the exalted-present Son of Man. The Spirit of the Son of Man was motivating expectation of the parousia, the charismatic intensified application of Torah, and the message of the near creator God.[48]   Accordingly, the earthly/human Jesus had no real significance for the first Q community. Jesus' significance lay entirely in his identity as the future Son of Man. The apocalyptic post-Easter enthusiasm was the primary characteristic of the group, and the environment from which all theology (and christology) sprung.[49] Christology was therefore of secondary importance to the earliest Q community, and what christology it had was future oriented. The Son of Man was a future figure who would bring in judgement.

The historical Jesus does not gain significance within Schulz's scheme until the emergence of the later Hellenistic community. From the enthusiastic prophetic sayings of the earlier community which foretold the imminent inbreaking of the Son of Man, now come the words of the earthly Jesus as a prophet of the endtimes before the approach of the Son of Man parousia. The process of recourse to the earthly Jesus took place in the layers of tradition, in the collection of Q, and in the Q redaction. Kerygmatic recourse to the words and deeds of Jesus was motivated by a decrease in prophetic enthusiasm, the delay of the parousia, and kerygmatic reaction to the Markan material.[50]   The Son of Man was, therefore, an eschatological figure in both the early and late Q communities.

---

[47] *Q–Die Spruchquelle*, 165.

[48] *Ibid.,*165.

[49] *Ibid.*, 165. Schulz agrees with Martin Dibelius that the origin of this theology exists in early Christian preaching. See M. Dibelius, *Die alttestamentlichen Motive des Petrus und Johannes dem Taufer untersucht,* BZAW 33 (1918) 146.

[50] *Q-Die Spruchquelle*, 482.

C. Dieter Lührmann

Dieter Lührmann also interprets the Son of Man passages within Q from an eschatological perspective, although he does not believe that the Son of Man emphasis sprang from charismatic enthusiasm, but rather from the opposition existing between the Gentile Q community and their Jewish counterparts. The Son of Man was to the Q community a figure who in the endtime would bring judgement against the Jews (whom they spoke of through the mouth of Jesus as "this generation") and reward to themselves (since they sided with the Son of Man). Lührmann claims that the Q passages which juxtapose the "coming" and the "has come" Son of Man prove the Son of Man is for Q the self-understanding of Jesus. Nevertheless, in agreement with Bultmann, Tödt, and F. Hahn, Lührmann's comparison of Jesus to the Son of Man does not fall back on an authentic saying(s) of Jesus.[51] He admits, though, that it is at least possible that the sayings about the future Son of Man go back partly to Jesus, and as a result the identification of Jesus with the coming Son of Man may fall back on the tradition of a Palestinian community.[52] In any case, Lührmann does not believe that the identification of Jesus with the Son of Man was originally the work of Q redaction, but instead the combination took place in a previous layer of tradition.

Most importantly, Lührmann sees continuity between Jesus and the Q community in eschatology—not in kerygma. Jesus is not the pronouncement; rather the content of pronouncement is the coming judgement in which Jesus will save his people as the Son of Man.[53]

D. Paul Hoffmann

Paul Hoffmann stresses the eschatological significance of the term Son of Man from an apocalyptic perspective. Hoffmann compares Jesus to the Ethiopic Enoch and claims that Jesus was raised to be the Son of Man status in Q in the same way as Enoch was exalted in the Similitudes (1 Enoch 71:14-17). Jesus' words became those of the future judge at the final judgement.[54] The resurrection was the apocalyptic means by which Jesus was exalted to Son of Man status.

---

[51] *Die Redaktion der Logienquelle*, 75. See R. Bultmann, *Die Geschichte der synoptischen Tradition*, (1957) 3rd ed., 133; H.E. Tödt, *Der Menschensohn in der synoptischen Uberlieferung* (1959) 45; F. Hahn, *Christologische Hoheitstitel*, (1963) 37.

[52] *Die Redaktion der Logienquelle*, 85.

[53] *Ibid.*, 96, 97.

[54] *Studien zur Theologie der Logienquelle*, 141.

Ultimately the endtime expectation of Q was anticipation of Jesus' coming as the Son of Man.

According to Hoffmann, the eschatological orientation of Jesus' sayings took place after Jesus' death through the influence of the surrounding apocalyptic environment which came into being as a result of the Jewish-Roman war of 70 A.D. The Son of Man phrase thus entered Q redactionally at a late stage in the same manner that it entered Mk. 13.[55] Whereas Jesus originally expected an immediate inbreaking of the kingdom of God through the completion of his work, the Q community expected a future (imminent) kingdom to be brought in with the return of Jesus as the Son of Man. While Hoffmann agrees that Jesus only spoke of a future Son of Man and never applied the term to himself, he stresses that later when Jesus was identified as the Son of Man, the association was made not in order to heighten Jesus' authority on earth, but rather to identify him as the endtime Son of Man. Thus, Hoffmann does not agree with Tödt that the earthly Son of Man sayings can be rendered separate in meaning from the future sayings because from the beginning the present sayings had in view the coming Son of Man. In this way Jesus' works came to have eschatological significance, and his pronouncements aroused anticipation of the coming Son of Man.[56]

Hoffmann then agrees with Lührmann that continuity between Jesus and the Q community exists primarily in eschatology. He asserts that it is possible to determine the peculiarity of Q in relation to the older tradition of the prophets who were sent to Israel by Wisdom, and also in relation to the tradition of John the Baptist. Likewise it is possible to identify the influence which the Son of Man confession had on later theological development even in the question of the meaning of Jesus' death. Jesus' fate falls in line with that of all messengers of wisdom—the prophets before him and the disciples after him—yet Q qualifies Jesus in a unique way in which he is identified as the Son of Man. Jesus' preaching of the Son of Man comes to fruition in judgement. The destiny of the world depends on its response to Jesus and his message. The sending and rejection of Jesus take on a new accent because they go beyond the traditional prophetic statement; through the identification of the rejected one with the Son of Man Jesus, those rejected also participate in the personal destiny of Jesus. Thus the last judgement is eagerly awaited by the Q community.[57]

---

[55] "QR und der Menschensohn. Eine vorläfige Skizze", in *The Four Gospels*, FS F. Neirynck; Leuven: Leuven U.P. (1992) 451-452. Hoffmann admits, however, that his theory is quite speculative: "Die vorausgehenden, manchem vielleicht allzu spekulativ erscheinenden Überlegungen, bilden eine Arbeitshypothese" (456).

[56] *Ibid.*, 142-147.

[57] *Ibid.*, 100, 102, 188, 189.

Thus Schulz, Hoffmann, and Lührmann maintain common ground in agreeing that the Q community placed primary significance on the future role of Jesus as the Son of Man. In doing so they make the same mistake characteristic of Tödt in that they overlook the extensive Q material which describes the present work and authority of Jesus on earth. This difficulty is not removed, but rather enhanced with the claim that the Q community created the present Son of Man sayings. It is not clear why the Q community felt the need to create present sayings when all they really were interested in was the future.

E. Athanasius Polag

In contrast to Hoffmann, Schulz, and Lührmann, Athanasius Polag approaches the Son of Man figure in Q philologically. In so doing he draws heavily from Carsten Colpe's article "ὁ υἱὸς τοῦ ἀνθρώπου" in *TDNT*,[58] though he disagrees with many of Colpe's conclusions. Polag begins with the common assumption that the Greek form ὁ υἱὸς τοῦ ἀνθρώπου originally developed from the Aramaic form בר נשא. He then claims that בר נשא had four possible meanings in its day (the second meaning having two variations of its own):

> 1) a collective meaning—a group of men, or men overall
> 2) a singular meaning—the man, a man
> 2.1) a pronominal use or generalizing use—some men (often with כל)
> 2.2) a qualified indefinite meaning—a certain man or a determined man
> (*bestimmter Mensch*)
> 3) a generic use—men as opposed to other beings (animals etc.)
> 4) man as the *terminus technicus* within apocalyptic texts—titular meaning.[59]

Since meanings 1 and 2.1 don't exist within the sayings of Jesus, only the generic use, the qualifying indefinite use, and the titular use can be considered as possible meanings for בר נשא within Q. From these three possibilities the qualified indefinite meaning emerges as the most likely candidate.

In support of this he argues that the indefinite epithet was used to mark the disguised speaker's well-known greatness; thus, the qualified indefinite places more emphasis on the function or activity of the person under consideration than on that person himself. The expression becomes in effect a suggestive and circumscribing way of talk. The translation could be read in the sense of "a certain man" (*ein gewisser Mensch*) or "a particular man" (*ein bestimmter Mensch*). Within the sayings of Jesus a circumlocution should not appear unusual if the

---

[58] C. Colpe, "ὁ υἱὸς τοῦ ἀνθρώπου", *TDNT* VIII, 403-481.

[59] *Die Christologie der Logienquelle*, 103.

activity of God and his function in the judgement event are in view. בר נשא sayings express that one man will participate in a decisive way in the endtime judgement.

How does בר נשא come to be associated with Jesus? Polag answers this question by connecting the kingdom pronouncements of Jesus and the future function of judgement. Because a judgement function is applied to Jesus with his present activity in bringing in the kingdom, it is natural that בר נשא should be used to specify Jesus' judgement function in the end. The inner connection between the "kingdom words" and the "judgement words" leads to the conclusion that the formal circumlocution, which already existed in the primary formation of the sayings, never meant other than Jesus himself.[60]

Why was the circumlocution used if it simply stood for Jesus? Again Polag stresses that the function or situation determines the distinction between Jesus and "the man": the proper name "Jesus" has one function, while "the man" has another. Thus Lk. 12:8, 9 is not a contradiction. The functionally required distinction allows for the acceptance of one identification for both the speaker and the hearer. The saying sets off a change in the function of the person in view of the hearer—not one common function for two different persons. In the present Jesus brings judgement with the kingdom pronouncement (man's acceptance or rejection of Jesus determines his inclusion or exclusion with regard to the kingdom); in the endtime he will bring judgement, but in the guise of בר נשא. "Jesus" represents a present function, "the man" represents a future function.

Thus, in contrast to Hoffmann, Tödt, Colpe, and Ferdinand Hahn,[61] Polag does not believe ὁ υἱὸς τοῦ ἀνθρώπου originated as a messianic title in a unique apocalyptic tradition. He plays down the apocalyptic influence citing the lack of any reference within Q to Jesus' preexistence—a key feature of the apocalyptic background. Moreover, he does not classify the images emerging from the coming Son of Man sayings as purely apocalyptic. All that can be stated from these sayings is that he will come (Mt. 10:23); he will appear (Mt. 24:27//Lk. 17:24); he will come in the midst of calamity and terminate persecution of the disciples (Mt. 24:37//Lk. 17:26); his judging function is hinted at (Lk. 21:36); and he has a sign, but it is unspecified (Mt. 24:30; diff. Mk. 13:26). Therefore, Polag claims that these passages portray solely an image of a particular figure who would appear in the endtime in order to save and to judge. He does not believe that a distinct self-contained apocalyptic image exists in Q.[62]

---

60 *Ibid.*, 114.

61 F. Hahn, *Christologische Hoheitstitel*, 25.

62 *Ibid.*, 102-117. See esp. pp. 109, 112, 114.

Polag does, however, recognize the influence of apocalyptic traditions within the development of Q, but only in the later stage of theological reflection within the *Hauptsammlung*. At this time when the smaller speech groups and individual traditions were being gathered into a larger composition, the form בר נשא ceased to be used as a circumlocution (*Umschreibungsformel*) and took on a titular application which expressed an apocalyptic expression of the eschatological Son of Man. But christological reflection within the development of Q did not stop with the apocalyptic interpretation of בר נשא; indeed, the late redaction of Q reveals traces of a scribal tradition whose christological influence can be seen clearly in those Q passages which focus on Jesus' relationship to God (esp. Lk. 10:21, 22; Mt. 11:25-27). The titles "Son of God" and "the Son" originated at this stage. The christology of Q, then, cannot be reduced to merely a Son of Man christology.[63]

The major weakness of Polag's christology is its three-tiered redactional scheme which forces the adoption of a very complex philological understanding of the origin of the phrase Son of Man. He may also underestimate the apocalyptic dimension of Q. To reject an apocalyptic background because Q lacks a reference to the preexistence of the Son of Man requires a narrow understanding of a very broad body of literature. If the title did originally derive from בר נשא it must be asked why the Greek translators chose ὁ υἱὸς τοῦ ἀνθρώπου unless an apocalyptic background was in view. Polag's philological solution is vague and not entirely convincing. Anton Vögtle justifiably questions whether the first-century audience could have understood Jesus' functional claims in the present and future as outlined by Polag.[64] It seems reasonable to suppose that at least the scribes and those educated in the synagogues would have associated the בר נשא figure with Dn. 7. But if Polag is correct in locating the origin of the titular use of Son of Man within the redaction of Q, then the question arises of Mark's references to ὁ υἱὸς τοῦ ἀνθρώπου? Did Mark use Q as a source, or did the Markan community also have an apocalyptic charismatic experience with christological consequences?

Conclusion

There is no positive evidence that a Q community proclaimed an esoteric Son of Man christology which in some manner competed with or varied from the orthodox christology of the early Church. That Q adhered strictly to a future Son

---

[63] *Ibid.*, 117, 198-199.

[64] Anton Vögtle, "Bezeugt die Logienquelle die authentische Redeweise Jesu vom <<Menschensohn>>?" In *Logia,* 80.

of Man christology is unlikely for a number of reasons: (1) the positive evidence that Q emphasizes the present activities of Jesus; (2) the diversity within Q (Jesus' teaching addresses much more than the Son of Man figure); (3) the lack of differentiation between Mark's and Q's use of the present and future Son of Man sayings; (4) the lack of evidence that the Q sayings originated in Q redaction; and (5), the conjecture with which the noted scholars are forced to rationalize the formation of the Son of Man sayings within: (a) a vague situation of apocalyptic enthusiasm; (b) an unclear apocalyptic event; (c) through the creative redaction of a hypothetical Q community; or (d), in response to Jewish persecution of the hypothetical Q community.

Recent assessments of the Son of Man within Q have fallen in line with each individual scholar's understanding of the redaction of Q. Tödt, Schulz, Lührmann, Hoffmann, Schmithals and Schenk [65] all agree that the title "Son of Man" never entered the mind of Jesus or crossed his lips except possibly in reference to another being who would come in the future. They uniformly locate the association of the Son of Man with Jesus in the redactional activity of the Q community. Such a position has recently been upheld by Leif E. Vaage who attributes Lk. 6:22-23; 11:30; 12:8, 9, 40; 17:24, 26-30 to Q redaction arguing that these secondary sayings are characterized by "use of biblical tradition and metaphors of violence."[66]

Not all NT scholars, however, are as convinced of the redactional production of the Son of Man within Q. Heinz Schürmann[67] argues that the Son of Man sayings existed in an early stage of tradition and were added as supplements to individual Q logia secondarily as introductions and conclusions. He describes Q as a collection of independent traditions rather than as a composition unified by one theological theme. If Schürmann's thesis is correct, the Son of Man references cannot be explained as the theological handiwork of a final redactor: "But with the greatest certainty one can state that the Son of Man words take their overall pattern from individual logia. There is no certainty that they can be spoken of as the final redaction of the saying source."[68] Thus, Schürmann asserts that the end redaction

---

[65] Wolfgang Schenk, "Der Einfluß der Logienquelle auf das Markusevangelium", *ZNW* 70 (1979) 141-163. Schenk believes the Son of Man sayings were created within the Q redaction.

[66] "The Son of Man Sayings in Q: Stratigraphical Location and Significance", *Semeia* 55 (1992) 121.

[67] Heinz Schürmann, "Beobachtungen zum Menschensohn-Titel in der Redequelle. Sein Vorkommen in Abschluß und Einleitungswendungen", in *Jesus und der Menschensohn,* FS Anton Vögtle; Freiburg: Herder (1975) 124-148. Schürmann classifies each of the ten Son of Man sayings within Q as a conclusion or an introduction.

[68] "Beobachtungen zum Menschensohn-Titel in der Redequelle. Sein Vorkommen in Abschluß und Einleitungswendungen" (140).

of Q merely passes on the Son of Man sayings—it did not create them.[69] Authenticity at this point becomes a question of personal judgement—the sayings were either created in an intermediate stage of Q's development, or they originated from the lips of Jesus himself. In our opinion, the former is an unnecessary conjecture. Individual logia which originate from a primitive Aramaic background warrant the greatest possible consideration as authentic Jesus tradition.

In addition to Schürmann's findings, scepticism of a creative end redaction stems from the sheer diversity of Q communities, layers of redaction, redactional motives, *Sitze im Leben*, carriers etc, as proposed by these authors. Indeed, when a hypothesis leads to a variety of inconclusive results, the hypothesis itself must be called into question. Such is the case with the hypothesis of a Q community whose activities included the manufacturing of the Son of Man sayings of Jesus. *In these views of tradition history, there is nothing which logically can be denied to Jesus.* Against Vaage for example, we fail to see how "biblical tradition and metaphors of violence" suggest redactional activity peculiar to Q. Do not Biblical traditions and images of violence coalesce in Jesus' statements about the coming of the Son of Man in Mk 13? On the basis of the criterion of multiple attestation an argument could be made that such images suggest dominical origin![70]

If the hypothesis of the creation of the Son of Man sayings within a final redaction of Q is poorly based, what about at an intermediate level of redaction? Adela Y. Collins, whose methodology is similar to Schürmann's, has recently concluded that Son of Man sayings appear at every stage of the formation of Q.[71] Yet, while the history of the combination of Jesus' sayings must have taken place in a compositional fashion, we fail to see how compositional investigations relate

---

[69] Schürmann's conclusions are not entirely convincing, however. That the Q SM sayings were "floating logia" secondarily inserted into their present locations does not necessarily suggest that the logia themselves are secondary. Elsewhere Schürmann argues that isolated logia are more likely to be authentic ("Das Zeugnis der Redenquelle für die Basileia-Verkündigung Jesu", *Logia*, 155). Furthermore, six Son of Man sayings exist in the middle of Q blocks (Lk 12:8, 9; 12:10; 12:39, 40; 17:24; 17:26, 27; 17:28-30 par.) and, therefore can only be said to be introductions or conclusions on the basis of Schürmann's speculative arrangement of the Q material.

[70] So C.M. Tuckett, "On the Stratification of Q, a Response", *Semeia* 55 (1992) 221: "At the very least, one must say that conflict, hostility and rejection seem endemic to the SM sayings in Q. In turn this makes the SM in Q not so dissimilar at one level from the SM in Mark who is above all a figure who "must" suffer and die (Mark 8:31, etc.). The terminology is not identical, but there is an underlying agreement here which makes it at least plausible that some such idea might be traceable back to Jesus."

[71] "The Son of Man Sayings in the Sayings Source", in *To Touch the Text*, FS Joseph A. Fitzmyer; New York: Crossroad (1989) 369-89. Collins perceives four compositional stages: (a) the oldest 'individual' sayings (Mt. 24:26-27//Lk. 17:23-24); (b) the stage at which individual sayings are linked (Mt. 24:44//Lk. 12:40); (c) the stage at which sayings were added as introductions or conclusions (Lk. 12:8-9); (d) the final compositional stage when larger speeches were created (Mt. 24:37-39//Lk. 17:26-27; Lk. 11:30).

to the rather different question of authenticity. For to say that a saying entered Q at an intermediate or final stage of composition does not necessarily suggest that saying's secondary origin. Clearly an authentic saying could be placed into a secondary context or arrangement. Hence we question Schürmann's sceptical conclusions on authenticity. Lack of evidence to support early church creation and the abundant Son of Man sayings throughout the Synoptics (in stark contrast to contemporary Jewish and Christian documents) remain persuasive support in our opinion for the likelihood that Jesus himself took up the phrase and applied it to himself. In any case, it can be stated confidently that no positive evidence points to a variant Son of Man christology within Q.

In chapters 3 and 4 we demonstrated that wisdom and prophecy complement one another as messianic attributes of Jesus and thus need not be considered signals of Q redaction or signs of independent compositional layers. The self-designation "Son of Man" is equally harmonious to Jesus' messianic identity and coheres with his wisdom teaching and his anointing with the Spirit. 4 Ezra 13:37, 52 and 1 En. 48:10; 52:4 identify the Son of Man as Messiah and assume the 'one like a son of man' in Dn. 7:13, 14 is an individual figure.[72] Hence there exists a historical relationship between the self-designation "Son of Man" and the Messiah. That Jesus could have identified himself with the figure of Dn. 7:13, 14 and been aware of the traditions behind 4 Ezra and 1 Enoch, which attributed Messianic connotations to the self-designation, opens the way to the probability that another apparent earmark of Q redaction—the Son of Man—actually finds its origin in the Messianic consciousness of Jesus himself. And in view of the broad parallels between Q and the book of Daniel, it appears likely that Jesus could have voiced Son of Man sayings which on the one hand conform to idiomatic Aramaic usage, but which on the other hand convey the veiled irony of Jesus' authority as the human and yet Danielic Son of Man (Lk. 7:34//Mt. 11:19; Lk. 9:58//Mt. 8:20). "This generation" in Q is foolish because it has rejected Jesus the Son of Man who mediates the wisdom concomitant with entering the kingdom of God. The close association of the Son of Man with the kingdom of God is not to be severed—the two concepts coexist in Daniel as they do in the Q sayings of Jesus.[73]

---

[72] See W. Horbury, "The Messianic Associations of 'The Son of Man'", *JTS* 36 (1985) 34-55; J.J. Collins, "The Son of Man in First Century Judaism", 457f.; C. Caragounis, *The Son of Man.*

[73] So I.H. Marshall ("The Synoptic Son of Man Sayings in Recent Discussion", *NTS* 12 [1965-66] 327-51) and more recently C. Caragounis (*The Son of Man*, 232-242). *Contra* P. Vielhauer, "Gottesreich und Menschensohn in der Verkündigung Jesu", *Festschrift für Gunther Dehn*, Neukirchen: Kreis Moers (1957) 51-79.

Chapter 7

The Kingdom of God in Q

I. Introduction

In this chapter we shall analyse the kingdom of God sayings in Q for the purpose of addressing five primary questions.

First, to clarify the eschatological contours of Q. Do the Q kingdom of God sayings reveal a characteristic Q perception of a present, imminently coming (P. Hoffmann), or delayed (D. Lührmann, S. Schulz) advent of the kingdom? U. Luz has written that Mark and Q differ significantly in their eschatological perspectives. Where Q emphasizes the presence of God's rule in Jesus' ministry, Mark's tradition, according to Luz, seems to lack eschatological orientation.[1] C. Mearns, in contrast, has recently argued that Q contains a thoroughly "futuristic eschatology."[2] In response to both scholars, we hope to clarify that the kingdom of God in Q has present and future dimensions—neither dimension requiring explanation on the basis of Q community *Tendenz*.

The use of a single eschatological phrase to designate fulfillment both in the present and in the future has historical precedent in the OT expression the Day of the Lord. In a few instances the classical prophets announce that the Day of the Lord already has come—especially in the historical disaster that befell Jerusalem and in the deportment to Babylon (Lam. 1:21; 2:22; 3:2; Eze. 7:2, 3, 6, 24; Obad. 15). In other instances expectation is in the near future: (Isa. 13:6, 9; 26:21; Jer. 4:9; Zph. 1:7) and in other cases the distant future (Amos 5:18; Isa. 24:21; 60:1f.; Micah 4:6; Mal. 3:5). Hence a first-century reader of the OT literary prophets could have interpreted the Day of the Lord as an event taking place in more than one place and time. Further, D. Allison has shown on the basis of Jubilees 23 and

---

[1] "Das Jesusbild der vormarkinischen Tradition", *Jesus Christus in Historie und Theologie,* FS H. Conzelmann, Ed. G. Strecker; Tübingen: JCB Mohr [Paul Siebeck] (1975) 359: "Die zunächst an den Q-Varianten im Markusevangelium festgestellte Tendenz zur Enteschatologisierung ist in der Markusüberlieferung weit verbreitet."

[2] "Realized Eschatology in Q? A Consideration of the Sayings in Luke 7.22, 11.20 and 16.16", *SJT* 40 (1987) 189: "The hypothesis I wish to maintain is that Q has a consistently futurist eschatology."

1 En. 91:12-17; 93 that "Jewish thinking could envision the final events—the judgement of evil and the arrival of the kingdom of God—as extending over time, and as a process or series of events that could involve the present."[3] Thus the scholarly dichotomy between the present and future dimensions in Q may be entirely unnecessary, not requiring explanation on the basis of the supposed eschatological enthusiasm which purportedly induced Q redaction. Because both present and future eschatology have Jewish precedents, historically it is possible that Jesus could have interpreted the kingdom of God as present in his acts and preaching while at the same time still future in the anticipated future consummation of the kingdom in the final judgement and in the final gathering of God's people for eschatological salvation. In the pages that follow we hope to support this possibility.

Second, in analyzing the kingdom of God sayings in Q, we address the question of the Q community idea and its relation to Jesus. We intend to show that in Q there is a clear portrait of Jesus' attempt to gather people into the saving grace of God's kingdom. The community element in Q appears through Jesus' own ministry where the kingdom of God is offered as eschatological salvation to people.[4] Those people who accept the saving benefits of Jesus' ministry become the people of God. Thus we hope to show that the concept of community is important in Q, but not in the sense often ascribed (see Ch. 2).

Third, we address the question of Q's christology. In response to scholars such as P.M. Casey and R.A. Horsley, who argue that the miracles and teachings in Q register Jesus as a prophet solely attempting the renewal of Israel,[5] we shall see that the kingdom of God sayings, in addition to what we have already said in Chs. 3 and 4, demand that Jesus be seen as something more than a prophet. In view of their OT background, the christological implications of Jesus' miracles in Q are profound, particularly as they relate to the kingdom of God.[6]

---

[3] *The End of the Ages Has Come*, Philadelphia: Fortress (1985) 17-19, 104-105; *idem*, Davies and Allison, *Matthew* I, 389-90.

[4] So R. Schnackenburg, *God's Rule and Kingdom*, ET Edinburgh: Nelson (1963) 217: "eschatological salvation can never be dissociated from the people of God and the community of God belongs necessarily to the kingdom of God."

[5] Richard A. Horsley, "Q and Jesus: Assumptions, Approaches, and Analyses", *Semeia* 55 (1992) 208, 209. P.M. Casey, *From Jewish Prophet to Gentile God*, 61. The weakness of Casey's study, in our opinion, is his failure to take into consideration the christological significance of Jesus' teachings and actions. Casey bases his conclusions on the late origin of the major christological titles.

[6] *Pace* U. Luz, "Das Jesusbild der vormarkinischen Tradition", 355: "In der Q-Tradition selbst haben – von Lk. 7,1ff abgesehen – die Wunder kein selbständiges Gewicht." See also p. 360. Similarly, E. Schillebeeckx, *Jesus*, 423: ". . . the Q tradition, which is therefore interested only in Jesus' preaching (logia) and hardly at all in his miracles."

Fourth, we address the question of Q redaction. Analyzing successively the kingdom of God passages which are parallel in Matthew and Luke, we will pay particular attention to the hypothesis that the Q materials were originally collected, arranged, edited and in some cases creatively composed by an early esoteric Christian community. H. Koester has written that the saying form, though most original to the Jesus tradition, became acceptable to the orthodox church only through radical critical alteration of form and theological intention: "Critical evaluation of the Gattung, *logoi*, was achieved by Matthew and Luke through imposing the Marcan narrative-kerygma frame upon the sayings tradition represented by Q."[7] From another perspective, C.M. Tuckett and D. Catchpole have asserted that the Lord's prayer and the Q section on cares (Lk. 12:22-31//Mt. 6: 25-33) "provide a specially clear window through which to view the concerns and commitments of the Q community."[8] In response to these assertions and others like them, we analyze the dominant theme within Q, the kingdom of God, to clarify how Matthew and Luke have altered Q. Are the "concerns and commitments" supposedly characteristic of Q different from those of Jesus himself? Do Matthew and Luke alter Q to bury its no longer acceptable "theological intention," or do they simply rephrase Q into language understandable to their listeners? Do the Q kingdom of God sayings reveal a community bias toward John the Baptist and Jesus and even developed concepts of soteriology, christology, law, eschatology, and salvation-history? We will see that a growing number of scholars postulate exactly that. What is their evidence?

And fifth, we address the question of authenticity. While we cannot prove the authenticity of sayings which were voiced nearly two thousand years ago, we shall add to the abundance of evidence which weighs in favour of the dominical origin of the Q kingdom of God sayings. Sayings whose authenticity was once nearly a scholarly consensus have been relegated to uncertainty most notably by the Jesus Seminar in America, which by vote has attempted to confirm among other things the following two propositions:

> Proposition 2: For Jesus, the kingdom of God was *not* an eschatological nor an apocalyptic phenomenon.

---

[7] "Gnomai Diaphoroi: The Origin and Nature of Diversification in the History of Early Christianity", *Trajectories through Early Christianity*, 135.

[8] "Q, Prayer, and the Kingdom: A Rejoinder", *JTS* 40 (1989) 377. Similarly C.M. Tuckett, "Q, Prayer, and the Kingdom", *JTS* 40 (1989) 367, 373.

Proposition 3: No kingdom saying in Mark, Q, or the Gospel of Thomas unequivocally and undoubtedly preserves what Jesus was referring to when he used the symbol of the kingdom of God and its associated conceptuality and images.[9]

We find these propositions remarkable.[10] *The kingdom of God cannot be separated from eschatology.* It is in its very essence an eschatological term. Eschatology is not out of view even in texts such as Mt. 6:33 where the kingdom relates to the sovereign ability of God to provide for man's basic needs.[11] Here, as in Lk. 6:20//Mt. 5:3 and Lk. 11:3//Mt. 6:11, God's present allotment is a foretaste of future salvation in the eschatological feast (Isa. 25). In the Synoptic Gospels, as J. Jeremias successfully affirmed, "the *basileia* is always and everywhere understood in eschatological terms."[12] And while few would identify Jesus as an apocalyptist or as the author of an apocalypse, James H. Charlesworth is certainly correct that "the impact of Jewish apocalypticism and apocalyptic thought upon Jesus is undeniable and pervasive."[13] In the pages that follow we will see that the polling of the Jesus Seminar does not represent a consensus within contemporary NT scholarship. Against those who interpret Q strictly against a Hellenistic background,[14] we will see that the kingdom of God sayings—which establish the primary theme of Q—are dependent upon the background of Biblical Judaism.

The centrality of the kingdom of God surfaces in the following chart which lists the major features and characteristics of Q in order of frequency. The bare data do not of course produce a conclusive portrait of the theological or

---

[9] For the results of this seminar, see: J. Butts, "Probing the Polling: Jesus Seminar Results on the Kingdom Sayings", *Forum* 3,1 (1987) 98-128. Representative of this perspective are the books of Marcus J. Borg: *Conflict, Holiness and Politics in the Teachings of Jesus*, New York/Toronto: Edwin Mellen (1984) and *Jesus: A New Vision*, San Francisco: Harper & Row (1987).

[10] Ben Witherington III, (*The Christology of Jesus* [1990] 192) rightly points out that a non-eschatological reconstruction of Jesus (1) requires the dismissal of all synoptic material referring to the future coming of the kingdom or the Son of Man; (2) requires the dismissal of all other eschatological teaching of Jesus (e.g., Lk. 17; Mk. 13); (3) requires "a reductionist approach" to parables which speak of future judgement; (4) renders difficult the eschatological acts of Jesus (cursing of the fig tree; cleansing the temple); and (5), renders difficult the relation of Jesus and John – John's message is clearly one of eschatological doom.

[11] So C.M. Tuckett, "Q, Prayer, and the Kingdom of God", *JTS* 40 (1989) 374.

[12] *New Testament Theology*, 102.

[13] *Jesus within Judaism*, 42.

[14] J. Kloppenborg, *The Formation of Q*. And more recently, Heinz O. Guenther, "The Sayings Gospel Q and the Quest for Aramaic Sources: Rethinking Christian Origins", *Semeia* 55 (1992) 41-76. See, however, Kloppenborg's recent article "Literary Convention, Self-Evidence and the Social History of the Q People," where he locates the "formative stratum" of Q in "the villages and large towns of Galilee" (100).

christological content of the Q material, but they do suggest its major emphases—
the kingdom of God and the Son of Man.

Major Theological and Christological Concepts of Q

ἡ βασιλεία τοῦ θεοῦ (τῶν οὐρανῶν).	11	(1) 6:20b//5:3f. (2) 7:28//11:11 (3)10:9//10:7 (4) 11:2// 6:9a,10a (5) 11:20//12:28 (6) 12:31//6:33 (7) 13:18f.// 13:31, 32 (8) 13:20, 21//13:33 (9) 13:28//8:12b, 11b, 12a (10) 13:29//8:11a (11) 16:16//11:12[15]
ὁ υἱὸς τοῦ ἀνθρώπου	11	(1) 6:22//5:11 (2) 7:34//11:19 (3) 9:58//8:20 (4) 11:30// 12:40 (5) 12:8//10:32 (6) 12:10//12:32 (7) 12:40//24:44 (8) 17:24//24:27 (9) 17:26//24:37 (10) 17:30//24:39 (11) 22:28//19:28[16]
ὁ πατήρ	8	(1) 6:36//5:48 (2) 10:21a//11:25 (3) 10:21b //11:26 (4) 10:22//11:27 [x3] (7) 11:2//6:9 (8) 11:13//7:11
ὁ ἐρχόμενος	3	(1) 3:16//3:11 (2) 7:20//11:3 (3) 13:35//23:39
{τὸ ἅγιον} πνεῦμα	3	(1) 3:16//3:11 (2) 4:1//4:1 (3) 12:10//12:32[17]
σοφία	3	(1) 7:35//11:19 (2) 11:31//12:42 (3) 11:49 diff. Mt. 23:34
ὁ υἱὸς τοῦ θεοῦ	2	(1) 4:3//4:3 (2) 4:6//4:9
ὁ υἱός	2	10:22//11:27 [x2]

A. The Grounds for Authenticity

On the basis of the criterion of dissimilarity from contemporary Judaism and later
Christian writings, and on the basis of the criterion of multiple attestation in nearly

---

[15] This is a conservative number. H. Schürmann ("Das Zeugnis der Redenquelle für die Basileia-Verkündigung Jesu", *Logia*, 121-200) counts fifteen KG sayings in Q. Those not listed above include: (1) 9:61 diff. Mt.; (2) 12:32 diff. Mt.; (3) Mt. 5:19; (4) Mt. 23:13 diff. Lk. 11:52. J. Schlosser (*Le Règne de Dieu dans les dits de Jésus*, 43) attributes eleven KG sayings to Q including Lk. 22:28-30/Mt. 19:28 which is not included in our list above. H. Merklein (*Die Gottesherrschaft als Handlungsprinzip, Untersuchung zur Ethik Jesu,* Würzburg: Echter Verlag [1981] 21) more conservatively identifies in Q ten sayings but adds that the idea of Kingdom occurs also in the Beelzebul controversy (Lk. 11:17, 18//Mt. 12:25, 26). A. Polag attributes twelve to Q (Lk. 6:20//Mt. 5:3; Lk. 7:28//Mt. 11:11; Lk. 9:62 *Sondergut*; Lk. 10:9//Mt. 10:7; Lk. 11:2//Mt. 6:10; Lk. 11:20//Mt. 12:28; Lk. 12:31//Mt. 6:33; Lk. 12:32 *Sondergut*; Lk. 13:18//Mt. 13:31; Lk. 13:20//Mt. 13:33; Lk. 13:28, 29//Mt. 8:11, 12; Lk. 16:16//Mt. 11:12). To these references, Polag adds two sayings which probably (*wahrscheinlich*) should be attributed to Q (Lk. 22:30 diff. Mt.; Mt. 5:19 *Sondergut*) and one saying which possibly belongs to Q (Lk. 14:15: *Sondergut*). He identifies Lk. 9:60b; 10:11; 19:11 as Lk. redaction and Mt. 7:21; 22:2; 23:13 as Mt. redaction. In *Christologie der Logienquelle*, 49 n. 143.

[16] Mt. 10:23 could also be a Q passage lacking a Q parallel.

[17] τὸ πνεῦμα τοῦ θεοῦ also occurs in Mt. 12:28 where Luke's parallel is ἐν δακτύλῳ θεοῦ.

every location of Jesus' teaching in the Synoptic Gospels,[18] and on the basis of multiple attestation in multiple forms in the Synoptic Gospels (parables, sayings, etc.), and on the basis of comparison to other important themes in Jesus' teaching at large,[19] the kingdom of God sayings in Q have *a priori* grounds for authenticity. In Q the phrase ἡ βασιλεία τοῦ θεοῦ occurs eight times exclusively on the mouth of Jesus,[20] while the phrase ἡ βασιλεία τοῦ πατρός occurs twice,[21] as does βασιλεία alone.[22] In Mark ἡ βασιλεία τοῦ θεοῦ appears thirteen times on the mouth of Jesus,[23] while βασιλεία appears four times.[24] Elsewhere in Mark the theme appears important both in the triumphal entry (11:10) and in the characterization of Joseph of Arimathea (15:43). In Matthew ἡ βασιλεία τῶν οὐρανῶν occurs thirty-two times[25] (6x from Mark;[26] 6x possibly 7x from Q).[27] Four times Matthew attests the phrase ἡ βασιλεία τοῦ θεοῦ;[28] five times the phrase ἡ βασιλεία τοῦ πατρός;[29] two or possibly three times Matthew refers to ἡ βασιλεία τοῦ υἱοῦ τοῦ ἀνθρώπου;[30] three times Matthew refers to the preaching of the gospel of the kingdom (κηρύσσειν τὸ εὐαγγέλιον τῆς βασιλείας);[31] once to the word (ὁ λόγος) of the kingdom (13:19); and twice to the sons of the kingdom.[32] In coherence with the other synoptic writers, Luke uses the phrase ἡ βασιλεία τοῦ θεοῦ thirty-two times[33] (8x possibly 9x from

---

[18] The simple evidence outlined by Jeremias (*New Testament Theology*, 96-108) has not yet been overturned.

[19] As compared with other theological concepts, the Kingdom of God is by far the most frequent on the lips of Jesus. See I.H. Marshall, "The Hope of a New Age: The Kingdom of God in the New Testament", *Jesus the Saviour*, 213, 236 n. 2.

[20] Lk. 6:20//Mt. 5:3; Lk. 7:28//Mt. 11:11; Lk. 10:9//Mt. 10:7; Lk. 11:20//Mt. 12:28; Lk. 13:18//Mt. 13:31; Lk. 13:20//Mt. 13:33; Lk. 13:29//Mt. 8:11; Lk. 16:16//Mt. 11:12

[21] Lk. 11:2//Mt. 6:10; Lk. 12:31//Mt. 6:33

[22] Lk. 11:17//Mt. 12:25; Lk. 11:18//Mt.12:26

[23] 1:15; 4:11, 26, 30; 9:1, 47; 10:14, 15, 23, 24, 25; 12:34; 14:25

[24] 3:24 (x2); 13:8 (x2)

[25] 3:2; 4:17; 5:3, 10, 19 (x2), 20; 7:21; 8:11; 10:7; 11:11, 12; 13:11, 24, 31, 33, 44, 45, 47, 52; 16:19; 18:1, 3, 4, 23; 19:12, 14, 23; 20:1; 22:2; 23:13; 25:1

[26] 4:17 (Mk. 1:15); 13:11 (Mk. 4:11); 13:31 (Mk. 4:30); 18:3 (Mk. 10:15); 19:14 (Mk. 10:14); 19:23 (Mk. 10:23)

[27] 5:3; 8:11; 10:7; 11:11, 12; 13:33 (13:31 also has affinities with Mk. 4:30, hence its origin is a matter of dispute).

[28] 12:28 (Q//Lk. 11:20); 19:24 (Mk. 10:25); 21:31, 43

[29] 6:10 (Q//Lk. 11:2); 6:33 (Q//Lk. 12:31); 13:43; 26:29; 25:34

[30] 13:41; 16:28; and possibly 20:21 diff. Mk. 10:37

[31] 4:23; 9:35; 24:14

[32] 8:12; 13:38

[33] 4:43; 6:20; 7:28; 8:1, 10; 9:2, 11, 27, 60, 62; 10:9, 11; 11:20; 13:18, 20, 28, 29; 14:15; 16:16; 17:20 (x2), 21; 18:16, 17, 24, 25, 29; 19:11; 21:31; 22:16, 18; 23:51

Mk.).[34] Twice Luke adopts the concept ἡ βασιλεία τοῦ πατρός,[35] three times the concept of the kingdom of the son,[36] and once Luke uses the absolute ἡ βασιλεία (12:32). Helmut Merklein represents the vast majority when he concludes from this data, on the basis of multiple attestation, that the "kingdom pronouncement" represents the authentic preaching of Jesus—"Die Verkündigung von der 'Gottesherrschaft'" does not commence with the preaching of the post-Easter church.[37] The burden of proof, therefore, rests upon those who would deny the authenticity of the Q kingdom of God sayings. Confidence in this assertion grows stronger when we observe that the Q sayings are doubly attested in Matthew and Luke. If Q is a valid hypothesis, the two evangelists independently valued the Q kingdom of God sayings as authentic Jesus tradition.[38] Would Matthew and Luke have valued Q if its content was somehow suspect? Second, we believe it is telling that sayings are not actually placed upon the lips of Jesus in Q in the manner in which they are in later documents—as they are for instance in the Gospel of Thomas. The name Jesus does not appear so that the sayings' dominical origin must have been assumed throughout the transmission process. Independently, Matthew and Luke attributed these sayings to Jesus without feeling the need to preface them with "Jesus said" as the editor of the

---

[34] 8:10 (Mk. 4:11); 9:27 (Mk. 9:1); 13:18 (Q but compare Mk. 4:30); 18:16 (Mk. 10:14); 18:17 (Mk. 10:15); 18:24 (Mk. 10:23); 18:25 (Mk. 10:25); 22:18 (Mk. 14:25); 23:51 (Mk. 15:43)

[35] 11:2; 12:31

[36] 1:33(?); 22:29, 30; 23:42

[37] *Die Gottesherrschaft als Handlungsprinzip: Untersuchung zur Ethik Jesu,* 25. Representative advocates of this general conclusion include: J. Jeremias, *New Testament Theology* I, 96; R. Schnackenburg, *God's Rule and Kingdom,* 77f.; G.E. Ladd, *Jesus and the Kingdom,* 118; R.T. France, *Divine Government,* 1; I.H. Marshall, "The Hope of a New Age: The Kingdom of God in the New Testament", 213, 214. H. Schürmann (*Gottes Reich –Jesu Geschick,* Freiburg: Herder, 1983) and N. Perrin (*Rediscovering the Teaching of Jesus,* New York: Harper &Row, 1967) represent more skeptical persuasions, yet both maintain a minimal number of authentic sayings (Perrin: Mt. 12:28//Lk. 11:20; Lk. 17:20; Lk. 16:16//Mt. 11:12; Schürmann, 135: Lk. 11:2-4; 6:20; 11:20; 12:31; and 13:18f. par). Two notable sceptics are W. Schenk ("Gefangenschaft und Tod des Täufers Erwängungen zur Chronologie und ihren Konsequenzen", *NTS* 29 [1983] 453-483 [456]) who, appealing to the kingdom perception of John the Baptist, discounts the uniqueness of Jesus' kingdom language, and E. Bammel ("Erwägungen zur Eschatologie Jesu", *Studia Evangelica III* ; Berlin: Akademie Verlag [1964] 3-32) who concludes: "*Βασιλεία* ist je und dann ein Ausgangspunkt, keinswegs aber der zentrale Begriffe in der Verkündigung Jesu gewesen" (18). However, Jesus' pronouncement of the kingdom stresses salvation, John's stresses judgement. Bammel's conclusion results from unwarranted scepticism. He underestimates the importance of the kingdom of God in Mark: "in der Darstellung der Verkündigung Jesu kommt es doch merkwürdig spärlich vor." Yet Pesch (*Markus* I, 107) says the opposite: "Gottes Herrschaft ist nach dem Bericht des Markus der zentrale Begriff von Predigt und Lehre Jesu . . ." In Q he claims only Mt. 12:28//Lk. 11:20 goes back to Jesus with certainty. The scholarly consensus is otherwise.

[38] See J.D.G. Dunn, *The Evidence for Jesus,* London: SCM (1985) 7, 8.

Gospel of Thomas did repeatedly. A lack of explicit references to Jesus suggests that the audience recognized the sayings' content to be dominical. Thus until there are convincing linguistic or conceptual reasons for denying these sayings to Jesus, we will continue to take their authenticity seriously.

With this broad body of evidence before us, it comes as a surprise that H. Schürmann believes only five kingdom sayings in Q represent the *ipsissima verba Jesu*.[39] Ten, according to Schürmann, are addition words (*Zusatzworten*) which reflect the secondary theological ideas of post-Easter preaching.[40] While Schürmann concedes that three *Zusatzworte* may be kerygmatic transformations of authentic sayings—thus containing the *vox Jesu* [41]—and one may even be a redactional transformation of an *ipsissimum verbum Jesu*,[42] we are left wondering how he is able to make such qualitative judgements. The answer lies primarily in his criteria for determining authenticity:

1. If a saying could have existed independently during its transmission it is likely to be dominical. If it is dependent upon its context it is likely to be secondary.
2. Evidence of Easter experience or kerygmatic coloring bespeaks secondary origin.
3. Church orientation according to ecclesiology, christology, pneumatology, salvation-history, law, a Gentile mission etc., argues for secondary origin.
4. Anti-Jewish polemic or anti-John the Baptist polemic indicates secondary community origin.
5. A saying which explicitly fulfils OT prophetic material (LXX or MT) is likely to be secondary.

---

[39] "Das Zeugnis der Redenquelle für die Basileia-Verkündigung Jesu." In *Logia*, 121-200 (177-79). Lk. 6:20//Mt. 5:3; Lk. 11:20//Mt. 12:28; Lk. 12:31//Mt. 6:33; Lk. 13:18f.//Mt. 13:31, 32; Lk. 11:2f//Mt. 6:9f. Schürmann's conclusions correlate with his conjecture concerning the history of composition behind the saying's source. According to Schürmann Q developed in successive stages: (1) *Grundworte* – isolated logia, (2) *Zusatzworte* – interpretive additions, (3) *Spruchreihen* – saying rows grouped according to theme or catch-phrase, 4) *frühe Kompositionen* – early compositions, and 5) *Sammlung* – the final collection (128-132). Each stage does not necessarily lead to the other. For instance a sayings pair could enter a later speech without having been part of a sayings group or row. We find Schürmann's thesis convincing in part; however, we are uncomfortable with the uncertainty that at first only minute sayings of Jesus could have been transmitted and only subsequently entered larger bodies of synoptic material. The unity within Schürmann's later compositional forms may suggest that that material may have been a unity from the beginning. Surely Jesus spoke in language broader than individual pithy sayings. Furthermore, we do not believe Schürmann's composition theory is a valid criterion for judging authenticity. That a composition is secondary in arrangement does not imply that its parts are secondary in origin. For a more recent but very similar statement of the composition of Q, see Schürmann's article "Zur Kompositionsgeschichte der Redenquelle. Beobachtungen an der lukanischen Q-Vorlage", *Der Treue Gottes Trauen*, FS G. Schneider; Freiburg: Herder (1991) 325-342.

[40] Lk. 7:28//Mt. 11:11; Lk. 9:61 diff Mt.; Lk. 10:9//Mt. 10:7; Lk. 12:32 *Sondergut*; Lk. 13:20//Mt. 13:33; Lk. 13:28//Mt. 8:11; Lk. 13:29//Mt. 8:12; Mt. 5:19; Lk. 16:16//Mt. 11:13, 12; Mt. 23:13

[41] Lk. 9:61f.; Lk. 10:9//Mt. 10:7; Lk. 13:20//Mt. 13:33

[42] Lk. 16:16//Mt. 11:13

6. A saying colored by apocalyptic imagery is likely secondary.

7. Criterion of Coherence: A kingdom of God saying which differs in orientation from an agreed upon authentic saying such as the Lord's prayer (Lk. 11:2f.) is secondary.

In the pages that follow we will question several of these criteria. Is there clear evidence of Easter experience or kerygmatic coloring in these sayings? Is there evidence of church orientation? Is there anti-Jewish polemic which could not be ascribed to Jesus? Is there evidence of anti-John polemic? Is it really valid to say that any saying that has apocalyptic coloring or which seems to fulfil OT prophecy is likely to be secondary? And is Schürmann following a valid procedure in weighing each saying against his interpretation of the Lord's prayer (Lk. 11:2)? Could Jesus have used the dynamic phrase "kingdom of God" with different emphases in different contexts? Confronting these questions, we believe it is quite possible that what has been often attributed to the *Tendenz* of the Q community may more validly be said of Jesus himself.

B.   The Meaning of the Kingdom of God in the Sayings of Jesus

The "kingdom of God" in the Synoptic Gospels in general and Q in particular is an enigmatic abstract phrase which defies systematic classification according to ethics, eschatology, or apocalyptic. However, three features characterize the kingdom of God in the Synoptic Gospels.

First, 'the kingdom', is 'of God': the mere phrase communicates the power, authority, justice, righteousness, eternal nature, and salvific plan of God. The "kingdom of God" calls to mind the cosmic rule or kingship which the Jews exclusively associated with their God YHWH. Hence, "the kingdom of God" has been defined in recent scholarship as "God's dynamic presence," "God in Strength," "Divine Government," "the sovereign activity of God," and "God's Kingship."[43] Equally apparent in the Synoptic Gospels, however, is the idea of the kingdom of God as the future realm to be set up by God at the end of the age. While the past, present, and future aspects of "the kingdom of God" in the sayings of Jesus may well relate directly to the eternal nature of God, the clear distinction between present and future sayings mandates an explanation of their relation— perhaps with the future being the fulfillment or consummation of the present.

Secondly, ἡ βασιλεία τοῦ θεοῦ is a Semitic phrase perhaps reflecting the Aramaic expression (מלכותא די־אלהא / מלכות אלהא) which recalls the character of

---

[43] B. Chilton, *God in Strength*, Linz: Plöchl (1979) 89, 283f; *idem*, "Introduction", *The Kingdom of God, Issues in Religion and Theology*, 5, 25, 26; R. Schnackenburg, *God's Rule and Kingdom*, 348; H. Schürmann, *Das Gebet des Herrn*, Freiburg: Herder (1958) 41f.; R.T. France, *Divine Government*, London: SPCK (1990) 12f.

God's universal rule over all creation, the nations of the earth, and His people Israel. "Kingdom of God" calls to mind God's action in the OT where God's rule benefits man in acts of salvation, but also where God's justice necessitates punitive judgement.[44] The fact that Jesus saturates his kingdom of God sayings with allusions to the OT confirms this point. The kingdom of God, therefore, was not a revolutionary idea on the lips of Jesus, but as R.T. France states: "already carried deeply significant connotations, and was well calculated to set his audience buzzing with enthusiastic expectation, however varied those expectations may have been."[45] The kingdom of God occasioned a response.

And thirdly, as noted above, the kingdom of God in the Synoptic Gospels is inextricably bound to the ministry of Jesus. While John the Baptist warns of the wrath he anticipates at God's coming, it is through Jesus' ministry that God's rule takes visible form in the announcement of good news to the poor, in salvific healings, and in the defeat of demonic powers. With these happenings in view, A. Polag defines the kingdom of God as a label for the eschatological rule of God which imparts a sphere of eschatological salvation whose beginning among men appears in the acts and preaching of Jesus.[46] While it is true that the kingdom of God is not a christological term, Jesus' relationship to the kingdom is commensurate with his unique relationship with God in that Jesus mediates God's saving power in a unique way. As the one who mediates God's saving rule, Jesus assumes unique authority in Q as he does in the Synoptic Gospels as a whole.

II. Lk. 6:20//Mt. 5:3

In Lk. 6:20//Mt. 5:3 Jesus fulfils the role of the anointed messenger of God prophesied to bring eschatological salvation to the poor. Jesus' words fulfil Isa. 61:1f. The first beatitude is Jewish in content and its location within a collection of beatitudes of varying form is Jewish, as the discovery of 4Q 525 has proven.[47] There exists no certainty that 6:20//5:3 ever existed in a "deconstructed" "de-edited" form. If it did, however, the distinctions between $αὐτῶν$[48] and $τῶν$

---

[44] See G.R. Beasley-Murray, *Jesus and the Kingdom of God*, 3-35; R. Schnackenburg, *God's Rule and Kingdom*, 11-75.

[45] *Divine Government*, 21.

[46] *Christologie der Logienquelle*, 56, 59.

[47] See J.A. Fitzmyer, "A Palestinian Collection of Beatitudes." In *The Four Gospels*, FS F. Neirynck; Leuven: Leuven U.P. (1992) 513: "For Jesus' utterance of beatitudes was not simply an imitation of a well-known Palestinian Jewish form, but the utterance of them in multiple form is now also seen as characteristic of that background."

[48] The third person appears prevalent among beatitudes in OT and Intertestamental Judaism, however, the second person also has witnesses.

οὐρανῶν,[49] on the one hand, and ὑμετέρα and τοῦ θεοῦ, on the other hand, do not greatly affect the beatitude's meaning. Matthew's τῷ πνεύματι only emphasizes what Luke implies.[50] The second clause requires a religious meaning for both texts: The poor are fortunate now because they are in fact receiving the good news which Jesus preaches and the healing blessings which Jesus administers. The three following beatitudes, which focus on the future, do not alter the present blessing but intensify it: because the poor have now received the kingdom as represented in Jesus' ministry, they will at the final judgement receive in full the saving grace of God's sovereignty.

The first three beatitudes follow the same form (μακάριος + subject + ὅτι clause). They divide into two parts: the first part addressing a situation of misery, and the second part announcing the reason why the identified audience is blessed. Scrupulous analysis of the beatitude form has resulted in the discovery of beatitudes both in wisdom literature, where the emphasis is on good fortune in this world often as a result of ethical behavior, and in apocalyptic writings where "the blessed" are people facing literal misfortune on earth and whose hope is fixed purely on future salvation which will come with the Day of the Lord (Isa. 30:18; 32:30; Dn. 12:12). In our context μακάριος denotes an announcement of good fortune toward the identified listeners who are counted as "blessed" as a result of their encounter with Jesus. In meeting Jesus the poor experience the saving benefits characteristic of God's saving rule.

---

[49] In determining which qualifying phrase represents the original ("of God" or "of heaven") most scholars have appraised τῶν οὐρανῶν as redactional as the phrase occurs thirty-two times in Matthew and nowhere else in the NT. Semantically, the distinction is slight if at all as Matthew uses both phrases interchangeably. Guelich, however, argues that Matthew broadens the meaning by transmitting the OT concept of heaven as God's realm "where, enthroned, he rules over all the world." Thus when τῶν οὐρανῶν fastens to the dynamic rule denoted by βασιλεία the result is a double reference to the sovereign rule or reign of God (*The Sermon on the Mount*, Waco: Word [1982] 77). M. Pamment ("The Kingdom of Heaven According to the First Gospel," *NTS* 27 [1981] 211-232) has made the case that in Matthew "the kingdom of heaven" refers to an imminent but entirely future reality while "the kingdom of God" refers to a present reality on earth where the will of God is performed (229, 232). We do not find Pamment's arguments to be fully convincing. The distinction requires that Mt. 6:10 (the second petition of the Lord's prayer) be understood in the present – a temporal understanding few would concede. Furthermore, we are not convinced that in Mt. the first beatitude (kingdom of heaven) refers to an exclusively future blessing. As the saving characteristics of Isa. 61:1f. are present in Jesus' ministry, so the kingdom of heaven is in some sense present as well. The distinction between the two phrases is difficult to maintain.

[50] J.H. Charlesworth (*Jesus within Judaism*, 68-70) notes that the Essenes of the Qumran community conceived of themselves as both the "poor" and the "poor in spirit." See 1QM 11:9, 13; 13:12-14 and elsewhere in the War Scroll.

The note of irony which clamors throughout the beatitudes appears immediately in the first breath "Blessed are the poor."[51] Is "the poor" a technical term for members of the Q community? The NT allows little evidence to suggest so.[52] In fact "the poor" fits the description of the church in Jerusalem as adequately as a hypothetical esoteric group in Galilee. Clearly Lk. 6:20//Mt. 5:3, as a saying of Jesus, would have brought comfort to the earliest Church in Jerusalem.

How do we identify οἱ πτωχοί—as the literal destitute[53] or as the religious poor—those who have turned in need to God? The evidence is mixed. πτωχός occurs one hundred times in the LXX: thirty-nine times for the adjective עָנִי[54] (poor, afflicted, humble);[55] twenty-one times for the adjective דַּל (low, weak, poor, thin, helpless);[56] ten times for the adjective אֶבְיוֹן (in want, needy, beggar, poor). πτωχός translates רָשׁ (in want, famished)[57] and less frequently מִסְכֵּן (poor, needy, beggar)[58] and חֵלְכָה (hapless, luckless, unfortunate, dejected).[59] Each Hebrew term denotes economic poverty. Frequently in the OT, however, πτωχός and its Hebrew equivalents take on a religious meaning. Especially in the Psalms

---

[51] The qualifying phrase "in spirit" has been identified as Matthean redaction by most commentators for four notable reasons: (1) poor occurs without qualification in Mt. 11:5//Lk. 7:22; (2) "in spirit" disrupts perfect parallelism; (3) Lk. 6:24 has "the rich" without a modifier "which implies an unqualified "the poor" in at least Qlk"; and (4), Matthew customarily adds qualifying phrases (5:6a, 32; 6:13b; 13:12b; 19:9; see Davies and Allison, *Matthew* I, 442). Yet, the "poor in spirit" has a Hebrew equivalent in 1QM 14:7 which allows the possibility that τῷ πνεύματι may have existed prior to Matthew's recording. Most importantly, if the religious nuance of "poor" exists in the Lukan version as I.H. Marshall (*Luke*, 250), Davies and Allison (*Matthew* I, 444), and R.A. Guelich (*The Sermon on the Mount*, 75) have argued, the differences between the two versions may be minimal with Luke implying what Matthew emphasizes.

[52] L.E. Keck, "The Poor Among the Saints in the New Testament", *ZNW* 56 (1965) 100-129.

[53] Representatives of an exclusively economic interpretation include: J. Lambrecht, *The Sermon on the Mount*, ET Wilmington: Glazier (1985) 55; J. Fitzmyer, *Luke* I, 631; U. Luz, *Das Evangelium nach Matthäus* I, Zürich: Benziger (1985) 205; S. Schulz, *Q–Die Spruchquelle*, 81.

[54] F. Hauck and E. Bammel, "πτωχός", *TDNT* VI, 889.

[55] *BDB*, 776, 777.

[56] *BDB*, 195.

[57] *BDB*, 930.

[58] *BDB*, 587.

[59] *BDB*, 319.

πτωχοί identifies the pious who admit need of God's help.[60]   And later in Jewish literature "the poor" is a designation for the oppressed people of God.[61]

Evidence supports an implicit religious interpretation of "the poor." First, the saying's content requires a Jewish rather than Greek background as a result of its climax—the blessing of the kingdom (the Greek background of πτωχός is purely economic).[62] Second, rich and poor have clear religious denotations in the OT. The rich are associated with wealth and sin (especially the breaking of God's law which demands the protection of the poor),[63] and the "poor," as we have noted, is the characteristic name in later OT writings for people who have turned in need to God for protection and provision.[64] Third, Luke communicates a religious sense both for the rich who have taken God for granted and for the poor who find their only hope in God (1:48, 53; 14:21-23; 16:25). There exists no evidence that the poor are blessed because of their poverty alone. Fourth, and perhaps most importantly, the parallels between πτωχοί in Lk. 6:20//Mt. 5:3 and πτωχοῖς in Isa. 61:1f. and between πενθοῦντε . . . παρακληθήσονται in Mt. 5:4 and παρακαλέσαι πάντας τοὺς πενθοῦντας in Isa. 61:2 seem to demand a religious interpretation.[65] The poor are specifically those who witness the arrival of the eschatological herald of good news.

In Isa. 61:1f., the poor are those who receive from the anointed herald the good news that freedom, liberty, the favorable year of the Lord, and "the day of vengeance of our God" have come.[66] Davies and Allison observe that like Lk. 6:20//Mt. 5:3 the association of a beatitude with the fulfillment of Isa. 61:1f. occurs elsewhere in Q in Lk. 7:22, 23//Mt. 11:4-6 where immediately after announcing to John's disciples that the poor have the gospel preached to them, Jesus voices the beatitude: "And blessed is he who keeps from stumbling over me." From this connection, they conclude "that Jesus associated the makarism

---

[60] Ps. 12:5; 14:6; 22:24; 37:14; 69:29; 70:5; 86:1; 88:15; Isa. 61:1. Davies and Allison note that in Ps. 35:10; 37:14; 40:17; 70:5; 86:1; and 109:22, "πτωχός καὶ πένης" is a fixed expression used of the attitude of one in prayer", *Matthew* I, 443 n. 19.

[61] Isa. 10:2; 26:6; Ps. Sol. 5:2, 11; 10:6; 15:1; 18:2; 1QpHab. 12:3; 1QM 14:7; 1QH 5:13-14; 4QpPs 2:9-10. See Davies and Allison, *ibid.*, 443.

[62] Guelich, *The Sermon on the Mount*, 68; F. Hauck and E. Bammel, "πτωχός", *TDNT* VI, 889.

[63] Georg Strecker, *The Sermon on the Mount: An Exegetical Commentary*, ET Nashville: Abingdon (1988) 31f.

[64] Ps. 25:9; 34:2; 37:11; 76:9; 147:6; 149:4. See Guelich, *The Sermon on the Mount*, 69.

[65] See Davies and Allison, *Matthew* I, 436-438, who ascribe Mt. 5:3-4, 6, and 11-12 to Q and 5:5, 7, 8, and 9 to Qmt. Among these, they find persuasive allusions to Isa. 61:1f. in 5:3, 4, and 5.

[66] Watts, *Isaiah* II, 302.

form with the OT text about good news for the poor."[67]   The poor are blessed because they have recognized their need for Jesus' ministry and have thus accepted the salvation offered to them. They are blessed because they have identified with Jesus. This image compares favorably with Jesus' commission of disciples in Q: "Carry no purse, no bag, no shoes" (Lk. 10:4a; Mt. 10:9, 10a; Mk. 6:8). For these, life's normal responsibilities have been replaced by the demands of following Jesus: "allow the dead to bury their own dead" (Lk. 9:60a//Mt. 8:22b). When this theme complements Jesus' self-witness elsewhere in Q ("a friend of tax collectors and sinners", 7:35b//11:19), it seems reasonable to identify the poor as both the economically poor who were attracted by Jesus' message and the religiously poor—who were in fact social and religious outcasts, "who stood empty-handed, without a power base and pretence, before God."[68]

A.   The Eschatological Significance of the First Beatitude

In contrast to the future orientation of the beatitudes which follow, both Matthew and Luke use the present tense ἐστίν to describe the blessing of the poor. Most commentators tread cautiously here defining ἐστί as a "futuristic present" which "denotes an event which has not yet occurred, but which is regarded as so certain that in thought it may be contemplated as already coming to pass."[69]   G.R. Beasley-Murray correctly stresses that the beatitudes evoke the prospect of future salvation,[70] yet Guelich is also correct in noting that the fulfillment of Isa. 61:1f includes the present.[71] Keeping both in view, A. Polag correctly underscores the importance of Jesus' acts:

> Die Heilaussage als solche, d.h. das Tun Jesus, wird in keiner Weise motiviert oder begründet; sie steht einfach als Faktum da. Durch sie wird aber eine besondere Situation verursacht, nämlich die der Heilszuwendung an die »Armen«, und diese hat in den Verheißungen der Schrift einen bestimmten Stellenwert: sie markiert den Beginn des endzeitlichen Heilshandelns Gottes.[72]

Indeed, by preaching good news to the poor, healing the sick (Lk. 7:22), and eating with sinners and tax collectors, Jesus fulfils Isa. 61:1f., so that the time of salvation has in effect begun. It is noteworthy that from a different perspective, S.

---

[67] *Matthew* II, 438.

[68] Guelich, *The Sermon on the Mount*, 71.

[69] Dana and Mantey, *A Manual Grammar of the Greek New Testament*, 185.

[70] *Jesus and the Kingdom of God*, 162.

[71] *The Sermon on the Mount*, 76.

[72] *Die Christologie der Logienquelle*, 42.

Schulz also takes the present tense at face value in asserting that through the salvation call of Jewish-Christian prophets an apocalyptic-future salvation has broken into the present.[73] Emphasizing the social character of the blessing, H. Merklein concurs: "Doch bleibt—im Vorgriff auf die weitere Untersuchung—zu betonen, daß Jesus das Heil der kommenden Gottesherrschaft für die nächste Nähe erwartet und sogar in die Gegenwart hineinragen sieht."[74] Lk. 6:20//Mt. 5:3 denotes the present fulfillment of Isa. 61:1f. and the advent though not consummation of eschatological salvation.[75] The poor are not blessed simply because of their economic status, but because "theirs is the Kingdom of God." The eschatological reign of God has commenced with Jesus' preaching and his ministry to the poor: The poor are blessed both because they are the recipients of Jesus' ministry now, and because they will receive the full benefits of God's favour in the future judgement. The salvific force of Lk. 6:20//Mt. 5:3, then, should not be confined exclusively to present or future soteriology. Salvation has begun though it has not yet consummated. The eschatological people of God have begun to be gathered by Jesus.

B. The Christological Significance of the First Beatitude

In Q Isa. 61:1f. is the only OT passage which Jesus directly adopts in interpreting his own ministry (Lk. 7:22//Mt. 11:5). The allusion is similar to Jesus' appeal to Isa. 61:1f. in Lk. 4:18,19. As a result H. Schürmann[76] and C. Tuckett[77] have both attempted to explain Lk. 4:18, 19 as a Q passage unused or unavailable to Matthew. Tuckett concludes "the application of Isa. 61 to Jesus was an important, and distinctive, feature of Q's christology."[78] Both Schürmann and Tuckett convincingly demonstrate that the full quotation of Isa. 61:1 in Lk. 4 is thematically uncharacteristic of Luke and therefore should not be registered as redaction. This likelihood does not demand that Lk. 4:18, 19 be classified as Q redaction, however, as it could just as logically be Q tradition. Indeed, it is unclear that Lk. 4:18, 19 should be ascribed to Q at all. The parallel usage of *Ναζαρά* in Lk. 4:16//Mt. 4:13 may be coincidental, while the supposed thematic links between

[73] *Q Die Spruchquelle,* 81.

[74] *Die Gottesherrschatft als Handlungsprinzip: Untersuchung zur Ethic Jesu,* 54.

[75] So also J. Dunn, *Jesus and the Spirit,* London: SCM (1975) 55: "Rather by their very style and content they seem to express an already established, deeply held and firm assurance of Jesus that the Isianic prophecy was being fulfilled in himself and his ministry."

[76] Der «Bericht vom Anfang». Ein Rekonstruktionsversuch auf Grund von Lk. 4,14-16, *Studia Evangelica* II (*TU*, 87), Berlin (1964) 242-258.

[77] "Luke 4,16-30, Isaiah and Q", *Logia,* 343-361.

[78] *Ibid.,* 354.

Lk. 4:18, 19 and Q are very general and could well be said of Jesus' synoptic preaching as a whole.[79] The best solution, in our view, on the basis of multiple attestation, is that Lk. 4:18, 19, Lk. 6:20//Mt. 5:3, and Lk. 7:22//Mt. 11:5 attest to Jesus' application of Isa. 61:1f to his own ministry. The authenticity of the first beatitude is agreed upon by Beasley-Murray,[80] J. Dupont,[81] E. Schweizer,[82] I.H. Marshall,[83] S. Schulz,[84] Davies and Allison,[85] A. Polag,[86] J. Lambrecht,[87] J. Jeremias,[88] and H. Schürmann.[89] If these scholars are correct, and if Isa. 61:1f. is the background to the first beatitude, we have, as Davies and Allison suggest, a very early testimony to Jesus' message of salvation:

> . . . if Jesus did utter the beatitudes, he must have done so conscious of being the eschatological herald who had been anointed by God and given the Spirit. And those who heard him would not have missed this. Interpreted against the background of Isa 61:1-2, Mt. 5:3, 4, and 6 with their Lukan parallels constitute a paradigmatic example of "eschatology in the process of realization". On the one hand, salvation is not yet. The hungry *will* be satisfied. Those who weep *will* laugh. The poor *will* enter the kingdom of God. On the other hand, the anointed, Spirit-bearing herald of Isa 61 has already appeared. He has already brought good tidings to the poor. He has already comforted those who mourn. Prophecy has been fulfilled. Eschatology has entered the present.[90]

J. Lambrecht comprehends a similar emphasis: "Although it is not explicit, there is a christological and salvation historical background to the first three beatitudes.

---

[79] Tuckett ("Luke 4,16-30, Isaiah and Q", 353) lists the following thematic links: (a) Jesus' referring to individuals and whole stories rather than isolated texts in the OT, (b) Jesus' combining a threat against the Jews with a promise to non-Jews, and (c) the references to Elijah and Elisha in 4:18 may link up with the miracles in Lk. 7:22//Mt. 11:5. However, (a) seems problematic as Jesus is here responding to an isolated text; (b) there is no evidence in 7:22//11:5 that Jesus is exclusively judging the Jews or blessing non-Jews; and (c), the link between the references to Elijah and Elisha in Lk. 4:18 and the miracles in Lk. 7:22//11:5 are speculative. The miracles in 7:22 are better explained as Jesus' fulfilment of Isa 29:18; 35:5, 6; 42:18; 26:19; and 61:1.

[80] *Jesus and the Kingdom of God*, 157.

[81] *Les Béatitudes* I, 210-212.

[82] *Matthew*, 86f.

[83] *Luke*, 247.

[84] *Q–Die Spruchquelle*, 78.

[85] *Matthew* I, 438.

[86] *Die Christologie der Logienquelle*, 129.

[87] *The Sermon on the Mount*, 57.

[88] Jeremias notes that the antithetic parallelism is pre-Lukan, *Die Sprache des Lukasevangeliums*, 138.

[89] Schürmann classifies Lk. 6:20//Mt. 5:3 a "Grundwort" and states: "Lk. 6,20 b . . . ist als eschatologischer Verheißungsruf Jesu mit größerer Wahrscheinlichkeit bereits vorösterliche Tradition", "Das Zeugnis der Redenquelle für die Basileia--Verkündigung Jesu", 140.

[90] *Matthew* I, 438, 439.

For only by means of the actions of Jesus in Galilee at that particular time did the beatitudes become possible. Christ himself belongs to the fulfillment of the promises."[91] The christological import of Lk. 6:20//Mt. 5:3, then, is that Jesus, in word and deed, has brought good news to the poor. Against the background of Isa. 61, this announcement denotes the commencement of the time of salvation: God's saving grace is now being proclaimed and administered in the ministry of Jesus. Jesus is more than a prophet. He is the fulfillment and the fulfiller of prophecy.

III.   Jesus the Herald of Eschatological Salvation:
Lk. 7:22-23//Mt. 11:4-6; Lk. 7:28//Mt. 11:11

Lk. 7:28//Mt. 11:11 occurs in the middle of a large block of Q material (Lk. 7:18-35//Mt. 11:2-19) whose unifying theme is the question of Jesus' relationship to John the Baptist. Throughout this section the two versions are closely parallel both in vocabulary and word order except for the obvious Lukan editorial insertions of 7:21, 29, 30 and Matthew's inclusion of 11:12, 13 (Lk. 16:16).[92] The fact that both Matthew and Luke retain the passage in largely unaltered forms suggests its traditional pedigree and unity. Because our interest lies in the kingdom of God in Q, we isolate 7:28//11:11 and the preceding verses which affect its meaning.

A.   The Study of Q and the Historicity
of Lk. 7:22, 23//Mt. 11:4-6

In answer to John's question "Are you the coming One", Jesus directs attention to the acts which characterize his ministry. He allows the observer to define his identity on the basis of his acts. The minor differences between the two versions do not affect the meaning of the text.

Despite the absence of christological terminology in Lk. 7:22, 23 par., major works on Q identify this passage as a secondary creation of the Q community. A. Polag, who identifies Lk. 7:18-26 as one of only five kernel fragments (*Kernstücke*) of Q,[93] asserts that ὁ ἐρχόμενος in 7:19//11:3 represents the christological witness of the late redaction of Q as the phrase is characteristic of Q and compares favorably with Lk. 3:16, 17//Mt. 3:11—a passage which Polag

---

91 *The Sermon on the Mount*, 58.

92 See J. Kloppenborg, *Q Parallels*, 52-61.

93 *Die Christologie der Logienquelle*, 129.

attributes to late Q redaction. The closing "blessing" (*Makarismus*) determines the meaning of the entire passage, and according to Polag, reveals the situation not of Jesus but of those who met him.[94] H. Schürmann renders the historical situation described by Matthew and Luke impossible as the early imprisonment and beheading of John would have prevented such an encounter.[95] Similarly, D. Zeller identifies here a post-Easter situation because John in his anticipation of the final judgement would not have had a perception of a human mediator of salvation. Hence Lk. 7:22, 23 par. probably represents a Christian insertion similar to Jn. 7:3 which attempts to prove the messiah through his actions.[96] S. Schulz, also detecting post-Easter authorship, claims 7:22f. reflects the theologically conscious reflection of the Hellenistic Q community. This origin is supported by the quotations of the LXX, the underlying polemic against the disciples of John the Baptist, and the prophetic-apocalyptic style form of the beatitude.[97] P. Hoffmann, meanwhile, follows Bultmann in perceiving a temporal discrepancy between John's question and Jesus' answer: while John and the historical Jesus emphasized the kingdom as the endtime event, Jesus' answer presupposes his earthly wonder deeds. As a result, Hoffmann argues that 7:22, 23 represents a community expansion of Lk. 10:23//Mt. 13:16. The emphasis of the beatitude, then, is upon Jesus' endtime function as the Son of Man. The community's anticipation of the parousia and their conviction of Jesus' function as judge lead the group to create a passage which designates Jesus as the hinge upon which salvation and damnation depend. For this community, 'the Coming One' is identical to the endtime Son of Man.[98] More recently, J. Kloppenborg has concluded: ". . . the entire pronouncement story is a post-Easter creation, arising in the effort to attract Baptist disciples into the Christian fold. The story deliberately invokes Baptist expectations in its use of the title 'the Coming One,' but infuses the title with specifically Christian content."[99]

However, despite the consensus among these scholars to the contrary, the authenticity of our passage is well grounded.[100] The presuppositions which form the foundations of the conclusions below are inherently weak. John's question does not presuppose a connection on John's part between Jesus' saving acts and

---

[94] *Ibid.*, 35 n. 99, 38, 145.

[95] *Lukas*, 414.

[96] *Kommentar zur Logienquelle*, 39f.

[97] *Q-Die Spruchquelle*, 195f.

[98] R. Bultmann, *History of the Synoptic Tradition*, 22; P. Hoffmann, *Studien zur Theologie der Logienquelle*, 200-214. In response to Hoffmann, see J. Dunn, *Jesus and the Spirit*, 58.

[99] *The Formation of Q*, 107.

[100] The authenticity of the passage has most recently been defended by W. Wink, "Jesus' Reply to John. Matt 11:2-6/Luke 7:18-23", *Forum* 5 (1, '89) 121-28.

his messiahship. On the contrary John's statement is a question implying ignorance. It is important to note that Q pictures Jesus not only as a wonder worker but also as a judge who pronounces woe. It is likely, therefore, that John paid particular attention to Jesus' words of judgement while overlooking the significance of his saving acts. Jesus, not denying the chaff will be burned, emphasizes that his present task is to gather the wheat into his barn (Lk. 3:17//Mt. 3:12). The elaborate nature of the novel explanations put forth to explain the passage's origin within hypothetical communities raises serious doubt about the conclusions of Hoffmann, Schulz, and Zeller. ὁ ἐρχόμενος is nowhere attested in pre-Christian Judaism or the NT as a specific christological designation. Nor is the phrase a christological title in Q. In Lk. 3:16//Mt. 3:11 neither Matthew nor Luke have the article and Luke merely has ἔρχεται. In Lk. 13:35//Mt. 23:39 ὁ ἐρχόμενος depends upon Ps. 118:26 where the phrase designates an individual distinctly different from the eschatological judge envisioned by John in Lk. 3:16; 7:20 par. Behind the two uses exist the different perspectives of Jesus and John— not one christological title peculiar to the Q community. Third, an underlying polemic between the followers of Jesus and John is more apparent that real. The positive statements about John in Lk. 7:26, 27, 28a, 33 par. render such an understanding improbable. Fourth, the allusions to Isa. 61:1f. are particularly characteristic of Jesus' speech (Lk. 4:18, 19; Lk. 6:20b//Mt. 5:3; Lk. 6:21a//Mt. 5:6; Lk. 7:22, 23//Mt. 11:5, 6; Mt. 5:5; Mk. 1:14, 15)—a fact which questions secondary origin here.[101] Fifth the quotations of the LXX do not necessarily prove the passage's origin in a Greek-speaking milieu. Assimilation to the LXX would have been acceptable in the translation process if it were an accurate translation of the Aramaic or Hebrew. As R.T. France has noted, the appropriateness of this quote does not depend on the LXX and thus its text-form does not prove its origin in a Greek-speaking community.[102] Further, the fact that

---

[101] Davies and Allison, *Matthew* I, 438: "So the farther back we go, the greater the impact of Isa. 61 seems to be. The implication? If, as seems overwhelmingly probable, the core of the beatitudes (5.3, 4, 6) be dominical, Jesus must have formulated them with Isa 61:1 in mind. Conversely, Matthew has not done much if anything to accentuate the connections between Isa 61 and Mt. 5:3-12", 438. On Mk. 1:14, 15, see R.A. Guelich, *Mark*, Waco: Word (1989) 46: "Taken in isolation this summary would suggest that Mark viewed Jesus as the eschatological messenger promised in Isa 52:7 and 61:1 who would announce the arrival of God's rule and deliverance, the "good news from God."

[102] ". . . it is only to be expected that someone translating Aramaic quotations into Greek would tend to assimilate his translations to the Greek version with which he was familiar. Thus where the LXX was a fair translation of the Aramaic, it would be pedantic to expect him to retain scrupulously the peculiarities of the Aramaic where nothing depended on the points of difference. Only where the use of the quotation depends on its LXX form, and could not have been based on the Hebrew or Aramaic text can text-form be admitted as evidence that the quotation was first

Lk. 7:27//Mt. 11:10, a text that exists within this same block of Q material, reflects a Semitic text-form rather than the LXX belies the conjecture that we have behind this material a conscious presentation of christology by a Greek speaking community.[103] Sixth, secondary origin gains little support from form critical presuppositions: the claim that the apophthegm in 7:22 and the beatitude in 7:23 betray community authorship unnecessarily constrains the authentic speech of Jesus.[104] Seventh, coherence to Lk. 10:23//Mt. 13:16 argues for the historicity of our saying and not vice versa. Eighth, Kloppenborg's comment that the story "infuses the title ('the Coming One') with specifically Christian content" simply is not true. As A. Polag has noted, "Der gesamte Wortlaut scheint unbeeinflußt von späterer christologischer Terminologie."[105] And finally, the Jewish pedigree of this passage is proven by the recent reconstruction of fragment 1 column 2 of 4Q 521[106]:

1. [הש] מים והארץ ישמעו למשיחו	(1) The Heavens and the earth will obey His Messiah, (2) [. . . and all th]at is in them. He will not turn aside from the Commandments of the Holy Ones. (3) Take strength in His service, (you) who seek the Lord. (4) Shall you not find the Lord in this, all you who wait patiently in your hearts? (5) For the Lord will visit the Pious Ones and the Righteous will He call by name. (6) Over the Meek will His Spirit hover, and the Faithful will He restore by His power. (7) He shall glorify the Pious Ones on the Throne of the Eternal Kingdom. (8) He shall release the captives, make the blind see, raise up the do[wntrodden.]. (9) For[ev]er will I
2. [וכל א]שר בם לוא יסוג ממצות קדושים	
3. התאמצו מבקשי אדני בעבדתו vacat	
4. הלוא בזאת תמצאו את אדני כל המיחלים	
" בלבם	
5. כי אדני חסידים יבקר וצדיקים בשם יקרא	
6. ועל ענוים דוחו תרחף ואמונים יחליף	
" בכחו	
7. יכבד את חסידים על כסא מלכות עד	
8. מתיר אסורים פוקח עורים זוקף כ[פופים]	
9. ל[עו]לם אדבק [בו]שלים ובחסדו [אבטח]	

---

made in a Greek speaking milieu", R.T. France, *Jesus and the Old Testament*, London: Tyndale (1971) 32.

[103] On 7:27//11:10, see Darrel L. Bock, *Proclamation from Prophecy and Pattern: Lucan Old Testament Christology*, Ph.D Dissertation, University of Aberdeen (1982) 166f.; K. Stendahl, *The School of St. Matthew*, Philadelphia: Fortress (1968) 49-52; R.T. France, *Jesus and the Old Testament*, 242-243.

[104] An apophthegm is simply a terse pointed saying, embodying an important truth in a few words. According to Bultmann, apophthegms were idealized constructions utilized in sermonic material within the Church. However, the failure of Bultmann and Dibelius to agree on the nature of the form suggests caution in ascribing validity to it as a means of determining the pedigree of Jesus' sayings. Schulz and Hoffmann, however, accept its validity outright.

[105] *Die Christologie der Logienquelle*, 38.

[106] The following reconstruction of 4Q 521 is that of Robert Eisenman and Michael Wise, *The Dead Sea Scrolls Uncovered*, Rockport: Element (1992) 21. Cf., Émile Puech, "Une Apocalypse Messianique (4Q521)", *RevQ* 60 (Oct., 1992), Tome 15, Fascicule 4, 485.

10. וט]ובו [ ] הקדש לוא יתאחר [ ]
11. ונכ ב דות שלוא היו מעשה אדני כאשר
" י[ ]
12. אז ירפא חללים ומתים יחיה ענוים יבשר
13. [ ].ש[קד]ושים ינהל ידעה [ב]ם יעשה
14. [ ] וכלו כ. [ ]

cling [to Him . . .], and [I will trust] in His Piety (*Hesed*, also 'Grace'), (10) and [His] Goo[dness . .] of Holiness will not delay . . (11) And as for the wonders that are not the work of the Lord, when He . . . (12) then He will heal the sick, resurrect the dead, and to the Meek announce glad tidings. (13) . . . He will lead the [Holy Ones; He will shepherd [th]em; He will do (14) . . . and all of it . . .

Line 8 shares with Lk. 7:22//Mt. 11:4f. the same anticipation of the *eschatological* fulfillment of Isa. 35:5; 42:7; 61:1, 2. The fragment as a whole has in common with Q an interest in the Kingdom of God (line 7), focus on the meek/poor (line 6), the Spirit (line 6), elements of apocalyptic (heaven/earth dualism, wonders, eschatological salvation for the faithful), and line 7, which has points of contact with Lk. 22:30//Mt. 19:28, even recalls the role of the one like a son of man in Dn. 7:13, 14, 18.[107] The juxtaposition of these themes in 4Q 521 renders unnecessary the hypothesis of multiple thematic strata in Q. Émile Puech finds in lines 6-8 and 10-13 eight points of verbal and conceptual contact between fragment 1 column 2 and verses regularly attributed to Q.[108]

Virtually proving the Jewish background of Lk. 7:22 par., 4Q 521 demonstrates how Jesus' acts as recorded in Q relate directly to the present accomplishment of events which signal the future hope for the kingdom of God on the part of a community historically contemporary with Jesus. It is even possible that the Qumran community expected the miraculous acts refered to in lines 11-13 to be accomplished by a messianic figure.[109] In any case, Jesus' acts clearly represent the present saving reality of the kingdom of God as anticipated by people at Qumran. 4Q 521 underscores the fact that in Lk. 7:22//Mt. 11:4 Jesus assumes in his acts a role far greater than that of a prophet attempting the renewal of Israel. Indeed, his acts are those expected of the Lord himself when he would come to visit his people. *Jesus is anointed by God with the Holy Spirit to bring eschatological salvation to the poor and afflicted. He acts in God's stead. Functionally, Jesus identifies himself as the Messiah come to fulfill the eschatological expectations of Isa. 61:1f.*

---

107 See Puech, "Une Apocalypse Messianique (4Q521)", 489. Interestingly, Eisenman and Wise describe the Messianic figure of line 1 as "a supernatural figure in the manner of Dan. 7's 'Son of Man coming on the clouds of Heaven' (p. 20).

108 "Une Apocalypse Messianique (4Q521)", 488-493: Lk. 6:20//Mt. 5:3 (line 6); Lk. 22:30//Mt. 19:28 (line 7); Lk. 7:22//Mt. 11:5 (line 8); Lk. 11:33-36//Mt. 5:16 (line 10); Lk. 7:22f.//Mt. 11:2f. (line 11); Lk. 10:9//Mt. 10:1, 8; Lk. 7:22c//Mt. 11:5c (Line 12); Lk. 6:21//Mt. 5:3 (line 13).

109 Eisenmen and Wise, *The Dead Sea Scrolls Uncovered*, 20.

If, then, there exists no great obstacle to perceiving the historicity of 7:22, 23//11:4-6, we may follow A.E. Harvey[110] in maintaining that the Isaianic background of Jesus' response to John indicates that Jesus understood his acts of healing as signs that the salvific rule of God had begun in his ministry. 4Q 521 verifies that first-century Jews would have understood the pattern and eschatological significance of Jesus' miracles.[111] The raising of the dead, the healing of the blind, the lame and the deaf do not exist in Isaiah as acts characteristic of a prophet (26:19; 29:18, 19; 35:5, 6; 42:7), but as events which signify the eschatological salvific work of God. The bringing of "good news" to the poor, likewise, represents the inauguration of the eschatological "year of jubilee" in Isa. 61:1f. Indeed, of the acts mentioned, only the cleansing of lepers lacks an Isaianic precedent, but this act like the others has great salvific significance against the background of the OT, where the Pentateuch clearly designates lepers as unclean and thus unfit for life both in the Hebrew community at large and in tabernacle worship in particular. Hence, against the OT background, to have leprosy was to be separated from God. In healing victims of the disease, Jesus brought outcasts into the realm of God's people where salvation could be secured. With these facts in mind, W.G. Kümmel writes,

> So Jesus' reply to the Baptist's question claims that the acts and the message are to be regarded as a proof of the beginning of the Kingdom of God, and it sees this beginning taking place exclusively in Jesus and his activity. It is shown once more that the proclamation of the good news of the future coming of the Kingdom of God, which was Jesus' talk, receives its particular and decisive character through the fact that the person of Jesus by his actions brings about already now what is expected from the eschatological future.[112]

The decisive "character of the kingdom" of which Kümmel speaks is its saving power inaugurated in Jesus' ministry. Jesus' allusion to Isa. 61:1f. implies that he

---

[110] *Jesus and the Constraints of History*, Philadelphia: Westminster (1982) 141f.

[111] *Contra* E.P. Sanders, *Jesus and Judaism*, Philadelphia: Fortress (1985) 163: ". . . subsequent Jewish literature does not indicate that Jews habitually looked for miracles as a sign of the coming end."

[112] *Promise and Fulfilment*, 111. Similarly, C. Schuppan, *Gottes Herrschaft und Gottes Wille: Eine Untersuchung zur Struktur der Rede von Gott in der Spruchquelle Q im Vergleich mit dem Frühjudentum und dem Matthäus-und Lukasevangelium*. Unpublished Ph. D. Dissertation, Ernst-Moritz-Arndt-Universität Greifswald (1978) 60: "Die Wundertaten sind gegenüber dem LXX-Text, dort steht das Futur, im Präsens der Erfüllung des AT im Mittelpunkt der Antwort: Die angekündigte und erhoffte Endzeit ist angebrochen." Also, C.H. Dodd, *The Parables of the Kingdom*, 38, 39; R.T. France, *Jesus and the Old Testament*, 95, 96; G.E. Ladd, *Jesus and the Kingdom. The Eschatology of Biblical Realism*, New York: Harper & Row (1964) 23-38; J.A.T. Robinson, *Jesus and His Coming*, London: SCM (1957) 101; J. Jeremias, ET *Jesus' Promise to the Nations*, London: SCM (1958) 46f.; I.H. Marshall, *Luke*, 291f.; J. Fitzmyer, *Luke* I, 668f.; A. Polag, *Christologie der Logienquelle*, 37.

is endowed with the Spirit of God. His acts are not those of a Hellenistic Divine-Man, but rather his authority stems from his relationship to God. In short, Jesus' endowment with the Spirit equips him to radiate God's saving power. With this perspective before us, the following beatitude, καὶ μακάριός ἐστιν ὃς ἐὰν μὴ σκανδαλισθῇ ἐν ἐμοί, designates the "Blessed" as those who do not stumble upon Jesus, because his message of the kingdom is authoritative. To reject Jesus equals defying the Spirit and refusing the saving benefits of the kingdom—a decision which has obvious eschatological consequences. Thus "the saying pronounces an eschatological verdict upon the people concerned; by their attitude to Jesus they will stand or fall at the last judgement."[113]

B.   John's Relation to Jesus and the Kingdom of God

The difference between Jesus and John in Q is clear. John is a prophet of judgement who warns that the kingdom of God will be bad news for the unrepentant (Lk. 3:7-9//Mt. 3:7-10; Lk. 3:16, 17//Mt. 3:11, 12). Jesus, on the other hand, while not contradicting John's pronouncement of doom, balances John's warning by heralding the good news of the kingdom. The kingdom of God will be good news for those who identify with Jesus. That Lk. 7:22, 23//Mt. 11:4-6 speaks of Jesus' inauguration of the kingdom is supported by Lk. 7:26, 27//Mt. 11:9, 10. The two versions of this saying parallel exactly except for the additional ἐγώ in Mt. 11:10. The agreement between the text-form of the second half of the quotation and the MT against the LXX suggests that the quotation represents a Semitic conflation of Ex. 23:20 and Mal. 3:1. The Semitic text-form coupled with the presence of the same composite quotation in Mk. 1:2 and Exodus Rabbah 23:20 suggest the traditional character of the citation. Its secondary creation within a layer of Q redaction is, hence, unlikely.[114]

The composite quotation holds in tension the image of God guiding and protecting his people through his angel (Ex. 23:20) with the image of the eschatological messenger who prepares the way for the Lord (Mal. 3:1) i.e., the one who comes before the great and terrible Day of the Lord (Mal. 3:23; 4:5, 6). Mal. 4:5f. implies that John is here identified with Elijah. Lk. 7:27a//Mt. 11:10a indicate that John is the one who will prepare the way, but less obvious is the identification of σου in 7:27//11:10. Does σου refer to the people of Israel (Ex. 23:20) or to Jesus as the representative of God (Mal. 3:1)? In favour of the latter option is the preceding evidence in Lk. 7:22, 23//Mt. 11:2, 3 where what was

---

113 I.H. Marshall, *Luke*, 292.

114 *Pace* D. Catchpole (*The Quest for Q*, Edinburgh: T&T Clark [1993] 66) who claims that "Q, unlike the midrash, causes the texts to interpenetrate and to form a new composite whole."

affirmed in reference to Yahweh in Isa. 35:5 is applied to Jesus in his present ministry in which his acts mark the commencement of God's salvific rule. Because John's question of Jesus' identity remains fresh, the alteration of Malachi's first person μου to Q's second person appears significant: σου refers to Jesus and associates him with the appearance of the "Day of the Lord" which is prepared for by John. As in Lk. 7:22, 23 par., the coming of Jesus replaces that of Yahweh. J. Fitzmyer states: "The purpose of the OT quotation is to identify John as a precursor of Jesus: in this he is "something more than a prophet."[115] To press Fitzmyer's statement further: John is greater than a prophet because of the magnitude of Jesus' message and ministry—in preparing the way for Jesus, John paves the way for the inception of God's eschatological rule.[116]

In another Q passage (Lk. 16:16//Mt. 11:12, 13) it is not clear whether John should be considered in or out of the kingdom because both μέχρι and ἕως can be taken inclusively or exclusively. It is attractive to view John as within the kingdom in light of three factors: (1) his violent death at the hands of Herod Antipas; (2) Luke's presentation of John as a preacher of good news (3:18); and (3), Luke's identification of John's ministry as the beginning of the Gospel (Acts 1:22). In Matthew John may be considered within the kingdom as Matthew most often uses ἀπό inclusively and frequently parallels the activities of Jesus and John. On the other hand, H. Merklein[117] has emphasized correctly the clear distinction between the ministries of Jesus and John—particularly in Q. While the preaching of John stresses eschatological judgement (Lk. 3:7-9 par.), Jesus' emphasizes salvation (Lk. 7:24 par.). While John looks to the immediate future, Jesus announces that the kingdom is present in his work (Lk. 11:20 par.). While John awaits the coming one (Lk. 3:16, 17 par.), Jesus is the coming one (Lk. 7:18f. par.). While John is qualified as "more than a prophet" and "the greatest among those born of women," he is also qualified as less than the least in the kingdom of God (Lk. 7:26, 28 par.). And if John's identification as Elijah in Mt. 11:14 alludes to Mal. 4:5, the figure there is a prophet who comes "*before* the great and terrible day of the Lord." And, most importantly in Q, John himself announces: "I baptize you with water; but One is coming who is mightier than I, and I am not fit to untie the thong of His sandals; He will baptize you with the Holy Spirit and with fire" (Lk. 3:16 par.). Hence if Lk. 16:16//Mt. 11:12, 13 portrays John within the kingdom his presence must be qualified as being on a very different plane from that of Jesus. Jesus fulfils the prophecy of John in a manner incomprehensible to

---

[115] *Luke* I, 674.

[116] So H. Schürmann, *Lukas*, 417.

[117] *Die Gottesherrschaft als Handlungsprinzip*, 85-87.

John himself. P. Hoffmann certainly goes too far in identifying John as the inaugurator of the endtime, who brings in the kingdom of God.[118] John announces coming judgement, but Jesus brings the salvific benefits of the kingdom—it is through Jesus that the poor are blessed and the battle with Satan is staged.

C. Salvation History in Q? Lk. 7:28//Mt. 11:11

R. Bultmann, M. Dibelius, W.G. Kümmel, P. Hoffmann, F. Hahn, D. Lührmann and S. Schulz[119] agree in perceiving diverse traditions behind Lk. 7:28a//Mt. 11:11a which they consider dominical and Lk. 7:28b//Mt. 11:11b which they consider a secondary attempt by the early Church to clarify the superiority of Jesus to John. According to W. Wink, the church behind Q was at pains to alter tradition in order to clarify John's subordinate position in relation to Jesus.[120] Such a distinction seems unwarranted, however, in view of the parallelism which unites the verse and the non-existence of evidence to document a separate *Sitz im Leben* for 7:28b. Furthermore, 7:28a, when standing by itself, appears awkward both in relation to this block of Q material and in relation to Jesus' statements about John elsewhere. H. Schürmann and S. Schulz[121] classify the saying as "Ecclesiastical" as a result of its "Salvation History" orientation. But this criterion appears unjustified as Lk. 7:22, 23 par. and Lk. 7:26, 27 par. demonstrate Jesus' knowledge that John's preaching has prepared for Jesus' own ministry in which God's rule has begun. Clearly the primary distinction rests between John's preaching which emphasized repentance and judgement and Jesus' ministry which brings a message of joy to the poor and healing to the sick—the events marking the beginning of the eschatological reign of God. A temporal distinction infused by the *heilsgeschichtlich* thought of the early Church is not apparent. Indeed, we

---

[118] *Studien zur Theologie der Logienquelle*, 50-79, esp. 62; Similarly V. Schönle (*Johannes, Jesus und die Juden*, Frankfurt am Main: Peter Lang [1982] 103): "Was aber nicht gesagt wird, ist, daß mit dem Täufer das Reich schon endgültig gekommen sei."

[119] R. Bultmann, *The History of the Synoptic Tradition*, 177; M. Dibelius, *Die urchristliche Überlieferung von Johannes dem Täufer*, Göttingen: Vandenhoeck & Rupprecht (1911) 13, 14; W.G. Kümmel, *Promise and Fulfillment*, 125 n. 75; P. Hoffmann, *Studien zur Theologie der Logienquelle*, 218, 220; F. Hahn, *Christologische Hoheitstitel*, 375; D. Lührmann, *Die Redaction der Logienquelle*, 27; S. Schulz, *Q–Die Spruchquelle*, 229, 230.

[120] *John the Baptist in the Gospel Tradition*, Cambridge: CUP (1968) 24: "the Q traditions reveal a situation in which the church is laboring to define John's relationship to the kingdom of heaven. Apparently Jesus' adulation of John in the verses that follow (Matt. 11:7-9[Q]) has become a source of embarrassment to the church."

[121] H. Schürmann, "Das Zeugnis der Redenquelle für die Basileia-Verkündigung Jesu", 142; S. Schulz, *Q–Die Spruchquelle*, 229, 230.

wonder if the early-Church could have comprehended twentieth-century conceptions of *Heilsgeschichte*.

The three comparatives μείζων ... μικρότερος ... μείζων are the key words in determining the meaning of the text. The first marks John as greater than anyone born of woman–i.e., by human merit he is the greatest.[122] Whether John's superior status results from his prophetic eminence, his moral discipline, or his strict adherence to Jewish orthopraxy is not stated, but among men he ranks at the top. Yet, "the least in the kingdom of God is greater than he." Controversy over the meaning of μικρότερος arises from the legitimacy of translating the term either as a superlative connoting a generic usage (least) or as a strict comparative denoting an individual (the lesser).[123] Dibelius, Suggs, Cullmann and Hoffmann, among others, support the second option in arguing that μικρότερος refers directly to Jesus as he was "the lesser" in respect to his previous discipleship to John.[124] This interpretation depends upon a specific relationship between Jesus and John that the Gospel texts themselves do not illuminate—we have no evidence elsewhere that Jesus was ever referred to as "the lesser" or "the younger" in relationship to John. Further, μικρότερος refers to "the lesser" or "the least" in relation to the kingdom not in regard to John. We take μικρότερος, whether superlative or comparative, as an indefinite reference to persons of low rank in the kingdom of God. The final μείζων is definitely a comparative as a result of the genitive of comparison that follows where αὐτοῦ clearly refers back to John: the lesser/least in the kingdom are greater than John—the greatest of men. The emphasis of the saying, then, is not so much on denigrating John, as on exalting the superiority of the kingdom—even its least stand superior to humanity's best.

ἐν τῇ βασιλείᾳ refers to the present inbreaking of God's eschatological rule which is taking place in Jesus' ministry.[125] The least in the kingdom are greater than John because they have encountered, in Jesus, God's saving power. As H. Merklein attests, kingdom here should be understood dynamically rather than

---

[122] "Born of woman" is an OT usage for "man" specifically in reference to mortality: Job 14:1; 15:14; 25:4; 1QS 11:21; 1QH 13:14; 18:12-13; 16:23-24. See F. Büchsel, "παραδίδωμι", *TDNT* II, 172.

[123] See Blass, Debrunner and Funk, *A Greek Grammar of the New Testament*, § 60, 244.

[124] F. Dibelius, "Zwei Worte Jesu", 190-192; M.J. Suggs, *Wisdom, Christology and Law in Matthew's Gospel*, 67; O. Cullmann, *The Christology of the New Testament*, 32; P. Hoffmann, *Studien zur Theologie der Logienquelle*, 220-224.

[125] The present orientation of the saying is supported by among others: H. Schürmann, "Das Zeugnis der Redequelle für die Basileia-Verkündigung Jesu", 141, 142; H. Merklein, *Die Gottesherrschaft als Handlungsprinzip*, 87; J. Schlosser, *Le Règne de Dieu dans les dits de Jésus*, 163; E. Schweizer, *Matthew*, 170; C.H. Dodd, *The Parables of the Kingdom*, 32; T.W. Manson, *The Sayings of Jesus*, 70; E. Percy, *Die Botschaft Jesu. Eine traditionskritische und exegetische Untersuchung*, 201.

statically; It is not the Church but God's saving power which is in view.[126] ἐν τῇ
βασιλείᾳ occurs twice elsewhere in the Gospels (Mk. 14:25; Lk. 13:28, 29//Mt.
8:11, 12) where the phrase refers specifically to the eschatological banquet. J.
Schlosser does not consider these passages as parallels to 7:28 par. as a result of
the temporal distinction.[127] Yet a relationship certainly does exist. Those who
experience now the salvific power of God in Jesus' ministry have a foretaste of the
blessings that will be theirs at the consummation of the kingdom. As John has not
yet had such an encounter, he remains with those still waiting.[128] Lk. 7:28//Mt.
11:11, then, in our opinion, does not appear to contain secondary community
fabrication of Salvation History. While the distinction between Jesus and John is
nuanced, the likelihood that Jesus would have reflected upon John's person and
ministry is logical. Though it is extremely unlikely that the early Church would
have understood the theories of *Heilsgeschichte* which have flourished in NT
theology this century, it is probable that Jesus himself and his teaching were the
impetus for the Church's understanding of salvation in history.[129]

IV.   Lk. 10:9//Mt. 10:7: The Mission Discourse in Q;
Evidence of a *Q Sitz im Leben*?

The mission section of Q has been crucial for scholars who have attempted to
define the character and *Sitz im Leben* of the so-called Q community. Dieter
Lührmann claims the harvest imagery (Lk. 10:2) depends on an OT background
(Joel 4:1; Isa. 27:11; Hos. 6:11) which presupposes a Gentile mission, while the
judgement sayings indicate the delay of the parousia (Lk. 10:11, 12 par.).[130] The
Q community has re-apocalyticized the preaching of Jesus in light of their own
situation. Paul Hoffmann writes that the Q version of Jesus' commissioning
address represents the incorporation of primitive sayings with newly formed
sending and instruction sayings with the result that primitive logia of Jesus have

---

[126] *Die Gottesherrschaft als Handlungsprinzip*, 87.

[127] *Le Règne de Dieu dans les dits de Jésus*, 164.

[128] Lk. 13:28//Mt. 8:11 rules out the possibility that this saying excludes John from
salvation at the ultimate consummation of the Kingdom. 7:28//11:11 is, in fact, silent on this
issue.

[129] The saying's authenticity is supported by: J. Schlosser, *Le Règne de Dieu dans des dits
de Jésus*, 160; E. Percy, *Die Botschaft Jesu. Eine traditionskritische und exegetische
Untersuchung*, Lund: Gleerup (1953) 201; R. Schnackenburg, *Gottes Herrschaft und Reich. Eine
biblisch-theologische Studie*, 91, 92; J.A. Sint, "Die Eschatologie des Täufers, die Täufergruppen
und die Polemic der Evangelien", *Vom Messias zum Christus*, Wien; Freiburg; Basel: Herder
(1964) 117, 118; G.E. Ladd, *The Presence of the Future*, 200, 201; I.H. Marshall, *Luke*, 293; E.
Schweizer, *Matthew*, 170; J. Dupont, *Le Christ et son Précurseur*, *AsSeign* 7 (1969) 22-25.

[130] *Redaktion der Logienquelle*, 60, 94.

been interpreted anew in light of the mission setting of the Q-group: "Heimatlosigkeit, eine *radikale Trennung* von der Familie, von der Sorge um Besitz und Unterhalt, die schon für Jesu Nachfolgeforderung typisch waren, gelten auch noch für die Q-Gruppe."[131] Rudolf Laufen addressing *"Der 'Sitz im Leben' der Q-Aussendungsrede"* identifies as unaltered primitive sayings of Jesus the equipping saying (Lk. 10:4 par.), the "Peace" greeting (Lk. 10:5-8 par.), the commands to heal the sick and pronounce the kingdom of God (Lk. 10:9 par.), and the command to "wipe off the dust" (Lk. 10:11, 12). To this material the Q-redactor has pasted Lk. 10:2, 3, 13-15, 16. The additions, according to Laufen, reveal the redactor's primary motives of sending and judgement.[132] Hence, for Laufen, this passage presupposes a secondary post-resurrection awareness that Jesus is the exalted figure on whom eschatological salvation and judgement depend. With different results, Risto Uro perceives four stages in the composition of the Q mission address: (A) the "Kernel" (Lk. 10:4-7ab par.); (B) the "Early Mission Code" (Lk. 10:4a-11a par.); (C) "the mission code enlarged by interpretive sayings" (Lk. 10:3, 12, 13-15, 16 par.), and (D) the final redaction of Q—the large thematic section from Lk. 9:57-11:13.[133] Behind each layer of composition, Uro identifies a different situation.[134] He concludes: "Q as a document of Jesus' sayings came into being as a community teaching in such a social situation around 70 C.E. "[135] D. Catchpole classifies as Q redaction Lk. 10:2; 10:7b; Mt. 10:5b; Lk. 10:13-15; 10:16 par. concluding that "this single extra stratum was what fitted the old Jesus-material for re-use in a context which was later but not altogether new, that of the post-Jesus mission to Israel."[136]

---

[131] *Studien zur Theologie der Logienquelle*, 329; italics Hoffmann's.

[132] *Die Doppelüberlieferungen der Logienquelle und des Markusevangeliums*, 290-291: "Sendungs- und Gerichtmotiv, diese zwei Aspekte ein und derselben Grundaussage, sind es also, die die Einheit der neuen Aussendungsrede schaffen: wie Gott Jesus gesandt hat, so sendet dieser seine Boten, die Missionare, zu den Menschen; wie im Verhältnis zu Ihm die Entscheidung des zukünftigen Gerichtes fällt, so auch beim Verhalten der Menschen gegenüber den Glaubensboten. Der Q-Redaktor hat diesen Gedankengang . . ."

[133] *Sheep Among the Wolves: A Study on the Mission Instructions of Q*, 97-116.

[134] The early "mission code" was shaped by wandering missionaries in the "first decades after Jesus' crucifixion; the "mission speech" reflects a later Jewish body of missionaries who extend the "mission code" at a later time to a more hostile audience; "The 'final redactor' of Q uses these polemic and missionary traditions, but applies them to his ecclesiastical and didactic purposes"; *Sheep Among the Wolves: A Study on the Mission Instructions of Q*, 160, 199, 241.

[135] *Sheep Among the Wolves: A Study on the Mission Instructions of Q*, 271.

[136] "The Mission Charge in Q", *Semeia* 55 (1992) 172. Catchpole supports Uro in ascribing Lk. 10:2//Mt. 9:37, 38 to a "church mission" (153). However, this saying coheres with Jesus' own mission to Israel. Its purpose, that of gathering the eschatological people of God, is essentially the same as that of the second petition of the Lord's prayer which calls for God to perform the act commensurate with the hallowing of his name, *viz.*, the gathering of people for salvation (Eze. 20:41, 44; 36:22-24). Furthermore, the secondary origin of Lk. 10:2 (and also

According to Catchpole, Lk. 10:3+11:39+16:16 and par. reveal the polemical situation in which the Q mission existed.

A host of other scholars put forth similar views in describing the social setting of the Q-Community as the very extension of the circumstances which the Evangelists apply to Jesus and his disciples.[137] While there is little doubt that the early Church reflected upon the teachings of Jesus as it developed its mission's methodology, it is unclear that any part of this text originated secondarily as a byproduct of the mission's movement. Is it not problematic that the passages which Catchpole assumes to be secondary fit very well the polemical context of Jesus' interaction with his opponents the Pharisees? And can we deny that Jesus sent out disciples? F. Hahn argues on the basis of multiple attestation that there can be no doubt: "On the basis of the commissioning words in Mk. 6:7-11 par., Lk. 9:1-5, as well as Lk. 10:1-12 and Mt. 9:37f; 10:5-16, there can be no doubt about it, however much the wording may have been influenced by later missionary experience."[138] If we take as our premise the fact that Jesus did actually send out disciples—an almost unavoidable conclusion[139]—we are left with the question of whether or not there exist sayings in Lk. 10:2-12 par., which are incompatible with what we know about Jesus and his followers outside of Q. Such is not the case to the extent outlined above—a Gentile mission is nowhere alluded to.[140]

10:7b; 10:13-15, 16) is a speculative presupposition. Each verse has an appropriate *Sitz im Leben Jesu.* See Davies and Allison, *Matthew* II, 149f.; F. Hahn, *Mission in the New Testament*, 40 n. 3; I.H. Marshall, *Luke,* 417; J. Fitzmyer, *Luke* II, 843 writes that the only prohibition against a dominical origin for the mission charge is "that such a preparation would suggest a greater allegiance to him than the disciples' eventual defection would seem to tolerate." However, the disciples' radical obedience to the earthly Jesus is well attested (Mk. 14.31; Mt. 19:27; 26:33, 35; Lk. 18:28) and only heightens the irony of their later denial.

[137] H.R. Balz. *Methodische Probleme der neutestamentlichen Christologie, WMANT* 25; Neukirchen-Vluyn: Neukirchener Verlag (1967) 169f.; E. Käsemann, *New Testament Questions of Today*, 119f.; H. Kasting, *Die Anfänge der urchristlichen Mission, BEvT* 55; München: Kaiser (1969) 97; W. Schenk, *Synopse zur Redequelle der Evangelisten*, 60; O.H. Steck, *Israel und das gewaltsame Geschick der Propheten*, 288.

[138] *Mission in the New Testament*, 32. So M. Hengel, *The Charismatic Leader and His Followers,* 74: "That Jesus did send forth the disciples can hardly be doubted in principle, even if it is impossible to reconstruct the circumstances in detail."

[139] See M. Hengel, *The Charismatic Leader and His Followers,* 76f. Similarly, T.W. Manson, *The Sayings of Jesus*, 73: "The mission of the disciples is one of the best attested facts in the life of Jesus."

[140] So J. Gnilka, *Mattäusevangelium* I, 352, 53: "Von diesen Vorgaben her ist man keinesfalls gezwungen, bei der Ernte an die Heidenmission zu denken." R. Uro admits these points despite his conclusions: "There is no doubt that in many respects the "itinerant radicalism" revealed in the synoptic sayings go back to the historical Jesus. It is a standard view that Jesus was a charismatic leader who led the life of a wandering preacher and called certain individuals to be with him, demanding separation from home, family, and daily work. This can hardly be disputed . . ." *Sheep Among the Wolves*, 132.

When we add Laufen's own admission of uncertainty in ascribing specific sayings to redaction, we are left with little or no evidence upon which to build a *Q Sitz im Leben*. [141]

A. Lk. 10:9//Mt. 10:7 and the Soteriology of Q

P. Hoffmann writes that the way to salvation for Q was obedience to furthering the work and words of Jesus.[142] Similarly, R. Uro claims, in reference to our present kingdom saying, that Q passes on the preaching of the kingdom as its focal proclamation even after Easter: "The kingdom of God did not cease to be a subject of proclamation after Easter. The command in Lk. 10:9 is an important proof of that. . . . Like the other early instructions, it reflects the situation of the early Christian preachers, their program and the style of mission."[143]

Certainly Uro is correct that the kingdom of God continued to be preached after Easter, however, it is far from certain that the kingdom was preached in isolation from the Easter faith. It is preferable to view the mission discourse as a collection of dominical instructions which the Evangelists have incorporated into their gospels as reliable authoritative guides to missionary practice. Mark and Q have differences in detail but the differences are not theological.[144] Both reflect the basic tradition that Jesus commissioned disciples to advance his ministry of healing and preaching. It is probable that the disciples, including the twelve, were aware of Jesus' mission instructions and valued them as directives for missionary practice after Easter. When Paul met Peter (Gal. 1:18) three years after his conversion, it seems incredible that Peter would not have shared Jesus' teachings—especially those which had to do with missionary practice, as Peter was fully aware of Paul's commission to preach Jesus Christ among the Gentiles (Gal. 1:16). It may not be coincidence, therefore, that four Pauline texts appear reminiscent of the mission discourse (1 Co. 9:4, 14; 10:27; 1 Th. 4:8). From this information, Davies and Allison conclude:

---

[141] "Ob diese Sprüche alle vom Redaktor der Logienquelle hinzugefügt wurden oder zum Teil schon vor der Bearbeitung durch ihn der Rede angehört haben, läßt sich nicht in jedem Fall mit Sicherheit sagen", *Die Doppelüberlieferungen der Logienquelle*, 270.

[142] "Der Weg zur Rettung im Gericht ist für Q also das Tun der Worte Jesu." *Studien zur Theologie der Logienquelle*, 309.

[143] *Sheep Among the Wolves*, 151.

[144] The two versions compare favorably in prohibiting the messengers from carrying a purse or a bag (Mk. 6:8; Lk. 10:4), but Mk. differs in allowing the disciples to take staff and sandals – items which Lk. and Mt. prohibit (Lk. 10:4; Mt. 10:10). Luke alone forbids the greeting on the way and while Lk. 10:1-12 addresses the seventy, Mk. 6:7-13; Lk. 9:1-6; and Mt. 9:37f. address the twelve.

Interestingly enough, the closest parallels belong to material found in Q's mission
discourse as we have reconstructed it (Lk. 10.7a, 7b, 8, 16). This is some reason for
inferring Paul's knowledge of a collection of logia not far from what we have contended
belonged to Q.[145]

While this conclusion is a bold one, the evidence does imply Paul's awareness of
Jesus' teaching, and suggests that Paul literally applied Jesus' instructions to his
own mission enterprise—a practice frequently associated exclusively with the Q
community.[146] In relation to this information, the obvious question to raise is
whether it is necessary to speculate that Lk. 10:1-16 par., reflects a unique
soteriological emphasis or mission's perspective of Q when in fact the missionary
Paul, the preacher of the cross, draws from the same tradition? We think not.
Rather, the Q material was valued as tradition at a very early stage and was used as
such in the Church at large.

B. Jesus the Sender of Disciples who Preach the Kingdom of God

Lk. 10:9//Mt. 10:7, 8[147] usually appears within discussions focusing on the
temporal nature of the kingdom. The question is whether *ἤγγικεν* means "to

---

[145] *Matthew* II, 164. See also D.C. Allison, "The Pauline Epistles and the Synoptic
Gospels: The Pattern of the Parallels, *NTS* 28 (1982) 1-32; D.L. Dungan, *The Sayings of Jesus
in the Churches of St. Paul*, Philadelphia: Fortress (1971) 3-80. *Contra* C.M. Tuckett, "Paul and
the Synoptic Mission Discourse?", *ETL* 60 (1984) 376-381. Tuckett argues that "the mere
existence of isolated allusions cannot establish Allison's theory that larger blocks of synoptic
material were as such known to Paul" (377) . . . It is just as likely that Paul knew this as an
isolated saying" (381). Allison responds to Tuckett's criticism in a second article ("Paul and the
Missionary Discourse", *ETL* 61 [1985] 369-375) claiming that the phenomenon that over half of
the Pauline-Synoptic parallels appear in only three synoptic blocks suggests a pattern in Paul's
use of traditional material (370). Allison further disagrees that 1 Tim. 5:18 and Did. 13:1-2
provide evidence that the sayings in Lk. 10 were originally isolated, since these two passages
were likely dependent upon Matthew (371). Allison remains convinced "the synoptic parallels to
1 Cor. 9, 1 Cor. 10, and 1 Thess 4 all appear in Lk. 10:1-16, which may be close to being
undiluted Q material. . . . Paul knew a form of the missionary discourse very close to what was
in Q" (375). For the parallels in vocabulary between Lk. 10 and 1 Cor 9, see Allison (*ETL* 61,
372).

[146] So T.W. Manson, *The Sayings of Jesus*, 180: "This principle, it may be noted, governs
the missionary work of Paul, who supported himself by manual labor in his evangelistic career."

[147] Mt. 10:7, 8 differs from Lk. 10:9 in order, length, and the addition of the concluding
phrase "give freely." Most scholars identify *πορεύομαι* and *κηρύσσετε* as Mt. redaction while
the *ὅτι* recitative may be an omission by Lk. for whom such usage is uncommon (*Blass,
Debrunner and Funk*, § 470,1). The origin of Luke's *ἐφ᾽ ὑμᾶς* is highly contested. H.
Conzelmann followed by S. Schulz and E. Grässer have identified the phrase as typical of Luke's
eschatological terminology; however, the existence of the exact same phrase in Lk. 11:20//Mt.
12:28, also a Q Kingdom saying, suggests that the phrase may be traditional. Luke's *τοὺς ἐν
αὐτῇ ἀσθενεῖς* has been taken by most scholars as the original wording in reference to *πόλιν* in

have come" in which case the translation would be similar to the meaning of ἔφθασεν in Lk. 11:20//Mt. 12:28, or whether ἤγγικεν means "to be near" which implies "close but not yet." Debate on this issue endures. Several facts require consideration. First, ἐγγίζειν is a fitting word within Jesus' kingdom pronouncement as we have described it to this point. In the LXX the word denotes both the approach of the time of salvation (Isa. 50:8; 51:5; 56:6) and the approaching day of judgement (Eze. 7:7; 22:4). Similarly, the adjective ἐγγύς denotes the proximity of judgement within the OT prophets (Joel 1:15; 2:1; Ob. 15; Zeph. 1:7, 14; Isa. 13:6; Eze. 30:3).[148] Second, ἤγγικεν in a kingdom context is not peculiar to Q. It appears in Mk. 1:15 in the introductory pronouncement of Jesus.[149] And third, ἤγγικεν in Lk. 10:9//Mt. 10:7 exists in tension with the healing ministry of the disciples just as ἔφθασεν exists in tension with Jesus' exorcism in Lk. 11:20//Mt. 12:28. There is a close association between Jesus' miracles and the present reality of the kingdom of God.

Mt. 3:2 and Lk. 21:8 preclude the possibility that ἤγγικεν denotes imminence exclusively. However, the relation of Lk. 10:9//Mt. 10:7, 8 to Lk. 11:20//Mt. 12:28 and Lk. 7:22f.//Mt. 11:4f. requires that we look at this saying not only from a temporal standpoint but also from a christological one. The works of Jesus alluded to in Lk. 7:22f//Mt. 11:4f. identify Jesus as the anointed one of Isa. 61:1f.

Lk. 10:8 despite the fact that Matthew's participial form ἀσθενοῦντας appears in Lk. 4:40; Ac. 19:12; and Mt. 25:43, 44. The additional healings in Matthew probably represent Matthew's assimilation of Jesus' works in Lk. 7:22//Mt. 11:5 to the disciples here. The first Evangelist acts similarly in Mt. 10:1 where he reports the twelve doing exactly what he has deemed characteristic of Jesus earlier in Mt. 4:23; 9:35. δωρεὰν ἐλάβετε, δωρεὰν δότε has also been presumed to be redactional as it fits Matthew's style in continuing the rhythm of the preceding couplets while forming a fitting transition to the new thought in Mt. 10:9, 10. It must be said, however, that the background of this phrase is thoroughly Semitic (*Strack Billerbeck* 1, 561-4), which suggests the phrase may have been originally an independent dominical saying subsequently placed in this context by Matthew. See S. Schulz, *ibid.*, 406, 407; R. Laufen, *ibid.*, 221, 222; P. Hoffmann, *ibid.*, 273; A. Polag, *ibid.*, 46, 47; H. Schürmann, *Lukas*, 407; H. Conzelmann, *Die Mitte der Zeit*, 98; E. Grässer, *Das Problem der Parusierverzögerung in den synoptischen Evangelien und in der Apostelgeschichte*, 140.

[148] See H. Preisker, *TDNT* II, "ἐγγύς, ἐγγίζω", 330-332.

[149] R. Uro (*Sheep Among Wolves*, 152) follows G. Dautzenburg and D. Georgi (*Die Gegner des Paulus im 2. Korintherbrief. Studien zur religiösen Propaganda in der Spätantike*, Neukirchen-Vluyn: Neukirchener Verlag [1964] 205-213) in perceiving a clear distinction between the meaning of ἤγγικεν in Mk. 1:15 where the word connotes temporal nearness and the meaning of the same word in Q where it specifies spatial and concrete dimensions - "the kingdom has come upon men in the activity of the disciples." This distinction should not be pressed, however, as Mk. 1:15 anticipates the healing and exorcism miracles which Jesus performs in the early chapters of Mark's Gospel. It is telling that Dautzenberg goes on to accept Mk. 1:15 and Lk. 10:9//Mt. 10:7, 8 as independent sayings which testify that the early Church's KG teaching was directly dependent upon the teaching of Jesus himself; "Der Wandel der Reich-Gottes-Verkündigung in der urchristlichen Mission", 30.

whose works signify the salvific presence of God's reign. Similarly, Jesus'
exorcism of the demon alluded to in Lk. 11:20//Mt. 12:28 proves, to Jesus'
satisfaction, that the kingdom is alive in Jesus' own ministry. Here in Lk.
10:9//Mt. 10:7, 8 the healing ministry of Jesus' messengers evidences the nearness
of the kingdom. These Q sayings suggest that we comprehend the kingdom not
exclusively as a temporal span, but as a manifestation of salvific power which
Jesus radiates in his own ministry. Representative of the kingdom is the power
which Jesus commissions his disciples to express both in word and deed. The
disciples' ministry, however, in no way elevates the disciples to the status of Jesus
because the recognition that they have been sent by Jesus remains in view—their
ministry is not their own but that commissioned them by Jesus. As a result, the
acceptance or rejection of Jesus' messengers bears the same consequences as the
acceptance or rejection of Jesus himself—ie., those who welcome the disciples
witness the salvific benefits of the kingdom as marked by the healings, while those
who rebuff the disciples face judgement.[150]

W. Thüßing has written that Jesus' proclamation of the kingdom of God
contains the starting point for christology, because Jesus' message reveals his
relationship to God—"the theme 'Jesus and the kingdom of God' is identical with
the theme 'Jesus and God.'"[151] Thüßing's statement is supported by the fact that
in Lk. 7:22//Mt. 11:5 Jesus performs the acts which the OT prophets and 4Q 521
expected from God (Isa. 29:18; 35:5, 6 ; 42:18). A similar oddity occurs here in
Lk. 10:9//Mt. 10:7 where Jesus displays unusual authority in sending out
disciples. O.H. Steck, P. Hoffmann, and J. Kloppenborg[152] have rightly noted
that Lk. 10:3, 16 par., place Jesus in the position of God or Sophia as the one who
initiates the eschatological harvest and who sends out eschatological envoys.
M.D. Johnson, however, has shown conclusively that Wisdom is not a figure in
pre-Christian literature who sends out "envoys"—rather Wisdom visits man

---

[150] So A. Polag, *Christologie der Logienquelle*, 69: "Auf diese zeichenhafte Erklärung der
Solidarität mit Jesus in einem Akt der Aufnahme seiner Boten kommt es anscheinend bei der
ganzen Aktion der Jungersendung an." See also W. Thüßing, *Neutestamentlichen Theologien 1*,
Dusseldorf: Patmos (1981) 80: "Die Stellungnahme der Menschen 'in den Städten Israels' für oder
gegen Jesus hat ihre futurisch-eschatologischen Auswirkung."

[151] *Ibid.*, 66.

[152] O.H. Steck, *Israel und das gewaltsame Geschick der Propheten*, 286 n. 9; J.
Kloppenborg, *The Formation of Q*, 197 n. 113, 319; P. Hoffmann, *Studien zur Theologie der
Logienquelle*, 139: "In Q-Logion tritt Jesus an die Stelle, die in der apokalyptischen Tradition
Jahwe oder die Weisheit einnehmen; gerade in dieser Funktion wird er der "Sohn" genannt. Er ist
es auch, nicht Gott oder die Weisheit, der die Jünger sendet und zu wirkmächtiger Ankündigung
der Nähe der Herrschaft Gottes bevollmächtigt. Dabei bleibt er als der Sohn dem Vater
untergeordnet, als der Gesandte dem, der ihn gesandt hat; dennoch ist deutlich: die Gruppe weiß
sich in ihrer Hoffnung und ihrer Wirksamkeit in einmaliger Weise an die Person Jesu gebunden,
dessen Menschensohnwürde sie bekennt."

herself.[153] Thus, as in Lk. 7:22//Mt. 11:5, we are left with the fact that Jesus in Luke 10:2-12 par. acts in place of God. What are we to make of this?

Jesus' authoritative commissioning address correlates with his *abba* address, his self-disclosure as the Son of Man, and his self-identification as "the Son" in Lk. 10:22//Mt. 11:27—which together with the preaching of the kingdom represent the genuine thought of Jesus. Jesus understands his authority as the prerogative of the Son of Man figure of Dn. 7:13, who in Dn. 7:14 receives eternal dominion (שָׁלְטָנֵהּ שָׁלְטָן עָלַם), an authority remarkably close to that associated with God in Dn. 3:33b and 6:27b and which is in fact exactly the same authority as that which describes God's eternal rule in 4:31 (שָׁלְטָנֵהּ שָׁלְטָן עָלַם). Furthermore, if the "sending out sayings" have a conceptual background in Daniel 7, difficulty no longer exists in comprehending why Jesus authorizes the disciples to wield the authority and message which characterizes his own ministry, because the combination of terms cited as unique to God and the "one like a son of man" are applied in Dn. 7 to the suffering saints. In Dn. 7:18 the "saints" receive a kingdom which they will rule forever, while in 7:22, following God's judgement, the saints take possession of the kingdom; and, in 7:27a, the sovereignty, the dominion, and the greatness of all the kingdoms under the heavens are given to the saints. Thus, the background of Dn. 7 makes comprehensible the disciples' healing ministry and their pronouncement of the kingdom of God in Lk. 10:9//Mt. 10:7, 8, as they are in solidarity with Jesus the Son of Man in whom resides the authority of Yahweh.

Lk. 10:21, 22//Mt. 11:25-27 communicates congenial thoughts by holding together the same three-way relationship between: (a) almighty sovereign God whom Jesus characteristically refers to as father (πάτερ, κύριε τοῦ οὐρανοῦ καὶ τῆς γῆς), (b) Jesus the Son who receives all things from the Father, and (c) Jesus' followers to whom he desires to reveal the Father (καὶ ᾧ ἐὰν βούληται ὁ υἱὸς ἀποκαλύψαι). In Lk. 10:9//Mt. 10:7, 8 the disciples are precisely the ones who have been commissioned by Jesus to heal the sick and to pronounce that the kingdom of God has come near. What can this mean except that the disciples have received directly from Jesus the knowledge that God's power is salvific and available to men through Jesus the Son. Lk. 10:9//Mt. 10:7, 8 cannot be read without presupposing a direct relationship between God and Jesus, and since Jesus characteristically refers to God as "Father" in Q, it remains only fitting that here we see Jesus speaking as the Son.

Finally, this interpretation of Lk. 10:9//Mt. 10:7, 8 gains support from the Lord's Prayer where Jesus teaches the disciples to pray to God with his customary *abba* address. It must not be overlooked that in the act of teaching the prayer Jesus

---

[153] "Reflections on a Wisdom approach to Matthew's Christology", 44-64.

reveals to his followers the very nature of the God to whom they are praying—his fatherhood, his sovereignty, his creatorship, and his holiness. Furthermore, Ro. 8:15 and Gal. 4:6 are evidence that *abba* was valued sacred by the earliest Christians as a usage of Jesus which implies intimate sonship not only for Jesus but for the early Christians themselves. These references suggest that at a very early period within the life of the Church, Christians were reflecting upon Jesus' sayings and drawing christological conclusions from them.[154] Lk. 10:9//Mt. 10:7, 8 exemplifies how the early church could have taken an authentic commissioning address of Jesus to his original disciples and applied it to their own post-Easter situation in which missionaries such as Paul were commissioned for missionary service by the exalted Lord Jesus.[155] There exists no reason to speculate that Jesus' Q sayings were valued exclusively at any point in time by a community which did not place significance upon Jesus' death and resurrection.

V. The Lord's Prayer: Lk. 11:2-4//Mt. 6:9-13

The Lord's prayer advances our argument that Q contains fragments of tradition which describe Jesus' intent to gather the people of God for the eschatological day of salvation. In coherence with other Q passages,[156] the Lord's Prayer confirms

---

[154] So W. Thußing, *Erhöhungsvorstellung und Parusieerwartung in der ältesten nachösterlichen Christologie*, Stuttgart: Katholisches Bibelwerk (1970) 55-82, esp. 57.

[155] S. Schulz (*Q-Die Logienquelle,* 409) identifies the entire mission section as conforming to a single secondary "Apophthegm" which was manufactured during the Hellenistic-Jewish phase of Q. H. Schürmann ("Das Zeugnis der Redenquelle für die Basileia-Verkündigung Jesu", 46-150) addresses the saying as a secondary addition (*Zusatzbildung*) to the mission tradition in conformity with Lk. 11:20//Mt. 12:28 which Schürmann claims to be authentic. Schürmann identifies ecclesiastical tainting behind Lk. 10:6 and 10:11b. He largely bases his conclusion on the comparison of Lk. 10:2-12 par., and Mk. 6:6-13 which does not contain a KG saying. Yet Mk. 6:6-13 is clearly a redactional abbreviation of traditional material. Further, Mk. 6:12, 13 does in fact compare quite closely with Lk. 10:9 par., in that the disciples call for repentance, cast out demons, and heal many. They perform the acts which characterize Jesus elsewhere. It is telling that in Mk. 1:15 Jesus' announcement of the Kingdom precedes his command to repent and believe in the Gospel. Thus, when in 6:12 the disciples preach repentance, it is a fair estimation that simultaneously they would have announced the nearness of the Kingdom as it was, in fact, the reason for repenting.

[156] The hypothesis of a Q original behind Mt. 6:9-13 and Lk. 11:2-4 is by no means problemless despite the vast number of scholars who judge the parallels between the two versions to be evidence of a Q *Vorlage* (See J. Kloppenborg, *Q-Parallels*, 84). Differences in wording and length prohibit certain proclamation of original form. Caution is appropriate despite attempts to see the differences in length as Matthew's expansion and the differences in tense and vocabulary as alterations typical of Luke's style. Jeremias originally resisted the redactional approach by citing the unlikelihood that the Gospel writers would have altered a sacred liturgical prayer well known to the intended audiences. To this warning, E. Lohmeyer adds that both versions of the prayer contain poetic structures – a fact that "serves as a warning against any assumption that one form arose from the other as a result of abbreviation or expansion", (*The Lord's Prayer*, London:

that Jesus in Q is more than a prophet. Jesus is a figure bearing uncommon authority who has set out to gather the eschatological people of God. Despite enormous controversy surrounding several key words and phrases in the Lord's Prayer, which perhaps may never be settled, several facts do surface. The prayer is "theocentric." In appealing to God as Father, the prayer invokes God's mercy together with his sovereignty and power. It seeks the salvific benefits of God's kingdom. The entreaty is a prayer to God: The ones praying recognize their need for God's intervention in their lives for daily provisions, for forgiveness, and for protection from evil. The prayer is characteristic of Jesus.[157] H. Schürmann goes so far as to argue that the Lord's Prayer is the key to understanding Jesus' teaching in its entirety: "Die Verkündigung Jesu muß das Vaterunser aufschlüsseln, und: das Vaterunser ist der Schlüssel für die Verkündigung Jesu";[158] and especially Jesus' teaching on the kingdom of God: "Hinter dem Gebetswunsch «Vater, es komme dein Reich» wird –wie wohl nirgendwo sonst—Jesu ureigenes Basileia-Verständnis deutlich."[159] The positive aspects of Schürmann's statement are secure. The Lord's prayer requests from God the successful completion of Jesus' ministry. It requests that God's people (those who have identified with Jesus) receive a new relationship with God—a relationship likened to sonship. It requests that God's kingdom be consummated in order that the saving benefits

---

Collins [1965] 30). Furthermore, word counts which often form the basis for ascribing a word or phrase to secondary redaction could be misleading in the case of the Lord's Prayer as the Evangelists could have adopted a form of speech from a known dominical teaching like the Lord's Prayer and subsequently repeated the usage elsewhere as characteristic of Jesus. Yet, despite the significant differences, a common Greek source seems probable in light of the parallels especially in regard to ἐπιούσιος – a word extremely rare in Greek literature but exactly parallel in the two versions of Jesus' prayer. If we seek a common source, Matthean priority falters on the fact that there are no Mattheanisms in Luke's prayer. In fact the petitions most characteristic of Matthew are absent from Luke. The expansion of the Lord's Prayer seems more likely than its reduction in light of known tendencies in later transmissions of Greek texts. Do we concede the prayer's background to Q? We hesitate. U. Luz has detected reminiscences of Matthew's version in Mk. 11:25 and 2 Ti. 4:18 and with less certainty Mk. 14:36, 38; Jn. 12:28; 17:15 (*Matthäus* I, 335). This evidence suggests that Matthew's greater length does not require redaction on the part of the first Evangelist, but rather the language may attest to the prayer as it existed at a very early stage. Cf. G. Schneider ("Das Vaterunser des Matthäus", *A Cause de L'Évangile*, FS J. Dupont; Cerf: Publications de Saint-André [1985] 69) who argues that Matthew did expand an original Q prayer.

[157] Davies and Allison (*Matthew* I, 593) reason it is unlikely that the Early Church would have created a prayer requesting the coming of God's kingdom when 1 Cor. 16:22, Rev. 22:20 and Didache 10:6 demonstrate that the church's cry was in fact μαραυα θα. Others supporting authenticity include among others: I.H. Marshall, *Luke*, 455; J. Fitzmyer, *Luke* II, 897 f.; U. Luz, *Matthäus* I, 336; J.D.G. Dunn, *Christology*, 27, 28; H. Schürmann ("Das Zeugnis der Redenquelle für die Basileia-Verkündigung Jesu", 153): "--Lk. 11,2-4 dürfte mit an Gewißheit grenzender Wahrscheinlichkeit Jesus zuzusprechen sein"; A. Polag, *Christologie der Logienquelle,* 59, 60; G.R. Beasley-Murray, *The Kingdom of God,* 147f., and the vast majority of scholars.

[158] *Das Gebet des Herrn,* 13.

[159] "Das Zeugnis der Redenquelle für die Basileia-Verkündigung Jesu", 153.

characteristic of heaven might be openly visible on earth. It requests divine forgiveness and calls for the defeat of Satan. In brevity and clarity, the Lord's Prayer expresses the theological content of Jesus' gospel of the kingdom (Mk. 1:15).

Schürmann claims five features of Jesus' perception of the kingdom of God can be gleaned from Lk. 11:1-4//Mt. 6:9-14. (1) Jesus' concept of *Basileia* is eschatological and still future. (2) The kingdom is the destiny of the praying Jesus and, as the three "We Petitions" suggest, those who follow Jesus in praying to God as *abba*. Those who pray have a present consciousness of God's reign. (3) Jesus' concept of the kingdom is eschatologically bound to God's eschatological gift of salvation. (4) The kingdom for Jesus means the full and final consummation of Jahweh's reign at the end of history. And (5), the salvific character of Jesus' kingdom address is deeply stamped by his own relationship to the Father.[160]

Schürmann's final point—that the *abba* address reveals Jesus' unique relationship to God—has been refuted by G. Vermes in his criticism of Jeremias's groundbreaking studies on the prayers of Jesus.[161] Vermes argues that the earliest use of Son of God related primarily to Jesus' activities as a miracle worker and exorcist and not to a filial relationship to God.[162] While few doubt that Jesus referred to God as Father in prayer, Vermes reminds us that the ancient Hasidim prayed for an hour each day to their Father in heaven (the Mishnah Berakhoth 5:1). Also undermining the uniqueness of Jesus' *abba* prayer is an ancient Jewish anecdote which refers to God as *abba* in heaven,[163] and Jeremias's own data which show that *abba* was used by adults as an address of affection to old men. And finally, wisdom texts exist in which God is addressed as Father with a degree of intimacy (Wisd. 14:3; Sir. 23:1, 4; 51:10; III Macc.6:3, 8). These objections, however, must be weighed carefully. If Vermes's objections are accepted as they stand, we are left with the fact that *abba* represents, if not the unique, at least the characteristic designation of God as Father in Jesus' prayers—a fact demonstrated by the special significance attested by Paul to *abba* in Ro. 8:15 and Ga. 4:6 and by

---

160 *Ibid.*, 153.

161 J. Jeremias, *The Prayers of Jesus,* ET London: SCM (1967) 53-54.

162 *Jesus the Jew,* London: Collins (1973) 210.

163 *Ibid.*, 210f. *Babylonian Ta' anit 23b,* the ancient Jewish anecdote, reads, according to Vermes, "Master of the Universe, do it for the sake of these who are unable to distinguish between the Father who gives rain and the father who does not." *M. Ber. 5,1* reads "The ancient Hasidim spent an hour (in recollection before praying) in order to direct their hearts towards their Father in heaven."

"all five strata of the Gospel tradition": Mark, Q, M, L, John.[164] It appears unlikely that Paul would have emphasized *abba* if it were a common prayer idiom. Yet more can be said in Jeremias's defense. Vermes' citations have historical weaknesses. J. Fitzmyer points out that Vermes' rendition of M. Ber. 5,1 depends upon a variant form of the Mishnaic statement which in all probability is not the most primitive. Also misleading is the fact that the literal translation of the Hebrew of m. Ber. 5,1 reads: ". . . to direct their heart to the Place" rather than Vermes' ". . . to direct their hearts towards their Father in heaven." In addition, Fitzmyer notes that the form in Vermes' citation is לַאֲבִיהֶם (to their father) and not *abba*. The ancient Jewish anecdote which Vermes cites (B. Ta'anit 23b) comes from the fifth-century Babylonian Talmud and hence cannot be taken as evidence for common first-century Palestinian usage.[165] The cited Wisdom texts do not in fact contain or emphasize the Aramaic name *abba* as it occurs in Mk. 14:36; Ga. 4:6; Ro. 8:15.[166] The Pauline references emphasize the filial implications of the term and indicate that at a very early stage sonship to God was understood to be a specific gift bestowed upon the followers of Jesus.[167] That *abba* does not necessarily mean "Daddy"[168] does not belittle the term's uniqueness in the prayers of Jesus. Thus after almost forty years of critical scrutiny, Jeremias' basic proposal remains sound—apart from Jesus' usage there is not forthcoming evidence in the literature of ancient Palestinian Judaism that *abba* is used as a personal address to God.

abba implies Jesus' personal familiarity with God the father, as Aramaic was the language of the people not the synagogue. J. Schlosser may also be correct that Jesus' use of *abba* is unique in regard to distance. In contrast to the references offered by Vermes in which *abba* is qualified as the "Father in heaven," Jesus' use of *abba* implies the direct accessibility of God. It is here, according to Schlosser, that "Nous touchons là l'originalité de Jésus."[169] The use of *abba* then insinuates a theological perspective which Jesus' entire prayer presupposes.

---

[164] Mk. 14:36; Mt. 6:9//Lk. 11:2; Mt. 11:25, 26//Lk. 10:21, 22; Lk. 23:34, 46; Mt. 26:42; John 11:41; 12:27f.; 17:1, 5, 11, 21, 24, 25; J. Jeremias, *The Prayers of Jesus*, 54.

[165] "Abba and Jesus' Relationship to God", 27, 29-30.

[166] *The Prayers of Jesus*, 29. J. Dunn (*Christology in the Making*, 27) also criticizes Jeremias' claim by citing Wis. 14:3; Sir. 23:1, 4; 51:10; 3 Macc. 6:3, 8. Ben Witherington III (*The Christology of Jesus*, Minneapolis: Fortress [1990] 216-21), however, rightly points out that 3 Macc. and Wisdom both go back to Greek, not Aramaic originals. Sir. 23:1, 4; 51:10, written in Hebrew, does not contain the word *abba* "much less *abba* in prayer language" (217).

[167] See R. Bauckham, "The Sonship of the Historical Jesus in Christology", *SJT* 31 (1985) 35-41.

[168] See James Barr, " 'Abba' isn't 'Daddy' ", *JTS* 39 (1988) 28-47.

[169] *Le Dieu de Jésus*, 207.

That *abba* reflects Jesus' filial relationship to God strengthens in view of Mt. 16:17; Mk. 13:32; Lk. 22:29; and Lk. 10:22//Mt. 11:27—passages which deal specifically with Jesus' relationship to God as the source of Jesus' authority and revelation. Of these, Lk. 10:22//Mt. 11:27 stands out for our present study of Q.

A. Jesus the Son, God the Father and the Kingdom of God in the Lord's Prayer and Lk. 10:21, 22//Mt. 11:25-27

J. Fitzmyer, after affirming J. Jeremias's basic conclusions that *abba* recalls a term used by Jesus himself in reference to God in prayer, isolates the references Jeremias identified as authentic (Lk. 11:2 par.; Lk. 10:21 par.; and Mk. 14:36) to reach the conclusion that "a cautious look at all aspects of the *abba* problem seems to call for the recognition that some part of the tradition was rooted in an attitude of Jesus in his historical ministry."[170] From this judgement, Fitzmyer turns to Jeremias's other famous conclusion that "'my father' on the lips of Jesus expresses a unique relationship with God."[171] It is in relation to Jesus' "uniqueness" that Lk. 10:21-22//Mt. 11:25-27 appears crucial. In this passage whose two Greek versions parallel almost exactly, Jesus' portrait of God the Father who reigns as "Lord of heaven and earth" parallels the Lord's Prayer where God's fathership coincides with the authority manifested in his will "on earth as it is in heaven." Similar to the humble attitude displayed before God by those who pray Jesus' prayer the recipients of God's gift in Lk. 10:21 par. are babes—those aware of their total dependence upon the Father. However, Lk. 10:21, 22 par. goes beyond the Lord's Prayer to state specifically that the children have received a gift of knowledge somehow hidden from the wise and understanding. "All things" ($\pi\acute{a}\nu\tau a$) refers to an exclusive authority given Jesus by the Father. The plain meaning of Lk. 10:22//Mt. 11:27 is that Jesus' authority comes specifically from his relation as son to God the Father. It is Jesus' sonship which allows him to reveal the Father, and to preach the nearness of the kingdom of God. When we compare this text with the burden of Jesus' teaching elsewhere in Q—namely teaching on the kingdom of God—the obvious inference to be made is that Jesus derives from God in a unique manner the authority which he assumes in heralding in the kingdom (Lk. 6:20//Mt. 5:3; Lk. 7:22//Mt. 11:5), in teaching authoritatively

---

[170] *"Abba and Jesus' Relationship to God"*, 33.

[171] *The Prayers of Jesus*, 83-84. So also J.D.G. Dunn, among others: "It is difficult therefore to escape the conclusion that Jesus said 'Abba' to God for precisely the same reason that (most of) his contemporaries refrained from its use in prayer – viz., because it expressed his attitude to God as Father, his experience of God as one of unusual intimacy", *Jesus and the Spirit*, 23.

about the kingdom, in proclaiming that the kingdom of God is somehow present in his acts (Lk. 7:22//Mt. 11:5; Lk. 11:20//Mt. 12:28), and in judging who will and who will not participate in the future eschatological banquet (Lk. 13:28, 29//Mt. 8:11, 12; Lk. 14:15-24//Mt. 22:1-10). It is, indeed, telling that in Q the following facts converge. (1) Jesus performs saving acts which the OT exclusively associates with God on the eschatological Day of the Lord (Lk. 7:22//Mt. 11:5: Isa. 26:19f.; 29:18f.; 35:5f.). (2) Jesus refers to God in an unusually intimate fashion in the Lord's Prayer. (3) Jesus refers to himself as son in relation to God in a non-titular manner (Lk. 10:21, 22 par.). (4) Jesus adopts the epithet Son of Man which implicitly alludes to Dn. 7:13, 14 where "the one like a Son of Man" appears in close proximity to "the Ancient of Days" and, like Jesus in Q, receives the same dominion, power, and kingdom which in earlier parts of Daniel describe the sovereignty of God (3:33; 4:31). (5) Jesus initiates in Q the eschatological harvest and sends out messengers—a function characteristic of God in the OT and in Wisdom texts.[172] (6) In Q Lk. 9:59f.//Mt. 8:21f., Jesus authoritatively demands his followers to break with Jewish custom. Such authority appears, according to M. Hengel, "in a way in which in the OT only God himself enjoined obedience on individual prophets in regard to the proclamation of his approaching judgment."[173] (7) And finally, in no less than nineteen cases does Jesus assume special authority in defiance of Jewish religious leaders by using the λέγω ὑμῖν (σοί) address in Q.[174] Thus characteristic of Q is the eschatological distinction of Jesus described in Lk. 10:23//Mt. 13:16, 17:

---

[172] So J. Kloppenborg: "While the metaphor of teacher or master is an important one, Q 10:3, 16 implies somewhat more. In these texts Jesus appears as the one who initiates the eschatological harvest and as the one whose message, as carried by his envoys, is equivalent to the voice of God. Steck rightly notes that 10:16 in effect places Jesus in the position of God or Sophia, as sender of the eschatological envoys", *The Formation of Q*, 319. Kloppenborg, however, believes the association of Jesus with the divine occurred in the second (polemical) stage of Q's literary development (320). Kloppenborg refers to O.H. Steck, *Israel und das gewaltsame Geschick der Propheten*, 286 n. 9. See also D. Catchpole, "The Mission Charge in Q", *Semeia* 55, 154.

[173] *The Charismatic Leader and His Followers*, 12.

[174] Lk. 6:27//Mt. 5:44; Lk. 6:29//Mt. 5:39; Lk. 7:9//Mt. 8:10; Lk. 7:26//Mt. 11:9; Lk. 7:28//Mt. 11:11; Lk. 10:12//Mt. 10:15; Lk. 10:14//Mt. 11:22; Lk. 10:24//Mt. 13:17; Lk. 11:51//Mt. 23:36; Lk. 12:3//Mt. 10:27; Lk. 12:4//Mt. 10:28; Lk. 12:22//Mt. 6:25; Lk. 12:27//Mt. 6:29; Lk. 12:24//Mt. 24:47; Lk. 12:51//Mt. 10:34; Lk. 12:59//Mt. 5:26; Lk. 13:24//Mt. 7:13; Lk. 13:35//Mt. 23:39; Lk. 15:7//Mt. 18:13. So J.D.G. Dunn (*Jesus and the Spirit*, 79): "When others in the tradition in which Jesus stood expressed the immediacy of their authority, they prefaced their words with "Thus says the Lord." But Jesus said, "Amen, I say to you" and, "But I say to you."

But blessed are your eyes, because they see; and your ears, because they hear. For truly I say to you, that many prophets and righteous men desired to see what you see, and did not see it; and to hear what you hear, and did not hear it.

In this passage, as in Lk. 10:21//Mt. 11:25, Jesus refers indefinitely to a blessing which his listeners have received. What is definite, however, is that the blessing is manifest in the appearance and ministry of the speaker—Jesus. Hence it is clear that within Q Jesus' uniqueness resides precisely in his relationship to God—a relationship which authorizes him to bring good news to the poor, heal the sick, cast out demons, and reveal the Father. In view of this evidence, is it necessary to speculate that the "Q community" collected, modified, and created sayings of Jesus as a byproduct of "prophetic enthusiasm" occasioned by a particular expectation of the parousia or some other unknown apocalyptic stimulus? It seems infinitely more plausible, rather, that Jesus created an atmosphere of "enthusiasm" in his acts and in his teaching about the kingdom, and that it was Jesus himself who attracted followers and who instilled hostility in religious authorities who rejected his arrogant teaching (Q: Lk. 11:37-52//Mt. 23:4, 6, 7, 13, 25-31, 34-36). Of the former group it is plausible that some recorded Jesus' teaching. Jesus himself was the motivation for them to do so. In the latter group we may see the early impetus for hostility towards Jesus—the form of hostility which eventually led to his execution. There exists no conclusive evidence to discredit the authenticity of Lk. 10:22//Mt. 11:27. Its conceptual background exists in the OT and in Jewish Wisdom Literature[175]—literature familiar to Jesus.[176] We have in Q the dominical

---

[175] The saying's background is clearly not in Hellenistic literature. The closest parallel appears to be Wisdom 2:10, 13, 16, 18. However, the function of Jesus elsewhere in Q together with his mediator role here require that his sonship be viewed as a role more significant than the "poor man" in Wisdom who places his trust in God.

[176] For extensive lists of scholars, past and present, who support or deny the authenticity of Lk. 10:22, see J. Fitzmyer, "Abba and Jesus' Relation to God", 37 n. 91, 92. Notable scholars not included in his list who support the saying's authenticity include I.H. Marshall, "The Divine Sonship of Jesus", 146; J.D.G. Dunn, *Christology in the Making*, 27, 28; J. Fitzmyer, *Luke* II, 870 ("substance as authentic"). J. Schlosser (*Le Dieu de Jésus*, Paris: Cerf [1987] 143-145) has recently discredited the saying's authenticity arguing that 10:22 is inconsistent with 10:21 on 5 counts: (1) the two differ as to genre – the one is a prayer of praise the other a theological statement; (2) v. 21 is Semitic; v. 22 is not; (3) the subject of revelation changes from the Father in v. 21 to the Son in v. 22; (4) the object of revelation changes from "these things" in v. 21 to "the Father" in v. 22; and (5), the image of Jesus in v. 22 is that of the exalted Christ (Mt. 28:18; 1 Cor 15:27). Such objections, however, are not decisive. While "the contrast of the Father and the Son, made explicit in v. 22, is already implicit in v. 21b" (Fitzmyer, *Luke* II, 866), we do not understand why Jesus could not have followed a prayer with a theological statement. The content of v. 22 is in fact Semitic (see Davies and Allison, *Matthew* II, 286-87). Finally Jesus' authority need not be viewed as transcendent. The parallels between Mt. 28:18 and 1 Cor. 15:27 are not impressive. In Q Jesus teaches authoritatively, heals authoritatively, casts out demons, and pronounces woes on the religious leaders of Judaism. He must have considered

origin of the later identification of Jesus as the Son of God—a filial relationship which authorizes Jesus to proclaim the kingdom of God on earth and a relationship which leads Jesus to instruct his disciples to pray to God as *abba* – father.[177] *In Q Jesus is more than a prophet attempting the renewal of Israel.*

B. "Hallowed be thy Name; Thy Kingdom Come"

The first "Thou Petition" (ἀγιασθήτω τὸ ὄνομά σου) exists in exact parallel in Matthew, Luke, and Didache 8:2 and in a similar form in the Jewish Kaddish prayer. The third person aorist passive imperative ἀγιασθήτω is a divine passive which, in view of the aorist tense and the OT background, calls upon God to act on behalf of his name to bring about justice and redemption for his people in the eschatological day of salvation (Isa. 48:11; 52:6; Eze. 20:9, 14, 22; 36:22; 39:27-28). As G. Lohfink has emphasized, the call for God to sanctify his name is, against the OT background of Eze. 20:41, 44; 36:22-24, a request for God to gather his people: "He will sanctify it by gathering Israel in the last days from all over the world, renewing it, and making it again into a holy people."[178]

The future orientaton of the Lord's prayer does not require that we deny to Jesus all "present" kingdom of God sayings. The second "Thou petition" of the Lord's prayer (ἐλθέτω ἡ βασιλεία σου) completes the opening call for God to hallow his name by fully establishing his reign upon earth. ἐλθέτω like ἀγιασθήτω is an aorist imperative connoting a once-for-all, point in time, action. The second "thou petition" is thus a request for the future coming of God's absolute rule.[179] It is likely, however, that the aorist tense refers to the completion or fulfillment of God's reign rather than the commencement of the kingdom. "Kingdom" as the subject of "come" does not exist in the OT, ancient Jewish texts,

---

his authority to have come from somewhere. For a recent defense of the authenticity of Lk. 10:22, see Ben Witherington III, *The Christology of Jesus*, 221-28.

[177] Jesus as revealer of hidden knowledge to the select few is not exclusive to Lk. 10:22 par., or a wisdom tradition unique to Q. Jesus exudes the same ability in Mk. 4:11-12 – a saying whose authenticity has recently been supported by G.R. Beasley-Murray, *Jesus and the Kingdom of God*, 103-107. In Mk. 4:11 τὰ πάντα refers indefinitely to the message of the Kingdom which Jesus teaches in parables to those "outside," while in Lk. 10:22 πάντα refers indefinitely to the secrets of the kingdom which have been given to Jesus the Son.

[178] *Jesus and Community*, 15-17. Eze. 36:23, 24: "And I will vindicate the holiness of my great name, which has been profaned among the nations, and which you have profaned among them; and the nations will know that I am the Lord, says the Lord God, when through you I vindicate my holiness before their eyes. For I will take you from the nations, and gather you from all the countries, and bring you into your own land."

[179] E. Lohmeyer's statement is representative: "The tense of the verb . . . allows only the idea of a single coming; The first and most obvious meaning of the sentence is that this kingdom comes once for all and that it is therefore final and eschatological", *The Lord's Prayer*, 102.

or the NT outside of the Gospels. The nearest background for "kingdom come" exists in the OT anticipation of the coming of God (Isa. 35:4; 40:9-10; Zech. 14:5; 1 En. 1:3-9; 25:3: Jub. 1:22-8; T. Levi 5:2; As. Mos. 10:1-12; Tg. to Zech. 2:14-15).[180] It is perhaps no coincidence then that Jesus interprets his role in Lk. 7:22//Mt. 11:5, 6 against the background of Isa. 26:19; 29:18; 35:5, 6; 42:18; and 61:1, while in the first beatitude fulfilling Isa. 61:1 with the blessing of the poor. If Jesus did see himself as the herald of the kingdom as multiple attestation in Mk. 1:14,15; Lk. 4:18,19; and Lk. 7:22//Mt. 11:5, 6 indicate, and if Jesus did interpret his acts as the events characteristic of God's coming—"the eyes of the blind will be opened, and the ears of the deaf will be unstopped" (Isa. 35:5)—then "Your kingdom come" may well request the universal manifestation or consummation of God's saving power as it has begun to be revealed in Jesus' ministry. The thrust of the Lord's prayer is different therefore from comparable Jewish prayers simply because of the identity of its speaker.[181] It was given special importance by early Christians who had foremost in their minds the salvific acts which God performed through their savior.[182]

Excursus: The Forgiveness of Sins in Q

Dieter Zeller has written that the direct plea to God for the forgiveness of sins in the Lord's Prayer represents the theology of the "Q community" which attached no atoning value to Jesus' death on the cross—an event they only faintly remembered.[183] For the Q community the earthly work of Jesus has little significance.[184] Zeller's statement addresses an enigma underlying the synoptics at large: How to explain Jesus' present proclamation of God's forgiveness (Mk. 2:5; Lk. 7:48) in light of the forgiveness which he achieves for man on the cross (Mk. 10:45; 1 Cor. 15:3). Does the Lord's Prayer present a conflicting understanding of forgiveness from that preached by Paul? In response to this question, we first point out that the two forms of forgiveness were not viewed as

---

[180] So Davies and Allison, *Matthew* I, 604; J. Schlosser, *Le Règne de Dieu dans les dits de Jésus* I, Paris: Gabalda (1980) 268-83.

[181] I.H. Marshall writes, "the Christian prayer is distinguished by the fact that those who pray it have been taught by Jesus that the kingdom of God is at hand. They look forward to the consummation of the promises of God", *Luke*, 457.

[182] As in the Didache where the Lord's Prayer is prayed just prior to Baptism.

[183] "In Q wird der Tod Jesu nur einmal als Entschwinden angedeutet (Lk. 13,35); er ist nicht als Sühnesterben verstanden, die Vergebung Gottes braucht nicht erst durch ihn erwirkt zu werden, sondern die Q-Gemeinde bittet den Vater im Himmel direkt darum (Lk. 11,4), freilich von Jesu Wort ermuntert, daß Gott barmherzig ist (vgl. 6,36)", *Kommentar zur Logienquelle*, 97.

[184] "Gemessen an den Evangelien berichtet die Logienquelle *wenig vom Wirken des irdischen Jesus . . .*", *Kommentar zur Logienquelle*, 96.

contradictory to one another by the first Christians as the inclusion of the Lord's prayer in the Didache suggests. In addition, an answer to this question may reside in Jesus' preaching of the kingdom as it unfolds in his ministry and in the Lord's Prayer. The force of the aorist tenses and the eschatological language of the prayer suggest that the forgiveness which is sought here is forgiveness from the wrath to come at the final judgement. However, ἡμέραν/σήμερον still applies: the prayer seeks tomorrow's forgiveness today or as E. Lohmeyer puts it, "The aorist, as hitherto, demands not only a single action, but an action that is once and for all: it asks for God to give us bread today because it is eschatological bread, and to forgive our sins today because they are eschatologically blotted out."[185] The crucial weakness with Zeller's position, we believe, is that he does not take seriously enough the Q passages which emphasize the acts of Jesus (Lk. 7:1b-10//Mt. 8:5-10,13; Lk. 7:18-23//Mt. 11:2-6; Lk. 10:13-15//Mt. 11:21-23; Lk. 10:23-24//Mt. 13:16-17). Lk. 7:18-23 par., in particular, designates Jesus as the herald of God's kingdom—his acts signal the present manifestation of God's salvific power upon earth—the very power which will characterize God's rule at the end of time. The forgiveness of sins, like the healing of the blind, the lepers, and the deaf, is a present sign of the saving power characteristic of God's rule which is now proclaimed by Jesus but which will be experienced fully at the end of time. Hence the present forgiveness which Jesus authoritatively confers in Mk. 2:5; Lk. 7:48, like that sought in the Lord's Prayer, is a present manifestation of eschatological forgiveness. It is important to note that none of these passages attempt to explain how forgiveness is achieved—it is only asked for and received as a benefit of the kingdom. How does the kingdom of God relate to Jesus' death on the cross? In Mk. 2:5; Lk. 7:48 and the Lord's Prayer, faithful believers receive in the present through Jesus the eschatological forgiveness which Jesus anticipates accomplishing in Mk. 14:24 through his death on the cross. Jesus anticipates his death and the pouring out of his blood "for many" in Mk. 14:24 as an event directly related with his entrance into the kingdom of God. Jesus, therefore, interprets his death in Mark as accomplishing the same end as intended for his acts in Q—to gather people for salvation in the kingdom of God. Jesus' death and resurrection, like his healings and exorcisms, make known the saving power of God which faithful believers anticipate at God's final coming (Isa. 25:8). Jesus' death and resurrection do not conflict with but vindicate his preaching of the kingdom.

---

[185] *The Lord's Prayer*, 179.

VI.   Lk. 11:20//Mt. 12:28: Jesus, the Spirit and the Kingdom of God

A. The Tradition History of the Beelzebul Controversy and the Unity of Lk. 11:19, 20 par.

Like Jesus' commissioning address to the disciples, "the Beelzebul controversy" exists in all three Synoptic Gospels: Mt. 12:22-30; Mk. 3:22-27; and Lk. 11:14 - 23. Multiple accounts of Jesus exorcizing demons (Mk. 1:23-26, 32; 5:1-5; 16:9; Mt. 4:24; 8:28-34; 9:32, 33; 12:22, 23; 15:22-28; 17:14-21) support the case for the historicity of this account. The three versions show significant parallels between Matthew and Mark and between Matthew and Luke but only negligible similarity between Mark and Luke. As a result, those who adhere to the Q hypothesis conceive that a common tradition has entered the Synoptics in Mk. 3:22-27 and Q (Lk. 11:14-23), while Matthew conflates Mark and Q.[186] The parallels exist as follows.

Q Luke	Q Matthew	Mark
11:14	12:22f (?)	
11:15	12:24	3:22
11:17, 18	12:25, 26	3:23-26
11:19, 20	12:27, 28	
11:21, 22	12:29	3:27
11:23	12:30	
		3:28-30//Mt.12:31f.
11:24-26	12:43-45	
11: 16, 29	12:38, 39	8:11, 12//Mt. 16:12a, 4
11:31, 32	12:41, 42	

Lk. 11:20//Mt. 12:28 does not have a counterpart in Mark and has thus been classified as a Q logion. The parallelism between Lk. 11:19 par., and 11:20 par., argues for the verses' unity and not the contrary. The apparent incongruity between the exorcisms of the sons of the Jews in v. 19 and the exorcisms of Jesus in v. 20 is explained by the implicit contrast between Jesus and his Jewish counterparts. In Lk. 11:19//Mt. 12:27 Jesus acknowledges the exorcisms of Jewish contemporaries, but he does not assume that the Jewish exorcisms are accomplished by the Spirit of God nor does he assume the Spirit of God is accomplishing these exorcisms in order to demonstrate eschatological salvation which is consonant with the advent of the kingdom of God. James Dunn observes

---

[186] Davies and Allison assess Matthew's redactional process thus: "In sum, then, 12:22-8 and 30 are from Q, 12:29 from Mark, and 12:31-2 draws upon both of Matthew's primary sources", *Matthew* II, 333.

that Jesus' exorcisms stand in contrast to the exorcistic practices of his contemporaries. Whereas contemporary exorcists cast out demons by means of physical aids (Tobit 8:2; Josephus *Ant.* 8:45-49) or the invocation of another power source (Mk. 9:38; Acts 19:13), Jesus used no aids (Mk. 1:25//Lk. 5:8; 9:55) but rather cast out demons directly through "the eschatological power of God." Jesus' exorcisms have special significance not because they are unique in themselves (others exorcised demons), but, like Jesus' healing miracles (other prophets had healed), Jesus' exorcisms bear witness of Jesus' authority to mediate the eschatological saving power of God. Just as the healings in Lk. 7:22//Mt. 11:5 signify the presence of God's saving rule in Jesus' ministry, so also do Jesus' exorcisms bear witness to the eschatological power of God at work in Jesus in direct confrontation with the powers of Satan. According to Dunn, "the saying would most likely evoke the Jewish expectation that Satan would be vanquished at the end of the age (Isa. 24:21-22; 1 Enoch 10:4f.; Jub. 23:29; 1QS 4:18-19; T. Mos. 10:1; T. Levi 18:12; T. Jud. 25:3; Rev. 20:2-3)."[187] Like Jesus' other miracles, Jesus' exorcisms are unique, because his works have eschatological significance and are brought about by the Spirit of God.

B. Lk. 11:20//Mt. 12:28

Scholars have argued both for Luke's ἐν δακτύλῳ θεοῦ and for Matthew's ἐν πνεύματι θεοῦ as the original Q wording. In favour of Matthew's reading, Harnack argued on the basis of Lk. 1:51, 66, 73 that Luke characteristically used anthropomorphisms and thus he may have added one here.[188] Others question whether Matthew would have retained kingdom "of God" rather than his characteristic "of heaven," while simultaneously omitting ἐν δακτύλῳ—an allusion to Moses typology seemingly attractive to Matthew.[189] As to whether Luke would have omitted a "Spirit" phrase, Hamerton-Kelly notes that a word count of πνεῦμα (Lk. 38x; Mt. 19x) is not conclusive, while "Luke changes 'ἐν τῷ πνεύματι τῷ ἁγίῳ' (Mark xii. 36 par. Matt. xxii. 43) to 'ἐν βίβλῳ ψαλμῶν'" in Lk. 20:42.[190] Hence it appears that, if Luke was following Mark as his source at this point, he does omit the word πνεῦμα in at least one instance. It is thus reasonable to see him following a similar procedure in 11:20.[191] In favour of Luke's reading, however, scholars have considered it more likely that Matthew

---

187 "Matthew 12:28/Luke 11:20 – A Word of Jesus?", 43.

188 *The Teaching of Jesus*, 82.

189 J. Dunn, *Jesus and the Spirit*, 44f.

190 "A Note on Matthew xii. 28 par Luke xi. 20", *NTS* 11 (1964, 65) 167-69.

191 So also C.S. Rodd, "Spirit or Finger", *ExpT* 72 (1961) 157-58.

would remove an anthropomorphism and assimilate the wording to Mt. 12:18, 31, 32, where πνεύμα is a key word. This explanation gains support from the fact that the Spirit is never attested as a means of exorcising demons in Jewish sources while "the finger of God" is. Finally, it is argued that Matthew would have omitted "finger" because it had magical connotations.[192] If so, Luke contains the original wording and we have a clear allusion to Ex. 8:19 (MT 8:15) where Pharaoh's magicians attribute the plagues in Egypt to the "finger of God." The important parallel between the plagues and Jesus' saying, we believe, exists not so much in a Moses typology, but rather in the simple realization that the same power (Yahweh's!) is present in Jesus as that which was present in awesome display at the Exodus. God's omnipotence is just as apparent in Jesus' ministry as it was in the revered story of the Exodus.[193] The variation of vocabulary does not greatly affect the meaning of the text. Hamerton-Kelly observes that in Eze. 8:1-3; 37:1; 1 Chr. 28:11-19 the two phrases mean essentially the same thing—the power of God.[194]

Lk. 11:20//Mt. 12:28 coheres with what we have seen elsewhere in Q. First, in his act of healing Jesus claims that God's power is at work in himself—the same power which repeatedly rescued Israel in the OT. Second, if Jesus was aware of the OT connection between the "finger of God" and the "Spirit"—not an unlikely possibility—Jesus here, regardless of the original vocabulary, is claiming to be anointed by the Spirit and may well be identifying himself as the anointed one of Isa. 61:1f., who has come to initiate the eschatological day of salvation. The conceptual parallels among Lk. 6:20; 7:22; 11:20 par., provide a core of evidence indicating that Jesus understood himself to be anointed by the Spirit of God. The result of this anointing was the manifestation of God's power in Jesus in the form of miraculous healings and exorcisms. The healings of Lk. 7:22//Mt. 11:4, 5 do not place Jesus in the line of OT prophets, but rather identify him doing the acts anticipated of God at his coming (Isa. 29:18: 35:5, 6). The exorcism in 11:20 has the same connotations—God's saving power has come in Jesus. As Dunn stresses, "the outpouring of the prophetic Spirit in plentiful supply upon Israel was commonly regarded as one of the chief blessings and hallmarks of the new age."[195] It is the direct action of the Spirit through Jesus which distinguishes him

---

[192] Davies and Allison, *Matthew* II, 340.

[193] C. Caragounis correctly warns of reading too much into the parallelism, "Kingdom of God, Son of Man, and Jesus' Self-Understanding", *TynB* 40 (1989) 9. *Contra* R.H. Fuller, *The Mission and Achievement of Jesus*, London: SCM (1954) 37f.

[194] *Ibid.*, 168. In Eze. 8:1-3 the "hand of God" and the "spirit of God" are synonymous as in Eze. 37:1 and 1 Chr. 28:11-19. See also the references supplied by Davies and Allison, *Matthew* II, 340 n. 35. Compare Psalm 8:3 with 33:6.

[195] *Jesus and the Spirit*, 47.

from contemporary Jewish exorcists, and more importantly, it is the endowment of the Spirit which implies that the kingdom is present in him.

With Jesus' miraculous deed being the subject of the protasis, ἄρα introduces the apodosis of the sentence by emphasizing the result of Jesus' act: "the Kingdom of God has come upon you." This phrase, as is well known, has been at the center of the enduring controversy surrounding the temporal nature of Jesus' kingdom preaching. In reaction to C.H. Dodd's claim that ἔφθασεν implies the arrival of the kingdom,[196] J.Y. Campbell, K.W. Clark and numerous others[197] have responded that ἔφθασεν connotes not "arrival" but "nearness" in which case the kingdom of God here, as elsewhere, refers to the future consummation. To summarize, most contemporary scholars, correctly we believe, have sided with Dodd in regard to Lk. 11:20//Mt. 12:28, though few have adopted his full scale version of "realized eschatology."[198] First, as G.R. Beasley-Murray points out, the linguistic evidence favours a present meaning: Liddell and Scott, Moulton and Milligan, Blass and Debrunner, Bauer, and G. Fitzer[199] in his article in *TDNT* all agree in citing Lk. 11:20//Mt. 12:28 with other NT references (1 Th. 2:16; 2 Co.

---

[196] *The Parables of the Kingdom,* 44. And later in response to Campbell, "The Kingdom of God has Come", *ExpT* 48 (1936-37) 138-142.

[197] J.Y. Campbell, *ibid.,* 91-94; K.W. Clark, 'Realized Eschatology ', *JBL* 59 (1940) 367-383; E. Grässer, *Das Problem der Parusieverzögerung in den synoptischen Evangelien und in der Apostelgeschichte,* Berlin: Topelmann (1960) 61f.; H. Conzelmann, "Gegenwart und Zukunft in der synoptischen Tradition", *ZTK* 54 (1957) 286-287; R.H. Fuller, *The Mission and Achievement of Jesus,* 37-38; R. Bultmann, *Theology of the New Testament,* Vol. 1, 7.

[198] W.G. Kümmel, *Promise and Fulfillment,* 99; G.E. Ladd, *The Presence of the Future,* 139; E. Jüngel, *Paulus und Jesus,* Tübingen: JCB Mohr [Paul Siebeck] (1964) 185; J. Fitzmyer, *Luke* 2, 919; I.H. Marshall, "The Hope of a New Age: The Kingdom of God in the New Testament", 219; Davies and Allison, *Matthew* II, 339f. *Pace* Chrys Caragounis ("Kingdom of God, Son of Man and Jesus' Self-Understanding", 19; *idem*, "Kingdom of God/Kingdom of Heaven", *Dictionary of Jesus and the Gospels*, 1992, 417-30) who claims Lk. 11:20 implies the advance but not the presence of the kingdom. Caragounis' conclusion, however, is based upon an atypical rendering of the aorist tense: "The aorist tense is *sometimes* used to emphasize the certainty and immediacy of an action that properly belongs to the future by describing it as though it had already transpired" (1992; 423). However, *most* of the time the aorist tense refers to an accomplished event having taken place at a point in time in the past. Moreover, Caragounis underestimates the correlation between Jesus' miracles and the presence of the kingdom: "Jesus' miracles are only the preliminaries, not the kingdom of God itself" (*ibid*). Yet, as we have seen, against the OT, Jesus' miracles are signs that the eschatological events expected of God on the eschatological day of the Lord are in fact taking place in Jesus' ministry in the present (Isa. 61:1; 35:5). Jesus' exorcisms express the same event. Finally, Caragounis' distinction between present and future is so marginal that we wonder if it is really apparent: "Ephtasen implies that the coming of the kingdom of God is so imminent that the kingdom of God may be considered as being virtually here" (1992: 423).

[199] G.R. Beasley-Murray, *Jesus and the Kingdom of God,* 78; J.H. Moulton and G. Milligan, *The Vocabulary of the Greek New Testament,* 667; F. Blass and A. Debrunner, *A Greek Grammar of the New Testament and Other Early Christian Literature,* 101; G. Fitzer, "φθάνω", *TDNT* IX, 92; W. Bauer, 856, 857.

10:14; Ro. 9:31; Php. 3:16) where the normative meaning of φθάνω is "to arrive" or "come." Meanwhile the only NT reference which has another meaning (come before; precede) is found in 1 Th. 4:15 (φθάσωμεν) which is clearly not a parallel to ἔφθασεν here. Second, the context of our saying requires a present setting as T.W. Manson pertinently put it, "the exit of the evil spirits is the *result* of the Divine presence, not the *preparation* for it."[200] Third, as J. Gnilka suggests, ἐφ' ὑμᾶς requires a present orientation.[201] And fourth, the historical likelihood that Jesus could have had a present perception of the kingdom of God has been proven by Heinz-Wolfgang Kuhn in his study of Qumran literature in which the combination of future and present eschatological salvation appears in temple symbolism, though Kuhn exposes a clear distinction between the presence of eschatological salvation in Qumran's temple symbol and Jesus' pronouncement that God's rule was present in his work.[202]

    H. Schürmann has made the following six conclusions in respect to the interpretation of the kingdom of God in Lk. 11:20//Mt. 12:28. (A) The kingdom pronouncement of Jesus is a salvation happening (*Heilschaffendes*). (B) It is the work of God. (C) It is dynamically present. (D) As the work of God, the kingdom is both a salvation rule (*Herrschaft*) and a kingdom or realm (*Reich*). (E) God's power is present in the work of Jesus; Jesus' work is God's work. And (F), 11:20//12:28 is motivated by soteriological and christological grounds rather than ethical ones. All this Schürmann states in regard to a saying which he identifies as containing at minimum the *vox Jesu* and with the greatest possibility the *ipsissimum verbum Jesu*.[203]

C. The Implications of Lk. 11:20//Mt. 12:28 for the Study of Q

The implications of Schürmann's conclusions have a decisive bearing on the question of the christological content of Q and its origin. If 11:20//12:28 is, indeed, an authentic saying of Jesus as most modern critics have agreed,[204] there

---

[200] *The Sayings of Jesus*, 86.

[201] *Das Matthäusevangelium* I, 458.

[202] Thus Kuhn concludes: "Die eschatologisch-gegenwärtigen Aussagen der untersuchten Qumrantexte gründen in der Heilsgegenwart Gottes auf Grund der "*Tempelssymbolik*" und die *Gemeinde* ist der Ort, an dem schon das künftige Heil präsent ist. Ganz anders bei Jesus: Die Verkündigung der Gegenwart der Gottesherrschaft gründet in dem Anspruch Jesu, daß *in seinem Wirken* Gottes Herrsein aufgerichtet wird", *Enderwartung und gegenwärtiges Heil: Untersuchungen zu den Gemeindeliedern von Qumran*, Göttingen: Vandenhoeck & Ruprecht (1971) 204. Italics Kuhn's.

[203] "Das Zeugnis der Redenquelle für die Basileia-Verkündigung Jesu", 157.

[204] On the authenticity of 11:20//12:28 Bultmann is commonly quoted: "the highest degree of authenticity which can make for any saying of Jesus: it is full of that feeling of eschatological

appears no way of getting around the fact that Jesus himself had an awareness of his own personal role in transmitting God's saving power to people. To that extent 11:20//12:28 is motivated by the soteriological and christological understanding of Jesus not a Q community or Q redactor. The claims of S. Schulz, D. Zeller, and D. Lührmann[205] that the Beelzebul controversy reveals evidence of polemic within the Q community ignores the friction which would have developed immediately in Jesus' ministry if he performed miracles, claimed to be anointed by the Spirit, and implied that the kingdom of God was active in his ministry. It is hard to imagine that pious Jews would not have reacted publicly to Jesus—some no doubt with open hostility. Furthermore, the magnitude of Jesus' claims would themselves have created "enthusiasm" among Jesus' followers before Easter. For if Lk. 11:20 is authentic, an unknown apocalyptic event is not needed to explain motivation for the composition of Q, because in Jesus himself God's saving power is revealed.

It is often observed that Q does not contain late christological titles such as Lord or Christ—a fact which has led some to defend the early origin of Q but which has convinced others that Q represents a variant christology. However, Lk. 11:20//Mt. 12:28 together with Lk. 7:22//Mt. 11:5 and Lk. 6:20//Mt. 5:3 indicate that the search for a peculiar Q christology or soteriology is misplaced. For instead of revealing the christological *Tendenz* of an esoteric community, these passages convey the fact that Jesus was anointed by the Spirit to bring eschatological salvation to people—acts consonant with messiahship.[206] Lk. 6:20//Mt. 5:3, by

---

power which must have characterized the activity of Jesus", *History of the Synoptic Tradition,* 162. So also: H.E. Tödt, *The Son of Man in the Synoptic Tradition,* 264; E. Käsemann, *Essays on New Testament Themes,* 39; *Contra* A. Fuchs who considers it unthinkable that Mk. would have omitted this saying had it been in the earliest form of the Beelzebul controversy, *Die Entwicklung der Beelzebulkontroverse bei den Synoptikern,* Freistadt: Plöchl (1978) 91, 92. However, Mark's brevity occasioned the omission of much traditional material. J.D.G. Dunn ("Matthew 12:28/Luke 11:20– A Word of Jesus?", 38-46) has recently defended authenticity (*contra* E.P. Sanders) on the basis of the criterion of double dissimilarity (contemporary Judaism and the early Church) and the criterion of cohesion to other synoptic material.

[205] Schulz (*Q - Die Logienquelle,* 212, 213) believes 11:20 was kerygmatically expanded within the Palestinian-Jewish Q community and contains early Christian apologetic and preaching. The Q-community is reacting on two fronts – against pre-Markan "Wonderman" Christology and simultaneously against Jews who accused Jesus of working with Beelzebul. D. Lührmann (*Die Redaktion der Logienquelle,* 42) considers the entire section an expanded apophthegm in which Q redaction underscores the pronouncement of judgment against "this generation (11:29//12:39)" – a phrase which earmarks the polemical interests of the Q community (Lk. 7:31; 11:29, 30, 31, 32, 50, 51 and par). However, ἡ γενεὰ αὔτη is just as characteristic of Jesus' speech in Mark: 8:12 (2x); 38; 9:19; 13:30. Similarly, D. Zeller (*Kommentar zur Logienquelle,* 60) states that polemical material already reflects problems within the Q-Community in the final redaction.

[206] So Otto Betz, "Jesus' Gospel of the Kingdom." In *The Gospel and the Gospels,* Ed. P. Stuhlmacher; ET Grand Rapids: Eerdmans (1991) 60: "It is by no means the case that no miracles

alluding to Isa. 61:1f., indicates that Jesus considered himself the Isianic herald of salvation, the one anointed by the Spirit to bring Good News to the poor. Lk. 7:22//Mt. 11:5 designates Jesus as anointed by the Spirit to bring Good News to the poor and to perform the salvific healing acts characteristic of Yahweh in the Day of the Lord.   And now in 11:20//12:28 Jesus identifies his power over demons as evidence that he himself is anointed by the finger of God (= Spirit) to bring God's salvific power to men.   Jesus' exorcisms fit him into the mold of a Davidic figure (see Wisd. 7:15-22 [20]; Josephus *Ant*. 8.2, 5; Ps.-Philo *Liber Antiquitatum Biblicarum* 60; 11QPsAp[a]),[207] as these acts recall the same ability Jewish tradition attributes to Solomon the literal Son of David.   It is more than noteworthy in our discussion of Q that the ability to expel demons, like other principle attributes of Jesus in Q (wisdom, anointing by the Holy Spirit, prophetic character), finds historical precedent in David (11QPsAp[a]) and Solomon (Wisd. 7:15-22; Josephus *Ant*. 8.2,5).   Jesus' expulsion of demons thus has messianic implications as does his healing, wise teaching and anointing by the Holy Spirit— "Something greater than Solomon is here" (Lk. 11:31//Mt. 12:42)!   When we add Lk. 12:10//Mt. 12:32b which implies that Jesus (as Son of Man) depends upon the Spirit, we have a body of authentic Q sayings in which Jesus identifies himself as a figure anointed by the Spirit of God both to radiate God's saving power to men and to defend God's universal reign against demonic aggressors.   The anointing of the Spirit occasions the question of Jesus' identity.   With this question before us, and with the recollection that others have perceived wisdom and prophetic christologies as determinative for Q, we cite Isa. 11:1-5:

---

were expected from the Jewish Messiah – on the contrary. The σημεῖα τῆς ἐλευθερίας (Josephus, *JB* 2.262) promised by the "prophets" (Jewish messianic pretenders) must be viewed as signals of the dawning year of release (Isa. 61:1f.) and of the eschatological jubilee. They will show that God is with such a redeemer– that he is "the one who was to come"; as "signs" they must correspond to the miracles done by Moses or Joshua. And the Targum on Isaiah 53, which interprets the servant as messianic, finds in v. 8 a description of the miracles "which take place for us in his days –who can tell them?" (cf. IV Ezra 13:49f.; 7:28).

[207] Wisd. 7:17a, 20b: "For it is he (God) who gave me (Solomon) unerring knowledge of what exists, . . . the powers of spirits and the reasonings of men."
Josephus *Ant*. 8.2,5: "God also enabled him (Solomon) to learn that skill which expels demons, which is a science useful and sanative to men."
In Ps. -Philo *LAB* 63 David plays a psalm to rebuke the demon troubling king Saul: "But let the new wonb from which I was born rebuke you, from which after a time one born from my loins will rule over you."
11QPs[a] XXVII: "In all, the songs which he (king David) uttered were 446, and 4 songs to make music on behalf of those stricken (by evil spirits)."
See: Klaus Berger, "Die königlichen Messiastraditionen des Neuen Testaments", *NTS* 20 (1974) 1-44; Dennis C. Duling, "Solomon Exorcism, and the Son of David", *HTR* 65 (1975) 235-252; E. Lövestam, "Jésus Fils de David chez les Synoptiques", *ST* 28 (1974) 97-109.

Then a shoot will spring from the stem of Jesse, and a branch from his roots will bear fruit. And the Spirit of the Lord will rest on Him, the spirit of wisdom and understanding, the spirit of counsel and strength, the spirit of knowledge and the fear of the Lord. And he will delight in the fear of the Lord, and he will not judge by what his eyes see, nor make a decision by what his ears hear; but with righteousness he will judge the poor, and decide with fairness for the afflicted of the earth; And he will strike the earth with the rod of his mouth, and with the breath of his lips he will slay the wicked. Also righteousness will be the belt about his loins, and faithfulness the belt about his waist.

We do not quote this passage because Jesus refers to it in Q (though Isa. 11:2 has parallels with Isa. 61:1f which Jesus does cite in Q), but we refer to it because the image of the prophesied messiah in Isa. 11 exudes many of the same characteristics which Jesus exercises in Q: the anointing of the Spirit, wisdom, an interest in the poor, and a focused priority on the fear of the Lord (cf. Lk. 12:31//Mt. 6:33). There is no explicit evidence within Q that Jesus interpreted his ministry against this passage, but his announcement of Good News, the nature of his acts, his anointing with the Spirit, the equality of his power with that of Yahweh, and his saving ministry to the sick, the poor and the demon possessed demand that we take seriously Jesus' messiahship in the Q material. There is indeed a pattern to what Jesus says and does in Q—a pattern that points to his messiahship. The messianic associations of the designation Son of Man in the *Similitudes* and 4 Ezra 13 fit into this pattern as do the messianic overtones of the act of gathering the people of God (*Psalms of Solomon* 17:26)—a feat which Jesus clearly attempts in Q (Lk. 10:2f//Mt. 9:37f; Lk. 13:34,35//Mt. 23:37-39).

VII. Seek the Kingdom of God! Lk. 12:29-31//Mt. 6:31-33

Lk. 12:29-31//Mt. 6:31-33 climaxes a block of Q material in which Jesus rationally exhorts his listeners to abandon the weight of human anxiety by focusing all hope upon the blessings of God's kingdom. The vast majority of scholars attribute the passage to Q despite notable differences in 12:24//6:26, 12:26//6:28, and 12:29//6:31. Because not all of the differences can be accounted for by the editorial activity of the Evangelists, the variation may suggest two variants of Q.[208] R. Bultmann,[209] D. Zeller,[210] and J. Kloppenborg[211] have broken down Lk. 12:22-31//6:25-33 into numerous independent sayings as a result of formal disparities and shifts in vocabulary and logic. Such fragmentation, however,

---

[208] I.H. Marshall, *Luke*, 525.

[209] *The History of the Synoptic Tradition*, 81, 88.

[210] *Die weisheitliche Mahnsprüche bei den Synoptikern*, Würzburg: Echter (1977) 86.

[211] *The Formation of Q*, 218.

seems forced in light of the unifying theme of Jesus' answer to human anxiety which pervades the entire section. Following the introductory λέγω ὑμῖν phrase, Jesus commences with the command not to worry (μὴ μεριμνᾶτε) about the necessities of food and clothing. Lk. 12:22, 23//Mt. 6:25 characterizes Jesus' train of thought throughout the argument which climaxes in the kingdom of God saying in Lk. 12:31//Mt. 6:33. The issue is human anxiety over the necessities of life. The tone is authoritative—Jesus speaks in the imperative. The perspective is redirected—from the audience's point of view to that of Jesus. The overriding question is posed—why should man not be anxious about what he needs to live? And the suggestion is made that there exists something greater (πλεῖον) to pursue—the kingdom of God.

The nature imagery drawn from the OT, the קל וחומר form of argument (Lk. 12:24//Mt. 6:26), the parallelism in Lk. 12:24, 27, 28, the antithetic parallelism in Lk. 12:29-31, and the emphasis of God's faithfulness clarify that this passage is thoroughly Jewish. Jesus rationally explains his command not to be anxious by drawing attention to the ravens/birds who manage to exist without apparent worry. Employing קל וחומר, the first rule of rabbi Hillel, [212] that "what applies in a less important case will certainly apply in a more important case,"[213] Jesus moves the audience to consider the benevolence of God the creator as evidenced in Ps. 147:9: "He gives to the beast its food, and to the young ravens which cry." Because God provides for the lesser creatures, Jesus argues it is illogical, by Hillel's principle, for man to be anxious because in God's eyes man is of far greater value than animals (Gn. 1:26).

A. Lk. 12:30//Mt. 6:32

Lk. 12:30 and Mt. 6:32 have thirteen words in common out of sixteen in Luke and seventeen in Matthew. ταῦτα γὰρ πάντα obviously refers directly back to the basic needs of food, drink, and clothing emphasized in 12:22//6:25f. The Gentiles (τὰ ἔθνη) supply a negative example to be avoided.[214] The phrase appears strange if indeed the supposed Q community was involved in a Gentile mission. The distinction does not appear ethnic but religious.[215] Because the Gentiles have no faith in God, they anxiously desire security in the form of material wealth.

---

[212] E. E. Ellis, *The Old Testament in Early Christianity*, Tübingen: JCB Mohr [Paul Siebeck] (1991) 131.

[213] R. Longenecker, *Biblical Exegesis in the Apostolic Period*, Grand Rapids: Eerdmans (1975) 34.

[214] Cf. 1 Ti. 4:5 , "not in lustful passion, like the Gentiles who do not know God."

[215] So R.T. France, *Matthew*, Leicester: Tyndale (1985) 141.

Because Jesus' audience lacks faith (ὀλιγόπιστοι; 12:28//6:30), their hope is no greater than that of the pagans. Luke's ἔθνη τοῦ κόσμου represents a frequent rabbinic designation for the non-Israelite world[216] and thus should not be attributed to Lucan redaction.[217] ἐπιζητέω (I search for / I seek after)[218] occurs twice in Luke (both times in Q passages) and three times in Matthew (2x in Q and 1x in Mk. par.).[219] The wording qualifies the kind of anxiety under scrutiny: it is an active search, a striving for material security. In the closing phrase, Gundry argues that the three words distinctive to Matthew are all the result of the Evangelist's redaction: γάρ in 32b is a Mattheanism (Mt.123-4x; Mk. 64x; Lk. 97x) replacing δέ; ὁ οὐράνιος provides a parallel to 6:26 thus re-emphasizing, in a manner characteristic of Matthew, the majesty of God's fatherhood;[220] while ἁπάντων provides a parallel to πάντα in v. 32a.[221] Although the word counts are not decisive, we find Lucan dependence on Matthew hardly credible. In any case, the closing phrase, "and/for your father knows that you need these things," provides the foundational logic underlying the preceding argument and the kingdom of God saying which immediately follows. Because God the father, as all-knowing creator (ὁ πατὴρ οἶδεν), provides the necessities of life for all creation, Jesus' audience does not need to be anxious. A. Polag cites ὁ πατήρ as a technical term in Q which connotes the disciples' unique relationship to God in which they depend solely on the father's mercy and care.[222] In emphasizing the role of the father, Jesus moves the listener's perspective from human despair to God's sovereignty. His call for absolute hope in God compares with the

---

[216] *Strack, Billerbeck* II, 191.

[217] I.H. Marshall, *Luke*, 529; W. Wrege, *Die Überlieferungsgeschichte der Bergpredigt*, Tübingen: JCB Mohr [Paul Siebeck] (1968) 122. Gundry, *Matthew*, Grand Rapids: Eerdmans (1983) 118, conjectures that Mt. omitted κόσμος in an attempt to prevent a slur on the Gentiles.

[218] Bauer, 292.

[219] Lk. 12:30//Mt. 6:32; Lk.11:29//Mt. 12:39; Mt. 16:4//Mk. 8:12

[220] οὐράνιος (Mt. 7x; Mk. 0; Lk. 1x); οὐρανός with πατήρ (Mt. 13x; Mk. 1x; Lk. 1x).

[221] Gundry (*Matthew*, 118) appeals to the frequency of πᾶς in Mt.; however, the usage here is ἅπας which is used only three times in Matthew in comparison to twenty appearances in Luke. This would be a strange occurrence if Luke were using Matthew.

[222] *Christologie der Logienquelle*, 62. "ὁ πατήρ" 6x (possibly 7x) in Q: Lk. 6:35//Mt. 5:44-45 (?); Lk. 6:36//Mt. 5:48; Lk. 10:21//Mt. 11:25-26; Lk. 10:22//Mt. 11:27; Lk. 11:2//Mt. 6:9; Lk. 11:11-13//Mt. 7:9-11; Lk. 12:30//Mt. 6:32. J. Schlosser has analyzed each of these sayings with the conclusion that except for Lk. 10:22 par., they all represent the authentic speech of Jesus; *Le Dieu de Jésus*, Paris: Cerf (1987) 150. On this passage he is supported by: D. Catchpole, "The Ravens, the Lilies and the Q Hypothesis. A Form-Critical Perspective on the Source-Critical Problem", *SNTU* 6-7 (1981-82) 87; M.G. Steinhauser, *Doppelbildworte in den synoptischen Evangelien. Eine form- und traditionskritische Studie*, Würzburg: Echter (1981) 233-234.

dependence upon God and the "fear of the Lord" characteristic of the Messiah of the Psalms of Solomon:

> The Lord himself is his king, the hope of the one who has a strong hope in God. (17:34)

> And the blessing of the Lord will be with him in strength, and he will not weaken; His hope will be in the Lord. Then who will succeed against him, mighty in his actions and strong in the fear of God? (17:38-40)

> Blessed are those born in those days, to see the good things of the Lord which he will do for the coming generation; (which will be) under the rod of discipline of the Lord Messiah, in the fear of his God, in wisdom of spirit, and of strength, to direct people in righteous acts, in the fear of God, to set them all in the fear of the Lord. A good generation living in the fear of God, in the days of mercy. (18:6-9)

Jesus' teaching falls in line with his other messianic attributes in Q.

B.   Lk. 12:31//Mt. 6:33

Mt. 6:33 contains at least six and possibly eight words not found in Lk. 12:31, while Luke varies only once from Matthew. Luke's introductory πλήν (however, but) serves to break off the preceding negative discussion to emphasize positively what is important—seek the kingdom.[223] As a result of the comparative word count (Mt. 5; Mk. 1; Lk. 15), most scholars classify πλήν as Lucan redaction.[224] Serving the same purpose, Matthew's δὲ πρῶτον places exclusive importance on Jesus' command to seek "first" the kingdom. Mt. 5:24; 13:30; 23:26 diff. Lk. 11:41 suggest that an introductory πρῶτον is characteristic of Matthew. Thus if both πλήν and πρῶτον betray redaction by the Evangelists, δὲ may have been the original introduction to the saying. What of the other variations? UBS 3 has bracketed [τοῦ θεοῦ] as a result of the diverse textual data and internal disagreement among the committee members. In our opinion, the minority view is favorable—*viz*., that the earlier variants א, (B), it[1,] bo; Eus., (which omit τοῦ θεου) represent the original Matthean reading because τοῦ θεοῦ would have been a natural supplement for a later editor, but not for Matthew who prefered τῶν οὐρανῶν.[225] βασιλεία without a noun modifier occurs elsewhere in Matthew in the Lord's prayer (6:10)—a passage which has numerous parallels with our

---

[223] Bauer, 669.

[224] J. Jeremias, *Die Sprache des Lukas Evangeliums*, 219. J. Dupont, *Les Beatitudes*, 3:32-34; S. Schulz, *Q- Die Spruchquelle*, 152; R.A. Guelich, *The Sermon on the Mount*, 341, *et al.*

[225] B.M. Metzger, *A Textual Commentary*, 18, 19; R.H. Gundry, *Matthew*, 119; *Pace* Davies and Allison, *Matthew* I, 660 n. 25.

present text. Matthean redaction probably also occurs in the phrase καὶ τὴν δικαιοσύνην.[226] δικαιοσύνη occurs five times in Matthew's Sermon on the Mount (5:6, 10, 20; 6:1, 33) without appearing once in Luke's Sermon on the Plain. Finally, Lk. 12:31 lacks πάντα which Matthew has possibly added in reference to ἁπάντων in Mt. 6:22.

If we remove each conjectural addition, the following hypothetical Q reconstruction appears: ζητεῖτε δὲ τὴν βασιλείαν αὐτοῦ,

καὶ ταῦτα προστεθήσεται ὑμῖν.

In antithetic parallelism to Lk. 12:29 (Mt. 6:31) where Jesus commands his audience not to seek food and drink, Jesus now commands positively that his listeners do seek the kingdom. The exclusivity of seeking the kingdom is the focus of Jesus' admonition. Is Jesus or the Q community advocating an ascetic lifestyle as the proper response to the impending rule of God? D. Zeller[227] and P. Hoffmann[228] place Lk. 12:31//Mt. 6:33 on the mouths of wandering radical preachers who were motivated by the expectation of the imminent breaking in of God's kingdom. However, such an understanding disorientates the context of our saying by reading in a pre-conceived concept of Q eschatology. The issue in this context, rather, is human anxiety and God's kingdom is the solution to that anxiety. The closing phrase ταῦτα προστεθήσεται ὑμῖν makes this clear. προστεθήσεται is a divine passive[229] with God as the implied subject; ταῦτα links to ἐπιζητοῦσιν in Lk. 12:30//Mt. 6:32 where the subject is food and drink. The focus of the phrase stands in perfect keeping with the preceding illustrations of the birds of the air and the grass of the field and with the prohibitions in Lk. 12:22, 29//Mt. 6:25, 28-31: Jesus' listeners need not be anxious like the unbelieving Gentiles because their basic needs have been met as one of the latent benefits of the kingdom. Like the first Beatitude, the pronouncement of the kingdom of God is the occasion and grounds for the exhortation not to worry.[230]

Because Jesus prescribes "seeking the kingdom" as the cure to present distress, it seems unlikely that "kingdom," in this context, refers *exclusively* to the

---

[226] R.A. Guelich, *The Sermon on the Mount,* 347; U. Lüz, *Matthäus* I, 370; G. Strecker, *The Sermon on the Mount,* 139; Davies and Allison, *Matthew* I, 661.

[227] *Kommentar zur Logienquelle,* 80. See, however, U. Luz (*Matthäus* I, 371) who argues that in Early Christianity no distinction was made between wandering radicals and settled followers of Jesus.

[228] *Studien zur Theologie der Logienquelle,* 41. Hoffmann speculates that this pericope was possibly bound in Q with Mt. 6:19-21 diff Lk. 12:33-34; Lk. 12:39f., 42-46//Mt. 24:43-51a.

[229] A. Polag lists the following theological passives in Q which serve as circumlocutions for the activity of God: Lk. 6:21, 37, 38; 11:2, 9, 10, 29; 12:2, 10, 31; 13:28, 35; 17:34, 35; 19:26 par. Mt.; Lk. 12:3, 9; 11:50, 51 diff. Mt.; Lk. 12:48b; 17:10 S diff. Mt.; Mt. 5:13 diff. Lk. = Mt. redaction; *Christologie der Logienquelle,* 63.

[230] So H. Merklein, *Die Gottesherrschaft als Handlungsprinzip,* 182.

future apocalyptic end-event.[231]   H. Schürmann concedes the difficulty of such a designation when he writes of this pericope: "Sachlich ist die Βασιλεία (τοῦ Θεοῦ) (1) zukünftige, jedoch auch irgendwie schon «gegebene»."[232]   In regard to the temporal setting, ζητέω implies an active "seeking" or "looking for" with the hope of finding.[233]   In the OT, ζητεῖν θεόν and ζητεῖν κύριον are frequently used to describe man's voluntary turning to God.[234]   It is in this sense that Jesus commands his audience to seek the kingdom in Lk. 12:31//Mt. 6:33.   The humiliating epithet ὀλιγόπιστοι in Lk. 12:28//Mt. 6:30 suggests that the anxious have not focused their faith in God's ability to provide.   Jesus counters that God's sovereignty is evident now as proven by his ability to provide for his creation. The kingdom, here, refers to the broader sense of God's sovereignty both present and future: the faithful to God need not fear because God as sovereign king of the universe will provide.   The divine passive προστεθήσεται does not mean that God will provide necessities, which are needed now, at the parousia; rather, the sense is that God will provide now as the needs arise.   God's provision now is a foretaste of salvation then.

The authenticity of 12:31//6:33 is contested by S. Schulz who attributes the saying to early Christian prophets in the oldest Q community of Syrian Palestine. He reaches this conclusion as a result of formal characteristics: Διὰ τοῦτο λέγω ὑμῖν (12:22/6:25); τίς δὲ ἐξ ὑμῶν (12:25//6:27); and, λέγω δὲ ὑμῖν (12:27b//6:29).   However, as we noted in Chapter 4, outside of Jesus' sayings David Aune[235] has located the λέγω ὑμῖν phrase in the LXX, Greek magic papyri, and the Pauline corpus, a fact which eliminates the possibility that the phrase is exclusive to prophetic origins.   τίς δὲ ἐξ ὑμῶν, meanwhile, has no contemporary parallels which suggests authenticity especially when attached to a *qal wahômer* argument.[236]   J. Kloppenborg,[237] and D. Zeller[238] locate 12:31//6:33 within a defined Wisdom tradition.   They note that "seeking" is frequently associated with the pursuit of Sophia in Wisdom literature, while the

---

[231] *Contra*: J. Dupont, *Les Beatitudes*, 3:293-95; J. Jeremias, *The Parables of Jesus*, ET London: SCM (1963) 215; W.G. Kümmel, *Promise and Fulfilment*, London: SCM (1957) 125-6; S. Schulz, *Q-die Spruchquelle*, 155; G. Strecker, *The Sermon on the Mount*, 139.

[232] "Das Zeugnis der Redenquelle für die Basileia-Verkündigung Jesu", 160.

[233] Bauer, 338.

[234] H. Greeven, "ζητέω", *TDNT* II, 893 n. 5.

[235] *Prophecy in Early Christianity and the Ancient Mediterranean World*, 164, 392.

[236] J. Jeremias, *The Parables of Jesus*, 103.

[237] *The Formation of Q*, 219.

[238] Zeller identifies Mt. 6:25-33 "Eine kunstvolle weisheitliche Mahnrede" (an artistic wisdom admonition), *Kommentar zur Logienquelle*, 78; *idem, Die weisheitliche Mahnsprüche bei den Synoptikern*, 86, 91. Zeller does, however, consider Mt. 6:25, 27 par. to be authentic (92).

structure of 12:31//6:33 is similar to Pr. 3:9-10. Kloppenborg notes that "Wisdom tradition is indeed familiar with the notion that those who seek Sophia first are rewarded with security and provisions."[239] However, $\sigma o\phi\acute{\iota}a$ is never referred to in this passage. The OT background is not Pr. 3, but Ps. 147 which is clearly alluded to in 12:24//6:26:

> He gives to the beast its food,
> And to the young ravens which cry.
> He does not take pleasure in the legs of a man.
> The Lord favours those who fear him,
> Those who wait for his lovingkindness. (147:9-11)

This passage, like Lk. 12:31//Mt. 6:33, addresses the sovereignty of God—those who wait upon God, who submit to His authority, will have their needs met. Certainly this saying contains a tenet truth of wisdom (that the wise seek God). Yet it is unclear how this truth suggests secondary Q *Tendenz*. On the other hand, the parallelism in Lk. 12:24, 27, 28, the antithetic parallelism in Lk. 12:29-31, the *qal wahômer* form of argument, and the fact that there exists no precise Jewish parallel to this saying supports the a dominical origin of 12:31//6:33 within Palestine.[240]

The content of Lk. 12:31//Mt. 6:33 has much in common with Jesus' teaching elsewhere both in Q and in Mark. As in the Lord's Prayer, here God is identified as both the bearer of the kingdom and the dispenser of daily food (Lk. 11:3; Mt. 6:10, 11). In both texts, Jesus places primary importance on man's devotion to God's sovereignty, while attributing secondary prominence to the request for daily bread. As in the first Beatitude, Jesus speaks as the herald of the kingdom: in Lk. 6:20//Mt. 5:3 Jesus pronounces the kingdom as the blessing of the poor, whereas in Lk. 12:31//Mt. 6:33 he identifies one aspect of why the kingdom is a blessing— it removes the impetus for worry. Further, in direct speech, Lk. 12:31//Mt. 6:33 teaches what Jesus performs in the temptation narrative where three times Jesus "seeks first the kingdom," by appealing directly to the sovereignty of God in his rebuke of Satan. The basic message of our text is the same as that found in Mk. 11:29-30:

---

[239] *The Formation of Q*, 219.

[240] H. Schürmann claims 12:31//6:33 contains the »vox Jesu«; "Das Zeugnis der Redenquelle für die Basileia-Verkündigung Jesu", 159; Davies and Allison, *Matthew* I, 659; I.H. Marshall, *Luke*, 525 f.; H. Merklein, *Die Gottesherrschaft als Handlungsprinzip*, 179; D. Aune, *Prophecy in Early Christianity and the Ancient Mediterranean World*, 166. Thus J. Jeremias writes, "Dieser Abschnitt weist nur minimale redaktionelle Eingriffe auf. Er zeigt besonders deutlich, wie zurückhaltend mit Eingriffen Lukas bei den Worten Jesu ist", *Die Sprache des Lukasevangeliums*, 219.

Truly I say to you, there is no one who has left house or brothers or sisters or mother or father or children or farms, for My sake and for the gospel's sake, but that he shall receive a hundred times as much now in the present age, house and brothers and sisters and mothers and children and farms, along with persecutions; and in the age to come, eternal life.

If in Mark "the gospel" equals the kingdom of God as 1:14, 15 indicates, 11:29-30 represents Markan evidence that Jesus identified man's present security as one benefit of seeking the kingdom—a teaching that corroborates Lk. 12:31//Mt. 6:33. Both passages represent what H. Merklein considers the central tenet of Jesus' teaching—the call for man to exclusively orient life (*Handlungsprinzip*) according to the kingdom of God as opposed to law or any other ethical institution.[241].

VIII. The Parables of the Mustard Seed and Leaven

A. The Parable of the Mustard Seed

The three synoptic versions compare the kingdom to a mustard seed.[242] Mark in part assimilates the parable's wording to the context of Ch. 4 which is unified by the seed image (4:3-8, 13-20, 26-29, 30-32). In Ch. 4 all 10 occurrences of the verb $\sigma\pi\epsilon\acute{\iota}\rho\omega$ appear in Mark. In light of the apparently less Semitic $\ddot{o}\varsigma$ $\ddot{o}\tau\alpha\nu$,[243] we may view the Markan phrase $\ddot{o}\varsigma$ $\ddot{o}\tau\alpha\nu$ $\sigma\pi\alpha\rho\hat{\eta}$ $\dot{\epsilon}\pi\grave{\iota}$ $\tau\hat{\eta}\varsigma$ $\gamma\hat{\eta}\varsigma$ as redactional in wording.[244] Meanwhile Mt. 13:31b is rightly understood to be Matthew's conflation of Mark and Q.[245] If Matthew's $\dot{\eta}$ $\beta\alpha\sigma\iota\lambda\epsilon\acute{\iota}\alpha$ $\tau\hat{\omega}\nu$ $o\dot{\upsilon}\rho\alpha\nu\hat{\omega}\nu$ is

---

[241] "Die von Jesus verkündete Gottesherrschaft stellt das entscheidende Prinzip für das menschliche handeln dar", *Die Gottesherrschaft als Handlungsprinzip*, 295.

[242] The parable of the mustard seed occurs in the Gospel of Thomas § 20: "The disciples said to Jesus, 'Tell us what the kingdom of heaven is like.' He said to them, 'It is like a mustard seed, smaller than all seeds. But when it falls on ground which is cultivated, it sends forth a great branch (and) becomes a shelter for birds of the sky.'" The Gospel of Thomas version is late and dependent on the Synoptic accounts. Thomas' "Kingdom of Heaven" probably depends on Matthew's characteristic $\dot{\eta}$ $\beta\alpha\sigma\iota\lambda\epsilon\acute{\iota}\alpha$ $\tau\hat{\omega}\nu$ $o\dot{\upsilon}\rho\alpha\nu\hat{\omega}\nu$, while the phrases "the smallest of all seeds," "produces a great branch," and "whenever" depend on the redactional work of Mark. The added introduction and the extra phrase "which is cultivated," a phrase which Fitzmyer claims "slightly allegorizes the parable," show that Thomas' parable derives from the Synoptic Gospels. See J. Fitzmyer, *Luke* II, 1015; Davies and Allison, *Matthew* II, 421; Harry Fleddermann, "The Mustard Seed and the Leaven in Q, the Synoptics, and Thomas", 229; C.M. Tuckett, "Thomas and the Synoptics", *NovT* 30 (1988) 148-53.

[243] Davies and Allison, *Matthew* II, 417.

[244] See, Guelich, *Mark* I, 247, 48; R. Pesch, *Markus* I, 260-64.

[245] *Pace* F. Kogler (*Das Doppelgleichnis vom Senfkorn und vom Sauerteig in seiner traditionsgeschichtlichen Entwicklung*, Würzburg: Echter Verlag, 1988) who defends A. Fuchs' view that the parables of the leaven and the mustard seed provide evidence of three layers of synoptic tradition: (1) canonical Mark; (2) Deutero-Mark; (3) Matthew/Luke redaction of Mark and Deutero-Mark. According to Kogler, "Dmk" made unimportant corrections to Mk., but also

identified as a Matthean insertion made necessary by Matthew's altered introduction, the first seven words in Matthew and Luke exist in exact parallel against Mark—thus the Q hypothesis. However, the final phrase in Mt. 13:31 differs in vocabulary from both Luke and Mark. Most likely Matthew has adopted Mark's verb $\sigma\pi\epsilon\iota\rho\omega$, rephrased it in the customary tense of a parable, the past tense, and altered Q's $\kappa\hat{\eta}\pi o\varsigma$ (a hapaxlegomenon) to $\dot{\alpha}\gamma\rho\dot{o}\varsigma$—a term frequent in Matthew (17x; 7x in Ch.13). In this case Luke's wording adheres to Q. Because neither Mark's $\gamma\hat{\eta}$ nor Matthew's $\dot{\alpha}\gamma\rho\dot{o}\varsigma$ are foreign to Luke or to his readers, it is hard to understand why Luke, if Mark and Matthew were his sources, would have replaced either term with the hapaxlegomenon $\kappa\hat{\eta}\pi o\varsigma$. Against those who isolate $\kappa\hat{\eta}\pi o\varsigma$ to a Hellenistic milieu and so the Q parable at large, it need only be noted that $\kappa\hat{\eta}\pi o\varsigma$ is documented as existing in pre-Christian papyri[246] and in the Theodotion text of Ezekiel 31:8, where it refers to God's garden in which great cedars exist. If the translator of Q chose to follow the reading of the Theodotion text as is quite evident in the closing OT allusion, the existence of $\kappa\hat{\eta}\pi o\varsigma$ here need not suggest an exclusively Hellenistic origin but only the preference of Greek text-type on the part of the translator.[247] Despite the variation in wording, the basic message is the same in each gospel. The kingdom ironically compares with a tiny mustard seed. The kingdom, like the seed, has a small beginning.

Following the kingdom's comparison to a mustard seed, Matthew and Mark add a comment absent in Luke—that the mustard seed is the smallest of all seeds. Matthew's variation from Mark (his added $\dot{o} \ldots \mu\dot{\epsilon}\nu \; \dot{\epsilon}\sigma\tau\iota\nu$ instead of $\ddot{o}\nu$ and the omission of $\dot{\epsilon}\pi\dot{\iota} \; \tau\hat{\eta}\varsigma \; \gamma\hat{\eta}\varsigma$) represent the first evangelist's improvement of Mark's

---

expanded Mk. according to later theological views of the early Church. Originally Jesus, in allusion to Eze. 17:23, contrasted the seed and its mature plant as an event comparable to the small emergence of the kingdom in his ministry and the kingdom's future universal consummation. Mk. took over the parable and applied it to the situation of his church. Dt-Mk. re-interpreted the parable according to the growth process, altered the allusion from Eze. to Daniel 4, interpreted the parable according to the Gentile mission, and added the leaven parable to create a double pericope. At the Dmk layer of tradition, the church became equated with the kingdom of God and the place and authority of Jesus was exalted. Matthew and Luke basically passed on the emphasis of Dmk (216-17). While Kogler is correct that Dmk is no more hypothetical than Q (223), the layers of theological development he proposes are not evident in the text. The growth process and the basic contrast between seed and mature plant exist in each version. The original OT background (Daniel or Ezekiel) is an uncertainty. The Gentile mission and early church *Sitz im Leben* are not evident. We do not think the Dmk theory successfully explains the phenomenon of Mk.-Q doublets (see J. Fitzmyer, *Luke* I, 81).

[246] Moulton and Milligan, 343.

[247] Fleddermann suggests that the appearance of $\kappa\hat{\eta}\pi o\varsigma$ in the Theodotion text of Eze. 31:8 may reinforce the concluding image of the tree "by placing the tree in God's garden" (222). This understanding, however, involves an allegorical understanding of the parable, while the great tree in Eze. 31 is in fact Assyria and not the eschatological kingdom of God.

grammar and his omission of unnecessary words.[248] The addition makes explicit what was already implied in Luke's comparison of the kingdom to the mustard seed, which was the proverbial image of the smallest seed in ancient Jewish folklore.[249] In all three accounts, then, Jesus compares the kingdom of God to a mustard seed to explain that the kingdom is like a seed whose beginning is tiny, unnoticed, and far from earth-shaking in appearance. Just as the seed's diminutive size disguises its immense organic potential, so too does Jesus' ministry contain, in embryonic form, the dynamic budding forth of God's rule among men.

If we are correct in viewing Matthew's parable as a conflation of Mark and Q, the first Evangelist takes ὅταν, μεῖζον, τῶν λαχάνων, γίνεται, and ὥστε from Mark and from Q αὐξάνω, καὶ δένδρον and the entire final phrase τὰ πετεινὰ . . . κλάδοις αὐτοῦ. Luke reproduces Q and Mark represents a dynamic translation of the same Aramaic parable. All three parables conclude by contrasting the kingdom's original form as a mustard seed to its final grandeur as a tree or a mature plant (Mk.). Each version recalls an OT text in which the tree symbolizes a great kingdom (Ps. 103:12; Dn. 4:10-12, 20f. LXX; Eze. 17:23; 31:5, 6). While Q appears closest to the Theodotion text of Dn. 4:21 (ὑποκάτω αὐτοῦ κατῴκουν τὰ θηρία τὰ ἄγρια καὶ ἐν τοῖς κλάδοις αὐτοῦ κατεσκήνουν τὰ ὄρνεα τοῦ οὐρανοῦ), Mark stands closer to Eze. 17:23 (καὶ πᾶν πετεινὸν ὑπὸ τὴν σκιὰν αὐτοῦ ἀναπαύσεται). However, both are allusions, not direct quotations. A mixed Aramaic allusion to the OT image of the Great Tree representing an immense kingdom may well stand behind both passages. The difference between δένδρον (Q) and μεῖζον πάντων τῶν λαχάνων (Mk.) does not counter such a suggestion. In growing great branch's which produce shade for the birds, Mark's plant bears the characteristics of a tree. And, since the terms δένδρον and λάχανον were related in ancient times, the terms are both suitable for the developed mustard plant.[250] The OT allusions, then, in both Mark and Q, accentuate the great size of the mature plant and thus strengthen the contrast between the minuscule seed and its fully developed form. In relation to the kingdom of God, the tree image indicates that though Jesus' ministry has begun on a small scale, its results will be an immense kingdom—the consummation of God's rule. The contrast could not be greater.

---

[248] *Matthew* II, 418.

[249] C.H. Hunzinger, *TDNT* VII, 288. In contrast, M. Black explains the structural difficulties as Mark's mistranslation of an Aramaic play on words: *An Aramaic Approach to the Gospels and Acts*, 165.

[250] See C.H. Hunzinger, "σίναπι", *TDNT* VII, 289.

B. The Parable of the Leaven

Uncertain is the question whether the leaven parable originally followed the parable of the mustard seed or whether it was originally independent and only secondarily attached to the mustard seed as a result of common theme. Mark's omission of the leaven parable cannot affect this question because it is easy to see why Mark would have omitted it from Ch. 4 which is built around the image of the seed. That the two parables parallel in structure accords with the hypothesis of their primitive association.[251]

Apart from the introductions, the Matthean and Lucan versions of the leaven are extremely close. Matthew's introduction which adheres closely in style to Mt. 13:3, 10, 13, and 24 probably indicates Matthean redaction as does Matthew's direct statement as opposed to Luke's question.[252] Luke's introduction, if word counts are indicative (πάλιν Lk. 2x; Mt. 17x; Mk. 28x), may have existed in Q. The difference between Luke's κρύπτω and Matthew's ἐγκρύπτω is slight.[253]

The leaven essentially makes the same impression as the mustard seed: the kingdom, though small and hidden at first, generates a massive end product. In contrast to the negative connotations of leaven in OT and NT literature,[254] leaven is here used positively by Jesus to describe the energetic productive nature of the kingdom of God. The leaven permeates a remarkably large amount of dough—far more than that usually associated with a woman's daily baking. σάτον, a large dry measure, is a Greek loanword from the Aramaic סָאתָא = Hebrew סְאָה.[255] In ancient Judaism three Sata apparently equalled an ephah which was enough grain to feed over one hundred people.[256] The parable, then, appears striking both in language and measure. The kingdom's small beginning has unthought of consequences.

Jesus, therefore, presents in these parables two descriptions of the kingdom of God which hold in tension the kingdom's present rule as it exists in his ministry on earth and as it will exist in the future consummation of the kingdom at the end

---

[251] Such is the conclusion of J. Dupont, "Le Couple parabolique du Sénevé et du Levain", *Jesus Christus in Historie und Theologie,* FS H. Conzelmann; Tübingen: JCB Mohr [Paul Siebeck] (1975) 345.

[252] So Davies and Allison, *Matthew* II, 422; H. Fleddermann, "The Mustard Seed and the Leaven", *SBL Seminar Papers,* Atlanta: Scholar's Press (1989) 223; S. Schulz, *Q-Die Spruchquelle,* 307.

[253] Against B K L N 892 1010 and 1424, many of the best manuscripts witness Lk. in exact parallel to Mt.: 𝔓75 ℵ A D W Θ Ψ 070 *f*13 1 𝔐.

[254] Ex. 12:15-20; 34:25; Lev. 2:11; Mt. 16:6; Lk. 12:1; 1 Cor. 5:6.

[255] Bauer, 745.

[256] So J. Jeremias, *The Parables of Jesus,* 147.

of history.[257] Despite the contrast in appearance, God's eschatological rule is alive in both events. The kingdom commences humbly in Jesus' preaching of the kingdom and in his ministry among the poor, the demon-possessed, and the sick. As a seed which contains the potential to produce a tree or a pinch of yeast which is able to swell an entire loaf, Jesus promises that his activities, though not sensational in the eyes of all, presently bear the blueprints for God's eschatological rule as it will manifest itself in the judgement and salvation of man at the end of history. The present and future manifestations of the kingdom are held in tension by God's power as revealed in Jesus.

C. The Mustard Seed and Leaven Parables: a Witness to the Situation of the Q Community?

R. Laufen argues that the Q community recognizes in these parables its own situation in relation to the fulfillment of the kingdom of God. Following Jeremias' remark that $\kappa\alpha\tau\alpha\sigma\kappa\eta\nu\acute{o}\omega$ was "an eschatological technical term for the incorporation of the Gentiles into the people of God," Laufen argues that the parable is both one of growth which emphasizes the ecclesiastical commissioning of the Q missionaries (Lk. 10:16//Mt. 10:40), and a parable of contrast which eschatologically juxtaposes the images of the seed and the tree. The Q community has in view the eschatological contrast between the community's present humble existence and the future consummation of the kingdom.[258] Similarly, H. Fleddermann writes that the parables: "help us to see the full scope of Q's eschatology." Fleddermann, among others, believes that Q's eschatology deals with the delay of the Parousia: "There can be no doubt that Q reckoned with the delay of the parousia. . . . The Mustard Seed and the Leaven assign a reason for the delay on a cosmic level. The delay allows the tiny, hidden kingdom to grow and permeate the whole world."[259] S. Schulz identifies the seed's growth as evidence that the parable originated in a Hellenistic-Jewish Q community whose members had to deal with the delay of the Parousia in contrast to the earlier Palestinian Q community which expected the immediate return of the Son of Man. The parables of the mustard seed and leaven, therefore, are positive reactions to the delay. Though the kingdom has not yet culminated in its final show of power, it has begun in microscopic form. First in the two messengers of Sophia—Jesus

---

[257] Here we differ from C.H. Dodd, *The Parables of Jesus*, 145: ". . . the eschaton, the divinely ordained climax of history, is here", and W.G. Kümmel, *Promise and Fulfilment*, 131. Both the beginning and end are in view.

[258] *Die Doppelüberlieferungen der Logienquelle und des Markusevangeliums*, 190-192, 200.

[259] *Ibid.*, 233.

and John the Baptist—and now in the members of the Hellenistic Q community, who further the kingdom's saving power in their missionary enterprise (Lk. 10:2-16). Thus, according to Schulz, the mustard seed and leaven reflect the kerygmatic thrust of the Hellenistic Q community.[260]

However, the fact of the historical Jesus is the major deterrent to interpreting the mustard seed and leaven parables against the hypothetical background of a Q group. While Fleddermann complains that H.K. McArthur "confuses the search for an original form of the parable in Jesus' ministry and the reconstruction of the Q text used by Matthew and Luke,"[261] one may well ask if Fleddermann and the other Q scholars noted above are not guilty of the exact reverse—seeking the biases of Q where there should be sought the teaching of Jesus. The Mustard Seed's authenticity is supported by its Palestinian coloring, the ease with which it can be translated into Aramaic, and the composite nature of its allusion to the OT (the allusions are neither direct quotations of the LXX nor are they dependent on one LXX text-type).[262] What is true of Mk.'s version is also true of Q. The indefinite nature of the OT allusion cautions against viewing it as a secondary insertion implemented in view of the Gentile Mission. In favour of the mustard seed's authenticity is its multiple attestation. Hence, Schürmann concludes that the parable's primitive features indicate the: "«größere Wahrscheinlichkeit » für einen «Sitz im Leben » der vorösterlichen Verkündigung Jesu und seiner Jünger." The parable, for Schürmann, represents the *vox Jesu.*[263]

On the basis of the criterion of coherence, the similarities between the parable of the mustard seed and the parable of the leaven argue for the latter's authenticity. Both have similar introductions, both portray the initial hiding of something tiny which in time becomes great, both deal with an organic process, both develop the theme of the kingdom of God as an event in Jesus' ministry which begins not with a catastrophic event but with a ministry to people. In the synoptic Gospels, Jesus

---

[260] *Q-Die Spruchquelle*, 298-306: "Der kerygmatische Rahmen der Traditionsschicht von Q ist allein der sachgemäße Interpretationsschlüssel dieses theologisch so zentralen Gleichnisses" (304). Schulz, however, does not agree that κατασκηνόω refers to the Gentile mission as the Gentile mission is clearly not the term's meaning in Daniel 4:9 Theodotion (p. 306).

[261] *Ibid.*, (221) in regard to H.K. McArthur's "The Parable of the Mustard Seed", *CBQ* 33 (1971) 198-201.

[262] R. Pesch, *Markus,* 263. So also Jeremias: "This does not, however, exclude the possibility that Jesus himself occasionally referred to Scripture in a parable. In at least two cases this is extremely probable: at the end of the parable of the Mustard Seed, and at the end of the parable of the Seed growing of itself . . .", *The Parables of Jesus,* 32.

[263] "Das Zeugnis der Redenquelle für die Basileia-Verkündigung Jesu", 162, 163.

frequently emphasizes the same point with different images.[264] As a result, we are confused by Schürmann's identification of the leaven as a Church creation secondarily placed on the lips of Jesus. Unapparent is the mission terminology and ecclesiastical understanding of kingdom which Schürmann cites as features distinctive from the authentic parable of the mustard seed.[265] On the contrary, the parable's authenticity is suggested by the pleonastic participle λαβοῦσα, a Semitism,[266] and the Semitic loanword σάτον. The imagery as a whole is appropriate to a Palestinian background.[267]

Important is the fact that both parables can be convincingly placed within the ministry of Jesus. The small beginning represents the coming of Jesus, the herald of the Good News, in whom the kingdom of God is alive and active as is evident in Jesus' healing ministries (Lk. 7:22//Mt. 11:4, 5) and exorcisms (Lk. 11:20//Mt. 12:28). This much must have been evident to Jesus' followers. However, the colossal end product of Jesus' ministry was less evident, as E. Fuchs remarks:

> The similitude chooses its image by contraries, as in fact Jesus often does. The relation between a tiny beginning and the miraculous conclusion is therefore certainly emphasized, but it is not self-evident in the case of the Basileia. On the other hand, it is self-evident and obvious that Jesus has in mind his own situation and that of his hearers, when he proclaims the Basileia to them.[268]

Following a similar train of thought, R.T. France reasons that within Jesus' ministry the mustard seed and leaven parables responded to the serious issue of disillusionment both by Jesus' disciples and by the crowds at large who heard Jesus' proclamation of the kingdom, but who saw little evidence of its reality: "for those outside the disciple group it affected the credibility of an announcement of God's reign which apparently had little to show for it; for the disciples there was the natural impatience to see God's kingdom in all its glory, and the total eradication of all that opposed it."[269] In response to this situation, Jesus voices as

---

[264] For instance the parables of the Hidden Treasure, the Costly Pearl, and the Dragnet in Mt. 13:44-50; the images of the unshrunk cloth and the old wineskin in Mk. 2:21, 22, and the parables of the Lost Sheep, the Lost Coin, and the Lost Son in Lk. 15:1-32.

[265] "Das missionsterminologische und ekklesiologische Verständnis von «Basileia» möchte man so Jesus nicht zusprechen", "Das Zeugnis der Redenquelle für die Basileia-Verkündigung Jesu", 164. Also arguing for secondary origin, S. Schulz places the Leaven parable, like the Mustard Seed, in the Hellenistic Q Community whose Kerygma was determined by the delay of the Parousia, *Q-Die Spruchquelle*, 309.

[266] See *Blass, Debrunner, and Funk*, §419 example (2): "Λαβών and other descriptive participles are common in pleonastic usage (using more words than necessary) following the Hebrew pattern", 216.

[267] So J. Jeremias, *The Parables of Jesus*, 146f.

[268] *Studies of the Historical Jesus*, ET London: SCM (1964) 92.

[269] *Matthew*, 228.

promise and encouragement the parables of the mustard seed and leaven. From Jesus' humble ministry will eventually result the universal consummation of God's kingdom in all its power.

Because the parables can be placed convincingly within Jesus' ministry, there exists no good reason for viewing them as evidence for the Q community's reaction to the delay of the parousia, especially in view of our lack of evidence that the early Church ever identified itself as the kingdom of God. It is telling that Schulz, immediately after discrediting the parable's authenticity, has the Hellenistic Q Community place the parable back onto the lips of the historical Jesus through kerygmatic recourse; and, in fact, goes on to explain the microscopic beginning of the kingdom against the background of Jesus' earthly ministry.[270] Is it not easier to see the exact reverse taking place? The parables of the mustard seed and leaven were retained on account of their dominical origin by Matthew, Mark, Luke and the compilers of Q. The parables continued to shed light on the significance of Jesus' ministry and expressed the reality that what Jesus started had not yet been completed. To that extent, the compilers of Q indeed would have applied the parables to their own situation.

A.M. Ambrozic has written that the mustard seed parable attempts to solve "the incongruity between the glorious kingdom expected by the contemporaries of Jesus and the humility and apparent insignificance which characterized his ministry."[271] It reveals Jesus' attempt to explain and defend the truth of his kingdom proclamation. In Q we have Jesus' self-identification as herald of the kingdom following Isa. 61 and his claim to cast out demons by the finger of God (Lk. 11:20//Mt. 12:28). We, on the other hand, also have humble depictions of Jesus as the Son of Man castigated as a glutton and drunkard—a friend of tax-collectors and sinners (Lk. 7:34//Mt. 11:19), and Jesus the homeless Son of Man, who unlike the birds and foxes has nowhere to sleep (Lk. 9:58//Mt. 8:20). There is, then, within Q an internal irony between these two depictions of Jesus—the one a figure of power, the other a figure of humility. To those confused by the incongruity between Jesus' radical proclamation and his humble lifestyle, the parable of the mustard seed represents the promise that within Jesus' lowly ministry exists the same power as that which will shatter the world in the endtime

---

[270] "Die Basileia wächst vielmehr irdisch-sichtbar aufgrund der Worte und Taten des irdischen Menschensohnes Jesus und der apokalyptischen Erntearbeit seiner Boten in Israel, und auf diesen unscheinbaren, wirklich wunderbaren Anfang richtet das Gleichnis die Aufmerksamkeit", *Q-Die Spruchquelle*, 305.

[271] *The Hidden Kingdom: A Redaction-Critical Study of the References to the Kingdom of God in Mark's Gospel,* Washington: Catholic Biblical Association of America (1972) 130.

manifestation of the kingdom of God.[272] The parables of the mustard seed and leaven call for faith in Jesus and the power at work in him.[273]

The attempt to explain the parallel sayings of Jesus against the eschatological perspectives of a hypothetical Q community is redundant. The problems created by P. Hoffmann's and D. Lührmann's disagreement as to whether the Q community expected the immediate or delayed appearance of the eschatological Son of Man, and S. Schulz's elaborate scheme which attaches an imminent expectation to his Palestinian Q community and a delayed perspective to the Hellenistic Q community seem unnecessary in view of the likelihood that Jesus himself understood the kingdom to be both present in his earthly ministry and also future in the eschatological climax of history. The Q parables have both events in view. Different levels of Q redaction seem unnecessary, at least on eschatological grounds, because of the likelihood that Jesus himself held present and future in tension.

IX. They will come from North and South: The Eschatological Banquet (Lk. 13:28, 29//Mt. 8:11, 12)

Lk. 13:28, 29//Mt. 8:11, 12 presents the kingdom of God as the eschatological banquet—the eschatological sphere of salvation in which the repentant and faithful enjoy the eternal rewards of their relationship to God which they have gained through their identification with Jesus. Those who follow Jesus on earth will receive their reward at God's banquet at the end of time. The kingdom, according to Jeremias, is the goal of the pilgrimage: "the scene of God's revelation of himself, Zion, the holy Mountain of God."[274] Or as Beasley-Murray puts it, the kingdom represents "the gladness that comes when God is known, the joy of fellowship and the life eternal that God bestows in the revelation of his saving sovereignty."[275]

Lk. 13:28, 29//Mt. 8:11, 12 presents the kingdom as God's "eschatological show of power,"[276] which will attract some but actively reject others. In voicing this warning Jesus assumes prophetic knowledge of how God will bless his

---

[272] So C. Caragounis (*The Son of Man*, 178), "But if Dan 4 could be used by Jesus to illustrate the tiny and humble beginning of the Kingdom of God, which eventually grows and fills the whole earth, why could it not also be used by him to illustrate the apparently insignificant and humble beginning of the Son of Man's work in proclaiming God's Kingdom, at a time when its future glory was still out of sight, but was nonetheless implicit in his message?"

[273] So R. Pesch, *Markus* I, 263.

[274] *Jesus' Promise to the Nations*, 60.

[275] *Jesus and the Kingdom of God*, 174.

[276] *Ibid.*, 70.

faithful. Indeed, he assumes the authority of God himself by announcing who will and who will not be saved. The decisive criterion which determines salvation or judgement is mankind's response to Jesus and the truth of his ministry. The recurring witness of Jesus in Q testifies to this truth (Lk. 10:12-15//Mt. 11:21-23; Lk. 10:16//Mt. 10:40; Lk. 11:31, 32//Mt. 12:41, 42; Lk. 11:23//Mt. 12:30). Those from "east and west" therefore are people who have put their trust unconditionally in Jesus' authority to share the saving power of God. They are the poor who will inherit the kingdom, who will be satisfied, and who will rejoice at God's eschatological banquet.[277] Lk. 13:28, 29//Mt. 8:11, 12 is not an explicit christological portrait of Jesus, but its implications are great—Jesus announces, describes, and is the means of salvation.[278]

A.   Lk. 13:28//Mt. 8:12

The opening phrase is a warning of the judgement awaiting those who do not seek first the kingdom. Their fate, as Polag puts it, is total disaster (*Unheil*).[279] Yet their misfortune is a calamity which they have brought upon their own heads. For in the endtime they are characterized not by repentance or remorse, but by rage, hatred, and "anger directed against the master."[280] No tragedy exceeds that which will be experienced by those envisioned here. Weeping and gnashing of teeth "describes the fate of those who receive the summons to the joy of God's kingdom but do not come to partake of it."[281]

Lk. 13:28b differs from Mt. 8:11b with the additional phrases ὅταν ὄψησθε, καὶ, πάντας τοὺς προφήτας, and τοῦ θεοῦ. Beasley-Murray, B. Chilton, and S. Schulz view ὅταν ὄψησθε as Luke's redactional link to Lk. 13:25-27.[282] In contrast, J. Schlosser argues that the phrase is traditional, while Davies and Allison suggest it was omitted by Matthew when he flipflopped the saying's

---

[277] Lk. 6:20b, 21//Mt. 5:3, 4, 6; Lk. 14:15-24//Mt. 22:1-10.

[278] So F. Hahn, *Mission in the New Testament*: "Thus Jesus' message and works in Israel became a witness among the Gentiles, and still more: as the eschatological event already began to be realized, salvation came within the direct reach of the Gentiles"(39) . . . "What is decisive for the missionary service of early Christianity is the work and message of Jesus. The Kingdom of God which has drawn near begins to be realized with his appearing, the new people of God is gathered, and in spite of the concentration on Israel, the Gentiles do not remain untouched by it. With the command to missionize and the conveying of his own authority, Jesus brings the disciples into his eschatological work" (164).

[279] *Christologie der Logienquelle*, 92.

[280] I.H. Marshall, *Luke*, 567.

[281] K.H. Rengstorf, "κλαυθμός", *TDNT* III, 726.

[282] G.R. Beasley-Murray, *Jesus and the Kingdom of God*, 170; B. Chilton, *God in Strength*, 194; S. Schulz, *Q-Die Spruchquelle*, 323.

order.[283] In favour of the traditional origin is the phrase's frequency in Jesus' eschatological language (Mt. 5:8; 24:30; 26:64; Mk. 13:26; Lk. 17:22; 21:27). The evidence, however, is not conclusive. How one reconstructs the sayings' original order clearly influences the manner in which a difficult phrase is attributed to the redaction of the Evangelists. Those favouring the original order of Luke are more likely to attribute ὅταν ὄψησθε to tradition, while those favouring Matthew's order will invariably identify the phrase as Lukan redaction. With more certainty, we may ascribe Luke's καὶ πάντας τοὺς προφήτας, a typical Lukan phrase (Lk. 11:50; 24:27; Acts 10:43), and Matthew's τῶν οὐρανῶν, a typical Matthean phrase, to redaction.[284]

The positive alternative to eternal teeth gnashing is entrance into the kingdom of God. The image of Abraham, Isaac, and Jacob in the kingdom of God is characteristic of Jesus (Mt. 22:32; Mk. 12:26; Lk. 20:37) and recalls the OT promise of God's eschatological protection for the children of Jacob (Isa. 29:22; 41:8; 51:2). The picture envisions a time when the Israelites will "sanctify the Holy One of Jacob, and stand in awe of the God of Israel" (Isa. 29:23b). It is the time of salvation for which Jesus has taught his disciples to pray when God's strength will serve as the salvation of Israel from all her enemies (Isa. 41:8f). It is this sphere of salvation which awaits those faithful to Jesus.

The image of the future appearance of the three Patriarchs and the images of eschatological damnation and eschatological salvation imply the anticipation of the resurrection of the dead.[285] It is in the future, following the resurrection, when the blessings of the kingdom will be fully realized and exclusion from the kingdom will be suffered. Those who follow Jesus now will be saved later. The one who rejects Jesus now will later be rejected from the kingdom of God. The image coheres with Q material elsewhere (Lk. 6:22//Mt. 5:11, 12; Lk. 12:8, 9//Mt. 10:32, 33).

Though the thought conveyed is identical, the vocabulary of Lk. 13:28c and Mt. 8:12a differ except for the common use of ἐκβάλλω. A good case can be put forth for the antiquity of both versions. While Matthew Black has argued

---

[283] J. Schlosser, *Le Règne de Dieu dans les dits de Jésus*, 605; Davies and Allison, *Matthew* II, 26. In this scenario, Matthew transposed the three patriarchs from Q 13:28b to Q 13:29 to form Matthew 8:28.

[284] So B. Chilton, *God in Strength*, 194; J. Fitzmyer, *Luke* II, 1026; I.H. Marshall, *Luke Historian and Theologian*, Exeter: Paternoster (1970) 170 n. 1; P. Hoffmann, "πάντες ἐργάται ἀδικίας: Redaktion und Tradition in Lk. 13:22-30", *ZNW* 58 (1967) 207; J. Schlosser, *Le Règne de Dieu dans les dits de Jésus*, 605; S. Schulz, *Q-Die Spruchquelle*, 323.

[285] The resurrection of the dead is a perception characteristic of Jesus: Mt. 12:41f.//Lk. 11:31f; Lk. 14:14; Mk. 12:18f.; Lk. 10:12; Mt. 11:22; Mt. 5:29; Mk. 9:45; Mt. 10:28; 23:33. See W.G. Kümmel, *Promise and Fulfillment*, 89; G.R. Beasley-Murray, *Jesus and the Kingdom of God*, 174; J. Schlosser, *Le Règne de Dieu dans les dits de Jésus*, 633-37.

forcefully for taking Luke's circumstantial clause as translation from an Aramaic original,[286] Matthew's phrase "sons of the kingdom" represents an equally Jewish form of speech.[287] The vast majority of scholars follow Black assuming that the author of Matthew was fluent in Semitic speech and was capable of transmitting the saying in a distinctively Jewish manner.[288] Because "sons of . . ." phrases are equally characteristic of Luke,[289] it appears difficult to explain why Luke would have omitted the epithet here. We cautiously consider Matthew's "sons of the Kingdom" a Matthean insertion and Luke's direct address ($\dot{v}\mu\hat{a}s$), which is characteristic of Q, as tradition.[290] Also redactional is the phrase "into the outer darkness" which is exclusive to Matthew (22:13; 25:30).[291] The use of $\xi\xi\omega$ with $\beta\dot{a}\lambda\lambda\omega$ in Mt. 13:48; Mk. 12:8; Lk. 4:29; 14:35; 20:15; Lk. 22:62//Mt. 26:75 suggests, by the criterion of multiple attestation, that Luke's wording here reflects Jesus' traditional judgement language.[292]

That Jesus directed this threat of eternal exclusion from the kingdom of God to a specific audience is certain. However, there exists no evidence of who this audience was. The inclusion of the three patriarchs in the kingdom and the implications of Jesus as speaker warn against identifying the audience as the Jewish people in total. As a prophetic statement of judgement this saying does not pronounce an irreversible verdict but describes the future penalty of rejecting Jesus' present kingdom message. Lk. 13:28 par., thus, is a warning advising listeners who have ears to hear to repent and change their ways in view of the future judgement.

B.   Lk. 13:29//Mt. 8:11

If Luke's order represents the original as we suggest, we may conjecture that Matthew has removed "Abraham, Isaac, and Jacob" from the Q beginning, switched the saying's beginning to the end and vice versa, and then reinserted the patriarchs phrase into the newly formed first half of 8:11. In the process Matthew has omitted one reference to the kingdom. This complicated manoeuvre is made

---

[286] *An Aramaic Approach to the Gospels and Acts*, 82; So also J. Jeremias, *Jesus' Promise to the Nations*, 55 n. 185.

[287] *Strack Billerbeck* I, 476f.

[288] Bruce Chilton, *God in Strength*, 192; J. Schlosser, *Le Règne de Dieu dans les dits de Jésus* II, 606; S. Schulz, *Q-Die Logienquelle*, 606; *Contra* P.D. Meyer ("The Gentile Mission in Q", *JBL* 89, 1970) who believes Lk. omitted the phrase (412).

[289] 1:16; 4:35; 6:8 (2x); 20:34; 20:36 (2x)

[290] B. Chilton, *God in Strength*, 192; S. Schulz, *Q-Die Spruchquelle*, 323, 324.

[291] Davies and Allison, *Matthew* II, 30; S. Schulz, 324; B. Chilton, *God in Strength*, 193.

[292] B. Chilton, *God in Strength*, 194.

necessary by Matthew's secondary placement of the pericope within the narrative on the Centurion's faith. Because Lk. 13:28 would be an awkward transition from Mt. 8:10b, Matthew has reversed the pericope's order and attached the λέγω δέ ὑμῖν phrase to the beginning of Q 13:29a.[293] In so doing he has created parallelism with Ἀμὴν λέγω ὑμῖν in Mt. 8:10//Lk.7:9 and thus a smooth transition into its new narrative setting.[294]

The origin of Matthew's πολλοί is contested. J. Schlosser, P.D. Meyer, and S. Schulz[295] argue that πολλοί is a Matthean addition inserted to heighten the contrast between the faithful coming from east and west and the unfaithful Sons of the kingdom. Matthew has created a link among the many who will experience eschatological salvation in the kingdom of God, the many who will be ransomed by the life of the Son of Man in Mt. 20:28, and the many whose sins will be forgiven as a result of Jesus' shed blood in Mt. 26:28. Of a different opinion, however, are B. Chilton, J. Jeremias, and J. Fitzmyer[296] who argue that πολλοί was originally in Q and was secondarily omitted by Luke as a result of his previous use of πολλοί in 13:24, where the adjective refers negatively to the many who seek to enter the narrow door but are not able. To avoid confusion with 13:25-27 as to who the "many" are, Luke has omitted the word in 13:29. Both views are plausible. If the latter is correct, we have here a synoptic verse which identifies the future recipients of kingdom salvation in much the same language as Jesus uses elsewhere in reference to the future recipients of Cross salvation (Mk. 10:45; 14:25 par.; Ro. 5:16). If Matthew made the insertion, the saying provides evidence of how closely the early Church associated Jesus' kingdom preaching with his death on the cross. Indeed, the latter fulfilled the former.

The positive foil to the outcasts are the many who come from east and west, north and south. The latter phrase, καὶ ἀπὸ βορρᾶ καὶ νότου, may be a Lukan addition as a result of its omission by Matthew and the Hellenistic spelling of βορέας.[297] However, both the longer and the shorter descriptions antedate our

---

[293] λέγω δέ ὑμῖν. Mt. 58x; Mk. 16x; Lk. 45x

[294] *Pace*, B. Chilton who argues that Luke here reverses the order and edits down: "In order to maintain his focus on those who are cast out, he must not only reverse the traditional order of vv. 28, 29, he must also truncate the sentence about those who will recline at table in the kingdom so that this "Drohwort" does not turn into a "Jubelruf", *God in Strength*, 188.

[295] J. Schlosser, *Le Règne de Dieu dans les dits de Jésus* II, 606f.; P.D. Meyer, "The Gentile Mission in Q", 412; S. Schulz, *Q-Die Spruchquelle*, 323, 24; P. Hoffmann, "πάντες ἐργάται ἀδικίας: Redaktion und Tradition in Lk. 13:22-30", 208f.

[296] B. Chilton, *God in Strength*, 199; J. Jeremias, *Jesus' Promise to the Nations*, 56; J. Fitzmyer, *Luke* II, 1026; W. Grimm, "Zum Hintergrund von Mt. 8:11f//Lk. 13:28", *BZ* 16 (1972) 255-56.

[297] So B. Chilton, *ibid.*, 190; J. Schlosser, *Le Règne de Dieu dans les dits de Jésus* II, 605.

saying in related passages in the OT.[298] The four points of the compass are mentioned in Ps. 107:3 in reference to the redeemed the Lord has gathered from the lands of the earth, while in Zch. 8:7 east and west refer to the whole world from which God will gather his remnant to live in Jerusalem. Both phrases have the same meaning.

It is a matter of debate whether east, west, north, and south refers to the eschatological inclusion of Gentiles into the kingdom of God or to the diaspora Jews whom God will bring to Zion from the ends of the earth. While the vast majority of scholars detect an allusion to the Gentiles,[299] they are not explicitly named in 13:29//8:11. Davies and Allison make a strong case against the Gentile interpretation in view of the saying's OT background in which "east and west" refers exclusively to the return of diaspora Jews to Jerusalem from Babylon and Egypt. While there exist no OT passages which portray Gentiles journeying from distant lands for God's eschatological feast, Ps. 107:3; Isa. 25-27; 49; and Eze. 37-39 do contain the theme of the pilgrimage of diaspora Jews. In view of this evidence, then, it would seem that the saved entering the kingdom are diaspora Jews if, indeed, Jesus' saying is totally dependent on the conventions of OT thought.[300]

The OT background, however, is complex. On the one hand, there are passages which describe the last days as a time when Gentiles will "stream" to the mountain of the Lord (Isa. 2:2f.), and there are, on the other hand, passages which include "all peoples" in God's eschatological banquet (Isa. 25:6f.). In view of Jesus' occasional ministry to Gentiles (Mk. 7:24f; Mt. 8:5f.//Lk. 7:1f.; Lk. 7:11; Mt. 25:31f.) and his statements which contrast Gentiles with the unfaithful of "this generation" (Lk. 11:31, 32//Mt. 12:41, 42), we should not be too hasty in excluding them from Jesus' perspective here. In any case the contrast is not ethnic but religious—between Jewish religious authorities who have rejected Jesus and hence the kingdom, and pagan Gentiles who have repented and as a result will be saved in the end.

ἀνακλίνω within a future kingdom saying clearly refers to reclining at the heavenly banquet. This image frequents the OT and Intertestamental Jewish

---

[298] W. Grimm argues that the closest OT parallel to our passage is Isa. 43:5b-6a which provides the motive for coming, the four directions, and the hope of salvation. However, the passage does not mention the eschatological banquet; "Zum Hintergrund von Mt. 8:11f.//Lk. 13:28", *BZ* 16 (1972) 255, 56.

[299] J. Jeremias, *Jesus' Promise to the Nations*, 60; G.R. Beasley-Murray, *ibid.*, 170; W.G. Kümmel, *Promise and Fulfilment*, 51, 83, 85, 89; F. Hahn, *Mission in the New Testament*, 39; A. Polag, *Christologie der Logienquelle*, 92; I.H. Marshall, *Luke*, 568.

[300] *Matthew* II, 27.

texts[301] where God in His eschatological rule prepares a "lavish banquet" for all peoples (Isa. 25:6). The event occasions festive joy, the swallowing up of death, the wiping away of tears, the removal of reproach, the salvation of God, and, indeed, with veil removed, direct fellowship with God himself (Isa. 25:6f.). The banquet scene describes Jesus' future promise in every level of the synoptic tradition: Q Lk. 13:29//Mt. 8:11; Mt. 22:2-14; Mk. 14:25; Lk. 14:15. The image is of eschatological salvation. The people of God, those who have responded positively to Jesus, have been gathered to receive their reward of eternal salvation.

C. The Implications of Lk. 13:28, 29//Mt. 8:11, 12
for the Study of Q

B. Chilton, D. Zeller, W. Trilling, and G. Strecker detect the so-called polemical theology of Q within Jesus' warning of the plight of those who will weep and gnash their teeth when they are excluded from the future kingdom.[302] The Q community, being at odds with contemporary Jewish leaders, has added the judgement phrase in reaction to their Jewish antagonists.[303] S. Schulz identifies Lk. 13:28, 29//Mt. 8:11, 12 as a secondary prophetic oracle which originated in the enthusiastic milieu of the late Syrian Q-community which dealt with the delay of the parousia through kerygmatic recourse on the earthly Jesus.[304] Similarly, P.D. Meyer writes: "The pericope reflects the Q-community's apprehension that Gentiles will participate in the eschatological banquet with the patriarchs, while Israelites will have excluded themselves."[305] Meyer conjectures that the Q

---

[301] Ps. 107:1-9; Isa. 25:6-8; 49:10-13; Eze. 39:17-20; 1 En. 62:14; 1QSa. For occurrences of the banquet image in post NT literature see Davies and Allison, *Matthew* II, 30.

[302] B. Chilton, *God in Strength*, 196; D. Zeller, "Das Logion Mt. 8,11f und das Motif der Völkerwallfahrt," *BZ* 16 (1972) 88, 89; W. Trilling, *Das Wahre Israel*, München: Kosel (1964) 88; G. Strecker, *Der Weg der Gerechtigkeit*, Göttingen: Vandenhoeck & Ruprecht (1971) 100 n. 2.

[303] Hence, Chilton concludes: "The announcement about the meal with the patriarchs has been glossed with a second verse imbued with the style and theology of Q to produce an eschatological polemic against Israel", *God in Strength*, 198. Chilton assigns to Q redaction the phrases: λέγω δὲ ὑμῖν ὅτι and ἐκεῖ ἔσται ὁ κλαυθμὸς καὶ ὁ βρυγμὸς τῶν ὀδόντων (179).

[304] *Q-Die Spruchquelle*, 323-330, esp. 328; D. Zeller likewise identifies our saying as a prophetic oracle: "Das Logion Mt. 8,11 / Lk. 13,28 und das Motiv der 'Völkerwallfahrt," *BZ* 16 (1972) 88-91.

[305] "The Gentile Mission in Q", *JBL* 89 (1970) 412.

community (which was itself Jewish) used the Gentile mission evangelistically to shame fellow Jews into repentance and hence into the kingdom.[306]

Does Lk. 13:28, 29//Mt. 8:11, 12 require explanation in light of the theological understanding of a Q community? Again, because a more likely *Sitz im Leben* exists within the life of Jesus, the answer must be no. When the Synoptic Gospels and John are saturated with evidence that Jesus faced hostility from Jewish religious leaders, particularly the Pharisees, it makes little sense to speculate that our saying or any part thereof originated as a result of Q polemic—a hypothesis which has no textual support. Like the Gospels at large, Jesus' adversaries in Q, when named explicitly, are Pharisees and lawyers—religious experts of renown who found Jesus' kingdom preaching abhorrent in the implications they made about Jesus and his relation to God.[307] Elsewhere in Q Jesus' adversaries are the Galilean cities of Chorazin, Bethsaida, and Capernaum—cities of Jesus' homeland which heard Jesus' message, rejected it, and as a result will, according to Jesus' warning, face the consequences in eternal judgement. When, therefore, we add the evidence from Q that Jesus believed salvation or damnation was to be determined on the last day according to the criterion of man's present acceptance or rejection of Jesus himself (Lk. 12:8, 9//Mt. 10:32, 33 diff. Mk. 8:38), it seems extremely likely that in Lk. 13:28, 29//Mt. 8:11, 12 Jesus is warning an audience which is hostile to his ministry that they will face exclusion from the eschatological feast which will take place in the kingdom of God.[308]

A strong case can be made for the dominical origin of Lk. 13:28, 29 par. While Schulz's two-phase community scheme is too elaborate to warrant credibility, H. Schürmann's scepticism seems based on ideological speculation rather than logical method.[309] There simply exists no evidence to suggest that Lk. 13:28 par. was a secondary expansion of Lk. 13:26f. to which was later appended Lk. 13:29 par.—an originally independent logion which interpreted the church's Gentile mission in terms of Ps. 107:3 (106:3).[310] On the contrary, the Aramaic

---

[306] *Ibid.*, 412, 417; S. Schulz, *Q-Die Spruchquelle*, (330) detects the same implications and argues that Q's theology, though at first radically different from Paul's kerygma, eventually became united with Paul in the hope that Israel might one day be saved (Ro. 9-11).

[307] Lk. 11:39b-41//Mt. 23:25-26; Lk. 11:42//Mt. 23:23; Lk. 11:43//Mt. 23:26, 27; Lk. 11:46//Mt. 23:4; Lk. 11:52//Mt. 23:13.

[308] J. Schlosser (*Le Règne de Dieu dans les dits de Jésus* II, 625) argues that the unusual combination of apocalyptic nationalism and prophetic universalism goes back to Jesus' original understanding: "L'eschatologie de Jésus pourrait bien n' être en première ligne ni apocalyptique ni prophétique mais 'jésuanique'!" Similarly, F. Hahn, *Mission in the New Testament*, 35 n. 1.

[309] The same could be said of V. Hasler's argument (*Amen*, 21f., 60, 62,132) that the saying refers not to adherence to the human Jesus but to the risen Lord.

[310] Schürmann ("Das Zeugnis der Redenquelle für die Basileia-Verkündigung Jesu", 164-168)

participle construction, the lack of a direct reference to Jesus, the divine passive,[311] the Jewish mode of thought, the frequency of Semitisms, the multiple attestation of the banquet image in Jesus' teaching on the future, together with Jesus' frequent inclusion of repentant Gentiles within the kingdom in contrast to unbelieving Jews all add up to forceful evidence in support of the saying's dominical pedigree. In this conclusion we support, among others, J. Schlosser, H. Merklein, F. Hahn, G. Dalman, B. Chilton (in part) and Davies and Allison.[312]

Lk. 13:28, 29//Mt. 8:11, 12 describes the kingdom of God as the future realm of salvation which will include members of every race who have responded positively to Jesus. This kingdom saying does not contain hints of creative editorial work on the part of a Q community who had a novel interpretation of Jesus and his work. Jesus, rather, in describing the consummation of the kingdom in terms of the eschatological banquet, adopts the OT image which he later uses to encourage his disciples at the Lord's Supper before his impending death (Mk. 14:25; Lk. 22:30). The form of salvation to be experienced in the future is the same in both contexts—eternal festal joy in communion with God and the saints. The wedding feast is Jesus' promise of hope to the poor who hear his call (Mt. 22:1-14; 25:1-12; Lk. 14:16-24). The penalty for rejecting Jesus' call is eternal judgement. The saying looks forward to the successful completion of Jesus' earthly mission—the time when the Lord's prayer will be answered in full; the time when all the people of God will be gathered for eternal salvation.

X. The Kingdom of God Suffers Violence:
Lk. 16:16//Mt. 11:12, 13

Rather than revealing the theological understanding of a hypothetical Q Community, Lk. 16:16//Mt. 11:12, 13 communicates Jesus' awareness that his opponents' rejection of himself is an act paramount to a direct assault against the kingdom of God. The concept of God's kingdom suffering violent attacks would have been extraordinary to Jesus' listeners who were submerged in the OT

---

identifies 13:28 par. and 13:29 par. as addition words "*Zusatzworte*" to the preceding context Lk. 13:23, 25, 26f. par. Because they could not have existed as isolated sayings, they do not represent pre-Easter pronouncements of Jesus.

[311] Divine passives are arguably a frequent characteristic of Jesus' speech. See J. Schlosser, *Le Règne de Dieu dans les dits de Jésus* II, 614, 615; A. Polag, *Christologie der Logienquelle*, 63.

[312] J. Schlosser, *ibid.,* II, 614; H. Merklein, *Die Gottesherrschaft als Handlungsprinzip*, 121; F. Hahn, *Mission in the New Testament*, 36; G. Dalman, *The Words of Jesus*, 110; B. Chilton, *God in Strength*, 179; Davies and Allison, *Matthew* II, 18, 28.

conviction of the sovereignty of God and the omnipotence of his rule. However, Lk. 16:16 par. matches the irony of Jesus' suffering Son of Man sayings and the enigmatic concept of a suffering Messiah. Lk. 16:16 par. anticipates the Passion narratives of the Synoptics as it juxtaposes Jesus' rejection with his administration of the kingdom of God. It contains evidence that in the Q material Jesus, the representative of the kingdom and the agent of God's saving grace, suffers hostility and rejection in the present.

A. The Synoptic Problem

The original context of the saying is unknown.[313] While Matthew places the logion in the Q block of material concerning Jesus' response to John (Mt. 11:2-19//Lk. 7:22-35), Luke inserts it between the parable of the unrighteous steward (16:1-13) and the story of Lazarus and the rich man (16:19-21). H. Schürmann has made a convincing case that Lk. 16:14-18 was originally a unity in Q—combined according to the common theme of law—which Matthew subsequently divided (Lk. 16:16 = Mt. 11:12, 13; Lk. 16:17 = Mt. 5:18; Lk. 16:18 = Mt. 5:32), placing 16:16 in Ch. 11 amidst other materials relating to John the Baptist.[314]

1. Mt. 11:12, 13

Because it is unlikely that Luke would have changed the context of 16:16 had he found it in 7:22-35, it is probable that Matthew made the change in context and in doing so reversed the saying's order to begin with Lk. 16:16b and added the

---

[313] Grounds exist for supposing that Lk. 16:16 and Mt. 11:12, 13 have their origin in a common Greek source. Luke's dependence upon Matthew is unlikely (D. Catchpole, "The Law and the Prophets in Q", 95) in view of the fact that four features of Mt. are less primitive than comparable features in Lk. ($\pi \acute{a} \nu \tau \epsilon \varsigma$, $\gamma \acute{a} \rho$, the order of prophets and law, and $\acute{\epsilon} \pi \rho o \phi \acute{\eta} \tau \epsilon v \sigma a \nu$). It seems unlikely that Mt. and Lk. would use $\beta \iota \acute{a} \zeta \epsilon \tau a \iota$ which occurs nowhere else in the NT in the same tense in the same saying, if they were not utilizing related Greek sources. Why would Lk. alter Mt.'s context? The two versions have 10/19 words in common for Luke (53%) and 10/28 for Matthew (36%). If to these figures one adds $\tau o \hat{v}$ $\theta \epsilon o \hat{v}$ and $\tau \hat{\omega} \nu$ $o \mathring{v} \rho a \nu \hat{\omega} \nu$ as synonymous terms and one removes $\epsilon \mathring{v} a \gamma \gamma \epsilon \lambda \acute{\iota} \zeta \epsilon \tau a \iota$ as Lukan redaction and $\delta \grave{\epsilon}$ $\tau \hat{\omega} \nu$ $\mathring{\eta} \mu \epsilon \rho \hat{\omega} \nu$ $\mathring{I} \omega \acute{a} \nu \nu o v$ $\tau o \hat{v}$ $\beta a \pi \tau \iota \sigma \tau o \hat{v}$ and $\acute{\epsilon} \pi \rho o \phi \acute{\eta} \tau \epsilon v \sigma a \nu$ as Mt. redaction, the percentages for parallels raise to 13/19 for Lk. (68%) and 12/21 for Mt. (57%). Though not decisive, these percentages suggest that Mt. and Lk. independently used a common literary source. D. Kosch, *Die Gottesherrschaft im Zeichen des Widerspruchs,* Frankfurt am Main: Peter Lang (1985) 14.

[314] *Traditionsgeschichtliche Untersuchungen zu den synoptischen Evangelien,* 126-136; *idem,* Das Zeugnis der Redenquelle für die Basileia -Verkündigung Jesu", 169, 170. P. Hoffmann (*Studien zur Theologie der Logienquelle,* 53-56), however, argues that Lk.'s context is entirely secondary despite the change in theme following v. 18.

customary Jewish phrase ἀπὸ δὲ τῶν ἡμερῶν as a transitional device.[315] Matthew probably altered Luke's τοῦ θεοῦ to τῶν οὐρανῶν and added the typically Matthean epithet τοῦ βαπτιστοῦ.[316] The other variant from Lk. 16:16b, ἕως ἄρτι, may also be a Matthean expansion, but such is uncertain as the phrase is not typical of Matthew and occurs nowhere else in the Synoptics.[317] The final phrase in Mt. 11:12a, βιάζεται, occurs only here and in Lk. 16:16 and is thus certainly original. In sum, then, if our thinking is correct, Mt. 11:12a with the exception of βιάζεται is an expansion of Lk. 16:16b made necessary by Matthew's change of context.

Mt. 11:12b (καὶ βιασταὶ ἁρπάζουσιν αὐτήν) is considered to be original by most authors as a result of the hapaxlegomenon βιαστής—a term which is extremely infrequent in ancient Greek literature and as such a seemingly unlikely creation of Matthew.[318] ἁρπάζω, however, occurs in the synoptics in Matthew alone (3x): here, once in the parable of the sower (13:19) in difference to αἴρω (Mk. 4:15; Lk. 8:12), and once in the parable of the Strong Man—also in difference to αἴρω (Mt. 12:29 diff. Lk. 11:22). Such evidence might lead to the conclusion that ἁρπάζω is a Matthean favorite and as such is an addition here. It is plausible, however, that Matthew has inserted ἁρπάζω in 13:19 because it is the word which describes the supernatural conflict between God's people and Satan in Matthew's traditional material elsewhere (12:29; 11:12b). This possibility is supported by the likelihood of redaction in Lk. 16:16b and the frequency of αἴρω in Matthew (20x; Mk. 21x; Lk. 20x). It is not axiomatic that Matthew followed the same process in 11:12b and 12:29 that he did in 13:19. If Luke added εὐαγγελίζεται in 16:16b, which is probable, he was forced to truncate either βιάζεται or ἁρπάζουσιν to refrain from having three verbs in a very short phrase.

---

[315] "The days of . . ." phrases are typical of Matthew (2:1; 3:1; 23:30; 24:37) though Semitic (Gn. 26:18; Judg. 5:6; 2 Sm. 21:1; Ezra 9:7; Isa. 1:1) and thus cannot be ruled out as original. So Davies and Allison, *Matthew* II, 253. Against Hoffmann (51), the vast majority of scholars consider the phrase Matthean. So P.S. Cameron, *Violence and the Kingdom*, Frankfurt am Main: Peter Lang (1988) 150, 51; H. Merklein, *Die Gottesherrschaft als Handlungsprinzip*, 84; S. Schulz, *Q-Die Spruchquelle*, 261; J. Schlosser, *Le Règne de Dieu dans les dits de Jésus* II, 513.

[316] Mt. 7x; Mk. 3x; Lk. 4x

[317] G.R. Beasley-Murray (*Jesus and the Kingdom of God*, 94) follows G. Dalman (*The Words of Jesus*, 141) in harmonizing Matthew's ἕως ἄρτι with Luke's ἀπὸ τότε through the suggestion that behind both unique phrases originally existed the Aramaic phrase min haka ulehala which translated into Greek renders ἀπὸ τότε ἕως ἄρτι. This hypothesis, however, requires the redactional omission of ἕως ἄρτι on the part of Lk., which is what P. Hoffmann (*Studien zur Theologie der Logienquelle*, 52) and J. Schlosser (*Le Règne de Dieu dans les dits de Jésus* II, 513) argue. Hoffmann's conclusion, however, is dictated by his conviction that the Lukan version is altered by Luke's view of salvation history.

[318] See G. Schrenk, "βιάζομαι, βιαστής", *TDNT* I, 614.

We speculate that he eliminated the latter which was originally in Q as found in Matthew.

In switching the saying's order, Mt. 11:13 concludes by expanding Lk. 16:16a. The introductory πάντες γάρ,[319] the reversed order of "the prophets and the law,"[320] and the verb προφητεύω[321] are probable alterations made by the first Evangelist. Luke's μέχρι is to be favored to Matthew's ἕως in view of the fact that μέχρι occurs only here in Luke while its one occurrence in Mark is omitted by both Matthew and Luke (Mk. 13:30 diff. Mt. 24:34; Lk. 21:32).[322] In sum, then, we conjecture that Matthew has reordered the saying to fit the context of Ch. 11 on John. In doing so he has significantly expanded the vocabulary in 11:12a and 11:13.

The violent connotations of Mt. 11:12b—(βιάζω, βιαστής, and ἁρπάζω are terms of violence which together imply criminal force)—support G. Schrenk's case that βιάζεται is a passive verb in the bad sense—"the Kingdom of God is attacked by contentious opponents."[323] A negative reading corresponds to the rejection which John and Jesus experienced in their ministries and to the negative use of ἁρπάζω in Mt. 13:19, where Satan takes away the word of the kingdom.

---

[319] πᾶς + γάρ (Mt. 6x; Mk. 2x; Lk. 2x); Davies and Allison, *Matthew* I, 79. So D. Kosch, *Die Gottesherrschaft im Zeichen des Widerspruchs*, 16. *Pace* B. Chilton (*God in Strength*, 212) who believes πάντες was originally in Mt.'s source but not in Lk.'s.

[320] While Lk.'s order represents the traditional phrase, Mt.'s is unique to extant literature. See Davies and Allison, *Matthew* I, 484. Scholars preferring the Lucan order include: J. Fitzmyer, *Luke* II, 1116; Davies and Allison, *Matthew* II, 257; P.S. Cameron, *Violence and the Kingdom*, 137; I.H. Marshall, *Luke*, 628; S. Schulz, *Q-Die Spruchquelle*, 261. Dissenting, however, is J. Kloppenborg (*The Formation of Q*, 114) who considers Mt.'s order original according to the criterion of difficulty.

[321] προφητεύω is a favorite term of Lk. and thus an unlikely omission on his part. More likely is Mt.'s addition in view of Mt. 11:9, 14. So P. Hoffmann, *Studien zur Logienquelle*, 52; D. Kosch, *Die Gottesherrschaft im Zeichen des Widerspruchs*, 16; I.H. Marshall, *Luke*, 628.

[322] *Pace* P. Hoffmann who follows H. Conzelmann in claiming that Lk. inserted both μέχρι Ἰωάννου and ἀπὸ τότε according to his salvation history scheme: *Studien zur Logienquelle*, 52. Other scholars argue for the originality of ἕως in view of its frequency in Q: H. Merklein, *Die Gottesherrschaft als Handlungsprinzip*, 81; S. Schulz, *Q-Die Logienquelle*, 261 n. 590; D. Catchpole, "On Doing Violence to the Kingdom", *IBS* 3 (1981) 95.

[323] "βιάζομαι, βιαστής", *TDNT* I, 611. Schrenk's article is still the best work on this subject. He weighs βιάζομαι in Mt. as an intransitive middle, a transitive middle, a passive in the good sense, and a passive in the bad sense. The final option he considers the best solution (609-614). He is followed by: J. Fitzmyer, *Luke* II, 1117; Davies and Allison, *Matthew* II, 256; J. Schlosser, *Le Règne de Dieu dans les dits de Jésus* II, 510, 524; R.T. France, *Matthew*, 195. However, numerous scholars have taken βιάζομαι here as a middle in the positive sense. So R. Schnackenburg: "men who believe the gospel and harness all their energies seek the kingdom of God and nothing else since the days of John the Baptist", *God's Rule and Kingdom*, 131. So also: I.H. Marshall, *Luke*, 629; G.R. Beasley-Murray, *Jesus and the Kingdom of God*, 93f.; B. Chilton, *God in Strength*, 218. The division among competent scholars suggests caution.

We take Mt. 11:12, 13, then, as a statement that the kingdom of God suffered violence at the hands of those who persecuted Jesus and John.

2. Lk. 16:16

As our analysis of Mt. 11:12, 13 implies, we take as original the order of Lk. 16:16 and the vocabulary of Lk. 16:16a. With many others, however, we detect Luke's editorial activity in 16:16b. While it is true that $\epsilon \dot{v} \alpha \gamma \gamma \epsilon \lambda \dot{\iota} \zeta \omega$ occurs elsewhere in Q (Lk. 7:22//Mt. 11:5), the frequency of the verb in Luke-Acts compared with Matthew and Mark (Lk.-Acts: 25x; Mt. 1x; Mk. 0x) together with the fact that Luke alone of the Evangelists uses the verb with the kingdom of God (Lk. 4:43; 8:1; Acts 8:12) suggests the term is a Lucan addition here. After inserting $\epsilon \dot{v} \alpha \gamma \gamma \epsilon \lambda \dot{\iota} \zeta \omega$, Luke added the final phrase "and all enter into it violently" in order to maintain the original verb $\beta \iota \dot{\alpha} \zeta \epsilon \tau \alpha \iota$. If this redactional hypothesis is correct, Luke applied a positive interpretation to a negative statement: where Matthew reads "the kingdom of God suffers violence," Luke writes "the kingdom of God is preached (as Good News); and where Matthew has "violent men are seizing it," Luke reads "every man is pressed into it." Perhaps Luke interpreted $\beta \iota \dot{\alpha} \zeta \epsilon \tau \alpha \iota$ in view of Lk. 13:24 where Jesus commands his audience to strive to enter the narrow gate—a feat which many will not be strong enough to accomplish. Or conceivably Luke recalls 14:23 where the servant forces, compels or urges ($\dot{\alpha} \nu \alpha \gamma \kappa \dot{\alpha} \zeta \omega$) the poor, crippled, and blind to enter the master's banquet. In either case $\beta \iota \dot{\alpha} \zeta \epsilon \tau \alpha \iota$ in Luke should be read in the middle voice in the good sense. The positive connotations of $\epsilon \dot{v} \alpha \gamma \gamma \epsilon \lambda \dot{\iota} \zeta \omega$ and the entrance phrase ($\pi \hat{\alpha} \varsigma \ \epsilon \dot{\iota} \varsigma \ \alpha \dot{v} \tau \dot{\eta} \nu$) support this view.

B. The Meaning of the Kingdom in its Context

P.S. Cameron in his detailed monograph on Mt. 11:12, 13 argues that the kingdom in Mt. 11:12 refers not to God's "reign" or "rule" but rather to "God's house" in the spatial or local sense of a fortress or stronghold. Cameron reaches this conclusion as a result of his thorough study of the possible Semitic background for Mt. 11:12 in which possible backgrounds are found in the words פָּרַץ (break through, in, open) for $\beta \iota \dot{\alpha} \zeta o \mu \alpha \iota$, פָּרִיץ (violent one, robber, murderer) for $\beta \iota \alpha \sigma \tau \dot{\eta} \varsigma$, and גָּזַל (tear away, seize, rob) or טָרַף (tear, seize) for $\dot{\alpha} \rho \pi \dot{\alpha} \zeta \omega$. Cameron searches the OT and finds this vocabulary used in contexts which portray violence against God's house (2 Chr. 24:7), his law (Eze. 22:23-31) and even God himself (Mal. 3:8f.). Finally, he notes that "God's House" is described eschatologically in Qumran literature and in the Targums, where in one case פָּרַץ is interpreted as referring to the eschatological revelation of the kingdom (Eze. 7:22).[324]

Cameron, however, is unclear as to what exactly Jesus meant if he referred to the kingdom as a stronghold which was being attacked or robbed. The spatial image does not seem entirely consistent with his contention that in Mt. 11:12 the kingdom of God suffers violence in the rejection of its representatives Jesus and John. When the kingdom is present in intangible terms within specific individuals, it is easier to see the kingdom of God as referring to a sphere of salvation which exerts the dynamic rule of God. Cameron, however, is certainly correct that Lk. 16:16//Mt. 11:12, 13 speaks of the kingdom as present and active in the ministry of Jesus.[325] In rejecting Jesus, Jesus' opponents affront the kingdom.

C. Lk. 16:16//Mt. 11:12, 13 a Suffering Kingdom of God Saying?

The striking feature of Lk. 16:16 par. is the paradox inherent in the idea of the kingdom of God suffering violence. The kingdom by representing the awesome rule and power of God logically seems out of place as the object of hostile force— especially antagonism which is to a degree successful. Indeed, the theory that the early church created such an idea is remarkable. However, for Jesus the very same paradox exists within Q in Jesus' statements that the Son of Man is considered a drunkard and glutton (Lk. 7:34 par.) and has no place to lay his head (Mt. 8:20 par.), and outside of Q in Jesus' suffering Son of Man sayings. While Mark makes it clear that Jesus' disciples could not understand the concept of a suffering messiah, the difficulties inherent in Lk. 16:16 par. and the differing contexts of its two versions suggest that the early church and the Evangelists similarly found this saying difficult to comprehend. The fact that the Synoptics intermix present, future, and suffering Son of Man sayings with present, future, and in this case suffering kingdom of God sayings exclusively on the lips of Jesus suggests that for Jesus the two phrases were related: where the Son of Man is there also is the kingdom of God; when the Son of Man comes in the future so too will come the kingdom of God; when the Son of Man suffers rejection the kingdom of God is violated. Perhaps Jesus never juxtaposed the two phrases because it would have been redundant for him to do so. Later, however, the relation between the two was acknowledged by Matthew as is seen by his expansion of Mk. 9:1 to "the

---

[324] *Violence and the Kingdom*, 141-154.

[325] The Kingdom is viewed as present by among others: W.G. Kümmel, *Promise and Fulfilment*, 123; G. Schrenk, "βιάζομαι, βιαστής", 613; R.T. France, *Matthew*, 196; Davies and Allison, *Matthew* II, 257.

Son of Man coming in His kingdom" (Mt. 16:28). Lk. 16:16 par. presents the kingdom of God as a present entity which suffers violence in the rejection of Jesus its herald and representative.[326]

D. Lk. 16:16//Mt. 11:12, 13 and the Study of Q

The myriad of difficulties associated with Lk. 16:16 par. has not prevented advocates of a creative Q community from speculating that the "*Stürmerspruch*" reveals the situation of the editors of Q. S. Schulz identifies the logion as the creative product of the late Syrian Q Community as a result of its christological motivation, its present kingdom understanding, its hint that the delay of the parousia is in view, and its intensified adherence to Torah.[327] From a different perspective, P. Hoffmann claims the saying reveals the Q-Group's eschatological understanding that John has fulfilled the role of Elijah (Mal. 3:1) in signaling the inbreak of the eschaton—the last period of history. Since the departure of John and Jesus, the Q-Group proclaims the kingdom is present in its messengers and waits expectantly for the imminent return of the Son of Man. Lk. 16:16 par. reveals the Group's conviction that the endtime in which they live is a period of spiritual suffering and persecution in which their affliction fulfils Jesus' prediction in Lk. 11:51, 52. Hence, the saying's background exists in the apocalyptic supposition of endtime suffering which precedes the time of salvation (1 En. 99:4; 100:1f.: Jub. 23:18; 1QS 1:18; 1QpHab. 5:7).[328]

Others assert that the saying relates the Q Community's understanding of OT law which has been received directly from Jesus. Its proximity to Lk. 16:17//Mt. 5:18 according to B.Chilton, H. Schürmann, and R. Laufen indicates that OT law remains valid for the Q community.[329] H. Merklein writes that Lk. 16:17//Mt. 5:18 is an interpretive addition by the Q community to prevent an antinomian

---

[326] Exactly who the aggressors were is not clear. Hypotheses include Herod Antipas (P.S. Cameron, *Violence and the Kingdom*, 152), Zealots (P. Hoffmann, *Studien zur Logienquelle*, 78, 79), Pharisees (A. Polag, *Christologie der Logienquelle,* 79; J. Schlosser, *Le Règne de Dieu dans les dits de Jésus* II, 521), and the last generation in Israel at the time of the Q community (S. Schulz, *Q-Die Spruchquelle*, 264-66).

[327] *Q-Die Spruchquelle*, 263, 264.

[328] *Studien zur Theologie der Logienquelle*, 50-79 esp. 63-75. Hoffmann locates the historical situation of this group in Palestine between 40 and 70 A.D. and states that the opponents of Q were probably Zealots (74-76). The group's conviction that OT prophecy is presently being fulfilled motivates them to expand the authentic word of Jesus Lk. 10:23f//Mt. 13:16f. to describe how Jesus fulfilled scripture Lk. 7:22//Mt. 11:5 – Isa. 26:19; 29:18f; 35:5; 61:1f. (p. 63).

[329] B. Chilton, *God in Strength*, 213, 230; H. Schürmann, *Traditionsgeschichtliche Untersuchungen zu den synoptischen Evangelien*, 136; R. Laufen, *Die Doppelüberlieferungen der Logienquelle und des Markusevangeliums*, 356.

misunderstanding of Lk. 16:16//Mt. 11:12, 13 which contains the authentic concept of Jesus that adherence to the kingdom replaces Torah as the decisive criterion for how men should live (*Handlungsprinzip*).[330]

V. Schönle isolates Lk. 16:16 par. as the key for understanding the "*heilsgeschichtliche Reflexion*" of the authors of Q. According to Schönle, the Q authors smoothed out the primitive polemical background of Jesus' sayings directed against John and his followers. By applying the composite allusion of Ex. 23:20/Mal. 3:1 to John in Lk. 7:27//Mt. 11:10, Q raises John to the eminent status of the eschatological Elijah figure who ushers in the Messiah. Q emends tradition by adding the statements that John is more than a prophet and the greatest born among women. Mt. 11:12, 13 was not originally a unity. The Q composers added Mt. 11:13 as a positive remedy to 11:12 in which John is excluded from the kingdom. The change elevates John to the figure who inaugurates the time of salvation.[331]

The presupposition, however, of Hoffmann, Schulz, and Schönle that Lk. 16:16 par. is a secondary composition of the Q community permits radical elaboration without taking into consideration the saying's suitable place within the ministry of Jesus. There exists no reason to doubt that John suffered hostile opposition from Jewish leaders and a violent death at the hands of Herod Antipas and that Jesus, surviving John, would have reflected on his predecessor's demise and related it to the rejection he experienced in his own ministry. In fact the weakness of the hypotheses of Hoffmann, Schulz, and Schönle alike, is the manner in which they project Jesus' situation directly onto the situation of the community which supposedly passed on and in some cases created his sayings.[332] They say of the Q Community what is more easily understood of Jesus. It seems in our opinion that rather than creating sayings to explain the present situation such a group would have interpreted their present situation in light of traditional material that they valued as genuine instruction of Jesus. Such was certainly the case for Luke in Acts where the disciples without once quoting a saying of Jesus follow a

---

[330] *Die Gottesherrschaft als Handlungsprinzip*, 94. D. Kosch (*Die eschatologische Tora des Menschensohnes*, Göttingen: Vandenhoeck & Ruprecht [1989] esp. 473-480) reaches a similar conclusion that Q essentially contains Jesus' understanding that the Kingdom in some sense fulfills the purpose of OT Torah and is "eschatological Torah."

[331] *Johannes, Jesus und die Juden: Die Theologische Position des Matthäus und des Verfassers der Redenquelle im Lichte von Mt. 11*, BET 17, Frankfurt am Main: Verlag Peter Lang (1982) 96-113, esp. 101-105: "Der Stürmerspruch erweist sich dann natürlich als ein Schlüssel für das heilsgeschichtliche Denken schon von Q" (117).

[332] P. Hoffmann, *Studien zur Logienquelle*, 76; S. Schulz, *Q-die Spruchquelle*, 265; V. Schönle, *Johannes, Jesus und die Juden*, 118: "Wie die explizite Gerichtsankündigung Jesu an das Volk in dem Zusammenhang steht, daß in gleicher Weise wie Jesus nun auch die Q-Gemeinde selbst für ihr Auftreten eschatologische Bedeutung in Anspruch nimmt."

pattern set forth by their Lord in the third Gospel. In contrast to their previous failures in the Gospel, in Acts the disciples follow faithfully the model of Jesus by speaking with authority in public debate, preaching the Gospel, and even performing miracles. Yet not once do Jesus' followers quote Jesus in a polemical situation. If such were a common practice in previous or contemporary community's—especially the one responsible for collecting the majority of extant dominical sayings—would not Luke have described the activity as characteristic of Christians in the early church?[333]

We fail to see the new intensified understanding of Torah, the mission's kerygma, the ecclesiastically determined kingdom pronouncement, and the advanced Salvation-History periodizing which leads H. Schürmann to identify the logion as a secondary composition.[334] The focus of 16:16 par. is not Salvation-History, the law, or John the Baptist, but the paradox of the kingdom suffering violence.[335] Paradox is characteristic of Jesus' speech[336] and the kingdom is the crux of Jesus' preaching. The sheer difficulty of the saying suggests that it was retained because of its dominical origin.[337]

XI. Conclusions

We set out in this chapter on the kingdom of God in Q with five objectives: (1) To detect whether the Q kingdom of God sayings reveal a characteristic Q perception of a present, imminently coming, or delayed parousia; (2) To see to what extent the community element in Q is tied to Jesus himself as opposed to the secondary orientation of an independent early Christian group; (3) To see if indeed Jesus in Q is only a prophet; (4) To investigate the redaction of Q to evaluate whether the kingdom of God sayings in Q bear evidence of an underlying Q community

---

[333] The same could be said of Paul who refrains from quoting Jesus in arguments with opposition.

[334] "Das Zeugnis der Redenquelle für die Basileia-Verkündigung Jesu", 169-173.

[335] So D. Kosch: *Die Gottesherrschaft im Zeichen des Widerspruchs* (Lk. 16,16), ". . . in Q ist also primär ihr Bezug zur eschatologischen Basileia-Erwartung und zur Person und Autorität Jesu zu beachten, während die Frage nach der Geltung des Gesetzes keineswegs im Vordergrund steht" (57); ". . . die Heilsgeschichte keineswegs im Zentrum des Logions steht und dass die Zuordnung des Täufers zur Zeit des AT keineswegs gesichert ist" (20).

[336] See E. Percy, *Die Botschaft Jesu. Eine traditionskritische und exegetische Untersuchung*, 197.

[337] Lk. 16:16 par. is considered as authentic by among others: J. Fitzmyer, *Luke* II, 1115; J. Jeremias, *Theology of the New Testament*, 46, 47; P.S. Cameron, *Violence and the Kingdom*, 126, 27; D. Kosch, *Die Gottesherrschaft im Zeichen des Widerspruchs (Lk. 16,16)* 93 n. 10; H. Merklein, *Die Gottesherrschaft als Handlungsprinzip*, 90; E. Käsemann, *The Problem of the Historical Jesus*, 210; Davies and Allison, *Matthew* II, 254; W.G. Kümmel, *Promise and Fulfilment*, 114f.; R. Schnackenburg, *God's Rule and Kingdom*, 130f.

Tendenz; and (5), To weigh the arguments which deny these sayings to the authentic speech of Jesus, to see if what often has been attributed to the *Tendenz* of the Q community may more validly be said of Jesus himself. As a result of our study, we are inclined to answer numbers 1, 3 and 4 in the negative. A lack of credible evidence demands more caution than Q scholars have used in attributing material to the hypothetical Q community. To #3 it is clear that in Q Jesus is certainly more than a prophet. To the fifth question we are inclined to say yes because there exist no solid literary or conceptual reasons for denying the core of these sayings to the historical Jesus.

We conclude that there exists no evidence to warrant the hypothesis that any of the sayings studied reflect the *Sitz im Leben* of a Q community. We are not impressed by the community preaching, the developed form of Salvation-History, the ecclesiology, the unique *Q perspective* of Jesus' saving benefits, and the Q Gentile Mission which others detect. It is not at all obvious that these sayings have been altered to meet ecclesiastical needs. They were retained, rather, because of their inherent value as sayings of Jesus.

What we do see in Q is Jesus attempting to gather people—sinners, the poor, the sick, and the outcasts into the kingdom of God: "O Jerusalem, Jerusalem, the city that kills the prophets and stones those sent to her! How often I wanted to gather your children together, just as a hen gathers her brood under her wings, and you would not have it!" (Lk. 13:34//Mt. 23:37). In Q those who desire and accept the saving benefits of Jesus' ministry are fortunate because in identifying with Jesus they have met the one criterion on which depends acceptance or rejection in the eschatological banquet. The act of gathering people for salvation is yet another characteristic of Jesus in Q which implies his messiahship on the basis of Jewish tradition.[338]

Jesus and community are inextricably bound in Q. Jeremias' statement that "the *only* significance of the whole of Jesus's activity is to gather the eschatological people of God"[339] is not contradicted by the Q material. In Q we see this gathering process taking place in the earthly ministry of Jesus (Lk. 11:23//Mt. 12:30; Lk. 10:2//Mt. 9:37, 38), and we also gain a glimpse of the gathered community as it will exist at the consummation of the kingdom of God (Lk. 13:28, 29//Mt. 8:11, 12). We do not see early Church kerygma, we see the

---

[338] Thus, in speaking of the Messiah (17:32), the Son of David (17:21), the one "powerful in the holy spirit" (17:37), the one "mighty in his actions and strong in the fear of God" (17:40), Psalms of Solomon 17:26 reads: "He will gather a holy people whom he will lead in righteousness."

[339] *New Testament Theology*, 170. Similarly G. Lohfink, *Jesus and Community*, ET Philadelphia: Fortress Press (1982) 26: "Jesus' preaching of the reign of God cannot be isolated from his turning to the people of God. It led necessarily to the gathering of Israel."

earliest response to Jesus, his message, and his ministry. P.M. Casey has observed correctly that the only specific identity factor of the Jesus movement was Jesus himself.[340] Jesus himself and not apocalyptic enthusiasm or a specific form of eschatology is the source of identity for Jesus' followers in both Mark and Q (Lk. 11:23//Mt. 12:30; Mk. 8:38; Lk. 12:8, 9//10:32, 33; Mk. 10:21b). Hence in Mark and Q the response to Jesus is the decisive factor determining salvation. Response to Jesus takes two forms: one of acceptance by social outcasts and sinners (Lk. 7:34//Mt. 11:19; Mk. 2:15-17), the other of rejection primarily by religious leaders of Judaism (Lk. 11:37-52 par.; Mk. *passim*). Despite the fact that Jesus' ministry brings the *basileia* near or even in some sense brings God's rule into the present, Jesus' ministry is not accomplished fully because the people of God has not been gathered completely for the day of salvation (Lk. 13:34, 35//Mt. 23:37-39). Q does not read like a finished story—a remaining event needs to take place to enable the gathering of all God's people. Therefore, though Q does not refer to Jesus' passion, the purpose of Jesus' earthly ministry in Q is in part exactly the same as the purpose for Jesus' death in Mark—namely to gather God's people together for the feast of salvation in the kingdom of God. The reign of God manifests itself in both events for the same purpose.

In contrast to H. Schürmann who attributes seven sayings to later Kerygmatic formulation, we judge all ten kingdom of God sayings in our study to be authentic. Clearly this conclusion will be radical to some. However, the sayings we have dealt with, kingdom of God sayings doubly attested in Matthew and Luke, have been too readily rejected on the basis of faulty criteria. We simply do not see the Kerygmatic coloring which is so apparent to Schürmann. His criteria for judgement as cited in our introduction are much too subjective in our opinion. Our judgements in regard to authenticity are supported by the vast majority of commentators on the Gospels of Matthew and Luke and by the majority of scholars who have written on the sayings of Jesus. The burden of proof still remains on those who would discredit the kingdom of God sayings voiced by Jesus in the Q material.

Jesus himself could have held in tension both a present and future understanding of the kingdom of God.[341] Q contains in tension one saying which

---

[340] *From Jewish Prophet to Gentile God*, Cambridge: James Clarke & Co. (1991) 73, 74.

[341] Representative: G.E. Ladd, *Jesus and the Kingdom*; R. Schnackenburg, *God's Rule and Kingdom;* L. Goppelt, *New Testament Theology* I. So Davies and Allison, *Matthew* I, 389, 90: "So the seeming contradiction between the presence of the kingdom and its futurity is dissolved when one realizes that Jewish thinking could envision the final events - the judgement of evil and the arrival of the kingdom of God - as extending over time, and as a process or series of events that could involve the present. When Jesus announces that the kingdom of God has come and is

views the kingdom of God as present and active in the ministry of Jesus (Lk. 11:20 par.), one saying which views the kingdom as the future manifestation of God's power which occasions both the eschatological feast and the eschatological sentence of judgement (Lk. 13:28, 29//Mt. 8:11, 12), and the parables of the mustard seed and leaven which hold in tension the kingdom present and future. There exists no evidence that Jesus saw in the present the consummation of the kingdom; rather, his appearance as the anointed herald indicates that in his present acts and preaching Jesus perceived the inauguration of God's eschatological saving power. The present and future exist in tension precisely in man's response to the kingdom: As man responds positively or negatively to the kingdom of God as manifested presently in Jesus, so will the kingdom be a positive or negative reality with blessing or woe at the consummation.[342] Present and future sayings, then, do not necessitate the suspect hypothesis that the Q community expected an imminent parousia at an early phase, while later coming to grips with the delay. Jesus, we suspect, held present and future in tension according to the timeless nature of God's sovereign rule.

These sayings demonstrate the burden of Jesus' message that man must subordinate all in view of the kingdom of God (Lk. 12:31//Mt. 6:33). In Q the kingdom of God is a dynamic term which Jesus adopts to identify the power of God which is exercised both in Jesus' ministry and in the eschatological day of festal joy/punitive judgement. The conceptual background for Jesus' understanding of the kingdom of God in Q is the OT and intertestamental Judaism. The frequency of allusions to the OT in each saying indicates this clearly. Hence in compliance with the sovereignty of God in the OT, the kingdom of God which Jesus speaks about in Q confers both saving benefits and woe. As the prophets warned Israel and Judah in the OT, so Jesus warns that in rejecting the saving benefits of the kingdom of God, man subjects himself to eternal damnation.

Though dependent on the image of God in the OT, the kingdom of God sayings in Q are unique in portraying the power of God as demonstrably active in one historical person—Jesus. In contrast to John the Baptist who preaches judgement and repentance, Jesus, though expressing words of eschatological judgement, emphasizes the saving power of God which is active and present in himself. The "Blessed" who receive the kingdom of God are the same as the "Blessed" who do not stumble over Jesus. In Q the kingdom of God does not

---

coming, this means that the last act has begun but not yet reached its climax: the last things have come and will come."

[342] Thus C. Schuppan (*Gottes Herrschaft und Gottes Wille*) writes of the kingdom of God in Q: "Heil und Unheil sind so gegenwärtig und zukünftig zugleich. Auf diese Weise sind die Gegenwartsaussagen mit den Zukunftserwartungen in eine feste Verbindung gebracht worden" (78).

exist on earth apart from the ministry of Jesus. The community element which exists in Q is directly tied to the person of Jesus and his mission. Those who receive now the saving benefits of Jesus' ministry—the poor, the blind, the lame, the deaf, the dumb, the lepers, the demon possessed—are the same as those who will experience the eternal bliss associated with the eschatological feast in Zion. Future salvation is prepared for and realized in Jesus' ministry.

In relation to the question of the origin of NT christology, Lk. 11:20//Mt. 12:28, whose authenticity is a scholarly consensus, describes Jesus both as anointed with the Spirit/Finger of God and as a figure who authoritatively mediates the power of God directly against Satan. In the first Beatitude (Lk. 6:20//Mt. 5:3) and in Jesus' response to John (Lk. 7:22f.//Mt. 11:4f), Jesus fulfils Isa. 61:1f. and assumes the role of the one anointed by the Spirit to bring eschatological salvation to the poor, sight to the blind, health to the sick, and life to the dead. In Lk. 12:10//Mt. 12:32 Jesus implies that the Holy Spirit is the source of his authority and power. When we link these observations with the knowledge that "the word 'messiah' retained the sense of 'anointed' and was used to refer to a person endowed with the Spirit for a particular purpose authorized by God,"[343] we are left with the fact that in Q Jesus bears the prominent characteristics of a Jewish Messiah.[344]

Furthermore, as we have stressed, Jesus' endowment with God's power stands in perfect relation to his address of God as Father both in the Lord's Prayer (Lk. 11:2f.//Mt. 6:9f.) and in Lk. 10:21, 22//Mt. 11:25-27, where Jesus refers to himself as the son. Jesus' anointing by the Spirit, his wise teaching, his miracles which fulfil the day of salvation anticipated in the OT (Isa. 26:19; 29:18; 35:5, 6), and his commissioning of disciples in view of the eschatological harvest (Lk. 10:2//Mt. 9:37)—an act associated with God in OT and Wisdom Texts—all correspond directly to his unique filial relationship with God. In Q Jesus is more than a prophet attempting the renewal of Israel!

---

[343] I.H. Marshall,"The Hope of a New Age: The Kingdom of God in the New Testament", 226.

[344] Jesus' sayings do not identify him as identical in character with the Messianic figures anticipated by the OT and apocalyptic writings but they do make connections. So G.R. Beasley-Murray (*Jesus and the Kingdom of God*, 146): "The Old Testament presents the Messiah not as the agent through whom the kingdom comes, but rather as the agent of the kingdom after God has established it. In some apocalyptic writings the Messiah has a role in the coming of the kingdom, but the function that Jesus assigns to himself in relation to the kingdom goes well beyond anything said of the Messiah in the Old Testament or in the apocalyptic and rabbinic teaching of his day. Since we would do well to have a term to denote the manifold function of Jesus with respect to the kingdom of God, and since the title Messiah is the acknowledged umbrella term to denote the representative of the kingdom, it is difficult to avoid appropriating it for Jesus."

Finally, we suggest that the powerful implications of Jesus' sayings themselves motivated the recording, collecting, and passing on of the Q material. Early Christian prophetic enthusiasm, the delay of the parousia, unknown apocalyptic events, and kerygmatic recourse to the historical Jesus in light of the emergence of the Gospel of Mark are less compelling stimulants for the collection of Q than the radical claims that Jesus himself made in these sayings. The claim that the kingdom of God was active in Jesus' personal ministry would have attracted enthusiastic support and aggressive opposition just as the Beelzebul controversy reports. In light of what we have said above, it seems quite apparent that the early Church would have been extremely interested in these sayings and would have used them as traditional material to support the belief that Jesus was the Messiah. While it is certainly true that the early Church anxiously awaited the return of Christ/the Son of Man, it is also true that the church was conscious of living in the era of fulfillment. As I.H. Marshall remarks, "Its hope for the future was based on what it already knew of the present working of God."[345] Further, the Church's teaching on Jesus' death and resurrection did not invalidate or render obsolete Jesus' own teaching. The motivation for collecting the sayings of Jesus was probably the simple conviction that Jesus' death and resurrection vindicated Jesus' pre-Easter claim that the kingdom of God was active in his personal ministry.

The sceptic may find our conclusions unsatisfactory because we have surveyed material from only one layer or body of Synoptic tradition. What we have attributed to Jesus may be true simply for the Jesus of Q. For this reason we next turn to the Gospel of Mark. How does Jesus' preaching of the kingdom in Q compare with his proclamation of the kingdom in Mark? Because Mark's Kerygma in its entirety is essentially the gospel of the kingdom (1:15), logically Mark's kingdom of God sayings should express striking dissimilarities from Q, if indeed the two traditions express different interpretations of Jesus' saving work. Do Mark and Q really contain incompatible Kerygmas or does Q differ from Mark only in extent as opposed to content? To answer these questions, we now turn to the kingdom of God in Mark.

---

[345] "The Hope of a New Age: The Kingdom of God in the New Testament", 231.

Chapter 8

The Kingdom of God in Mark
Compared with the Kingdom of God in Q

I. The Problem

In analyzing the 13 kingdom of God sayings which are attributed to Jesus in Mark, we intend to further evaluate the hypothesis that Q bears witness to a radically different "kerygmatic" response to Jesus as opposed to Mark which orients around the preaching of the cross. Comparison of an important shared theme should accentuate the biases of both sources if indeed the two are kerygmatically inconsistent.

The problem we address is illustrated by the recent studies of Heikki Räisänen and Walter Schmithals who independently hypothesize that Mark transformed the unacceptable Q-tradition by means of the "Messianic Secret." Schmithals argues that the Messianic Secret was motivated by the need to combine an unchristological Q^1 with the Passion and Easter stories.[1] Räisänen, in contrast to W. Kelber and E. Boring,[2] claims that Mark opposed Q not because Q's authority resided in prophets of the risen Jesus, but "with the aid of the secrecy theme, Mark tries to reject the claims of people like the bearers of the Q-tradition who appealed to the authority of the historical Jesus."[3] In short Räisänen asserts: (1) whereas in Q Jesus' exorcisms signify the nearness of the kingdom of God, in Mark the exorcisms specify the majesty of the person of Jesus; (2) while in Q the title Christ is missing and Jesus is not understood as a divine being, in Mark Jesus is the Hellenistic Divine Man; (3) where Q lacks a Passion Narrative and understands Jesus' death as the typical fate of a prophet according to the Deuteronomistic

---

[1] "... daß Markus seine Geheimnis Theorie benutzt, um die unmessianische Überlieferung der Tradenten der Spruchüberlieferung Q^1 mit der christologischen Grundschrift zu verbinden. Dazu dienen ihm die folgenden einzelnen Motive seiner Geheimnistheorie", *Einleitung in die drei ersten Evangelien*, 424-427 (424).

[2] See Ch. 1: pp. 12, 13.

[3] *The 'Messianic Secret' in Mark*, ET Edinburgh: T&T Clark (1990) 254; German edition 1976.

tradition, "the theology of the cross constitutes a central feature in Mark's theology"; and (4), whereas Q made the future parousia the basis for its christology, Mark "seems more like a representative of realized eschatology." Finally, as a result of his perceived distinction between Palestinian Q and Hellenistic Mark, Räisänen concludes: "It is just these Hellenistic features which constitute to a large extent post-Easter developments. It is at these points that Mark and Q contradict each other. It is also precisely here that the secrecy theme occurs."[4]

However, are these conclusions the result of valid methodology? Schmithals' thesis hinges on his understanding of the relationship between Mark and the two phases of Q (Q^1 and Q). In his scheme Q^1 was composed prior to Mark around A.D. 75. Mark at a later date took over the Q^1 material in an attempt to win over the Q^1 group to the christological kerygma of the early Church. The Messianic Secret motif was motivated by the need to combine the unchristological Q^1 with the Passion and Easter stories of Mark. When Mark's purpose was achieved, christological elements were added to Q^1 by the redactor of Q.[5]

The weakness of Schmithals' elaborate theory is its dependence upon manifold hypotheses which are not altogether convincing. Instead of identifying the authority of the historical Jesus as the *raison d' être* for the early collection of Jesus' teaching, Schmithals conjectures that the circle responsible for transmitting Q^1 was motivated by an apocalyptic experience which erupted when Caligula placed his statue in the Jerusalem temple (A.D. 40). However, the Caligula event is altogether absent in Q.[6] Furthermore, the divide between Q^1 and Q is artificial at best. While Schmithals attributes Jesus' teaching on the kingdom of God to the earliest phase of Q, it is important to note that Jesus' kingdom of God teaching is not entirely without christological relevance: Lk. 11:20//Mt. 12:28 specifies that Jesus is empowered by the Spirit of God, while Lk. 6:20//Mt. 5:3 presents Jesus functioning as the eschatological herald who is anointed by the Spirit to bring good news to the poor on the eschatological day of the Lord (Isa. 61:1f.). Both sayings

---

[4] *Ibid.*, 253.

[5] *Einleitung*, 424-427; 'Evangelien', *Theologische Realenzyklopädie*, Band X, Berlin: Walter de Gruyter (1982) 625: "Das beherrschende Interesse der Redaktion des Evangelisten drückt sich in seiner Messiasgeheimnis-Theorie aus. Vermutlich begegnete der Evangelist im Anschluß an die Wirren des jüdischen Krieges den Tradenten der noch unchristologischen Logienüberlieferung Q^1. Er stellt sich dem für ihn rätselhaften Problem, wie es zu einer Jüngerschaft Jesu ohne österliches Christusbekenntnis kommen konnte. Die Lösung des Rätsels bringt die Messiasgeheimnis-Theorie, deren verschiedene Motive er im Anschluß an Ansätze der Grundschrift entfaltet und mit der Grundschrift verbindet. Das auf diese Weise redigierte und herausgegebene Mk.Ev diente vermutlich dazu, die Gruppe um Q^1 für das christliche Bekenntnis zu gewinnen."

[6] *Pace* G. Theissen; see p. 25 n. 31.

complement Jesus' role as Messiah. Finally, Schmithals is not consistent in his methodology. After asserting that the Mk./Q doublets represent the earliest contents of Q[1],[7] his logic seems faulty when later he identifies as late Q redaction all other cases of Mark/Q agreement. Dual attestation would seem to support the early origin of the latter just as clearly as it does the former.

Räisänen's conclusions are no more convincing than those of Schmithals. While θεῖος ἀνήρ christology has been refuted almost overwhelmingly,[8] Jesus' divine sonship emerges just as explicitly in Q (Lk. 4:1-13//Mt. 4:1-11; Lk. 10:21, 22//Mt. 11:25-27) as it does in Mark. Räisänen is correct that Jesus' miracles do mark the nearness of the kingdom of God in Q, but the phenomenon does not contradict Mark, where Jesus opens his Galilean ministry with the call: Πεπλήρωται ὁ καιρὸς καὶ ἤγγικεν ἡ βασιλεία τοῦ θεοῦ μετανοεῖτε καὶ πιστεύετε ἐν τῷ εὐαγγελίῳ. As this pronouncement of Jesus is programmatic for the entire Gospel of Mark, we are safe in assuming that its message is confirmed by Jesus' miracles which occur in the ensuing chapters. Further, it is telling that the very same phrase appears in Q (Lk. 10:9//Mt. 10:7): Ἤγγικεν ἐφ' ὑμᾶς ἡ βασιλεία τοῦ θεοῦ. Hence the nearness of the kingdom of God is a feature of Jesus' teaching in Mark and Q and as such does not support Räisänen's claim. In fact, as we will argue further in this chapter, Jesus' miracles in Mark correlate well with the arrival of God's saving rule in Q, where in response to John's question of Jesus' identity Jesus answers with the composite quotation of Isa. 26:19; 29:18; 35:5, 6; 42:18; 61:1f.: "the blind receive sight, the lame walk, the lepers are cleansed, and the deaf hear, the dead are raised up, the poor have the gospel preached to them." This passage, of course, cannot be pressed to detail every miracle Jesus performs in Mark—it does not mention nature miracles—but its parallels are indeed striking especially in consideration of the fact that Jesus performs in Mark all of the miracles spoken of by Jesus in this Q passage. Even the cleansing of lepers, the one healing miracle which does not allude to Isaiah 35 or 61 in Q 7:22//11:4f., has a parallel in Mk. 1:42.

It is our thesis that a comparison between the kingdom of God sayings in Q and Mark will reveal not diverse but similar traditions with compatible conceptual and background features. To the extent that we are able to substantiate this thesis,

---

[7] *Einleitung*, 399-402.

[8] Numerous scholars have demonstrated that 'divine man' was a rare term in ancient Greek literature. In the cases where it does occur it appears dissimilar to the NT usage of 'Son of God'. See C.R. Holladay, *Theios Aner in Hellenistic Judaism: A Critique of the Use of this Category in New Testament Christology*, SBLDS 40; Missoula: Scholars Press, 1972; Wülfing von Martitz, "υἱός", TDNT 8 (1972) 334-40; David L. Tiede, *The Charismatic Figure as Miracle Worker*, SBLDS 1; Missoula: Scholars Press, 1972; Barry Blackburn, *Theios Aner and the Markan Miracle Traditions*, WUNT 2. Reihe 40; Tübingen: J.C.B. Mohr (Paul Siebeck) 1991.

we will be able to support the likelihood of the Q/Mk. sayings' dominical origin. Our thesis, then, is diametrically opposite to that of Dieter Lührmann who emphasizes the differences between Mark and Q in his article "The Gospel of Mark and the Sayings Collection Q" :

> The differences, however, cannot be neglected in favour of a unifying picture of early Christianity or of a historical Jesus as the unique origin of the traditions about him. He did not leave authentic words or even writings. It is second-hand information which we have about him or texts which reflect the effects that he produced on those whom he met. It is these effects with which a comparison of Mark and Q has to deal.[9]

Lührmann is certainly correct that the differences cannot be neglected, but neither can the similarities. For Lührmann the kingdom of God is a different entity for Mark as opposed to Q: "So, whereas in Q the nearness of the kingdom of God is the content of the disciples' preaching, who directly continue Jesus' preaching, in Mark this nearness is bound to the gospel which they have to proclaim."[10] While in Q the coming of the kingdom of God means the *coming* of the Son of Man, in Mark the nearness of the kingdom of God is bound to the *past* of Jesus which remains valid for the present.[11]

But are these differences real? In our study of the kingdom of God in Q, particularly with regard to Lk. 6:20//Mt. 5:3 and Lk. 7:22f.//Mt. 11:5f., we saw that in Q Jesus fulfills Isa. 61:1f. as the anointed herald of good news who performs the saving acts commensurate with the arrival of the Day of the Lord. Against this framework the famous saying Lk. 11:20//Mt. 12:28 fits perfectly—"If I by the Spirit/Finger of God cast out demons then the kingdom of God has come upon you." The Isaiah background, the presence of the Spirit, and Jesus' miraculous acts suggest that the kingdom has arrived in Jesus' ministry. Is not the same true for Jesus in Mark? In Mark are Jesus' miracles the work of the Hellenistic Divine Man as Räisänen supposes, or are they eschatological acts performed by Jesus the herald of eschatological salvation—the one anointed by the Spirit of God to bring the saving benefits of the eschatological Day of the Lord? It is our thesis that traditional material in Mark, like Q, associates Jesus' preaching and acts with the fulfilment of the Isaianic promises concerning the arrival of the kingdom of God. Jesus is the Isaianic herald of salvation in both.

---

[9] Lührmann admits the weakness of his own methodology: "I will obviously have to overemphasize differences between Mark and Q for reasons of methodology, for only by doing so can a comparison become profitable." In "The Gospel of Mark and the Sayings Collection Q", *JBL* 108 (1989) 62.

[10] *Ibid.*, 68.

[11] *Ibid.*, 67-68.

The purpose of Mark's Gospel is christological. But for Mark the question is not so much who is Jesus—for he answers that question immediately in 1:1: Jesus is the Messiah the Son of God—but rather the question which Mark seeks to answer is how did Jesus show himself to be the Messiah and Son of God? It is our intention to show that Mark vindicates his title by first appealing to traditions which support Q in identifying Jesus as the herald and initiator of God's rule upon earth. This established, Mark's passion narrative verifies the implications of Jesus' Galilean ministry. Mark no more contradicts Q than he does the first eight chapters of his own Gospel. For Mark as for Q, the kingdom of God has arrived in the ministry of Jesus.

II. Mk. 1:1-13

Mark's introduction addresses in a sequence identical to Q the role of John as forerunner to Jesus, John's attestation of Jesus' greatness, Jesus' baptism, and the temptation narrative. Throughout these verses Jesus' ministry is set against the background of Isaiah. Following Mark's title, "The beginning of the gospel of Jesus Christ, the Son of God" (1:1), Mark's introduction follows a two-part structure: (1) the ministry of John the Baptist (1:2-8); and (2), the beginning of Jesus' earthly ministry (1:9-15). The first section on John begins with a composite citation (1:2-3) of three OT passages (Ex. 23:20; Mal. 3:1; Isa. 40:3) which anticipate the coming of one who will prepare the way for the Lord. Mark's emphasis on Isaiah (1:2) and the quotations of Mal. 3:1 and Isa. 40:3 are important in that they shift the image from that of the angel of the Exodus to the prophetic figure who will prepare the way for the eschatological Day of the Lord. In view of the parallel quotations in Mt. 3:3 and Lk. 3:4-6 which cite only Isa. 40:3f., W. Schmithals has taken Mark's composite quotation as redactional and even strategic to his Messianic Secret motif.[12] However, it is striking that the same composite quotation which exists in Mk. 1:2bc exists in a Q saying (Lk. 7:27//Mt. 11:10) which refers to John and holds in tension the arrival of the kingdom of God (Lk. 7:28//Mt. 11:11) with the image of Jesus as the Herald, the one who imparts eschatological salvation following Isa. 29:18; 35:5; 42:18; 61:1 (Lk. 7:22// Mt. 11:5f.). The congruence between the Q and Mark quotations and the existence of the same composite quotation in Rabbinic literature (Exod. Rab. 23:20) suggests the traditional pedigree of the combination of Ex. 23:20 and Mal. 3:1. In Mk. 1:2

---

[12] *Markus* I, Gütersloh: Mohn (1979) 75. See also W. Marxsen, ET *Mark the Evangelist: Studies on the Redaction History of the Gospel*, Nashville: Abingdon (1969) 37 n. 28.

and in Lk. 7:27//Mt. 11:10 the quotation designates John as the precursor of the
the eschatological Day of the Lord which has arrived in the ministry of Jesus.[13]

A. John the Baptizer

Following the OT quotation, vv. 4-6 identify John as the prophetic figure who
fulfills vv. 2-3 and prepares the way for the Lord.[14] Here Mark supports Q in
identifying John as calling all Israel to repent.[15] V. 4 describes John's ministry as
"preaching a baptism of repentance for the forgiveness of sins." This description
of John has a Q counterpart in Mt. 3:7-10//Lk. 3:7-9 which exclusively identifies
John as a preacher of repentance and judgment while not mentioning the
forgiveness of sins. R. Laufen and R.A. Guelich take this distinction as evidence
of Mark's redactional modification of John as the preparer for the Gospel rather
than judgment. J. Lambrecht, presupposing that Mark had the entire body of Q
before him, argues that Mark intentionally omitted Lk. 3:7-9, 17//Mt. 3:7-10, 12:
"every threat with judgment, every reference to punishment is out of place and,
therefore, left out."[16] While Guelich claims Mark's John prepared for the good

---

[13] *Pace* D. Catchpole (The Quest for Q, Edinburgh: T&T Clark [1993] 60-78) and J.
Lambrecht ("John the Baptist and Jesus in Mark 1.1-15: Markan Redaction of Q?", *NTS* 38
[1992] 357-384) who argue that Mark's citation is dependant on Q. Lambrecht argues that Mark,
using Q, actually took Mal 3.1 from Lk. 7:27//Mt. 11:10: "The fact that Mark inserts this
Malachi quotation seems to prove that he knows Jesus' eulogy of John from Q 7.24-28 . . ."
(372). However, while Mark's knowledge of Q material cannot be categorically denied, Markan
use of Q 7:24-28 is a bold conjecture. The contexts of the two passages are different, Mark lacks
Q's ἔμπροσθέν σου, and there is no reason to confine the interpretation of John against Mal. 3:1
to Q alone. Mk. 1:5, which does not have a Q parallel, was probably known by Mark to fulfil
Mal. 3:4. Catchpole attempts to establish Mark's dependence on Q by: 1) analyzing Q (Lk.)
7:24-28 for layers of secondary Q tradition; 2) examining Mk. 1:1-11 for matching layers of the
same traditions; and 3), establishing the reasonability that correspondence between Q redaction and
Markan redaction indicates Markan dependence upon Q. Using these procedures Catchpole
reconstructs the beginning of Q from Mk. 1:2-5. However, his conclusions depend on his
sensational ability to identify hidden features of Markan and Q redaction, and the great uncertainty
that conjectural layers of Q redaction (Lk. 7:27) were created *ad hoc* by a historically uncertain Q
group.

[14] D. Catchpole (*The Quest for Q*, 68) identifies two distinct John traditions: First, that
maintained by John himself and his followers that he was the prophetic preparer for the Lord
(God); Second, the corrective Christian tradition generated in Q redaction that saw John as the
preparer for Jesus: "The shift from God to Jesus in the identity of 'the coming one' is carried out
equally by the framing of (Lk.) 7:18-23 around 7:22 and by the insertion of 7:27." However, the
two apparent traditions are not unharmonious. In Q (Lk. 7:22) Jesus appears as the coming one
preforming the very acts of God anticipated by the prophets. In preparing the way for the day of
the Lord, John in fact prepares for the kingdom of God as manifested in the ministry of Jesus.

[15] So R. A. Guelich, *Mark* I, 20: "The reference to Judea (cf. 3:7) and Jerusalem implies
what the Q tradition (Mt. 3:7-10//Lk. 3:7-9) states."

[16] "John the Baptist and Jesus in Mark 1.1-15: Markan Redaction of Q?", 373f.

news of God's eschatological salvation,[17] Laufen goes so far as to say that Mark designates John as the first pronouncer of the Christian Gospel of Jesus the Messiah and Son of God.[18] In other words, the repentance and forgiveness to which John beckons is the same as that preached by the early Church. However, this distinction, though real in part, is not absolute in every detail. Mark and Q agree that John preached essentially a message of repentance: while in Mark John preaches a "baptism of repentance for the forgiveness of sins", in Q (Lk. 3:8//Mt. 3:8) John challenges his listeners to "bring forth fruits in keeping with repentance." It should not be overlooked that even in Q John's preaching is not entirely pessimistic: those who repent and act accordingly will be spared from the ensuing judgment. Keeping in mind the fact that the term repentance denotes a 'change of mind', a 'turn around', and a 'complete change in conduct' especially (in biblical texts) with a view towards sin, it is important to note that Jewish baptism contemporary with John presupposed a true transformation on the part of the repentant.[19] In Mark John's baptism does not forgive sins directly, but as Guelich correctly states: "the ultimate goal of repentance-baptism was the forgiveness of sins and acceptance by God in the coming day of salvation."[20] John's baptism prepares for future salvation. How different, then, is the repentance for forgiveness which John calls for in Mark from John's baptism of men who repented in order that they might escape judgment in Q? The distinction, if pressed, is one of nuance.

B. The Coming One

In any case, John's baptism contrasts clearly with that of Jesus and the early Church in vv. 7, 8 where John prophesies of the coming one: "After me one is coming who is mightier than I, and I am not fit to stoop down and untie the thong of his sandals. I baptized you with water, but he will baptize you with the Holy Spirit." As in Q (Lk. 3:16//Mt. 3:11), John's baptism in Mark is not empowered by the Holy Spirit in contrast to the "Coming One" who will baptize with "the

---

[17] *Mark* I, 17.

[18] "Er steht mit seiner 1,7.8 überlieferten Botschaft ganz in Dienst der christlichen Predigt. Er steht damit am Anfang einer Geschichte, die erst an ihr Ziel gekommen sein wird, wenn alle Völker das Evangelium von Jesus dem Christus und Gottessohn vernommen haben (vgl. Mk. 13,10)", *Die Doppelüberlieferungen*, 125.

[19] G.R. Beasley-Murray, *Baptism in the New Testament*, Grand Rapids: Eerdmans (1962) 34, 35.

[20] *Mark* I, 27.

Holy Spirit and Fire."[21]   The Mark and Q versions of this passage stand remarkably close except for Mark's omission of "fire."[22] The distinction raises the question of originality. Five possibilities exist: the 'coming one' will baptize: (1) with fire only—meaning judgment, (2) with the spirit/wind only (Mk.)—meaning judgment, (3) with the Holy Spirit only—meaning salvation (Mk.), (4) with fire and the spirit—a hendiadys meaning judgment,[23] or (5), with fire and the Holy Spirit—meaning judgment and salvation (Q). Of these 1, 2, and 4 lack textual support as fire does not exist alone in either account and spirit is qualified by 'holy' in both accounts. 3 requires for Q to have added "fire" perhaps to emphasize John's role as a preacher of judgement, but this procedure seems unnecessary in view of the Q context which is already saturated by images of the wrath to come.[24] Hence we prefer 5. While no previous texts designate any but God as the giver of the Holy Spirit, it is not unreasonable to think that John would have been aware of the expectation of a Messiah anointed with the Spirit (Isa. 11:2; 61:1), the expectation of the Spirit as a sign of the endtimes, and the expectation of the Spirit as an agent of cleansing from sins (1QS 4:20; 1QH 16:11; Eze. 36:25).[25] This solution, then, requires that Mark omitted Q's 'fire' (if he was using the exact same tradition) perhaps with the purpose of playing down John's warning of judgment while emphasizing his role as preparer for the one soon to bring eschatological salvation (1:2, 3). If so, Mark merely stresses one aspect of John's prediction which was already in Q: "He will *gather his wheat* into the barn, but he will burn up the chaff with unquenchable fire" (Lk. 3:17//Mt. 3:12). At this point it is interesting to note that while many exegetes interpret several kingdom of

---

[21] *Pace* Arland D. Jacobson, "The Literary Unity of Q", *JBL* 101/3 (1982) 380-381: "The basic difference is that in Q John appears as a prophet in his own right but in Mark he has been subordinated to Jesus. . . . Thus neither in Mark nor in the pre-Marcan tradition was John a prophet in his own right. But in Q, John is independent, a preacher of repentance before the imminent judgment of Yahweh." However, in Mark John is clearly a prophet while in Q he is clearly subordinate to Jesus: Lk. 3:16b//Mt. 3:11: Ἐγὼ μὲν ὕδατι βαπτίζω ὑμᾶς ἔρχεται δὲ ὁ ἰσχυρότερός μου, οὗ οὐκ εἰμὶ ἱκανὸς λῦσαι τὸν ἱμάντα τῶν ὑποδημάτων αὐτοῦ αὐτὸς ὑμᾶς βαπτίσει ἐν πνεύματι ἁγίῳ καὶ πυρί (cf. Lk. 7:28//Mt. 11:11).

[22] Mt. and Lk. agree against Mk.: (1) in the order of clauses, (2) the use of μέν. . . δέ, (3) the use of a present tense rather than an aorist for baptize, (4) the placing of ὑμᾶς, (5) the addition of καὶ πυρί. So J. Kloppenborg, *Q Parallels*, 12. For a discussion of these technical differences see R. Laufen, *Die Doppelüberlieferungen*, 108.

[23] So Davies and Allison, *Matthew* I, 317, 318; J.D.G. Dunn, "Spirit and Fire Baptism", *NovT* 14 (1972) 81-92. This view is persuasive in that Spirit in ancient texts was associated with judgment (Isa. 4:4; 40:24; 41:16; Jer. 4:11-16; 23:19; 30:23; Eze. 13:11-13), and thought of as a purifying agent (1QS 4.21).

[24] R. Laufen supports #3 as a result of the dispute with the disciples of John: *Die Doppelüberlieferungen*, 109. However, we fail to see how Mark's omission of fire would have achieved a polemical end.

[25] R.A. Guelich, *Mark* I, 28.

God sayings in Q against the supposition that there was a growing tendency in the early Church to belittle the role of John as a result of the apparent polemic taking place between the Church and John's followers, we see in Mark exactly the opposite taking place: John is consciously designated as the forerunner and herald of Jesus—his role is heightened with time rather than played down.[26]

C. Jesus' Baptism

It is a matter of debate whether or not the baptism account in Mk. 1:9-11 had a counterpart in Q (Lk. 3:21, 22//Mt. 3:13, 17).[27] In favour of inclusion in Q, Kloppenborg cites the following textual agreements between Matthew and Luke against Mark: (1) the use of the participial form $\beta\alpha\pi\tau\iota\sigma\theta\tilde{\eta}\nu\alpha\iota$, (2) the use of $\dot{\alpha}\nu o\dot{\iota}\gamma\omega$ instead of $\sigma\chi\dot{\iota}\zeta\omega$, (3) the use of $\dot{\epsilon}\pi$ ' $\alpha\dot{\upsilon}\tau\dot{o}\nu$ in place of $\epsilon\dot{\iota}\varsigma$ $\alpha\dot{\upsilon}\tau\dot{o}\nu$, and (4), the location of $\kappa\alpha\tau\alpha\beta\alpha\dot{\iota}\nu\omega$ before $\dot{\omega}\varsigma$ ($\epsilon\dot{\iota}$) $\pi\epsilon\rho\iota\sigma\tau\epsilon\rho\dot{\alpha}\nu$.[28] While these agreements may be attributed to the similar editing of Mark by Matthew and Luke, it is telling that in Q John's statement about the greatness of the "Coming One" immediately precedes the temptation narrative which three times identifies Jesus as the Son of God—the status imposed upon Jesus by God at the baptism. Thus it is logical that between Lk. 3:7-9//Mt. 3:7-12 and Lk. 4:1-13//Mt. 4:1-11 there was a baptism account in Q. Furthermore, Jesus' succession of John, his endowment with the Spirit, his sonship (non-titular), and the association of his work with the prophecies of Isaiah are all images central to the Q material (Lk. 12:10//Mt. 12:32; 11:20//12:28; 7:18-23//11:2-6; 10:21, 22//11:25-27). Meanwhile the Markan baptism account is certainly not a creation of Mark: the anarthrous references to Jesus and John, the absolute use of "the Spirit," and reference to the Jordon contrast to comparable Markan usage in 1:4-8.[29] Two major events take place at Jesus' baptism in Mark: first, God identifies Jesus as his son, and second, the Spirit equips Jesus for his ministry—an event which corresponds to the OT hope for the age of salvation (Isa. 11:2; 42:1; 61:1; 63:10-64:1), and which verifies the

---

[26] See A.E.J. Rawlinson, *Mark*, London: Methuen (1947) 8.

[27] Representative of those who attribute a baptism text to Q: A. Harnack, *The Sayings of Jesus*, 254; H. Schürmann, *Lukasevangelium* I, 197; U. Luz, *Matthäus* I, 150-51; I.H. Marshall, *Luke*, 152; P. Hoffmann, *Studien zur Logienquelle*, 4; A Polag, *Christologie der Logienquelle*, 2 (vermutlich); W. Schmithals, *Lukas*, Zürich: Theologischer Verlag (1980) 54; Davies and Allison, *Matthew* I, 329. *Pace* J. Kloppenborg, *The Formation of Q*, 84-85; J. Fitzmyer, *Luke* I, 479.

[28] *Q-Parallels*, 16.

[29] Pesch, *Markus* I, 88; Guelich *Mark* I, 30.

superiority which John attributes to the baptism of the "greater one" (1:8).[30] In each of these aspects Mark's emphases parallel Q exactly.[31]

D. Jesus' Temptation

Immediately following the baptism account, Mark and Q bear witness to Jesus' temptation.[32] While it is possible that Q (or the pre-Mt./Lk. tradition) expanded Mark, or that Mark abbreviated Q,[33] it is more probable that Mark and Q independently drew from a primitive tradition concerning Satan's temptation of Jesus at the beginning of his ministry.[34] Apart from the general difference in length, Matthew and Luke agree against Mark in the naming of Jesus, the citing of three temptations, the triple quotation of the OT,[35] the use of $\delta\iota\acute{\alpha}\beta o\lambda o\varsigma$ instead of $\sigma\alpha\tau\alpha\nu\tilde{\alpha}\varsigma$, the identification of Jesus as the Son of God, and the image of Jesus

---

[30] So Guelich, *Mark* I, 35.

[31] *Pace* P. Vassiliadis, "The Nature and Extent of the Q Document", *NovT* 20 (1978) 49-73: "However, the structure of the Marcan Version of Jesus' Baptism, as well as the 4th evangelist's opposition to the overestimation of John which was directed, in our view, not against the fictitious Baptist sect but against the Q-community located at Ephesus, makes us believe that the Q version of Jesus' Baptism differed widely from that of the canonical synoptics; perhaps the role of John in it was somewhat overtoned at the expense of Jesus" (73). Vassiliadis' argument is based upon speculation and a comparison of Q and the fourth Gospel – a comparison that has obvious difficulties.

[32] The verbal agreement between Mt. 4:1-11 and Lk. 4:1-13 especially in the speeches suggests a Q background. While the themes of Mt. 4:1-11 are at home in Mt., Luke sometimes (4:2, 3, 4, 7) presents the more primitive or original wording (see Davies and Allison, *Matthew* I, 350f.). Further, scriptural quotations, narrative material, and Jesus' struggle with Satan are all found elsewhere in Q (Lk. 7:27//Mt. 11:10; 13:35//23:39; 7:1-10//8:5-13; 11:14-23//12:22-30; 11:24-26//12:43-45). Scholars attributing Lk. 4:1-13//Mt. 4:1-11 to Q include H. Schürmann, *Lukas* I, 218; I. H. Marshall, *Luke*, 165; J. Fitzmyer, *Luke* I, 506f; Davies and Allison, *Matthew* I, 351; A. Polag, *Christologie der Logienquelle*, 2; S. Schulz, *Q - Die Spruchquelle*, 177f.; J. Kloppenborg, *The Formation of Q*, 246-62; *Contra*: D. Lührmann, *Redaktion der Logienquelle*, 56.

[33] So J. Lambrecht ("John the Baptist and Jesus in Mark 1.1-15: Markan redaction of Q?", 377) who claims $\kappa\alpha\grave{\iota}$ $o\grave{\iota}$ $\check{\alpha}\gamma\gamma\epsilon\lambda o\iota$ $\delta\iota\eta\kappa\acute{o}\nu o\upsilon\nu$ $\alpha\grave{\upsilon}\tau\tilde{\wp}$ betrays Mark's knowledge of Q. However, this phrase does not have a Q counterpart. The closest parallel is Lk. 4:10//Mt. 4:6 (Ps 91:11), but the vocabulary, speaker (Satan), and context of the Q passage are dissimilar to Mk. 1:13.

[34] So Davies and Allison, *Matthew* I, 357; R.A. Guelich, *Mark* I, 37; V. Taylor, *Mark*, London: Macmillan (1949) 162-63; P. Pokorny, "The Temptation Stories and Their Intention", *NTS* 20 (1973-74) 115-17.

[35] C.M. Tuckett ("The Temptation Narrative in Q", *The Four Gospels*, FS F. Neirynck; Leuven: Leuven U.P. [1992] 479-507): "One important aspect of the Q story, in contrast to the Markan account, is the fact that Jesus is portrayed as citing scripture and being obedient to scripture" (487). However, the contrast does not hold up to Mark as a whole where Jesus repeatedly cites and advocates obedience to scripture. See Mk. 7:10 (Ex. 20:12; Dt. 5:16; Ex. 21:17); Mk. 10:6-8 (Gn. 1:27; 5:2; 2:24); Mk. 10:19 (Ex. 20:12-16; Dt. 5:16-20); Mk. 11:17 (Isa. 56:7); Mk. 12:29-30 (Dt. 6:4-5); Mk. 12:31 (Lev. 19:18).

hungering (ἐπείνασεν) and fasting. While Mark's temptation narrative may point to an Adam-Christ typology,[36] its Q counterpart has been convincingly attributed to an Exodus typology.[37] Hence evidence does not suggest the dependence of one upon the other.

However, these distinctions should not undermine the major conceptual parallels between the two accounts: (A) Jesus is led by the Spirit, (B) into the wilderness, (C) forty days, (D) to be tempted by Satan/the Devil, (E) but Jesus resists and is in the end victorious. Further, while Mark does not mention Jesus' fasting, the image of the angels ministering to Jesus implies as much. Likewise Exodus-typology is not entirely foreign to Mark as a result of the reference to forty days. And while Satan does not refer to Jesus as the Son of God in Mark's account as the Devil does in Q, it is interesting to note that the Son of God designation is central to Mark's christology and, except for God and the centurion at the cross, demons alone refer to Jesus as the Son of God during the period of his earthly ministry in Mark (3:11; 5:7).[38] The same is true of Q where only the devil calls Jesus the Son of God and where Jesus alone refers to himself as the son (Lk. 10:22 par.).

Finally, the themes inherent to the temptation narrative befit both Mark and Q where Jesus as the stronger one binds Beelzebul (Mk. 3:27; Q Lk. 11:21, 22//Mt. 12:29), casts out demons (Mk. 5:8; Q Lk. 11:19, 20//Mt. 12:27, 28), and attributes first priority to following God's will (Mk. 10:17-31; Q Lk. 12:31//Mt. 6:33). Though not containing a kingdom of God saying, Jesus' initial resistance of Satan in the temptation narrative sets the standard for his administration of the kingdom of God as it exists in conflict with Satan and the demons in Mark and in

---

[36] So J. Gnilka, *Markus* I, Zürich/Neukirchen-Vluyn: Benzinger/Neukirchener Verlag (1978,79) 58; J. Jeremias, " 'Aδάμ", *TDNT* I, 141; R.A. Guelich, *Mark* I, 39. Jesus like Adam lived at peace with the wild animals (Gn. 1:28; 2:19-20; Mk. 1:13b), and was tempted by Satan, but whereas Adam sinned Jesus resisted thereby restoring harmony to creation. See Ro. 5:12-21; 1 Cor. 15:22, 45-49.

[37] Davies and Allison, *Matthew* I, 352: "Having passed through the waters of a new exodus at his baptism, he enters the desert to suffer a time of testing, his forty days of fasting being analogous to Israel's forty years of wandering. Like Israel, Jesus is tempted by hunger. And, like Israel, Jesus is tempted to idolatry."

[38] Mk. 1:1 is obviously editorial and Mk. 14:61 implies a lack of knowledge on the part of the high priest. The centurion's statement occurs after Jesus' death. On the rôle of "Son of God" in Mark, J.D. Kingsbury (*The Christology of Mark*, Philadelphia: Fortress [1983] 140-41) writes: "'Son of God' is thus the sole title in Mark's story to be expressly applied to Jesus by transcendent beings. When observed also from this angle, therefore, this title can be seen to lie at the heart of the motif of the secret of Jesus' identity and to dominate the story line of Mark's Gospel. In content, the distinctiveness of the title "Son of God" lies in the fact that, in a way the other titles do not, it highlights the unique filial relationship that Jesus has to God and the soteriological implications associated with this."

Q. The temptation narrative does not indicate significant disparity between Mark and Q, but in fact shows double attestation to the primitive conviction that Jesus, while empowered by the Spirit, successfully began his ministry by resisting Satan.[39] If Mark's wilderness motif (1:12, 13) alludes to the paradisaical conditions for the age of salvation which characterizes the promises of Isaiah (11:6-9; 32:14-20; 65:25), then Mark views Jesus as fulfilling the Isaianic promises in a manner which corresponds with the Q material (Lk. 7:22f.//Mt. 11:4f.), where Jesus fulfills Isa. 61:1f. in heralding in the blessings of the age of salvation. In both hypothetical sources Jesus' objective is the same.

III. Mk. 1:14, 15

Mk. 1:14, 15 marks the beginning of Jesus' ministry with the historical report that Jesus commenced his work after John was handed over. According to this report, Jesus began his earthly ministry in Galilee with the spirited charge that "the time is fulfilled and the kingdom of God has come near, repent and believe in the Gospel." Like Mark, both Matthew and Luke locate Jesus' public emergence immediately following his temptation, but Matthew and Luke go beyond Mark to make explicit that Jesus' ministry fulfilled the eschatological hope prophesied by Isaiah (Mt. 4:14-17; Isa. 8:23-9:1/Lk. 4:16-21; Isa. 61:1f.). Luke, in contrast to Matthew and Mark, does not identify Jesus' first address as a direct statement of the nearness of the kingdom of God, but rather embarks with the claim that Jesus' work fulfills Isa. 61:1f.:

> The Spirit of the Lord is upon me, because he anointed me to preach the gospel to the poor. He has sent me to proclaim release to the captives, and recovery of sight to the blind, to set free those who are downtrodden, to proclaim the favorable year of the Lord. (Lk. 4:18, 19)

Hence Matthew, Mark, and Luke agree that Jesus saw his ministry as the fulfilment of OT promise, but whereas Matthew and Mark locate fulfilment in the

---

[39] *Pace* E. Best, (*The Temptation and the Passion: The Markan Soteriology*, SNTSMS 2, 1965) who argues that Jesus' temptation in Mark is a contest as opposed to the temptation in Q which is a test. Best sees as important the discrepancy between Mk. and Q as to the time of the temptation: "In Mark, unlike Q, there is no suggestion that the time of temptation fell at the end of the forty-day period. The temptation rather took place within the period of the forty days and may indeed, so far as Mark is concerned, have lasted throughout that period" (6). Best's conclusion is based upon taking the circumstantial participle νηστεύσας in Mt. 4:2 "after he had fasted" as the Q reading. However, Lk. 4:2 which has an equal claim to be the Q reading, clearly states that Jesus faced temptation during the 40 days: ἡμέρας τεσσεράκοντα πειραζόμενος ὑπὸ τοῦ διαβόλου. How important this temporal uncertainty is to the portrait of Jesus presented in Mark and Q is unclear.

arrival of the kingdom of God, Luke identifies Jesus' saving acts as the saving benefits which fulfill Isaiah's promise for the arrival of the eschatological Day of the Lord.[40] Luke thus implies what is explicit in Matthew and Mark.

Conversely it is our purpose to show that what Luke makes explicit was already implicit in Mark—namely that Jesus' proclamation of 1:15 in Mark fulfills Isa. 61:1f. and explains the character of Jesus' ministry as it unfolds in the ensuing narrative of Mark's gospel. The arrival of the saving benefits championed in Isa. 61:1f. (35:5) essentially equals the arrival of the kingdom of God. If our argument proves sound, we will lay the foundation for the assertion that Mark and Q agree on the major aspects which characterize Jesus' relation to the kingdom of God and its arrival: that the kingdom's arrival coincides with Jesus' endowment with the Spirit, that the kingdom is manifested in Jesus' acts, that Jesus emphasized the kingdom's arrival as a message of good news, that the kingdom arrived in Jesus to face direct opposition from Satan and his demons, and that the kingdom's arrival in Jesus fulfills the Isaianic promise concerning the events which will characterize the advent of God's coming. To the degree that Mark and Q agree on the crucial details of Jesus' ministry, we may raise our confidence in the likelihood that Jesus himself interpreted his mission as the arrival of God's rule and the fulfilment of Isa. 61:1f.

Before approaching Mk. 1:15 exegetically, it is important to our argument to restate the implications of Mk. 1:1-14. First, the "good news of Jesus" for Mark is the fulfilment of Isaiah. Against the background of Isa. 40:3, John prepares the way for the good news (Isa. 40:5, 9) which comes not in Jahweh as in the OT, but in Jesus. Thus as the successor of John, Jesus is the good news prophesied by Isaiah. Second, Jesus' authority is directly related to his endowment with the Spirit—a union which coincides with God's declaration of Jesus' sonship and an authority which enables Jesus to successfully confront the aggression of Satan. And third, it is significant that Mark and Q have in common the exact OT quotation Isa. 40:3, Jesus' baptism, Jesus' temptation by Satan, the role of the Spirit, the forerunner role of John, and the Galilean location of Jesus' ministry—parallels which differ only in nuance. Thus, *a priori*, Jesus' endowment with the Spirit and his role as fulfiller of the "good news" place him in a position commensurate with the herald figure of Isa. 61:1f.

---

[40] We do not believe Lk. 4:16-21 originally belonged to Q. See p. 160.

A. Mk. 1:15

Mk. 1:15 can be broken down into five parts: a connecting phrase introducing a quotation (ὅτι recitative), two declarative statements, and two commands. The two imperatives exist in synthetic parallelism and supplement or complete the thought of the declarative statements.

The authenticity of this saying is held in question by not a few as a result of its "programmatic" form—its surface appearance as a short Markan statement of the essence of Jesus' message. Because the thoughts conveyed by the fulfilment of time (ὁ καιρός), the call to repent, and the call to believe in the Gospel reflect the vocabulary of early Church preaching, many view this saying as Mark's placement of later kerygma upon the lips of the historical Jesus (cf. Ro. 13:11, 12). However, as we shall see, such reasoning obscures the distinctiveness of Mk. 1:15 and underestimates the probability that Mark has selected a traditional saying to serve a programmatic purpose. And as we shall see, the vocabulary represented here not only conforms to the interests of the church, but also to the primary emphases of Jesus' ministry.

The perfect passive form of πληρόω and the qualified meaning of ὁ καιρός as the "appointed time" indicate that the first declaration announces the "fulfilment" or "coming to pass" of a decisive moment in time whose significance continues into the present.[41] The passive voice implies God's action in this process. The tension between this phrase and the following statement addressing the nearness of the kingdom verifies that Jesus is here referring to a strategic time corresponding to the expectation of prophetic/apocalyptic texts (Dn. 7:22, 25; 9:27; 11:14; Eze. 7:12; 9:1). However, R. Pesch correctly stresses that Jesus' message differs from the typical apocalyptic concept of time. Where apocalyptic writings explain time change as a result of a cataclysmic historical event, in Jesus' saying time is fulfilled because the kingdom of God has come near.[42] In favour of the traditional pedigree of this phrase, B. Chilton cites its un-Markan syntax, vocabulary, and Mark's diverse use of καιρός.[43] In addition, this context compares favourably with Jesus' usage in Lk. 12:56//Mt. 16:3 where Jesus refers to the signs of the

---

[41] The context demands this use of καιρός. See: O. Cullmann, *Christ and Time*, ET Philadelphia: Fortress Press (1964) 39-44; G. Delling, "καιρός", *TDNT* III, 456-65; J. Barr, *Biblical Words for Time*, SBT 33; London: SCM, 1969.

[42] *Markus* I, 102. So also in Mk. 4:29 where the KG, like the harvest, appears at the decisive moment in time.

[43] *God in Strength*, 59: ". . . when neither syntax nor vocabulary seems Markan, and when the material in question appears in a logion, it is appropriate to conclude that the redactor is transmitting a traditional construction."

times ($τῶν καιρῶν$) in an eschatological sense, which like 1:15 demands a proper response from man.[44]

The synthetic parallelism between the nearness of the kingdom and the fulfilment of time and the fact that 1:2-13 identifies Jesus' ministry as the fulfilment of OT prophecy suggests that $ἤγγικεν$ here refers to the arrival in the present of God's rule. A host of scholars adhere to this position with the condition that $ἤγγικεν$ holds in tension the present and future, so that the kingdom is viewed as present in power with time fulfilled, but the completion or consummation yet to come.[45] This understanding correlates with the perfect tense of the verbs. Mk. 1:15b has a direct Q parallel in Q $ἤγγικεν ἐφ᾽ ὑμᾶς ἡ βασιλεία τοῦ θεοῦ$ (Lk. 10:9//Mt. 10:7). In 10:9//10:7 Jesus' disciples do the same things and preach the same message as Jesus preaches in 1:15 and does in Mk. chs. 1-6. The mission of the twelve in Mk. 6:6b-13 verifies, however, that this phenomenon is not unique to Q or the supposed Q community. For here the disciples extend John's and Jesus' repentance preaching (1:4, 15; 13:10) and perform the eschatological acts of healing and exorcism which in Q vindicate Jesus' claim that the kingdom of God has come ($ἔφθασεν$: Lk. 11:20//Mt. 12:28). As a result, weight should not be placed on the lack of a kingdom of God saying in Mk. 6:13. Both texts correspond to the conceptual background of Isa. 35:5; 61:1f.—that acts of healing mark the advent of God's eschatological saving rule. But in Mk. 1:15 it is Jesus himself who inaugurates the new age—his ministry fulfills OT expectation and brings near the kingdom of God.

Jesus' declaration that the time is fulfilled and the kingdom of God has come near requires a specific response from his listeners—"repent and believe in the Gospel." The phrase has no NT parallel. Its Semitic syntax[46] and the un-Markan features of using $πιστεύω$ with an object in combination with $ἐν$ as opposed to $εἰς$[47] argue strongly for taking the phrase as traditional. $ἐν τῷ εὐαγγελίῳ$, then,

---

[44] See: I.H. Marshall, *Luke*, 550; Davies and Allison, *Matthew* II, 582.

[45] The kingdom is viewed as present in 1:15 by R. Schnackenburg, *God's Rule and Kingdom*, 141-142; A.M. Ambrozic, *The Hidden Kingdom*, Philadelphia: Fortress (1973) 21-23; W. Kelber, *The Kingdom in Mark*, 7-11; G.R. Beasley-Murray, *Jesus and the Kingdom of God*, 72-73; G.E. Ladd, *The Presence of the Future*, 145f; R.A. Guelich, *Mark* I, 44,45; R. Pesch, *Markus*, 102; M. Black, "The Kingdom of God has Come", *ExpT* 63 (1951-52) 289-290. *Contra*: W.G. Kümmel, *Promise and Fulfillment*, 19-24; W. Marxsen, *Mark*, 132-134.

[46] Moulton, Howard, Turner, *Grammar of New Testament Greek* II, 464; C.E.B. Cranfield, *Mark*, Cambridge: CUP (1963) 68; B. Chilton, *God in Strength*, 93.

[47] $πιστεύω$ occurs 26x in Mk., but only twice with an object outside of 1:15: in 9:42 where [$εἰς ἐμέ$] is bracketed by UBS 3 and NA 26 because the phrase is omitted by ℵ *D* and *Δ*, and in 11:31, where "believe" is used in a non-religious sense without a preposition in reference to John the Baptist. Cf. B. Metzger, *Textual Commentary*, 101, 102; J. Gnilka, *Markus* I, 65. Scholars who consider the phrase traditional include: R. Pesch, *Markus* I, 103, 104; J. Gnilka, *Markus* I, 65; R.A. Guelich, *Mark* I, 44, 45.

need not have originally referred in the technical sense to the Gospel of 1:1 or the Gospel of Jesus' death and resurrection.[48] Noting the variety of contexts for εὐαγγέλιον/εὐαγγελίζω in the NT, many scholars have reached the conclusion that εὐαγγέλιον in the earliest phase referred to the "Good News" of God's coming to bring salvation to men.[49] The context of 1:15, a kingdom of God saying, is fitting for this usage. In addition, such a usage compares favourably with the concept of good news advocated by Jesus in Lk. 4:16-30; Mt. 5:3//Lk. 6:20; Lk. 7:18f.//Mt. 11:2f. where Jesus fulfills Isa. 61:1f. as the herald of good news by pronouncing eschatological blessings corresponding to the arrival of God's salvation. According to Mark, then, the Church at an early stage identified the good news of the kingdom of God as originally voiced by the historical Jesus to be the advent of the Gospel. The call to repent places Jesus within the prophetic tradition. However, the urgency of Jesus' call, as we have stressed, relates directly to the arrival of the kingdom of God.[50] In this regard, Mk. 1:15 contains the same combination of wisdom/prophetic thought as characterizes much of the Q material. On the basis of a past understanding or conviction of the gravity of the events and circumstances associated with the arrival of God's rule, Jesus challenges his listeners to repent now.

In our comparison of Mark and Q, it is important to observe that Q contains conceptual parallels to Jesus' call to repent and believe as a result of the news of the fulfilment of time and the arrival of the kingdom of God.

Woe to you, Chorazin! Woe to you, Bethsaida! For if the miracles had been performed in Tyre and Sidon which occurred in you, they would have repented long ago, sitting in sackcloth and ashes. (Lk. 10:13//Mt. 11:21)

The men of Nineveh shall stand up with this generation at the judgment and condemn it, because they repented at the preaching of Jonah; and behold, something greater than Jonah is here. (Lk. 11:32//Mt. 12:41)

---

[48] *Pace* J. Schlosser, (*Le Règne de Dieu dans les Dits de Jésus*, Vol 1, 96, 104) who after arguing for the traditional pedigree of the first three phrases of Mk. 1:15 attributes the final one to the mission language of the Hellenistic-Jewish Christian community. However, if 1:15 is "programmatic" for the material which follows in Mark, ἐν τῷ εὐαγγελίῳ does not refer to the "Gospel of Christ", but rather to the Good News (Isa. 61:1f.) which is present in Jesus' ministry.

[49] P. Stuhlmacher, *Das paulinische Evangelium* I, Göttingen: Vandenhoeck & Ruprecht (1968) 243; H. Merklein, *Die Gottesherrschaft als Handlungsprinzip*, 18f.; B. Chilton, *God in Strength*, 63; R. Pesch, *Markus* I, 103; R. Schnackenburg, "'Das Evangelium' im Verständnis des ältesten Evangelisten", *Orientierung an Jesus: zur Theologie der Synoptiker*, FS J. Schmid; Freiburg: Herder (1973) 320, 321; V. Taylor, *Mark*, 167; A.E. J. Rawlinson, *Mark*, 13.

[50] See J. Gnilka, *Markus* I, 67.

Jesus' perspective in both Mark and Q is that his preaching and his miraculous acts should compel a decisive response from those who see and hear the impact of his ministry.

B. The Isaiah Background of Mk. 1:15

R.A. Guelich argues that Mark presents Jesus as the fulfilment of Isaianic promise: "Jesus' ministry in Galilee clearly reflects the setting of Isa. 52:7; 61:1. Jesus is introduced 'as proclaiming' or 'heralding' the good news from God."[51] Further, Guelich points out that what is true of Mark's introduction in general is particularly true of Mk. 1:15: "Taken in isolation this summary would suggest that Mark viewed Jesus as the eschatological messenger promised in Isa. 52:7 and 61:1 who would announce the arrival of God's rule and deliverance, the "good news from God."[52] Guelich, of course, is not alone in this observation.[53] Morna Hooker, for instance, writes that Jesus' miracles of restoration and exorcism demonstrate against the background of Isa. 35 and 61 the process initiated in Mark's prologue: "the time of salvation has arrived in the person of Jesus, in whom the renewing, creative Spirit of God is at work."[54] Along the same lines Barry Blackburn notes that in Mk. 7:32, where Jesus heals the man with the speech impediment, $\mu o\gamma\iota\lambda\acute{a}\lambda o\varsigma$ is used—a word only occuring in Mk. 7:32 and Isa. 35:6 in all the Greek Bible.[55] It is likely then that Mark interprets Jesus' teaching and work against the exact same OT background (Isa. 35:5; 61:1f.) as that which Jesus alludes to in Q (Lk. 6:20//Mt. 5:3; Lk. 7:22f//Mt. 11:4f.).[56] That this is true, however, is hard to prove because 1:15 does not contain a direct quotation of the OT.

---

[51] *Mark*, 45-46.

[52] *Mark*, 46.

[53] G.R. Beasley-Murray, *Jesus and the Kingdom of God*, 75; J. Gnilka, *Markus* I, 66; M. Hooker, *The Message of Mark*, London: Epworth (1983) 42, 43.

[54] *Ibid.*, 43.

[55] *Theios Aner and the Markan Miracle Traditions*, 242.

[56] So Burton L. Mack, "Q and the Gospel of Mark: Revising Christian Origins", *Semeia* 55 (1992) 27: "This saying (Lk. 7:22) could not be used as such, but may have triggered Mark's choice of the miracles stories he used to create Jesus' character." Here we differ from the following scholars who attribute little or no significance to Jesus' fulfillment of Isaiah in Mark: K. Koch, *Die Bedeutung der Wundererzählungen für die Christologie des Markusevangelium*, Berlin: Walter der Gruyter, 1975; K. Kertelge, *Die Wunder Jesu im Markusevangelium*, StANT 23, München: Kösel, 1970; L. Schenke, *Die Wundererzählungen des Markusevangeliums*, Stuttgart: Katholisches Bibelwerk, 1974. We are supported, however, by K. Kertelge (201) who agrees that Jesus' acts are signs of the presence of the kingdom in Mark: "Jetzt schon, in der Geschichte Jesu, bricht in den Wundern die $B\alpha\sigma\iota\lambda\epsilon\acute{\iota}\alpha$ $\tauo\hat{\upsilon}$ $\theta\epsilon o\hat{\upsilon}$ an, die von Jesus selbst angekündigt wird (1,14f.)."

Nevertheless, B. Chilton's study of 1:15 indicates that Targum Isaiah provides the closest linguistic and textual background to this verse. In particular Chilton finds the closest background to Mark's καιρός in Targum Isa. 60:22 (נמו : a determined time) and the nearest parallel to πληρόω in Targum Isa. 60:20 (מלש: days actually completed).[57] The proximity of these two verses is indeed striking both to one another and to Isa. 61:1 which immediately follows 60:22 if chapter and verse divisions are removed as they would have been in ancient texts. In short, Chilton's study leads to the conclusion: "The logion is not a citation; it rather uses scriptural language innovatively to proclaim God's dynamic presence in clear familiar diction. In this use of language, the saying strongly commends itself as dominical."[58] If indeed this is the case, Mk. 1:15 supports the Q material in attesting that Jesus saw the arrival of God's rule in his ministry as the fulfilment of Isa. 61:1f—a text correlating the fulfilment of time, the anointing of the spirit, and the arrival of God's eschatological salvation in the form of "Good News" to the poor and healing to the sick. Hence the background of Isa. 61:1f. corresponds perfectly to the interests of Mark and Q.

C. The Significance of Jesus' Miracles in Mark

Mk. 1:14, 15 has been regarded by some as the work of an early Christian prophet, a passage which reveals Jesus/John polemic, which bears evidence of the early Church's concept of salvation history, which originated as the result of a certain expectation of the parousia, and which was occasioned by an unstated crisis in history.[59] In these respects Mark has been analyzed with the same scholarly presuppositions as has the Q material. In fact, however, Mk. 1:15 shows how Jesus' original message was valued as the beginning of the Gospel by the early Church. Like the Q material, Mark's introduction depicts Jesus' endowment with the Spirit and defeat of Satan as evidence that the kingdom of God arrived in Jesus' ministry. As in Q, in Mark Jesus himself occasions "apocalyptic enthusiasm" through the radical nature of his message ("the kingdom is near"),

---

[57] *God in Strength*, 85-89.

[58] *Ibid.*, 95. Scholars reaching the same conclusion: R. Pesch, *Mark* I, 103; R.A. Guelich, *Mark* I, 41f; W. Egger, *Frohbotschaft und Lehre*, Frankfurt: Knecht (1976) 56-61. Others attribute it to the earliest Church which correctly passed on Jesus' message: R. Schnackenburg, "Das Evangelium", 318-321; F. Mussner, "Gottesherrschaft und Sendung Jesu nach Markus 1,14f." In *Praesentia Salutis: Gesammelte Studien zu Fragen und Themen des Neuen Testaments.* Dusseldorf: Patmos (1967) 82, 83; J. Gnilka, *Markus* I, 64-65. Others assign 1:15 directly to Mark: R. Bultmann, *History of the Synoptic Tradition*, 118; W. Marxsen, *Mark*, 132-34; A.M. Ambrozic, *The Hidden Kingdom*, 4-6.

[59] See L.E. Keck, "The Introduction to Mark's Gospel", *NTS* 12 (1965-66) 361, 369; W. Marxsen, *Mark the Evangelist*, 88f., 135.

through the power of his acts, through the followers he attracts, and through the disciples he commissions.[60] The historical event creating crisis is stated explicitly; it is the message and ministry of Jesus.

The likelihood that Mark patterns much of Jesus' ministry after the same Isaiah passages which underlie Q gains support from the nature of Jesus' Galilean ministry. While Jesus does not voice a single kingdom of God saying between 1:15 and 4:11, we must remember that 1:15 serves a programmatic role in Mark, so that the content of 1:15 ("the time is fulfilled; the kingdom of God has come near") remains the understood content of Jesus' preaching and teaching in passages where Mark emphasizes Jesus' preaching/teaching role but refrains from providing the explicit content of that teaching (1:22, 27, 38, 39). It is important in this respect that in Mark Jesus' authoritative teaching goes hand in hand with his miracles of exorcism and healing. It is as if Mark first presents Jesus' claim "the time is fulfilled; the kingdom has come" and then goes on to display how the kingdom has come, while all the time inquiring what Jesus' relation to the arrival of the kingdom means.

Hence immediately following Jesus' charge in 1:15, he calls his disciples and begins his ministry in Capernaum (1:21f.), where Jesus' teaching is vindicated by his successful exorcism of an unclean spirit. In embryo form, 1:22-28 combines two leading motifs of Mark's narrative: the amazement response to Jesus' teaching and acts (vv. 26, 27), and the messianic secret (v. 25). In view of 1:15, the exorcism is Mark's first piece of evidence that God's rule has indeed arrived in Jesus' ministry (cf. Lk. 11:20//Mt. 12:28).[61] Though the crowd responds with amazement ("What is this? A new teaching with authority! He commands even the unclean spirits, and they obey him"), they do not fully comprehend what they have seen and heard. The result, however, is the spread of enthusiasm: "immediately the news about him went out everywhere."

---

[60] So R. Pesch, *Markus* I, 102: "Das Nahegerücht = Angekommensein der Gottesherrschaft (ἤγγικεν) entspricht Jesus Auffassung von Gottes Königtum als einem machtvollen, dynamischen Geschehen, in dem Gott seine Heilsherrschaft universal aufrichtet: Gottes Herrschaft bricht herein. Mit der Verkündigung dieser grundlegenden Botschaft, dieses Evangeliums, sendet Jesus auch seine Jünger in die Palästinamission (Mt. 10,7; Lk. 10,9.11). Der Heroldsruf spricht in gedrängtester Form Jesu Gotteserfahrung und die darin begründete Heils – Zukunftserwartung enthusiastisch aus."

[61] *Pace* G. Dautzenberg ("Mk. 4,1-34 als Belehrung über das Reich Gottes", *Biblische Zeitschrift* 34 [1990] 58): "Im Unterschied zu Q (Lk. 11,20) hebt Markus nicht auf einen verborgenen Anbruch der Basileia im Wirken Jesu ab; es ist wenigstens zweifelhaft, ob die Gleichnisse 4,26ff.30ff. von ihm im Sinne einer Gegenüberstellung von Anfang und Vollendung der Basileia verstanden worden sind, wenn sie je eine solche Aussage gehabt haben sollten. Die mk Basileiakonzeption auf die Zukunft ausgerichtet, . . ."

The answer to the crowd's question "What is this?" is the arrival of God's saving rule in Jesus in a manner corresponding to the promises of Isaiah: good news has come to the afflicted, liberty to the captives (Isa. 61:1, 2). Such is confirmed if our conjecture is correct that the unclean spirits' identification of Jesus as the "Holy One of God" corresponds in function to the frequent role taken by the "Holy One of Israel" or the "Holy One of Jacob," who is the recipient of Israel's rejoicing on that day, when "the deaf shall hear" and " the blind shall see" (Isa. 29:18, 19). In the OT, this epithet is often used with or substituted for YHWH and, according to J.D.W. Watts, "conjures up all the memories of God's acts of salvation in Israel's behalf from the Exodus onward."[62] When we recall that Jesus fulfills the place of God in Mark's opening quotation of Isa. 40:3, this exalted name need not occasion alarm—especially when elsewhere the demons in Mark identify Jesus directly as the Son of God.

Following this incident, Mark continues to display the arrival of God's saving rule in additional exorcisms and in healings which directly fulfill the eschatological expectations and hopes of Isaiah. After Mark's summarizing statement, "And he healed many who were ill with various diseases, and cast out many demons" (1:34a), Mark's Jesus proceeds to cleanse a leper (1:39f.), heal a paralytic (2:3f.), exorcise the Gerasene demoniac (5:1f.), heal the hemorrhaged woman (5:25-34), restore the life of the synagogue official's daughter (5:35-43), feed the 5000, still the storm, heal the sick at Gennesaret (6:53), cast out the demon from the Syrophoenician woman's daughter (7:29), feed the 4000 (8:1), heal the deaf and dumb man in Decapolis (7:32-39), cast out a demon from a mute boy (9:25), and heal Bartimaeus the blind man (10:46). In short the healings of the blind, the deaf, the lame, and the dumb correspond to the eschatological saving benefits associated with God's coming in Isa. 35:5, 6: "then the eyes of the blind will be opened, and the ears of the deaf will be unstopped. The the lame will leap like a deer, and the tongue of the dumb will shout for joy" (cf. 29:18; 42:18). Jesus' restoring to life of the little girl corresponds to the new life expected at God's coming in Isa. 26:19: "Your dead will live; their corpses will rise." Likewise the feeding of the 4000 and 5000 correspond to eschatological blessings associated with the arrival of God's rule: "They will not hunger or thirst, neither will the scorching heat or sun strike them down; For he who has compassion on them will lead them" (Isa. 49:10; cf. 55:1-2; 65:13; Ps. 107:5-9). And finally, the stilling of the storm corresponds to the alteration of nature expected in the day of salvation: "You will winnow them, and the wind will carry them away and the storm will scatter them; but you will rejoice in the Lord, you will glory in the Holy One of Israel" (Isa. 41:16).

---

[62] *Isaiah* II, 105.

Such an understanding of Jesus' miracles in Mark correlates perfectly with the arrival of God's saving rule in Q where in response to John's question of Jesus' identity Jesus answers with the composite quotation of Isaiah (26:19; 29:18; 35:5, 6; 42:18; 61:1f.): "the blind receive sight, the lame walk, the lepers are cleansed, and the deaf hear, the dead are raised up, the poor have the gospel preached to them." This passage, of course, cannot be pressed to detail every miracle Jesus performs in Mark—it does not mention nature miracles—but its parallels are indeed striking especially in consideration of the fact that Jesus performs in Mark all of the miracles spoken of by Jesus in Q. The one healing miracle which does not allude to Isaiah 35 or 61 in Q 7:22f.//11:4f. (the cleansing of lepers) does have a parallel in Mk. 1:42. Further, while Jesus' exorcisms are not grounded in Isaiah passages which identify the defeat of Satan as a sign of the arrival of God, the eschatological implication of Jesus' exorcism of demons is explicit in Q (11:20//12:28), while in Mark Jesus' exorcisms supply evidence of his true identity (the Son of God) and are in fact redactionally coupled with healing miracles by Mark to hint that exorcisms, like healing miracles, testify both to the action of God in Jesus and to Jesus' true identity: "And he healed many who were ill with various diseases, and cast out many demons; and he was not permitting the demons to speak, because they knew who he was" (1:34).

But what of the feeding of the 4000 and the 5000? These miracles bear evidence that Mark presented Jesus' miraculous works as pointers to the eschatological work of God which was present in Jesus' earthly ministry. For in the feeding of the crowds in Mark, Jesus' Q pronouncements are realized: "Blessed are you who hunger now, for you shall be satisfied" (6:20a//5:6); "Give us this day our daily bread" (11:3//6:11). Thus, in Mark as in Q, Jesus' acts validate his charge that the "Good News" has come to the poor and the time has been fulfilled—the kingdom of God has come near.

While there is a growing tendency in scholarship to emphasize the theological aspect of the kingdom of God in the teaching of Jesus and as a result disassociate the kingdom of God from christology, a comparison between Q and Mark indicates that the arrival of the kingdom of God in Jesus' ministry as accompanied by the Spirit relates directly to Jesus' identity.[63] In other words, the arrival of the kingdom in Jesus implies something special about Jesus himself. In this regard it is important to observe that major christological features of Mark correspond with

---

[63] *Pace* B. Chilton, "Introduction", *The Kingdom of God*, IRTh 5; London: SPCK (1984) 26: "We need to bear in mind that the kingdom, not the messiah, was the burden of Jesus' preaching and (first of all) that of his disciples. Radical immanence, side by side with radical transcendence, appears to be basic to the kingdom of God, and not a subsidiary development of Jesus' messianic self-consciousness (whatever that may have been)."

the power of God breaking forth in Jesus: the Messianic secret corresponds with
the secret inbreaking of the kingdom (1:24, 25, 34, 43, 44; 3:10, 11; 6:2f.; 7:32-
37; 8:21; 10:46),[64] and amazement at Jesus corresponds with "Seeing and
Hearing" what is taking place (1:27; 2:12; 5:20, 42; 6:2f.; 7:32-37; 10:32;
11:18)—namely the miracles and the preaching of Good News (events which
according to Isa. 35 and 61 mark the dawn of God's saving rule). It is clear, then,
that just as Jesus expected John to reach an accurate conclusion as to his identity
on the basis of his eschatological preaching of Good News and acts of healing in Q
7:22//11:4f., so also in Mark Jesus is confounded by his disciples' inability to
make a connection between the events taking place and the eminence of Jesus
himself.

Nowhere is the tension between Jesus' acts/God's rule and the question of his
identity more apparent than in the sequence of events taking place in Mk. 7:24-
8:26—the events leading up to Peter's confession. Here Mark presents the
expulsion of the demon from the Gentile woman's daughter (7:24-30), the healing
of the deaf and dumb man (7:31-36), and the editorial statement: "And they were
utterly astonished, saying, 'He has done all things well; He makes even the deaf to
hear and the dumb to speak' " (7:37). Against the background of Isa. 35:5; 61:1f.,
the people are amazed at Jesus, whether they understand it or not, because God's
saving rule is presently revealing itself. After this event, Mark proceeds to present
the feeding of the 4000—an event that has eschatological relevance and requires a
response from those who see and hear. Conceptually the feeding corresponds to
the eschatological promise of God in Isa. 41:17f.:

> The afflicted and needy are seeking water, but there is none,
> And their tongue is parched with thirst,
> I, the Lord, will answer them myself,
> As the God of Israel I will not foresake them. (41:17)

> That they may see and recognize,
> And consider and gain insight as well,
> That the hand of the Lord has done this,
> And the Holy One of Israel has created it. (41:20)

Thus, it is not an arbitrary ordering of events when Mark's Jesus, following the
feeding of the 4000, responds in frustration to the disciples' despair in not having
bread, "Why do you discuss the fact that you have no bread? Do you not yet see

---

[64] So J. Gnilka, *Markus* I, 165: "Darum muß mit dem μυστήριον τῆς Βασιλείας ihre
noch nicht offenbare Präsenz gemeint sein, die mit Jesu Wirken gegeben ist. Ist diese Deutung
bereits für das vormarkinische Wort anzunehmen, so artikuliert sich die christologische
Implikation der Gottesherrschaft bei Markus dadurch, daß Jesus der Messias und Gottesohn ist.
Es ist darum zutreffend, vom Messias – oder Gottessohngeheimnis zu sprechen."

or understand? Do you have a hardened heart? Having eyes, do you not yet see or understand? And having ears, do you not hear? . . . Do you not yet understand?" (8:17, 18, 21). With the feeding miracle in view, Jesus' disciples are insensitive to the reality of God's power which is presently at work in Jesus himself. The connection has not yet been made between the arrival of God's rule in Jesus and Jesus' christological identity. Ironically the disciples, like the crowds at large, have seen and heard Jesus' acts and preaching of good news and even been amazed by it, but they have not yet understood the immense eschatological import which seeing and hearing Jesus should occasion. Again this scenario compares favourably with Jesus' instruction in Q where the wise are contrasted with fools who do not hear and act in response to Jesus' words (Lk. 6:46//Mt. 7:24-27).[65] The seeing and hearing motif is equally characteristic of Q: "Go and report to John what you have seen and heard," which is followed by a veiled hint of the correlation between Jesus' healing, good news preaching and his christological identity, "And blessed is he who keeps from stumbling over me" (Lk. 7:23//Mt. 11:6). This Q passage conceptually parallels Mark's secrecy theme as it concludes with Jesus' address of his generations' inability to comprehend the reality of God's work in John and in Jesus the Son of Man:

> To what then shall I compare the men of this generation, and what are they like? They are like children who sit in the market place and call to one another; and they say, 'We played the flute for you, and you did not dance; we sang a dirge, and you did not weep.' For John the Baptist has come eating no bread and drinking no wine; and you say, "He has a demon!" The Son of Man has come eating and drinking; and you say, 'Behold, a gluttonous man, and a drunkard, a friend of tax-gatherers and sinners!' Yet wisdom is justified by all of her children. (Lk. 7:31-35//Mt. 11:16-19; cf. 10:12-15//11:14, 21-23; 10:23, 24//13:16, 17).

Thus, Mark and Q together attest to the initial inability of Jesus' audience, both hostile and receptive, to see and hear with understanding the eschatological importance of Jesus' acts and preaching. Before Mark's redaction, it was this inability to see and hear the eschatological import of Jesus' ministry which gave rise to the Messianic Secret.

---

[65] Thus C. Schuppan (*Gottes Herrschaft und Gottes Wille*) writes: "Im Vergleich zum Judentum dieser Zeit ist im Wirken Jesu etwas Neues da: die Verbindung von Wunder und endzeitlicher Verkündigung. Ein entscheidender Zug im Wirken Jesu ist damit zum besonderen Anliegen der in Q gesammelten Traditionen geworden: *Machttaten* und *Verkündigung, Hören* und *Sehen* gehören zur Wirksamkeit Jesu und seiner Boten. Die Gegenwart des Wirkens Jesu erweist sich als der Anbruch der erwarteten Endzeit" (62; italics ours). Clear in Mark is the uniqueness which Schuppan observes in Q.

IV. Mk. 4:11-12

The motif of seeing and hearing holds in tension the arrival of the kingdom of God and Jesus' identity in the second kingdom of God saying in Mark. Here as before, it is our intention to show that Mark's secrecy theme appears compatible with the Q material and in fact supports the traditional nature of the wisdom and apocalyptic features which some scholars have attributed to Q redaction. The majority of scholars identify the contrast in form and style between 4:11-12 and its environment in ch. 4 as evidence that 4:11-12 was a product of pre-Markan tradition which was secondarily inserted into its present context between the parable of the sower (4:3-9) and its explanation (4:13-20).[66] The antithetic parallelism in v. 11, the presence of Semitisms,[67] the divine passives ($\delta\acute{\epsilon}\delta o\tau a\iota$, $\gamma\acute{\iota}\nu\epsilon\tau a\iota$, $\dot{a}\phi\epsilon\theta\tilde{\eta}$), the synoptic hapaxlegomenon $\tau\grave{o}$ $\mu\nu\sigma\tau\acute{\eta}\rho\iota o\nu$, and the agreement of the quotation of Isa. 6:9 in 4:12 with Targum Isa. against both the LXX and the MT suggest the saying's Palestinian origin and supports the probability of its authenticity.[68]

The internal contrast between those "inside" who have received the mystery of the kingdom of God and those "outside" who receive "all things" in parables is qualified in v. 12 by Jesus' quotation of Isa. 6:9. While those who receive the mystery of the kingdom are given the ability to see and hear with understanding, those outside receive all things in parables or riddles in order that they may not see with perception and not hear with understanding even though they see and hear with physically capable eyes and ears. Thus, those outside are prevented by God from repenting and experiencing forgiveness. While this interpretation is unacceptable to most scholars, it is the most natural translation of the Greek and adheres to the manner in which God gradually hardened Pharaoh's heart before the

---

[66] V. Taylor, *Mark*, 254, 255; J. Jeremias, *The Parables of Jesus*, 14; R. Pesch, *Markus* I, 236; J. Gnilka, *Die Verstockung Israels*, München: Kösel Verlag (1961) 23-24; K.H. Schelkle, "Der Zweck der Gleichnisreden (Mk. 4,10-12)", *Neues Testament und Kirche,* FS R. Schnackenburg; Freiburg: Herder (1974) 71f.; *Contra:* A. M. Ambrozic, *The Hidden Kingdom,* 52-53, and R. Bultmann, *History of the Synoptic Tradition,* 199, who categorize the 4:11, 12 as Markan redaction.

[67] Antithetic parallelism, the redundant demonstrative $\dot{\epsilon}\kappa\epsilon\acute{\iota}\nu o\iota\varsigma$, and the threefold use of circumlocution for God's action are features of Semitic speech: cf. J. Jeremias, *The Parables of Jesus,* 15. See also R.E. Brown, *The Semitic Background of the term 'Mystery' in the New Testament,* Philadelphia: Fortress Press, 1968.

[68] So J. Jeremias, *The Parables of Jesus,* 15; T.W. Manson, *The Teaching of Jesus,* 76-80; V. Taylor, *Mark,* 257; J. Gnilka, *Die Verstockung Israels,* 24; W. Marxsen, *Der Exeget als Theologe: Vorträge zum Neuen Testament,* Güttersloh: Mohn (1968) 27; S. Brown, "The Secret of the Kingdom of God (Mark 4:11)", *JBL* 92 (1973) 63; K.H. Schelkle, "Der Zweck der Gleichnisreden (Mk. 4,10-12)", 74, 75; J. Fitzmyer, *Luke* I, 707; G.R. Beasley-Murray, *Jesus and the Kingdom of God,* 107; H. Schürmann, *Lukas,* 461.

Exodus when Egypt's king failed to respond to the wonders performed through
Moses and Aaron.   Further, G. Bornkamm is correct when he states: "The
decision effected by the mode of instruction presupposes already in the people a
state which makes it ripe for the judgment of hardening,"[69] because v. 11
presumes that those inside have already responded positively to Jesus while those
outside have rejected him—despite seeing his miracles and hearing his message of
good news.

What is the mystery of the kingdom of God which Jesus' followers receive?
The description of the kingdom of God as a mystery which God himself reveals
has its background in Jewish apocalyptic and wisdom literature where God reveals
the secret of his eschatological rule through the wisdom he has given to the faithful
few.   The concept that God reserves his secrets for the wise exists as early as
Psalm 25:14 (24:14): "The Secret of the Lord is for those who fear him," where
the Theodotion text uses μυστήριον to translate the Hebrew word סוֹד (secret
council, intimacy).[70]   However, the majority of scholars cite the LXX and
Theodotion texts of Daniel (2:18f., 27, 28, 29, 30, 47, θ 4:9) as the background
for μυστήριον in Mk. 4:11, where μυστήριον renders the Aramaic word רָז
(Secret):[71]

> Daniel answered before the King and said, 'As for the mystery (τὸ μυστήριον/רָזָה)
> about which the king has inquired, neither wise men, conjurers, magicians, nor diviners
> are able to declare it to the king.   However, there is a God in heaven who reveals
> (ἀποκαλύπτων/גָּלֵא) mysteries (μυστήρια/רָזִין) and He has made known to King
> Nebuchadnezzar what will take place in the latter days.' (ἐσχάτων τῶν ἡμερῶν/
> בְּאַחֲרִית יוֹמַיָּא : Dn. 2:27, 28}

> The King answered Daniel and said, 'Surely your God is a God of gods and a Lord of
> kings and a revealer of mysteries (ὁ ἀποκαλύπτων μυστήρια/וְגָלֵה רָזִין, since
> you have been able to reveal this mystery' (ἀποκαλύψαι τὸ μυστήριον/לְמִגְלָא
> רָזָה: Dn. 2:47)

The secret which God reveals through Daniel is the sequence of events which
culminates in the disclosure of God's eschatological rule ("And in the days of
those kings the God of heaven will set up a kingdom which will never be
destroyed"; 2:44f.).   It is wisdom revealed by God independent of human
understanding (2:30).[72]

---

[69] "μυστήριον", *TDNT* IV, 818.

[70] BDB, 691.

[71] BDB, 1112.

[72] Davies and Allison, *Matthew* II, 389, cite as comparable 1QH 1.21: "these things I know
by the wisdom which comes from thee, for thou hast unstopped my ears to marvellous
mysteries."

As in Daniel 2, the mystery Jesus speaks of in Mk. 4:11 is a *secret* pertaining to God's endtime rule which is revealed to the few by God. Mark's secrecy theme itself has eschatological implications: God is revealing through Jesus the dawn of his reign. Thus, the mystery of the kingdom of God in 4:11, according to scholarly consensus,[73] is the presence of the kingdom of God in Jesus' ministry. Whereas in late apocalyptic "mystery" came to denote God's revelation of endtime events, in Mark the secrecy theme holds in balance Jesus' Messiahship and God's revelation of his eschatological rule through Jesus. Thus, C.E.B. Cranfield, commenting on Mk. 4:11, is able to say, "The secret of the kingdom of God is the secret of the person of Jesus."[74] Because those around Jesus with the twelve had responded positively to Jesus' ministry and as a result were with Jesus, they now were in a position to see and hear with understanding: (A) what Jesus' ministry meant—the kingdom has come—and (B), what Jesus' ministry meant about Jesus—He is the Messiah (8:27). How does this interpretation of Mark compare with Q?

In Q, as in Mark, the inside/outside motif correlates seeing and hearing with understanding the gravity of Jesus' message: "Woe to you, Chorazin! Woe to you, Bethsaida! For if the *miracles* had been performed in Tyre and Sidon which occurred in you, they would have *repented* long ago (11:13//11:21); "The men of Nineveh shall stand up with this generation at the judgment and condemn it, because they *repented* at the *preaching* of Jonah; and behold, something greater than Jonah is here (11:32//12:41); "The Queen of the South shall rise up with the men of this generation at the judgment and condemn them, because she came from the ends of the earth to *hear* the wisdom of Solomon; and behold, something greater than Solomon is here" (11:31//12:42). Q, then, supports Mark's emphasis that Jesus' preaching and his acts have eschatological relevance in themselves— enough significance in fact to provoke repentance and motivate the question as to who Jesus is, if Jesus indeed is greater than the prophet Jonah and greater than the wise King Solomon, the son of David and heir apparent to the Messiah of Israel.

However, the closest parallel to Mk. 4:11, 12 in Q is Lk. 10:21, 22//Mt. 11:25-27:

I praise thee, O Father, Lord of heaven and earth, that you hid these things from the wise and intelligent and revealed them to babes. Yes, father, for thus it was well-

---

[73] A.M. Ambrozic, *The Hidden Kingdom*, 92; G.R. Beasley-Murray, *Jesus and the Kingdom of God*, 364; Davies and Allison, *Matthew* II, 389; R. Schnackenburg, *God's Rule and Kingdom*, 189; G. Bornkamm, "μυστήριον", *TDNT* IV, 818, 819; W. Grundmann, *Markus*, Berlin: Evangelische Verlagsanstalt (1977) 92; R. Pesch, *Markus* II, 239; H. Schürmann, *Lukas*, 461; J. Gnilka, *Die Verstockung Israels*, 44; C.E.B. Cranfield, *Mark*, 153.

[74] *Mark*, 153.

pleasing in your sight. All things have been handed over to me by my father, and no knows who the son is except the father, and who the father is except the son, and anyone to whom the son wills to reveal him.

This saying differs from Mk. 4:11-12 in two aspects: its first part is a prayer to God as opposed to a direct statement to Jesus' disciples, and its second part is a statement of rejoicing rather than a statement of judgment. Beyond these differences, 10:21, 22//11:25-27, like Mk. 4:11-12: (1) contains the inside/outside distinction; (2) portrays God as the revealer of understanding to the few who constitute the group of Jesus' followers; (3) contains the secrecy motif (all things are hidden ($\dot{\alpha}\pi\acute{\epsilon}\kappa\rho\upsilon\psi\alpha\varsigma$ $\tau\alpha\hat{\upsilon}\tau\alpha$); (4) identifies Jesus as the mediator of God's hidden wisdom; and (5), has a wisdom/apocalyptic background. Further, it is not unlikely that "these things" ($\tau\alpha\hat{\upsilon}\tau\alpha$) which are hidden from the wise in Lk. 10:21//Mt. 11:25 corresponds to "all things" ($\tau\acute{\alpha}$ $\pi\acute{\alpha}\nu\tau\alpha$) in Mk. 4:11—the mystery of the kingdom of God which is concealed in parables from Jesus' enemies. And finally, if Luke represents the original order of Q as most scholars believe (who adhere to the Q-hypothesis), this Q saying like Mk. 4:11 is followed immediately by another saying which picks up the seeing/hearing motif:

Blessed are the eyes which *see* the things you *see*, for I say to you, that many prophets and kings wished to *see* the things which you *see*, and did not *see* them, and to *hear* the things which you *hear*, and did not *hear* them. (Lk. 10:23, 24//Mt. 13:16, 17)

What are the things which the kings and prophets could not see or hear but which Jesus' followers are blessed to perceive? If Q is our guide, there is only one location where seeing and hearing is connected with a beatitude and that is in Jesus' response to John where he fulfills Isaiah's promises for endtime salvation (35:5f.; 61:1f.): "report to John what you have *seen* and *heard*: the blind receive sight, the lame walk, the lepers are cleansed, and the deaf hear, the dead are raised up, the poor have the Gospel preached to them. And *blessed* is he who keeps from stumbling over me" (7:23//11:6).

Herein, we believe, exists the origin of the so-called "Messianic Secret." In Mark as in Q, Jesus' contemporaries were unable to evaluate intelligently the eschatological pertinence of Jesus' announcement of good news to the poor (Mk. 1:15; Lk. 7:22//Mt. 11:4), his healing acts and his exorcisms. They failed to understand that Jesus' ministry signaled the dawn of God's eschatological rule. And, most importantly, they failed to comprehend the significance of Jesus himself as the one mediating the saving benefits of God's rule. Ironically, the few, those inside, who responded to the good news and followed Jesus—the poor, the sick, the babes—received the opportunity to understand Jesus' ministry and ultimately his Messiahship/Sonship, while those who rejected Jesus—the wise, the Pharisees and Lawyers—were prevented from perceiving the arrival of the kingdom and its agent—Jesus, the Messiah, Son of God. It is of course an underlying irony within Mark that Jesus responds in disbelief even at the insiders, the disciples, who were not able to make the most of the evidence provided them by Jesus' miracles (Mk. 6:52; 8:17, 21). However, the insiders at least are given the opportunity to understand. Lk. 10:21, 22//Mt. 11:25f. indicates first that the stimulus for the Messianic Secret existed independently from Mark and so was not Mark's literary invention, and second that Mark's development of the Messianic Secret was in no way occasioned by a need to correct the portrait of Jesus as advocated by the Q material (*contra* H. Räisänen and W. Schmithals). While Q, like the central section of Mark, never identifies Jesus as the Christ, Q like Mark does: (A) identify Jesus as anointed by the Spirit; (B) presents Jesus as the herald of good news after Isa. 61:1f.; (C) presents Jesus' acts as the fulfilment of Isa. 35:5; 61:1—the events which signal the dawn of God's eschatological rule; and (D), Q (11:4//6:9; 10:21//11:25), like Mark (14:36), places Jesus in an intimate Father/Son relationship with God. On the one hand, because Jesus' antagonists could not make the connection between A, B, and C they could not comprehend D, while on the other hand Jesus' followers did see their good fortune as a result of A, B, and C, and so were counted as insiders and given the blessing of understanding D. For the one, rejecting Jesus leads to the failure to repent and the judgment which ensues, for the other acceptance of Jesus stimulates repentance and results in blessing.

V. One Must Enter The Kingdom of God Like a Child

Appropriate to this section of our comparison of Mark and Q is Jesus' teaching on children in Mk. 10:13-16.[75] The two Markan kingdom of God sayings in these verses correlate with the Q material on several fronts.

First, Jesus' statement that the kingdom of God belongs to children (10:14) and his stipulation that the kingdom must be received by the child-like (10:15), appear consonant with Jesus' words of thanks in Lk. 10:21//Mt. 11:25 where he praises the Father that "these things" have been hidden from the wise and

---

[75] Mk. 10:13-14,16 is frequently described as an apophthegm into which v. 15 has been secondarily inserted by the Evangelist by means of catch-word association ($\beta\alpha\sigma\iota\lambda\epsilon\acute{\iota}\alpha$ $\tauο\hat{υ}$ $\thetaεο\hat{υ}$, $\pi\alpha\hat{\iota}\varsigma$). V. 15, however, hardly destroys the flow of thought between vv. 14 and 16, but merely challenges adults to emulate the child's faith. The historicity of 10:15 and the passage as a whole is a present day consensus: R. Bultmann, *History of the Synoptic Tradition*, 105, 110; E. Schweizer, *Mark*, 206; A.M. Ambrozic, *The Hidden Kingdom*, 138, 39; V. Taylor, *Mark*, 424; C.E.B. Cranfield, *Mark*, 322; J. Dupont, *Les Béatitudes* I, 158; M. Black, *An Aramaic Approach to the Gospels and Acts,* 219f.; R. Pesch, *Markus* I, 130f., 133 n. 9; J. Gnilka, *Markus* I, 80: "belongs to Jewish Christian Palestinian tradition." *Contra*, R. Schnackenburg, *God's Rule and Kingdom*, 142.

intelligent and revealed to babes (νηπίοις).[76] The kingdom of God is not gaine through human intellect or gnostic insight, but rather as a free gift to those wh accept with innocent child-like faith the truth of Jesus' ministry.[77]

Second, Mk. 10:13-16 corresponds in thought with the reversal of valu spoken of by Jesus in the beatitudes and woes in Q. Surely as the poor, th hungry, and those who mourn receive present blessing in view of their futu habitation in the kingdom of God, so too do children have a part in the futu kingdom of God who receive now in innocence the blessing of Jesus' ministry. And as Jesus rebukes the intelligent and the wise who would prevent the simp from entering the kingdom (Lk. 11:52//Mt. 23:13; Mk. 10:31), so he also rebuke those who would prevent children: "It would be better for him if a millstone we hung around his neck and he were thrown into the sea, than that he should cau one of these little ones to stumble" (Lk. 17:2//Mt. 18:7). Hence Jesus came to th aid of children just as he came to bring the blessings of the kingdom of God to th poor, the sick, and the sinful. He received children not only for the purpose illustrating a proper faith, but also in order to receive children into the savir power of God. Consequently, Jesus commanded his listeners to respect the valu of children. The image corresponds to the paradox which characterizes Jesu teaching in general: "the last will be first and the first will be last" (Lk. 13:30//M 20:16). The target group of Jesus' ministry includes the poor, the sick, the lam

---

[76] Independently, A.M. Ambrozic (*The Hidden Kingdom*, 151, 152), K. Berger (*Die Ame Worte Jesu*, 43, 44), and Gerhard Ringshausen ("Die Kinder der Weisheit zur Auslegung von M 10:13-16par", *ZNTW* 77 [1-2, 1986] 34-63) trace the pedigree of Mk. 10:15 to a wisdo background (Pr. 8:4-36; 18:12; 29:23; Sir. 3:18; 10:20, 28; 11:12f.) comparable to L 10:21//Mt. 11:25: "Mk. 10:15 is thus a sapientially colored torah of entry. It expresses the san thought as the Q logion Mt. 11:25/Lk. 10:21", (Ambrozic,152). If these scholars are correct, th passages under review strengthen more firmly the compatibility of Q's wisdom background wi Mark. However, the evidence, in our opinion, is not strong. It is very hard to see how M 10:15 depends on the wisdom passages cited. The term wisdom is not used. Furthermore, v cannot accept Ambrozic's claim that δέξηται "is to be seen as a technical term which describes willing and understanding acceptance of wisdom in its various manifestations" (144). Jesus' u of δέχομαι in the synoptics (28x) is too frequent and too varied to postulate a confine background on the basis of the word alone. Ringshausen's claim (52, 53, 61) that Mk. 10:13-1 implies the wisdom christology of the wandering prophets who originally pronounced the wor sounds strangely familiar to what others have written about the hypothetical Q community. Bo claims, however, rest entirely upon speculation.

[77] So J. Dupont (*Les Béatitudes*, II, 216) who argues that Mk. 10:14, 15 and Lk. 10:21//M 11:25 have in common the perspective that God's revelation comes not to close observers of th law but to the simple who benefit most from God's rule.

[78] So J. Schlosser, *Le Règne de Dieu dans les Dits de Jésus*, Vol 2, 491, 92: "Jésus accueil les enfants parce que Dieu leur trouve l'explication ultime de la prérogative eschatologique donne aux enfants comme aux autres marginaux de l'institution judaïque."

the sinful and children—whoever would accept his announcement of good news.[79]

And third, Mk. 10:15 promotes the father-child relationship advocated by Jesus in the Lord's Prayer. Whereas in the Lord's Prayer Jesus teaches his disciples to appeal to God as Father and to pray "Thy kingdom Come," here Jesus flatly states: "whoever does not receive the kingdom of God like a child shall not enter it at all." Like the children received by Jesus, the one who prays in the manner taught by Jesus must do so entirely dependent upon God's sovereign ability to meet every need both physical "give us our daily bread" and spiritual "forgive us our debts . . . lead us not into temptation." The one who prays for God's eschatological salvation must do so as a child—utterly aware of complete dependence upon God.

Hence Jesus teaches about children and the kingdom of God in Mk. 10:13-16 in a manner entirely consistent with the Q kingdom of God sayings.[80]

VI. Mark Chapter 4

Chapter 4 is the first of only two extensive examples of Jesus' teaching in Mark's Gospel (the other being Ch. 13). Its contents, therefore, demonstrate what Mark considered to be the hallmarks of Jesus' message. While much debate exists as to whether the present structure or order of ch. 4 represents the editorial handiwork of the evangelist or the tradition which preceded him, only extreme sceptics, because of un-Markan vocabulary and synoptic variants, deny the traditional pedigree of at least the parable of the sower and the soils (4:3-9), the five wisdom sayings (4:21-25), the parable of the "Seed Growing Secretly" (4:26-29), and the parable of the Mustard Seed (4:30-32). Further, as we have noted, many scholars count as genuine the kingdom of God saying (4:11-12), while a growing number accept as dominical the explanation to the parable of the sower and the seeds (4:13-20).

The recurring command to see and hear, the inside/outside motif, the contrast between what is hidden and what is revealed, the tension between the present manifestation of the kingdom and its future consummation, and the challenge to faith in Jesus constitute the themes which dominate and unify Jesus' teaching in

---

[79] So J. Dupont, *Les Béatitudes*, II, 151-81: "C'est cette mission qui rend actuel le privilège que vant aux παιδία et aux νήπιοι, comme aux pauvres, aux affligés et aux affamés, la sollicitude miséricordieuse et toute gratuite que Dieu leur port" (218).

[80] So also R. Pesch, *Markus* II, 133: "Jesu an vielleicht übliche Wendungen anknüpfende Formulierung ist in der Nähe der Vorstellungen vom Suchen (Mt. 6,33; Lk. 12,31) and glüchlichen Finden (Mt. 13, 44-46) der Gottesherrschaft anzusiedeln."

Mk. 4. Here as in Q the main thrust of Jesus' teaching is the kingdom of God. The parable of the Sower and the Soils and its explanation, though not containing a reference to the kingdom, are given kingdom orientation by the intersecting kingdom saying in 4:11, 12. The seeing/hearing, secret/revelation motifs in vv. 21-25 likewise conform to the kingdom perspective of 4:11, 12. The parable of the Seed Growing Secretly and the parable of the Mustard Seed are both explicit kingdom parables. And the stilling of the sea (4:35-41) is a sign which against the background of Isa. 41:16 identifies the arrival of God's saving rule in Jesus—a sign which calls for a response of faith in Jesus and which raises the question of Jesus' identity: "Who then is this, that even the wind and the sea obey him?" (4:41). While the entire chapter remains untainted by later Christian preaching of the cross and resurrection, each theme has counterparts in Q. Double attestation between Mark and Q undermines the logic of those who make much of the lack of passion emphasis in Q, and suggests that traditional material originally served as the impetus for the direction which Mark's narrative follows.

A.   The Parable of the Sower and the Soils (4:3-9)

Despite debate as to the focal image of this parable—the ower, the seed, or the various soils—the basic contrast clearly exists between the bad soils which do not bear fruit and the good soil which does. It is clear that v. 9, "He who has ears to hear, let him hear," elicits the challenge that Jesus' listeners must emulate the good soil as opposed to the bad and so receive the seed which is given by Jesus with full devotion and singleness of interest. In recent study two interpretations of the parable predominate. The first isolates the primary theme in the contrast between present and future: though Jesus' preaching has not produced universal repentance or the arrival of God's kingdom in apocalyptic glory, as a seed Jesus' preaching has germinated and will in the end produce a harvest visible to all. Thus, the purpose of the parable was to produce faith in the midst of disillusionment with Jesus' ministry.[81] The second more simple interpretation is that the parable challenges men to hear and carry out fully what Jesus teaches.[82] In our opinion the second interpretation is more convincing because it adheres more closely to the interpretation which follows (vv. 13-20), the earliest interpretation of the parable which we have, while the first seems to force 4:3-9 into the framework of the

---

[81] So J. Jeremias, *The Parables of Jesus*, 149-151; N. Perrin, *Rediscovering the Teaching of Jesus*, New York: Harper & Row (1967) 155-7; R.A. Guelich, *Mark* I, 197, et al.

[82] So I.H. Marshall, *Luke*, 323-4; G.R. Beasley-Murray, *Jesus and the Kingdom of God*, 131; Davies and Allison, *Matthew* II, 376, et al.

parable of the Seed Growing Secretly and the parable of the Mustard Seed. However, both interpretations are consistent with Jesus' teaching in Q.

If we adopt the first postion, the ironic contrast between the present arrival of the kingdom of God in Jesus' rejected ministry and the kingdom's future glorious consummation exists not only in the Q parables of the Mustard Seed and Leaven where the kingdom is likened to minute embryos which slowly but certainly produce magnificent results, but also in the Q portrait of Jesus at large where despite Jesus' claim that the kingdom has come (Lk. 11:20//Mt. 12:28), Jesus as the agent of the kingdom exists as a rejected figure considered "a gluttonous man, and a drunkard, a friend of tax-gatherers and sinners" (Lk. 7:34 par.), who has "no place to lay his head" (Lk. 9:58 par.), and whose miracles fail to bring about repentance in his homeland (Lk. 10:12-15 par.). Even more striking is the fact that in the face of contemporary expectations of the kingdom as a cataclysmic event, Q Lk. 16:16//Mt. 11:12, 13 describes the kingdom as an entity which suffers violence (Mt.) or force (Lk.).

However, if Mk. 4:3-9 is interpreted as Jesus' challenge to his followers to listen and to obey (position 2), the parable stands consistent with Jesus' contrast between the two foundations in Q Lk. 6:46-49//Mt. 7:24-27:

> Therefore everyone who hears these words of mine, and acts upon them, may be compared to a wise man, who built his house upon the rock. And the rain descended, and the floods came, and the winds blew, and burst against that house; and yet it did not fall, for it had been founded upon the rock. And everyone who hears these words of mine, and does not act upon them, will be like a foolish man, who built his house upon the sand. And the rain descended, and the floods came, and the winds blew, and burst against that house; and it fell, and great was its fall.

Here the wise man, like the good soil in Mk. 4:3-9 and its interpretation 4:13-20, withstands the elements which seek his destruction and so acts positively on the word which he receives. The same contrast exists between those who receive the word "and act upon them" (Q) / "and accept it, and bear fruit" (Mk.), and those who hear the word but do not act upon them and so "fall" Q / "fall away" and "become unfruitful" (Mk.).[83]

---

[83] Furthermore, the same wisdom motif (good soil produces good fruit) undergirds Mk. 4:3-9 as that expressed in Q Lk. 6:43//Mt. 7:17: "For there is no good tree which produces bad fruit; nor, on the other hand, a bad tree which produces good fruit."

B. The Explanation of the Sower and the Soils 4:13-20

Mk. 4:13-20 maintains the preceding parable's emphasis (4:3, 9) on successfully hearing the word (4:15, 16, 18, 20). The three bad soils—that beside the road, the rocky ground, and that among the thorns—correspond to listeners who have heard the word yet have neither retained it nor nurtured it. Some listeners are like the soil along the road in that they almost immediately surrender the word to Satan who comes to take it away. Others are like the rocky soil, who receive the word with joy and yet fall away when affliction or persecution arrives. And still others are like soil with thorn bushes, who allow anxiety or worry to choke out the word. Finally, those who hear the word and retain it are like the good soil: "they hear the word and accept it, and bear fruit, thirty, sixty, and a hundredfold" (4:20).

While the interpretation would have served as a warning to members of the early Church to be wary against falling away from the faith, Mk. 4:11, 12 demands that "the word" (ὁ λόγος 4:14, 15[2], 16, 17, 18, 19, 20) be taken in this context as "the mystery of the kingdom of God" i.e.—the good news about the presence of God's saving power in Jesus' ministry. Hence in 1:45 Mark describes the leper who has just been healed by Jesus: ὁ δὲ ἐξελθὼν ἤρξατο κηρύσσειν πολλὰ καὶ διαφημίζειν τὸν λόγον, and in 4:33, immediately following the explicit kingdom parables of the Seed Growing Secretly and the Mustard Seed, Mark writes: καὶ τοιαύταις παραβολαῖς πολλαῖς ἐλάλει αὐτοῖς τὸν λόγον καθὼς ἠδύναντο ἀκούειν. Contrast in 4:13-20 exists between those who reject Jesus' message of the good news of the kingdom (1:14, 15) and those who accept it, follow Jesus, and in turn bear fruit. At the earliest stage, for Mark and for Q, the fruit which the disciples bore was not the gospel of Jesus' death and resurrection (1 Cor. 15:3) but the advancement of Jesus' earthly ministry (Mk. 6:7-13; Lk. 10:2-11//Mt. 9:37, 38, 10:7f., 9-13, 16a): "And they went out and preached that men should repent. And they were casting out many demons and were anointing with oil many sick people and healing them (Mk. 6:13).

Mark's parable of the Sower and the Soils is consistent with the theological thrust of Jesus in Q not only in the parable of the Two Foundations cited above but also in the Lord's Prayer and in the extended section on earthly cares (Lk. 12:22-31//Mt. 6:25-33). In each passage Jesus compels his listeners to place trust exclusively in God as the provider both of earthly needs and eschatological salvation. The Lord's Prayer corresponds to the needs of listeners who have witnessed a falling away and ask how they can avoid the trap of Satan, persecution, and earthly cares. The prayer provides for the disciples a vehicle for focusing upon the sovereignty of God in beseeching God to consummate his kingdom, to provide for daily needs, and to deliver from temptation, or, if modern commentators are correct, to provide strength in order to prevent the yielding to temptation which leads to falling away.[84]

Likewise the worries of the world, the deceitfulness of riches, and the desires for other things which choke the word in Mk. 4:19 have Q counterparts in Lk. 12:22-31//Mt. 6:25-33, where Jesus similarly directs his listeners to the sovereignty of God by means of observations drawn from everyday life—the characteristic procedure of wisdom thought. Surely as God provides for the ravens and the lilies, so will he meet the needs of his people. As a result, Jesus commands his listeners not to be anxious (μέριμνα: Lk. 12:22, 25, 26 par.; cf. Mk. 4:19: καί αἱ μέριμναι τοῦ αἰῶνος καί ἡ ἀπάτη τοῦ πλούτου καί αἱ περὶ τὰ λοιπὰ ἐπιθυμίαι εἰσπορευόμεναι συμπνίγουσιν τὸν λόγον),[85] but to "seek the kingdom of God" (Lk. 12:31//Mt. 6:33). We see in this passage (Lk. 12:28//Mt. 6:30) an amazement on the part of Jesus at the listeners' lack of faith ("how much more will he clothe you, O men of little faith!"), which is similar to the end of Mk. 4 where Jesus appears amazed by his audiences' failure to take into account the power already demonstrated in Jesus' own ministry: "Why are you so timid? How is it that you have no faith?" (Mk. 4:40). The passages differ primarily as to the recipient of faith: in Q Lk. 12:2-32//Mt. 6:25-33 Jesus calls for faith in God, whereas Mk. 4:40 beckons for faith in Jesus himself. The same logic, however, underlies both: Jesus challenges his audience to base faith on things seen and heard and in turn to act appropriately in seeking the kingdom or accepting the word—the mystery of the kingdom.

Beyond these similarities we are wary of pressing for parallels for fear of obscuring the rich variety of Jesus' teaching in the synoptic gospels. However, our observations, we hope, have at least demonstrated that Jesus' teaching in Mark follows a similar pattern and heads in the same direction as does Jesus' teaching in Q. Variety yes, incompatibility no.

---

[84] J. Carmignac (*Recherches sur le 'Notre Père',* Paris: Letouzey & Ané [1969] 437-445) is followed by many.

[85] Cf. also Q Lk. 16:13//Mt. 6:24: "No servant can serve two masters; for either he will hate the one, and love the other, or else he will hold to one, and despise the other. You cannot serve God and mammon."

C.   Mk. 4:21-25[86]

Following the interpretation of the parable of Sower and the Soils and preceding the kingdom parables of the Seed Growing Secretly and the Mustard Seed, Mark presents five short sayings of Jesus which conform to the kingdom motifs that unify ch. 4: the call to see and hear (4:23, 24), the image of a future revealing of what was once or is presently hidden (4:21, 22), and the contrast between the insiders "those who have" and the outsiders "those who have not" (4:25).   In Mark's context, 4:21, 22 present the kingdom of God as a lamp under a bushel which (cf. 4:26-29, 30-32), despite its present hiddeness, will in the future fulfill its purpose and radiate light where all can see.   4:24, 25, following Jesus' commands to see and hear (vv. 23, 24a), present a challenge to Jesus' audience to accept his teaching about the kingdom. Those who have accepted Jesus' teaching on "the mystery of the kingdom" (4:11) will be given more understanding, while those who have rejected Jesus will receive all things in parables and even what they have will be taken away.[87]

For our purposes, the presence of these sayings in Mk. 4 demonstrates the consistency of Mark with Q in a number of aspects.   First, as sayings which make a point by reflecting on observations drawn from everyday life, these sayings by definition fit the classification of wisdom logia.[88]   They contain the blend of wisdom thought (reflection on past experience), apocalyptic (the motif of revelation), and prophecy (the call to hear in view of future blessing or judgment), which Q scholars claim as characteristic of Q.   Hence these sayings weaken W. Kelber's assertion that Mark and Q are incompatible in form.   And further, E. Boring's hypothesis that Mark is essentially an attempt to correct the oral tradition of early Christian prophecy seems odd in light of 4:24, which according to E. Käsemann fits the form of a "Sentence of Holy Law"[89]—one of the forms associated with early Christian prophecy.   Mark 4:21-25, according to recent form

---

[86] For extended treatment of Mk. 4:21-25 in comparison to its Q parallels in Lk. 11:33//Mt. 5:15, Lk. 12:2//Mt. 10:26, Lk. 6:38//Mt. 7:2, Lk. 19:26//Mt. 25:29 see: J. Dupont, "La Transmission des Paroles de Jésus sur la Lampe et la Mesure dans Marc 4,21-25 et dans la Tradition Q", *Logia*, 201-236. Dupont's thorough exegetical comparison is followed by the conclusion that Mk. 4:21-25 is coherent with the thought of Mk. 4:1-34. While the sayings unit in Mark is more recent than the scattered sayings in Q, segments of Mk. 4:25 and 4:22 appear more ancient than their counterparts in Q. Considering this, the hypothesis of one document's dependence upon the other is not convincing (235-36).

[87] Here we follow the interpretation of R.A. Guelich, *Mark* I, 236-237.

[88] These sayings are classified as wisdom sayings by the following: R. Bultmann, *History of the Synoptic Tradition*, 79-108; R. Pesch, *Marcus* I, 247f.; R.A. Guelich, *Mark* I, 227; J. Fitzmyer, *Luke* II, 957; Davies and Allison, *Matthew* I, 670.

[89] *New Testament Questions of Today*, 77.

critical studies, contains five aphoristic units—the form most commonly associated with oral tradition.[90]

Second, Mk. 4:21-25 demonstrate that Mark incorporated traditional sayings of Jesus without orienting those sayings to the preaching of the cross.[91] Why, then, should we be surprised at the lack of cross emphasis in Q when Mark, despite its passion narrative, does not kerygmatically transform traditional material?

Third, R. Pesch, K. G. Reploh, A.M. Ambrozic, G. Schneider, and R. Laufen identify these sayings as Mark's mission challenge to his community to make known in public the secret reign of God which began in Jesus' pre-Easter ministry.[92] If these scholars are correct, 4:21-25 testifies to the fact that mainstream early Christian preaching advanced Jesus not only as the figure who died to forgive sins, but also as the figure to whom man must unite in order to experience the hope of the future salvific blessings associated with the kingdom of God. And if the early Church combined faith in the death of Jesus with the hope of the consummation of God's kingdom, as it obviously did, there can be no doubt that the Q material would have been valued for its own content by the early Church.

---

[90] Four short collections of aphorisms exist in Mk.: 2:19-22; 4:21-25; 8:34b-38; 9:42-50. In total there are 44 aphorisms in Mark compared to 49 in Q. See David Aune, "Oral Tradition and the Aphorisms of Jesus", *Jesus and the Oral Gospel*, JSNTSS 64; Sheffield: JSOT Press (1991) 250-266. See also: J.D. Crossan, *In Fragments: The Aphorisms of Jesus*, San Francisco: Harper & Row (1983) 330-41; *idem, Sayings Parallels: A Workbook for the Jesus Tradition*, Philadelphia: Fortress Press (1986) 21-131.

[91] Among the following scholars exists the consensus that for Mark and his readers the consummation of the Kingdom was a future event which was unaffected by the cross and resurrection: W. Wrede, *The Messianic Secret,* ET London: James Clark (1971) 70-71; C.E.B. Cranfield, *Mark*, 164-65; J. Gnilka, *Markus* I, 181; R.A. Guelich, *Mark* I, 232; C.E. Carlston, *The Parables of the Triple Tradition*, Philadelphia: Fortress Press (1975) 155; J. Marcus, *The Mystery of the Kingdom of God*, Atlanta: Scholars Press (1986) 150-151.

[92] R. Pesch, *Marcus* I, 254: "Markus bezieht sie wie die vorangehenden Sprüche auf das Mysterium der Gottesherrschaft, das den Jüngern verborgen gegeben ist; sie sollen auf das Gehörte achten, an die Zukunft von Gottes Herrschaft glauben und diesen Glauben das Maß ihres missionarischen Engagements sein lassen. Das Maß, nach dem die Jünger gemessen werden, kann nur ihr Verhalten bei der Offenbarmachung und Verkündigung des Geheimnisses des Gottesreiches sein." So also R. Laufen, *Die Doppelüberlieferungen der Logienquelle*, 168: "Es ist die Aufgabe der Christen, das Geheimnis der Βασιλεία, das Evangelium von Jesus Christus als dem Bringer der Gottesherrschaft, allen Völkern bekannt zu machen." Similarly, A.M. Ambrozic, *The Hidden Kingdom*, 104; K.-G. Reploh, *Markus–Lehrer der Gemeinde*, Stuttgart: Katholisches Bibelwerk (1969) 70-71; G. Schneider, "Das Bildwort von der Lampe. Zur Traditionsgeschichte eines Jesus-Wortes", *ZNW* 61 (1970) 183-209.

Finally, Mk. 4:21, 22, 24, 25 have not only direct parallels in Matthew and Luke, but also Q variants three of which exist as doublets in Luke.[93] The fact that these parallels and variants exist in different contexts in each gospel suggests that at a very early stage the precise original meaning of these sayings was lost with the result that the Evangelists themselves were forced to grapple with their import. Hence the simplest answer to why the Gospel writers retained these difficult sayings at all was because they valued them as dominical. In turn we can apply the same reasoning to many of the difficult sayings in Q: the Church retained and passed on sayings not only because of their content but in some cases primarily because of the source of their origin.

D.   The Parable of the Seed Growing Secretly: Mk. 4:26-29

In the parable of the Seed Growing Secretly, Jesus explicitly likens the kingdom of God to a seed which after being planted grows on its own ($a\mathit{\dot{v}}\tau\acute{o}\mu\alpha\tau o\varsigma$) without human interference or understanding until the seed produces a fruit bearing plant which occasions a harvest. In keeping with the surrounding content of Mk. 4, the parable maintains the contrast between the enigmatic commencement of the kingdom of God in Jesus' ministry (that which is vulnerable, hidden, mysterious (vv. 3-8, 11-12, 14-20, 21, 22, 30) and the future consummation of the kingdom of God (that which will be revealed openly vv. 8, 20, 21, 22, 32). As the minute seed bears the blueprint for the future harvest, so does Jesus' humble ministry set in motion the process which will consummate God's rule. As continuity exists between the seed and the harvest, so the present manifestation of the kingdom in Jesus' ministry links to the future universal arrival of God's judgment and blessing.[94] In Mark's context, the parable consoles the listener that the kingdom has indeed arrived and the time has indeed been fulfilled (1:15), though not initially

---

[93] J. Fitzmyer, *Luke* I, 81. Mk. 4:21=Lk. 8:16; Q Lk. 11:33//Mt. 5:15; Mk. 4:22=Lk. 8:17; Q Lk.12:2//Mt. 10:26; Mk. 4:25 = Lk. 8:18; Q Lk. 19:26//Mt. 25:29. Mk. 4:24 has a Q parallel in Lk. 6:38//Mt. 7:2. Representative scholars attributing the Mt./Lk. parallels to Q: J. Fitzmyer, *Luke* I, 956; R. Laufen, *Die Doppelüberlieferungen der Logienquelle*, 165; I.H. Marshall, *Luke*, 487, 512, 708; Davies and Allison, *Matthew* I, 471, 670; R. Pesch, *Markus* I, 250f.; H. Schürmann, *Lukas* I, 363; S. Schulz, *Q–Die Spruchquelle*, 146, 474. The parallels, however, are complex: Lk. 12:2//Mt. 10:26 agrees decisively against Mk. 4:22. Lk. 11:33//Mt. 5:15 agree against Mk. 4:21 being declarative statements as opposed to Mark's question. Mt. 7:2 is closer to Mk. 4:24 than its supposed Q parallel (Lk. 6:38), and Mt. 25:29 agrees with Lk. against Mk. ($\pi\alpha\nu\tau\grave{\iota}$ $\tau\hat{\omega}$ $\check{\epsilon}\chi o\nu\tau\iota$ . . . $\delta\grave{\epsilon}$ $\tau o\hat{\upsilon}$ $\mu\grave{\eta}$ $\check{\epsilon}\chi o\nu\tau o\varsigma$), but also agrees with Mk. against Lk. ($\mathit{\dot{a}}\pi$ $a\mathit{\dot{v}}\tau o\hat{\upsilon}$). Thus, if using Q, Mt. has conflated his two sources.

[94] So A.M. Ambrozic, *The Hidden Kingdom*, 119: "Jesus is not merely affirming that the Kingdom is coming; no one in his audience had doubts about that. What Jesus is affirming is that his coming and activity are intimately linked with this glorious manifestation of the Kingdom in the future, that his ministry is the first step of its arrival."

in the way expected—i.e., by a cataclysmic or an apocalyptic end-event. The presence of the kingdom in Jesus' ministry, though disappointing in scale, verifies that God's purposes will be accomplished especially in regard to future salvation and judgment.[95]

The parable of the Seed Growing Secretly has no parallel in Matthew or Luke. However, its climaxing identification of the fulfilment of the kingdom as a harvest ($\theta\epsilon\rho\iota\sigma\mu\acute{o}\varsigma$) does have a counterpart in Q Lk. 10:2//Mt. 9:37b, 38, where Jesus commands his disciples to beseech the Lord of the harvest to send workers into his harvest because the harvest is great and the workers are few. At first glance it may appear that whereas in Mk. 4:29 the harvest focuses on judgment and is yet to come, in Q the harvest is a present undertaking with the focus on salvation. However, Lk. 10:2//Mt. 9:37b, 38 does not describe the arrival of the endtime.[96] The saying, rather, focuses awareness on the greatness of the task ($\acute{o}$ $\mu\grave{\epsilon}\nu$ $\theta\epsilon\rho\iota\sigma\mu\grave{o}\varsigma$ $\pi o\lambda\acute{u}\varsigma$)—the harvest has hardly begun much less been completed.[97] Furthermore, while the allusion to Joel 3:13 in Mk. 4:29 clarifies that that harvest refers to eschatological judgment, eschatological judgment is not totally out of view in the Q commissioning address where Jesus prophesies that it will be better for Sodom on the day of judgment than for those cities which reject his messengers (Lk. 10:12//Mt. 10:15). On the other hand, the kingdom of God for Mark, like Q, is a message of good news (1:15).[98] The parable of the Seed Growing Secretly is, then, in no way inconsistent with the Q material.

E. The Parable of the Mustard Seed

Mark's parable of the Mustard Seed 4:30-32, as we have studied in detail, differs in three aspects from its direct parallel in Q (Lk. 13:18-19//Mt. 13:31-32): (1) Mk. 4:30-32 is set in the present tense and thus technically represents a similitude as

---

[95] This interpretation is agreed upon by: W. Kelber, *The Kingdom in Mark*, 39, 41; A.M. Ambrozic, *The Hidden Kingdom*, 119; R. Pesch, *Markus* I, 262, 263; J. Gnilka, *Markus* I, 185; J. Jeremias, *The Parables of Jesus*, 152, 53; R.A. Guelich, *Mark* I, 244f.; V. Taylor, *Mark*, 266; J. Crossan, "The Seed Parables of Jesus", *JBL* 92 (1973) 265; R.T. France, *Divine Government*, 27; G.R. Beasley-Murray, *Jesus and the Kingdom of God*, 126, 127.

[96] So P. Hoffmann (*Studien zur Logienquelle*, 289-293) and S. Schulz (*Q-Die Spruchquelle*, 411).

[97] So I.H. Marshall, *Luke*, 416.

[98] In the OT judgment and salvation are flip sides of the same coin. In Joel 3:13 the harvest of judgment is followed in 3:18 by a statement of the eschatological blessings expected at the day of the Lord. So also in Isa. 27:12 where the harvest of judgment is followed by the trumpeting of salvation (27:13). In Ps. 126:5, 6 the harvest image applies to future blessing: "Those who sow in tears shall reap with joyful shouting. He who goes to and fro weeping, carrying his bag of seed, shall come again with a shout of joy, bringing his sheaves with him."

opposed to the Q version which being a literal parable exists in the past tense; (2) Mk. 4:31 goes beyond Q to emphasize the extreme smallness of the seed (μικρότερον ὂν πάντων τῶν σπερμάτων); and (3) Mark concludes with an allusion to Eze. 17:23 as opposed to the Q parable which concludes with an allusion to the Theodotion text of Dn. 4:12, 21. However, these distinctions appear immaterial to the parables' interpretations in light of the major features which the two versions have in common. Both compare the kingdom of God to a mustard seed. Both focus on the contrast between the kingdom's small beginning and its colossal consummation. Both follow the form of a double question. And both use different but conceptually compatible OT texts to accentuate hyperbolically the size of the mature mustard plant.[99]

As a result of these obvious parallels in thought, the parable of the Mustard Seed provides conclusive evidence that Mark and Q have in common the perception of the kingdom of God as a power which enters the world in a small hidden form and yet eventually matures into an immense visible show of sovereignty. For Mark the parable of the Mustard Seed coheres with the preceding seed parables of ch. 4 which describe the surprising presence of the kingdom in contrast to its future glory (4:3-8, 26-29). The parable further advances the image of the kingdom as a mystery (4:11, 12) which though presently unseen will be revealed (4:21, 22, 26-29). Like the parable of the Seed Growing Secretly, the parable of the Mustard Seed counters the listeners' failure to comprehend the presence of God's rule in Jesus' ministry despite the absence of an immediate show of cataclysmic apocalyptic power.

Implicit in the Mark and Q versions of the Mustard Seed parable, Mark's parable of the Seed Growing Secretly, and the Q parable of the leaven (Lk. 13:20-21//Mt. 13:33) is the correlation between the kingdom of God as it exists in Jesus' present small-scale ministry which encounters rejection, and the future invincible manifestation of the kingdom which will come at the eschaton. Herein lies part of the mystery of the kingdom of God—it has come but not as expected (4:11).

While in both Mark and Q Jesus heralds that the kingdom of God has come or at least has come near, in neither source does he claim that he has arrived to inflict the final judgment. Instead both Mark and Q present Jesus fulfilling the eschatological promises of Isa. 35:5 and 61:1—Jesus preaches good news to the poor, heals the sick, raises the dead. Against this background, the parables of the Seed Growing Secretly, the Mustard Seed, and the Leaven clarify that Jesus' preaching and healing ministry provides a foretaste of the good things which will

---

[99] G. Dautzenberg ("Mk. 4,1-34 als Belehrung über das Reich Gottes", *Biblische Zeitschrift* 34 [1990] 52) describes the Q version as a paradox as opposed to Mark's contrast. If so the distinction remains slight.

come. But those who reject Jesus' ministry in the present cannot expect to experience salvation at the eschaton. As the present binds to the future, so the future partially reflects the present.

The same scenario underlies the parable of the great supper which many commentators attribute to Q (Lk. 14:16-24//Mt. 22:1-10).[100] In this context the future members of the eschatological banquet are presented as an extension of the blessed people who accept and experience the saving power of Jesus' earthly ministry. When those invited do not accept the invitation, the poor, the maimed, the blind, and the lame are given a share in the eschatological banquet.[101] Jesus, then, foresees the future time of salvation as the composite fulfilment of Isa. 61, 35, and 25:6-12. The people who will enjoy the eschatological banquet on God's holy mountain (Isa. 25) will bear the same traits as those who receive the eschatological blessings of the Isaianic Herald of good news—they will be the poor, the blind, the deaf, the lame, the dumb. As in Q Lk. 7:22//Mt. 11:4f., Lk. 6:20//Mt. 5:3f., and the miracles of Mark, the eschatological blessing and judgment described in Q (Lk. 14:15-24//Mt. 22:1-10) fulfills Isa. 35:5f. and Isa. 61:1f., so that the future arrival of the kingdom correlates with its present manifestation in Jesus' ministry.

Multiple Markan and Q texts that hold in tension the present arrival of God's eschatological rule in Jesus' ministry with the future consummation of God's kingdom in universal glory make weak the foundation of hypotheses which are based upon the conjecture that the supposed Q community went through progressive stages of eschatological or apocalyptic expectation. Jesus' own ministry was the stimulus for present excitement (enthusiasm) and future expectation.

F. Jesus Stills the Storm (Mk. 4:35-41)

Mark 4 closes with a miracle story which describes Jesus performing an act of power which OT and Jewish texts reserve as the prerogative of God (Ps. 104:7; 107:23-31; Jonah 1; 2 Macc. 9:8). The story essentially makes the same point as Q Lk. 11:32//Mt. 12:41—"here is something greater than Jonah!"[102] The story's

---

[100] See J. Kloppenborg (*Q-Parallels*, 166) for an extensive list of scholars who attribute this passage to Q.

[101] καὶ τοὺς πτωχοὺς καὶ ἀναπείρους καὶ τυφλοὺς καὶ χωλοὺς εἰσάγαγε ὧδε (Lk. 14:21).

[102] So R. Pesch, *Markus* I, 272, 3: "Jesus handelt selbst, wie in der Jonaerzählung Gott handelt. . . . Der christliche Erzähler zeigt Jesus als den, der in Gottes Vollmacht handelt: Hier is mehr als Jona!"; R.A. Guelich, *Mark* I, 267:"the parallel with Jonah shows him to be greater than Jonah." Linguistic parallels between the Jonah story and Mk. 4:35-41 exist in κοπάζειν

contacts with Jonah 1 are striking: both Jesus and Jonah fall asleep during a life threatening storm, both awaken to cries of despair, both receive requests to calm a storm, and both occasion a response of fear when the sea is calmed (Jonah 1:16). However, Jesus appears greater than Jonah in that he follows God's call where Jonah disobeys, Jesus personally rebukes the winds while Jonah's shipmates pray to God for help, and Jesus' act produces the astonished response, "Who then is this, that even the wind and the sea obey him?," whereas Jonah's mates respond to the calm with fear in God (1:16). In performing an act which in the OT only God could do, Jesus again demonstrates that the kingdom of God is present in his own ministry. Yet the disciples, despite having been given the mysteries of the kingdom (4:11), still do not have eyes to see and so fail to make the connection. Again Jesus' dismay at the disciples' lack of faith correlates with Q, where Jesus pronounces woes when his works of power fail to engender repentance (Lk. 10:13//Mt. 11:21). Despite the miracles, the presence of God in Jesus remains a mystery (cf. Lk. 10:21, 22//Mt. 11:25-27).

Conclusion

The major motifs of Mark ch. 4 are consistent with the Q material. The kingdom of God in both Mark and Q is a mystery which challenges people to see and hear and to make a response to what is taking place in Jesus' ministry. In both Mark and Q the secret of the kingdom is inextricably bound to the person of Jesus. Those who accept Jesus' ministry acquire in advance the blessings of the kingdom of God, while those who refuse Jesus preclude themselves from the salvation which could be theirs and so make their own punitive judgment inevitable. As there are insiders and outsiders in Mk. 4, there are blessings and woes in Q. Furthermore, Mk. 4 and Q have in common images of growth which express the continuity between the present outpouring of the kingdom in Jesus' ministry and the future fulfilment of the kingdom at the eschaton. The events taking place in Jesus' ministry verify that God's rule is present in Jesus, though his audience in neither Mark nor Q could fully detect it or comprehend what it meant about Jesus himself.

VII. Seek the Kingdom of God!

In the Q sayings which we have analyzed, Jesus places absolute importance upon seeking the kingdom of God (Lk. 12:31//Mt. 6:33). The first phrase the disciples

---

(Mk. 4:39; Jonah 1:11, 12) and ἐφοβήθησαν φόβον μέγαν (Mk. 4:41; Jonah 1:10, 16). See Pesch, *Markus* I, 273.

are taught to pray "Father hallowed be your name, let your kingdom come" (Lk. 11:2//Mt. 6:9) characterizes this burden of Jesus' call to discipleship—man must place all hope in the Father's ability to save. Jesus explicitly prohibits indecisive obedience to God: "you are not able to serve God and mammon" (Lk. 16:13b//Mt. 6:24b). Jesus calls his disciples to the same singleness of purpose which he himself displayed in the temptation narrative (Lk. 4:1-13//Mt. 4:1-11). All hope resides in God's ability to provide for man's basic needs and ultimately for man's eschatological salvation (Lk. 12:22f.//Mt. 6:25f.). Thus Jesus commands his followers to forsake all but the barest necessities (Lk. 10:4-7//Mt. 10:9-13) and to advance his own ministry by healing the sick and proclaiming "the kingdom of God has come near to you" (Lk. 10:9//Mt. 10:7). Entrance into the kingdom is the ultimate blessing for those obedient to Jesus' call, while exclusion from the kingdom is the penalty for rejecting Jesus' ministry (Lk. 13:28, 29//Mt. 8:11, 12). Hence the listener's response to the kingdom of God in Jesus' ministry is *the* factor determining the individual's future salvation or damnation (cf. Lk. 12:8, 9//Mt. 10:32, 33).

In Mark Jesus' teaching about the kingdom of God has a similar emphasis. The presence of the kingdom of God in Jesus' ministry warrants a decisive response on the part of the listener: "the time is fulfilled, the kingdom of God has come near, *repent* and *believe* in the gospel" (1:15). Here Jesus' teaching commands a literal "change of mind" a laying aside of an old lifestyle and a new belief in the good news that the time is fulfilled and the kingdom of God has come near in Jesus' ministry.

A. Mk. 9:47, 48

As in Q, Jesus teaches his listeners in Mark to forsake all in view of the utter consequences of falling outside the the kingdom. Like Q Lk. 13:28, 29//Mt. 8:11, 12, Mk. 9:47 presents the eschatological division between those who will enter the kingdom of God and those who will be cast into Gehenna. In both Lk. 13:28, 29 par. and Mk. 9:47, eternal life is the reward for seeking the kingdom of God with unwavering singleness of purpose[103] (Lk. 13:28: ἐν τῇ βασιλείᾳ τοῦ θεοῦ / Mk. 9:47: εἰς τὴν βασιλείαν τοῦ θεοῦ), while the punishment for stumbling is perpetual anguish (Lk. 13:28 par.: ἐκεῖ ἔσται ὁ κλαυθμὸς καὶ ὁ βρυγμὸς τῶν ὀδόντων / Mk. 9:48; Isa. 66:24: ὅπου ὁ σκώληξ αὐτῶν οὐ τελευτᾷ καὶ τὸ πῦρ οὐ σβέννυται).

---

[103] εἰς τὴν βασιλείαν τοῦ θεοῦ completes and qualifies the phrase εἰς τὴν ζωήν which occurs in 9:43 and 45.

The fear of this future divide is the motivating factor for the only negative petition of the Lord's Prayer: "and lead us not into temptation." To enter into temptation is to stumble and to fall away from the saving benefits of the kingdom and hence into judgment. To enter temptation diametrically opposes seeking the kingdom. Thus in Q Jesus teaches his disciples what to fear: "fear the one who after death has the authority to cast into Gehenna" (Lk. 12:5//Mt. 10:28).

Common, then, to Mark[104] and Q is Jesus' command that all effort exclusively focus upon seeking God's rule now because the consequences of seeking or not seeking could not be more severe; they are the basis for future salvation and judgment. Surely it is significant that Jesus' description of eschatological salvation ($\dot{\epsilon}\nu$ $\tau\hat{\eta}$ $\beta\alpha\sigma\iota\lambda\epsilon\dot{\iota}\alpha$ $\tau o\hat{v}$ $\theta\epsilon o\hat{v}$) and eschatological damnation ($\epsilon\dot{\iota}\varsigma$ $\tau\dot{\eta}\nu$ $\gamma\dot{\epsilon}\epsilon\nu\nu\alpha\nu$) are exactly parallel in Mark and Q.[105]

B. Mk. 10:23, 24, 25

The dilemma of the rich man in Mk. 10:17-22 and Jesus' statements about the rich in Mk. 10:23-27 present the converse of the first beatitude in Q: "Blessed are the poor for theirs is the kingdom of God" (Lk. 6:20//Mt. 5:3).[106] Logically those who chase after earthly gain cannot simultaneously seek wholeheartedly the kingdom of God. The rich man while keeping the law has stumbled upon the anxieties of his age (Lk. 12:22//Mt. 6:25; Mk. 4:7, 19) and has failed to trust in the Father's ability to provide for his needs. As a result he refuses to follow Jesus' command that he sell his possessions, give to the poor, and follow Jesus. The rich man consciously chooses earthly treasure in preference to treasure in heaven.

---

[104] The majority of scholars accept Mk. 9:47, 48 as authentic tradition as a result of its Semitic syntax, its poetic form, and its similarity to other sayings of Jesus which focus on the gravity of judgment and entrance into the KG: V. Taylor, *Mark*, 411; C.E.B. Cranfield, *Mark*, 314; M. Black, *An Aramaic Approach to the Gospels and Acts*, 127f.; K. Beyer, *Semitische Syntax im Neuen Testament* I, Göttingen: Vandenhoeck & Ruprecht (1962) 78f.; R. Pesch, *Markus* II, 113, 116; J. Gnilka, *Markus* II, "daß Markus die Logien 9,42-50, deren Grundbestand auf Jesus zurückgeht, wiederum in einer mehr zersagten, weiterentwickelten Form überliefert hat" (67). A.M. Ambrozic (*The Hidden Kingdom*, 176) dissents, however, arguing that rabbinic parallels to 9:47 suggest the saying was originally taken over from Jewish materials, slightly reworded and placed on the lips of Jesus by early Christians. Ambrozic's argument, however, is not persuasive. The rabbinic sources he refers to (Strack-Billerbeck I, 302-303) are all dated significantly later than the time of Jesus and are in fact not parallels to Jesus' saying as they do not speak of the kingdom of God. What the rabbinic sources do suggest is that Jesus adopted a Jewish idiom popular in his day and applied it to his kingdom of God teaching.

[105] Heaven / Hell dualism occurs in one other place in Q (Lk. 10:15//Mt. 11:23) where the term $\dot{q}\delta\eta\varsigma$ is used.

[106] So J. Schlosser, *Le Règne de Dieu dans les Dits de Jésus*, Vol 2, 557: "Le logion qui déclare impossible l' entrée des riches dans la Basileia répond exactement au macarisme des pauvres, dont il représente en quelque sorte l'antithèse."

The rich man's failure to make the right decision and to seek foremost the kingdom of God compels Jesus to reflect on the plight of the rich in general as they respond to the requirements for entrance into eternal life (10:17). He remarks twice how difficult ($\delta \acute{v}\sigma\kappa o\lambda o\varsigma$) it is for the rich to enter the kingdom (10:23, 24) and qualifies that "it is easier for a camel to go through the eye of a needle than for a rich man to enter the kingdom of God" (10:25).

The rich man provides the negative contrast to obedient discipleship. He is unwilling to lay aside earthly provisions (Lk. 10:4f.//Mt. 10:9f.), and take up his cross (Q Lk. 14:25-27//Mt. 10:37, 38; Mk. 8:34),[107] but more importantly, he refuses to follow Jesus (cf. Mk. 1:17f., 20; 2:14) as the figure knowing the way to eternal life (10:17), the way into the kingdom of God, and the way to be saved (10:26). The Markan passage presupposes, then, that Jesus speaks with divine wisdom (cf. Mk. 6:2). Jesus knows the way to salvation.

The Markan passage is entirely consistent with the Q material:

Strive to enter by the narrow door; for many, I tell you, will seek to enter and will not be able. (Lk. 13:24//Mt. 7:13)

Some are last who will be first and some are first who will be last. (Lk. 13:30//Mt. 20:16; cf. Mk. 10:31)

No servant can serve two masters; for either he will hate the one, and love the other, or else he will hold to one, and despise the other. You cannot serve God and mammon. (Lk. 16:13//Mt. 6:24)

Sell your possessions and give to charity; make yourselves purses which do not wear out, an unfailing treasure in heaven, where no thief comes near, nor moth destroys. For where your treasure is, there will your heart be also. (Lk. 12:33, 34//Mt. 6:20, 21; cf. Mk. 10:21)

The unity of thought behind these Q sayings of Jesus and Mk. 10:17-27 is indisputable. The burden of Jesus' teaching about the kingdom of God and man's proper response to it focuses in Mark and Q upon man's obligation to lay aside all stumbling blocks and to seek the kingdom of God, the treasure in heaven, actively by following Jesus. To do otherwise is to reject God's gift of salvation.

Mk. 10:17-31 renders suspect the theory that at some point in time Mark and Q were in some fashion kerygmatically incompatible. The disciples' question in 10:26, "Then who can be saved," implies that if the rich man had laid aside everything and followed Jesus, he would have entered the kingdom of God (10:23, 24, 25), gained eternal life (10:17) and gained salvation. Like the Q material, this passage does not refer to Jesus' death on the cross. Yet Mark

---

[107] Mk. 10:21 was interpreted in this light as early as A ,W, f1.13, 𝔐 which interpolated $\alpha\rho\alpha\varsigma$ $\tau o v$ $\sigma\tau\alpha v\rho o v$ into the text.

obviously did not consider it to be contradictory to the passion narrative or else he would not have included it within his Gospel. Therefore, in light of these sayings of the Markan Jesus which deal specifically with salvation but do not mention the cross, there seems little basis for the special significance so often associated with the lack of passion emphasis in Q. Jesus' earthly ministry and his death both offered saving benefits according to the Gospel writers. That the Q material supports the one does not logically imply that it contradicts the other.

Furthermore, Jesus' command that the rich man lay aside his riches and follow questions the validity of the hypothetical Q community which scholars describe as a band of travelling ascetics who exclusively preached the teachings of the earthly Jesus. It is telling that in amazingly similar terms as those used to describe the Q group, J. Gnilka traces Mk. 10:23f. to a community expression: "Hinter dieser erweiterten Überlieferung steht eine asketisch geprägte Gemeinde, die das Armutsideal ernstnimmt."[108] What conclusions are we to draw? Do Mark and Q draw material from the same community tradition? Or do they draw material from two different but amazingly similar communities? Or did Mark create a story on the basis of material known to him from Q? Or do both Mark and Q independently draw from complementary traditions traceable to the historical Jesus? When no tangible historical or literary evidence can be found to support the existence of these theoretical communities, and when only Mk. 10:24a, 26 bear traces of Markan redaction,[109] only the last, in our opinion, is an acceptable option.

C. Mk. 12:34

"Seek the kingdom of God!" is again the focus of Jesus' answer to the scribe's question in Mk. 12:28f., "What is the first commandment of all?" In pronouncing the *Shemá* (Dt. 6:4, 5) as the greatest commandment, Jesus challenges the scribe to seek God's will above all else as Jesus did in his temptation experience in the wilderness, where at Satan's enticement, Jesus affirmed "You shall worship the Lord your God and serve him only" (Dt. 6:13; 10:20). Likewise the command to love God with heart, soul, mind, and strength correlates with the desired relationship with God which Jesus lays out in the Lord's Prayer: "Your kingdom Come, Your will be done." The focused emphasis on seeking God exclusively is the same.

For our purposes, it is important to observe that there exist only two explicit statements of Jesus in the Synoptic Gospels which speak of man's love of God—

---

[108] *Markus* II, 85.
[109] See J. Gnilka, *Markus* II, 84.

this one in Mark and the other in Q (Lk. 11:42//Mt. 23:23), where Jesus similarly places maximum priority on loving God at the expense of the Pharisees' traditions:

> But woe to you Pharisees! For you pay tithe of mint and rue and every kind of garden herb, and yet disregard *justice* and *the love of God*; but these are the things you should have done without neglecting the others.

Indeed, if we take justice ($\kappa\rho\iota\sigma\iota\varsigma$) here to refer to fair relations to other men, Lk. 11:42//Mt. 23:33 combines the same components of Mk. 12:29-31—the love of God and man. On the basis of the conceptual parallel, there appears to be little distinction between Jesus' liberal approach to the law in Mark and Q.[110]

While Jesus does not identify Lev. 19:18, "love your neighbor as yourself,"[111] as the second most important command in Q, he does command his disciples in an extended Q passage to love fellow man in a radical fashion (Lk. 6:27-38//Mt. 5:39b-42, 44-48; 7:1, 2, 12):

> But I say to you who hear, love your enemies, do good to those who hate you, bless those who curse you, pray for those who mistreat you. Whoever hits you on the cheek, offer him the other also; and whoever takes away your coat, do not withhold your shirt from him either. (Lk. 6:27-29//Mt. 5:44, 39b-41)

> And just as you desire men to do to you, do to them likewise. (Lk. 6:31//Mt. 7:12)

> And if you love those who love you, what credit is that to you? For even sinners love those who love them. (Lk. 6:32//Mt. 5:46)

> But love your enemies, and do good, and lend, expecting nothing in return; and your reward will be great, and you will be sons of the Most High; for He Himself is kind to ungrateful and evil men. (Lk. 6:35//Mt. 5:45)

> Be merciful, just as your Father is merciful. (Lk. 6:36//Mt. 5:48)

Jesus commands his disciples to love others, particularly enemies, in a manner commensurate with the love God has shown to them. The love which Jesus

---

[110] As opposed to the conservative adherence to tradition as outlined in Lk. 11:42 par.

[111] While the majority of scholars agree that the combination of Dt. 6:5 and Lev. 19:18 probably goes back to Jesus, not all agree that the story of the scribe's question is historical: G. Bornkamm, "Das Doppelgebot der Liebe", *Neutestamentliche Studien für Rudolf Bultmann zum siebzigsten Geburtstag*, BZNW 21 (1954) 85-93; R. Pesch, *Markus* II, 244f.; J. Gnilka, *Markus* II, 167f. G. Bornkamm is followed by many with the claim that this story had its original *Sitz* in the early Christian mission to the Hellenistic world, which had a plurality of gods. It is important to note, however, that the background of this passage is entirely Jewish while reminiscence to a Gentile mission is entirely lacking. To interpret Mk. 12 against the scenario of Acts 10:34 and Acts 17, as Bornkamm does (42, 43), is hardly a valid methodology. On the other hand, the positive description of the Scribe cuts against the grain of the synoptics where Scribes and Pharisees are generally seen in a negative light. Such reduces the likelihood of post-Easter origin.

commands in these Q sayings fully accords with the background of Mk. 12:29-31 in Lev. 19:17-18: "You shall not hate your fellow countryman in your heart" . . . "You shall not take vengeance, nor bear any grudge against the sons of your people, but you shall love your neighbor as yourself; I am the Lord."

The scribe, then, being in one mind with Jesus on the extreme importance of loving God and man is identified by Jesus as "not far from the kingdom of God." The love of God and the love of fellow man stand as prerogatives presupposed by Jesus as attributes characteristic of those who would be his disciples and who would enter the kingdom. It is important, however, that Jesus qualifies that the scribe is "not far from the kingdom." While he has not made the mistake of the rich man, he too has not followed Jesus.

In declaring that the scribe is not far from the kingdom of God, Jesus assumes supernatural knowledge as he does earlier in Mark where he assumes such knowledge in claiming that one must enter the kingdom as a child and without preoccupation with material affluence. As J. Gnilka notes, the authority which Jesus assumes in making such statements tacitly raises the questions of where Jesus gets his knowledge and who Jesus is, "Er bedarf der Brand—und Schlachtopher als weg zu Gott nicht mehr, sondern muß sich die Frage stellen, wer den dieser Jesus ist."[112] And as E. Lohmeyer observes, such authority could hardly have gone unnoticed: "Hier spricht Einer, der weiss wer dem Königreich Gottes nahe und wer ihm fern ist."[113] In this regard, Jesus is no less a mediator of supernatural knowledge in Mark, than he is in Lk. 10:21//Mt. 11:25 (Q), where he expresses knowledge of those to whom God has given "these things." In Mark and in Q Jesus expresses knowledge of the advent of the kingdom and he identifies specifically who will and who will not be members of the kingdom. As in Lk. 10:21, 22//Mt. 11:25-27, such knowledge begs the question of Jesus' identity, though Mark in this instance leaves implicit the significance of Jesus' knowledge. Yet, because Mk. 1:1 is presupposed throughout the second Gospel, there can be no doubt that in Mark Jesus' knowledge is commensurate with Jesus' sonship, as it is in Lk. 10:22//Mt. 11:26, 27.[114]

---

[112] *Markus* II, 167.

[113] *Markus*, 260.

[114] K. Berger (*Die Gesetzeauslegung Jesu*, WMANT 40, Tiel I; Neukirchen: Neukirchener Verlag, 1972, 177-92) argues that Mk. 12:28-34 is to be understood against a Wisdom background (Wisdom of Solomon 2:13, 18; 5:4f; 6:17b, 18a; Proverbs 8:17, 21; 28:4; Psalms 119; Daniel 4:27), so that the scribe here is seeking after the wisdom which Jesus mediates and which is near in the KG: "Wer diese Weisheit von Jesus empfängt, ist nicht fern vom Reiche Gottes" (187). Adherence to Jesus' teaching is the measure for nearness to the KG and the criterion for belonging to the Jewish-Christian mission. While such an interpretation of Mk. 12:34 would further unify the thought behind Mk. and Q, Berger's argument is not convincing as σοφία is not mentioned in Mk. 12:28-34 and there is no evidence to suggest that Jesus here is

Conclusion

The kingdom of God sayings in Mk. 9:47, 10:23, 24, 25, and 12:34 compare favorably to Jesus' emphasis in Q Lk. 12:31//Mt. 6:33; Lk. 11:2-4//Mt. 6:9-13, where man's first priority is to seek to obey the will of God. Further, Mk. 9:47; 10:23-25 and Q Lk. 13:28, 29//Mt. 8:11, 12 have in common Jesus' identification of the kingdom of God as the ultimate blessing for those who do earnestly seek first God's rule and who respond positively to Jesus' ministry. On the other hand, the two also have in common Jesus' warning that the penalty for deviating from God's will, specifically by refusing to follow Jesus, is exclusion from the kingdom. Agreement between Mark and Q on these crucial themes renders implausible the hypothesis that originally the two were kerygmatically incompatible.

VIII. Jesus and the Future

The seed parables have shown that as in Q, so also in Mark Jesus anticipates a future manifestation of the kingdom of God which is to be characterized by power and visibility. In our study of the two remaining Markan kingdom of God sayings which orient towards the future (9:1; 14:25), we intend to demonstrate that *Mark is eschatologically consistent with the Q material.* Furthermore, we hope to show that the contexts of these sayings argue for the consistency of Q with Mark's passion emphasis.

A. Mk. 9:1

Mk. 9:1 is an isolated logion which provides a transition between a string of sayings which focus on discipleship (8:34b-38) and Mark's account of the transfiguration (9:2-8). In form the saying bears the traits of a prophetic oracle ($Aμὴν \ λέγω \ ὑμῖν$ + future proclamation)[115]—a fact which severely damages E.

---

referring to a wisdom oriented version of the Shema. Berger's conclusions, though, do show that Jesus' teaching in Mark is open to the same misunderstanding as is his teaching in Q. Scholars have thus been able to interpret Mark against the same wisdom background that others have claimed as unique to Q. Cf. Gerhard Ringshausen, "Die Kinder der Weisheit. Zur Auslegung von Mk. 10,13-16 par", *ZNTW* 77 (1-2, 1986) 34-63.

[115] G. Bornkamm ("Die Verzögerung der Parousie", *Geschichte und Glaube: Erster Teil: Gesammelte Aufsätze* III, Müchen: Kaiser, 1968, 46-55, esp. 48), and E. Grässer (*Das Problem der Parousieverzögerung in den synoptischen Evangelien und in der Apostelgeschichte*, Berlin: Topelmann, 1957, 133-36) argue that Mk. 9:1 is an early Christian oracle pronounced in the name of the exalted Jesus.

Boring's claim that Mark was written to correct prophetic Q. The string of sayings 8:34-9:1 proves, as did 4:21-25, that Mark has no aversion to sayings material.

The explicit suffering Son of Man saying which initiates this section of Mark (8:31) should activate a movement of thought which strikingly deviates from the contours of Q, if indeed Mark and Q were originally incompatible in their responses to Jesus. However, the opposite is true. Mark incorporates sayings, two of which have direct parallels in Q, which express Jesus' command that his disciples share the path of suffering which Jesus himself experienced during his ministry. With 8:31 fresh on the readers mind, Mk. 8:34b qualifies that Jesus' disciples must follow the pattern of suffering lived by Jesus: "If anyone desires to come after me, let him deny himself, and take up his cross, and follow me." The call to suffering seemingly stands in sharp contrast to the authoritative form of discipleship displayed in Mk. 6:7-13, where the twelve receive authority to cast out demons, heal the sick, and preach the message of repentance. In both cases, however, the disciples are called to emulate Jesus.

The same tension between authority and suffering exists in the Q call to discipleship. Jesus commissions his disciples to "heal the sick" and proclaim "the kingdom of God has come near" (Lk. 10:9//Mt. 10:7), but he also prepares his disciples for the rejection which they will inevitably face: "but whatever city you enter and they do not receive you, go out into its streets and say, 'even the dust of your city which clings to our feet, we wipe off in protest against you' " (Lk. 10:11//Mt. 10:14). Ironically, rejection and suffering, not power, are the direct results of proclaiming the authority of Jesus: "Blessed are you when men hate you, and ostracize you, and cast insults at you, and spurn your name as evil, for the sake of the Son of Man" (Lk. 6:22//Mt. 5:11). Hence the call to discipleship in Q is consistent with that in Mark as is proven by the variant call to take up the cross in Lk. 14:27//Mt. 10:38: "Whoever does not carry his own cross and come after me cannot be my disciple."

Mk. 8:38, which immediately precedes the kingdom of God saying in 9:1, likewise has affinity to the Q material in general and a variant parallel in Q (Lk. 12:8, 9//Mt. 10:32, 33). Like the woes in Q (Lk. 11:37-52 par.), Mk. 8:38 is essentially a statement of judgment registered against the present "adulterous and sinful generation" which has rejected Jesus and his call to repent and receive the gospel (1:15). As in Q Lk. 12:8, 9//Mt. 10:32, 33, this saying correlates this generation's future salvation or judgment with its present acceptance or rejection of Jesus and his ministry. Like the parables of the mustard seed and leaven, here are evident the present humility and the future glory which characterize God's rule through Jesus. The rejected figure of Jesus corresponds ironically to the exalted Son of Man just as the present minuscule arrival of the kingdom of God corresponds to the future consummation of the kingdom in glory. Mk. 8:38, therefore, and its Q parallel assert that the way of suffering, i.e., following Jesus, is the way to vindication and eschatological salvation.

Against the context of the verses which have proceeded, Mk. 9:1[116] is a statement of consolation and comfort to the disciples that their suffering is not in vain—some of them at least "will not taste death until they see the kingdom of God after it has come with power." For the majority of scholars, this saying clearly refers to the parousia.[117] The qualification of the kingdom's coming "with power" coupled with its proximity to 8:38 which refers to the coming of the Son of Man seems to make the parousia the natural meaning of the kingdom. The phrase "some of those standing here" apparently indicates the parousia's delay.

Accepting this meaning, G.R. Beasley-Murray and Anton Vögtle argue that 9:1, being relevant to Mark's day, is a community modification of the dominical saying in 13:30. The basis for this conclusion is the conviction that Mk. 13:30 adheres more closely than 9:1 to the overall message of Jesus represented by sayings such as Lk. 11:51//Mt. 23:36 which express extreme urgency in view of the coming judgment.[118]

Internal evidence, however, does not suggest the secondary creation of Mk. 9:1. The likelihood that the saying was an originally isolated logion, its $\dot{\alpha}\mu\dot{\eta}\nu$ $\lambda\acute{\epsilon}\gamma\omega$ $\dot{\nu}\mu\hat{\imath}\nu$ formulation, the Jewish expression "shall not taste death," the Semitic phrase $o\dot{\nu}$ $\mu\acute{\eta}$ ... $\ddot{\epsilon}\omega\varsigma$, the fact that the phrase $\ddot{\epsilon}\omega\varsigma$ $\ddot{\alpha}\nu$ $\ddot{\iota}\delta\omega\sigma\iota\nu$ $\tau\dot{\eta}\nu$ $\beta\alpha\sigma\iota\lambda\epsilon\dot{\iota}\alpha\nu$ $\tau o\hat{\nu}$ $\theta\epsilon o\hat{\nu}$ is a hapaxlegomenon in the NT, and the sheer difficulty of the saying all point to an early origin.[119] It is unclear how 9:1 is any less urgent than 13:30.

In addition there is no certainty that the kingdom's coming with power refers to the parousia. The kingdom of God in Jesus' teaching is a dynamic term which refers to the eschatological manifestation of God's power in a variety of ways—the defeat of Satan, the healing of the sick, the eschatological banquet. Hence it is not outside the realm of possibility that the coming of the kingdom of God "in power"

---

[116] For extended treatment of the variety of interpretations of this saying see: A.M. Ambrozic, *The Hidden Kingdom*, 203-240; K. Brower, "Mark 9:1 Seeing the Kingdom in Power", *JSNT* 6 (1980) 17-41; G.R. Beasley-Murray, *Jesus and the Kingdom of God*, 187-193. For the history of the saying's interpretation see M. Künzi, *Das Naherwartungslogion Markus 9.1 par.*, BGBE 21; Tübingen: J.C.B. Mohr [Paul Siebeck], 1977.

[117] M. Künzi, *ibid.*, 120f., lists the majority of contemporary scholars who hold this position.

[118] G.R. Beasley-Murray, *Jesus and the Kingdom of God*, 192-93; A. Vögtle, "Exegetische Erwägungen über das Wissen und Selbstbewußtsein Jesu", *Gott in Welt*, FS K. Rahner; Freiburg: Herder (1964) 644.

[119] See R. Pesch, *Markus* II, 66-67; *Strack-Billerbeck* I, 751f.; J. Behm, *TDNT* I, 675-7; K. Beyer, *Semitische Syntax im Neuen Testament* I, 132f.; Moulton, Howard, and Turner, *Grammar of New Testament Greek* I, 187-192. For an extensive list of scholars claiming the authenticity of Mk. 9:1, see A.M. Ambrozic, *The Hidden Kingdom*, 215 n. 60.

could be referring to a subsequent event or sequence of events in Jesus' ministry such as the crucifixion or the resurrection,[120] or to an event subsequent to the resurrection such as Pentecost or the destruction of Jerusalem, as many have speculated. If referring to Jesus' death and resurrection, 9:1 completes the line of thought begun in 8:31: "the Son of Man must suffer many things . . . be killed . . . and after three days rise again."[121]

Another possibility is that the saying refers to a visionary experience on the part of those who will not taste death, because 9:1 speaks of "seeing the kingdom of God" as opposed to physically experiencing the world's cataclysmic end. This possibility is attractive if Mk. 8:38 refers to the enthronement of the Son of Man as opposed to his parousia as R.T. France argues.[122] In this case the kingdom's coming in power may refer to the transfiguration which immediately follows 9:1 or to an experience such as occurs in Acts 7:56, where literally before tasting death Stephen sees "the heavens opened up and the Son of Man standing at the right hand of God"—a vision of the Son of Man's enthronement.

We cannot ascribe the coming of the kingdom in 9:1 to a definite historical reference, because it was originally an isolated logion open to a variety of possible interpretations. Whether an explicit prediction of the parousia or not, Mk. 9:1, we believe, represents one of the many veiled and mysterious sayings of Jesus which—similar to Jesus' parables and miracles—motivates, through seemingly radical speech, thought on the part of the listener as to the mystery of the kingdom of God (Mk. 4:11) and to Jesus' identity as the one who speaks authoritatively about the kingdom (cf. Mk. 13:2; 14:58; 15:29). Who is it that can predict the coming of the kingdom of God with power?

The thrust of Mk. 9:1 is consistent with the Q material. The longing to see the kingdom of God recalls the Lord's Prayer (Lk. 11:2//Mt. 6:10) and the indefinite claim for the future likens to that of Lk. 13:35//Mt. 23:39: "I say to you, you shall not see me until the time comes when you say, Blessed is he who comes in the name of the Lord." While Matthew and Luke saw this saying fulfilled in the

---

[120] So H. Giesen ("Mk. 9.1 – ein Wort Jesu über die nahe Parousie?", *TTZ* 92, 1983, 134-48) who argues that Mk. 9.1 coheres with the inside/outside motif in Mk. 1:14,15 and 4:11 which do not refer to the parousia. 9:1, he argues, presupposes the resurrection as a result of its preceding verse (8:38) which is post-resurrection in function. "In power" compares to the same phrase in Ro. 1:4 which refers to the resurrection. And further, if the parousia were in view, the present participle "coming" would be used in 9.1 as opposed to the perfect "has come" (135, 139, 146).

[121] So K. Brower, "Mark 9:1 Seeing the Kingdom in Power", *JSNT* 6 (1980) 40: "Mk. sees the whole sequence of death/resurrection/exaltation/parousia as part of a continuous whole, inextricably bound up with the person of Jesus. In each of these facets of the same whole, there is to be seen the kingdom in power."

[122] *Divine Government*, 75.

triumphal entry to Jerusalem, in Q it occurs in the context of judgment and refers "to the final consummation when the promise of the coming of the Messiah is fulfilled."[123] We cannot be certain how this saying would have been understood by Jesus' audience, but like Mk. 9:1 it certainly would have drawn a sharp reaction from those listening. In addition to these material parallels to Mk. 9:1, H. Schürmann has argued persuasively that Mt. 10:23 should be classified a Q logion: "But whenever they persecute you in this city, flee to the next; for truly I say to you, you shall not finish going through the cities of Israel, until the Son of Man comes."[124] If Schürmann's conjecture is correct, there is in Q a saying which follows a similar structure to Mk. 9:1 and which similarly informs the disciples of what will not happen until the Son of Man/kingdom of God comes.[125] Both express comfort to disciples experiencing rejection.

B. The Parousia: Mark 13 and the Q Apocalypse

There is little doubt that Mk. 13 has in view the final judgment. For even if the signs spoken of are identified with the destruction of Jerusalem in AD 70, it seems extremely difficult to remove the endtime significance of Mk. 13:10, 19, 25, 26, 27. V. 27, "he will send forth the angels, and will gather together his elect from the four winds, from the farthest end of the earth, to the farthest end of heaven," verifies that the Son of Man saying in v. 26 refers to the parousia.

In Mark there are three Son of Man sayings which could possibly refer to the parousia: 8:38; 13:26; 14:62. Common to each saying is dependence upon Dn. 7:13, 14, the emphasis of judgment, and the temporally indefinite prophecy of a

---

[123] I.H. Marshall, *Luke*, 577.

[124] *Traditionsgeschichtliche Untersuchungen zu den Synoptischen Evangelien*, 150-55. Schürmann argues: (a) that while it is hard to perceive Matthew creating this saying it is conceivable that he incorporated it as respected tradition; (b) Mt. could have found Lk. 12:11f.//Mt. 10:19 + Mt. 10:23 combined in Q as the content of 10:23 connects with the commissioning address; (c) Lk. 12:11f. and Mt. 10:23 are comfort words *"Trostworte"*; (d) Mt. 10:23 conforms by stitchword "Son of Man" with Lk. 11:10, 8f.; (e) Mt. 10:23 compares favorably to Q Lk. 6:23//Mt. 5:11; (f) Mt. 10:23 speaks of the cities of Israel–so also Lk. 11:12f., and (g), Luke would have omitted 10:23 because the cities of Israel were no longer the focus of his church's mission (p. 154). In this conjecture, Schürmann agrees with H.E. Tödt, *The Son of Man in the Synoptic Tradition*, 47-48; R. Schnackenburg, *God's Rule and Kingdom*, 204; and A. Polag, *Christologie der Logienquelle*, 4.

[125] Mt. 10:23, like Mk. 9:1, has generally been regarded as referring to the parousia. However R.T. France (*Matthew*, 184) argues: "The Son of Man comes is an echo of the language of Daniel 7:13, which does not speak of the 'son of man' coming to earth, but rather coming to God to receive authority, and Jesus' frequent uses of such language show that he applied it to his own future glory in times and situations varying from his vindication after the resurrection to the final judgment." It is apparent that however one interprets Mt. 10:23 and Mk. 9:1, the two are consistent with one another.

future revelation of the Son of Man. Each aspect has a parallel in Q. While Lk. 17:24//Mt. 24:27 contains a likely allusion to Dn. 7:13,[126] a certain reference to Dn. 7:13 occurs in Lk. 12:40//Mt. 24:44.[127] The comparison of the coming of the Son of Man to Jonah in Lk. 11:30//Mt. 12:40 and to Noah in Lk. 17:26//Mt. 24:37 clearly qualifies that the day of the Son of Man will be a day of judgment. And while Lk. 17:24//Mt. 24:27 indicates that the Son of Man will come as stars falling from the sky, Lk. 12:40//Mt. 24:44 parallels Mk. 13:32, 33 in stating explicitly that "the Son of Man is coming at an hour that you do not expect." We fail to see any contradiction between the Markan and Q sayings in regard to the imminence or delay of the parousia.

The fact that Q contains sayings which anticipate the return of the Son of Man Jesus implies the Q redactor's conviction of Jesus' death and resurrection. There is no extant tradition that Jesus ascended directly into heaven after the pattern of Enoch.

In addition to the compatibility of the Mark and Q parousia sayings, Q is entirely consistent with Mk. 13.[128] While it has been said that the so-called Q apocalypse (Lk. 17:22-24, 26-35//Mt. 24:26-28, 37-39, 17, 18; 10:39; 24:40, 41) has an aversion for the signs which characterize Mk. 13, it must be noted that the basis for this claim is a Q saying, "This generation is a wicked generation; it seeks for a sign, and yet no sign shall be given to it but the sign of Jonah" (Lk. 11:29//Mt. 12:39), which has a direct counterpart in Mk. 8:12. However, Mk. 8:12 differs from the Q version by qualifying that *no sign* at all will be given to this generation. On the other hand, Jesus does, in fact, offer signs in the Q apocalypse of what the day of the Son of Man will be like: it will be like lightning, it will be like the days of Noah, it will be like the days of Lot: "There will be two men in bed; one will be taken, and the other will be left" (17:34//24:40).[129] In both Mark

---

[126] So G. Vermes, "Appendix E" in M. Black, *An Aramaic Approach to the Gospels and Acts*, 321-328.

[127] So M. Casey, *The Son of Man*, 190: "Matt. 24:44//Lk. 12:40 is a Q saying containing the collocation of 'Son of Man' and 'coming' which is a sign of the influence of Dan. 7:13. The event referred to is clearly the parousia of Jesus. The sentence does not contain any features that make it unacceptable. The last three words constitute a brief quotation from Dan. 7:13, and for this reason the reference to this text seems clear enough to be satisfactory and the use of בר אנש is sound Aramaic."

[128] So G.R. Beasley-Murray, *Jesus and the Future*, London: Macmillan (1954) 230-231: "The views of the two writers are not to be opposed, as has been the fashion so long: in respect of details they are complementary; and fundamentally they are united."

[129] *Pace* J. Jeremias, *New Testament Theology*, 124: "Thus the two synoptic apocalypses have quite different themes. In Mark 13 all the emphasis is on the preliminary signs; in Luke 17.20-37 it is on the suddenness of the end. . . . It is beyond question that the theme of Lk. 17.20-37 is a nucleus of the proclamation of Jesus, whereas Mark 13 is a theme that belongs to the early church."

and Q, therefore, Jesus does in fact offer signs while resisting his adversaries who attempt to provoke him into performing miracles spontaneously for improper reasons. The presence or absence of signs is a difficult criterion upon which to build a dichotomy between Mark and Q.

Q and Mark 13 have in common Jesus' warning that his disciples not be misled in the final days (Mk. 13:5-7; Lk. 17:23//Mt. 24:26), apocalyptic orientation, the identification of the parousia as a time of eschatological judgment, the call to vigilance (Mk. 13:33-37; Lk. 17:24//Mt. 24:27), eschatological warning to "this generation" (Mk. 13:30; Lk. 11:29-32, 50-51//Mt. 12:39, 41-42; 16:4; 23:36), the woe form (Mk. 13:17; Q passim), the motif of the ingathering of God's elect on the eschatological day (Mk. 13:27; Lk. 13:28, 29//Mt. 8:11, 12), and both explicitly refrain from projecting a specific date for the parousia. Neither alludes to Jesus' death and resurrection.[130] Hence, if Mark is a reliable foil to Q, we have little evidence that the Q community advanced an eschatology which was uniquely their own. The material parallels between Mark and Q suggest dependence upon a common tradition, and the burden of weight rests upon those who would discredit that tradition as dominical.[131]

---

[130] *Contra* S. Schulz, "Mark's Significance for the Theology of Early Christianity", *The Interpretation of Mark*, IRTh. 7, London: SPCK, 158-167: "Mark 1 begins with the Baptist and Mark 13 closes with the parousia of the Son of Man, but this Q catechism framework has been mutilated beyond recognition by Mark. He not only includes between these two points the mass of controversy material and Hellenistic miracle stories which Q has willfully negated, but has added to ch. 13 the dogmatic conclusion of the Aramaic speaking early church, the passion narrative -i.e., the passion kerygma of Hellenistic Christianity" (165). We, however, fail to see how Q has negated Jesus' miracles or his rejection by the Jewish leaders. Neither Mark 13 nor Q Lk. 17 par. have anything to do with Jesus' passion experience.

[131] S. Schulz (*Q - Die Spruchquelle*, 282-83) argues that the Q-apocalypse in Lk. 17 par. is the handiwork of the Hellenistic-Jewish Q community as a result of: (1) its use of the LXX; (2) the call to alertness which presupposes the delay of the parousia; (3) the mixture of kerygma with apocalyptic thought; (4) the uniqueness of the form (*Gattung*) apocalyptic prophecy to this part of Q; (5) the wisdom interpretation of the OT which displays an advanced layer in Q; (6) difference to the oldest Q material which speaks only of the judgment function of the Son of Man whereas in Lk. 17 the endtime is thematized; (7) multiple Semitisms which display Jewish origin; and (8), the fact of similarity with Mark which suggests late origin. Thus, according to Schulz, the Q-apocalypse appeared in a late layer of Q in reaction to the Markan tradition. However, Schulz's reasoning reflects a desperate attempt to make this section of Q congenial to a guiding presupposition that Q represents a distinctly different tradition, a distinctly different kerygmatic recourse upon Jesus, and a distinctly different community orientation (p. 5). Allusive use of the LXX may simply reflect the translator's preferred OT text. The call to alertness hardly represents a late awareness of the delay. Wisdom, prophecy, the KG, the Son of Man, and judgment are all subjects and modes of thought traceable to the book of Daniel and clearly congenial to the apocalyptic thought which was in the air during Jesus' day. Multiple Semitisms (M. Black, *Aramaic Approach to the Gospels and Acts*, 41, 91; K. Beyer, *Semitische Syntax im Neuen Testament* I, 96, 237) raise the likelihood of dominical origin as does congeniality with the book of Mark. Hence the dominical origin of the substance of this material is advocated by: I.H.

IX. Mk. 14:25:[132] Mark, Q, Jesus' Death
and the Kingdom of God

The content of Mark's final dominical kingdom of God saying underscores the continuity between Jesus' proclamation of the nearness of the kingdom of God (1:15), and the anticipation of Jesus' death which pervades Jesus' perspective as he approaches Jerusalem and prepares for his crucifixion.[133] Mk. 14:25 clarifies that the preaching of the kingdom of God and the preaching of Jesus' death are not two contradictory expressions of God's means of salvation, but rather two phases of Jesus' ministry whose unifying purpose was to bring mankind into saving covenant with God. The fact that Q contains material stemming from the first phase of Jesus' ministry does not suggest that it contradicts other sources which focus on Jesus' death and resurrection, but rather Q correlates with that later material as both phases adhere to the same whole.

In Mark, as in Q, Jesus appears on the scene with the intention of bringing the Jewish nation into saving fellowship with God. As we have shown, in both sources Jesus heralds the message of Good News which recalls the eschatological blessings consummate with the coming of God. Jesus offers salvation. In Mark and Q, however, Jesus' message and his eschatological works empowered by the Spirit are sharply rejected by the people best equipped to comprehend his message—Jewish leaders trained in the scriptures. Hence it is easy to see how the rejection of Jesus' Galilean ministry in Q and in the first part of Mark paves the way for Jesus' ultimate death in Jerusalem.

Mk. 14:25 distinguishes three primary aspects in which Jesus' death completes what his Galilean ministry began. In each aspect Q is consistent with Mark.

First, Mk. 14:25 is set in the context of Jesus' table fellowship with his disciples. The meal which takes place in the days immediately preceding Jesus'

Marshall, *Luke*, 657; J. Jeremias, *New Testament Theology*, 124; and R. Schnackenburg, *Schriften zum Neuen Testament*, München: Kösel (1971) 220-243.

[132] The authenticity of Mk. 14:25 is supported by its multiple Semitisms (Jeremias counts seven; *The Eucharistic Words of Jesus*, 182-184), the typically Jewish ideas contained in the saying, the multiple attestation of the saying in Mt. 26:29 and Lk. 22:16,18, and the multiple attestation of the eschatological banquet image in the teaching of Jesus (Lk. 13:29//Mt. 8:11; Lk. 14:15-24//Mt. 22:2-8; Mt. 22:9-13; 25:10; Lk. 22:29). Hence the vast majority of scholars classify Mk. 14:25 as authentic. See A.M. Ambrozic, *The Hidden Kingdom*, 196 n. 71 for an extensive list of supporting scholars.

[133] So H. Merklein, *Die Gottesherrschaft als Handlungsprinzip*, 154: "Positiv bringt das Wort nur zum Ausdruck, daß Jesus auch im Angesicht des zu erwartenden Todes an der Geltung seiner Basileia-Ansage festhält, indem er darauf hinweist, daß er den Wein, den er von jetzt an nicht mehr trinken kann, neu trinken wird in der Basileia."

death on the cross preserves the design which characterized Jesus' first meals with sinners and tax-collectors in Galilee. As Jesus' meals with tax-collectors and sinners in Mk. 2:15,16 and Q Lk. 7:34//Mt. 11:19 anticipated future communion with God at the eschatological feast, so also at the last supper Jesus looks beyond his death to the time of vindication, when "I drink it new in the kingdom of God."

Second, the image in Mk. 14:25 of the kingdom of God as an eschatological feast is coherent with the portrait of the kingdom which Jesus prophesies in Q (Lk. 13:29//Mt. 8:11; Lk. 14:15-24//Mt. 22:2-8) where Jesus forecasts that his opponents will be cast out while others "will come from east and west, and from north and south, and will recline at the table in the kingdom of God." Hence at the close of his ministry, the focus of Jesus' hope remains the salvation to be experienced in God's eschatological dominion—the same hope that characterized the early phase of his earthly ministry.

And third, the purpose of Jesus' death remains the same as the original purpose of his earthly ministry—to bring man into saving covenant with God (Jer. 31:31).[134] His blood is the blood of the covenant which is poured out for many. The covenantal relationship with God is the same as that envisioned by Jesus in his lament in Lk. 13:34b//Mt. 23:37b: "How often I wanted to gather your children together, just as a hen gathers her brood under her wings, and you would not have it." Because of Jesus' rejection by his generation in Q and in the Galilean section of Mark, his death is required as the means of establishing covenant with God. As table fellowship with Jesus gave sinners a preview of God's saving grace, and as obedient discipleship coalesced with advancing Jesus' preaching and healing ministry, so now identification with Jesus' death brings Jesus' disciples into a covenant relationship which offers to the disciples the hope of fellowship with God at the eschatological banquet through the forgiveness of sins. The purpose of the forgiveness of sin is the exact same as the purpose of Jesus' entire ministry—to defeat Satan and to enable the unfortunate, the poor, the sick and sinners, to align themselves with the eschatological saving sovereignty of God and to share in the feast Jesus envisions in Mk. 14:25b.

---

[134] See R. Schnackenburg's chapter "The Reign of God and Jesus' Community" in *God's Rule and Kingdom*, 215-256: "Eschatological salvation can never be dissociated from the people of God and the community of God belongs necessarily to the kingdom of God. The future achievement of salvation is to be the consummation of all God's action throughout history, and this includes the choice of Israel as his people (217) . . . Because the teaching of Jesus and his apostles was rejected by the people, contemporary Israel could no longer be considered as the eschatological community, or as its root. . . . The redemptive power of Jesus' atoning death provides both the possibility and the existence of a new people of God" (218). So also J. Jeremias, *New Testament Theology*, 170: "Indeed, we must put the point even more sharply: the only significance of the whole of Jesus' activity is to gather the eschatological people of God."

Mk. 14:25, then, is consonant with the general thrust of the Lord's Prayer (Lk. 11:2-4//Mt. 6:9-13)—"thy kingdom come", "Give us each day our daily bread", "And forgive our sins"—where Jesus teaches that the disciples are to pray in the kingdom and the forgiveness of sins—the features of salvation which Jesus anticipates in the days leading to his death. Jesus' ambition to consolidate the eschatological people of God provides the impetus for his preaching and miracles, his calling of disciples, his commission of disciples to reap the eschatological harvest,[135] his death on the cross as the means for the forgiveness for sin, and his prophecy of the future kingdom as the endtime gathering of God's people (Lk. 13:29//Mt. 8:12).[136] Thus Jesus' ministry as envisioned in Q (Lk. 12:8, 9//Mt. 10:32, 33; Lk. 11:23//Mt. 12:30; Lk. 13:34//Mt. 23:37) is consistent with the purpose for Jesus' death in Mark—both are meant to bring sinful man into community with God.

Thus with the essential consistency of Mark and Q in view, can we suppose with others that there is reason to suppose a form of kerygmatic diversity between the two? Our findings suggest that the answer to this question must be no. Jesus' death on the cross in Mark is fully consistent with the purpose of Jesus' ministry in Q and the fact of Jesus' rejection by his people in Q. The salvation imparted by Jesus' death cannot be fully understood apart from Jesus' earthly ministry. The end effect of Jesus' teaching, his miracles, his crucifixion, his resurrection, his exaltation, and his parousia as the Son of Man are all related as each phase demonstrates the power of God at work in Jesus, the figure on whom depends mankind's destiny either in punitive judgment or in God's eschatological feast.

Conclusion

Jesus' teaching about the kingdom of God in Mark is fully compatible with his teaching about the kingdom of God in Q. Mark, like Q, does not bear evidence of secondary "kerygmatic" orientation in view of Jesus' death and resurrection. Accord between Mark and Q in their respective witnesses to the central theme of Jesus' ministry, the kingdom of God, supports the primitive origin of both while

---

[135] So A. Polag, *Christologie der Logienquelle*, 46: "Das Handeln Jesu ist im Ansatz ausgerichtet auf die Sammlung des Volkes zur Konstituierung des endzeitlichen Gottesvolkes." On Covenant theology in Q see Polag, *ibid.*, 37, 43-46, 71, 119f., 138f., 154, 167f., 175, 177f., 179-81.

[136] So R. Pesch, *Markus* II, 361: "Jesu Jünger werden durch seine besonderen Gaben beim Paschalmahl, das Brot und den Wein, die Jesus deutet, schon vorweg zu Teilhabern am messianischen Festmahl gemacht. Jesus, der Messias, hat ihnen Gemeinschaft mit sich selbst, Gemeinschaft mit Gott im neuen Bund geschenkt, den Gott aufgrund des Sühnetodes seines Gesalbten in Kraft setzt."

undermining the contemporary hypothesis that Mark and Q were originally kerygmatically incompatible. The two are compatible because they are both dependent upon authentic Jesus tradition.

In Mark and in Q the heart of Jesus' teaching is the kingdom of God. Jesus' role as teacher of the kingdom of God is emphasized in both.[137] In both Jesus mediates the saving power of the kingdom of God through his teaching and through his healings and exorcisms. Jesus' role as mediator of the kingdom of God presumes his matchless authority and his unique relation to God. In Mark Jesus openly objects to the established religious authorities of his day, he authoritatively rebukes demons, and he calls disciples to follow himself. It is no surprise, therefore, that the crowds and the disciples respond to Jesus in wonderment, "What is this? A new teaching with authority! He commands even the unclean spirits, and they obey him" (1:27; cf. 6:2). Similarly, in Q Jesus sends disciples with the claim that his commissioning authority is identical with the authority of God: "The one who listens to you listens to me, and the one who rejects you rejects me; and he who rejects me rejects the one who sent me" (Lk. 10:16//Mt. 10:40). Throughout Q Jesus articulates authoritative control through his characteristic use of the imperative[138] and the λέγω ὑμῖν phrase. Thus A. Polag identifies Jesus' authority as the trait which summarizes the primary stratum of Q.[139] It is significant that in Mark and Q Jesus' authority becomes apparent foremost in his ministry of the kingdom of God (Lk. 11:20//Mt. 12:28; Mk. 1:14, 15).

In Mark and in Q Jesus speaks of the kingdom of God as the ultimate realm of salvation. Omission from the kingdom, in contrast, is the ultimate sentence

---

[137] The establishment of two different christological traditions behind Mark and Q which views Q as a collection of teaching, and Mark as a gospel of action focused on the Passion fails to take into account Mark's major emphasis on Jesus' teaching role. Mark exceeds Mt. and Lk. in using the verb "to teach" (διδάσκειν) 15 times and identifies Jesus 12 times with the noun "teacher" (διδάσκαλος). The name rabbi is applied 3 times to Jesus in Mark. Clearly, then, Mark stresses teaching as a major function of the earthly Jesus. See C.F. Evans, *The Beginning of the Gospel*, London: SPCK (1968) 47; R.T. France, "Mark and the Teachings of Jesus", *Gospel Perspectives* I, Sheffield: JSOT Press (1980) 101-136. *Contra* Charles E. Carlston ("On 'Q' and the Cross", *Scripture, Tradition, and Interpretation*, Ed. W. Gasque and W.S. LaSor, Grand Rapids: Eerdmans, 1978, 29-30): ". . . Q reflects a tendency, known elsewhere in early Christian literature but particularly clear in Gnosticism, to concentrate not on the death of Jesus but on his teaching . . ."

[138] The following list includes only imperatives used as commands by Jesus: Lk. 6:23[2], 27[2], 28[2], 29, 30[2], 35[3], 36, 37[2], 38, 42; 7:22, 59; 9:60[2], 10:2, 3, 4, 5, 7[2], 8, 9, 10, 11; 11:2, 9[3], 35, 41; 12:1, 7, 22, 32, 33[3], 35, 40; 13:24, 30; 14:35; 17:3[3], 6[2], 31[2], 32 and par.

[139] *Christologie der Logienquelle*, 117, 118: "Ein zusammenfassender Überblick erlaubt aber, einigermaßen adäquat darzustellen, was nach der primären Formung des Q-Materials unter »Vollmacht Jesu« inhaltlich zu verstehen ist."

charged against those who reject Jesus. As a result, Jesus isolates the kingdom of God as the primary hope and focus of human endeavor. Jesus' charge is that man seek first the kingdom of God. As God has offered the blessings of the kingdom to man through Jesus, so man must respond passionately to God by loving God and by loving fellow man.[140] The kingdom of God occasions enthusiasm.

In Mark and in Q the mystery of the kingdom of God comes to those who see and hear with faith the ministry of Jesus.[141] The kingdom of God is a gift to those attracted to Jesus' ministry—sinners, tax-collectors, children, the sick, but in Mark as in Q, the mystery of the kingdom of God is hidden from those most capable intellectually to receive it—the wise, the lawyers, the Pharisees and Scribes who are the very figures who reject Jesus. In turn those who follow Jesus will enter the kingdom in the future, while those who reject Jesus will be unsuitable for future salvation in the eschatological banquet.

Both Mark and Q, then, exhibit a dichotomy between insiders and outsiders. The concept of community (*Gemeinschaft*) is similar in both. Those who belong to the community of salvation are those who have left all and followed Jesus and have perpetuated his ministry.

In Mark and in Q the kingdom of God is a dynamic phrase which has present and future dimensions. Both present the kingdom as an entity which has a small beginning and a colossal consummation.

Q conceals the Messianic character of Jesus in a manner that is consistent with the phenomenon of the "Messianic Secret" in Mark (*pace* W. Schmithals and H. Räisänen). The Q temptation narrative is conceptually consistent with the secrecy motif.

---

[140] Cf. H. Merklein, *Die Gottesherrschaft als Handlungsprinzip*, "Die Gottesherrschaft ist für Jesus das entscheidende Handlungsprinzip", 221 and passim.

[141] Christopher D. Marshall (*Faith as a Theme in Mark's Narrative*, Cambridge: CUP, 1989) distinguishes two main expressions or applications of faith in Mark: (A) "Kerygmatic faith" which "denotes the believing acceptance of Jesus' proclamation of the dawning kingdom, a response entailing ethical conversion and a commitment of reliant trust upon Jesus as bearer of the Kingdom (1:15). The main form this takes in Mark is the commitment of discipleship" (228), and (B) "Petitionary Faith" which "denotes the concrete act of believing trust required of those who seek the operation of Kingdom power in Mark." According to Marshall, there are four types of petitionary faith in Mk.: (1) faith for miraculous help for oneself (2:1-12; 5:24-34; 6:5; 10:46-52); (2) faith in seeking aid for a third party (5:21-24, 35-43; 7:24-30; 9:14-29); (3) faith required of those who seek to perform miracles (9:28f; 11:23); and (4), faith for all petitionary prayer (11:25f.). Applying Marshall's scheme to Q, we find that Q contains elements of both "Kerygmatic Faith" (in virtually all Q passages which deal with the KG and in Lk. 14:27//Mt. 10:38 in particular) and "Petitionary Faith" (Lk. 17:5, 6//Mt. 17:20; Lk. 7:1b-10//Mt. 8:5-10, 13). Mark and Q, therefore, not only share faith as a theme, but even speak of the same kind of faith.

Jesus employs wisdom modes of thought in his pedagogical style within Mark as he does within Q. Isolated sayings like those which characterize Q appear frequently in Mark and occur strung together in sayings' chains. The fact that Mark adopts sayings material into his Gospel expresses the value Mark placed on Jesus' traditional sayings. There is no evidence that Mark attempted to correct sayings tradition.

The "Insider/Outsider" motif in Mark discloses Jesus' polemic against Scribes and Pharisees. Hence the Jesus of Mark and the Jesus of Q exist in opposition to the very same antagonists. Such accord renders implausible the hypothesis that Jesus' woe sayings in Q were originally voiced by a Q community which existed in conflict with contemporary Judaism as represented by the phrase "this generation." The phrase ἡ γενεὰ αὕτη is equally characteristic of Mark (8:12[2], 38; 9:19; 13:30), where Jesus adopts it as an inclusive term for his contemporaries who fail to believe by utterly refusing to grasp the eschatological significance of his teaching and healing ministry.[142]

Hence Mark and Q are consistent with one another in their respective usages of 'the kingdom of God,' the most important theme which they share.

---

[142] *Contra* D. Lührmann (*Die Redaktion der Logienquelle*, 24-48) who argues that "dieses Geschlecht" represents a characteristic theme of Q and the recipient of the polemical material in Q.

Chapter 9

Is Q from a 'Second Sphere' of Christianity?

I. Introduction

The purpose of our final chapter is to complete our evaluation of the apparent christological and soteriological disparity between Mark and Q and to apply a final test to the hypothesis that Mark and Q represent opposing kerygmas.[1] In our comparison of the kingdom of God sayings in Mark and Q, we found the two sources utterly compatible with one another. Similarly, we believe there are good textual grounds for claiming that Mark and Q have compatible (not parallel, but compatible) christological and soteriological emphases. Therefore, in this chapter we will analyze the appropriate texts to see if indeed diverse incompatible streams of tradition originally shaped the form and content of Mark and Q. Is it a valid assumption that behind Mark and Q there originally existed two different historical communities who responded in different ways to Jesus of Nazareth? Do Mark and Q contain separately self contained kerygmas—that is, two sets of preaching which differ in their assessment of Jesus' achievement and which disagree in their interpretation of the benefits Jesus bestowed upon his followers? In view of what we have said thus far in our thesis, is Q still to be classified as a collection stemming from a 'second sphere' of Christianity?

---

[1] E.g., Burton L. Mack, "Q and the Gospel of Mark: Revising Christian Origins", *Semeia* 55 (1992) 19: "The Q people were not Kerygmatic Christians. . . . If Mark is right about Christian origins, the tradents of Q certainly got it wrong" (21). Similarly, J. Kloppenborg, " 'Easter Faith' and the Sayings Gospel Q", *Semeia* 49 (1990) 71: ". . . it has become quite usual to speak of 'the community of Q' as a definable and autonomous group within primitive Christianity and to assume that the Q document reflects in some important way the theology of a "second sphere" of primitive Christianity uninfluenced by the kerygmatic assertion of the saving significance of Jesus' death and resurrection. Implicit in this is the suggestion that Q represents the main and guiding theological statement of a particular community or group of communities"; Jack D. Kingsbury, *Jesus Christ in Matthew, Mark, and Luke,* 1: "Because the "passion kerygma" is so central to early Christian proclamation, scholars have questioned whether there could have arisen within nascent Christianity any theological document of importance that did not, as Mark, highlight the death and resurrection of Jesus. It may be that in Q one has just such a document, for in place of proclaiming the cross, Q lays stress on the imminent return of Jesus, Son of Man, for judgment."

II. Q and the Synoptic Gospels

Q does not contain a passion narrative. In sharp contrast, NT scholars of all persuasions agree that Mark focuses upon the cross as the decisive event which reveals Mark's answer to Jesus' identity and his significance. Q, therefore, is silent on the very theme, Jesus' passion, which climaxes the christology of Mark. Our question, as a result, is this: Is Q's silence valid evidence of a variant early Christian kerygma?

In order to answer this question, first we will evaluate the passion narratives' impact on gospel material outside of Q. Is Q's apparent silence a stark contrast to its synoptic environment?

We first observe that despite the fact that the synoptic Gospels contain passion narratives, the atonement does not surface as the consistent explicit emphasis of Matthew, Mark, or Luke. Matthew and Mark each contain only two direct references to the atoning value of Jesus' death (Mk.10:45; 14:22-24; Mt. 20:28; 26:28). Luke, meanwhile, speaks the least on Jesus' death as Lk. 22:27 omits the ransom clause of Mk. 10:45 leaving only Lk. 22:19f. which associates Jesus' death with the new covenant of Jer. 31:31. Outside of this handful of references, the atoning value of Jesus' death is implied primarily in the association of Jesus with the Suffering Servant of Isaiah. With Lk. 22:37 being the only direct quotation of Isa. 53:12 in the synoptics, the degree, however, to which the Gospel writers compare Jesus with the Suffering Servant is a continuing subject of controversy. In our opinion Morna Hooker,[2] C.K. Barrett,[3] C.F.D. Moule[4] and others have underestimated the importance of the allusions to the Suffering Servant in the synoptic gospels,[5] but we do agree that the servant allusions are implied and can hardly be identified as clear statements of early church kerygma.[6]

---

[2] *Jesus and the Servant,* London: SPCK, 1959.

[3] "The Background of Mark 10:45", *New Testament Essays: Studies in Memory of T.W. Manson,* Ed. A.J. B. Higgins, Manchester: Manchester U.P., 40-53.

[4] "From Defendant to Judge–and Deliverer: an Enquiry into the Use and Limitations of the Theme of Vindication in the New Testament", *Studiorum Novi Testamenti Societas Bulletin* (1959) 1-18.

[5] The one formal quotation (Lk. 22:37) and the two allusions (Mk. 10:45; 14:24) to Isa. 53:12 are few and complex in their linguistic relation to the LXX and MT. However, the linguistic parallels do exist and provide a better solution, in our opinion, to the background of these synoptic sayings than does the hypothesis that Mk. 10:45 alludes to Daniel 7 where the SM is an exalted worshipped figure. On the linguistic debate see: R.T. France, "Servant of the Lord in the Teaching of Jesus", *TynB* 19 (1968) 26-52; *pace* C K. Barrett, "The Background of Mark 10:45."

[6] We concur with Chrys Caragounis: "Thus, though affinities between Mk. 10:45 and Isa. 53 are recognized, these are not strong enough to warrant the theory that the logion is the creation of the Palestinian Church on the basis of Isa. 53", *The Son of Man: Vision and Interpretation* , 191.

The purpose of making these general observations is to illustrate that Q's failure to interpret explicitly the cross is quite characteristic of the synoptic gospels as a whole. When Matthew, Mark, and Luke only seldomly present direct references to the atoning benefits of Jesus' death, should we find it remarkable that Q is silent on the same issue? On the contrary, it would seem abnormal if Q did frequently refer to the cross in qualifying terms.[7] The refusal of Matthew, Mark, and Luke to place on Jesus' lips sayings which explicate the salvific benefits of Jesus' death suggests the synoptic writers' allegiance to the historical material at their disposal.

III. Q and "Deuteronomistic Theology"

If Q's silence does not raise our suspicions, what can we say to the positive evidence supporting an "unorthodox" interpretation of Jesus' death within Q? Charles E. Carlston,[8] Paul Hoffmann,[9] Arland D. Jacobson,[10] John Kloppenborg,[11] James Robinson,[12] Siegfried Schulz,[13] Richard A. Edwards,[14]

---

[7] The same could be said about Q in respect to the Pauline letters; hence A.D. Nock's statement: "It is very striking that Paul so seldom uses the actual phrase 'forgiveness of sins'; the idea is in his mind, but he is filled with the idea of the positive creative activity of Christ . . .", *St. Paul*, London: Thornton Butterworth (1938) 80. Similarly, B. Gerhardson, *The Origins of the Gospel Tradition*, Philadelphia: Fortress (1979) 40. And more recently, D. Allison ("The Pauline Epistles and the Synoptic Gospels", *NTS* 28 [1982] 16): "Although the words of institution and the kerygmatic statement in 1 Cor 15 held a fundamental meaning for Paul and his communities, they occur only once in his writings and are not even clearly alluded to outside of 1 Corinthians. Had this epistle not survived, surely some scholars would have confidently avowed that the Pauline churches did not celebrate the Lord's Supper."

[8] "On 'Q' and the Cross", 30.

[9] "Die Deutung des Todes Jesu unter dem Einfluß der Propheten–Tradition und des Menschensohn-Bekenntnisses", *Studien zur Theologie der Logienquelle*, 187-190. Hoffmann claims that there is probably in Q a witness for an older understanding of Jesus' death which goes back to the early Jewish Christian community (189). He conjectures that the Q group associated their own rejection with the rejection of Jesus the Son of Man. The identification of the Q group's rejection with the rejection of Jesus assures the Q group that they will participate in the personal destiny of Jesus, who has assumed, since his death, the exalted status of the Son of Man. Herein lies (for Hoffmann) the soteriology of Q (190).

[10] "The Literary Unity of Q", *JBL* 101 (1982) 365-89; *idem*, "The Literary Unity of Q: Lc. 10:2-16 and Parallels as a Test Case", *Logia*, 420.

[11] John S. Kloppenborg, *The Formation of Q*, 27; *idem*, " 'Easter Faith' and the Sayings Gospel Q", 92.

[12] "The Gospels as Narrative", *The Bible and the Narrative Tradition*, New York: Oxford UP (1986) 107.

[13] *Q–Die Spruchquelle*, 483. Schulz agrees with O.H. Steck that Jesus' death in Q implies the motif of the violent death of the prophets.

[14] *A Theology of Q*, 149, 150.

Dieter Lührmann[15] and Dieter Zeller[16] agree that Q interprets Jesus' death against the background of the "deuteronomistic tradition" outlined by O.H. Steck.[17] According to Steck the "deuteronomistic tradition" follows a four phase pattern: (1) Israel's history is a story of rebellion; (2) God sent his prophets to call the disobedient people to repent in order to avoid judgment; (3) Israel rejected, persecuted, and killed the prophets sent to her; (4) hence Israel faces destruction as it did in 722 and 586 B.C. Fitting into this pattern, Jesus' death within Q has the same significance as that of the OT prophets who died before him—and no more. Jack D. Kingsbury represents this view when he writes:

> A remarkable feature of Q is that no direct mention is made of the cross of Jesus. The one time the word "cross" occurs is in a saying of Jesus which speaks of the cost of discipleship: "Whoever does not bear his own cross and come after me, cannot be my disciple" (Lk. 14:27). What can be inferred about Jesus from this passage, however, is clear: the community of Q conceives of his death in terms of martyrdom. In its eyes, Jesus has suffered the fate of John the Baptist and all the prophets (Luke 11:47-51; 13:34). In stark contrast to Mark's Gospel, therefore, the cross is not the locus of salvation in Q.[18]

In reaching this conclusion, Kingsbury makes a methodological jump characteristic of the perspective we are criticizing. After correctly demonstrating that ὁ σταυρός occurs once in Q in a saying dealing with discipleship, he then illogically applies the pertinence of Lk. 14:27 par. exclusively to the hypothetical Q community who apparently viewed Jesus as a typical martyr. But Lk. 14:25-27//Mt. 10:37-38, while possibly alluding to Jesus' eventual death, does not qualify the meaning of Jesus' execution any more than does its doublet in Mk. 8:34; Lk. 9:23; Mt. 16:24. The burden of each version is discipleship. And suffering, even martyrdom, is consonant with discipleship not only in Q and Mark, but also in Acts (Appendix A), in the Pauline corpus (Appendix B) and indeed throughout the NT.

Nevertheless the "deuteronomistic tradition" is said to pervade the Q material[19] and three Q passages purportedly fit Jesus' death into the deuteronomistic mold.[20]

---

[15] "The Gospel of Mark and the Sayings Collection Q", 64.

[16] *Kommentar zur Logienquelle*, 96, 97.

[17] *Israel und das gewaltsame Geschick der Propheten*, 266-268. The OT background for the deuteronomistic pattern unfolds as follows: (1) Israel's disobedience (Ne. 9:26-30; 2 Chr. 30:7, 8; 2 Kgs. 17:11-12); (2) warning to repent (Ne. 9:26, 30; 2 Kgs. 17:13); (3) Israel's refusal to repent (Ne. 9:26, 29-30; 2 Kgs. 17:14-17, 19); (4) God's Judgement (Ne. 9:30; 2 Kgs. 17:18, 20).

[18] *Jesus Christ in Matthew, Mark and Luke*, 24-25.

[19] Arland Jacobson, "The Literary Unity of Q" (384), isolates Q passages which fit each of Steck's phases: (1) Lk. 6:23; 11:47-51; 13:34-35; 14:16-24 and par.; (2) Lk. 6:23; 11:47-51; 13:34-35; 14:16-24; (3) Lk. 3:7-9, 16-17; 6:20-49; 7:31-35; 10:2-12; 11:29-32; 11:39-52; and (4), Lk. 10:10-12, 13-15, 16; 12:10.

[20] Dieter Lührmann, cites also (Lk. 6:23//Mt. 5:12) as identifying Jesus' death as the typical fate of the prophets: "The Gospel of Mark and the Sayings Collection Q", 64. He argues that

A.   Lk. 11:47-51//Mt. 23:29-31, 34-36

In the first Q passage which possibly foreshadows Jesus' death, Jesus warns his opposition that they are guilty of the same crimes which their ancestors committed when they murdered and persecuted the prophets and apostles (Mt. has prophets and wise men and scribes). Because of their part in these crimes, this generation will be punished—justice is required of them. The sense is that Jesus' opponents are completing the evil task which their forefathers began; therefore, they are responsible for all the innocent blood which has been shed from Abel to Zechariah.

Our interest lies in the latter part of this passage, Lk. 11:49-51//Mt. 23:34-36, for it is in these verses that recent scholars have found allusions to Jesus' martyrdom within Q. At the outset, however, it should be noted that Jesus' death is nowhere mentioned. Those who discover here a statement on Jesus' death must maintain that the Q community included Jesus among those who were killed between the time of Abel and that of Zechariah. As a result, Zechariah can neither be identified as Zechariah, the son of Jehoiada, who was stoned in the court of the temple (2 Chr. 24:20-22) or Zechariah the writing prophet (Zch. 1:1), because both figures died well before the time of Jesus. To maintain that this passage alludes to Jesus' death, one must identify Zechariah as Zechariah the son of Bareis (compare with the Mt. account which reads Zechariah the son of Barachias), who was slain by zealots in the temple in AD 67.[21] This reading, however, is very unlikely[22] as it depends on the double hypothesis that Luke omitted υἱοῦ Βαραχίου from the original Q reading, while Matthew retained the original form. In a parallel which is generally characterized by Matthean redaction[23] rather than Lukan omission,[24] it is more likely that Luke's Ζαχαρίου is the original form and refers to Zechariah the son of Jehoida. In this case Q (Lk. 11:49-51//Mt. 23:34-

---

while the phrase "their fathers used to treat the prophets" in Lk. 6:23 distinguishes between the time of the prophets and now, the Matthean phrase "the prophets which were before you" does not make a temporal distinction and therefore identifies both Jesus and Jesus' followers with the prophets. The Matthean phrase (for Lührmann) is original to Q (64 n. 65). Such reasoning is highly speculative. See Davies and Allison, *Matthew* I, 463 n. 55.

[21] Jos. Bel. 4:334-344. So O. H. Steck, *Israel und das gewaltsame Geschick der Propheten*, 37-40.

[22] Most agree that it is very improbable that υἱοῦ Βαραχίου originally stood in Q. See A. Harnack, *Sayings*, 104; S. Schulz, *Q–Die Spruchquelle*, 338; Ernst Haenchen, "Matthäus 23", *ZTK* 48 (1951) 45; D. Lührmann, *Redaktion der Logienquelle*, 47; P. Hoffmann, *Theologie der Logienquelle*, 165.

[23] Possible redaction within the Mt. version include: ἐγώ (v. 34); σταυρώσετε καὶ ἐξ αὐτῶν μαστιγώσετε ἐν ταῖς συναγωγαῖς ὑμῶν καὶ διώξετε ἀπὸ πόλεως εἰς πόλιν (v. 34); and δίκαιον (two occurrences in v. 35).

[24] I.H. Marshall, *Luke*, 506.

36) does not present Jesus' death as the fate common to prophets. The clear comparison, rather, is between Jesus' opponents and their ancestors.

Images of martyrdom and the basic contours of the "deuteronomistic tradition," therefore, do color this Q passage,[25] but it is the prophets of old, the righteous, who surface as the martyr figures. While Lk. 11:49-51//Mt. 23:34-36 may implicitly refer to Jesus' death, it does not qualify the meaning of his crucifixion. To claim that it is a statement by a certain community which attached no significance to Jesus' death is to argue what the text does not support.

B.   Lk. 13:34-35//Mt. 23:37-39

The second Q passage which is said to refer to Jesus' death originally may have existed side by side with Lk. 11:47-51//Mt. 23: 29-36 in which case Matthew's order would represent the original arrangement of Q.[26] The Lukan vocabulary, however, probably adheres closer to the Q original.[27] We cite the "Lament over Jerusalem" with the primary question in mind: Does this saying clearly qualify Jesus' death as the death of a martyr and no more? In Luke Jesus' death is definitely in view as a result of its proximity to 13:33: "because it is not possible for a prophet to die outside of Jerusalem." Lk. 13:33 provides evidence that Luke at least did not perceive discontinuity between Jesus' death as a prophet and his death as the suffering Messiah. Can we be sure that what was true for Luke was not also true for the transmitters of the Q material?

Like the preceding passage, the "Lament over Jerusalem" fails to present an explicit statement which interprets Jesus' death or even identifies it. Again the allusion to Jesus' fate is revealed through the association of Jesus with the prophets and "those sent" to Jerusalem. While the comparison between Jesus and

---

[25] On the conception of martyrdom behind (Lk. 11:49-51//Mt. 23:34-36), Ethelbert Stauffer states, "Behind the strictly final ἵνα of Lk. 11:50 is a conception of the murder of the righteous common to the theology of martyrdom, namely, that by such murder the enemies of God fill up the measure of their sins and bring the judgment day upon themselves", "ἵνα", *TDNT* III, 328 n. 46.

[26] For an exhaustive study of this passage, see O.H. Steck, *Israel und das gewaltsame Geschick der Propheten*, 40-58. Steck argues Lk. 13:34 reflects the original form–the Mt. version being largely redactional (p. 50); Lk. 13:35b (par.) is a Christian addition (p. 53); the "Jerusalem Word" is not an authentic pronouncement of Jesus (p. 56); and the form of the passage is the prophetic judgement word (p. 58). The weakness of Steck's theory lies in the lack of evidence that the "Jerusalem word" ever existed in a late Jewish piece of tradition whose form was isolated to the content of prophetic judgement immediately preceding the fall of Jerusalem (p. 238). Indeed, such a late date for the conception of one fragment of Q is very unlikely as it would force the composition of Q into the mid 70's–80's A.D. and the composition of Luke and Matthew to an extremely late date.

[27] Steck argues this point extensively: "Tradition und Redaktion im Jerusalemwort (Mt. 23, 37-39 par)", *Israel und das gewaltsame Geschick der Propheten*, 48-50.

the prophets is understood, it is not clear that Lk. 13:34//Mt. 23:37 understands Jesus to be on par ontologically with the prophets killed and messengers stoned in Jerusalem.[28]   More likely the passage represents Jesus' free use of wisdom terminology[29] in administering judgment to the Jerusalem authorities who share the responsibility for killing the prophets and messengers of God.[30]   As Jerusalem refused to repent and to seek God's protection at the preaching of ancient prophets, so she has now refused to repent at the preaching of Jesus. As the prophets' murderers will be punished, so those who reject Jesus will face eschatological judgment (cf. Lk. 11:47//Mt. 23:29).

When emphasis does turn to Jesus as speaker in Lk. 13:34b//Mt. 23:37b, the subject moves from Jerusalem's guilt in murdering God's messengers to Jerusalem's rejection of Jesus' personal offer of protection.[31]   In identifying himself as the figure on whom depends the Jews' unification and salvation, Jesus assumes authority which surpasses that of the OT prophets.   Thus in Lk. 13:35//Mt. 23:38 Jerusalem's house is left desolate because it has rejected Jesus' offer of salvation—not because it has murdered Jesus. In saying, "How often I wanted to gather your children together the way a hen gathers her chicks under her wings," Jesus assumes exalted status as the figure intended to occasion the gathering of God's eschatological people into the kingdom of God. According to Psalms of Solomon 17:26, 30f., the task attempted by Jesus was that expected of the Messiah.[32]   Further, Jerusalem's rejection of Jesus paves the way for the synoptic passion narratives where Jesus describes his death as "the blood of the covenant which is poured out for many" (Mk. 14:22-26).[33]   In the end Jesus' death accomplishes the feat originally intended by his call to repentance and his preaching of the kingdom of God.   Finally, Lk. 13:35b//Mt. 23:39, "You will not

---

[28] Eduard Lohse notes the unlikelihood of such a reading, "Mt. 23:37 par. Lk. 13:34 speaks of stoning and putting to death, not crucifying; hence it cannot be called vaticinium ex eventu." In "Sayings of Jesus about Jerusalem", *TDNT* VII, 329 n. 236.

[29] So I.H. Marshall, *Luke*, 574.

[30] Calling the saying "a good Palestinian metaphor", E. Lohse notes, "Jesus can hardly have been saying that He himself had often wanted to gather Jerusalem as a hen gathers her chickens under her wings", *TDNT* VII, 329.

[31] J. Fitzmyer goes so far as to say that the authorities have rejected Jesus' offer of God's salvation: "Jesus uses a readily understood figure for his own love and concern for his contemporaries, manifesting thereby in a new way the salvific interest of God himself, which he has sent to proclaim", *Luke* II, 1035.

[32] "He will gather a holy people whom he will lead in righteousness (17:26a) . . . And he will purge Jerusalem (and make it) holy as it was even from the beginning, (for) nations to come from the ends of the earth to see his glory, to bring as gifts her children who had been driven out, and to see the glory of the Lord with which God has glorified her" (17:30b-31).

[33] So R. Schnackenburg, *God's Rule and Kingdom*, 250: "After the failure of his preaching to the Jews, Jesus regards his Passion as a necessary precondition for the coming of the perfect kingdom."

see me until you say 'Blessed is he who comes in the name of the Lord'", appears to be a strange conclusion to a saying which alludes to Jesus' martyrdom. Temporally the saying points to the future rather than to the past, and focuses on Jesus' exaltation rather than his demise. Indeed, this saying also may well be an implicit identification of Jesus' messiahship.[34] In any case, "Blessed is he who comes in the name of the Lord" is anomalous to descriptions of OT prophets and John the Baptist.

C. Lk. 14:27//Mt. 10:38

The final Q passage which possibly alludes to Jesus' death is a statement which Matthew and Luke both use to describe the cost of discipleship.[35] Jesus warns the audience, the twelve or more likely the crowd at large, that obedience to himself must be unconditional—even to the point of death. To refuse to suffer is to fail the test of discipleship.

The inclusion of τὸν σταυρόν in both the Matthean and Lukan versions presents historical difficulties for commentators and suggests to some scholars an after the fact allusion to Jesus' death. Again, however, it must be stressed that this passage, like the previous two we have discussed, is neither a description of Jesus' death, nor an interpretation of why Jesus died. It is the audience which is advised to take up the cross.[36] If, therefore, the saying refers to Jesus' death at all, it does so faintly without a hint of the Q community *Tendenz*.[37]

Moreover, it is very unlikely that this saying reflects a unique perspective of the Q community because it repeats teaching found in Lk. 9:23, 18:29f., and is in fact a "Q doublet" to Marcan teaching (8:34). This problem is not removed with the claim that Mark used Q. Mk. 8:34 is equally primitive and also focuses on the

---

[34] Thus Fitzmyer, "The saying preserved in "Q" and even as used in Matthew undoubtedly referred to Jesus' parousiac coming, his coming as judge", *Luke* II, 1035. I.H. Marshall remarks that Jesus spoke similarly of the future coming of the Son of Man: "Here, however, the symbolism is messianic (perhaps as a result of assimilation of the two figures) and contains an implicit identification as the coming One, the Messiah", *Luke*, 577.

[35] D. Seely ("Blessings and Boundaries: Interpretations of Jesus' Death in Q", *Semeia* 55 [1992] 132f.) argues that Lk. 14:27 is the earliest interpretation of Jesus' death within Q. According to Seely, the style and thought of this verse parallels comparable traits of Cynic and Stoic philosophy, where students often re-enacted the heroic deaths of their great teachers. There are parallels with the Cynic and Stoic models. However, Seely's argument has difficulties. The most prominent are the five stages (144, 45) of conceptual development which he deciphers behind the Q sayings on death (see C.M. Tuckett, "On the Stratification of Q a Response", 217-18) and the great disparity in content between Jesus' teaching and that of Cynic and Stoic philosophy.

[36] "It presents to the disciple the challenge of readiness for martyrdom", J. Fitzmyer, *Luke* I, 787.

[37] A unique perspective or bias of the Q community does not present itself in this saying.

theme of discipleship. An equally valid argument could be used to support Marcan originality.[38]

The argument that Lk. 14:27//Mt. 10:38 alludes to Jesus' martyrdom is not strengthened if the assumption is made that the saying is secondary.[39] For it is one thing to say that this logion alludes to Jesus' death on the cross, and it is another to argue that it denies the "orthodox" interpretation of the cross and presents a separate tradition in which Jesus' crucifixion is categorized as typical martyrdom. Such appraisals are made entirely from silence. For if this saying advances a view of Jesus' death which is in some way incompatible with the Marcan passion narrative, it is hard to understand why the author or editor of Mark included 8:34 in his narrative. If his objective was to "correct" a heretical christology or soteriology, would not his task have been easier and more effective if he had simply left out the saying all together? We agree with Kingsbury that such corrective tendencies are not evident in Mark.[40] Mark's inclusion of 8:34 verifies the saying's compatibility with Mark's understanding of discipleship and with the passion narrative which follows. We are not persuaded, therefore, that Lk. 14:27//Mt. 10:38 offers an unorthodox perspective of Jesus' death.

D. Further Considerations

Together these passages reflect the historical perspective that the prophets and the righteous of old died characteristically violent deaths. The image permeates the OT (Ne. 9:26; 1 Kgs. 18:4, 13; 19:10, 14; 2 Chr. 24:20, 21; 36:15-21; Jer. 2:30; 26:20-24) and exists in Intertestamental and extra-biblical literature (Lives of the Prophets; Jubilees 1:12; 4 Qp Hos 2.3-6; Josephus, *Antiquities* 10:38; Ascension

---

[38] So H. Schürmann, "Daß die Nachfolge bei Mk. gleich einleitend als Ziel genannt ist, könnte durchaus auch ursprünglich sein", *Das Lukasevangelium* I, 542. R. Laufen argues that Mark's use of ἀκολουθείτω μοι as opposed to Q's ἔρχεται ὀπίσω μου does not prove a Marcan alteration as Mark uses ἀκολουθέω in 1:18 where Simon and Andrew follow Jesus, and ὀπίσω αὐτοῦ in 1:20 where James and John come after him. The two phrases are synonymous: *Die Doppelüberlieferungen der Logienquelle und des Markusevangeliums*, 308.

[39] This is the position of J. Fitzmyer, "Since it is only the joining of Jesus' own messiahship with the cross on which he was crucified that makes the metaphor have any sense, the saying, as we now have it, must come from the early Christian community", *Luke* I, 785. Fitzmyer, however, obviously is not arguing that the phrase refers to Jesus' death as the common fate of a martyr. Further, a plausible case can be made for authenticity: "It is by no means necessary to suppose that the metaphor is 'Christian' in the sense that the Crucifixion of Christ is implied. If the idea of cross-bearing is not found in the older Rabbinic literature (cf. Billerbeck, I, 587), death by crucifixion under the Romans was a sufficiently familiar sight in Palestine to be the basis of the saying (cf. Josephus, BJ, ii.12. 6, ii. 14.9, V. II. I, Ant. xvii. 10.10)." V. Taylor, *Mark*, 381. Taylor's reasoning on Mk. 8:34 is similarly valid for the Q version.

[40] *The Christology of Mark's Gospel*, 33f.

of Isaiah 2:16; 5.1-14; *Paraleipomena Jeremiou* 9.21-32; Targum on Isaiah 28.1).[41]

But do the Q passages mentioned contradict the early church's proclamation that Jesus died as an atoning sacrifice for the forgiveness of sins (1 Cor. 15:3f.)? Several general observations suggest that we approach these passages with extreme caution. First, and most obviously, these passages do not in themselves directly speak of or interpret the meaning of Jesus' death and, therefore, cannot be said to deny or contradict the passion kerygma. We are dealing with an argument from silence. Because the sayings under question are allusive and are three in number out of a collection of roughly 230 verses, we must question the bold and perhaps radical claim that they earmark a variant early Christian response to Jesus' death. Third, it may be a pertinent question to ask whether or not the martyr image satisfies the christological implications of the surrounding Q material. For even if we speculate that Tödt is correct—that it was the Q community which originally associated the exalted Son of Man with the earthly Jesus; even then, we are still left with the question of how or why the supposed community came to make such an association.[42] Is it conceivable that a body of Gospel literature which identifies Jesus as the Son of God in the temptation narratives, which anticipates Jesus as the future Son of Man, and which presents Jesus speaking to God as a son to a father (Lk. 10:22//Mt. 11:27), is consistent in the end when it reduces itself to categorize Jesus' death as the fate typical of all the prophets? Fourth, we are hesitant to accept the martyr image as peculiar to Q owing to the motif's frequent appearance in the NT (Mk. 6:4; 12:2-5; Jn. 4:44; Acts 7:51-2; Ro. 11:3; Heb. 11:32-38; Jas. 5:10-11; Rev. 11:6-7; 16:16; 18:24) where suffering and martyrdom are consonant with Christian discipleship.[43] Just as these passages obviously do not suggest that the disciple's death has the same saving ramifications as did Jesus' death on the cross, so there are no grounds for the claim that the transmitters of Q equated

---

[41] On this tradition see: O Michel, *Prophet und Märtyrer*, BFTh 37, 2 Gütersloh: Mohn, 1932; H.J. Schoeps, *Aus früchristlicher Zeit*, Tübingen: J.C.B. Mohr [Paul Siebeck] 1950; H.A. Fischel, "Martyr and Prophet", *JQR* 37 (1946-7) 265-80, 363-86; B.H. Amaru, "The Killing of the Prophets: Unraveling a Midrash", *HUCA* 54 (1983) 153-80.

[42] Tödt concedes this point: "The community which resumed Jesus' preaching concerning the coming of the kingdom must nevertheless have attributed a fundamental meaning to the events of the passion and resurrection. Without recognizing this foundation a community would not have been established at all. Considered thus it is even more conspicuous that it was not the passion and resurrection which had to be preached according to the understanding of this community. They wanted to go on preaching what Jesus had preached", *Son of Man*, 250. However, is it necessary to claim that Jesus' sayings were preached in variance to or instead of the passion kerygma – is it really "conspicuous?

[43] See also: Mk. 4:17; 8:34; 10:30; Acts 5:40, 41; 7:54-60; 11:19; 12:2-4; 13:50; 14:22; 16:22f.; 17:6f.; 21:13, 27-40; 23:12-22; 2 Cor. 1:5; 4:8-12; 1 Th. 1:6; 3:3; 2 Th. 1:4, 5; 2 Ti. 3:12; Heb. 10:32-34; Rev. 1:9; 2:9, 10.

Jesus' death with that of his prophetic forebears. When martyr motifs exist within NT documents which address the redemptive significance of Jesus' death, we fail to see how its presence in Q suggests christological variance. And finally, martyr terminology—if indeed alluded to—does not necessarily contradict the redemptive value of Jesus' death. In Dn. 11:35, 2 Macc. 7:37-38,[44] and 4 Macc. 17:22,[45] it is the death of the martyrs which effectively delivers Israel from its sin and sin's consequences.[46] The martyr, therefore, does exist within Jewish literature as a figure which expresses redemptive ideas.[47]

Rather than contradict, Lk. 11:47-51, 13:34-35, and 14:27 and par. anticipate and support the passion narratives. In the first two passages, which originally may have been united, Jesus appears in conflict with a representative group of Jewish authorities—the group which condemns Jesus to death in the passion narratives. When he sharply accuses the authorities as being responsible with their fathers for the murder of the prophets and righteous figures of Israel's history, Jesus administers a humiliating insult to the Jews—one which forecasts a future retaliation. In a similar light, Jesus' assumption of the authority to judge and to predict future judgment must have repulsed the Jews. And while it is true that the lament over Jerusalem presents Jesus bemoaning the plight of the prophets, the passage accentuates more strongly Jesus' grief that his people have rejected his own offer of protection. In this passage Jesus identifies himself as the final chance for Israel. He says in effect: "because you have rejected me, your house is left to you desolate." The rejection of Jesus, therefore, has unprecedented consequences.

---

[44] "I, like my brothers, give up body and life for the laws of our fathers, appealing to God to show mercy soon to our nation and by afflictions and plagues to make you confess that he alone is God, and through me and my brothers to bring to an end the wrath of the Almighty which has justly fallen on our whole nation."

[45] "And through the blood of those devout ones and their death as an expiation, divine Providence preserved Israel that previously had been afflicted."

[46] See D. Hill, *Greek Words and Hebrew Meanings*, SNTSMS 5; Cambridge: C.U.P. (1967) 23-48; esp. 41-48. Hill claims that the language of 4 Maccabees may have had a direct influence on Paul in passages where the cost of redemption is the death of Christ (Ro. 3:24; 6:16-23; 7:14; Gal. 3). See also: I.H. Marshall, "The Development of the Concept of Redemption in the New Testament", *Reconciliation and Hope: Presented to L.L. Morris*, Ed. R.J. Banks, Exeter: Paternoster Press (1975) 153-169; Martin Hengel, *The Atonement,* Tr. John Bowden; London: SCM (1981) 60-65. Hengel (64) in response to Klaus Wengst (*Christologische Formeln und Lieder des Urchristentums*, StNT 7, Gütersloh, 1972) presents sources which show that "the vicarious atoning effect of the death or even the suffering of a righteous man was not unknown in the Palestinian Judaism of the first century AD." Thus, Wengst's claim that the vicarious interpretation of Jesus' death came out of Hellenistic Jewish Christianity is unfounded. On the evidence within rabbinic writings, see E. Lohse, *Märtyrer und Gottesknecht,* Göttingen: Vandenhoeck & Ruprecht, 1963.

[47] T. Baumeister, *Die Anfänge der Theologie des Martyriums,* Munster (1980) 12f., concedes that Israel did not have a "theology of martyrdom" other than Isa. 53:12 even in connection with the murder of the prophets.

Consequences, however, which befit those foolish enough to reject the salvation offered by God's anointed Messiah, who came to gather the people of Israel for salvation in the kingdom of God (Ps. Sal. 17:26, 30). Finally, the quotation of Ps. 118:26 in the closing phrase: "you shall not see me until the time comes when you say, "Blessed is he who comes in the name of the Lord", clearly anticipates the triumphal entry in Lk. 19:38 and Mt. 21:9, which quote the same OT passage. In summary, it is plausible that orthodox early Christians showed interest in these passages and indeed interpreted them in light of the passion narrative. Images of rejection, the cross, and Jerusalem have irrepressible connotations, and the reference to Ps. 118:26 identifies Jesus as a figure of no common merit.[48]

E. Mk. 12:1-11: The Parable of the Vineyard and the Tenants

The interpretation of Jesus within the pattern of "deuteronomistic tradition" cannot be isolated to the *Tendenz* of the Q community because, as J. Blank has shown,[49] it is Mark and not Q which provides the clearest portrait of Jesus as the consummation of Israel's rejection of the prophets.[50] While Mk. 6:4 affirms Mark's identification of Jesus as a prophet, the parable of the vineyard and the tenants gives prominence to Jesus' implied death as the climax to the "deuteronomistic" pattern.

The parable of the vine-growers bears witness to every "deuteronomistic" phase proposed by Steck. The owner of the vineyard represents God, the vine-growers represent disobedient Israel, the messengers represent the prophets sent to summon repentance, and the "beloved son" the heir of the vineyard, who is rejected, killed, and thrown out of the vineyard, represents Jesus. The parable concludes with an enraged sentence of judgment (v. 9). Mk. 12:1-11 traces back

---

[48] Arland J. Hultgren (*Christ and His Benefits, Christology and Redemption in the New Testament*, Philadelphia: Fortress, 1987, 21) claims the parable of the minas (Lk. 19:12//Mt. 25:15) "most certainly has allegorical overtones of the crucifixion and parousia." If Hultgren is correct, we have another Q passage to support our case. However, the passages more clearly refer to Jesus' exaltation and parousia rather than to the crucifixion – allegorical overtones of the crucifixion are very hard to detect in both the Mt. and Lk. versions. Moreover, Mt. does not contain the element of rejection found in Lk. 19:12, 14, 15a, 27. Thus, we are hesitant to cite the parable of the minas//talents, whose Mt.//Lk. comparison is very complex, as textual support for our argument though we do support Hultgren's conclusions in general.

[49] "Die Sendung des Sohnes. Zur christologischen Bedeutung des Gleichnisses von den bösen Winzern Mk. 12,1-12", *Neues Testament und Kirche*, FS R. Schnackenburg, Ed. J. Gnilka; Freiburg: Herder (1974) 11-41. The burden of Blank's article was to discount the consensus that Mk. 12:1-11 originated in a late phase of Hellenistic-Jewish Christianity. *Contra*, F. Hahn, *Christologie Hoheitstitel*, 315f.; and E. Schweizer, "υἱός", *TDNT* VIII, 334-97.

[50] *Contra* B. Mack, "Q and the Gospel of Mark: Revising Christian Origins", 27: ". . . Mark does not, indeed, could not follow Q in associating either the persecution of Jesus' followers or Jesus' own death with the Deuteronomistic motif of the killing of the prophets."

to the conceptual background of Isa. 5:1-7 and Jer. 7:21-28—prototypes for Steck's deuteronomistic pattern. The parable is thoroughly Jewish and untainted by later reinterpretation in light of the Passion and Resurrection kerygma.[51]

The conceptual parallels between Jesus' parable of the vine-growers in Mark and two of the Q passages considered above (Lk. 11:49-51//Mt. 23:34-36; Lk. 13:34-35//Mt. 23:37-39) are striking. In Mark and Q Jesus accuses his Jewish contemporaries of sharing in the guilt resulting from Israel's refusal to conform to the demands of God as voiced by the prophets. In each the prophetic tradition consummates in Jesus' rejection, and each closes with a strong statement of judgment. And while Lk. 13:35//Mt. 23:39 concludes with a quotation of Ps. 118:26, Mk. 12:10 concludes with a quotation of Ps. 118:22, 23. Whereas in the OT the condition for God's protection from political enemies was Israel's repentance, in Mark and in Q the condition for the Jews' salvation from eschatological judgment is adherence to Jesus himself (Lk. 12:8, 9//Mt. 10:32, 33; Lk. 11:23//Mt.12:30).[52]

In response to these similarities one could argue that Mk. 12:1-12 goes beyond Q by exalting Jesus as the "beloved son" (12:6). However, the parable setting of Mk. 12:6, the non-titular use of "son," and the likely dependence of not only 12:6 but also Mk. 1:9-11 and 9:7 upon Psalms 2 and 110 undermine arguments that we are dealing with a product of Hellenistic tradition. The "son" in Mk. 12:6, like the "one who comes in the name of the Lord" in Lk. 13:34//Mt. 23:39, is a figure whose christological significance is not explicitly laid out. Furthermore, Jesus' divine sonship is a concept familiar to Q both in the temptation narratives and in Lk. 10:21, 22//Mt. 11:25-27 where Jesus speaks in prayer to God as Father as he does in Mk. 14:36.

From this evidence we may conclude that the "deuteronomistic tradition" is no more characteristic of Q than Mark. In each the prophetic pattern of the rejection of the prophets culminates in Jesus.

Thus far, then, the theory of a variant kerygma in Q lacks supporting evidence. First, the argument from silence fails to startle us as a result of similar silence within Matthew, Mark, and Luke. Second, the positive evidence of a contrary interpretation of Jesus' death falters upon the allusive character of the few Q passages which are said to present Jesus as a common martyr figure—a figure

---

[51] Recent defenders of the authenticity of this parable include: James H. Charlesworth, *Jesus within Judaism*, 139-156; Ben Witherington III, *The Christology of Jesus*, 213-215; Klyne Snodgrass, *The Parable of the Wicked Tenants*, WUNT 27; Tübingen: J.C.B. Mohr (Paul Siebeck) 1983, 112.

[52] Such similarities led J. Blank ("Die Sendung des Sohnes", 24) to conclude: "Die beiden Q-Texte spiegeln genau dieselben Anschauungen wider, wie der Mk.-Text 12,1-12. Die traditionsgeschichtlichen Denkmodelle sind genau die gleichen. Wir haben es mit zwei verscheiden Ausprägungen ein und derselben Grundvorstellung zu tun . . ."

which itself has complex connotations and which does not necessarily challenge "orthodox kerygma." And finally, the "deuteronomistic tradition" is a paradigm which Q shares with Mark.

IV. The Resurrection in Q

As there are no Son of Man sayings in Q which refer specifically to Jesus' death, so there are also no sayings like Mk. 9:9, 31; 10:33, 34 which anticipate Jesus' resurrection. Seeing significance in this, J. Kloppenborg writes: "The notion of resurrection is absent from Q, not because Q already presupposes the resurrection and exaltation of Jesus to the right hand of God as a narrative event, but because this metaphor is fundamentally inappropriate to the genre and theology of Q."[53] We think differently. Belief in the general resurrection is presupposed by Jesus in three places within Q:

> But it will be more tolerable for Tyre and Sidon in the judgment, than for you. And you, Capernaum, will not be exalted to heaven, will you? You will be brought down to Hades! (Lk. 10:14, 15//Mt. 11:22, 23)

> The Queen of the South shall rise up with the men of this generation at the judgment and condemn them, because she came from the ends of the earth to hear the wisdom of Solomon; and behold, something greater than Solomon is here. The men of Nineveh shall stand up with this generation at the judgment and condemn it, because they repented at the preaching of Jonah; and behold, something greater than Jonah is here. (Lk. 11:31, 32//Mt. 12:41, 42)

> There will be weeping and gnashing of teeth there when you see Abraham and Isaac and Jacob and all the prophets in the kingdom of God, but yourselves being cast out. And behold, some are last who will be first and some are first who will be last. (Lk. 13:28, 29//Mt. 8:11, 12)

These Q sayings have in common the expectation that following the resurrection of the dead judgment will take place with acceptance or rejection of Jesus being the decisive factor determining inclusion or exclusion from the kingdom of God. In administering these proleptic sentences of woe, Jesus assumes for himself authority as the one equipped by God to condemn the guilty in view of the final day. The implication is clear that if "the Queen of the South" and the "men of Nineveh" shall rise up at the judgment, so shall Jesus as the one "Greater than Solomon" and "Greater than Jonah."

Such passages, however, only prove that in Q Jesus takes for granted the general resurrection—a belief not unique to Jesus but common to most orthodox

---

[53] "'Easter Faith and the Sayings Gospel Q'", 90. Similarly B. Mack, "Q and the Gospel of Mark: Revising Christian Origins", 20.

Jews including the Pharisees. But in addition to the Q passages which presuppose the general resurrection, there are also future Son of Man sayings in Q which refer to the parousia of Jesus as the Son of Man. Whether or not Jesus originally identified himself with that figure is not important here—those who transmitted the sayings definitely championed him to be Son of Man—no one doubts that. Hence between the earthly teaching of Jesus as recorded in Q, and the future appearance of the Son of Man Jesus as projected in Lk. 17:22, 24, 30 par., Jesus' resurrection has to be presupposed. The resurrection, though not elaborated, is as appropriate to the genre and theology of Q as it is to Mark's passion narrative.

V. Quotations and Allusions to the Old Testament within Q

A final positive argument we raise to support the compatibility of Mark and Q stems from the quotations and allusions to the OT within Q. Athanasius Polag lists 23 quotations from the LXX within Q: nine from Isaiah; five from the Psalms; three from Deuteronomy; two from Jeremiah; and one each from Genesis, Exodus, Micah and Malachi.[54] The UBS[3] confirms six of Polag's references as quotations, and identifies thirty-seven additional allusions and verbal parallels to the OT within Q. The margins of Nestle-Aland[26] expand this count further for a total of eighty-five for the combined existence of OT quotations, allusions, and verbal parallels.

Our purpose in analyzing the OT quotations and allusions is to seek to find any evidence that there exists a conceptual pattern in the OT references which might betray the christological or kerygmatic bias of the supposed Q community. While one searches in vain for even the slightest allusions to ancient Egyptian and Near Eastern sayings collections, Cynic literature, pre-Byzantine gnomologia, and later chreiai collections,[55] a bird's eye view of Aland's references reveals that Q may allude to as many as nineteen different OT books ranging from Genesis to Malachi and possibly to three extra-biblical intertestamental writings. The conceptual background of the Q material, then, is entirely Jewish. Further, Q does not interpret Jesus in light of a tradition isolated in one OT book or even in a set of books such as the Penteteuch, the Prophets, or the Wisdom books proper. Hence, if Q contains a variant tradition, and if that tradition draws from the OT, which it must considering its quotations and allusions, then that tradition must interpret Jesus against a broad OT background. Thus, prevalent OT themes such as

---

[54] *Fragmenta Q*, Neukirchen-Vluyn: Neukirchener Verlag (1979) 100-102.

[55] J. Kloppenborg's strict form critical methodology produces parallels between Q and other ancient sayings despite the impossibility of tracing the linguistic or conceptual pedigree of a single saying of Jesus to such backgrounds. See "Appendix 1", *The Formation of Q*, 329-341.

prophecy and wisdom are said to represent the variant conceptual background of Q.

But after going through the allusions and quotations individually, and then considering them as a whole, we are left with no sense of the unusual. Twelve categories represent the use of the OT in Q:

1) General allusions to OT historical figures and locations.[56]
2) Strictly verbal allusions.[57]
3) Allusions which cite OT backgrounds for NT customs and orthopraxy.[58]
4) Allusions to OT pictorial images.[59]
5) Direct Quotations of the OT in which Jesus defends his ministry against the temptations of Satan.[60]
6) Allusions which cite OT terminology in reference to God.[61]
7) a. Sayings of Jesus rooted in OT teaching.[62]
7) b. Jesus' instructions to his followers which reflect OT precursors.[63]
8) Allusions in which Jesus assumes the role played by God in the OT.[64]
9) OT quotations which Jesus claims to fulfil in his ministry.[65]
10) Allusions to the rejection of the prophets and righteous figures of Israel.[66]
11) OT allusions which John the Baptist fulfils.[67]

---

[56] E.g., (1) Lk. 9:61, 62//diff Mt.: 1 Kgs. 19:20; Gn. 19:17, 26; (2) Lk. 10:13-15//Mt. 11:21-23: Jonah 3:5; Dn. 9:3; Est. 4:3; (3) Lk. 11:32//Mt. 12:42: Jonah 3:5; (4) Lk.17:27//24:37f.: Gn. 6:11-13; 7:7; 17:21; (5) Lk. 17:28-30//Mt. 24:39b: Gn. 18:20; 19:15, 24; (6) Lk. 17:31, 32//Mt. 24:17,18: Gn. 19:17, 26.

[57] E.g., (1) Lk. 10:21, 22//Mt. 11:25-27: Ps. 136:26; (2) Lk. 12:6, 7//Mt. 10:29-31: 1 Sm. 14:45; 2 Sm. 14:11; (3) Lk. 12:53//Mt. 10:34-36: Mic. 7:6.

[58] E.g., Lk. 14:20: Dt. 24:5.

[59] E.g., (1) Lk. 7:24//Mt. 11:7-9: 1 Kgs. 14:15; (2) Lk. 12:54//Mt. 16:2, 3: 1 Kgs. 18:44; (3) Lk. 13:19//Mt. 13:32: Dn. 4:9, 18; Eze. 17:23; 31:6; Ps. 103:12 (LXX); (4) Lk. 13:28, 29//Mt. 8:11, 12: Ps. 107:3; Mal. 1:11.

[60] E.g., Lk. 4:1-13//Mt. 4:1-11: Dt. 8:3; 6:13, 16; 10:20; Eze. 8:3; Ps. 91:11,12; Isa. 7:12; 1 Kgs. 10:9.

[61] E.g., (1) Lk. 11:20//Mt. 12:28: Ex. 8:19; (2) Lk. 12:5//Mt. 10:28: Ps. 119:120; (3) Lk. 15:3-7//Mt. 18:12-14: Eze. 34:11.

[62] E.g., (1) Lk. 6:20b//Mt. 5:3-10: Isa. 61:1, 2; 65:18; (2) Lk. 6:33//Mt. 5:45-47: Lv. 25:35; (3) Lk. 10:21, 22//Mt. 11:25-27: Isa. 29:14; (4) Lk. 12:31//Mt. 6:25-33: Isa. 41:14; (5) Lk. 17:3, 4//Mt. 18:21, 22: Lv. 19:17; Ps. 119:164.

[63] E.g., (1) Lk. 10:4-7//Mt. 10:9-13: 2 Kgs. 4:29; 1 Sm. 25:5; Nu. 18:31; (2) Lk. 14:25-27//Mt. 10:37,3 8: Dt. 33:9.

[64] E.g., (1) Lk. 6:46//Mt. 7:21: Mal. 1:6; (2) Lk. 7:22, 23//Mt. 11:4-6: Isa. 29:18; 35:5, 6; 42:18; 26:19; 61:1; (3) Lk. 13:34, 35//Mt. 23:37-39: Isa. 31:5; Dt. 32:11; Ps. 91:4; 1 Kgs. 9:7; Jer. 12:7; 22:5.

[65] E.g., (1) Lk. 7:18-20//Mt. 11:23: Ps. 118:26; (2) Lk. 11:21, 22//Mt. 12:19: Isa. 49:24; 53:12; (3) Lk. 13:34, 35//Mt. 23:37-39: Ps. 118:26.

[66] E.g., (1) Lk. 6:23//Mt. 5:11: 2 Chr. 36:16; (2) Lk. 11:51//Mt. 23:34: Gn. 4:8, 10; 2 Chr. 24:20-23: Zch. 1:1.

[67] E.g., Lk. 7:27//Mt. 11:10: Ex. 23:20; Mal. 3:1.

12) Eschatological expectations which parallel expectations of OT passages.[68]

Drawn from a variety of OT sources, the quotations and allusions serve specific purposes in the sayings in which they exist. An overarching framework, however, which might be constructed to present a variant portrait of Jesus is not apparent. For even M. Sato who perceives Q to be analogous to OT prophet books agrees to the fact that in Q Jesus is a figure of exceptional authority.[69]

On the other hand, the OT background does provide hints that the Q material may, in fact, complement Mark's portrait of Jesus and the "orthodox" kerygma which Mark represents. Hints emerge from the multiple quotations and allusions to the book of Isaiah in Q. Two Q pericopes in particular suggest that Jesus interpreted himself in light of Isaiah.

A. Lk. 11:21, 22//Mt. 12:29

Past commentators including K.H. Rengstorf,[70] J.M. Creed,[71] W. Grundmann,[72] W. Manson,[73] A. Plummer,[74] and Barnabas Lindars[75] have identified this passage as a direct allusion to Isa. 53:12—the only verse in the Servant Songs which directly identifies the vicarious suffering and death of the servant. Lindars claimed, for example, that in Lk. 11:22//Mt. 12:29, "A saying of Jesus has been given messianic application and linked to the 'plot' of Isa. 53. The Passion is not mentioned, but is assumed in the struggle with the strong man."[76] Recently, however, scholars have been hesitant to make this connection for three primary reasons: (1) the verbal similarities are limited between the Q passage and Isa. 53:12;[77] (2) there is not a clear conceptual parallel between the two passages; and

---

[68] E.g., Lk. 13:28, 29//Mt. 8:11, 12: Isa. 43:5; 49:12; 59:19.

[69] *Q und Prophetie*, 95: "Der wichtigste Punkt jedoch, der Q über die Makrogattung 'Prophetenbuch' hinausrücken wird, besteht vor allem in der Gestalt des Sprechers Jesus selbst: Jesus in Q nimmt als für das Heil am Eschaton entscheidende Person die göttliche Stellung ein. Daraus stammt auch die einmalige christologische Gliederung der Stoffe in der Quelle. Diese exklusive Erhöhung der Stellung des Propheten ist in den alttestamentlichen Prophetenbüchern nicht geschehen."

[70] *Das Evangelium nach Lukas*, Göttingen: Vandenhoeck & Ruprecht (1958) 149.

[71] *Luke*, 161.

[72] *Das Evangelium nach Lukas*, Berlin: Evangelische Verlagsanstalt (1961) 239.

[73] *The Gospel of Luke*, London: Hodder and Stoughton (1930) 130.

[74] *The Gospel According to St. Luke*, Edinburgh: T&T Clark (1901) 303.

[75] *New Testament Apologetic*, London: SCM (1961) 85.

[76] *Ibid.*

[77] Verbatim agreements between the Mt. and Lk. sayings are limited to only four words: Mt.: τοῦ ἰσχυροῦ, καί, τήν, αὐτοῦ; Lk. ὁ ἰσχυρός, καί, τά, αὐτοῦ. The majority of commentators, however, identify this as a Q passage: So J. Kloppenborg: "The main argument

(3), "the strong" are the recipients rather than the conquerors in the Hebrew text. For these reasons, R.T. France,[78] J. Jeremias,[79] I.H. Marshall,[80] and J. Fitzmyer[81] have cited this text as a possible reference to Isa. 53:12, but have not pressed the connection for christological conclusions.

We likewise do not want to go beyond the evidence, but we find it sufficient in our present argument to point out that the verbal parallels to Isa. 53:12, though scant, do exist[82] (enough for NA[26] to record it as an allusion). Further, the most probable conceptual background for Lk. 11:22//Mt. 12:29 is a combination of Isa. 49:24f. and 53:12. In 49:24 it is the mighty man's prey which is taken: "Can the prey be taken from the mighty man, or the captives of a tyrant be rescued?", while the verbal parallel to the spoils (σκῦλα) in 53:12 is closer. Even Morna Hooker, who consistently rejects the association of Jesus with the servant, concedes the conceptual imagery of 49:24 when she writes, "Although there is no verbal correspondence between the Greek text and the LXX version of Isa. 49:24f., the similarity in meaning is so great that there is little doubt that Jesus had this passage in mind when he spoke these words . . ."[83] We do have, then, at minimum, a Q passage which presents Jesus interpreting his work in light of Isa. 53, if not in direct reference to Isa. 53 itself. This evidence does not prove that Jesus interprets his impending death in light of Isa. 53:12 (the death of the servant is not alluded to), but it does suggest that in Q Jesus interprets his work according to an OT passage which appears important to Jesus in Mk. 10:45 and elsewhere in the

---

for the inclusion of the parable in Q is that the agreement of Matthew and Luke in independently placing the parable of the strong man between Q 11:20 and 11:23 cannot be coincidental, but indicates that the parable also stood in Q at this point. Matthew preferred Mark to Q at this point", *Q Parallels*, 92. Kloppenborg lists as supporters of this conclusion: R. Bultmann, *History of the Synoptic Tradition*, 13-14; Creed, *Luke*, London: Macmillan (1930) 161; R. Edwards, *Theology of Q*, 110; J. Fitzmyer, *Luke* II, 918, 922 (probably); A.M. Hunter, *The Work and Words of Jesus*, 137; R. Laufen, *Die Doppelüberlieferung der Logienquelle und des Markusevangeliums*, 30; E. Käsemann, "Lukas 11:14-28", *Exegetische Versuche und Besinnungen*, vol. 2, Göttingen: Vandenhoeck & Ruprecht (1964) 242-248; J. Kloppenborg, *The Formation of Q*, 125; T.W. Manson, *Sayings*, 84; I.H. Marshall, *Luke*, 476-477; A. Polag, *Fragmenta Q*, 52; W. Schmithals, *Luke*, 134 (perhaps); E. Schweizer, *Luke*, 128; *Matthew*, 184-185; P. Vassiliadis,"The Nature and Extent of the Q Document," *NovT* (20) 49-73; D. Zeller, *Kommentar zur Logienquelle*, 59. Those who claim the saying was not in Q include: D. Lührmann, *Redaktion der Logienquelle*, 33; W. Schenk, *Synopse zur Redenquelle*, 136; S. Schulz, *Q–die Spruchquelle*, 203. Schulz claims Luke is here re-writing Mark rather that using Q.

[78] "The Servant of the Lord in the Teaching of Jesus", 43.

[79] *TDNT* V, 713.

[80] *Luke*, 477.

[81] *Luke* I, 923.

[82] Lk. 11:22 τὰ σκῦλα τοῦ ἰσχυροῦ διαδίδωσιν // LXX Isa. 53:12 τῶν ἰσχυρῶν μεριεῖ σκῦλα.

[83] *Jesus and the Servant*, London: SCM (1959) 74.

synoptic gospels. To this extent Lk. 11:21, 22//Mt. 12:29 questions the variant nature of Q.

B.   Lk. 7:22, 23//Mt. 11:4-6

Lk. 7:22, 23//Mt. 11:4-6 presents Jesus answering John the Baptist's question "Are you the coming one?" without a simple yes or no. Instead, Jesus tells John's messengers to report back that in Jesus' ministry the blind receive their sight, the lame walk, lepers are cleansed, the deaf hear, the dead are raised up, and the poor hear good news. Together these acts of Jesus represent the fulfilment of Isa. 26:19; 29:18f.; 35:5f.; 61:1f.

To be sure, none of these passages represent Servant Songs or the suffering servant in particular, but close similarities do exist between the figure of Isa. 61:1-3 and the mission of the servant in Isa. 42:1-7.[84] Both for instance are anointed with the Spirit (42:11; 61:1), and both proclaim freedom to prisoners (42:7; 61:1). In addition, the restoration of fortunes in 61:1 is reminiscent of the task of the servant in 49:6. Further, it is important to observe that the first person is used to describe the mission of Isa. 61:1 and that of the second and third Servant Songs, but nowhere between Isa. 40 and 66 does the writing prophet use the first person to describe his own work. Such evidence suggests a link between Isa. 61 and the Servant Songs. There is a hint within Q, therefore, that Jesus interpreted his ministry in terms of the suffering servant of Isaiah. Addressing this possibility, R.T. France writes:

> Certainly, Jesus can hardly have failed to notice the similarity of these two figures, which stand so close together in the same book of the OT, and the fact that He so emphatically applied the one to His own work must therefore strongly suggest, though it cannot prove, that He would have regarded the other as no less applicable.[85]

To France's comment we may add that it is very unlikely that Jesus would have perceived a contradictory distinction between Isa. 61 and the Servant Songs so that by applying one passage to his mission he somehow rejected the other. We are

---

[84] F.F. Bruce, *This is That,* Exeter: (1969) 90; C.H. Dodd, *According to the Scriptures,* London: Nisbet (1952) 94; E.E. Ellis, *Luke,* Grand Rapids: Eerdmans (1981) 97, 119, 120; I.H. Marshall, *Luke,* 183; M.D. Hooker (*Jesus and the Servant,* 84) agrees that the two figures were likely to have been joined in Jesus' time. M. de Jonge and A.S. van der Woude ("11Q Melchizedek and the New Testament", *NTS* 12 [1965-66] 301-326) note that Isa. 52:7 and 61:1f. are linked together in 11QMelch. On the Qumran material see also: David Hill, "The Rejection of Jesus at Nazareth (Luke IV 16-30) *NovT* 13 (1971) 161-180; James Sanders: "From Isaiah 61 to Luke 4", *Christianity, Judaism and other Greco-Roman Cults,* FS Morton Smith, Ed. J. Neusner; Leiden: E.J. Brill (1975) 75-106. For numerous, more dated advocates of this position see R.T. France, "The Servant of the Lord in the Teaching of Jesus", *TynB* 19 (1968) 43.

[85] "The Servant of the Lord in the Teaching of Jesus", 43.

left, then, with the important fact which cannot be questioned that Jesus does indeed interpret his mission in Q in light of Isa. 61—a passage very close in context to the Servant Songs. Though this fact does not prove our argument that Q complements the passion kerygma of Mark, it does provide confirmatory evidence.

On the other hand, there can be no doubt that in fulfilling the role of the Isaianic herald of Good News, Jesus in the Q material embarks on a ministry characterized by the very same attributes which set Jesus apart in the Galilean ministry of Mark: the anointing of the Spirit, the proclamation of Good News to the poor, and the successful performance of miracles to the blind, lame, deaf, and dumb. In both Mark and Q the burden of Jesus' message is his proclamation that the eschatological saving power of God is present in his own ministry.

Summary: The Q Material is Synoptic in Character

The absence of references to Jesus' death does not constitute evidence that Q contains a kerygma stemming from a 'second sphere' of Christianity because Q's silence is understandable in light of similar silence on the part of the Gospel writers themselves; because Jesus is, in fact, a rejected figure in Q; and, because there are Q allusions to passages in Isaiah which complement rather than contradict Mark's portrait of Jesus as the suffering Son of Man. Despite these arguments it remains true that Q does not contain an explicit suffering Son of Man saying or a single statement which qualifies the meaning of Jesus' death. Why is this the case if a variant community is not responsible? We close with four possible reasons. First, it is likely as J. Jeremias suspected, that the limited number of references to Isa. 53 in the synoptic Gospels reflects the fact that Jesus did not express the Servant role publicly, but only identified himself with the Servant before his disciples.[86] Following this argument, we may reason that if Q was addressed to a broad audience as its contents generally suggest, then we should not expect to find within Q references to the Suffering Servant. Second, despite recent arguments to the contrary, it is probable that the sayings of Jesus were utilized in teaching or preaching situations in the life of the early church in which knowledge of Jesus' death and resurrection were understood.[87] Third, passion allusions are few and

---

[86] *TDNT* V, 717.

[87] This is the conclusion of T.W. Manson, "The most probable explanation is that there is no Passion-story because none is required, Q being a book of instruction for people who are already Christians and know the story of the Cross by heart", *The Sayings of Jesus*, 16. Those reaching similar conclusions include: E. Käsemann, "On the Subject of Primitive Christian Apocalyptic", *New Testament Question of Today*, London: SCM, 1969, 119; W.G. Kümmel, *Introduction to the New Testament*, (1975) 73; O.H. Steck, *Israel und das gewaltsame Geschick der Propheten*, 288; P. Vielhauer, *Geschichte der urchristlichen Literatur: Einleitung in das Neue Testament, die Apokryphen und die Apostolischen Väter*, Berlin and New York: De Gruyter

interpretative statements of Jesus' death are absent in Q possibly because Jesus did not emphasize his own death until relatively late in his ministry. Matthew, Mark, and Luke agree in locating all of their suffering Son of Man sayings after Peter's confession at Caesarea Phillipi. Is there sufficient reason to doubt the Evangelist' placement of this material?[88] If the *Sitz im Leben Jesu* of the Q material was early or midway into Jesus' ministry, we would hardly expect it to include passion terminology, if its transmitters were conservative redactors, as we believe they were. Fourth, and last, there may be a clue to our puzzle in Jesus' answer to John: "the blind receive sight, the lame walk, the lepers are cleansed, the deaf hear, the dead are raised, and the poor are evangelized" (Lk. 7:22, 23//Mt. 11:4-6). In this passage, Jesus allows his mighty acts rather than an affirmative 'yes' or a contradictory 'no' to determine his identity. So it may well be with his death and resurrection. On infrequent occasions he openly anticipated his death, but in the end he allowed his actual crucifixion, resurrection, and exaltation speak for themselves, so that Tödt was correct when he wrote:

> The resurrection is God's affirmation of Jesus' *exousia*. Thereby the resurrection also is the confirmation before God of the fellowship bestowed by Jesus in his exousia on his own. Thus it is comprehensible why Jesus' teaching was taken up again and continued by the community; what Jesus had said had been confirmed by God.[89]

Final Conclusions

We conclude that evidence supporting a variant kerygma in Q does not stand up to critical evaluation. We have found the content of the Q passages which are said to bear witness to variant thought to be characteristic of the synoptics as a whole. The argument from silence is weak. In closing, therefore, the caveat expressed long ago by Adolf Harnack is worth repeating:

> A sceptic acquainted with the comparative history of religions will perhaps find even more here. He will argue as follows: The most ancient source which we possess for the life of Jesus knows nothing of His death upon the cross. . . . I regard it as quite possible that we shall very soon have to listen to this or to similar absurdities. The beginning is already made. In fact, there are far too many possible explanations of this

---

(1975) 328; U. Wilckens, "The Tradition-history of the Resurrection of Jesus", *The Significance of the Message of the Resurrection for Faith in Jesus Christ*, SBT 2/8, Ed. C.F.D. Moule; London: SCM (1968) 72.

[88] Kloppenborg's scepticism is unwarranted: "Easter Faith and the Sayings Gospel Q", 89: "Our inclination to read Q as a collection of pre-Easter sayings of Jesus derives from our knowledge of the latter evangelists' placement of Q. It may be doubted whether Q intended such a reading." What, we ask, is the basis for such doubt? How does Kloppenborg know what Q intended?

[89] *The Son of Man*, 252 as quoted in Kloppenborg, "Easter Faith and the Sayings Gospel Q", 83.

remarkable limitation of Q, and above all, our knowledge of Q and of its conclusion is far too uncertain to allow of the building up a critical theory upon such a foundation.[90]

Unfortunately, Harnack's fear has been realized in the growing number of critical works which presuppose Q to be the literary production of an esoteric community, as opposed to a simple collection of Jesus' sayings and teachings composed by eyewitness followers of Jesus, who passed on their memory of what Jesus said and did during his earthly ministry. The Q material is Jewish in background, synoptic in context, and dominical in origin according to the documents in which Q exists.

Therefore, to those who emphasize the silence of Q the alternative question must be raised. If the Q material contains authentic material from the early and middle stages of Jesus' earthly ministry where Matthew and Luke agree in placing it, why should Q contain explicit or even allusive references to Jesus' passion experience? On the other hand, in the postresurrection situation of the early Church, there is every reason to perceive why early followers of Jesus retained and valued the Q material as they sought to identify with and follow their Lord in an atmosphere of persecution.

---

[90] *The Sayings of Jesus*, n.1, 233, 234.

Summary and Conclusions

(1) *Comparison between Q and Mark indicates that Q is not from a "second sphere of Christianity."*

There are such close similarities between Q and Mark as to suggest that both sources rest ultimately on traditions about the historical Jesus handed down in the same or closely related Christian communities. A fresh study of the material shows that the alleged disparity between Mark and Q does not stand up to examination.[1] We have found the sayings materials which collectively compose Q to be compatible with the Gospel of Mark in regard to the primary theme which the two have in common—Jesus' sayings about the kingdom of God. Substantial textual evidence leads us to the conclusion that Mark and Q are consistent at least in their treatment of this theme, because the two are both dependent upon authentic Jesus tradition. Less detailed treatment of other shared themes—the Son of Man, eschatology, discipleship—cause us to strongly suspect that the same conclusion may be reached in regard to these subjects.

This does not imply that there was a vacuum in theological development from Jesus to the composition of Mark and Q. The evidence we have suggests that the earliest Jesus traditions were collected, arranged, edited, connected to one another secondarily and even shaped according to the needs of the church and the prevalent oral traditions in existence about Jesus. Yet while the editors of Mark and Q may have modified Jesus' teaching according to their particular situations, the overriding similarity between the two belies the presumption that Mark or the supposed Q community created dominical logia *ex nihilo.* Similarly, there is no evidence that Q sayings were originally voiced by prophets inspired by the risen

---

[1] Similarly, R. Laufen, *Die Doppelüberlieferungen der Logienquelle und des Markusevangeliums,* 386: "Die Einzeluntersuchungen haben nicht nur - bei aller Modifizierung und Aktualisierung - ein Höchstmaß an Kontinuität innerhalb der christlichen Traditionsgeschichte eines Jesuslogions aufgewiesen, sondern darüber hinaus gezeigt, daß die christliche Überlieferung von Herrenworten in der Geschichte Jesu selbst wurzelt, wenn auch bei einem einzelnen Logion immer nur die Möglichkeit, nicht die Tatsächlichkeit von Historizität ausgesagt werden kann. Selbstverständlich soll damit die Existenz von "Gemeindebildungen" nicht geleugnet werden. Aber sie spielen bei weitem keine so große Rolle, wie zum Beispiel R. Bultmann und ein Teil seiner Schule meinen."

Jesus;[2] in the foreground of Q stands entirely the Messianic authority of Jesus himself. The sayings were treasured, transmitted, and valued as athoritative within the early church because they were recognized as words spoken by the Messiah during his earthly ministry before his death, resurrection, and exaltation.

Although there are points of disparity between Mark and Q, the differences are minor in regard to content. Recent scholarly works which assign Q to an isolated community which orientated its traditional manuscripts around its particular proclivity for wisdom or the prophetic fail to recognize the same traits in Mark. In regard to these themes, Q's witness to what Jesus said and taught is christologically compatible with Mark's witness to what Jesus said and did (chs. 3, 4). This result causes us to wonder if in the scholarly zeal to discover the unique biases of the Gospel writers and the rather vague synoptic traditions which preceded them, redaction critics have not underestimated in some cases the importance of the enormous amount of material which the synoptic Gospels and their various hypothetical sources have in common.

Yet, form critics will ask, if Mark and Q are so compatible, why is there so little narrative in Q in contrast to Mark? We believe the substance of this distinction is exaggerated in view of the fact that in the temptation narrative and in the healing of the centurion's servant, Q does contain some narrative. Elsewhere we fail to see why there should be extensive narrative in Q, if the compiler's intention was to report, in its purest and most memorable form, the teaching of Jesus. In answering "What did Jesus teach?," Q recounts Jesus' memorable teachings with short pithy sayings and parables, forms which Q shares with Jesus' teaching in Mark, and forms befitting such a question. Mark's passion narrative, on the other hand, was stimulated by an entirely different question—what were the events that led up to Jesus' death and how did he die? Short pithy sayings of Jesus obviously could not respond appropriately or adequately to this question. Here an informed narrator would be needed. What were the events that led up to Jesus' death and how did he die? "Now the Passover and the Unleavened Bread was two days off; and the chief priests and the scribes were seeking how to seize him by stealth, and kill him" (Mk. 14:1). The formal disparities between Q and Mark are to be explained by the different questions which they answer.

Similarly, we have found the theory of a variant or "heretical" kerygma in Q to lack supporting evidence (Ch. 9).[3] Scholars are wrong to draw far-reaching

---

[2] There is no prophetic *Sitz im Leben* alluded to in Q. *Erhöhungschristologie* has to be read into the text.

[3] So J. Gnilka, *Neutestamentliche Theologie ein Überblick*; Würzburg: Echter Verlag (1989) 27: "Ob der Tod Jesu als Heilstod gedeutet wurde, verrät uns die Quelle nicht. Aus dem Schweigen darüber wird man keine besonderen Schlüsse ziehen dürfen."

conclusions from the absence of passion emphasis in Q. Q, a body of Jesus'
teaching, should not be pressed to contain all that is found in an entire Gospel.[4]
Although some scholars think that we can reach theological or historical
conclusions on the basis of what is not stated in Q, our observations indicate
otherwise. First, the apparent refusal of Q to interpret the meaning of Jesus' death
is not significant in the light of similar silence within Matthew, Mark, and Luke.
Second, the alleged evidence of an interpretation of Jesus' death which contradicts
Mark falters upon the allusive character of the few Q passages which are said to
present Jesus as a common martyr figure—a figure which itself has complex
connotations and which does not necessarily challenge "orthodox kerygma."
Third, the "deuteronomistic tradition" is a paradigm which Q shares with Mark
(Ch. 9), Acts (Appendix A), and the theological orientation of the apostle Paul
(Appendix B). Fourth, Jesus in Q is a rejected figure (Lk. 7:34//Mt. 11:19; Lk.
10:13-15//Mt.11:21-23; Lk. 13:34, 35//Mt. 23:37-39; Lk. 14:27//Mt. 10:38).
Such evidence anticipates Jesus' own death and corroborates the rejection Jesus
experiences in the Galilean section of Mark (2:6, 7, 18, 23, 24; 3:1, 2, 22, 30; 6:4;
7:1-5; 8:11f.). Jesus' death, therefore, is not a topic of striking dissimilarity
between Mark and Q.

(2) *Q and Mark are compatible in areas where they can be compared validly, that
is, in the themes and concepts which they have in common.*

In addition to the general consonance between Mark and Q on the subject of the
kingdom of God, there is positive correspondence between them in Q Lk.
7:22f.//Mt. 11:4f., which we believe to be a critical key to interpreting the
significance of Jesus' miracles in Mark. In Mark Jesus performs the exact same
miracles as are reported to John the Baptist in Q. In both Mark and Q, Jesus'
miracles relate directly to his proclamation of the Gospel—the Good News that
eschatological salvation has come through Jesus himself to those desiring the
benefits of his ministry. In Mark, as in Q, Jesus' miracles are strategic because
they identify him to be the eschatological herald of salvation (Isa. 61:1f.).

---

[4] If V. Taylor's simple reasoning is maintained, there is no reason to suspect that Q should
have alluded to Jesus' passion: "The simplest and most natural view is that Q began as a sayings-
source pure and simple. The fragmentary narrative element in most reconstructions of its
contents suggests this, and the inference is supported by the broad probabilities of the case. Q
was an innovation prompted by the needs of catechetical instruction. The times demanded a
compend of the Lord's oracles, similar in form to the wise sayings of the Book of Proverbs.
Such a collection could take its rise only out of that which already existed, and it was compiled
from Pronouncement-Stories, sayings-groups, and words of Jesus in free circulation" (*The
Formation of the Gospel Tradition*, 182, 83).

Both Mark and Q exhibit a dichotomy between insiders and outsiders. The concept of community (*Gemeinschaft*) is similar in both. Those who belong to the community of salvation are those who have left all and followed Jesus and have perpetuated his ministry. For these the kingdom of God occasions enthusiasm as God's rule through Jesus is the hope for human salvation both now and in the final judgement. In contrast, both Mark and Q present the kingdom of God as a mystery which is hidden from those most capable intellectually to receive it—the wise, the lawyers, the Pharisees and Scribes, who are the very figures who reject Jesus. A clear distinction exists, therefore, between those, on the one hand, who follow Jesus and as a result will enter the kingdom in the future and those, on the other hand, who reject Jesus and therefore will be found unsuitable for future salvation in the eschatological banquet. In Mark and Q Jesus' antagonists are the same.

The community concept in both Mark and Q occurs through Jesus' ministry where the kingdom of God is offered as eschatological salvation to people. Those who accept the saving benefits of Jesus' ministry become the people of God. In Q we see the gathering of the eschatological people of God in the earthly ministry of Jesus (Lk. 11:23//Mt. 12:30; Lk. 10:2//Mt. 9:37, 8), and we also gain a glimpse of the gathered community as it will exist at the consummation of the kingdom of God (Lk. 13:28, 29//Mt. 8:11, 12). We do not see early Church kerygma, we see the earliest response to Jesus, his message, and his ministry. Jesus himself and not 'apocalyptic enthusiasm' or a specific form of eschatology is the source of identity for Jesus' followers in both Mark and Q (Lk. 11:23//Mt. 12:30; Lk. 12:8-9//Mt. 10:32; Mk. 8:38; Lk. 12:8, 9//Mt. 10:32, 33; Mk. 10:21b). The hearers' response to Jesus himself is in both sources the decisive factor determining salvation. Response to Jesus takes two forms: one of acceptance by social outcasts and sinners (Lk. 7:34//Mt. 11:19; Mk. 2:15-17), the other of rejection primarily by religious leaders of Judaism (Lk. 11:37-52 par.; Mk. *passim*). Despite the fact that Jesus' ministry brings the *basileia* near, or even in some sense brings God's rule into the present, Jesus' ministry is not accomplished fully because the people of God has not been gathered completely for the day of salvation (Lk. 13:34, 35//Mt. 23:37-39). Thus the purpose of Jesus' earthly ministry in Q is in part exactly the same as the purpose for Jesus' death in Mark— namely, to gather God's people together for the feast of salvation in the kingdom of God (Mk. 14:24, 25). The reign of God manifests itself in both events for the same purpose.

Mark shares with Q the tension between present and future in the sayings of Jesus about the kingdom of God. Both support the likelihood that Jesus himself held in tension a present and future understanding of the kingdom of God.[5] Q contains one saying which views the kingdom of God as present and active in the ministry of Jesus (Lk. 11:20 par.), one saying which definitely views the kingdom as the future manifestation of God's power which occasions both the eschatological feast and the eschatological sentence of judgement (Lk. 13:28, 29//Mt. 8:11, 12), and the parables of the mustard seed and leaven which hold in tension the kingdom present and future. Similarly, Mark contains one present saying (1:15), two future sayings (9:1; 14:25), and two parables which draw attention to the kingdom both present and future (4:26-29, 30-32). There exists no evidence that Jesus saw the kingdom's consummation taking place in the present. Rather, his appearance as the anointed Isaianic Herald indicates that in his present acts and preaching Jesus perceived the inauguration of God's eschatological saving power. Present and future exist in tension precisely in man's response to the kingdom. As man responds positively or negatively to the kingdom of God as manifested presently in Jesus, so will accord man's salvation or damnation at the consummation of the kingdom of God. Present and future sayings, then, do not necessitate the suspect hypothesis that the Q community expected an imminent parousia at an early phase while later coming to grips with the delay.

(3) *The Q material, like Mark, is unified by the person and work of Jesus.*

Q and Mark show correspondences because both draw heavily from the authentic teaching of Jesus, and strong evidence indicates that the teachings and actions of Jesus in Q support post-Easter Christian acclamations that Jesus was the Messiah, the Son of God. While Q, in not containing the $Χριστός$ title, conceals the Messianic character of Jesus in a manner that is consistent with the phenomenon of the "Messianic Secret" in Mark, it also supports Jesus' messiahship (Mk. 1:1) in multiple ways. The plain meaning of Lk.10:22//Mt. 11:27 is that the source of Jesus' authority resides specifically in his relation as son to God the Father. It is Jesus' sonship which allows him to reveal the Father, and to preach the nearness of the kingdom of God and the saving power of the kingdom. Comparison of this text with the burden of Jesus' teaching elsewhere in Q implies that Jesus derives from God, in a unique manner, the authority which he assumes in heralding in the kingdom (Lk. 6:20//Mt. 5:3; Lk. 7:22//Mt. 11:5), in teaching authoritatively about the kingdom, in proclaiming that the kingdom of God is somehow present in his acts (Lk. 7:22//Mt. 11:5; Lk. 11:20//Mt. 12:28), and in judging who will and who

---

[5] Representative: G.E. Ladd, *Jesus and the Kingdom*; R. Schnackenburg, *God's Rule and Kingdom*; L. Goppelt, *New Testament Theology* I; Davies and Allison, *Matthew* I, 389, 90.

will not participate in the future eschatological banquet (Lk. 13:28, 29//Mt. 8:11, 12; Lk. 14:15-24//Mt. 22:1-10). It is, indeed, telling that in Q the following facts converge: (1) Jesus performs specific saving acts which the OT exclusively associates with God in the eschatological Day of the Lord (Lk. 7:22//Mt. 11:5: Isa. 26:19f.; 29:18f.; 35:5f.; Jer 31:7-9); (2) with the address *abba*, Jesus refers to God in an unusually intimate fashion in the Lord's Prayer; (3) Jesus refers to himself as son in relation to God in a non-titular manner (Lk. 10:21, 22 par.); (4) Jesus adopts the self-designation 'Son of Man' which implicitly alludes to Dn. 7:13, 14, where "the one like a Son of Man" appears in close proximity to "the Ancient of Days" and who, like Jesus in Q, receives the same dominion, power, and kingdom which in earlier parts of Daniel describe the sovereignty of God (3:33; 4:31); (5) Jesus initiates in Q the eschatological harvest and sends out messengers—a function characteristic of God in the OT and in Wisdom texts;[6] (6) in Q Lk. 9:59f.//Mt. 8:21f., Jesus authoritatively demands his followers to break with Jewish custom—an authority which appears, according to M. Hengel, "in a way in which in the OT only God himself enjoined obedience on individual prophets in regard to the proclamation of his approaching judgment;"[7] (7) and finally, in no less than nineteen cases does Jesus assume special authority in defiance of Jewish religious leaders by using the λέγω ὑμῖν (σοί) address in Q— a phrase which can be attributed to Jesus with confidence (see ch. 4).

With this body of material before us, we regard Q as a critical part of the foundation of synoptic evidence upon which to view Jesus as the chosen Messiah of God. Q shares the conviction of Mk. 1:1. Lk. 10:23//Mt. 13:16, 17 makes this clear:

> But blessed are your eyes, because they see; and your ears, because they hear. For truly I say to you, that many prophets and righteous men desired to see what you see, and did not see it; and to hear what you hear, and did not hear it.

In this passage, as in Lk. 10:21//Mt. 11:25, Jesus refers indefinitely to a blessing which his listeners have received. What is definite, however, is that the blessing is manifest in the appearance and ministry of the speaker—Jesus. Hence it is clear that within Q Jesus' uniqueness resides precisely in his relationship to God—a relationship which authorizes him to bring good news to the poor, heal the sick, cast out demons, and reveal the Father. In view of this evidence, it is not necessary to speculate that the Q community collected, modified, and created sayings of Jesus as a by-product of "prophetic enthusiasm" occasioned by a

---

[6] So J. Kloppenborg, *The Formation of Q*, 319; O.H. Steck, *Israel und das gewaltsasme Geschick der Propheten*, 286 n. 9; D. Catchpole, "The Mission Charge in Q", *Semeia* 55, 154.

[7] *The Charismatic Leader and His Followers*, 12.

particular expectation of the parousia or some other unknown apocalyptic stimulus. It is more plausible, rather, that Jesus created an atmosphere of "enthusiasm" in his own acts and in his teaching about the kingdom, and that it was Jesus himself who attracted followers and who instilled hostility in religious authorities who rejected his arrogant teaching (Q: Lk. 11:37-52//Mt. 23:4, 6, 7, 13, 25-31, 34-36). It is plausible that some of the former group recorded Jesus' teaching. Jesus himself was the motivation for them to do so. In the latter group we may see the early impetus for hostility towards Jesus—the form of hostility which eventually led to his execution.

Hence it is not necessary to speculate about an unknown apocalyptic event as the *raison d'être* for Q because Jesus' prophetic language, his assumption of wisdom terminology, the messianic connotations of his work, his proclamation of the "Good News" of the kingdom of God and his self-association with God would have created an atmosphere of crisis characterized both by enthusiasm among his followers but also by hostility among those pious Jews who recognized but rejected the authority which he assumed. The content of Jesus' sayings and indeed the mere identity of their speaker would have created the impetus for their being recorded, transmitted, arranged, and eventually integrated within the Synoptic Gospels.[8]

Furthermore, Jesus speaks and acts in Q in a manner concomitant with Messiahship. He is God's son (Lk. 4:3, 9//Mt. 4:6, 9; Lk. 10:22//Mt. 11:27). He is greater than the son of David (Lk. 11:31//Mt. 12:41). He is anointed by the Spirit (Lk. 7:22f.//Mt. 11:4f.; Isa. 61:1f.; Lk. 11:20//Mt. 12:28). He speaks with wisdom—an attribute expected of the Messiah (Isa. 11:2; See Ch. 3). He performs a specific combination of miracles which set him in the place of God and the Isaianic herald of eschatological salvation according to OT attestation (Isa. 29:18; 35:5, 6; 42:18; 26:19; 61:1; Jer. 31:7-9).[9] He defeats Satan and casts out demons (Lk. 4:1-13//Mt. 4:1-11; Lk. 11:20//Mt. 12:28). He authoritatively pronounces eschatological judgement upon the religious authorities of his day (Lk. 11:42, 43, 46//Mt. 23:23, 26, 27, 4). He proclaims that eschatological salvation has come in and through his ministry to the socially and religiously undeserving (Lk. 7:22f.//Mt. 11:4f.). He refers to himself with the self-designation Son of Man, which in I Enoch (48:10; 52:4) and 4 Ezra (13:37, 52) is a messianic

---

[8] So R. Riesner, *Jesus als Lehrer*, 352: "Wenn Jesus von sich als messianischem Weisheitslehrer sprach und infolgedessen seinen Worten höchste Autorität zuschrieb, so lag darin zumindest für den engsten Jüngerkreis, darüberhinaus aber auch für alle, die seinen—wenn auch verhüllten — Hoheitsanspruch ernstnahmen, ein außerordentliches Tradierungsmotiv."

[9] Miracles were expected of the Messiah in Judaism (Targum Isaiah 53:8f.; 4 Ezra 7:26-28; 13:49f. See O. Betz, "Jesus' Gospel of the Kingdom", *The Gospel and the Gospels* (1991) 60.

appellation.[10]   He sets out to gather the people of God in Jerusalem for eschatological salvation (Lk. 10:2f.//Mt. 9:37f.; Lk. 11:23//Mt. 12:30; Lk. 13:34, 35//Mt. 23:37-39)—an act to be performed by the Messiah according to Psalms of Solomon 17:26, and an act expected of God himself in Isa. 60:3; 62:10-12; Jer. 31:7-9. And finally, Jesus identifies himself as the decisive factor upon which man's salvation or damnation will depend in the final judgement (Lk. 12:8, 9//Mt. 10:32, 33; Lk. 13:28, 29//Mt. 8:11, 12). *Hence Q supports Mark's concept of the Gospel of Jesus Christ, the Son of God* (1:1).

(4) *The overwhelming evidence of OT allusions and quotations in Q demand that Q's conceptual background be classified as Jewish.*[11]

While quotations and allusions to the OT frequent Q, Q does not contain one allusion to an ancient Greek document (other than the LXX). This is a serious problem for scholarly hypotheses which attempt to trace Q to a predominantly Greek background (e.g., the theories of J. Kloppenborg and B. Mack). It is worth noting in this respect that the phrase 'son of man', the mere concept of the kingdom of God, the form of theological wisdom found in Q, and Q's prophetic features all reflect a Jewish background which Q shares with Mark. The primary conceptual background for Q is the book of Daniel which contains the same cluster of themes which characterize Q (ch. 5).

(5) *The content of Q does not provide landmarks for its division into separate strata of community contemplation.*

Whether Q is primarily orientated around apocalyptic, or wisdom, or eschatology, or prophecy is too simplistic a question in view of pre-Christian Jewish documents—particularly Daniel—where these themes and ways of communication converge and buttress one another (ch. 5). Wisdom, prophecy, and the performance of miracles were not mutually exclusive at the time of Jesus as can be seen in the apocryphal psalm 11QPs[a] XXVII. Neither do they represent technically rigid forms of literature. In view of the images which converge in Daniel, it would have been possible for Jesus to draw together the concepts of the Son of Man, the kingdom of God, judgement, prophecy, wisdom and various

---

[10] See W. Horbury, "The Messianic Associations of 'The Son of Man' ", *JTS* 36 (1985) 34-55; J.J. Collins, "The Son of Man in First Century Judaism", *NTS* 38 (1992) 457f.; C. Caragounis, *The Son of Man.*

[11] So C. Schuppan, *Gottes Herrschaft und Gottes Wille,* 28: "Die Spruchquelle reiht sich mit ihrem Sprachgebrauch in den Rahmen des Frühjudentums ein."

apocalyptic figures of speech and apply them to his mission. These themes are not unique to Jesus in Q, but appear in his teaching throughout the synoptic Gospels. Each is appropriate to his teaching on the kingdom of God. With Daniel as a historical precedent to Q, Jesus himself could have combined these concepts in his endeavour to preach the Good News of the kingdom of God.[12] The combination of attributes links Jesus to the Davidic ideal and hence insinuates his messianic identity. The prevalent theories that wisdom, prophecy and apocalyptic demarcate the different layers of Q redaction is, therefore, unsubstantiated and artificial.

We agree with Graham Stanton in his judgement that "Reconstructions of possible stages in the development of Q traditions are likely to be influenced by the investigator's presuppositions concerning the transmission and development of Gospel traditions, and even by views on the development of earliest Christianity."[13] The Q Community, the supposed strata of Q tradition, and the hypothetical, multifaceted redactional layers of Q represent presuppositional foundations for the majority of recent scholarly works on Q. While we recognize the value of scholarly hypotheses and realize the impossibility of suppressing entirely our own presuppositions, we find many aspects of the present Q campaign quite unconvincing. Our study leads us to conclude that the existence of an isolated distinct Q community is not a compelling hypothesis (ch. 2) primarily because of a basic lack of historical and textual evidence and because the Q material has great affinity in content with the Synoptic Gospels as a whole. It is safe to say that the Q *Tradents* shared one fundamental objective which in part motivated the writing of Mark's Gospel—namely the motive of passing on the Good News of what Jesus spoke and did. Convincing, we believe, is the possibility that Q was recorded, translated, and passed on through the channels of the first Christian congregations in Jerusalem. It will not be surprising, following this conjecture, that we have found dubious the many attempts to precipitate Q community *Tendenz* from its record of the sayings of Jesus. While the sayings of Jesus had to have been recorded and passed on by someone, the anonymity of that person, group, or community is important. Whoever they were, they did not desire to pass on memory of themselves, and we believe scholars err in speculating that these *Tradents* desired to reorient qualitatively or theologically the authoritative teaching of their master. It may not be too much to say that it is impossible to discover an unique Q christology or theology both because of our lack of extant evidence to warrant such conclusions (we do not know the entirety of what the Q transmitters

---

[12] As H.W. Attridge ("Reflections on Research into Q", *Semeia* 55, 1992, 233) writes, "the originating figure himself was a much more complex individual than Q1 gives him credit for being."

[13] "Q", in *Dictionary of Jesus and the Gospels*, (1992) 649.

believed) and because of the nature of the Q material that we do have, which complements rather than varies from the Synoptic tradition as a whole. In seeking an unique Q christology or theology, we may be striving for what cannot be found and indeed never existed. Indeed, we may be asking the wrong questions!

All this is emphatically not to deny the credibility or validity of the composition critical enterprise. Clearly the various fragments of Q did not come together at one point in time. An editor, a group of editors or even a series of editors must have played an important role in the recording, collecting, arranging and transmitting of the Jesus tradition present in Q. What we do deny, however, is a direct link between compositional layers and traditional pedigree. Authentic material may have entered the Q collection at a late stage just as easily as at its inception. Along the same lines, we hesitate to accept the growing consensus that authentic Jesus material is limited to isolated "floating logia." This criterion restricts, unreasonably we believe, the abilities of ancient transmitters of historical dialogue. Extended discourses attributed to Jesus in the Synoptics may have a better claim to authenticity than is often recognized (as in the case of Mk. 12:1-11). We must leave this question to further study.

We conclude, therefore, that a very simple but powerful impetus compelled the first compilers of the Jesus tradition: the desire to pass on to other believers the content and message of what the risen Lord Jesus said and did during his earthly ministry. We have shown that the content of this material would have caused excitement on the part of its readers because Jesus' earthly acts and teachings implied his identity as the eschatological herald of salvation—the anointed wise Messiah, who had come to defeat Satan and gather God's people for salvation in the kingdom of God. The Jesus tradition in Mark supports the Q material in confirming the historical probability that these were implications of Jesus' authentic teaching.

(6) *The Relationship and Historical Development of Mark and Q.*

There remains the problem of explaining the relationship and historical development of Mark and Q. How can we explain the coexistence of two apparently independent streams of Jesus tradition? How can we explain the similarities and the differences between Mark and Q if they are not, as many scholars conjecture, representatives of two different spheres of early Christianity? And why is it that Q knows so little of the other traditions that went into Mark?

These questions cannot, of course, be answered with anything close to certainty because of the lack of historical evidence to document the formation of the synoptic gospels and the sources and traditions that proceeded them. Yet a way may be open to a positive hypothesis if we take seriously the earliest Christian

traditions that we do have. As is implied by Lk. 1:1-4, there existed sources and
bits of tradition which the Gospel writers valued to such a degree that they
incorporated them into their Gospels without modifying them to the point where
they were no longer distinguishable from their own vocabularies and styles. If we
take the historical Jesus seriously and agree to the overwhelming probability that
Jesus' followers, and the disciples in particular, held in their memories specific
things that Jesus said and did, the historical judgement may be secure that Mark
and Q represent basically conservative redactions of orthodox or mainstream
tradition.[14]

In view of the early Christian testimonies that we do have, the best
explanation, in our opinion, for the development and relation of Mark and Q is to
be found in Papias' controversial statements (Eusebius *H.E.* 3:39:15-16) which
associate the disciple Peter with Mark and the disciple Matthew with a collection of
oracles (τὰ λόγια) which were put together and composed in Hebrew/Aramaic.
We do not, of course, maintain that all the material in Mark came via Peter; nor do
we suggest that the disciple Matthew is responsible for the entire collection of Q as
modern scholars have reconstructed it. But we are inclined to take Papias
seriously. His testimony is extremely early (100-150 AD) and was without doubt
taken in earnest by Eusebius and probably also by the later Church fathers who
linked Matthew and Peter with the first two Gospels respectively.

Furthermore, T.W. Manson was probably correct that Papias' statements
reflect not Papias' personal opinion, but the traditions of an earlier generation.[15]
The fact that Eusebius transmits very little of Papias, together with Eusebius'
apparently low view of Papias' intellect, suggests that Eusebius included the
selections of Papias which he did, because they were dependent upon tradition
which appeared to him to be trustworthy.

Is it possible that τὰ λόγια refers to oracles which the disciple Matthew
compiled or collected (συνετάξατο) in the Hebrew/Aramaic language ('Εβραΐδι
διαλέκτῳ) and which later Christian scribes independently translated into their own
language (presumably Greek) as best they could (ἡρμήνευσεν δ' αὐτὰ ὡς ἦν
δυνατὸς ἕκαστος)? Does τὰ λόγια refer to a collection of dominical traditions
something like Q? And if so, is it possible that Matthew, as the compiler of these
oracles, came to be associated in time with a Gospel not composed by him but
which contained in part dominical traditions which he collected or even composed?

---

[14] Cf. R. Pesch, *Markus* I, 2; M. Hengel, *Studies in the Gospel of Mark*, ET London: SCM
(1985) 31-41; C.E. B. Cranfield, *Mark, passim*; I.H. Marshall, *Luke*, 33 and *passim*.

[15] *The Sayings of Jesus*, 17.

Although many scholars have rejected this conjecture,[16] other prominent scholars have defended it.[17]

J. Kloppenborg, perhaps the most formidable opponent to the idea, ardently opposes the Matthew-Q connection arguing that Papias' statements on Matthew must be interpreted in the context of his statements on Mark. He reasons that Papias' remark about Mark not making "an orderly arrangement of τὰ κυριακὰ λόγια . . . implies that the elder considered Mark to be λόγια."[18] Though the primary definition of the term is oracle (especially at the time of Papias!), it had a wide range of reference among the Fathers including OT verses, sayings of Jesus and even the OT as a whole. τὰ λόγια, then, could be used in reference to a whole Gospel. Further, the use of τῶν . . . λογίων in connection with τὰ πραχθέντα in 3:39:15 indicates that Papias used λόγια as an inclusive term not only for sayings but also acts: "for him it included τὰ πραχθέντα, i.e., narratives." And finally, the title of Papias' own work Λογίων κυριακῶν ἐξηγήσεις confirms, for Kloppenborg, that in 3:39:15-16 λόγια refers to a finished product including sayings and narratives—"by λόγια he meant canonical Matthew."[19]

However, several observations indicate that Kloppenborg has not dealt a decisive blow to the Manson line of thinking. First, as M. Black has recently noted, it may not be valid methodology to insist that Papias' statement on Matthew be interpreted in light of his statements on Mark. In *H.E.* 3:39:15-16 the two are separated by an editorial comment by Eusebius and may, therefore, be considered two independent Papias traditions secondarily juxtaposed by Eusebius. If so the Matthew statement must be interpreted in isolation.[20] Second, even if both statements are taken together, we are not convinced that Papias uses τῶν κυριακῶν

---

[16] W. G. Kümmel's skepticism is representative: "Rather, as "the first Christian man of letters," Papias applies to the Gospels a false standard, so that it is in order to leave the Papias references out of consideration—in spite of their great age—when studying the literary relationships between the Gospels", *Introduction to the New Testament*, 53f.

[17] Most notably: F. Schleiermacher, "Über die Zeugnisse des Papias von unsern beiden ersten Evangelien," *TSK* 5 (1832) 735-68; T.W. Manson, *The Sayings of Jesus*, 17-20; David Hill, *Matthew*, 22-34; W.D. Davies, "Matthew, Gospel According To", in *Hasting's Dictionary of the Bible*, 2nd ed., Edinburgh: T&T Clark (1963) 631-33; C.F.D. Moule, *The Birth of the New Testament*, 3rd ed., London: Adam & Charles Black (1981) 105, 126, 127, 277; M. Black, "The Use of Rhetorical Terminology in Papias on Mark and Matthew", *JSNT* 37 (1989) 38.

[18] *The Formation of Q*, 53.

[19] *Ibid.*, 54. Thus Kloppenborg concludes: "Papias' testimony, consequently, is of no probative worth in the quest for an Aramaic Q. His claims are apologetically motivated, and they refer to the canonical Gospels, not to their sources."

[20] *JSNT* 37 (1989), 32: "We cannot, therefore, be certain that the two statements were juxtaposed in this way by anyone other than Eusebius, nor can we assume (as many have done) that both are 'traditions' of the elder'. Pap[mt] may preserve a tradition independent of Pap[mk], and is not just to be understood in the light of Pap[mk]."

ποιούμενος λογίων as a flat reference to the Gospel of Mark. The use of the genitive plural suggests that Papias is defending the collective value of the contents of Mark—he is not necessarily adopting λόγια as a technical synonym for Gospel.[21] It is not at all clear that Papias' Λογίων κυριακῶν ἐξηγήσεις was a compilation of traditions similar to Matthew, Mark or Luke. And third, we do not find compelling the assumption that Papias' phrase τὰ πραχθέντα (acts), is synonymous with "narrative" in the modern sense. Action is not necessarily narrative bound. As we have noted earlier, Q is not absolutely silent on Jesus' miracles (Lk. 7:22//Mt. 11:5; Lk. 11:20//Mt. 12:28), nor for that matter is Q totally devoid of narrative (Lk. 7:1-10//Mt. 8:5-13; Lk. 4:1-13//Mt. 4:1-11). Hence, the Matthean collection of λόγια referred to by Papias may have been something comparable to Q even if the λόγια are not restricted to short pithy sayings or even sayings chains.

Papias' statement still fits the contents of Q better than the Gospel of Matthew if λόγια is taken to refer to dominical oracles or to a Chriae collection—an ancient collection of sayings, maxims, and/or aphorisms of a prominent person structured around catchword, formal analogy and subject matter.[22] Manson's conclusion remains attractive: ". . . the statement of Papias which cannot be made to fit the Gospel of Matthew except by a forced and unnatural interpretation, does, when taken in its simple and natural meaning, fit a document such as Q like a glove."[23] And ironically, as Black has noted, "Kloppenborg's identification of Q with a Chriae collection would strongly support the well-known thesis which identifies τὰ λόγια in Pap^mt with the source Q . . ."[24]

If Q, whether in its final arrangement or in an intermediate state, was composed or collected by the apostle Matthew, its most plausible *Sitz im Leben* would be the earliest Jewish church in Jerusalem where Jesus' teaching would

---

[21] Here Kloppenborg's rendering of Eusebius is slightly misleading. 3:39:15 does not read τὰ κυριακὰ λόγια as he reproduces it, but "τῶν κυριακῶν ποιούμενος λογίων." Hence it is not a certainty that τὰ λόγια has an antecedent in the Markan statement even if the two are taken together.

[22] Kloppenborg (*ibid.*, 306-16) concludes that Q had become a Chriae collection by its second stage of development.

[23] *The Sayings of Jesus*, 17.

[24] *JSNT* 37 (1989) 35. *Pace* J. Kloppenborg, *The Formation of Q*, 263: "Two factors in particular suggest that any attempt to discuss the genre of Q should consider non-Jewish parallels. Q contains several chriae, a form which is not indigenous to Jewish (or Near Eastern) collections, but very common in Greek circles. Second, the very fact that Q was composed in Greek, not Hebrew or Aramaic, makes it *a priori* likely that resonances with Greek wisdom or sentence collections will be found." Kloppenborg has fallen short of proving that Q was composed in Greek. He, therefore, could be charged with arguing in a circle. Furthermore, he has not considered the great probability that Jews of the first century may have syncretized Jewish thought with Hellenistic literary forms. And as we have argued throughout this book, the content of Q represents thought steeped in Jewish theological wisdom—not Hellenistic philosophy.

have been of critical importance for the education of new converts primarily on the meaning, rewards and costs of discipleship (Acts 2:42). It is hard to imagine, however, that a single element of Q would have been outside the interests of the first converts to Christianity. After a period of oral transmission, the need inevitably arose for a written record of Jesus' teaching, and the apostle Matthew, a former tax-collector and eyewitness to Jesus' ministry, was the ideal person to assume the task.

At a later point in time, the conversion of Hellenistic Jews in Jerusalem would have stimulated the desire to translate Matthew's oracles into Greek. While most Hellenistic Jews in Palestine were probably bilingual in Greek and Hebrew/Aramaic, it is not difficult to imagine that the Hellenistic Jews of Acts 6:1-6 would have undertaken this task as the primary means of sharing the apostolic witness to Jesus' teaching among Greek-speaking converts who, despite their exposure to the Semitic languages, found Jesus' sayings difficult to translate and interpret. Hence translators adept at both languages were chosen and at a very early phase of the growth of Christianity, Q may have existed in two languages— Greek and Hebrew/Aramaic.

The subtle and often complicated differences we detect in the variant sayings shared by Mark and Q are to be explained by Mark's use of oral and written Aramaic traditions which originated from the memories of Jesus' disiciples and which thus corroborate the content of Q. The parallels in Greek terminology between Mark and Q are to be explained by the same choice of vocabulary on the part of the independent translators and the development of technically Christian vocabulary which was commonly understood to be the correct Greek rendering of Jesus' original Aramaic words (hence shared words such as $\epsilon\dot{v}a\gamma\gamma\dot{\epsilon}\lambda\iota o\nu$, $\dot{o}$ $\upsilon\dot{i}\grave{o}\varsigma$ $\tau o\hat{v}$ $\dot{a}\nu\theta\rho\dot{\omega}\pi o\upsilon$, $\dot{\eta}$ $\beta a\sigma\iota\lambda\epsilon\acute{\iota}a$ $\tau o\hat{v}$ $\theta\epsilon o\hat{v}$). The frequency of Aramaic and Hebrew words in the short space of Mark's Gospel suggests that Mark was a Greek speaking Jewish Christian who understood Aramaic.[25] His knowledge of both languages would have enabled him to translate Aramaic sayings of Jesus (which would have been of extreme value to his church) into written Greek. For example, as many have suggested, it is attractive to view Mk. 3:28 and Lk. 12:10 as two variant Greek renditions of one common underlying Aramaic saying. We propose that the author of Mark was translating by memory into Greek this logion, which came to him through Aramaic oral tradition as it was passed on to the church by the early apostles of the historical Jesus. The author of Luke, on the other hand, at a later time, took up the logion as he found it in his Greek source Q—a document

---

[25] See M. Hengel, "Problems in the Gospel of Mark", *The Gospel and the Gospels*, Ed. Peter Stuhlmacher, Grand Rapids: Eerdmans (1991) 229f. = *Das Evangelium und die Evangelien*, Tübingen: J.C.B. Mohr (Paul Siebeck) 1983.

which did not contradict preceding oral traditions, though it differed from them in minor details. The same procedure may also explain the variant endings of the Mustard Seed parable. While both recognized the tree metaphor, the author of Mark assimilated his translation to Eze. 17:23 in contrast to the translator of Q, who assimilated his text to the Theodotion text of Dn. 4:21.

Hence we may have in Q and Mark two independent and parallel but related streams of tradition. The doublets in Luke indicate that the author of the third Gospel absorbed both—one as he found it in Greek Mark, the other as he found it in Greek Q.[26]

The author of Matthew undertook a more complex procedure. As most commentators suspect, he conflated his sources; not only Mark and Q but also, being bilingual,[27] both the Greek and the Aramaic versions of Q. He conflated material common to Greek Mark and Greek Q, taking the elements from each which he considered truest to the original. He recognized the overlaps between Mark and Q and hence eliminated at least five doublets.[28] The doublets that remain result from the author's desire to buttress his special interests with dominical tradition.[29] While he primarily depended on the Greek translation of Q, he conferred with the original Aramaic and sometimes opted to provide a new Greek version, when he believed a better interpretation could be achieved (e.g., in cases where the Aramaic was ambiguous). This could explain the very complicated discrepancies between sayings such as Lk. 16:16 and Mt. 11:12, 13.

Why is it that Q knows so little of the other traditions that went into Mark? M. Hengel has presented a solid case for taking seriously the Papias tradition that associates the apostle Peter with Mark the author of the second Gospel.[30] He argues that internal Markan evidence supports Papias.[31] First, given its shorter length, Mark mentions Simon Peter more frequently than either Matthew or Luke.

---

[26] See J. Fitzmyer, *Luke* I, 81-82.

[27] Davies and Allison, *Matthew* I, 33: "Matthew, it would seem, lived in a bilingual or trilingual milieu, was familiar with Jewish traditions, had much more interest in and familiarity with the OT than Luke, and knew the OT both in Greek and Hebrew."

[28] *Ibid.*, 120 n. 74.

[29] *Ibid.*, 119.

[30] *Studies in the Gospel of Mark*, 47-53: "The dependence of the author on Peter, which plays a very important role in establishing the priority of Mark, but which today is usually completely ignored or even abruptly rejected, should be maintained: it makes a substantial contribution to our understanding of the Gospel. It is also confirmed, independently of Papias, by Justin in his reference to Mark 3.16f. as supposed 'recollections of Peter'. There are good historical reasons for what at first sounds an unusual piece of information, that Mark was Peter's interpreter" (50). Such a position has been advocated more recently by Morna Hooker, *The Gospel According to St. Mark*, London: A&C Black (1991) 6, 7.

[31] This paragraph is dependent upon Hengel's, "Problems in the Gospel of Mark", esp. pp. 238-43.

Second, Peter appears at strategic places within the Gospel—he is both the first (1:16) and the last (16:7) disciple mentioned. Dependence on Peter may be implied by the personal account of the healing of Simon's mother-in-law (1:29), the manner in which the disciples are described as "Simon and those with him" (1:36), and the prominent place given to Peter at the head of every list of the disciples, the twelve, the three and the four (Mk. 3:16f.; 5:37; 9:2; 13:3). Further, Peter is the last disciple spoken to by Jesus in Gethsemene (14:37) and the last to accompany him to the courtyard of the high priest (14:54). Particularly conspicuous is the reference to him at the end where the angels command the women, "Go and say to his disciples *and to Peter.*" All this underlines the fact that the unique significance of Peter in Mark's Gospel is what we would expect if Peter was to some extent the origin of Mark's tradition about Jesus, as Papias instructs. We perceive no historical reason to deny it. If, then, Hengel is correct that Peter traditions underlay select portions of Mark, we have a partial solution to the relation of Mark and Q. Mark differs from Q partly because it presents a second apostolic witness to the Jesus tradition. Peter related to Mark events and teachings of Jesus' career which Matthew did not think to record. Yet in some cases Mark received from Peter general impressions of Jesus' ministry which corroborated Matthew's (Q) teaching. Such may explain the teachings loosely common to Mark and Q, that Jesus ate with tax-collectors and sinners (Mk. 2:17; Lk. 7:34//Mt. 11:19) and demanded that compassion be extended to children (Mk. 10:13-16; Lk. 17:2//Mt. 18:17). Other differences may be explained by Mark's redaction and his inclusion of additional traditions, both oral and written, which came to him apart from Peter.

On the other hand, it is easy to perceive that Mark being a short, fast-moving Gospel does not contain all the dominical tradition that was at its author's disposal. The author of Mark selectively chose dominical traditions according to particular images and themes. It is easy to see, for example, why he would have omitted the leaven parable (if he knew it), when he composed ch. 4. He retained the Mustard Seed parable which fit the controlling image of the context and omitted the leaven, which would have introduced a new metaphor. In other cases Markan redaction is more difficult to comprehend.

We leave to further study the refinement or modification of our theory. But our tentative speculations, and that is all they are, help explain the overlaps between Mark and Q, the linguistic variations in the texts they share, and the presence in Q of materials not found in Mark (and vice versa). Taking seriously the results of contemporary redaction and tradition criticism, we have provided a theory which also does justice to the ancient associations of the disciples Matthew and Peter with the composition of the first two Gospels. A simple solution to the apparent absense of Passion emphasis in Q could be that the original recorder of the Q material was an eyewitness to the teaching he recorded but not an eyewitness to the events recorded in the latter chapters of the Synoptic Gospels. If Peter was the most respected witness to Jesus' passion, as the Gospels plainly suggest, it stands to reason that Petrine tradition would undergird the traditional framework of the passion accounts, as many have argued. Matthew's testimony to the crucifixion is largely absent because he was one of those who scattered at Jesus' arrest.

Whether our conjectures can be sustained or not, the existence of the sayings tradition is best explained by the certainty that Jesus had disciples who became after his death authoritative reporters of the Messiah's teaching and acts. The presence of at least some authentic dominical tradition in the Synoptic Gospels is doubted by very few contemporary scholars. If not from the disciples, from where do these traditions come?

Appendix A

Q and Discipleship in Acts

J. Kloppenborg's recent book *The Formation of Q* subtitled *Trajectories in Ancient Wisdom Collections* furthers the proposal of J.M. Robinson that Q fits into a trajectory of wisdom collections which extends from Proverbs through the Gospel of Thomas and into later Gnostic writings. We have not found this thesis convincing. It fails to take note of the similarity between the Q material and the synoptic material at large, while at the same time exaggerating wisdom influence in Q where out of roughly 230 verses the word σοφία occurs only three times. The words σοφία, σοφός, συνετός and συνίημι never appear in the Gospel of Thomas.[1] Furthermore, a strict comparison of form shows Q does not fit the description of a pure sayings' collection. Q does not have a prologue comparable to that of Thomas.[2] Q nowhere begins a pericope as Thomas always does with the phrase "Jesus said", or "His disciples asked him" or "the disciples said to Jesus." Q contains not only short pithy sayings but also the temptation narrative (Lk. 4:1-13//Mt. 4:1-11) and the narrative of the Centurion's servant (Lk. 7:1b-10//Mt. 8:5-10, 13). The shades of gnostic thought present in the Gospel of Thomas (§ 29, 50, 77) are totally lacking in Q. On the other hand, Q's emphasis of the eschatological identification of Jesus as the coming Son of Man is foreign to the Gospel of Thomas. Further, the Gospel of Thomas contains sayings entirely foreign to Q[3] in addition to sayings parallels with Mark and the material unique to Matthew (M) and Luke (L).[4] And finally, there does not exist a direct link

---

[1] According to A. Fuchs and F. Weissengruber, *Konkordanz zum Thomasevangelium*, SNTU Serie B, Band 4, Druck: Plöchl, Freistadt, 1978.

[2] "These are the secret sayings which the living Jesus spoke and Didymos Thomas wrote down. And he said, "Whoever finds the interpretation of these sayings will not experience death." "The Gospel of Thomas", Tr. H. Koester and T.O. Lambdin; *The Nag Hammadi Library in English*, Ed. James M. Robinson, Leiden: E.J. Brill (1977) 9.

[3] Representative is §6: "Blessed is the lion which the man shall eat, and the lion will become man; and cursed is the man whom the lion shall eat, and the lion will become man."

[4] §9 is representative which contains a variant version of the synoptic parable of the Sower and the Soils.

between the Gospel of Thomas and pre-synoptic Q material.[5]   Such a link would seem to be required for there to be a literary relationship between the two.

Instead of following a "wisdom trajectory" we believe the importance of the Q material resides partly in its value as a dominical source for the early Church's understanding of discipleship. Both Mark and Q contain traditional material which transmit instructions where Jesus commands his disciples to go out and further Jesus' mission through preaching the kingdom of God and through miraculous acts (Mk. 6:7-13; Lk. 10:1-16//Mt. 9:37-38; 10:16a, 5b, 6, 9-13, 7f., 11, 14f.; 11:21-23; 10:40). In Q Jesus states directly that the disciples have claim to Jesus' own authority as they go out (Lk. 10:16//Mt. 10:40). In Mark and in Q Jesus makes it clear that discipleship has direct consequences: persecution in the present (Lk. 6:22, 23//Mt. 5:11, 12; Lk. 14:25-27//Mt. 10:37, 38; Mk. 8:34, 35) but blessing in the future (Lk. 12:8//Mt. 10:32; Mk. 9:1). *Hence in the post-Easter situation, the early Church retained the Q material partly because of its value as a source for Jesus' instruction for discipleship.* We seek to support this observation by exposing the conceptual parallels between Jesus' instructions for discipleship in Q and the lifestyle of discipleship displayed by Stephen and Paul in the book of Acts and in 1 Thessalonians (Appendix B).

M. Casey has recently contended that Jesus' teaching ministry was formative for the disciples' own identity after Easter as early Christianity distinguished itself from orthodox Judaism. According to Casey the single identity factor differentiating the disciples from the rest of Judaism was Jesus himself: "He led the movement and taught his followers. He was himself the visible embodiment of Jewish identity, and the source of the Jewish identity of his disciples. Consequently, the disciples could not abandon Jesus' view of Judaism when he was put to death."[6] Here Casey is certainly correct. In Q Jesus himself is the identity factor for his followers: "He who is not with me is against me; and he who does not gather with me, scatters" (Lk. 11:23//Mt. 12:30); "And I say to you, everyone who confesses me before men, the Son of Man shall confess him also

---

[5] So C.M. Tuckett, *Nag Hammadi and the Gospel Tradition* , Edinburgh: T&T Clark (1986) 9: ". . . no firm evidence for the use of pre-synoptic sources (Q or otherwise) is found in these texts. Practically all the tractates appear to presuppose the synoptic gospels in their present final form." Hence radically speculative is the understanding of Thomas advocated by Steven L. Davies, *The Gospel of Thomas and Christian Wisdom*, (1983) 3: "It is a collection of sayings used to instruct newly-baptized Christians. It appears to reflect an early form of Johannine preaching and probably came into being at about the same time as the Q document. . . . Thomas should be dated ca. A.D. 50-70." The earliest datable fragments of the Gospel of Thomas (from which the Coptic was translated) are dated to about 200 A.D. Where and how early the document was originally composed is a matter of conjecture. See H. Koester's "Introduction", *The Nag Hammadi Library in English*, 117.

[6] *From Jewish Prophet to Gentile God*, 74.

before the angels of God; but he who denies me before men shall be denied before the angels of God" (Lk. 12:8, 9//Mt. 10:32, 33); "Whoever does not carry his own cross and come after me cannot be my disciple" (Lk. 14:27//Mt. 10:38). It is not wisdom but Jesus himself whom we find at the center of the Q material. Identification or rejection of Jesus is what matters.

There is within the synoptic gospels the conception that Jesus' teaching and miracles fail to occasion a response of repentance because they are not understood by the hearer. Jesus' teaching, his wisdom, and his miracles instead occasion rejection on the part of his learned enemies and amazement but not full comprehension on the part of the crowds and even Jesus' disciples. Despite this general lack of understanding, within Mark and Q Jesus' ministry stimulates a division between those attracted to Jesus, on the one hand, and those repelled by him on the other. To those who follow Jesus the mystery of the kingdom of God is given while those outside get everything in parables "in order that while seeing, they may see and not perceive; and while hearing, they may hear and not understand lest they return and be forgiven" (Mk. 4:11, 12 par.; Isa. 6:9; Jer. 5:21). While the gravity of Jesus and his ministry is hidden from the wise and intelligent "these things" are revealed to babes i.e., those who innocently identify with Jesus (Lk. 10:21//Mt. 11:25). As the gospels progress the former group—the Scribes and Pharisees in Mark and Q—intensifies opposition to Jesus thereby aborting the value of its knowledge: "Woe to you lawyers! For you have taken away the key of knowledge; you did not enter in yourselves, and those who were entering in you hindered" (Lk. 11:52//Mt. 23:13). For these "outsiders" the odds for true understanding decreases as opposition to Jesus increases. They belong with those who murdered the prophets (Lk. 11:49-51//Mt. 23:34-36) and so represent a tradition of *Unheilsgeschichte* or punitive judgement. Thus their sentence is one of woe.

For the disciples, on the other hand, it must be admitted that their understanding of Jesus and his ministry does not come about instantaneously. However, it is clear that the disciples' potential for understanding depends solely on their continued identification with Jesus. One purpose for Jesus' teaching (Mk. 6:1-6; 7:14; 11:18; 15:10) and his miracles (Mk. 6:52; 8:17, 18, 21; Lk. 7:22/Mt. 11:4-5) was to impart understanding by calling attention to Jesus himself and to raise the question of his identity. However, beyond Peter's confession in Mk. 8:29, the Synoptic Gospels do not identify the disciples as acquiring understanding before Easter either in regard to Jesus' miracles or in regard to his ensuing death (Lk. 18:34; Mk. 8:10; 9:32). It is not until after Easter in Lk. 24:27, 45 that the resurrected Jesus opens the disciples' minds to understand the scriptures in relation to his death and resurrection.

In the synoptic gospels, therefore, there is no evidence in Q or in Mark that Jesus mediates a wisdom or an esoteric teaching which imparts salvation. *Eternal blessing as opposed to damnation depends rather upon one's association with Jesus or one's rejection of Jesus—i.e., upon obedient discipleship.* The poor, the lame, the blind and the deaf are blessed because in their despair they have recognized their need for Jesus' ministry. In uniting with Jesus the saving power of God's rule has come to them.

Thus Jesus' earthly ministry produces disciples and antagonists. One group advances Jesus' ministry, the other attacks it. The one faces persecution but receives blessings. The other persecutes but receives a curse of *Unheilsgeschichte*—"they will keep on hearing and not understand, they will keep on seeing and not perceive."

I.   Discipleship in Acts

NT scholarship has successfully delineated a pattern of correspondence between Jesus' ministry in Luke and the design for Christian discipleship advocated in the book of Acts: Jesus' anointing with the spirit, his mission, suffering and rejection in Luke provides the literary paradigm for the spirit anointing, the performance of miracles, the suffering and rejection experienced by the early followers of Jesus in Acts.[7] As Jesus' rejection corresponds to the rejection experienced by OT prophets, so the disciples' rejection in Acts corresponds to the fate of Jesus. We cite these parallels to illustrate that the Deuteronomistic pattern proposed by O.H. Steck conforms not with a trajectory of wisdom thought leading through Q, the Gospel of Thomas and later Gnostic texts, but rather with the pattern of rejection repeated in the lives of the prophets, experienced by Jesus and emulated by Jesus' followers. Thus even in regard to the question of literary development, the Q materials which fit Jesus and his followers into the Deuteronomistic pattern of the rejection of the prophets do not require explanation by means of a variant development within early Christianity. Jesus' rejection in Q is the model for Christian discipleship in Acts. Hence the claim that the Gospel writers incorporated Q in order to suppress its supposed Gnostic proclivities is unsound in

---

[7] See Robert C. Tannehill, *The Narrative Unity of Luke-Acts*, Philadelphia: Fortress Press (1986) vol. 1, 285-89; (1990) vol. 2; 84, 87, 94-101, 176-182, 355; David P. Moessner, " 'The Christ must suffer' , New Light on the Jesus–Peter, Stephen, Paul Parallels in Luke-Acts", *NovT* 28 (1986) 220-56 (226, 56); Robert F. O'Toole, *The Unity of Luke's Theology: An Analysis of Luke-Acts*, Wilmington: Michael Glazier (1984) 82-86; Robert L. Brawley, *Luke-Acts and the Jews: Conflict, Apology, and Conciliation,* Atlanta: Scholars Press (1987) 25; Richard J. Dillon, *From Eye-Witnesses to Ministers of the Word: Tradition and Composition in Luke 24,* Rome: Biblical Institute Press (1978) 279-80.

view of the manner in which Luke uses Q as an integral component within his portrait of normative Christian discipleship.

A.   Stephen the Disciple of Jesus: Acts 6 and 7

The paradigm of the rejection of the prophets in the OT, in Q, and in Mk. 12:1-12 forms an important foundation for the early Christian concept of *Unheilsgeschichte*, on the one hand, and Christian discipleship on the other.   In Acts 6 Stephen comes from the original "congregation of the disciples," speaks "in wisdom" (6:10: τῇ σοφίᾳ), and faces rejection because of his obedient discipleship to Jesus.   Do such characteristics mark Stephen as a rejected messenger of Sophia?   Like the disciples Jesus commissioned in Mk. 6:13 and in Q Lk. 10:9//Mt. 10:7-8, Stephen's ministry is characterized by "great wonders and signs among the people" (6:8).   And upon his rejection as a disciple of Jesus the Nazarene (6:14), Stephen voices a sentence of woe in the face of his accusers which recalls Jesus' statements in Q (cf. Lk. 13:34//Mt. 23:37; Lk. 6:23//Mt. 5:12):

> You men who are stiff-necked and uncircumcised in heart and ears are always resisting the Holy Spirit; you are doing just as your fathers did.   Which one of the prophets did your fathers not persecute?   And they killed those who had previously announced the coming of the Righteous One, whose betrayers and murderers you have now become; you who received the law as ordained by angels, and yet did not keep it. (Acts 7:51-53)

And finally, like Jesus, Stephen is put to death in Jerusalem.   However, in furthering Jesus' acts and in exuding the Spirit and Wisdom, and in facing death in Jerusalem, Stephen does not fit into a trajectory of Wisdom's sages.   Stephen fulfils the discipleship role laid out by Jesus during his earthly ministry in Mark and in Q (Mk. 8:34; Lk. 14:27//Mt. 10:38).   In keeping with Q where Jesus is distinguished from his disciples as the Son and as the Son of Man, in Acts Stephen upon his death, as one who has remained loyal to Jesus to the end, sees before his death the fulfilment of Jesus' teaching in Q Lk. 12:8//Mt. 10:32.   He has furthered Jesus' ministry as an obedient disciple, he has faced rejection, and now before his death he sees "the Son of Man standing at the right hand of God" (7:56).   Meanwhile, it is not coincidental that Luke describes Stephen's antagonists as "gnashing their teeth at him" (ἔβρυχον).   The image recalls Jesus' description of the future dilemma of his adversaries in Lk. 13:28//Mt. 8:11, where he pronounces: "There will be weeping and gnashing of teeth there when you see Abraham and Isaac and Jacob and all the prophets in the kingdom of God, but yourselves being cast out."   The situation is similar in Acts 7 where the Jewish antagonists are cut to the quick and gnash their teeth.   In contrast Stephen, in the fullness of the Spirit, sees Jesus standing at the right hand of God as the Son of Man who reigns in power (7:55, 56). The distinction is not between Stephen, a figure of Wisdom, and his antagonists, but between the offended Jews and Stephen the follower of Jesus. Identification with Jesus is the issue, not wisdom.

B. Acts 13

The same paradigm for discipleship occurs in Acts 13 where Paul warns the Jews in Antioch not to assume the guilt of the Jewish forefathers who rejected the prophets:

> Take heed therefore, so that the thing spoken of in the Prophets may not come upon you: 'Behold, you scoffers, and marvel, and perish; for I am accomplishing a work in your days, a work which you will never believe, though someone should describe it to you. (Acts 13:40, 41; Hab. 1:5; cf. Isa. 6:9)

Here Paul warns his audience not to make the mistake characteristic of those who rejected the prophets and those who killed Jesus in Jerusalem (13:27). They must not underestimate the decision they make when they accept or reject Paul the apostle of Jesus. Hence a dichotomy develops between those who follow Paul and Barnabas (13:43) and those who contradict them (13:45). The latter group, according to Paul, has judged itself "unworthy of eternal life" (13:46) in contrast to the former which receives the message of salvation (13:47-49). Paul and Barnabas, following the pattern of discipleship required by Jesus, face persecution and rejection (13:50) before being driven out of the district. Before departing, however, they pronounce the verdict required by Jesus in such situations: "they shook off the dust of their feet in protest against them" (Acts 13:51; Q Lk. 10:10, 11//Mt. 10:14; Mk. 6:11; Lk. 9:5). Hence Paul and Barnabas fulfil the role of disciple as outlined by Jesus in Q and Mark.

C. Acts 14

A similar sequence of events develops in Iconium and Lystra in Acts 14. Paul's preaching stimulates a division between those who believe (both Jews and Greeks v. 1) and those who disbelieve (the Jews v. 2), so that "the multitude of the city was divided; and some sided with the Jews, and some with the apostles" (14:5). Paul and his entourage continue the ministry of the earthly Jesus as outlined in Lk. 10//Mt. 10; Mk. 6 by speaking boldly "with reliance upon the Lord" and by performing signs and wonders (14:3) including the healing of the lame man in Lystra (14:8-10). Once again the apostles face persecution as a result of their preaching of the Gospel (14:7) and their miraculous works. Paul is stoned and dragged out of the city (14:19). Like Stephen, Paul personifies obedient discipleship so that following this event Luke summarizes the basic thrust of the apostles' ministry:

> And after they had preached the gospel to that city and had made many disciples, they returned to Lystra and to Iconium and to Antioch, strengthening the souls of the disciples, encouraging them to continue in the faith, and saying, "Through many tribulations we must enter the kingdom of God. (14:21, 22)

For Luke the passage follows the paradigm for Christian discipleship as laid out by Jesus during his earthly ministry. The disciples follow Jesus' call to reap the harvest and learn to endure tribulation as a consequence (Lk. 10:3, 10//Mt. 10:16a, 14). Yet the prize (entrance into the kingdom of God) motivates endurance. Such teaching recalls Jesus' beatitudes where the poor are blessed because theirs is the kingdom of God (Lk. 6:22, 23//Mt. 5:11, 12). As Jesus strengthened the souls of his disciples by encouraging them to endure persecution in lieu of their stake in the kingdom and in view of their relation to the great men of faith, so Paul and Barnabas encourage new believers in the same way.

D. Paul and the Fate the Prophets in Jerusalem: Acts 20 and 21

As an obedient disciple of Jesus, Paul like Stephen follows the pattern set by the prophets and articulated by Jesus (Lk. 13:34//Mt. 23:37) when upon leaving Ephesus he anticipates his own demise in Jerusalem:

> You yourselves know, from the first day that I set foot in Asia, how I was with you the whole time, serving the Lord with all humility and with tears and with trials which came upon me through the plots of the Jews; how I did not shrink form declaring to you anything that was profitable, and teaching you publicly and from house to house, solemnly testifying to both Jews and Greeks of repentance toward God and faith in our Lord Jesus Christ. *And now, behold, bound in spirit, I am on my way to Jerusalem not knowing what will happen to me there, except that the Holy Spirit solemnly testifies to me in every city, saying that bonds and afflictions await me. But I do not consider my life of any account as dear to myself, in order that I may finish my course, and the ministry which I received from the Lord Jesus, to testify solemnly of the gospel of the grace of God.* And now, behold, I know that all of you, among whom I went about preaching the kingdom, will see my face no more. Therefore I testify to you this day, that I am innocent of the blood of all men. For I did not shrink from declaring to you the whole purpose of God. (Acts 20:18b-27)

Here again Paul interprets his persecution at the hands of the Jews as being the direct result of the ministry which he received as an apostle from the Lord Jesus ($\tau\grave{\eta}\nu$ $\delta\iota\alpha\kappa o\nu\acute{\iota}\alpha\nu$ $\mathring{\eta}\nu$ $\mathring{\epsilon}\lambda\alpha\beta o\nu$ $\pi\alpha\rho\grave{\alpha}$ $\tauο\hat{\upsilon}$ $\kappa\upsilon\rho\acute{\iota}o\upsilon$ $\,\mathring{I}\eta\sigmaο\hat{\upsilon}$). He foresees "bonds and afflictions" in Jerusalem despite his innocence. Like the prophets, Jesus, and Stephen, Paul faces rejection because he "did not shrink from declaring the whole purpose of God." Such a line of tradition, however, does not obscure Jesus' distinctive placement in God's plan as Luke obviously did not consider Paul to be on a par ontologically with Jesus. But as the prophets were martyred for declaring the will of God before an obstinate people, and as Jesus was crucified as a result of his staunch stand against the Jewish authorities who rejected the power of God as it manifested itself within his ministry, so too Paul must face rebuke as one who furthers the ministry of the earthly Jesus and as one who declares the "purpose of God" as it has been revealed to him by the risen Jesus. Paul's rejection results directly from his identification with Jesus.

E. Acts 28

Acts concludes with Paul the Apostle repeating the verdict of Isaiah, Jesus, and Stephen:

> The Holy Spirit rightly spoke through Isaiah the prophet to your fathers, saying,"Go to this people and say, 'You will keep on hearing, but will not understand; And you will keep on seeing, but will not perceive; For the heart of this people has become dull, and with their ears they scarcely hear, and they have closed their eyes; Lest they should see with their eyes, And hear with their ears, and understand with their heart and return, and I should heal them. '" (Acts 28:26, 27; Isa. 6:9, 10)

In rejecting Paul the apostle of Jesus, the Jewish antagonists have incurred the same judgement as did Jesus' enemies in Galilee (Mk. 4:11, 12)—in rejecting Paul they have rejected Jesus and the saving benefits flowing from Jesus' own ministry. In contrast to the poor, the blind, the lame, the lepers, the deaf, and the dead who received in full the salvific blessings of Jesus' mediation of kingdom power, and in contrast to the believers who heard and responded positively to Paul's preaching about Jesus, the Jewish antagonists who reject Paul lose precisely what "those who hear" gained—hearing, sight, perception and healing— "the salvation of God" (28:28).

Conclusion

There is material agreement between the kind of discipleship Jesus demands in Mark and Q and the discipleship displayed by Stephen and Paul in the book of Acts. Likewise the tradition of *Unheilsgeschichte*—the tradition of guilt facing those who rejected the prophets and those sent by God which incurs a curse of spiritual numbness (Isa. 6:9)—represents in Acts a foil to obedient discipleship as it does in Mark and Q. Most importantly the distinguishing factor between salvation and judgement remains consistent. The one who identifies with Jesus either through Jesus himself (the Gospels) or through Jesus' apostles (Acts) is saved; the one who rejects Jesus or his apostles faces a sentence of judgement which incurs a numbing of the heart. Jesus is unique to the Deuteronomistic pattern. In Q Jesus fulfils the prophetic pattern as the one anointed to bring eschatological salvation (Lk. 7:22//Mt. 11:5). In Acts Jesus is the means of salvation offered by the prophet-apostles. In both, to reject Jesus is to refuse salvation and to incur wrath.

Appendix B

Paul and the Q Material

Does the Q material counter Pauline teaching? Historically the inquiry into Paul's use of Jesus' sayings has given rise to a scholarly rift between sceptics who largely deny Paul's knowledge of Jesus' teaching and supporters who cite explicit references and implicit allusions to Jesus' teaching within the Pauline corpus as evidence of continuity between Paul and the bearers of the Jesus tradition.[1] If the latter could be proven in regard to Q sayings, the theological alienation of the Q material would be rendered suspect.

Dale Allison, a supporter of the interplay between Jesus and Paul, has identified a pattern of dependence emerging from the location of parallels in four defined portions of the Pauline corpus (Ro. 12-14, 1 Th. 4-5, Col. 3-4, 1 Cor. *passim*) coupled with a density of parallels in three synoptic blocks (Mt. 10 par.; Mk. 9:33-50 par.; Lk. 6:27-38 par.). Arguing that "If Paul knew nothing more than isolated sayings, then we would not anticipate finding any pattern at all,"[2] Allison defends the linguistic and conceptual parallels between Lk. 10 and 1 Cor. 9, 10, and 1 Th. 4 in order to reach the conclusion: "Paul knew a form of the missionary discourse very close to what was in Q."[3]

While Allison openly declares that his conclusions are reached by way of "inference" and "probability" as opposed to certainty, he has been heavily criticized just the same.[4] In response to Allison's 1982 article in *NTS,*[5] C.M. Tuckett wrote that Allison's theory was illfounded: "The mere existence of isolated allusions cannot establish Allison's theory that larger blocks of synoptic material were as such known to Paul . . . All that seems certain is that Paul knew and used one

---

[1] For the history of this discussion, see Victor Paul Furnish, "The Jesus-Paul Debate: from Baur to Bultmann", *Paul and Jesus*, JSNTSS 37, Ed. A.J.M. Wedderburn; Sheffield: JSOT Press (1989) 17-51.

[2] "Paul and the Missionary Discourse", *ETL* 61 (1985) 370.

[3] *Ibid.,* 375.

[4] Allison has found supporters, however. See Peter Stuhlmacher, "Jesustradition im Römerbrief? Eine Skizze", *TB* 14 (1983) 240-250.

[5] "The Pauline Epistles and the Synoptic Gospels: The Pattern of Parallels", 1-32.

saying, the workman saying, from this discourse."[6] Also sceptical of Allison's theory, F. Neirynck reduces Pauline dependence on sayings of Jesus to 1 Cor. 7:10-11 and 9:14 with the conclusion:

> Elsewhere in the Pauline letters there is no certain trace of a conscious use of sayings of Jesus. Possible allusions to gospel sayings can be noted on the basis of similarity of form and context but a direct use of gospel sayings in the form it has been preserved in the synoptic gospels is hardly provable. Paul's knowledge of a pre-synoptic gospel, of the source Q or pre-Q collections has not yet been demonstrated.[7]

With Neirynck's negative conclusion we agree—certainly there exists no conclusive evidence that Paul knew of or used Q. However, if we agree that we are without factual evidence relating to the transmission of Jesus' sayings from their point of origin to their inclusion into the Gospels, it is noteworthy that the earliest point of contact between the Q material and early Christianity exists in the letters of Paul as opposed to an esoteric community. Both Neirynck and Tuckett concede 1 Cor. 9:14 as an allusion to at least Lk. 10:7b//Mt. 10:10b—a Q saying.[8] When we add to this point of contact the possibility of other contacts[9] and the occasional nature of Paul's letters and hence the extreme unlikelihood that Paul in his extant letters reproduces his entire knowledge of the historical Jesus, the possibility that Paul was corroborative with the transmission of Jesus' teaching certainly seems superior to the blind conjecture that Q material developed in

---

[6] "Paul and the Synoptic Mission Discourse", *ETL* 60 (1984) 377, 381.

[7] "Paul and the Sayings of Jesus", *L'Apôtre Paul*, Ed. A. Vanhoye; Leuven: Leuven UP (1986) 320.

[8] So J. Kloppenborg, *Q-Parallels*, 72; S. Schulz, *Q–Die Spruchquelle*, 404-07; A. Polag, *Die Christologie der Logienquelle*, 3.

[9] Michael Thompson (*Clothed with Christ: The Example and Teaching of Jesus in Romans 12.1-15.13*, JSNTSS 59; Sheffield: JSOT Press, 1991) considers Ro. 12:14 to be "a virtually certain echo" of Lk. 6.27-36//Mt. 5:38-48: "The influence of dominical teaching here is clear . . ." (105). Further, Thompson sees "a highly probable echo" of Lk. 6:37a//Mt. 7:1 in Ro. 14:13a (172, 73, 237). Thompson concludes that the example of Jesus was more compelling for Paul than Jesus' words. W. Schenk (*Synopse zur Redenquelle der Evangelien. Synopse und Rekonstruktion in deutscher Übersetzung mit kurzen Erläuterungen*, Düsseldorf: Patmos, 1981, 86, 87, 132) provides an extensive list of Q-Pauline parallels which he subjects to the theory that Paul was aware of a Q-*Vorlage*. Accordingly, Q material not mirrored by Paul falls into the category of Q redaction which came into being after Paul's letters were written. N. Walter ("Paul and the Early Christian Jesus–Tradition", *Paul and Jesus*, JSNTSS 37; Sheffield: JSOT Press, 1989, 51-80) lists the following indirect references to Q material in Paul: Ro. 12:14: Lk. 6:28a//Mt. 5:44b; Ro. 12:17a (1Th. 5:15a): Lk. 6:29//Mt. 5:39b-41; Ro. 12:19-21: Lk. 6:27a + 35//Mt. 5:44a; 1 Cor. 4:11a : Lk. 6:21a//Mt. 5:6; 1 Cor. 4:12b-13: Lk. 6:27-28//Mt. 5:44; Lk. 6:22-3//Mt. 5:11-12. Allison, *NTS* 28 (1982) 20, lists the following Q--Paul parallels: Ro. 8:15; Lk. 11:2//Mt. 6:9; Ro. 12:14; Lk. 6:28//Mt. 5:44; Ro. 12:17; Lk. 6:27-36//Mt. 5:38-48; Ro. 12:21; Lk. 6:27-36//Mt. 5:38-48; Ro. 14:10-11; Lk. 6:37//Mt. 7:1-2; 1 Cor. 4:14; Lk. 6:28//Mt. 5:44; Col. 3:13; Lk. 11:4//Mt. 6:12; 1 Th. 5:2, 4; Lk. 12:39-40//Mt. 24:43-44; 1 Th. 5:15; Lk. 6:27-36//Mt. 5:38-48. The parallels vary in credibility and most are controversial.

isolation from orthodox early Christianity as represented by Paul and Mark. Inconsistency in method marks the process whereby some scholars scrupulously deny Pauline interest in the historical Jesus while at the same time asserting as valid the hypothesis of an esoteric community for which we have no historical allusions whatsoever.

I. Paul the Apostle of Jesus according to Paul's Letters

The historical verisimilitude of the brand of apostleship personified by Paul in Acts (Appendix A) is largely supported by what we find as characteristic of Paul's mission in the Pauline corpus itself. Like the earthly Jesus, Paul was a wandering preacher who suffered homelessness and rejection.[10] Like the disciples Jesus commissioned to go out into Galilee, Paul vindicates his apostleship "by signs and wonders and miracles" (2 Cor. 11:12). As Jesus commanded his disciples to be servants of all (Mk. 9:35; Lk. 14:11//Mt. 23:12; Lk. 13:30//Mt. 20:16), so Paul makes himself "a slave to all" (1 Cor. 9:19). As poverty was a characteristic of those who chose to follow Jesus during his earthly ministry,[11] so Paul is counted among the poor (1 Cor. 4:9-13). Here Paul's humble lifestyle is commensurate with his role as an apostle. The same equation repeats itself frequently in the Pauline corpus where Paul as a messenger of the Gospel faces various forms of persecution and imprisonment.[12] In these respects Paul conforms to the violent fate of Jesus, so that in 2 Cor. 4:10 he claims to carry about in his body "the dying of Jesus." Similarly, in Phil. 3:10 he writes that he has fellowship with "his sufferings, being conformed to his death."

In view of the material correspondence between Paul's ministry and the instructions for discipleship voiced by the earthly Jesus,[13] the supposed unorthodox nature of Q seems all the more remarkable. Paul fits the description of

---

[10] Q Lk. 9:58//Mt. 8:20; 1 Cor. 4:11-12; 2 Cor. 6:5; 11:27; Phil. 4:12; 1 Th. 2:9.

[11] Lk. 6:20-22//Mt. 5:3, 4, 6, 11; Mk. 1:16-20//Mt. 4:18-22; Mk. 10:21//Mt. 19:21; Lk. 18:22; Mk. 10:28-31//Mt. 19:27-30; Lk. 18:28-30; Mk. 6:8-9//Mt. 10:9-10; Lk. 9:3; Lk. 14:33

[12] 1 Cor. 15:32; 2 Cor. 1:5-6, 8-10; 4:9; 6:5, 8, 9; 11:23-25, 32-33; Ga. 5:11; 6:17; Phil. 1:7, 13-17; Ro. 8:36; Philemon 1:9, 23; Col. 1:24; 4:3, 18

[13] For more detailed treatment of the correspondence between Paul's ministry and the form of discipleship taught by the historical Jesus see Christian Wolf, "Humility and Self-Denial in Jesus' Life and Message and in the Apostolic Existence of Paul", *Paul and Jesus* (1989) 145-160. For the pre-Easter origin of "following Jesus", see E. Gräßer, "Nachfolge und Anfechtung bei den Synoptikern", *Der Alte Bund in Neuen: exegetische Studien zur Israelfrage im Neuen Testament*, Tübingen: J.C.B. Mohr (Paul Siebeck), 1985, 171; H.D. Betz, *Nachfolge und Nachahmung Jesu Christi im Neuen Testament*, BHT 37; Tübingen: JCB Mohr (Paul Siebeck), 1967, 13; M. Hengel, *The Charismatic Leader and His Followers, passim*.

a wandering poverty stricken persecuted messenger of Jesus—a description which compares Paul with descriptions of the early Jesus movement.[14]

II. Implicit Parallels between 1 Thessalonians 2:7-16 and Lk. 11:47-51//Mt. 23:29-36

There are three parallels in language between 1 Th. 2:7-16[15] and Mt. 23:29-36 which deserve observation. The first occurs in 1 Th. 2:7 where Paul reflects on his previous ministry to the Thessalonians: "But we proved to be gentle among you, as a nursing mother tenderly cares for her own children." Paul's statement recalls Jesus' cry to Jerusalem in Lk. 13:34b//Mt. 23:37b: "How often I wanted to gather your children to together, just as a hen gathers her brood under her wings, and you would not have it." The second parallel exists between Jesus' and Paul's common adoption of the "violent death of the prophets" motif within statements condemning Jewish aggressors (Lk. 11:47-51//Mt. 23:29-31, 34-36; 1 Th. 2:14-16). The third parallel occurs with Paul's remark in 1 Th. 2:16 that the Jews "always fill up the measure of their sins" ($\epsilon l \varsigma$ τὸ ἀναπληρῶσαι αὐτῶν τὰς ἁμαρτίας πάντοτε) which agrees in meaning and in context—that of guilt

---

[14] Thus compare J.M. Robinson's description, "The Gospels as Narrative" (106): "The pre-literary Jesus movement took place in the native hamlets of Galilee, among predominantly Aramaic-speaking peasants and fisherfolk, largely illiterate and poverty-struck, ultimately dependent on Diaspora cosmopolitan Christianity for their fate . . . Originally these itinerant radicals had renounced home, family, possessions and protection, a life style that ultimately was tolerated in mainline Christianity only as the exceptional status of monasticism, an ideal to be honored but not enforced on the church at large."

[15] 1 Th. 2:13-16 has been viewed by many to be an anti-Jewish interpolation from a period of time after A.D. 70: Birger A. Pearson, "1 Thessalonians 2:13-16: A Deutero-Pauline Interpolation", *HTR* 64 (1971) 79-94; Daryl Schmidt, "1 Thess. 2:13-16: Linguistic Evidence for an Interpolation", *JBL* 102 (1983) 269-79; H. Koester, *Introduction to the New Testament,* Vol. 2; Philadelphia: Fortress Press (1982) 113. However, 2:13-16 is found in all extant texts of the letter and the interpolation theory recently has been refuted. 2:13-16 has been defended as a necessary component of the letter; its style has been found consistent with other authentic Pauline letters; other historical events satisfy the text—the event alluded to need not be the destruction of Jerusalem in AD 70; and, Paul's chastisement of the Jews does not diametrically contradict Ro. 9-11. Paul here may be taking over a traditional set of ideas: so, O.H. Steck, *Israel und das gewaltsame Geschick der Propheten,* 275f.; R. Schippers, "The Pre-Synoptic Tradition in 1 Thessalonians II 13-16", *NovT* 8 (1966) 223-34; W.D. Davies, "Paul and the People of Israel", *NTS* 24 (1977-78) 4-39. Recent works defending the authenticity of the passage include: Jon A. Weatherly, "The Authenticity of I Thessalonians 2:13-16: Additional Evidence", *JSNT* 42 (1991) 79-98; C.A. Wanamaker, *The Epistles to the Thessalonians,* Grand Rapids: Eerdmans (1990) 29-33; T. Holtz, *Der erste Brief an die Thessalonicher,* EKK 13; Neukirchen-Vluyn: Neukirchener Verlag (1986) 27, 110-12; R. Jewett, *The Thessalonian Correspondence: Pauline Rhetoric and Millenarian Piety,* Philadelphia: Fortress (1986) 36-41; I. H. Marshall, *1 and 2 Thessalonians,* London: Marshall, Morgan and Scott (1983) 8-9; G.E. Okeke, "I Thessalonians 2:13-16: The Fate of the Unbelieving Jews", *NTS* 27 (1981) 127-36.

incurred through association with the murderers of the prophets—with Jesus' judgement against his Jewish adversaries in Mt. 23:32: "Fill up the measure 'of the guilt' of your fathers" ($\pi\lambda\eta\rho\acute{\omega}\sigma\alpha\tau\epsilon$ $\tau\grave{o}$ $\mu\acute{\epsilon}\tau\rho o\nu$ $\tau\^{\omega}\nu$ $\pi\alpha\tau\acute{\epsilon}\rho\omega\nu$ $\acute{\upsilon}\mu\^{\omega}\nu$).

While we succumb to the lack of adequate proof needed to persuade sceptics of interplay between Jesus and Paul, we find it plausible that Paul had Jesus' teaching in mind when he wrote to encourage the Thessalonians in their attempt to remain true to their Lord while facing persecution from Jewish opponents.[16]

In view of Paul's lifestyle as an apostle, it is not surprising that in agreement with what we have seen in Acts a concept of discipleship and *Unheilsgeschichte* appears in 1 Thessalonians where Paul seeks to encourage his Thessalonian audience which has passed through tribulation and has become "imitators" of Paul's group and of the Lord (1:6). Paul speaks as an apostle; one "entrusted with the Gospel," having faced "much opposition" (2:1-4).

The Thessalonian church, in receiving the gospel from Paul as "the word of God" (2:3) successfully identifies with Christ Jesus' sufferings. By unifying with Paul the apostle of Christ "as a nursing mother tenderly cares for her children" (2:7), the Thessalonians have done exactly what Jesus claims Jerusalem refused to do in Lk. 13:34b//Mt. 23:37b. The Thessalonian believers fall into the lineage of the prophets and the messengers of God as Jesus describes in Lk. 13:34a//Mt. 23:37a; Lk. 6:23//Mt. 5:12; Lk. 11:47-49//Mt. 23:29f.: Mk. 12:1-9:

> For you, brethren, became imitators of the churches of God in Christ Jesus that are in Judea, for you also endured the same sufferings at the hands of your own countrymen, even as they did from the Jews, who both killed the Lord Jesus and the prophets, and drove us out. They are not pleasing to God, but hostile to all men, hindering us from speaking to the Gentiles that they might be saved; with the result that they always fill up the measure of their sins. But wrath has come upon them to the utmost. (1 Th. 2:14-16)

---

[16] The parallels in theme between Mt. 23 and 1 Th. 2 have of course not gone unnoticed by past NT scholars. See D.Garland, *The Intention of Matthew 23*, Leiden: E.J. Brill (1979) 169-170, who notes that the similarities are "too unusual to be coincidental" (169), but goes on to expose three major differences between the two: (1) a different mission is in view—the one pagan the other to Israel; (2) the reference to filling the measure of sin in Mt. occurs as an imperative while in 1 Th. 2:15-16 it completes a result clause; and (3), in Paul "the filling up of sin" has already occured "proleptically" in contrast to Mt. where 23:32 refers to the "final allotment of time." These distinctions do not alter our argument. Both statements of judgment are directed to unbelieving Jews. Paul is writing in a new situation. The temporal distinction is hardly apparent for elsewhere in Q Jesus' charge is equally proleptic: "in order that the blood of all the prophets, shed since the foundation of the world, may be charged against this generation" (Lk. 11:50//Mt. 23:35, 36). See also R. Schippers, "The Pre-Synoptic Tradition in I Thessalonians II 13-16", 223-234; Birger A. Pearson, "I Thessalonians 2:13-16: A Deutero-Pauline Interpretation", 79-94. For the parallels between 1 Th. 2:13-16 and Mk. 12:1-5b, see O.H. Steck, *Israel und das gewaltsame Geschick der Propheten*, 276.

A tradition of discipleship has developed. The Thessalonians have obediently received the Gospel, and have become "imitators" (μιμηταί) of the churches in Judea who in turn imitated Jesus' own sufferings. By enduring persecution from the Jews, the Thessalonians follow the pattern of persecution set by Jesus and the prophets and now followed by Paul and his colleagues. The Thessalonians have taken up their cross.

The reverse situation arises for the Jewish adversaries of the Thessalonians who fall into the same line of *Unheilsgeschichte* which represents the foil to obedient discipleship through Mark, Q and Acts. They assume the guilt of those who killed the prophets and Jesus: "They are not pleasing to God, but hostile to all men . . . with the result that they always fill up the measure of their sins. But wrath has come upon them to the utmost."

Hence Paul transmits an understanding of discipleship and *Unheilsgeschichte* in Acts and in the Pauline corpus which parallels in language and in concept the radical vision of discipleship and judgment as Jesus speaks of in the Q material. When, therefore, Paul the figure most closely associated with "orthodox" early Christianity, fits Jesus into the tradition of Israel's rejected prophets, there appears little reason to suspect variant teaching in Q where Jesus identifies himself in such terms.

Bibliography

Aland, Kurt and Barbara. ET. *The Text of the New Testament.* Tr. E.F. Rhodes. Grand Rapids/Leiden: Eerdmans/E.J. Brill, 1987.

Allison, D. *The End of the Ages has Come.* Philadelphia: Fortress Press, 1985.

____. "The Pauline Epistles and the Synoptic Gospels: The Pattern of the Parallels", *NTS* 28 (1982) 1-32.

____. "Paul and the Missionary Discourse", *ETL* 61 (1985) 369-375.

Amaru, B.H. "The Killing of the Prophets: Unraveling a Midrash", *HUCA* 54 (1983) 153-80.

Ambrozic, A.M. *The Hidden Kingdom: A Redaction-Critical Study of the References to the Kingdom of God in Mark's Gospel.* CBQMS II. Washington: The Catholic Biblical Association of America, 1972.

Attridge, Harold W. "Reflections on Research into Q", *Semeia* 55 (1992) 233-234.

Aune, David. "Oral Tradition and the Aphorisms of Jesus." In *Jesus and the Oral Gospel*, Ed. Henry Wansbrough, JSNTSS 64, Sheffield: JSOT Press (1991) 211-266.

____. *Prophecy in Early Christianity and the Ancient Mediterranean World.* Grand Rapids: Eerdmans, 1983.

Bacon, B.W. "The Nature and Design of Q, the Second Synoptic Source", *HibJ* 22 (1922, 23) 674-88.

Balz, Horst R. *Methodologische Probleme der neutestamentliche Christologie.* WMANT 25. Neukirchen-Vluyn: Neukirchener Verlag, 1967.

Bammel, E. "Erwägungen zur Eschatologie Jesu." In *Studia Evangelica III*, TU 88, Ed. F.L. Cross; Berlin: Akademie-Verlag (1964) 3-32.

Barr, J. "Abba isn't Daddy", *JTS* 39 (1988) 24-47.

____. *Biblical Words for Time.* SBT 33. London: SCM, 1969.

____. "Jewish Apocalyptic in Recent Scholarly Study", *BJRL* 58 (1975-76) 9-35.

Barrett, C.K. *Jesus and the Gospel Tradition.* Philadelphia: Fortress Press, 1968.

____. "The Background of Mark 10:45." In *New Testament Essays: Studies in Memory of T.W. Manson*, Ed. A.J.B. Higgins; Manchester: Manchester U.P., 40-53.

Baumeister, T. *Die Anfänge der Theologie des Martyriums.* Munster: Aschendorff, 1980.

Bauckham, R. "The Sonship of the Historical Jesus in Christology", *SJT* 31 (1985) 35-41.

____. "The Son of Man: 'A Man in my Position' or 'Someone' ", *JSNT* 23 (1985) 35-41.

Bayer, Hans F. *Jesus' Predictions of Vindication and Resurrection.* WUNT 2. Reihe 20; J.C.B. Mohr (Paul Siebeck) 1986.

Beale, G.K. *The Use of Daniel in Jewish Apocalyptic Literature and in the Revelation of St. John.* New York: Lanham, 1984.

Beardslee, W.A. "The Wisdom Tradition and the Synoptic Gospels", *JAAR* 35 (1967) 231-240.

Beasley-Murray, G.R. *Jesus and the Kingdom of God.* Grand Rapids: Eerdmans, 1986.

____. *Baptism in the New Testament.* Grand Rapids: Eerdmans, 1962.

____. *Jesus and the Future. An examination of the criticism of the eschatological discourse, Mark 13 with special reference to the Little Apocalypse theory.* London: Macmillan, 1954.

Behm, J. "γεύομαι", *TDNT* I, 675-77.

Bergant, Dianne. *What are they saying about Wisdom Literature?* New York/Ramsey: Paulist Press, 1984.

Berger, Klaus. *Die Amen-Worte Jesu.* Berlin: Walter de Gruyter, 1970.

____. *Die Gesetzesauslegung Jesu.* WMANT 40 Teil I. Neukirchen: Neukirchener Verlag, 1972.

_____. "Die königlichen Messiastraditionen des Neuen Testaments", *NTS* 20 (1974) 1-44.

_____. "Zum Traditionsgeschichtlichen Hintergrund Christologischer Hoheitstitel", *NTS* 17 (1971) 391-425.

_____. "Zur Frage des traditionsgeschichtlicher Wertes apokryphen Gleichnisse", *NovT* 17 (1975) 58-76.

Best, Ernst. *The Temptation and the Passion: The Markan Soteriology.* SNTSMS 2. Cambridge: CUP, 1965.

Betz, H.D. "Jesus as Divine Man." In *Jesus and the Historian*, FS E.C. Colwell, Ed. F.T. Trotter, Philadelphia: Westminster (1968) 114-133.

_____. *Nachfolge und Nachahmung Jesu Christi im Neuen Testament.* BHT 37, Tübingen: J.C.B. Mohr (Paul Siebeck), 1967.

_____. "On the Problem of the Religio-historical Understanding of Apocalypticism", *JTC* 6 (1960) 134-56.

Betz, Otto. "Jesus' Gospel of the Kingdom." In *The Gospel and the Gospels*, Ed. P. Stuhlmacher, Grand Rapids: Eerdmans (1991) 53-74.

Beyer, K. *Semitische Syntax im Neuen Testament.* Göttingen: Vandenhoeck & Ruprecht, 1962.

Black, M. *An Aramaic Approach to the Gospels and Acts*, 3d ed. Oxford: Clarendon Press, 1967.

_____. "Aramaic Barnâshâ and the Son of Man", *ET* 95 (1984) 200-06.

_____. "The Aramaic Dimension in Q with Notes on Luke 17:22 and Matthew 24:26 (Luke 17:23)", *JSNT* 40 (1990) 33-41.

_____. *The Book of Enoch.* Leiden: E.J. Brill, 1985.

_____. "The Christological Use of the Old Testament in the New Testament", *NTS* 18 (1971, 72) 1-14.

_____. "The Eschatology of the Similitudes of Enoch", *JTS* 3 (1952) 1-10.

_____. "The Kingdom of God has Come", *ExpT* 63 (1951-52) 289-90.

_____. "The Son of Man Passion Sayings in the Gospel Tradition", *ZNW* 60 (1969) 1-8.

_____. "The Throne-Theophany Prophetic Commission and the 'Son of Man': A Study in Tradition-History." In *Jews, Greeks and Christians*, FS. W.D. Davies, Ed. R. Hamerton-Kelly and R. Scroggs, Leiden: E.J. Brill, 1976.

_____. "The Use of Rhetorical Terminology in Papias on Mark and Matthew", *JSNT* 37 (1989) 31-41.

Blackburn, Barry. *Theios Aner and the Markan Miracle Traditions.* WUNT 2. Reihe 40; Tübingen: J.C.B. Mohr [Paul Siebeck] 1991.

Blank, Josef. "Die Sendung des Sohnes. Zur christologischen bedeutung des Gleichnisses von den Bösen Winzern Mk 12,1-12." In *Neues Testament und Kirche*, FS R. Schnackenburg, Ed. J. Gnilka; Freiburg: Herder (1974) 11-41.

Blank, S.H. "Wisdom." In *The Interpreter's Dictionary of the Bible*, Ed. G.A. Buttrick; New York: Abingdon (1962) 852-861.

Bock, Darrel L. *Proclamation from Prophecy and Pattern; Lucan Old Testament Christology.* Ph. D. Thesis, The University of Aberdeen, 1982.

Bonnard, P. *L'Évangile selon saint Matthieu.* Neuchâtel: Delachaux & Niestle, 1970.

Borg, Marcus J. *Conflict, Holiness and Politics in the Teachings of Jesus.* New York/Toronto: Edwin Mellen, 1984.

_____. *Jesus: A New Vision.* San Francisco: Harper & Row, 1987.

_____. "Portraits of Jesus in Contemporary North American Scholarship", *HTR* 84:1 (1991) 1-22.

Boring, M. Eugene. *Sayings of the Risen Jesus: Christian Prophecy in the Synoptic Tradition.* SNTSMS 46; Cambridge: CUP, 1982.

_____. "The Kingdom of God in Mark." In *The Kingdom of God in 20th-Century Interpretation.* Peabody: Hendrikson (1987) 131-147.

_____. *The Continuing Voice of Jesus.* Lousiville: Westminster/John Knox Press, 1991.

Bornkamm, Günther. "Das Doppelgebot der Liebe." In *Neutestamentliche Studien für Rudolf Bultmann zum siebzigsten Geburtstag*, BZNW 21 (1954) 85-93.

_____. "Die Verzögerung der Parousie." In *Geschichte und Glaube: Erster Teil; Gesammelte Aufsätze III*, München: Kaiser (1968) 46-55.

_____. "Evangelien, synoptische", RGG Bd. 2; Tübingen: J.C.B. Mohr [Paul Siebeck] (1958) 759.

_____. "End Expectation and Church in Matthew." In *Tradition and Interpretation in Matthew*, Eds. G. Bornkamm, G. Barth, H.J. Held; Philadelphia: Westminster (1963) 15-57.

_____. "μυστήριον", *TDNT* IV, 802-828.

Borsch, F.H. *The Son of Man in Myth and History*. London: SCM, 1967.

Boston, James R. "The Wisdom Influence Upon the Song of Moses", *JBL* 87 (1968) 198-202.

Bovon, François. *Das Evangelium nach Lukas*. EKK III/1; Zürich/Neukirchen-Vluyn: Benziger Verlag/ Neukirchener Verlag, 1989.

Brawley, Robert L. *Luke-Acts and the Jews: Conflict, Apology, and Conciliation*. Atlanta: Scholars Press, 1987.

Brettler, Marc Zvi. *God is King*. JSOTSS 76; Sheffield: Sheffield Academic Press, 1989.

Brower, K. "Mark 9.1, Seeing the Kingdom in Power", *JSNT* 6 (1980) 17-41.

Brown, R.E. *The Gospel According to John*. Vol 1. New York: Doubleday, 1966.

_____. *The Semitic Background of the Term "Mystery" in the New Testament*. Philadelphia: Fortress Press, 1968.

Brown, S. "The Secret of the Kingdom of God (Mk. 4:11)", *JBL* 92 (1973) 60-74.

Bruce, F.F. "Qumrân and Early Christianity", *NTS* 2 (1955/56) 176-190.

_____. *This is That*. Exeter: Paternoster, 1969.

Bryce, Glendon E. *A Legacy of Wisdom: The Egyptian Contribution to the Wisdom of Israel*. Lewisburg: Bucknell U.P., 1979.

Büchsel, F. "παραδίδωμι", *TDNT* II, 169-173.

Bultmann, R. *Jesus and the Word*. Tr. L.P. Smith and E. H. Lantero; New York: Scribners, 1958.

_____. *The History of the Synoptic Tradition*. 2d ed. Tr. John Marsh; Oxford: Basil Blackwell, 1968.

_____. *Theology of the New Testament*, 2 Vol. Tr. Kendrick Grobel; New York: Scribner's, 1951.

Burkitt, F.C. *The Earliest Sources of the Life of Jesus*. Boston: Houghton Mifflin, 1910.

_____. *The Gospel History and Its Transmission*. Edinburgh: T&T Clark, 1906.

Butts, J. "Probing the Polling: Jesus Seminar on the Kingdom Sayings", *Forum* 3,1 (1987) 98-128.

Cameron, P.S. *Violence and the Kingdom: The Interpretation of Matthew 11:12*. ANTJ 5. Frankfurt am Main: Peter Lang, 1984.

Campbell, J.Y. "The Kingdom of God has Come", *ExpT* 48 (1936-37) 91-94.

Caragounis, Chrys C. "Kingdom of God, Son of Man and Jesus' Self-Understanding", *TynB* 40 (1989) 3-23; 223-238.

_____. "Kingdom of God/Kingdom of Heaven." In *Dictionary of Jesus and the Gospels*, eds. Joel Green, Scott McKnight, I.H. Marshall; Downers Grove/Leicester: Intervarsity Press (1992) 417-30.

_____. *The Son of Man: Vision and Interpretation*. Tübingen: J.C.B. Mohr (Paul Siebeck) 1986.

Carlston, Charles E. "On Q and the Cross." In *Scripture, Tradition, and Interpretation*, Ed. W. Gasque and W.S. LaSor; Grand Rapids: Eerdmans (1978) 27-33.

_____. *The Parables of the Triple Tradition*. Philadelphia: Fortress Press, 1975.

Carmignac, J. *Recherches sur le 'Notre Père'*. Paris: Letouzey & Ané, 1969.

Casey, Maurice. *From Jewish Prophet to Gentile God*. Cambridge: James Clarke & Co, 1991.

_____. "General, Generic and Indefinite: The Use of the Term 'Son of Man' in Aramaic Sources and in the Teaching of Jesus", *JSNT* 29 (1987) 21-56.

_____. *Son of Man The Interpretation and Influence of Daniel 7*. London: SPCK, 1979.

_____. "The Jackals and the Son of Man", *JSNT* 23 (1985) 3-22.

_____. "The Use of the Term 'son of man' in the Similitudes of Enoch", *JSJ* VII (1976) 11-29.

Catchpole, D. "On doing Violence to the Kingdom", *IBS* 3 (1981) 77-91.

_____. "Q, Prayer, and the Kingdom: A Rejoinder", *JTS* 40 (1989) 377-88.

_____. "The Mission Charge in Q", *Semeia* 55 (1992) 147-174.

_____. *The Quest for Q.* Edinburgh: T&T Clark, 1993.

_____. "The Ravens, the Lilies and the Q Hypothesis", *SNTU* 6-7 (1981-2) 77-87.

Charles, R.H. *A Critical and Exegetical Commentary on the Book of Daniel.* Oxford: Clarendon, 1929.

_____. *The Book of Enoch.* Oxford: Clarendon, 1912.

Charlesworth, J. *Jesus within Judaism.* London: SPCK, 1988.

_____. "Seminar Report. The SNTS Pseudepigrapha Seminars at Tübingen and Paris on the Books of Enoch", *NTS* 25 (1978-9) 315-23.

Chilton, Bruce. *God in Strength.* SUNT 1; Linz: Plöchl, 1979.

_____. "Introduction." In *The Kingdom of God,* Issues in Religion and Theology 5, Ed. B. Chilton, Philadelphia/London: Fortress/SPCK (1984) 1-27.

_____. *The Isaiah Targum.* The Aramaic Bible Vol. II; Edinburgh: T&T Clark, 1987.

Christ, F. *Jesus Sophia: die Sophia-Christologie bei den Synoptikern.* Zürich: Zwingli-Verlag, 1970.

Clark, K.W. "Realized Eschatology", *JBL* 59 (1940) 367-383.

Collins, Adela Yarbro. "The Son of Man in the Sayings Source." In *To Touch the Text,* FS Joseph A. Fitzmyer, Ed. M.P. Horgan and P.J. Kobelski; New York: Crossroad (1989) 369-89.

Collins, John J. "Introduction: Towards the Morphology of a Genre", *Semeia* 14 (1979) 1-20.

_____. *The Apocalyptic Vision of the Book of Daniel.* Missoula: Scholars Press, 1977.

_____. *"The Kingdon of God in the Apocrypha and Pseudepigrapha."* In *The Kingdom of God in 20th-Century Interpretation,* Peabody: Hendrikson (1987) 81-97.

_____. "The Son of Man and the Saints of the Most High in the Book of Daniel", *JBL* 93 (1974) 50-66.

Colpe, C. "ὁ υἱὸς τοῦ ἀνθρώπου", *TDNT* VIII, 400-77.

Conzelmann, H. *Die Mitte der Zeit. Studien zur Theologie des Lukas.* BHTh 17; Tübingen: J.C.B. Mohr (Paul Siebeck) 1964.

_____. "Present and Future in the Synoptic Tradition", *JTC* 5 (1968) 26-44.

_____. "History and Theology in the Passion Narratives of the Synoptic Gospels", *Int* 24 (1970) 178-97.

Coxon, P.W. "The Great Tree of Daniel 4." In *A Word in Season,* FS W. McKane, eds. J.D. Martin and P.R. Davies, JSOTSS 42; Sheffield: JSOT Press (1986) 91-111.

Cranfield, C.E. B. *The Gospel According to Saint Mark.* CGTC; Cambridge: CUP, 1963.

Creed, J.M. *St. Luke.* London: Macmillan, 1930.

Crenshaw, James L. "Prolegomena." In *Studies in Ancient Israelite Wisdom,* Ed. J.L. Crenshaw, New York: KTAV (1976) 1-45.

Crossan, J.D. *In Fragments: The Aphorisms of Jesus.* San Francisco: Harper & Row, 1983.

_____. *Sayings Parallels: A Workbook for the Jesus Tradition.* Philadelphia: Fortress Press, 1986.

_____. "The Seed Parables of Jesus", *JBL* 92 (1973) 244-266.

_____. *The Historical Jesus; The Life of a Mediterranean Jewish Peasant.* San Francisco: Harper & Row, 1991.

Cullmann, Oscar. *The Christology of the New Testament.* Tr. Shirley C. Guthrie and Charles A. M. Hall; Philadelphia: Westminster, 1963.

_____. *Christ and Time.* Philadelphia: Fortress Press, 1964.

Dalman, G. *The Words of Jesus.* Edinburgh: T&T Clark, 1909.

Dautzenberg, Gerhard. "Der Wandel der Reich-Gottes-Verkündigung in der urchristlichen Mission." In *Zur Geschichte des Urchristentums,* Ed. G. Dautzenberg, H. Merklein, K. Müller; Freiburg: Herder (1979) 11-32.

_____. "Mk 4,1-34 als Belehrung über das Reich Gottes. Beobachtungen zum Gleichniskapitel." *BZ* 34 (1990) 38-62.

Davies, P.R. *Daniel.* Sheffield: JSOT Press, 1985.

352   *Bibliography*

Davies, W.D. and Dale Allison. *The Gospel According to Saint Matthew*. 3 vols, ICC; Edinburgh: T & T Clark, vol. 1 (1988), vol. 2 (1991).

Davies, W.D. "Knowledge in the Dead Sea Scrolls and Matthew 11:25-30", *HTR* 46 (1953) 113-139.

_____. "Matthew, Gospel According To." In *Hasting's Dictionary of the Bible*, 2nd ed., Edinburgh: T&T Clark (1963) 631-33.

_____. "Paul and the People of Israel", *NTS* 24 (1977-78) 4-39.

_____.*The Setting of the Sermon on the Mount*. Cambridge: CUP, 1964.

Davies, Stephen L. *The Gospel of Thomas and Christian Wisdom*. New York: The Seabury Press, 1983.

De Villiers, P.G.R. "Revealing the Secrets. Wisdom and the World in the Similitudes of Enoch." In *Studies in I Enoch and the New Testament*, (Neotestamentica 17; Annual Publication of the NT Society of South Africa); Stellenbosch (1983) 50-68.

de Jonge, Marinus. *Christology in Context*. Philadelphia: Westminster Press, 1988.

de Jonge, Marinus and A.S. van der Woude. "11Q Melchizedek and the New Testament", *NTS* 12 (1965-66) 301-26.

Delling, G. "καιρός", *TDNT* III, 455-64.

Deutsch, Celia. *Hidden Wisdom and the Easy Yoke*. JSNTSS 18; Sheffield: JSOT Press, 1987.

Devisch, M. "La relation entre l' évangile de Marc et le document Q." In *L' Évangile Selon Marc*, BETL 34, Ed. M. Sabbe; Leuven: Leuven UP (1976) 59-91.

Di Lella, Alexander A. *The Wisdom of Ben Sira*. New York: Doubleday, 1987.

Dibelius, Martin. *Die altestamentlichen Motive des Petrus-und Johannes dem Taufer untersucht*. BZAW 33; Berlin: Walter de Gruyter, 1918.

_____. *Die urchristliche Überlieferung von Johannes dem Täufer*. FRLANT 15, Göttingen: Vandenhoeck & Rupprecht, 1911.

_____. *From Tradition to Gospel*. Tr. B.L. Woolf; Cambridge: James Clarke & Co, 1971.

_____. "Zwei Worte Jesu", *ZNW* 11 (1910) 188-192.

Dillon, Richard J. *From Eye-Witnesses to Ministers of the Word: Tradition and Composition in Luke 24*. Rome: Biblical Institute Press, 1978.

Dodd, C.H. *According to the Scriptures*. London: Nisbet, 1952.

_____. *The Parables of the Kingdom*. 5th ed. Glasgow: Collins, 1988.

Duling, Dennis C. "Solomon, Exorcism, and the Son of David." *HTR* 65 (1975) 235-252.

Dungan, D.L. *The Sayings of Jesus in the Churches of Paul*. Philadelphia: Fortress Press, 1971.

Dunn, J.D.G. *Christology in the Making*. 2nd ed. London: SCM, 1989.

_____. *The Evidence for Jesus*. London: SCM, 1985.

_____. *Jesus and the Spirit*. London: SCM, 1975.

_____. "Matthew 12:28/Luke 11:20 – A Word of Jesus?" In *Eschatology and the New Testament*, FS G.R. Beasley-Murray, Ed. W. Hulitt Gloer; Peabody: Hendrickson (1988) 29-49.

_____. "Prophetic 'I' - Sayings and the Jesus Tradition: The importance of testing prophetic utterances within early Christianity", *NTS* 24 (1978) 175-198.

_____. "Spirit and Fire Baptism", *NovT* 14 (1970) 81-92.

Dupont, Jacques. "La Transmission des Paroles de Jésus sur La Lampe et La Mesure dans Marc 4,21-25 et dans la Tradition Q." In *Logia*, FS J. Coppens, Ed. F. Neirynck; Louven: Louven UP (1982) 201-236.

_____. *Les Béatitudes*. Brugge: Leuven, 1958 (Tome I); Études bibliques: Paris, 1969 (Tome II), 1973, (Tome III).

_____. "Le Christ et son précurseur (Mt 11,2-11): troisième dimanche de l'Avent", *AsSeign* 7 (1969) 16-26.

_____. "Le Couple parabolique du Sénevé et du Levain." In *Jesus Christus in Historie und Theologie*, FS H. Conzelmann, Ed. G. Strecker; Tübingen: J.C.B. Mohr [Paul Siebeck] (1975) 331-347.

Edwards, Richard A. *A Theology of Q*. Philadelphia: Fortress, 1976.

____. "Christian Prophecy and the Q Tradition." In *SBL 1976 Seminar Papers*, Ed. George MacRae; Missoula: Scholars Press (1976) 119-126.

____. "The Eschatological Correlative as *Gattung* in the New Testament", *ZNW* 60 (1969) 9-20.

Egger, W. *Frohbotschaft und Lehre: Die Sammelberichte des Wirkens Jesu im Markusevangelium*. FTS 19; Frankfurt: Knecht, 1976.

Eichhorn, Johann Gottfried. *Einleitung in das Neue Testament*. 5 vol. Leipzig (1804).

Eichrodt, W. ET *Theology of the Old Testament*. Vol I. Tr. J.A. Baker; Philadelphia: The Westminster Press, 1961.

Eisenman, Robert and Michael Wise. *The Dead Sea Scrolls Uncovered*. Rockport: Element, 1992.

Ellis, E. Earle. *The Gospel of Luke*. London: Nelson, 1966.

____. *The Old Testament in Early Christianity*. Tübingen: J.C.B. Mohr (Paul Siebeck), 1991.

Evans, C.F. *The Beginning of the Gospel*. London: SPCK, 1968.

Ewalds, H. *Die drei ersten Evangelien*. Göttingen: Vandenhoeck & Ruprecht, 1850.

Farmer, William R. "The Church's Stake in the Question of 'Q' ", *Perkins Journal* 39 (1986) 9-19.

Ferch, A.J. *The Son of Man in Daniel 7*. Berrien Springs, MI: Andrews UP, 1983.

Fichtner, J. "Isaiah among the Wise." In *Studies in Ancient Israelite Wisdom*, Ed. James L. Crenshaw; New York: KTAV (1979) 421-438.

Fiorenza, Elisabeth Schüssler. *The Book of Revelation: Justice and Judgment*. Philadelphia: Fortress, 1985.

Fischel, H.A. "Martyr and Prophet", *JQR* 37 (1946-7) 265-80, 363-86.

Fitzer, G. "$\phi\theta\acute{a}\nu\omega$", *TDNT* IX, 88-93.

Fitzmyer, J. "A Palestinian Collection of Beatitudes." In *The Four Gospels*, FS F. Neirynck, Ed. F. Van Segbroeck, C.M. Tuckett, G. Van Belle, J. Verheyden; Leuven: Leuven U.P. (1992) 509-515.

____. "Abba and Jesus' Relation to God." In *À Cause de L'Évangile: Études sur les Synoptiques et les Actes*, FS J. Dupont; Paris: Cerf, 1985. 14-38.

____. *A Wandering Aramean*. SBLMS 25; Missoula: Scholars Press, 1979.

____. *The Gospel According to Luke*. Garden City: Doubleday, vol. 1 (1981), vol. 2 (1983).

Fleddermann, Harry. "The Mustard Seed and the Leaven in Q, the Synoptics, and Thomas." In *Society of Biblical Literature 1989 Seminar Papers*, Ed. David J. Lull; Atlanta: Scholars Press (1989) 216-236.

Fohrer, Georg. ET *Introduction to the Old Testament*. Tr. David Green; New York: Abingdon, 1968.

Fohrer, Georg and U. Wilckens. "$\sigma o\phi\acute{\iota}a$", *TDNT* VII, 465-526.

France, R.T. *Divine Government*. London: SPCK, 1990.

____. *Jesus and the Old Testament*. London: Tyndale, 1971.

____. "Mark and the Teachings of Jesus." In *Gospel Perspectives I*, Ed R.T. France and D. Wenham; Sheffield: JSOT Press (1980) 101-36.

____. *Matthew--Evangelist & Teacher*. Exeter: Paternoster Press, 1989.

____. "The Servant of the Lord in the Teaching of Jesus", *TynB* 19 (1968) 26-52.

Friedlander, Gerald. *The Jewish Sources of the Sermon on the Mount*. New York: KTAV, 1969.

Frost, S.B. *Old Testament Apocalyptic*. London: Epworth, 1952.

Fuchs, Albert. *Die Entwicklung der Beelzebul Kontroverse bei den Synoptikern*. SNTU Serie B, Band 5; Freistadt: Plöchl, 1979.

Fuchs, Albert and Franz Weissengruber. *Konkordanz zum Thomasevangelium*. SNTU Serie B, Band 4. Freistadt: Plöchl, 1978.

Fuchs, Ernst. *Studies of the Historical Jesus*. Tr. Andrew Scobie, London: SCM, 1964.

Fuller, R.H. *The Foundations of New Testament Christology*. New York: Scribner's, 1963.

____. *The Mission and Achievement of Jesus*. SBT 12. London: SCM,1954.

____. *Interpreting the Miracles*. London: SCM, 1963.

Furnish, Victor P. "The Jesus-Paul Debate: from Baur to Bultmann." In *Paul and Jesus*, Ed. A.J.M. Wedderburn, JSNTSS 37; Sheffield: JSOT Press, 1989.

Gammie, J.G. "On the intention and sources of Daniel i-vi", *Vetus Testamentum* 31 (1981) 282-292.

Garland, David E. *The Intention of Matthew 23*. Leiden: E.J. Brill, 1979.

Geldenhuys, N. *Commentary on the Gospel of Luke*. London: Marshall, Morgan & Scott, 1965.

Georgi, Dieter. *Die Gegner des Paulus im 2. Korintherbrief.* WMANT 11; Neukirchen-Vluyn: Neukirchener Verlag, 1964.

Gerhardson, B. *The Origins of the Gospel Tradition*. Philadelphia:Fortress, 1979.

Gese, H. "Wisdom, Son of Man, and the Origins of Christology: The Consistent Development of Biblical Theology", *Horizons in Biblical Theology* 3 (1981) 23-57.

Giesen, H. "Mk 9.1 -- ein wort Jesü über die nahe Parousie?", *TTZ* 92 (1983) 134-48.

Gnilka, J. *Das Evangelium nach Markus*. EKK; Zürich: Benzinger/Neukirchen-Vluyn: Neukirchener Verlag, vol. 1 (1978), vol. 2 (1979).

_____. *Das Matthäusevangelium*. HTKNT I/1,2; Freiburg: Herder, vol. 1 (1986), vol. 2 (1988).

_____. *Die Verstockung Israels*. SANT band III; München: Kösel-Verlag, 1961.

_____. *Jesus Christus Nach Frühen Zeugnissen Des Glaubens*. München: Kösel-Verlag, 1970.

_____. *Neutestamentliche Theologie Ein Überblick*. Würzburg: Echter Verlag, 1989.

Gohrer, Georg. "σοφια", *TDNT* VII, 465-496.

Goldingay, John E. *Daniel*. WBC 30. Waco: Word, 1989.

Goppelt, L. *Theology of the New Testament*. Grand Rapids: Eerdmans, vol. 1. (1975).

Gräßer, E. *Das Problem der Parusieverzögerung in den synoptischen Evangelien und in der Apostelgeschichte*. NZNW 22; Berlin: Topelmann, 1957.

_____. "Nachfolge und Anfechtung bei den Synoptikern." In *Der Alte Bund im Neuen: exegetische Studien zur Israelfrage im Neuen Testament*; Tübingen: J.C.B. Mohr (Paul Siebeck) 1985.

Greeven , H. "ζητέω", *TDNT* II, 892-893.

_____. "'Wer unter euch...?'" In *Wort und Dienst*, vol 3 (1952) 86-101.

Grimm, W. "Zum Hintergrund von Mt. 8:11f//Lk 13:28", *BZ* 16 (1972) 255-6.

Grundmann, W. *Das Evangelium nach Lukas*. THKNT 3. 10th ed. Berlin: Evangelische Verlagsanstalt, 1984 (1961).

_____. *Das Evangelium nach Markus*. THKNT 2; Berlin: Evangelische Verlagsanstalt, 1977.

Guelich, R.A. *Mark 1-8:26*. WBC 34a; Waco: Word, 1989.

_____. *The Sermon on the Mount*. Waco: Word, 1982.

Guenther, H.O. "The Sayings Gospel Q and the Quest for Aramaic Sources: Rethinking Christian Origins", *Semeia* 55 (1992) 41-76.

Gundry, R.H. *Matthew: A Commentary on his Literary and Theological Art*. Grand Rapids: Eerdmans, 1982.

_____. *The Use of the Old Testament in St. Matthew's Gospel, with special reference to the Messianic Hope*. Leiden: E.J. Brill, 1967.

Haenchen, E. "Matthäus 23", *ZTK* 48 (1951) 38-63.

Hahn, F. *Mission in the New Testament*. London: SCM, 1965.

_____. *The Titles of Jesus in Christology: their History in Early Christianity*. London: Lutterworth, 1969.

Hamerton-Kelly, R.G. "A Note on Matthew xii 28par. Luke xi 20", *NTS* 11 (1964,65) 167-69.

_____. *Pre-Existence, Wisdom, and the Son of Man*. SNTSMS 21; Cambridge: CUP, 1973.

Hanson, P.D. *The Dawn of Apocalyptic*. Philadelphia: Fortress, 1975; 2nd ed., 1979.

Hare, Douglas R.A. *The Son of Man Tradition*. Minneapolis: Fortress Press, 1990.

Harnack, Adolf von. *The Sayings of Jesus*. Tr. J.R. Wilkinson, New York: Putnam's Sons, 1908.

Hartman L.F. and A.A. Di Lella. *The Book of Daniel*. New York: Doubleday, 1978.

Harvey, A. E. *Jesus and the Constraints of History*. Philadelphia: Westminster, 1982.

Hasler, V. *Amen. Redaktionsgeschichtliche Untersuchung zur Einführungsformel der Herrenworte "Wahrlich ich sage euch."* Zürich: Hotthelf-Verlag, 1969.

Hauck F. and E. Bammel. "πτωχός", *TDNT* VI, 885-915.

Havener, Ivan. *Q The Sayings of Jesus.* Good News Studies 19; Collegeville: The Liturgical Press, 1987.

Hawthorne, Gerald. "The Role of Christian Prophets in the Gospel Tradition." In *Tradition and Interpretation in the New Testament*, FS E.E. Ellis, Eds. Gerald Hawthorne and Otto Betz; Grand Rapids/Tübingen: Eerdmans/ JCB Mohr [Paul Siebeck] (1987) 119-133.

Heaton, E.W. *The Book of Daniel.* London: SCM, 1956.

_____. *The Hebrew Kingdoms.* Oxford: Oxford University Press, 1968.

Hengel, Martin. "Jesus als Messianischer Lehrer der Weisheit und die Anfänge der Christologie", in *Sagesse et Religion*, Colloque de Strasbourg (Oct. 1976), Vendôme (1979) 147-188.

_____. *Judaism and Hellenism.* 2 Vols. Tr. John Bowden; London: SCM Press, 1974.

_____. "Kerygma oder Geschichte", *TQ* 151 (1971) 323-336.

_____. *Studies in the Gospel of Mark.* Tr. John Bowden, London: SCM, 1985.

_____. *The Atonement.* Tr. John Bowden, London: SCM, 1981.

_____. *The Charismatic Leader and His Followers.* Edinburgh: T & T Clark, 1981.

_____. *The 'Hellenization' of Judaea in the First Century after Christ.* Philadelphia: Trinity Press International, 1990.

Higgins, A. J. B. *Jesus and the Son of Man.* London/Philadelphia: Lutterworth Press/ Fortress Press, 1964.

Hill, D. *Greek Words and Hebrew Meanings.* SNTSMS 5; Cambridge: CUP, 1967.

_____. *New Testament Prophecy.* London: Marshall, Morgan & Scott, 1979.

_____. "On the Evidence for the Creative Role of Christian Prophets", *NTS* 20 (1974) 262-274.

_____. *The Gospel of Matthew.* NCBC; London: Marshall, Morgan and Scott, 1972.

_____. "The Rejection of Jesus at Nazareth (Luke IV 16-30)", *NovT* 13 (1971) 161-180.

Hirsch, Emanuel. "Fragestellung und Verfahren meiner Frügeschichte des Evangeliums", *ZNW* 41 (1942) 106-24.

Hoffmann, Paul. "Die Anfänge der Theologie in der Logienquelle." In *Gestalt und Anspruch des Neuen Testaments*, Ed. J. Schreiner and G. Dautzenberg; Würzburg: Echter-Verlag (1969) 147-151.

_____. "Jesu »Vorbot des Sorgen« und seine Nachgeschichte in der synoptischen Überlieferung." In *Jesu Rede von Gott und ihre Nachgeschicte in frühe Christentum*, FS Willi Marxsen, Ed. Dietrich -Alex Koch, Gerhard Selling and Andreas Lindemann; Gütersloh: Gütersloher Verlagshaus Gerd Mohn (1989) 116-142.

_____. "Πάντες ἐργάται ἀδικίας: Redaktion und tradition in Lk 13:22-30", *ZNW* 58 (1967) 188-214.

_____. "QR und der Menschensohn. Eine vorläufige Skizze." In *The Four Gospels*, FS F. Neirynck, Ed. F. Van Segbroeck, C.M. Tuckett, G. Van Belle, J. Verheyden; Leuven: Leuven U.P. (1992) 421-456.

_____. *Studien zur Theologie der Logienquelle.* Münster: Verlag Aschendorff, 1972.

Holladay, Carl H. *Theios Aner in Hellenistic Judaism: A Critique of the Use of This Category in New Testament Christology.* SBLDS 40; Missoula: Scholars Press, 1977.

Holtz, T. *Der erste Brief an die Thessalonicher.* EKK 13; Neukirchen-Vluyn: Neukirchener Verlag, 1986.

Holtzmann, Heinrich. *Die synoptischen Evangelien, ihr Ursprung und geschichtlicher Charakter.* Leipzig: 1863.

Hooker, Morna. *Jesus and the Servant: the Influence of the Servant Concept of Deutero-Isaiah in the New Testament.* London: SPCK, 1959.

_____. *The Gospel According to Mark.* London: A&C Black, 1991.

_____. *The Message of Mark.* London: Epworth Press, 1983.

_____. *The Son of Man in Mark.* London: SCM, 1967.

Horbury, W. "The Messianic Associations of the 'Son of Man'", *JTS* 36 (1985) 34-55.

Horsley, Richard A. "Q and Jesus: Assumptions, Approaches, and Analyses", *Semeia* 55 (1992) 175-209.

Hultgren, A.J. *Christ and His Benefits.* Philadelphia: Fortress Press, 1987.

Hunter, A.M. "Crux criticorum -- Matt. xi. 25-30--A Reappraisal", *NTS* 8 (1961-1962) 241-249.

_____. *The Work and Words of Jesus.* London: SCM Press, 1950.

Hunzinger, C.-H. "Aussersynoptisches Traditionsgut in Tomas-Evangelium", *TZ* 85 (1960) 843-846.

_____. "σίαπι", *TNDT* VII, 287-291.

Jacobson, Arland D. "Apocalyptic and the Synoptic Sayings Source Q." In *The Four Gospels*, FS F. Neirynck, Ed. F. Van Segbroeck, C.M. Tuckett, G. Van Belle and J. Verheyden; Leuven: Leuven U.P. (1992) 403-419.

_____. "The Literary Unity of Q", *JBL* 101 (1982) 365-89.

Jeremias, J. " 'Aδάμ", *TDNT* I, 141-143.

_____. *The Parables of Jesus.* London: SCM, 1963.

_____. "Die älteste Schicht der Menschensohn-Logien", *ZNW* 58 (1967) 159-72.

_____. *Die Sprache des Lukasevangeliums. Redaktion und Tradition im Nicht-Markusstoff des dritten Evangeliums.* KEK; Göttingen: Vandenhoeck & Ruprecht, 1980.

_____. *New Testament Theology.* Vol. 1, Tr. J.S. Bowden; London: SCM, 1971.

_____. *The Prayers of Jesus.* London: SCM, 1967.

_____. *Jesus' Promise to the Nations.* Tr. S.H. Hooke; SBT 24, London: SCM, 1958.

_____. *The Eucharistic Words of Jesus.* Tr. N. Perrin; London: SCM, 1966.

Jewett, R. *The Thessalonian Correspondence: Pauline Rhetoric and Millenarian Piety.* Philadelphia: Fortress, 1986.

Johnson, Marshall D. "Reflections on a Wisdom Approach to Matthew's Christology", *CBQ* 36 (1974) 44-64.

Jülicher, Adolf. *Einleitung in das Neue Testament.* Leipzig: J.C.B. Mohr (Paul Siebeck) 1894.

Jüngel, E. *Paulus und Jesus: Eine Untersuchung zur Präzierung der Frage nach der Aufsprung der Christologie.* Tübingen: J.C.B. Mohr (Paul Siebeck) 1962.

Kalugila, Leonidas. *The Wise King: Studies in Royal Wisdom as Divine Revelation in the Old Testament and Its Environment.* Lund: Gleerup, 1980.

Käsemann, E. "The Beginnings of Christian Theology." In *New Testament Questions of Today.* London: SCM (1969) 82-107.

_____. *Essays on New Testament Themes.* SBT 41; London: SCM, 1964.

_____. "Lukas 11:14-28." In *Exegetische Versuche und Besinnungen.* Vol 2; Göttingen: Vandenhoeck & Ruprecht (1964) 242-48.

_____. "On the Subject of Primitive Christian Apocalyptic." In *New Testament Questions of Today,* London: SCM Press, 1969.

_____. "Sätze heiligen Rechts in NT", *NTS* 1 (1954-5) 248-60.

Kasting, H. *Die Anfänge der urchristlichen Mission. Eine historische Untersuchung,* BEvTh 55; München: Kaiser, 1969.

Keck, Leander E. "The Poor Among the Saints in the New Testament", *ZNW* 56 (1965) 100-129.

_____. "Mark 3:7-12 and Mark's Christology", *JBL* 84 (1965) 341-358.

_____. "The Introduction to Mark's Gospel", *NTS* 12 (1966) 352-70.

Kelber, Werner. *The Kingdom in Mark.* Philadelphia: Fortress Press, 1973.

_____. *The Oral and Written Gospel: The Hermeneutics of Speaking and Writing in the Synoptic Tradition, Paul, Mark and Q.* Philadelphia: Fortress Press, 1983.

Kertelge, K. *Die Wunder Jesu im Markusevangelium.* SANT 23; München: Kösel, 1970.

Kim, Myung-Soo. *Die Trägergruppe von Q.* Ammersbek bei Hanburg: Verlag an der Lottbek, 1990.

Kim, Seyoon. *"The 'Son of Man'" as the Son of God.* Tübingen: J.C.B. Mohr (Paul Siebeck) 1983.

Kingsbury, Jack D. *Jesus Christ in Matthew, Mark, and Luke.* Philadelphia: Fortress Press, 1981.

____. *The Christology of Mark's Gospel.* Philadelphia: Fortress Press, 1983.

Kloppenborg, J. "'Easter Faith' and the Sayings Gospel Q", *Semeia* 49 (1990) 71-100.

____. "Literary Convention, Self-Evidence and the Social History of the Q People", *Semeia* 55 (1992) 77-102.

____. *Q Parallels.* Sonoma: Polebridge Press, 1988.

____. *The Formation of Q.* Philadelphia: Fortress Press, 1987.

____. "Wisdom Christology in Q", Laval théologique et Philosophique 34 (1978) 129-147.

Koch, D.A. *Die Bedeutung der Wundererzählungen für die Christologie des Markusevangeliums.* Berlin: Walter de Gruyter, 1975.

Koch, Klaus. "Is Daniel Also Among the Prophets?" In *Interpreting the Prophets*, Ed. J.L. Mays and Paul J. Achtemeir; Philadelphia: Fortress Press (1987) 237-248.

Koester, Helmut. *Ancient Christian Gospels.* London: SCM, 1990.

____. "Gnomai Diaphoroi: The Origin and Nature of Diversification in the History of Early Christianity." In *Trajectories through Early Christianity*, Ed. H. Koester and J.M. Robinson; Philadelphia: Fortress Press (1971) 114-157.

____. *Introduction to the New Testament.* Vol. 2; Philadelphia: Fortress Press, 1982.

____. "One Jesus and Four Primitive Gospels." In *Trajectories through Early Christianity*, Ed. H. Koester and J.M. Robinson; Philadelphia: Fortress Press (1971) 158-204.

____. "The Structure and Criteria of Early Christian Beliefs." In *Trajectories through Early Christianity*, Ed. H. Koester and J.M. Robinson; Philadelphia: Fortress Press (1971) 205-231.

Kogler, Franz. *Das Doppelgleichnis vom Senfkorn und vom Sauerteig in seiner traditionsgeschichtlichen Entwicklung.* Würzburg: Echter Verlag, 1988.

Kosch, D. *Die Gottesherrschaft im Zeichen des Widerspruchs: Traditions- und redaktionsgeschichtlich Untersuchung von Lk 16.16, Mt 11.12f bei Jesus, Q und Lukas.* Frankfurt am Main: Peter Lang, 1985.

____. *Die eschatologische Tora des Menschensohnes: Untersuchungen zur Rezeption der Stellung Jesu zur Tora in Q.* NTOA 12; Göttingen: Vandenhoeck & Ruprecht, 1989.

Kuhn, H.W. *Ältere Sammlungen im Markusevangelium.* SUNT 8; Göttingen: Vandenhoeck & Ruprecht, 1971.

____. *Enderwartung und gegenwartiges Heil: Untersuchungen zu den Gemeindeliedern von Qumran mit einem Anhang über Eschatologie und Gegenwart in der Verkündigung Jesu.* Göttingen: Vandenhoeck & Rupprecht, 1966.

Kümmel, W.G. *Die Theologie des Neuen Testaments nach seinen Hauptzeugen Jesus, Paulus, Johannes.* Göttingen: Vandenhoeck & Ruprecht, 1969.

____. *Introduction to the New Testament.* Tr. H.C. Kee; New York/Nashville: Abingdon, 1975.

____. *Promise and Fulfilment.* London: SCM, 1957.

Kunzi, M. *Das Naherwartungslogion Markus 9.1 par.* BGBE 21; Tübingen: J.C.B. Mohr (Paul Siebeck) 1977.

Lachmann, Karl. "De ordine narrationum in evangeliis synopticis", *ThStK* 8 (1835) 570-590.

Lacocque, André. *The Book of Daniel.* Tr. D. Pellauer. London: John Knox, 1979.

Ladd, G.E. "Apocalyptic." In *Evangelical Dictionary of Theology.* Ed. Walter Elwell; Grand Rapids: Baker (1984) 62-65.

____. *The Presence of the Future.* Grand Rapids: Eerdmanns, 1974.

____. *Jesus and the Kingdom.* New York: Harper & Row, 1964.

Lambrecht, J. "John the Baptist and Jesus in Mark 1.1-15: Markan Redaction of Q?", *NTS* 38 (1992) 357-384.

____. *The Sermon on the Mount: Proclamation and Exhortation.* GNS 14; Wilmington: Glazier, 1985.

Lang, Bernhard. *Wisdom and the Book of Proverbs: An Israelite Goddess Redefined.* New York: Pilgrim Press, 1976.

Laufen, Rudolf. *Die Doppelüberlieferungen der Logienquelle und des Markusevangeliums*. BBB 54; Bonn: Hanstein, 1980.

Lindblom, J. "Wisdom in the Old Testament Prophets", *VTS* (1955) 192-204.

Lindars, Barnabas. "Enoch and Christology." *ExpT* 92 (1981) 295-299.

_____. *Jesus Son of Man*. London: SPCK, 1983.

_____. *New Testament Apologetic: the Doctrinal Significance of the Old Testament Quotations*. London: SCM, 1961.

Lohfink, G. *Jesus and Community*. Tr. John P. Galvin. ET Philadelphia/New York: Fortress Press/ Paulist Press, 1984.

Lohmeyer, E. *Das Evangelium des Markus*. Göttingen: Vandenhoek &Ruprecht, 1963.

_____. *'Our Father': An Introduction to the Lord's Prayer*. ET London: Collins, 1965.

Lohse, E. *Märtyrer und Gottesknecht*. Göttingen: Vandenhoeck & Ruprecht, 1963.

_____. "Sayings of Jesus about Jerusalem", *TDNT* VII, 328-333.

_____. "Σιών", *TDNT* VII, 329-38.

Longenecker, Richard N. *Biblical Exegesis in the Apostolic Period*. Grand Rapids: Eerdmans, 1975.

Lövestam, Evald. "Jésus Fils de David chez les Synoptiques." *ST* 28 (1974) 97-109.

Lührmann, Dieter. *Die Redaktion der Logienquelle*. WMANT 33. Neukirchen-Vluyn: Neukirchener Verlag, 1969.

_____. "Jesus und Seine Propheten." In *Prophetic Vocation in the New Testament and Today*, Ed. J. Panagopoulos; NovTSup. 45; Leiden: E.J. Brill (1977) 210-217.

_____. "The Gospel of Mark and the Sayings Collection Q", *JBL* 108 (1989) 51-71.

Luz, U. "Das Jesusbild der vormarkinischen Tradition." In *Jesus Christus in Historie und Theologie*, FS H. Conzelman; Tübingen: J.C.B. Mohr [Paul Siebeck] (1975) 347-374.

_____. "Das Geheimnis motiv und die markinische Christologie", *ZNW* 56 (1965) 9-30.

_____. *Das Evangelium nach Matthaus*. 1. Teilband: Mt 1-7, EKK; Zürich: Benziger, 1985.

_____. "Sermon on the Mount/Plain: reconstruction of Q Mt and QLk." In SBLSPS 22 (1983) 473-479.

Mack, Burton L. "Q and the Gospel of Mark: Revising Christian Origins", *Semeia* 55 (1992) 15-39.

_____. *The Lost Gospel: The Book of Q & Christian Origins*. Rockport: Element, 1983.

Manson, T.W. *The Sayings of Jesus*. London: SCM, 1949.

Manson, W. *Jesus the Messiah*. London: Hodder and Stoughton, 1948.

_____. *The Gospel of Luke*. MNTC; London: Hodder & Stoughton, 1930.

Marcus, J. *The Mystery of the Kingdom of God*. SBLDS 90; Atlanta: Scholars Press, 1986.

Marshall, C.D. *Faith as a Theme in Mark's Narrative*. SNTSMS 64; Cambridge: CUP, 1989.

Marshall, I.H. *1 and 2 Thessalonians*. London: Marshall, Morgan and Scott, 1983.

_____. *Luke*. NIGTC; Grand Rapids: Eerdmans, 1978.

_____. *Luke, Historian and Theologian*. Exeter: Paternoster, 1970.

_____. "Palestinian and Hellenistic Christianity: Some Critical Comments", *NTS* 19 (1972-3) 271-87.

_____. "The Development of the Concept of Redemption in the New Testament." In *Reconciliation and Hope: Presented to L.L. Morris*, Ed. R.J. Banks; Exeter: Paternoster Press, 1975.

_____. "The Hope of a New Age: The Kingdom of God in the New Testament." In *Jesus the Saviour*; London: SPCK (1990) 213-239.

_____. "The Son of Man and the Incarnation", *Ex Auditu* 7 (1991) 29-43.

_____. "The Synoptic Son of Man Sayings in Recent Discussion", *NTS* 12 (1965-6) 327-51.

Martin, R.E. *Syntax Criticism of the Synoptic Gospels*. Lewiston/Queenston: Edwin Mellen Press, 1987.

Martitz, Wülfing von. "υἱός", *TDNT* 8 (1972) 334-40.

Marxsen, Willie. *Mark the Evangelist: Studies on the Redaction History of the Gospel*. Tr. J. Boyce; Nashville: Abingdon Press, 1969.

McArthur, H.K. "The Parable of the Mustard Seed", *CBQ* 33 (1971) 198-201.

____. *Der Exeget als Theologe: Vorträge zum Neuen Testament.* Gütersloh: Mohn, 1968.

McKane, William. *Prophets and Wise Men.* SBT 44; London: SCM, 1965.

Mearns, Chris. "Realized Eschatology in Q? A Consideration of the Sayings in Luke 7.22, 11.2 and 16.16", *SJT* 40 (1987) 189-210.

Merklein, Helmut. *Die Gottesherrschaft als Handlungsprinzip.* FZB 34; Würzburg: Echter Verlag, 1981.

____. *Jesu Botschaft von der Gottesherrschaft.* SBS 111; Stuttgart: Verlag Katholisches Bibelwerk, 1983.

Metzger, B. *A Textual Commentary on the Greek New Testament.* UBS Corrected ed., 1975.

Meyer, P.D. "The Gentile Mission in Q", *JBL* 89 (1970) 405-417.

Miller, M.P. "The Function of Isa 61:1-2 in 11 Q Melchizedek", *JBL* 88 (1969) 467-69.

Miller, Robert J. "The Rejection of the Prophets in Q", *JBL* 107/2 (1988) 225-240.

Michel, O. *Prophet und Märtyrer.* BFTh 37, 2 vol; Gütersloh: Mohn, 1932.

Morgan, Donn F. "Wisdom and the Prophets." In *Studia Biblica* I; Berlin: Akademie Verlag (1978) 209-244.

Moule, C.F. D. "As we forgive...': A Note on the Distinction between Deserts and Capacity in the Understanding of Forgiveness." In *Essays in New Testament Interpretation,* Cambridge: CUP (1982) 278-86.

____. "From Defendant to Judge--and Deliverer: an Enquiry in to the Use and Limitations of the Theme of Vindication in the New Testament." In *Studiorum Novi Testamenti Societas Bulletin* (1959) 1-18.

____. *Essays in New Testament Interpretation.* Cambridge: CUP, 1982.

____. *The Birth of the New Testament.* London: Black, 1962.

____. *The Origin of Christology.* New York and Cambridge: CUP, 1977.

Moessner, David P. " 'The Christ must suffer' New Light on the Jesus–Peter, Stephen, Paul Parallels in Luke-Acts", *NovT* 28 (1986) 220--56

Muilenburg, James. "The Son of Man in Daniel and the Ethiopic Apocalypse of Enoch", *JBL* 79 (1960) 197-209.

Murphy, R.E. "Wisdom Theses." In *Wisdom and Knowledge*, FS Papin, Ed. J. Armenti; Philadelphia: Villanova Press (1976) 187-200.

Mussner, F. "Gottesherrschaft und Sendung Jesu nach Markus 1,14f." In *Praesentia Salutis: Gesammelte Studien zu Fragen und Themen des Neuen Testaments*, Dusseldorf: Patmos (1967) 81-98.

Neirynck, Frans. *Duality in Mark: Contributions to the Study of the Markan Redaction.* Louvan: Leuvan U.P., 1989.

____. "Paul and the Sayings of Jesus." In *L' apôtre Paul: Personnalité, style et conception du ministère*, BETL 73, Ed. A. Vanhoye; Leuven: University & Peeters (1986) 265-321.

____. "The Symbol Q (= Quelle)", *ETL* 54 (1978) 119-125.

Neugebauer, F. "Geistsprüche und Jesuslogien", *ZNW* 80 (1962) 218-28.

Nock, A.D. *St. Paul.* London: Thornton Butterworth, 1938.

Okeke, G.E. "I Thessalonians 2:13-16: The Fate of the Unbelieving Jews", *NTS* 27 (1981) 127-36.

Osten-Sacken, P. von der. *Die Apokalyptik in ihrem Verhältnis zu Prophetie und Weisheit.* TExH 157; Munich: Kaiser, 1969.

O'Toole, Robert F. *The Unity of Luke's Theology: An Analysis of Luke-Acts.* Wilmington: Michael Glazier, 1984.

Pamment, M. "The Kingdom of Heaven According to the First Gospel", *NTS* 27 (1981) 211-232.

Parker, K.I. "Solomon as Philosopher King? The Nexus of Law and Wisdom in 1 Kings 1-11", *JSOT* 53 (1992) 75-91.

Pearson, Birger A. "I Thessalonians 2:13-16: A Deutero-Pauline Interpretation", *HTR* 64 (1971) 79-94.

Percy, E. *Die Botschaft Jesu. Eine traditionskritische und exegetische Untersuchung.* Lund Universitets Årsskrift; Lund: C.W.K. Gleerup, 1953.

Perrin, Norman. *Rediscovering the Teaching of Jesus.* New York/London: Harper & Row/SCM, 1967.

_____. "The Christology of Mark: A Study in Methodology." In *A Modern Pilgrimage in New Testament Christology,* Philadelphia: Fortress Press (1974) 104-121.

_____. *The New Testament. An Introduction. Proclamation and Parenesis, Myth and History.* New York: Harcourt Brace Jovanovich, 1982.

_____. "The Son of Man in Ancient Judaism and Primitive Christianity: a Suggestion", *BR* 11 (1966) 17-28.

Pesch, R. *Das Markusevangelium.* HTKNT II/1, 2; Freiburg: Herder, 1977.

_____. "Voraussetzungen und Anfänge der urchristlichen Mission." In *Mission im Neuen Testament,* QD 93; Freiburg: Herder, 1982.

Piper, R. *Wisdom in the Q Tradition: the Aphoristic Teaching of Jesus.* SNTSMS 61; Cambridge: CUP, 1989.

Plummer, A. *A Critical and Exegetical Commentary on the Gospel according to St. Luke.* ICC; Edinburgh: T&T Clark, 1922.

Pokorny, Peter. "The Temptation Stories and Their Intention", *NTS* 20 (1973-74) 115-27.

Polag, Athanasius. *Die Christologie der Logienquelle.* Neukirchen-Vluyn: Neukirchener Verlag, 1977.

_____. *Fragmenta Q: Textheft zur Logienquelle.* Neukirchen-Vluyn: Neukirchener Verlag, 1979.

Puech, Émile. "Une Apocalypse Messianique (*4Q521*)", RevQ 60 (Oct., 1992) 475-522.

Rad, Gerhard von. *Old Testament Theology.* 2 vol. Edinburgh: Oliver & Boyd, 1962-65.

Räisänen, Heikki. *The 'Messianic Secret' in Mark.* Tr. Christopher Tuckett, Edinburgh: T & T Clark, 1990.

Rawlinson, A.E. J. *St. Mark.* London: Metheun, 1947.

Reike, Bo. "πᾶς, ἅπας", *TDNT* V, 892-896.

Rengstorf, K. *Das Evangelium nach Lukas.* NTD 3. 10th ed.; Göttingen: Vandenhoeck & Ruprecht, 1965.

_____. "κλαυθμός", *TDNT* III, 725-26.

Reploh, K.G. *Markus--Lehrer der Gemeinde: Eine rekaktionsgeschichtliche Studie zu den Jüngerperikopen des Markusevangeliums.* SBM 9; Stuttgart: Katholisches Bibelwerk, 1969.

Riesner, Rainer. *Jesus als Lehrer.* WUNT 2. Reihe 7; Tübingen: J.C.B. Mohr (Paul Siebeck) 1981.

Ringshausen, Gerhard. "Die Kinder der Weisheit zur Auslegung von Mk 10, 13-16par", *ZNTW* 77 (1-2, 1986) 34-63.

Robinson, J.A.T. *Jesus and His Coming. The Emergence of a Doctrine.* London:SCM, 1957.

Robinson, J.M. "Logoi Sophon: On the Gattung of Q." In *Trajectories through Early Christianity,* Eds. H. Koester and J.M. Robinson, Philadelphia: Fortress Press (1971) 71-113.

_____. The Gospels as Narratives." In *The Bible and the Narrative Tradition,* Ed. Frank McConnell; New York: Oxford UP, 1986.

_____. *The Nag Hammadi Library in English.* Leiden: E.J. Brill, 1977.

_____. "The Sermon on the Mount/Plain: Work Sheets for the Reconstruction of Q." SBLSPS 22 (1983) 451-54.

_____. "The Recent Debate on the 'New Quest' ", *JBR* 30 (1962) 198-208.

Rodd, C.S. "Spirit or Finger", *ExpT* 72 (1961) 157-158.

Rosenthal, L.A. "Die Josephsgeschichte mit den Büchern Ester und Daniel verglichen", *ZAW* 15 (1895) 278-84.

Rowland, John. *The Open Heaven.* London: SPCK, 1982.

Russell, D.S. *The Method and Message of Jewish Apocalyptic.* London: SCM, 1964.

_____. *The Old Testament Pseudepigrapha. Patriarch & Prophets in Early Judaism.* London: SCM, 1987.

Sanders, E.P. *Jesus and Judaism.* Philadelphia: Fortress Press, 1985.

Sanders, James A. "From Isaiah 61 to Luke 4." In *Christianity, Judaism, and other Greco-Roman Cults*. FS Morton Smith, Ed. J. Neusner; Leiden: E.J. Brill (1975) 75-106.

____. "Isaiah in Luke." In *Interpreting the Prophets*, Eds. J.L. Mays and Paul J. Achtemeir, Philadelphia: Fortress Press (1987) 75-85.

Sato, Migaku. *Q und Prophetie*. WUNT 2/29; Tübingen: J.C.B. Mohr (Paul Siebeck) 1988.

Schelkle, K.H. "Der Zweck der Gleichnisreden (Mk 4,10-12)." In *Neues Testament und Kirche*, FS R. Schnackenburg; Freiburg: Herder (1974) 71-75.

Schenk, Wolfgang. "Der Einfluß der Logienquelle auf das Markusevangelium", *ZNW* 70 (1979) 141-163.

____. "Gefangenschaft und Tod des Täufers Erwängungen zur Chronologie und ihren Konsequenzen", *NTS* 29 (1983) 453-483.

____. *Synopse zur Redenquelle der Evangelien: Q Synopse und Rekonstruktion in deutscher Übersetzung mit kurzen Erläuterungen*. Düsseldorf: Patmos, 1981.

Schenke, L. *Die Wundererzählungen des Markusevangeliums*. SBB. Stuttgart: Katholisches Bibelwerk, 1974.

Schillebeeckx, Edward. *Jesus*. Tr. H. Hoskins; New York: Seabury, 1979.

Schippers, R. "The Pre-Synoptic Tradition in I Thessalonians II 13-16", *NovT* VIII (1966) 223-234.

____. "The Son of Man in Matt. 12:32 = Luke 12:10 compared with Mark 3:28." In *Studia Evangelica* IV, TU 102; Berlin: Töpelmann (1968) 231-235.

Schleiermacher, Friedrich Daniel Ernst. "Über die Zeugnisse des Papias von unsern beiden ersten Evangelien", *TSK* 5 (1832) 735-768.

Schlosser, J. *Le Dieu de Jesus*. LD 129. Paris: Cerf, 1987.

____. *Le Règne de Dieu dans les dits de Jésus*. EB, 2 vols.; Paris: Gabalda, 1980.

Schmidt, D. "The LXX Gattung 'Prophetic Correlative' ", *JBL* 96 (1977) 517-522.

____. "1 Thess. 2:13-16: Linguistic Evidence for an Interpolation", *JBL* 102 (1983) 269-79.

Schmidt, K.L. "βασιλεία", *TDNT* I, 579-593.

Schmithals, W. *Das Evangelium nach Lukas*. Zurich: Theologischer Verlag, 1980.

____. *Das Evangelium nach Markus*. OTNT 2/1-2. Gütersloh: Mohn, 1979.

____. *Einleitung in die drei ersten Evangelium*. Berlin: Walter de Gruyter, 1985.

____. "Evangelien." In *Theologische Realenzyklopädie* Band X; Berlin: Walter de Gruyter (1982) 571-626.

Schnackenburg, Rudolf. "'Das Evangelium' im Verständnis des ältesten Evangelisten." In *Orientierung an Jesus: zur Theologie der Synoptiker*, FS J. Schmid, Ed. P. Hoffmann; Freiburg: Herder (1973) 309-24.

____. *God's Rule and Kingdom*. Tr. John Murray; Edinburgh/London: Nelson, 1963.

____. *Schriften zum Neuen Testament. Exegese in Fortschritt und Wandel*. München: Kösel, 1971.

Schneider, Gerhard. "Das Bildwort von der Lampe. Zur Traditionsgeschichte eines Jesus - Wortes", *ZNW* 61 (1970) 183-209.

____. "Das Vaterunser des Matthäus." In *A Cause de L'Évangile*, FS J. Dupont; Paris: Cerf (1985) 57-90.

Schnider, Franz. *Jesus der Prophet*. Orbis Biblicus et Orientalis 2; Göttingen: Vandenhoeck & Ruprecht, 1973.

Scholer, David M. "Q Bibliography: 1981-1988." *SBL Seminar Papers* 27, Ed. David J. Lull; Atlanta: Scholars Press (1988) 483-495.

Schönle, V. *Johannes, Jesus, und die Juden: Die Theologische Position des Matthäus und des Verfassers der Redenquelle im Lichte von Mt 11*. BET 17; Frankfurt Am Main: Peter Lang, 1982.

Schrenk, G. "βιάζομαι, βιαστής", *TDNT* I, 609-614.

____. "πᾶς, ἅπας", *TDNT* V, 892-96.

Schulz, Siegfried. *Die Stunde der Botschaft*. Hamburg: Furche, 1967.

____. *Q, Die Spruchquelle der Evangelisten*. Zürich: Theologischer Verlag, 1972.

____. "Mark's Significance for the Theology of Early Christianity." In *The Interpretation of Mark*, IRTh.7. Ed. William Telford; London: SPCK (1985) 158-167.

Schuppan, Christoph. *Gottes Herrschaft und Gottes Wille: Ein Untersuchung zur Struktur der Rede von Gott in der Spruchquelle Q im Vergleich mit dem Frühjudentum und dem Matthäus- und Lukasevangelium.* Unpublished Ph.D. Dissertation, Ernst-Moritz-Arndt-Universität Greifswald, 1978.

Schürmann, H. "Beobachtungen zum Menschensohn-Titel in der Redenquelle. Sein Vorkommen in Abschluß und Einleitungswendungen." In *Jesus und der Menschensohn.* FS A. Vögtle; Freiburg: Herder (1975) 124-148.

____. *Das Gebet des Herrn.* Freiburg: Herder, 1958.

____. *Das Lukasevangelium. Erster Teil. Kommentar zu Kapitel 1,1-9,50.* 2nd ed., HThKNT 3/1; Freiburg: Herder, 1982.

____. "Das Zeugnis der Redenquelle für die Basileia-Verkündigung Jesu." In FS J. Coppens, *Logia*, Ed. J. Delobel, Leuven: Leuven University Press (1982) 121-200 = *Gottes Reich - - Jesu Geschick: Jesu ureigener Tod im Licht seiner Basileia - Verkündigung,* Freiburg/Basel/Vienna: Herder (1983) 65-152.

____. "Der «Bericht vom Anfang». Ein Rekonstruktionversuch auf Grund von Lk 4,14-16." In *Studia Evangelica* II, TU 87; Berlin: Akademie Verlag (1964) 1242-258; = *Traditionsgeschichtliche Untersuchungen zu den synoptische Evangelien,* Düsseldorf: Patmos Verlag (1968) 69-80.

____. *Gottes Reich-Jesu Geschick: Jesu ureigener Tod im Licht seiner Basileia-Verkundigung.* Freiburg/Basel/Vienna: Herder, 1983.

____. *Traditionsgeschichtliche Untersuchungen zu den synoptischen Evangelien.* KBANT, Düsseldorf: Patmos Verlag, 1968.

____. "Zur Kompositionsgeschichte der Redenquelle. Beobachtungen an der lukanischen Q-Vorlage." In *Der Treue Gottes Trauen,* FS G. Schneider, eds. C. Bussmann und Walter Radl; Freiburg: Herder (1991) 325-342.

Schweizer, E. "Der Menschensohn", *ZNW* 50 (1950) 185-209.

____. *The Good News According to Mark.* Tr. D.H. Madvig; Richmond: John Knox Press, 1970.

____. *The Good News According to Matthew.* Atlanta: John Knox Press, 1975.

____. "υἱός", *TDNT* VIII, 334-97.

Scott, R.B.Y. "Priesthood, Prophecy, Wisdom, and the Knowledge of God", *JBL* 80 (1961) 1-15.

____. "Solomon and the Beginning of Wisdom in Israel." In *Wisdom in Israel and in the Ancient Near East,* VT Sup 3, eds. M. Noth and D.W. Thomas; Leiden: Brill (1960) 262-79.

Seebass, H. "אַחֲרִית", *TDOT* I, 207-212.

Seeley, David. "Blessings and Boundaries: Interpretations of Jesus' Death in Q", *Semeia* 55 (1992) 131-146.

Seitz, O.J. "The Rejection of the Son of Man: Mark Compared with Q." *Studia Evangelica* VII; Berlin: Akademie Verlag (1982) 451-65.

Selman, M. "The Kingdom of God in the Old Testament", *TynB* 40.2 (1989) 161-184.

Sint, J.A. "Die Eschatologie des Täufers, die Täufergruppen und die Polemik der Evangelien." In *Vom Messias zum Christus. Die Fülle der Zeit in religionsgeschichtlicher und theologischer Sicht.* Ed. K. Schubert; Wien/Freiburg/Basel: Herder (1964) 55-163.

Sjöberg, Erik. *Der Menschensohn im Äthiopischen Henochbuch.* Lund: Gleerup, 1946.

____. *Der verborgene Menschensohn in den Evangelien.* Lund: Gleerup, 1955.

Snodgrass, Klyne. *The Parable of the Wicked Tenants.* WUNT 27 Tübingen: J.C.B. Mohr (Pauls Siebeck) 1983.

Stanton, Graham M. "On the Christology of Q." In *Christ and Spirit in the New Testament,* FS C.F.D. Moule, Eds. B. Lindnars and S.S. Smalley; Cambridge: CUP (1973) 25-40.

____. "Q". In *Dictionary of Jesus and the Gospels,* eds. Joel Green, Scott McKnight, I.H. Marshall; Downers Grove/Leicester: Intervarsity Press (1992) 417-30.

Staufer, E. "ἵνα", *TDNT* III, 323-33.

Steck, Odil Hannes. *Israel und das gewaltsame Geschick der Proheten.* WMANT 23; Neukirchen-Vluyn: Neukirchener Verlag, 1967.

Steinhauser, M.G. *Doppelbildworte in den synoptischen Evangelien.* FB 44; Würzburg: Echter Verlag, 1981.

Stendahl, K. *The School of St. Matthew and its Use of the Old Testament.* Philadelphia: Fortress Press, 1968.

Strecker, Georg. *Der Weg der Gerechtigkeit.* FRLANT 82; Göttingen: Vandenhoeck & Ruprecht, 1971.

_____. *The Sermon on the Mount: an exegetical Commentary.* Nashville: Abingdon, 1988.

Streeter, B.H. *The Four Gospels.* London: Macmillan, 1924.

Stuhlmacher, Paul. *Das paulinische Evangelium.* vol 1, FRLANT 95; Göttingen: Vandenhoeck & Ruprecht, 1968.

_____. "Jesustradition im Römerbrief? Eine Skizze", *TB* 14 (1983) 240-50.

Sugirtharajah, R.S. "Wisdom, Q, and a Proposal for a Christology", *ExpT* 102 (1990) 42-45.

Suggs, M. Jack. *Wisdom, Christology, and Law in Matthew's Gospel.* Cambridge: Harvard U.P., 1970.

Tannehill, Robert C. *The Narrative Unity of Luke-Acts.* Philadelphia: Fortress Press, vol. 1 (1986) vol. 2 (1990).

Taylor, Vincent. *The Formation of the Gospel Tradition.* London: Macmillan, 1949.

_____ *The Gospel According to St. Mark.* London: Macmillan, 1966.

_____. "W. Wrede's The Messianic Secret in the Gospels", *ET* 65 (1954) 246-50.

Theison, J. *Der auserwählte Richter. Untersuchungen zum traditionsgeschichtlichen Ort der Bilderreden des äthiopischen Henoch.* SUNT 12; Göttingen: Vandenoeck & Ruprecht, 1975.

Theissen, G. *The First Followers of Jesus, A Sociological Analysis of the Earliest Christianity.* London: SCM, 1978.

_____. *Studien zur Soziologie des Urchristentums.* Tübingen: JCB Mohr (Paul Siebeck) 1983.

_____. *The Gospels in Context.* Tr. Linda M. Maloney; Edinburgh: T & T Clark, 1992.

Thompson, Michael. *Clothed with Christ: The Example and Teaching of Jesus in Romans 12.1-15.13.* JSNTSS 59; Sheffield: JSOT Press, 1991.

Thußing, W. *Die Neutestamentlichen Theologien und Jesus Christus.* Dusseldorf: Patmos, 1981.

_____. *Erhöhungsvorstellung und Parusieerwartung in der ältesten nachösterlichen Christologie.* SBS 42; Stuttgart: Katholisches Bibelwerk, 1970.

Tiede, David L. *The Charismatic Figure as Miracle Worker.* SBLDS 1; Missoula: Scholars Press, 1972.

Tödt, H.E. *The Son of Man in the Synoptic Tradition.* Tr. D.M. Barton, London: SCM, 1963 = *Der Menschensohn in der synoptischen Tradition*, Gütersloh: Mohn, 1959.

Toy, C.H. *Proverbs.* ICC; Edinburgh: T&T Clark, 1899.

Trilling, W. *Das Wahre Israel.* SANT 10; Munich: Kösel, 1964.

Tuckett, C.M. "Luke 4,16-30, Isaiah and Q." In FS J. Coppens, *Logia*, Ed. J. Delobel; Leuven: Leuven University Press (1982) 343-354.

_____. *Nag Hammadi and the Gospel Tradition.* Edinburgh: T&T Clark, 1986.

_____. "On the Stratification of Q, A Response", *Semeia* 55 (1992) 213-222.

_____. "Paul and the Synoptic Mission Discourse?", *ETL* 60 (1984) 376-381.

_____. "Q, Prayer, and the Kingdom", *JTS* 40 (1989) 367-376.

_____. "The Present Son of Man", *JSNT* 14 (1982) 58-82.

_____. "The Temptation Narrative in Q." In *The Four Gospels*, FS F. Neirynck, Ed. F. Van Segbroeck, C.M. Tuckett, G. Van Belle, and J. Verheyden; Leuven: Leuven U.P. (1992) 479-507.

Uro, R. *Sheep Among the Wolves.* Helsinki: Suomalainen Tiedeakatemia, 1987.

Vaage, Leif E. "The Son of Man Sayings in Q: Stratigraphical Location and Significance", *Semeia* 55 (1992) 103-129.

Vassiliadis, Petros. "Prolegomena to a Discussion on the Relationship Between Mark and the Q Document", *Deltion Biblikôn Meletôn* 3 (1975) 31-46.

_____. "The Nature and Extent of the Q Document", *NovT* 20 (1978) 49-73.

Vermes, Geza. *Jesus the Jew*. London: Collins, 1973.

_____. "The Use of bar nash/bar nasha in Jewish Aramaic." In M. Black, *An Aramaic Approach to the Gospels and Acts*; Oxford: Oxford UP (1967) 310-30.

Vielhauer, P. "Gottesreich und Menschensohn in der Verkündigung Jesu." In *Festschrift für Gunther Dehn*, Ed. W. Schneemelcher; Neukirchen: Kreis Moers (1957) 51-79.

_____. "Erwägungen zur Christologie des Markusevangeliums." In *Aufsätze zum Neuen Testament*; Münich: Kaiser (1965) 199-214.

_____. *Geschichte der urchristlichen Literatur: Einleitung in das Neue Testament, die Apokryphen und die Apostolischen Väter*. Berlin: Walter de Gruyter, 1975.

Vögtle, A. "Bezeugt die Logienquelle die authentische Redeweise Jesu vom <<Menschensohn>>?" In *Logia*, FS J. Coppens, Leuven: Leuven UP (1982) 77-79.

_____. "Der 'eschatologische' Bezug der Wir-Bitten des Vaterunser." In *Jesus und Paulus*, Eds. E.E. Ellis and E. Grässer, Göttingen: Vandenhoeck & Ruprecht (1975) 344-362.

_____. "Exegetische Erwägungen über das Wissen und Selbstbewusstsein Jesu." In FS K. Rahner, *Gott in Welt*; Freiburg: Herder, 1964.

Wallace, R.S. *The Lord is King: The Message of Daniel*. Downers Grove: Intervarsity Press, 1979.

Walter, N. "Paul and the Early Christian Jesus-Tradition", *Paul and Jesus*, JSNTSS 37; Ed. A.J.M. Wedderburn, Sheffield: JSOT Press, 1989.

Wanamaker, C.A. *The Epistles to the Thessalonians*. NIGTC; Grand Rapids: Eerdmans, 1990.

Watts, John D. *Isaiah*. 2 vols, WBC 24,25, Waco: Word, vol. 1 (1985), vol. 2 (1987).

Weatherly, Jon A. "The Authenticity of I Thessalonians 2:13-16: Additional Evidence", *JSNT* 42 (1991) 79-98.

Wegner, Uwe. *Der Hauptmann von Kafarnaum*. WUNT 2. Reihe 14; Tübingen: J.C.B. Mohr (Paul Siebeck) 1985.

Weiß, Bernhard. *A Manual of Introduction to the New Testament*. Tr. A.J.K. Davidson, 2 vol. New York: Funk & Wagnalis, 1887-89.

Weiße, C.H. *Die evangelische Geschichte Kritisch und philosophisch bearbeitet*. 2 Bd. Leipzig, 1838.

_____. *Die Evangelienfrage in ihrem gegenwärtigen Stadium*. Leipzig, 1856.

Wellhausen, J. *Einleitung in die drei ersten Evangelien*. Berlin: 1905.

Wengst, Klaus. *Christologische Formeln und Lieder des Urchristentums*. StNT 7; Gütersloh: Gerd Mohn, 1972.

Westermann, Claus. *Basic Forms of Prophetic Speech*. Tr. H. White; London: Lutterworth, 1967.

Whybray, R.N. *The Intellectual Tradition in the Old Testament*. ZAW 135; Berlin: Walter de Gruyter, 1974.

Wilke, Ch. G. *Der Urevangelist oder exegetisch kritische Untersuchung über das Verwandschaftsverhältnis der drei ersten Evangelien*. Dresden-Leipzig, 1838.

Wilckens, Ulrich. "Jesusüberlieferung und Christus kerygma: zwei Wegurchristlicher Überlieferungsgeschichte." In *Theologia Viatorum* 10 (1965,66) 310-319.

_____. "σοφία", TDNT VII, 496-526.

_____. "The Tradition-history of the Resurrection of Jesus." In *The Significance of the Message of the Resurrection for Faith in Jesus Christ*. SBT 2/8, Ed. C.F.D. Moule; London: SCM (1968) 51-76.

_____. "Tradition de Jésus et Kerygma du Christ: la double historie de la tradition au sein du christianisme primitif", *RHPR* 47 (1967) 1-20.

Wink, Walter. "Jesus' Reply to John. Matt 11:2-6/Luke 7:18-23", *Forum* 5 (1,1989) 121-28.

_____. *John the Baptist in the Gospel Tradition*. SNTSMS 7; Cambridge: CUP, 1968.

Winston, David. *The Wisdom of Solomon: A New Translation with Introduction and Commentary*. New York: Doubleday, 1979.

Witherington III, Ben. *The Christology of Jesus*. Minneapolis: Fortress, 1990.

Wolf, Christian. "Humility and Self-Denial in Jesus' Life and Message and in the Apostolic Existence of Paul." In *Paul and Jesus*, JSNTSS 37, Ed. A.J.M. Wedderburn; Sheffield: JSOT Press (1989) 145-160.

Wood, J. *Wisdom Literature*. London: Duckworth, 1967.

Wrege, H. -T. *Die Überlieferungsgeschichte der Bergpredigt*. WUNT 9. Tübingen: J. C.B. Mohr (Paul Siebeck) 1968.

Zeller, Dieter. *Die weisheitlichen Mahnsprüche bei den Synoptikern*. FB 17. Würzburg: Echter, 1977.

_____. *Kommentar zur Logienquelle*. Stuttgart: Verlag Katholisches Bibelwerk, 1984.

_____. "Das Logion Mt 8,11f//Lk. 13:28 und das Motiv der 'Volkerwallfahrt' ", *BZ* 15 (1971) 222-237.

Ziener, G. *Die Theologische Begriffssprache im Buche der Weisheit*. BBB 11; Bonn: Hanstein, 1956.

Index of Biblical and Other Ancient Sources

I. Old Testament

II. Old Testament Apocrypha

III.   Pseudepigrapha

IV. Qumran Writings

VI. Rabbinic Writings

VII. Hellenistic-Jewish Writings

VIII. Early Christian and Gnostic Writings

Index of Modern Authors